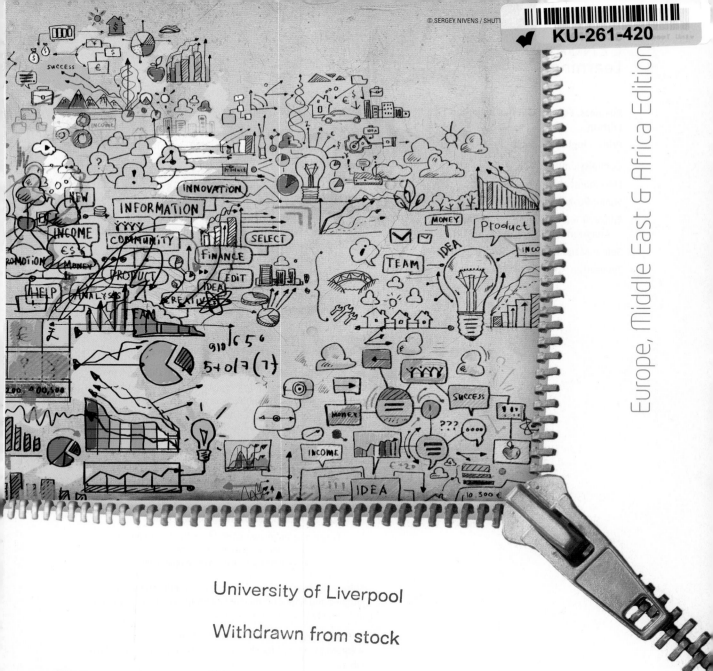

Business

Pride • Hughes • Kapoor

CENGAGE
Learning

Australia • Brazil • Japan • Korea • Mexico • Singapore • Spain • United Kingdom • United States

Business, Europe Middle East and Africa Edition

Pride, Hughes, Kapoor

Commissioning Editor: Annabel Ainscow

Development Editor: Felix Rowe

Senior Production Editor: Alison Burt

Editorial Team: Abbie Jones, Jenny Grene, Ana Arede

Senior Manufacturing Buyer: Eyvett Davis

Typesetter: CENVEO Publisher Services

For product information and technology assistance, contact **emea.info@cengage.com**.

For permission to use material from this text or product, and for permission queries, email **emea.permissions@cengage.com**

This work is adapted from *Business*, 12th Edition by Pride, Hughes and Kapoor published by South-Western, a division of Cengage Learning, Inc. © 2014.

British Library Cataloguing-in-Publication Data
A catalogue record for this book is available from the British Library.

ISBN: 978-1-4737-0476-3

Cengage Learning EMEA
Cheriton House, North Way, Andover, Hampshire, SP10 5BE
United Kingdom

Cengage Learning products are represented in Canada by Nelson
Education Ltd.

For your lifelong learning solutions, visit **www.cengage. co.uk**

Purchase your next print book, e-book or e-chapter at **www.cengagebrain.com**

Printed in China by RR Donnelley
1 2 3 4 5 6 7 8 9 10 – 16 15 14

To Nancy, Allen, Mike, Ashley, and Charlie Pride

To my wife Peggy and to my mother Barbara Hughes

To my wife Theresa; my children Karen, Kathryn, and Dave;
and in memory of my parents Ram and Sheela Kapoor

BRIEF CONTENTS

CONTENTS

v

Part 6
ACCOUNTING, FINANCE AND INVESTMENT 457

ABOUT THE AUTHORS

WILLIAM M. PRIDE
TEXAS A&M UNIVERSITY

William M. Pride (Texas A&M University) is professor of marketing, Mays Business School at Texas A&M University. He received his PhD from Louisiana State University. He is the author of Cengage Learning's *Marketing*, 15th edition, and a market leader. Dr. Pride's research interests are in advertising, promotion, and distribution channels. Dr. Pride's research articles have appeared in major journals in the fields of advertising and marketing, such as *Journal of Marketing, Journal of Marketing Research, Journal of the Academy of Marketing Science*, and the *Journal of Advertising*. Dr. Pride is a member of the American Marketing Association, Academy of Marketing Science, Association of Collegiate Marketing Educators, Society for Marketing Advances, and the Marketing Management Association. Dr. Pride has taught principles of marketing and other marketing courses for more than 30 years at both the undergraduate and graduate levels.

ROBERT J. HUGHES
RICHLAND COLLEGE, DALLAS COUNTY COMMUNITY COLLEGES

Robert J. Hughes (EdD, University of North Texas) specialises in business administration and college instruction. He has taught Introduction to Business for more than 35 years both on campus and online for Richland College—one of seven campuses that are part of the Dallas County Community College District. In addition to *Business* and *Foundations of Business*, published by Cengage Learning, he has authored college textbooks in personal finance and business mathematics; served as a content consultant for two popular national television series, *It's Strictly Business* and *Dollars & Sense: Personal Finance for the 21st Century*; and is the lead author for a business math project utilising computer-assisted instruction funded by the ALEKS Corporation. He is also active in many academic and professional organisations and has served as a consultant and investment advisor to individuals, businesses, and charitable organisations. Dr. Hughes is the recipient of three different Teaching in Excellence Awards at Richland College. According to Dr. Hughes, after 35 years of teaching Introduction to Business, the course is still exciting: "There's nothing quite like the thrill of seeing students succeed, especially in a course like Introduction to Business, which provides the foundation for not only academic courses, but also life in the real world."

JACK R. KAPOOR
COLLEGE OF DUPAGE

Jack R. Kapoor (EdD, Northern Illinois University) is professor of business and economics in the Business and Technology Division at the College of DuPage, where he has taught Introduction to Business, Marketing, Management, Economics, and Personal Finance since 1969. He previously taught at Illinois Institute of Technology's Stuart School of Management, San Francisco State University's School of World Business, and other colleges. Professor Kapoor was awarded the Business and Services Division's Outstanding Professor Award for 1999–2000. He served as an Assistant National Bank Examiner for the U.S. Treasury Department and as an international trade consultant to Bolting Manufacturing Co., Ltd., Mumbai, India.

Dr. Kapoor is known internationally as a coauthor of several textbooks, including *Foundations of Business*, 3rd edition (Cengage Learning), has served as a content consultant for the popular national television series *The Business File: An Introduction to Business*, and developed two full-length audio courses in business and personal finance. He has been quoted in many national newspapers and magazines, including *USA Today, U.S. News & World Report,* the *Chicago Sun-Times, Crain's Small Business,* the *Chicago Tribune*, and other publications.

Dr. Kapoor has traveled around the world and has studied business practices in capitalist, socialist, and communist countries.

ACKNOWLEDGEMENTS

The quality of this book and its supplements programme has been helped immensely by the insightful and rich comments of a special set of instructors. We are also indebted to all the reviewers and their respective contributions to this and previous editions. Their suggestions have helped us improve and refine the text as well as the whole instructional package.

We also wish to acknowledge Colette Wolfson and Linda Hoffman of Ivy Tech Community College and Julie Boyles of Portland State University for their contributions to the digital resources. We would again like to thank Julie Boyles as well as LuAnn Bean of the Florida Institute of Technology, Amit Shah of Frostburg State University, Ashli Lane of Texas State University, and our Digital Consultant, Martin Karamian. We thank the R. Jan LeCroy Center for Educational Telecommunications of the Dallas County Community College District for their Telecourse partnership and for providing the related student and instructor materials. Finally, we thank the following people for their professional and technical assistance: Stacy Landreth Grau, Marian Wood, Amy Ray, Elisa Adams, Courtney Bohannon, Jamie Jahns, Whitney Pearce, Laurie Marshall, Clarissa Means, Theresa Kapoor, David Pierce, Kathryn Thumme, Margaret Hill, Nathan Heller, Karen Tucker, and Dave Kapoor.

Many talented professionals at Cengage Learning have contributed to the development of Business. We are especially grateful to Mike Schenk, Jason Fremder, Kristen Hurd, Joanne Dauksewicz, Emily Nesheim, Holly Henjum, Stacy Shirley, Kristen Meere, and Megan Fischer. Their inspiration, patience, support, and friendship are invaluable.

PUBLISHER'S ACKNOWLEDGEMENTS

The content of this edition for Europe, the Middle East and Africa is predominantly adapted from the twelfth edition of Pride, Hughes and Kapoor's *Business* but also includes some examples and cases adapted from the following Cengage Learning EMEA textbooks:

- Ashwin, A. *et al, Business Studies* (2010)
- Dibb, S.; Simkin, L.; Pride, W.M.; Ferrell, O.C., *Marketing: Concepts & Strategies* Sixth Edition (2012)
- Doole, I. & Lowe, R., *International Marketing Strategy: Analysis, Development and Implementation* Sixth Edition (2012)
- Drury, C., *Management Accounting for Business* Fifth Edition (2013)
- Kelly, P. & Ashwin, A., *The Business Environment* (2013)
- Mankiw, N.G., & Rashwan, M., *Principles of Economics* Middle East Edition (2013)
- Mankiw, N.G. & Taylor, M., *Economics* Second Edition (2013)
- Mankiw, N.G. & Taylor, M., *Economics* South Africa Edition (2014)
- Mowen, M.; Hansen, D.; Heitger, D., *Cornerstones of Managerial Accounting* South Africa Edition (2014)
- Pride, W.M., *Marketing* Middle East Edition (2009)
- Thompson, T.; Scott, J.M.; Martin, F., *Strategic Management: Awareness and Change* Seventh Edition (2014)
- Verhage, B., *Marketing: A Global Perspective* (2014)
- Warnich, S. *et al, Human Resource Management in South Africa* Fifth Edition (2015 - not yet published)
- Witcher, B. & Chau, V.S., *Strategic Management: Principles and Practice* Second Edition (2014)

Full copyright details and acknowledgements appear in the aforementioned publications.

DIGITAL RESOURCES

A range of additional study tools is available online. **Lecturers:** please register here for access: http://login.cengage.com. **Students:** please search for *Business* on: www.cengagebrain.co.uk.

PART 1
THE BUSINESS ENVIRONMENT

In Part 1 of *Business*, we begin by examining the world of business and how the economy affects your life. Next, we discuss ethical and social responsibility issues that affect business firms and our society. Then we explore the increasing importance of international business.

1   **Introduction to Business**

2   **Responsible Business**

3   **Global Business**

1

INTRODUCTION TO BUSINESS

LEARNING OBJECTIVES

Once you read this chapter, you should be able to:

- Discuss what you must do to be successful in the world of business
- Define *business* and identify potential risks and rewards
- Define *economics* and describe the two types of economic systems: capitalism and command economy
- Identify the ways to measure economic performance
- Examine the different phases in the typical business cycle
- Outline the four types of competition
- Summarise the factors that affect the business environment and the challenges that businesses will encounter in the future

BUSINESS FOCUS

Toyota – growing too fast?

In the first few years of the new millennium the future prospects of the leading car makers changed. The U.S. car makers lost out as high fuel costs hit demand hard for 4-wheel drive Sports Utility Vehicles and other large cars. The firms were crippled by very high healthcare costs and as the recession hit hard, they were all kept afloat by the U.S. government. Chrysler only narrowly avoided bankruptcy.

By contrast Toyota had focused on being profitable and responding quickly to market changes and had developed a policy of manufacturing cars to suit the markets where they sell. However, even Toyota tried to become global too fast. Akio Toyoda, in written evidence to the US Congress, admitted that Toyota may have grown too quickly in its quest to become the world's number one car maker and put quantity before quality.

In the summer of 2006 Toyota's apparently perfect image was starting to become a little tarnished as the company recalled 2.2 million vehicles to correct faults, including potential power steering failure in its hybrid car, tyres bulging and possibly bursting in their small pick-up, and the possibility that air bags would not inflate in a crash. Worse was to follow when in 2010 it recalled around 10 million vehicles for various faults including faulty floor mats, sticking accelerator pedals, braking software problems and steering malfunctions.

Toyota's competitive advantage had always been built around quality and reliability, but of course as the development and manufacture of products was increasingly outsourced, it became more difficult to maintain high quality standards. Fast growth places considerable strain on effectively managing the supply chain especially where, as in Toyota's case, it constitutes such a high proportion of the car's value.

How can Toyota maintain control of its reputation and brand image and build the capability and capacity to be leader in the sector?

References: Maynard, M. and Fackler, M. (2006) 'A Rise in Defects at Toyota Puts its Reputation at Stake', *New York Times*. 5 August. Clark, A. (2010) 'Toyota Boss Akio Toyota Apologises Ahead of US Grilling, www.guardian.co.uk, 23 February.

Wow! What a challenging world we live in. Just for a moment, think about the economic problems listed here and how they affect not only you, but also businesses in the country where you live as well as in the wider global economy.

- Relatively high unemployment rates in many countries
- Reduced spending by worried consumers
- Increased government spending to stimulate a troubled economy that created large national debt in many countries across the world
- A volatile stock market and concerns about banks and financial institutions
- Reform movements in the West and several uprisings across the Middle East protesting against differences in wealth, income, power and human rights

In fact, just about every person around the globe was affected in some way by the economic crisis that began in late 2007. Despite the efforts of world governments to provide the economic stimulus needed to stabilise the economy, it took nearly four years before the economy began to improve. Today, even with signs of modest improvement, people still worry about their economic future and the future of their nation. Hopefully, by the time you read this material, the world economy will be much stronger. Still, it is important to remember the old adage, "History is a great teacher." Both nations and individuals should take a look at what went wrong to avoid making the same mistakes in the future.

In addition, it helps to keep one factor in mind: Economies continue to adapt and change to meet the challenges of an ever-changing world and to provide opportunities for those who want to achieve success. The Western economic system provides an amazing amount of freedom that allows businesses like Zynga for example—an Internet gaming company—to adapt to changing business environments. Despite troubling economic times and a weak economy, Zynga—and its 3,000 employees—is a success because it was able to introduce new games that players love, earn a profit, and sell stock to the general public.

Within certain limits, imposed mainly to ensure public safety, the owners of a business can produce any legal good or service they choose and attempt to sell it at the price they set. This system of business, in which individuals decide what to produce, how to produce it, and at what price to sell it, is called **free enterprise**. This free-enterprise system ensures, for example, that Amazon.com can sell everything from televisions, toys, and tools to computers, cameras, and clothing. This system gives Amazon's owners and stockholders the right to make a profit from the company's success. It gives Amazon's management the right to compete with bookstore rival Barnes & Noble and electronics giant Sony. It also gives consumers the right to choose.

> **free enterprise** the system of business in which individuals are free to decide what to produce, how to produce it, and at what price to sell it

In this chapter, we look briefly at what business is and how it became that way. First, we discuss what individuals and companies can do to be successful in the world of business and explore some important reasons for studying business. Then we define *business*, noting how business organisations satisfy their customers' needs and earn profits. Next, we examine how capitalism and command economies answer four basic economic questions. Then our focus shifts to how the nations of the world measure economic performance, the phases in a typical business cycle, and the four types of competitive situations. Next, we look at the events that helped shape today's business system, the current business environment, and the challenges that businesses face.

YOUR FUTURE IN THE CHANGING WORLD OF BUSINESS

The key word in this heading is *changing*. When faced with both economic problems and increasing competition not only from other domestic firms but also from international firms located in other parts of the world, employees and managers began to ask the question: What do we do now? Although this is a fair question, it is difficult to answer. Certainly, for a university student taking business courses or an employee just starting a career, the question is even more difficult to answer. Yet there are still opportunities out there for people who are willing to work hard, continue to learn, and possess the ability to adapt to change. Let's begin our discussion in this section with three basic concepts.

- What do you want?
- Why do you want it?
- Write it down!

Whether you want to obtain part-time employment to pay for university and living expenses, begin your career as a full-time employee, or start a business, you must *bring* something to the table that makes you different from the next person. Employers and the economic system are more demanding than ever before. Ask yourself: What can I do that will make employers want to pay me a salary? What skills do I have that employers need? With these two questions in mind, we begin the next section with another basic question: Why study business?

Why study business?

The potential benefits of higher education are enormous. To begin with, there are economic benefits. Over their lifetimes, university graduates on average earn much more than high school graduates. Although lifetime earnings are substantially higher for university graduates, so are annual income amounts (see Figure 1.1). In addition to higher income, you will find at least five compelling reasons for studying business.

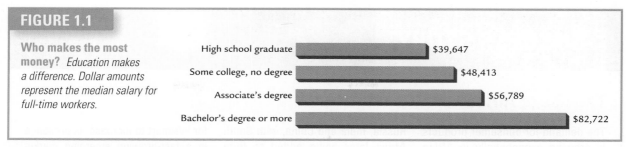

FIGURE 1.1

Who makes the most money? *Education makes a difference. Dollar amounts represent the median salary for full-time workers.*

High school graduate	$39,647
Some college, no degree	$48,413
Associate's degree	$56,789
Bachelor's degree or more	$82,722

Source: The 2012 Statistical Abstract of the U.S. Web site at www.census.gov (accessed January 10, 2012). Salary amounts were obtained from Table 692.

For help in choosing a career What do you want to do with the rest of your life? At some time in your life, someone probably has asked you this same question. Like many people, you may find it a difficult question to answer. This business course will introduce you to a wide array of employment opportunities. In private enterprise, these range from small, local businesses owned by one individual to large companies such as Unilever and Carrefour that are owned by thousands of stockholders. There are also employment opportunities with local and national governments and with charitable organisations such as the Red Cross and Save the Children.

To click your career into high gear, you can use online networking to advance your career. Web sites like Facebook, Twitter, LinkedIn, and other social media sites can help you locate job openings, help prospective employers to find you, and make a good impression on current and future bosses. To make the most of online networking, begin by identifying and joining sites where you can connect with potential employers, former classmates, and others who may have or may hear of job openings. Next, be sure your online profiles, photographs, and posts communicate your abilities and interests without being offensive or overly revealing. Finally, be ready to respond quickly when you spot a job opening.

One thing to remember as you think about what your ideal career might be is that a person's choice of a career ultimately is just a reflection of what he or she values and holds most important. What will give one individual personal satisfaction may not satisfy another. For example, one person may dream of a career as a corporate executive and becoming a millionaire before the age of 30. Another may choose a career that has more modest monetary rewards but that provides the opportunity to help others. What you choose to do with your life will be based on what you feel is most important. And *you* are a very important part of that decision.

To be a successful employee Deciding on the type of career you want is only the first step. To get a job in your chosen field and to be successful at it, you will have to develop a plan, or a road map, that ensures that you have the skills and knowledge the job requires. You will also be expected to have the ability to work well with many types of people in a culturally diverse workforce. **Cultural (or workplace) diversity** refers to the differences among people in a workforce owing to race, ethnicity, and gender. These skills, together with a working knowledge of accepted business practices, both locally further afield, and an appreciation for a culturally diverse workplace, can give you an inside edge when you are being interviewed by a prospective employer.

cultural (or workplace) diversity differences among people in a workforce owing to race, ethnicity, and gender

This text, your lecturer, and all of the resources available at your university can help you to acquire the skills and knowledge you will need for a successful career. But do not underestimate your part in making your dream a reality. In addition to the job-related skills and knowledge you'll need to be successful in a specific job, employers will also look for the following characteristics when hiring a new employee or promoting an existing employee:

 Honesty and integrity
● Willingness to work hard

SUCCESS STORY

The rise of Africa

© KATHY DEWITT / ALAMY

The demand for consumer products is growing exponentially in Africa and for companies around the world, Africa's attractiveness is increasing. The continent has survived the global downturn well and is growing faster than most non-BRIC emerging markets (BRIC stands for Brazil, Russia, India and China, with South Africa later being added to form BRICS). It is therefore no wonder that this enormous growth opportunity is attracting global companies such as Intel. Marcin Hejka, the EMEA Managing Director for Intel believes that "Africa will produce billion-dollar companies in the next ten years" and is "very confident in the growth in the continent".

Walmart, the biggest retailer in the world, has also been convinced by the lucrative opportunities available in Africa. It acquired a 51% stake in Massmart, a company with a strong presence of wholesale and retail stores in South Africa and in 13 other countries in Africa. This partnership will enhance Massmart's ability to reach more middle-class consumers in Africa, will provide a starting point for Walmart to increase its presence in a fast-growing emerging market and will likely signal to other foreign companies the accessibility of African markets. For African price-conscious consumers, this may translate into lower prices, as few retailers in the world could hope to compete with Walmart's well-known strengths in volume-based low pricing and logistics of suppliers and distribution.

Entering or expanding a business in Africa may seem difficult because of the continent's diverse nature. But Africa, in particular South Africa, may not be much more challenging than most other emerging markets. As growth in other developing markets appears to be slowing down, South Africa may be the "next best place on Earth" to explore new growth opportunities.

- Dependability
- Time management skills
- Self-confidence
- Motivation
- Willingness to learn
- Communication skills
- Professionalism

Employers will also be interested in any relevant work experience you may have had, internships or part-time jobs during the academic year. These things can make a difference when it is time to apply for the job you really want.

To improve your management skills   Often, employees become managers or supervisors. In fact, many employees want to become managers because managers often receive higher salaries. Although management obviously can be a rewarding career, what is not so obvious is the amount of time and hard work needed to achieve the higher salaries. For starters, employers expect more from managers and supervisors than ever before. Typically, the heavy workload requires that managers work long hours, and most do not get paid overtime. They also face increased problems created by the economic crisis, increased competition, employee downsizing, the quest for improved quality, and the need for efficient use of the firm's resources.

To be an effective manager, managers must be able to perform four basic management functions: planning, organising, leading and motivating, and controlling. To successfully perform these management functions, managers must possess four very important skills.

- *Interpersonal skills*—The ability to deal effectively with individual employees, other managers within the firm, and people outside the firm.
- *Analytic skills*—The ability to identify problems correctly, generate reasonable alternatives, and select the "best" alternatives to solve problems.
- *Technical skills*—The skill required to accomplish a specific kind of work being done in an organisation. Although managers may not actually perform the technical tasks, they should be able to train employees and answer technical questions.
- *Conceptual skills*—The ability to think in abstract terms in order to see the "big picture." Conceptual skills help managers understand how the various parts of an organisation or idea can fit together.

In addition to the four skills just described, a successful manager will need many of the same characteristics that an employee needs to be successful.

To start your own business Some people prefer to work for themselves, and they open their own businesses. To be successful, business owners must possess many of the same characteristics that successful employees have, and they must be willing to work hard and put in long hours.

It also helps if your small business can provide a product or service that customers want. For example, Steve Demeter, the CEO and founder of the software development firm Demiforce, began his career by creating the *Trism* application for the Apple iPhone. *Trism* was an immediate sensation and sold 50,000 copies at $4.99 in its first two months on Apple's AppStore. Now Demeter and the employees at Demiforce are working with a number of promising ideas in the works all with one goal in mind: to provide games and applications that people want.*

Unfortunately, many small-business firms fail: Approximately 70 per cent of them fail within the first ten years. Typical reasons for business failures include undercapitalisation (not enough money), poor business location, poor customer service, unqualified or untrained employees, fraud, lack of a proper business plan, and failure to seek outside professional help. Selected topics and examples throughout this text will help you to decide whether you want to open your own business. This material will also help you to overcome many of these problems.

To become a better informed consumer and investor The world of business surrounds us. You cannot buy a home, a new Volkswagen Polo Vivo, a pair of jeans at Gap Inc., or a fresh kebab from a street vendor without entering a business transaction. Because you no doubt will engage in business transactions almost every day of your life, one very good reason for studying business is to become a more fully informed consumer.

Many people also rely on a basic understanding of business to help them to invest for the future. According to Julie Stav, Hispanic stockbroker-turned-author/radio personality, "Take $25, add to it drive plus determination and then watch it multiply into an empire."* The author of *Get Your Share* believes that it is important to learn the basics about the economy and business, stocks, mutual funds, and other alternatives before investing your money. She also believes that it is never too early to start investing. Although this is an obvious conclusion, just dreaming of being rich does not make it happen. In fact, like many facets of life, it takes planning and determination to establish the type of investment programme that will help you to accomplish your financial goals.

BUSINESS: A DEFINITION

Business is the organised effort of individuals to produce and sell, for a profit, the goods and services that satisfy society's needs. The general term *business* refers to all such efforts within a society (as in "European business"). However, *a business* is a particular organisation, such as Nestlé S.A. or the Carrefour supermarket chain. To be successful, a business must perform three activities. It must be organised, it must satisfy needs, and it must earn a profit.

business the organised effort of individuals to produce and sell, for a profit, the goods and services that satisfy
   society's needs

The organised effort of individuals

For a business to be organised, it must combine four kinds of resources: material, human, financial, and informational. *Material* resources include the raw materials used in manufacturing processes as well as buildings and machinery. For example, Nestlé needs flour, sugar, butter, eggs, and other raw materials to produce the food products it sells worldwide. In addition, this Swiss company needs human, financial, and informational resources. *Human* resources are the people who furnish their labour to the business in return for wages. The *financial* resource is the money required to pay employees, purchase materials, and generally keep the business operating. *Information* is the resource that tells the managers of the business how effectively the other three resources are being combined and used (see Figure 1.2).

FIGURE 1.2

Combining resources *A business must combine all four resources effectively to be successful.*

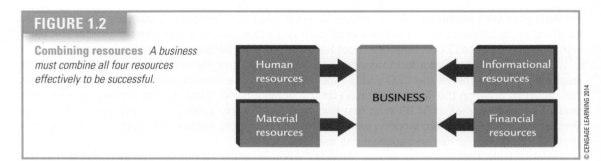

© CENGAGE LEARNING 2014

Today, businesses are usually organised as one of three specific types. *Service businesses* produce services, such as haircuts, legal advice, or tax preparation. *Manufacturing businesses* process various materials into tangible goods, such as delivery lorries, towels, or computers. Intel, for example, produces computer chips that, in turn, are sold to companies that manufacture computers. Finally, some firms called *marketing intermediaries* buy products from manufacturers and then resell them. Sony Corporation is a manufacturer that produces stereo equipment, televisions, and other electronic products. These products may be sold to a marketing intermediary such as Carrefour or Makro, which then resells the manufactured goods to consumers in their retail stores.

Satisfying needs

The ultimate objective of every firm must be to satisfy the needs of its customers. People generally do not buy goods and services simply to own them; they buy goods and services to satisfy particular needs. Some of us may feel that the need for transportation is best satisfied by an air-conditioned BMW with navigation system, stereo system, heated and cooled seats, automatic transmission, power windows, and remote-control side mirrors. Others may believe that a manual Peugeot 307 will

Organisation when it counts. Imagine what would happen if the medical professionals in a hospital operating room weren't organised— especially if you were the patient. Like a surgical operating room, a business must be organised in order to meet the needs of its customers and earn a profit.

© ANTON GVZDIKOV/SHUTTERSTOCK

do just fine. Both products are available to those who want them, along with a wide variety of other products that satisfy the need for transportation.

When firms lose sight of their customers' needs, they are likely to find the going rough. However, when businesses understand their customers' needs and work to satisfy those needs, they are usually successful. Back in 1962, Sam Walton opened his first discount store in Arkansas, in the U.S. Although the original store was quite different from the Walmart Superstores you see today, the basic ideas of providing customer service and offering goods that satisfied needs at low prices are part of the reason why this firm has grown to become the largest retailer in the world. Although Walmart has over 10,000 stores across 28 countries, this highly successful discount-store organisation continues to open new stores to meet the needs of its customers around the globe.*

Business profit

A business receives money (sales revenue) from its customers in exchange for goods or services. It must also pay out money to cover the expenses involved in doing business. If the firm's sales revenues are greater than its expenses, it has earned a profit. More specifically, as shown in Figure 1.3, **profit** is what remains after all business expenses have been deducted from sales revenue.

profit what remains after all business expenses have been deducted from sales revenue

FIGURE 1.3

The relationship between sales revenue and profit *Profit is what remains after all business expenses have been deducted from sales revenue.*

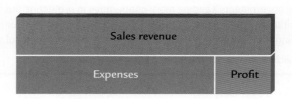

© CENGAGE LEARNING 2014

A negative profit, which results when a firm's expenses are greater than its sales revenue, is called a *loss*. A business cannot continue to operate at a loss for an indefinite period of time. Management and employees must find some way to increase sales revenues and reduce expenses to return to profitability. If some specific actions are not taken to eliminate losses, a firm may be forced to close its doors or file for bankruptcy protection. Although many people—especially stockholders and business owners—believe that profit is literally the bottom line or most important goal for a business, many stakeholders may be just as concerned about a firm's social responsibility record. The term **stakeholders** is used to describe all the different people or groups of people who are affected by the policies, decisions, and activities made by an organisation. Many corporations, for example, are careful to point out their efforts to sustain the planet, participate in the green ecological movement, and help people to live better lives in an annual social responsibility report. In its 86-page social responsibility report, General Mills describes how it contributed $100 million in 2010—a 10 per cent increase when compared to 2009—to a wide variety of causes, including support for programmes that feed the hungry and non-profit organisations in the United States and around the globe.* Although stockholders and business owners sometimes argue that the money that a business contributes to charitable causes could have been used to pay larger dividends to stockholders or increase the return on the owners' investment, the fact is that most socially responsible business firms feel social responsibility is the right thing to do and is good for business.

stakeholders all the different people or groups of people who are affected by the policies and decisions made by an organisation

RESPONSIBLE PRACTICE   Green is good for business

The concept of sustainability implies that businesses responsibly attempt to satisfy consumers' wants and needs without impairing future generations' ability to do the same. Once a mere trendy buzzword for developing greener business practices, "green" social responsibility is now becoming part of the very "DNA" of global corporations worldwide. Previously, sustainability efforts have been viewed with suspicion but nowadays, with stricter environmental regulations, green thinking is becoming essential to global companies that wish to remain competitive.

Firstly, there are considerable cost savings to be gained by introducing innovative measures to make products and production processes more "green". A leading potato chip maker in England adopted an interesting strategy by encouraging its potato growers to water their potatoes less frequently, thereby making the potatoes less expensive to transport, and even faster to bake. This resulted in a cost saving in growing and shipping the product, an environmentally-friendly reduction in water consumption and a streamlining of the company's production process.

Furthermore, creating new markets in industrialised countries is proving less effective than seeking out new markets in developing countries. When Unilever's efforts in India help grow women-owned micro-businesses, or its markets in Bangladesh enjoy free health care from floating clinics or potential consumers in Ghana enjoy clean water, this becomes part of the company's strategy to gain a sustainable competitive advantage in developing countries.

Managers worldwide now see various other benefits from pursuing sustainability strategies. Such strategies may help avert environmental catastrophes, as companies such as Shell in Nigeria or BP on the U.S. Gulf Coast had to deal with. Relations with foreign governments can also improve; GlaxoSmithKline found that their efforts in introducing low-priced drugs for developing markets had the parallel benefit of having those governments become more cooperative in protecting the company's patents there.

Analysts often point at the relationship between sustainability practices and management quality, arguing that green corporations are more likely to successfully compete in today's global markets.

References: B. Verhage (2014) *Marketing: A Global Perspective*

The profit earned by a business becomes the property of its owners. Thus, in one sense, profit is the reward business owners receive for producing goods and services that customers want. Profit is also the payment that business owners receive for assuming the considerable risks of business ownership. One of these is the risk of not being paid. Everyone else—employees, suppliers, and lenders—must be paid before the owners.

A second risk that owners undertake is the risk of losing whatever they have invested into the business. A business that cannot earn a profit is very likely to fail, in which case the owners lose whatever money, effort, and time they have invested.

To satisfy society's needs and make a profit, a business must operate within the parameters of a nation's economic system. In the next section, we define economics and describe two different types of economic systems.

TYPES OF ECONOMIC SYSTEMS

Economics is the study of how wealth is created and distributed. By *wealth,* we mean "anything of value," including the goods and services produced and sold by business. *How wealth is distributed* simply means "who gets what." Experts often use economics to explain the choices we make and how these choices change as we cope with the demands of everyday life. In simple terms, individuals, businesses, governments, and society must make decisions that reflect what is important to each group at a particular time. For example, suppose you want to take a weekend trip to some exotic holiday spot, and you also want to begin an investment programme. Because of your financial resources, though, you cannot do both, so you must decide what is most important. Business firms, governments, and to some extent society face the same types of decisions. Each group must deal with scarcity when making important decisions. In this case, *scarcity* means "lack of resources"—money, time, natural resources, and so on—that are needed to satisfy a want or need.

economics the study of how wealth is created and distributed

Today, experts often study economic problems from two different perspectives: microeconomics and macroeconomics. **Microeconomics** is the study of the decisions made by individuals and businesses. Microeconomics, for example, examines how the prices of homes affect the number of homes individuals will buy. On the other hand, **macroeconomics** is the study of the national economy and the global economy. Macroeconomics examines the economic effect of national income, unemployment, inflation, taxes, government spending, interest rates, and similar factors on a nation and society.

microeconomics the study of the decisions made by individuals and businesses
macroeconomics the study of the national economy and the global economy

The decisions that individuals, business firms, government, and society make, and the way in which people deal with the creation and distribution of wealth determine the kind of economic system, or **economy**, that a nation has.

economy the way in which people deal with the creation and distribution of wealth

Over the years, the economic systems of the world have differed in essentially two ways: (1) the ownership of the factors of production and (2) how they answer four basic economic questions that direct a nation's economic activity.

Factors of production are the resources used to produce goods and services. There are four such factors:

factors of production resources used to produce goods and services

- *Land and natural resources*—elements that can be used in the production process to make appliances, automobiles, and other products. Typical examples include crude oil, forests, minerals, land, water, and even air.
- *Labour*—the time and effort that we use to produce goods and services. It includes human resources such as managers and employees.
- *Capital*—the money, facilities, equipment, and machines used in the operation of organisations. Although most people think of capital as just money, it can also be the manufacturing equipment in a Pepperidge Farm production facility or a computer used in the corporate offices of McDonald's.

© MICHAEL RUBIN/SHUTTERSTOCK

Saving natural resources one bus at a time. *"Green" has taken on a whole new meaning. For consumers, the government, and businesses, green means a new way to save natural resources, to protect the environment, and often to reduce our dependence on oil from foreign countries.*

- *Entrepreneurship*—the activity that organises land, labour, and capital. It is the willingness to take risks and the knowledge and ability to use the other factors of production efficiently. An **entrepreneur** is a person who risks his or her time, effort, and money to start and operate a business.

> **entrepreneur** a person who risks time, effort, and money to start and operate a business

A nation's economic system significantly affects all the economic activities of its citizens and organisations. This far-reaching impact becomes more apparent when we consider that a country's economic system determines how the factors of production are used to meet the needs of society. Today, two different economic systems exist: capitalism and command economies. The way each system answers the four basic economic questions listed here determines a nation's economy.

1. *What* goods and services—and how much of each—will be produced?
2. *How* will these goods and services be produced?
3. *For whom* will these goods and services be produced?
4. *Who* owns and who controls the major factors of production?

Capitalism

Capitalism is an economic system in which individuals own and operate the majority of businesses that provide goods and services. Capitalism stems from the theories of the 18th-century Scottish economist Adam Smith. In his book *Wealth of Nations*, published in 1776, Smith argued that a society's interests are best served when the individuals within that society are allowed to pursue their own self-interest. According to Smith, when individuals act to improve their own fortunes, they indirectly promote the good of their community and the people in that community. Smith went on to call this concept the "invisible hand." The **invisible hand** is a term created by Adam Smith to describe how an individual's own personal gain benefits others and a nation's economy. For example, the only way a small-business owner who produces shoes can increase personal wealth is to sell shoes to customers. To become even more prosperous, the small-business owner must hire workers to produce even more shoes. According to the invisible hand, people in the small-business owner's community not only would have shoes but also would have jobs working for the shoemaker. Thus, the success of people in the community and, to some extent, the nation's economy is tied indirectly to the success of the small-business owner.

> **capitalism** an economic system in which individuals own and operate the majority of businesses that provide goods and services
>
> **invisible hand** a term created by Adam Smith to describe how an individual's personal gain benefits others and a nation's economy

Adam Smith's capitalism is based on the following fundamental issues—also see Figure 1.4.

1. The creation of wealth is properly the concern of private individuals, not the government.
2. Private individuals must own private property and the resources used to create wealth.
3. Economic freedom ensures the existence of competitive markets that allow both sellers and buyers to enter and exit the market as they choose.
4. The role of government should be limited to providing defence against foreign enemies, ensuring internal order, and furnishing public works and education.

One factor that Smith felt was extremely important was the role of government. He believed that government should act only as rule maker and umpire. The French term *laissez faire* describes Smith's capitalistic system and implies that there should be no government interference in the economy. Loosely translated, this term means "let them do" (as they see fit).

Adam Smith's laissez-faire capitalism is also based on the concept of a market economy. A **market economy** (sometimes referred to as a *free-market economy*) is an economic system in which

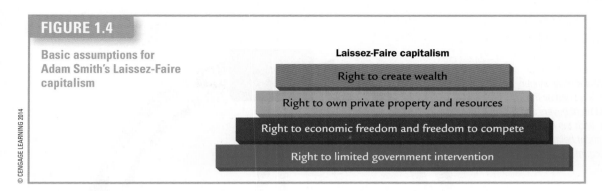

FIGURE 1.4

Basic assumptions for
Adam Smith's Laissez-Faire
capitalism

Laissez-Faire capitalism

Right to create wealth

Right to own private property and resources

Right to economic freedom and freedom to compete

Right to limited government intervention

© CENGAGE LEARNING 2014

businesses and individuals decide what to produce and buy, and the market determines prices and quantities sold. The owners of resources should be free to determine how these resources are used and also to enjoy the income, profits, and other benefits derived from ownership of these resources.

> **market economy** an economic system in which businesses and individuals decide what to produce and buy, and the market determines quantities sold and prices

Capitalism throughout the world

The capitalist economic system is rooted in the laissez-faire capitalism of Adam Smith. However, in practise the real-world economy is not as laissez-faire as Smith would have liked because governments participate as more than umpires and rule makers. Countries such as the United Kingdom, the United States and South Africa, for example, are all considered to have a **mixed economy**, one that exhibits elements of both capitalism and socialism.

> **mixed economy** an economy that exhibits elements of both capitalism and socialism

In a mixed economy, the four basic economic questions discussed at the beginning of this section (*what, how, for whom,* and *who*) are answered through the interaction of households, businesses, and governments. The interactions among these three groups are shown in Figure 1.5.

© KATHERINE WELLES/SHUTTERSTOCK

An apple a day . . . *Regarded as one of the most successful and profitable businesses in the very competitive technology industry, Apple has a history of introducing state-of-the-art consumer products like the iPhone and iPad. Although there are many ways to obtain Apple products, one way to "try out" the latest products is to visit one of their retail stores.*

FIGURE 1.5

The circular flow in a mixed economy
The "Western" economic system is guided by the interaction of buyers and sellers, with the role of government being taken into account.

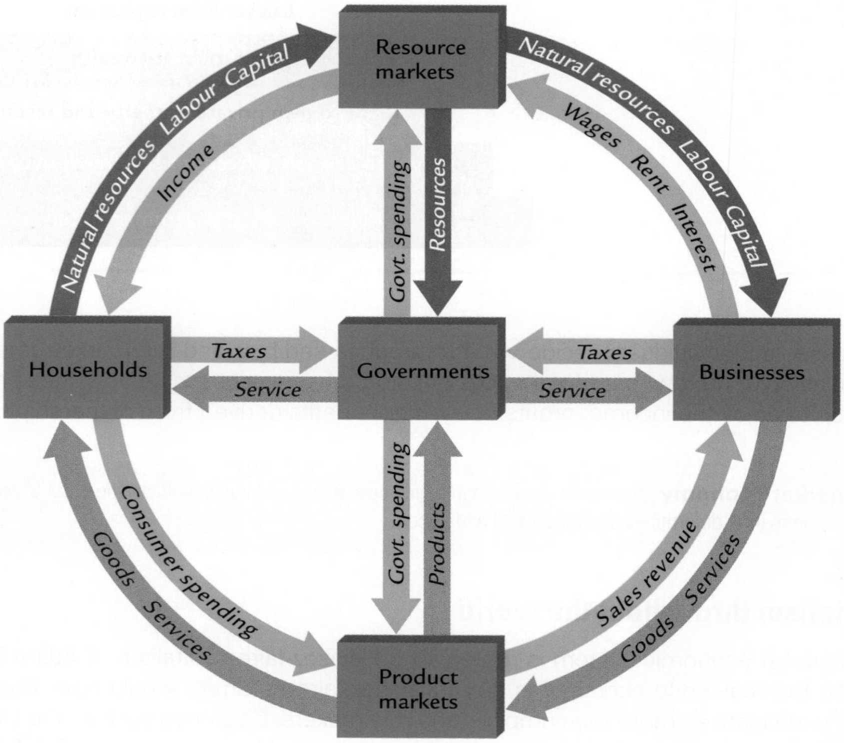

© CENGAGE LEARNING 2014

Households   Households, made up of individuals, are the consumers of goods and services as well as owners of some of the factors of production. As *resource owners,* the members of households provide businesses with labour, capital, and other resources. In return, businesses pay wages, rent, and dividends and interest, which households receive as income.

As *consumers,* household members use their income to purchase the goods and services produced by business. Today, approximately 70 per cent of total production in the U.S. consists of **consumer products**—goods and services purchased by individuals for personal consumption.* This means that consumers, as a group, are the biggest customers of American business. In other countries which are rich in natural minerals, such as South Africa, the extraction, processing and export of raw materials, including gold, diamonds, chrome and manganese, accounts for a significant proportion of business.

> **consumer products** goods and services purchased by individuals for personal consumption

Businesses   Like households, businesses are engaged in two different exchanges. They exchange money for natural resources, labour, and capital and use these resources to produce goods and services. Then they exchange their goods and services for sales revenue. This sales revenue, in turn, is exchanged for additional resources, which are used to produce and sell more goods and services.

Along the way, of course, business owners would like to remove something from the circular flow in the form of profits. When business profits are distributed to business owners, these profits become household income. (Business owners are, after all, members of households.) Households try to retain some income as savings. But are profits and savings really removed from the flow?

Usually not! When the economy is running smoothly, households are willing to invest their savings in businesses. They can do so directly by buying stocks issued by businesses, by purchasing shares in mutual funds that purchase stocks in businesses, or by lending money to businesses. They can also invest indirectly by placing their savings in bank accounts. Banks and other financial institutions then invest these savings as part of their normal business operations. Thus, business profits, too, are retained in the business system, and the circular flow in Figure 1.5 is complete. How, then, does government fit in?

Governments   It is the responsibility of a country's government to protect and promote public welfare, and the numerous government services are important. Typical services include national defence, police, fire protection, education, the construction and maintenance of roads, and, in some nations such as the U.K., a National Health Service. To pay for all these services, governments collect a variety of taxes from households (such as personal income taxes and sales taxes) and from businesses (corporate income taxes).

Figure 1.5 shows this exchange of taxes for government services. It also shows government spending of tax revenues for resources and products required to provide these services.

Actually, with government included, the circular flow looks more like a combination of several flows. In reality, it is. The important point is that together the various flows make up a single unit—a complete economic system that effectively provides answers to the basic economic questions. Simply put, the system works.

Command economies

Before we discuss how to measure a nation's economic performance, we look quickly at another economic system called a command economy. A **command economy** is an economic system in which the government decides *what* goods and services will be produced, *how* they will be produced, *for whom* available goods and services will be produced, and *who* owns and controls the major factors of production. The answers to all four basic economic questions are determined, at least to some degree, through centralised government planning. Today, two types of economic systems—*socialism* and *communism*—serve as examples of command economies.

> **command economy** an economic system in which the government decides what goods and services will be produced, how they will be produced, for whom available goods and services will be produced, and who owns and controls the major factors of production

Socialism   In a socialist economy, the key industries are owned and controlled by the government. Such industries usually include transportation, utilities, communications, banking, and industries producing important materials such as steel. Land, buildings, and raw materials may also be the property of the state in a socialist economy. Depending on the country, private ownership of smaller businesses is permitted to varying degrees. Usually, people may choose their own occupations, although many work in state-owned industries.

What to produce and how to produce it are determined in accordance with national goals, which are based on projected needs and the availability of resources. The distribution of goods and services—who gets what—is also controlled by the state to the extent that it controls taxes, rents, and wages. Among the professed aims of socialist countries are the equitable distribution of income, the elimination of poverty, and the distribution of social services (such as medical care) to all who need them. The disadvantages of socialism include increased taxation and loss of incentive and motivation for both individuals and business owners.

Today, many of the nations that have been labelled as socialist nations traditionally, including France, Sweden, and India, are transitioning to a free-market economy. Currently, many countries that were once thought of as communist countries are now often referred to as socialist countries. Examples of former communist countries often referred to as socialists (or even capitalists) include most of the nations that were formerly part of the Union of Soviet Socialist Republics, China, and Vietnam.

Communism   If Adam Smith was the father of capitalism, Karl Marx was the father of communism. In his writings during the mid-19th century, Marx advocated a classless society whose citizens together owned all economic resources. All workers would then contribute to this *communist* society according to their ability and would receive benefits according to their need.

Since the breakup of the Soviet Union and economic reforms in China and most of the Eastern European countries, the most prevalent remaining examples of communism are North Korea and Cuba. Today these so-called communist economies seem to practice a strictly controlled kind of socialism. The basic four economic questions are answered through centralised government plans. Emphasis is placed on the production of goods the government needs rather than on the products that consumers might want, so there are frequent shortages of consumer goods. Workers have little choice of jobs, but special skills or talents seem to be rewarded with special privileges.

MEASURING ECONOMIC PERFORMANCE

Today, it is hard to turn on the radio, watch the news on television, use the Internet, or read the newspaper without hearing or seeing something about the economy. Consider for just a moment the following questions:

- Is the gross domestic product of your country of residence increasing or decreasing?
- Why is the unemployment rate important?
- Are workers there as productive as workers in other countries?

The information needed to answer these questions, along with the answers to other similar questions, is easily obtainable from many sources. More importantly, the answers to these and other questions can be used to gauge the economic health of the nation. For individuals, the health of a nation's economy can affect:

- the financing you need to continue your education;
- your ability to get a job; and
- the amount of interest you pay for credit card purchases, automobiles, homes, and other credit transactions.

The importance of productivity in the global marketplace

One way to measure a nation's economic performance is to assess its productivity. **Productivity** is the average level of output per worker per hour. An increase in productivity results in economic growth because a larger number of goods and services are produced by a given labour force. To see how productivity affects you and the economy, consider the following three questions:

productivity the average level of output per worker per hour

One way to reduce costs is to manufacture products in a foreign country. In this photo, a Chinese worker assembles an electronic keyboard. To compete with foreign competition, manufacturers in the United States use sophisticated equipment and the latest technology to reduce costs, increase profits, and improve productivity.

© HE YUAN/EPA/LANDOV

Question: *How does productivity growth affect the economy?*

Answer: Because of increased productivity, it now takes fewer workers to produce more goods and services. As a result, employers have reduced costs, earned more profits, and sold their products for less. Finally, productivity growth helps businesses to compete internationally more effectively in a competitive world.

Question: *How does a nation improve productivity?*

Answer: Reducing costs and enabling employees to work more efficiently are at the core of all attempts to improve productivity. For example, productivity is expected to improve dramatically as more economic activity is transferred onto the Internet, reducing costs for customer service and handling routine ordering functions between businesses. Other methods that can be used to increase productivity are discussed later in the book.

Question: *Is productivity growth always good?*

Answer: Fewer workers producing more goods and services can lead to higher unemployment rates. In this case, increased productivity is good for employers but not good for unemployed workers seeking jobs in a very competitive work environment. Because employers had been able to produce more goods and services with fewer employees during the recent economic crisis, they did not want to increase the firm's salary expense by hiring new employees after the economy began to improve.

Gross domestic product

In addition to productivity, a measure called *gross domestic product* can be used to measure the economic well-being of a nation. **Gross domestic product (GDP)** is the total monetary value of all goods and services produced by all people within the boundaries of a country during a one-year period. For example, the values of motorcars produced by employees in an German-owned BMW plant and a U.S.-owned Ford factory in Germany are both included in the GDP for Germany. The U.S. GDP was $15.1 trillion in 2011.*

> **gross domestic product (GDP)** the total unit value of all goods and services produced by all people within the boundaries of a country during a one-year period

The GDP figure facilitates comparisons between one country and another because it is the standard used in international guidelines for economic accounting. It is also possible to compare the GDP for one nation over several different time periods. This comparison allows observers to determine the extent to which a nation is experiencing economic growth.

To make accurate comparisons of the GDP for different years, we must adjust the dollar amounts for inflation. **Inflation** is a general rise in the level of prices. (The opposite of inflation is deflation.) **Deflation** is a general decrease in the level of prices. By using inflation-adjusted figures, we are able to measure the *real* GDP for a nation. In effect, it is now possible to compare the products and services produced by a nation in constant dollars—dollars that will purchase the same amount of goods and services. Figure 1.6 depicts the GDP of the United States in current dollars and the real GDP in inflation-adjusted dollars. Note that between 1990 and 2011, America's real GDP grew from $8 trillion to $13.3 trillion.*

> **inflation** a general rise in the level of prices
> **deflation** a general decrease in the level of prices

Important economic indicators that measure a nation's economy

In addition to productivity, GDP, and real GDP, other economic measures exist that can be used to evaluate a nation's economy. Because of the recent economic crisis, one very important statistic

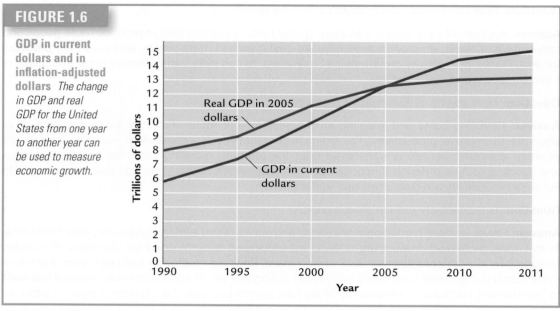

FIGURE 1.6

GDP in current dollars and in inflation-adjusted dollars *The change in GDP and real GDP for the United States from one year to another year can be used to measure economic growth.*

Source: U.S. Bureau of Economic Analysis Web site at www.bea.gov (accessed January 30, 2012).

that is in the news on a regular basis is the unemployment rate. The **unemployment rate** is the percentage of a nation's labour force unemployed at any time. According to the Bureau of Labour Statistics in the U.S., when workers are unemployed, they, their families, and the country as a whole lose. Workers and their families lose wages, and the country loses the goods or services that could have been produced. In addition, the purchasing power of these workers is lost, which can lead to unemployment for yet other workers.*

unemployment rate the percentage of a nation's labour force unemployed at any time

The **consumer price index (CPI)** is a monthly index that measures the changes in prices of a fixed basket of goods purchased by a typical consumer in an urban area. Goods listed in the CPI include food and beverages, transportation, housing, clothing, medical care, recreation, education, communication, and other goods and services. Economists often use the CPI to determine the effect of inflation on not only the nation's economy but also individual consumers. Another monthly index is the producer price index. The **producer price index (PPI)** measures prices that producers receive for their finished goods. Because changes in the PPI reflect price increases or decreases at the wholesale level, the PPI is an accurate predictor of both changes in the CPI and prices that consumers will pay for many everyday necessities.

consumer price index (CPI) a monthly index that measures the changes in prices of a fixed basket of goods purchased by a typical consumer in an urban area
producer price index (PPI) an index that measures prices that producers receive for their finished goods

Some additional economic measures are described in Table 1.1. Like the measures for GDP, real GDP, unemployment rate, and price indexes, these measures can be used to compare one economic statistic over different periods of time.

TABLE 1.1 Common measures used to evaluate a nation's economic health

Economic measure	Description
1. Balance of trade	The total value of a nation's exports minus the total value of its imports over a specific period of time.
2. Consumer confidence index	A measure of how optimistic or pessimistic consumers are about the nation's economy. This measure is usually reported on a monthly basis.
3. Corporate profits	The total amount of profits made by corporations over selected time periods.
4. Inflation rate	An economic statistic that tracks the increase in prices of goods and services over a period of time. This measure is usually calculated on a monthly or an annual basis.
5. National income	The total income earned by various segments of the population, including employees, self-employed individuals, corporations, and other types of income.
6. New housing starts	The total number of new homes started during a specific time period.
7. Prime interest rate	The lowest interest rate that banks charge their most credit-worthy customers.

© Cengage Learning 2014

THE BUSINESS CYCLE

All industrialised nations of the world seek economic growth, full employment, and price stability. However, a nation's economy fluctuates rather than grows at a steady pace every year. In fact, if you were to graph the economic growth rate for a nation like the United Kingdom or South Africa, it would resemble a roller coaster ride with peaks (high points) and troughs (low points). These fluctuations are generally referred to as the **business cycle**, that is, the recurrence of periods of growth and recession in a nation's economic activity. At the time of publication, many experts believed that the economy was showing signs of improvement. However, the recent economic crisis that began in the autumn of 2007 caused a recession that will require more time before the world experiences a complete recovery. Global unemployment rates are still high. People are reluctant to spend money on many consumer goods. Stock prices, although improving, are still below the record values experienced a few years ago. Although respective governments have enacted a number of stimulus plans designed to help unemployed workers, to protect banks and large firms both sides of the Atlantic, to reduce the number of home foreclosures, and to free up credit for both individuals and businesses, many experts still believe that we have serious financial problems. For many countries, the size of the national debt—a topic described later in this section—is a concern. Another problem—the inequality of income and wealth—has also become evident as a result of the Occupy Wall Street protestors and similar groups of discontented people across the globe. The recent economic crisis affected the economies of countries around the world in various ways.

business cycle the recurrence of periods of growth and recession in a nation's economic activity

During the recent economic crisis, unemployment rates were over 10 per cent and millions of workers lost their jobs. While economists still debate if we were in a recession or a depression, the global economy is now improving and the unemployment rate is beginning to decline.

© LUNA VANDOORNE / SHUTTERSTOCK

The changes that result from either economic growth or economic downturn affect the amount of products and services that consumers are willing to purchase and, as a result, the amount of products and services produced by business firms. Generally, the business cycle consists of four phases: the peak (sometimes called prosperity), recession, the trough, and recovery (sometimes called expansion).

During the *peak period* (prosperity), the economy is at its highest point and unemployment is low. Total income is relatively high. As long as the economic outlook remains prosperous, consumers are willing to buy products and services. In fact, businesses often expand and offer new products and services during the peak period to take advantage of consumers' increased buying power.

Generally, economists define a **recession** as two or more consecutive three-month periods of decline in a country's GDP. Because unemployment rises during a recession, total buying power declines. The pessimism that accompanies a recession often stifles both consumer and business spending. As buying power decreases, consumers tend to become more value conscious and reluctant to purchase frivolous or nonessential items. And companies and government at all levels often postpone or go slow on major projects during a recession. In response to a recession, many businesses focus on producing the products and services that provide the most value to their customers. And yet, there are still opportunities out there for business firms that are well managed and provide goods and services that their customers need. For example, Caterpillar, a global company that produces earth moving and construction equipment has profited from the ongoing building boom in developing nations, where many basic infrastructure improvements move ahead regardless of what the economic conditions are in the rest of the world.

 recession two or more consecutive three-month periods of decline in a country's GDP

Economists define a **depression** as a severe recession that lasts longer than a typical recession and has a larger decline in business activity when compared to a recession. A depression is characterised by extremely high unemployment rates, low wages, reduced purchasing power, lack of confidence in the economy, lower stock values, and a general decrease in business activity.

 depression a severe recession that lasts longer than a typical recession and has a larger decline in business activity when compared to a recession

The third phase of the business cycle is the *trough*. The trough of a recession or depression is the turning point when a nation's production and employment bottom out and reach their lowest levels. To offset the effects of recession and depression, governments can use both monetary and fiscal policies. **Monetary policies** are the decisions that determine the size of the supply of money in the nation and the level of interest rates. Through **fiscal policy**, a government can influence the amount of savings and expenditures by altering the tax structure and changing the levels of government spending.

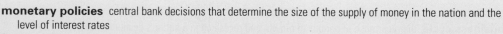 **monetary policies** central bank decisions that determine the size of the supply of money in the nation and the level of interest rates
fiscal policy government influence on the amount of savings and expenditures; accomplished by altering the tax structure and by changing the levels of government spending

Since World War II, business cycles have lasted from three to five years from one peak period to the next peak period. During the same time period, the average length of recessions has been 11 months.* Some experts believe that effective use of monetary and fiscal policies can speed up recovery and reduce the amount of time the economy is in recession. *Recovery* (or *expansion*) is the movement of the economy from recession or depression to prosperity. High unemployment rates decline, income increases, and both the ability and the willingness to buy rise.

Unfortunately, many of the problems that caused the recent economic crisis are still there, and they will take years to correct and resolve.

TYPES OF COMPETITION

The capitalist system ensures that individuals and businesses make the decisions about what to produce, how to produce it, and what price to charge for the product. The Lego Group of Denmark, for instance, can introduce new sets of its famous Lego toy construction bricks, license the Lego name (for example, to computer game developers), change their pricing strategies and method of distribution, and attempt to produce and market Lego in other countries or over the Internet. This system also allows customers the right to choose between Lego products and those produced by competitors.

As a consumer, you get to choose which products or services you want to buy. Competition like that between Lego and other toy manufacturers is a necessary and extremely important by-product of capitalism. Business **competition** is essentially a rivalry among businesses for sales to potential customers. In a capitalistic economy, competition also ensures that a firm will survive only if it serves its customers well by providing products and services that meet needs. Economists recognise four different degrees of competition ranging from ideal, complete competition to no competition at all. These are perfect competition, monopolistic competition, oligopoly, and monopoly. For a quick overview of the different types of competition, including numbers of firms and examples for each type, look at Table 1.2.

competition rivalry among businesses for sales to potential customers

Perfect competition

Perfect (or pure) competition is the market situation in which there are many buyers and sellers of a product, and no single buyer or seller is powerful enough to affect the price of that product. For perfect competition to exist, there are five very important concepts.

perfect (or pure) competition the market situation in which there are many buyers and sellers of a product, and no single buyer or seller is powerful enough to affect the price of that product

Competition often gives consumers a choice. *Different manufacturers use product differentiation to develop and promote the differences between their products and all similar products. Not only does product differentiation help their products stand out from the competition, it gives you—the consumer—a choice.*

© MONKEY BUSINESS IMAGES / SHUTTERSTOCK

TABLE 1.2 **Four different types of competition** *The number of firms determines the degree of competition within an industry.*

Type of competition	Number of business firms or suppliers	Real-world examples
1. Perfect	Many	Maize, wheat, peanuts
2. Monopolistic	Many	Clothing, shoes
3. Oligopoly	Few	Automobiles, cereals
4. Monopoly	One	Software protected by copyright, many local public utilities

© Cengage Learning 2014

- We are discussing the market for a single product, such as bushels of wheat.
- There are no restrictions on firms entering the industry.
- All sellers offer essentially the same product for sale.
- All buyers and sellers know everything there is to know about the market (including, in our example, the prices that all sellers are asking for their wheat).
- The overall market is not affected by the actions of any one buyer or seller.

When perfect competition exists, every seller should ask the same price that every other seller is asking. Why? Because if one seller wanted 50 cents more per bushel of wheat than all the others, that seller would not be able to sell a single bushel. Buyers could—and would—do better by purchasing wheat from the competition. On the other hand, a firm willing to sell below the going price would sell all its wheat quickly. However, that seller would lose sales revenue (and profit) because buyers are actually willing to pay more.

In perfect competition, then, sellers—and buyers as well—must accept the going price. The price of each product is determined by the actions of all buyers and all sellers together through the forces of supply and demand.

The basics of supply and demand   The **supply** of a particular product is the quantity of the product that producers are willing to sell at each of various prices. Producers are rational people, so we would expect them to offer more of a product for sale at higher prices and to offer less of the product at lower prices, as illustrated by the supply curve in Figure 1.7.

> **supply** the quantity of a product that producers are willing to sell at each of various prices

The **demand** for a particular product is the quantity that buyers are willing to purchase at each of various prices. Buyers, too, are usually rational, so we would expect them—as a group—to buy more of a product when its price is low and to buy less of the product when its price is high, as depicted by the demand curve in Figure 1.7.

> **demand** the quantity of a product that buyers are willing to purchase at each of various prices

The equilibrium, or market, price   There is always one certain price at which the demand for a product is exactly equal to the quantity of that product produced. Suppose that producers are willing to *supply* two million bushels of wheat at a price of $7 per bushel and that buyers are willing to *purchase* two million bushels at a price of $7 per bushel. In other words, supply and demand are in balance, or in equilibrium, at the price of $7. Economists call this price the *market price*. The **market price** of any product is the price at which the quantity demanded is exactly equal to the quantity supplied.

> **market price** the price at which the quantity demanded is exactly equal to the quantity supplied

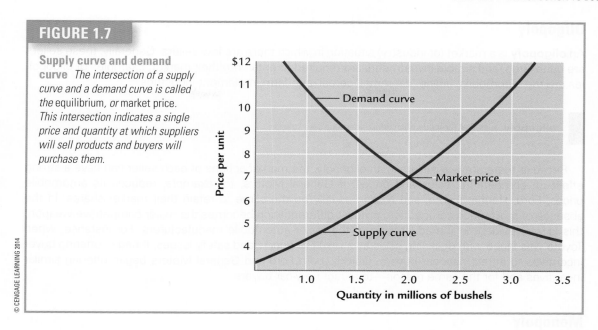

FIGURE 1.7

Supply curve and demand curve *The intersection of a supply curve and a demand curve is called the* equilibrium, *or* market price. *This intersection indicates a single price and quantity at which suppliers will sell products and buyers will purchase them.*

In theory and in the real world, market prices are affected by anything that affects supply and demand. The *demand* for wheat, for example, might change if researchers suddenly discovered that it offered a previously unknown health benefit. Then buyers would demand more wheat at every price. Or the *supply* of wheat might change if new technology permitted the production of greater quantities of wheat from the same amount of acreage. Other changes that can affect competitive prices are shifts in buyer tastes, the development of new products, fluctuations in income owing to inflation or recession, or even changes in the weather that affect the production of wheat.

Perfect competition is quite rare in today's world. Many real markets, however, are examples of monopolistic competition.

Monopolistic competition

Monopolistic competition is a market situation in which there are many buyers along with a relatively large number of sellers. The various products available in a monopolistically competitive market are very similar in nature, and they are all intended to satisfy the same need. However, each seller attempts to make its product different from the others by providing unique product features, an attention-getting brand name, unique packaging, or services such as free delivery or a lifetime warranty.

> **monopolistic competition** a market situation in which there are many buyers along with a relatively large number of sellers who differentiate their products from the products of competitors

Product differentiation is the process of developing and promoting differences between one's products and all competitive products. It is a fact of life for the producers of many consumer goods, from soaps to clothing to furniture to shoes. A furniture manufacturer such as Thomasville sees what looks like a mob of competitors, all trying to chip away at its share of the market. By differentiating each of its products from all similar products produced by competitors, Thomasville obtains some limited control over the market price of its product.

> **product differentiation** the process of developing and promoting differences between one's products and all competitive products

Oligopoly

An **oligopoly** is a market (or industry) situation in which there are few sellers. Generally, these sellers are quite large, and sizable investments are required to enter into their market. Examples of oligopolies are the automobile, airline, car rental, cereal, and farm implement industries.

 oligopoly a market (or industry) in which there are few sellers

Because there are few sellers in an oligopoly, the market actions of each seller can have a strong effect on competitors' sales and prices. If General Motors, for example, reduces its automobile prices, Ford, Honda, Toyota, and Nissan usually do the same to retain their market shares. In the absence of much price competition, product differentiation becomes the major competitive weapon; this is very evident in the advertising of the major automobile manufacturers. For instance, when Toyota was faced with declining sales as a result of quality and safety issues, it began offering buyer incentives to attract new-car buyers. Quickly, both Ford and General Motors began offering similar incentives and for the same reason—to attract new-car buyers.

Monopoly

A **monopoly** is a market (or industry) with only one seller, and there are barriers to keep other firms from entering the industry. In a monopoly, there is no close substitute for the product or service. Because only one firm is the supplier of a product, it would seem that it has complete control over price. However, no firm can set its price at some astronomical figure just because there is no competition; the firm would soon find that it has no customers or sales revenue either. Instead, the firm in a monopoly position must consider the demand for its product and set the price at the most profitable level.

 monopoly a market (or industry) with only one seller, and there are barriers to keep other firms from entering the industry

Classic examples of monopolies in the United States are public utilities, including companies that provide local gas, water, or electricity. Each utility firm operates in a **natural monopoly,** an industry that requires a huge investment in capital and within which any duplication of facilities would be wasteful. Natural monopolies are permitted to exist because the public interest is best served by their existence, but they operate under the scrutiny and control of various state and federal agencies. Although many public utilities are still classified as natural monopolies, there is increased competition in many areas of the country. For example, there have been increased demands for consumer choice when selecting a company that provides electrical service to both homes and businesses.

 natural monopoly an industry requiring huge investments in capital and within which any duplication of facilities would be wasteful and thus not in the public interest

A legal monopoly—sometimes referred to as a *limited monopoly*—is created when a government entity issues a franchise, license, copyright, patent, or trademark. For example, a copyright exists for a specific period of time and can be used to protect the owners of written materials from unauthorised use by competitors that have not shared in the time, effort, and expense required for their development. Because Microsoft owns the copyright on its popular Windows software, it enjoys a legal-monopoly position. Except for natural monopolies and legal monopolies, antitrust laws in several countries prohibit both monopolies and attempts to form monopolies.

BUSINESS TODAY

Standard of living is a loose, subjective measure of how well off an individual or a society is, mainly in terms of want satisfaction through goods and services.

> **standard of living** a loose, subjective measure of how well off an individual or a society is, mainly in terms of want satisfaction through goods and services

To understand the current business environment and the challenges ahead, it helps to understand how business developed.

Early business development

The capitalist business system we are familiar with has early roots. It arguably started with **bartering**, a system of exchange in which goods or services are traded directly for other goods or services without using money. There is evidence that bartering in some form was used in many ancient economies, such as Ptolemaic Egypt. Today, bartering is still in use and often takes place online (for example at barter bay).

> **barter** a system of exchange in which goods or services are traded directly for other goods or services without using money

Once trade (both internal and external) became the norm, the *domestic system* of production became popular – and still is in many countries. The **domestic system** was a method of manufacturing in which an entrepreneur distributed raw materials to various homes, where families would process them into finished goods. The merchant entrepreneur then offered the goods for sale.

> **domestic system** a method of manufacturing in which an entrepreneur distributes raw materials to various homes, where families process them into finished goods to be offered for sale by the merchant entrepreneur

In Britain, the domestic system was well suited to the textile industry. However, from the eighteenth century onwards, the **factory system** of manufacturing began to become widespread in Britain. In the factory system, all the materials, machinery and workers required to manufacture a product are assembled in one place. This system arguably saw its prototype – and first "modern factory" – in 1769 when Richard Awkwright patented the water frame and established Cromford Mill.

> **factory system** a system of manufacturing in which all the materials, machinery, and workers required to manufacture a product are assembled in one place

The Industrial Revolution had begun. Soon, a manufacturing technique called *specialisation* was used to improve productivity. **Specialisation** is the separation of a manufacturing process into distinct tasks and the assignment of the different tasks to different individuals.

> **specialisation** the separation of a manufacturing process into distinct tasks and the assignment of the different tasks to different individuals

The eighteenth and nineteenth centuries were the golden age of invention and innovation in machinery in Europe and the United States. At the same time, new means of transportation (for example, the network of canals and railways in Britain) greatly expanded the domestic markets. Certainly, many basic characteristics of our modern business system took form during this time period.

Business development in the 1900s

Industrial growth and prosperity continued well into the 20th century. The moving assembly line, which brought the work to the worker, refined the concept of specialisation and helped spur on the mass production of consumer goods. Fundamental changes occurred in business ownership and management as well. No longer were the largest businesses owned by one individual; instead, ownership was in the hands of thousands of corporate shareholders who were willing to invest in—but not to operate—a business.

Many countries were hit by an economic depression in the wake of the First World War. In the United States, the economic retreat was hindered by the depression of 1920-1921, although it began to rise throughout the twenties.

However, 1930 saw the start of the Great Depression, a severe worldwide economic depression which originated in the U.S. The majority of economic historians believe that the Great Depression only truly ended with the onset of the Second World War, when governments were forced to spend on industry and unemployment was reduced.

The global economy after the Second World War was also shaped by the following events:

- The aftermath of the Second World War up until the early 1970s saw a "long boom", particularly in Western European and East Asian countries.
- The collapse of the Bretton Woods system; oil crisis; and stock market crash of the 1970s
- The rise of many East Asian economies in the 1980s coupled with high inflation, high interest rates and reduced business profits for Western European countries
- Sustained economic growth in the 1990s

During the last part of the 20th century, the Internet became a major force in the economy. e-Business—a topic we will continue to explore throughout this text—became an accepted method of conducting business. **e-Business** is the organised effort of individuals to produce and sell *through the Internet*, for a profit, the products and services that satisfy society's needs.

 e-business the organised effort of individuals to produce and sell *through the Internet*, for a profit, the products and services that satisfy society's needs

Unfortunately, by the last part of the 20th century, a larger number of business failures and declining stock values were initial signs that larger economic problems were on the way.

A new century: 2000 and beyond

According to many economic experts, the first part of the 21st century might be characterised as "the best of times and the worst of times" rolled into one package. On the plus side, technology became available at an affordable price. Both individuals and businesses could now access information with the click of a button. They also could buy and sell merchandise online.

In addition to information technology, the growth of service businesses also changed the way firms do business in the 21st century. Because service businesses employ a large percentage of the workforce in nations such as the U.S. and the U.K., they are deemed to have a service economy.* A **service economy** is an economy in which more effort is devoted to the production of services than to the production of goods. Typical service businesses include restaurants, laundries and dry cleaners, estate agents, cinemas, repair companies, and other services that we often take for granted.

 service economy an economy in which more effort is devoted to the production of services than to the production of goods

On the negative side, it is hard to watch television, surf the Web, listen to the radio, or read the newspaper without hearing some news about the economy. Because many of the economic indicators described in Table 1.1 indicate troubling economic problems, there is still a certain amount of pessimism surrounding the economy.

The current business environment

Before reading on, answer the following question:

In today's competitive business world, which of the following environments affects business?

a. The competitive environment
b. The global environment
c. The technological environment
d. The economic environment
e. All of the above

Correct Answer: e. All the environments listed affect business today.

The competitive environment   Businesses operate in a competitive environment. As noted earlier in this chapter, competition is a basic component of capitalism. Every day, business owners must figure out what makes their businesses successful and how the goods and services they provide are different from the competition. Often, the answer is contained in the basic definition of business provided earlier. Just for a moment, review the definition:

Business is the organised effort of individuals to produce and sell, for a profit, the goods and services that satisfy society's needs.

In the definition of business, note the phrase *satisfy society's needs.* These three words say a lot about how well a successful firm competes with competitors. If you meet customer needs, then you have a better chance at success.

The global environment   Related to the competitive environment is the global environment. Not only do businesses have to compete with other domestic businesses, but they also must compete with businesses from all over the globe. According to global experts, China is one of the fastest-growing economies in the world. And China is not alone. Other countries around the world also compete with domestic firms. According to Richard Haass, president of the Council on Foreign Relations in the U.S., "There will be winners and losers from globalisation. We win every time we go shopping because prices are lower. Choice is greater because of globalisation. But there are losers. There are people who will lose their jobs either to foreign competition or [to] technological innovation."*

However, it is a two-way process. Globalisation does not only create competition; it also creates new customers. In fact there are many "potential" customers in developing nations that will buy goods and services manufactured by established domestic firms. For example, Procter & Gamble sells laundry detergent, soap, and nappies in Nigeria and has plans to do business in more than 50 African countries.* And Procter & Gamble is not alone. Unilever, DuPont, Johnson & Johnson, Philips, and many more companies are also selling goods and services to customers in countries all over the globe. The world is, in fact, a much smaller place than many business leaders once thought.

The technology environment   Although increased global competition and technological innovation has changed the way we do business, the technology environment for businesses has never been more challenging. Changes in manufacturing equipment, distribution of products, and communication with customers are all examples of how technology has changed everyday business practices. For example, many businesses are now using social media to provide customers with information about products and services. If you ask different people, you will often find different definitions for social media, but for our purposes **social media** is defined as online interaction that allows people and businesses to communicate and share ideas, personal information, and information about products or services. To illustrate how popular social media is, consider that Facebook with 800 million current users was launched in 2004 and Twitter with 300 million current users was launched in 2006. Because of rapid developments in social media and the increased importance of technology and information, businesses will need to spend additional money to keep abreast of an ever-changing technology environment and even more money to train employees to use the new technology.

> **social media** the online interaction that allows people and businesses to communicate and share ideas, personal information, and information about products or services

The economic environment The economic environment must always be considered when making business decisions. This fact is especially important when a nation's economy takes a nosedive or an individual firm's sales revenue and profits are declining. For example, both small and large business firms reduced both spending and hiring new employees over the last four years because of the recent economic crisis.

In addition to economic pressures, today's socially responsible managers and business owners must be concerned about the concept of sustainability. **Sustainability** means meeting the needs of the present without compromising the ability of future generations to meet their own needs.* Today there is an emphasis on doing *green* business; an approach to business practices that considers the environmental impact and long-term sustainability of such practices. Increasingly a combination of forces, including economic factors, growth in population, increased energy use, and concerns for the environment, is changing the way individuals live and businesses operate.

> **sustainability** meeting the needs of the present without compromising the ability of future generations to meet their own needs

When you look back at the original question we asked at the beginning of this section, clearly, each different type of environment—competitive, global, technological, and economic—affects the way a business does *business*. As a result, there are always opportunities for improvement and challenges that must be considered.

The challenges ahead

When it works well, the business system described above provides jobs for those who are willing to work, a good standard of living, and many opportunities for personal advancement. However, like every other system devised by humans, it is not perfect. It may provide prosperity, but equally it brought about the Great Depression of the 1930s, the economic problems of the 1970s and the early 1980s, and the economic crisis that began in the autumn of 2007.

Obviously, the system can be improved. However, there are many conflicting opinions, even amongst experts, on how this might be achieved.

The experts do agree, however, that several key issues will challenge the respective economic systems of many nations, and indeed the world economy itself, over the next decade. Some of the questions to be resolved include:

- How can we create a more stable economy and create new jobs for the unemployed?
- How can we regulate banks, savings and loan associations, credit unions, and other financial institutions to prevent the type of abuses that led to the recent economic crisis?
- How do we reduce national debt and still maintain a healthy economy and stimulate business growth?
- How can we use technology to make domestic workers more productive and firms more competitive in the global marketplace?
- How can we preserve the benefits of competition and small business in our economic system?
- How can we encourage economic growth and at the same time continue to conserve natural resources and sustain our environment?
- How can we meet the needs of two-income families, single parents, an ageing population, and the less fortunate who need health care and social programmes to exist?
- How can we resolve conflict with other countries throughout the world?

The answers to these questions are anything but simple. As we continue the journey through the 21st century, we need to exercise both ingenuity and creativity not only to solve our current problems but also to compete in the global marketplace and to safeguard the economy for future generations.

SUMMARY

- Discuss what you must do to be successful in the world of business.

  For many years, people in business—both employees and managers—assumed that prosperity would continue. When faced with both economic problems and increased competition, a large number of these people began to ask the question: What do we do now? Although this is a fair question, it is difficult to answer. Certainly, for a university student taking business courses or an employee just starting a career, the question is even more difficult to answer. And yet there are still opportunities out there for people who are willing to work hard, continue to learn, and possess the ability to adapt to change. The kind of career you choose ultimately will depend on your own values and what you feel is most important in life. By studying business, you can become a better employee or manager or you may decide to start your own business. You can also become a better consumer and investor.

- Define *business* and identify potential risks and rewards.

  Business is the organised effort of individuals to produce and sell, for a profit, the goods and services that satisfy society's needs. Four kinds of resources—material, human, financial, and informational—must be combined to start and operate a business. The three general types of businesses are service businesses, manufacturers, and marketing intermediaries. Profit is what remains after all business expenses are deducted from sales revenue. It is the payment that owners receive for assuming the risks of business—primarily the risks of not receiving payment and of losing whatever has been invested in the firm. Although many people believe that profit is literally the bottom line or most important goal for a business, many corporations are careful to point out their efforts to sustain the planet, participate in the green ecological movement, and help people to live better lives.

- Define *economics* and describe the two types of economic systems: capitalism and command economy.

  Economics is the study of how wealth is created and distributed. An economic system must answer four questions: *What* goods and services will be produced? *How* will they be produced? *For whom* will they be produced? *Who* owns and who controls the major factors of production? Capitalism is an economic system in which individuals own and operate the majority of businesses that provide goods and services. Capitalism stems from the theories of Adam Smith. Smith's pure *laissez-faire* capitalism is an economic system in which the factors of production are owned by private entities and all individuals are free to use their resources as they see fit; prices are determined by the workings of supply and demand in competitive markets; and the economic role of government is limited to rule maker and umpire.

  Our economic system today is a mixed economy. In the circular flow that characterises our business system (see Figure 1.5), households and businesses exchange resources for goods and services, using money as the medium of exchange. In a similar manner, the government collects taxes from businesses and households and purchases products and resources with which to provide services.

  In a command economy, government, rather than individuals, owns many of the factors of production and provides the answers to the three other economic questions. Socialist and communist economies are—at least in theory—command economies.

- Identify the ways to measure economic performance.

  One way to evaluate the performance of an economic system is to assess changes in productivity, which is the average level of output per worker per hour. Gross domestic product (GDP) can also be used to measure a nation's economic well-being and is the total currency unit value of all goods and services produced by all people within the boundaries of a country during a one-year period. It is also possible to adjust GDP for inflation and thus to measure real GDP. In addition to GDP, other economic indicators include a nation's balance of trade, consumer confidence index, consumer price index (CPI), corporate profits, inflation rate, national income, new housing starts, prime interest rate, producer price index (PPI), and unemployment rate.

- Examine the different phases in the typical business cycle.

  A nation's economy fluctuates rather than grows at a steady pace every year. These fluctuations are generally referred to as the business cycle. Generally, the business cycle consists of four states: the peak (sometimes called prosperity), recession, the trough, and recovery (sometimes called expansion). Some experts believe that effective use of monetary policy (the decisions that determine the size of the supply of money and the level of interest rates) and fiscal policy (the government's influence on the amount of savings and expenditures) can speed up recovery.

A deficit occurs when the government spends more than it receives in taxes and other revenues.

- Outline the four types of competition.

Competition is essentially a rivalry among businesses for sales to potential customers. In a capitalist economy, competition works to ensure the efficient and effective operation of business. Competition also ensures that a firm will survive only if it serves its customers well by providing products and services that meet their needs. Economists recognise four degrees of competition. Ranging from most to least competitive, the four degrees are perfect competition, monopolistic competition, oligopoly, and monopoly. The factors of supply and demand generally influence the price that customers pay producers for goods and services.

- Summarise the factors that affect the business environment and the challenges that businesses will encounter in the future.

From the beginning of the Industrial Revolution to the phenomenal expansion of industry in the 19th and early 20th centuries, governments including that of Americ maintained an essentially laissez-faire attitude toward business. However, during the Great Depression of the 1930s, the federal government began to provide a number of social services to its citizens.

To understand the major events that shaped the world during the remainder of the 20th and 21st century, it helps to remember that the economy was compared to a roller coaster ride earlier in this chapter—periods of economic growth followed by periods of economic slowdown. Events and a changing business environment including wars, rapid economic growth, the social responsibility movement, a shortage of crude oil, high inflation, high interest rates, reduced business profits, increased use of technology, e-business, and social media all have shaped business and the economy.

Now more than ever before, the way a business operates is affected by the competitive environment, global environment, technological environment, and economic environment. As a result, business has a number of opportunities for improvement and challenges for the future.

EXERCISE QUESTIONS

1   What is the difference between capitalism and communism and how might each system affect the way in which you do business?

2   If unemployment were to increase, how might this affect the Consumer Price Index and the Producer Price Index of a certain country?

3   Describe the business cycle and how each stage affects the economy.

4   Give two examples of an oligopoly and two examples of a monopoly.

5   How might the development of a new operating system affect a software design company? What are the wider implications for the technology environment?

CASE 1.1

James Dyson

James Dyson is an entrepreneur who challenged the industry giants, in his case with a revolutionary vacuum cleaner. His dual cyclone cleaner built a U.K. market share in excess of 50 per cent and international sales are blooming. A Hoover spokesman has said on the BBC Money Programme: "I regret Hoover as a company did not take the product technology of Dyson … it would have been lain on a shelf and not been used." Dyson has been compared by Professor Christopher Frayling, Rector of the Royal College of Art, with "the great Victorian ironmasters … a one-man attempt to revive British manufacturing industry

through design". Dyson is creative, innovative, totally focused on customers and driven by a desire to improve everyday products. His dedication and drive is reflected in the following comment: "the only way to make a genuine breakthrough is to pursue a vision with a single-minded determination in the face of criticism …" and this is exactly what he has done. Clearly a risk taker, he invested all of his resources in his venture. In the end his rise to fame and fortune came quickly, but the preceding years had been painful and protracted, and characterised by courage and persistence. They reflect the adage that "instant success takes time".

James Dyson's schoolmaster father died when he was just 9 years old. The public school to which he was then sent "made him a fighter". At school he excelled in running, practising by running cross-countries on his own; and it was on these runs that he began to appreciate the magnificence of the railway bridges constructed by Brunel in the nineteenth century, an experience which helped to form his personal vision. An early leap in the dark came when he volunteered to play bassoon in the school orchestra, without ever having seen a bassoon! Naturally artistic, he won a painting competition sponsored by the Eagle comic when he was 10 years old. Art became a passion and he later went on to complete a degree in interior design. Dyson may be an inventor, but he has no formal engineering background.

Dyson's first successful product and business was a flat-bottomed boat, the Sea Truck. At this time he learnt how a spherical plastic ball could be moulded, an idea that he turned to good use in the wild garden of his new home. His wheelbarrow was inadequate as the wheels sunk into the ground, so he substituted the wheel with a light plastic ball and thus invented the Ballbarrow. Backed by his brother-in-law on a 50:50 basis, Dyson invested in his new idea. Made of colourful, light plastic the barrow was offered to garden centres and the building trade, both of whom were less than enthusiastic. With a switch to direct mail via newspaper advertisements, the business took off. A new sales manager was appointed but his renewed attempt to sell the barrow through more traditional retail channels was again a failure. The financial penalty was the need for external investors, who later persuaded Dyson's brother-in-law to sell the business. A second painful experience came when the sales manager took the idea and design to the U.S., where Dyson later failed with a legal action against him.

Dyson's idea for a dual cyclone household cleaner came in 1979, when he was 31 years old. Again, it was a case of a need creating an opportunity. He was converting his old house and becoming frustrated that his vacuum cleaner would not clear all of the dust that he was creating. Particles were clogging the pores of the dust bags and reducing the suction capability of the cleaner. He needed something to collect paint particles. For his plastic spraying operation for the ballbarrows, Dyson had developed a smaller version of the large industrial cyclone machines, which separate particles from air by using centrifugal forces in spinning cylinders. He believed that this technology could be adapted for home vacuum cleaners, removing the need for bags, but his partners in the Ballbarrow business failed to share his enthusiasm. Out of work when the business was sold, his previous employer, Jeremy Fry (for whom he had developed the Sea Truck), loaned him £25,000. Dyson matched this by selling his vegetable garden for £18,000 and taking out an additional £7000 overdraft on his house. Working from home, risking everything and drawing just £10,000 a year to keep himself, his wife and three children, he pursued his idea. Over the years he produced 5000 different prototypes.

When he ultimately approached the established manufacturers his idea was, perhaps predictably, rejected. Replacement dust bags are an important source of additional revenue. A series of discussions with potential partners who might license his idea brought mixed results. Fresh legal actions in the U.S. for patent infringement – "with hindsight I didn't patent enough features" – were only partially offset by a deal with Apex of Japan. Dyson designed the G-Force upright cleaner which Apex manufactured and sold to a niche in the Japanese market for the equivalent of £1200 per machine, from which Dyson received just £20. At least there was now an income stream, but this had taken 7 years to achieve. Finally, in 1991 Lloyds Bank provided finance for the design and manufacture of a machine in the U.K. Several venture capitalists and the Welsh Development Agency had turned him down. Dyson was determined to give his latest version the looks of NASA technology, but further setbacks were still to occur. Dyson was let down by the plastic moulder and assembler with whom he contracted, and was eventually forced to set up his own plant. Early sales through mail-order catalogues were followed by deals with John Lewis and eventually (in 1995) with Comet and Curry's. In this year a cylinder version joined the upright. Dyson continues to improve the designs to extend his patent protection. By 1999 his personal wealth was estimated to be £500 million.

Dyson has always seen himself as more of an inventor than a businessman. He established two separate businesses, both in Malmesbury, Wiltshire (U.K.), and he kept Dyson Manufacturing and Dyson Research (design and patenting) apart. The dress code for employees is perpetually informal and communications are predominantly face-to-face. Memos are banned and even emails discouraged. Every employee is encouraged to be creative and contribute ideas. Most new employees are young – "not contaminated by other employers" – and they all begin by assembling their own vacuum cleaner, which they can then buy for £20. Designers work on improvements to the dual cyclone cleaners as well as new product ideas.

In early 2000 Dyson launched a robot version of the dual cyclone cleaner, which is battery-powered, self-propelled and able to manoeuvre itself around furniture. It retailed at some £2500, which limited it to a select segment of the market and it was slow to take off. He has since launched "The Ball", a version which has a large ball instead of wheels to make the cleaner more versatile. Later in 2000 Dyson launched a revolutionary super-fast washing machine with short wash cycles and an ability to spin clothes almost dry, presenting a challenge to the manufacturers of both washing machines and tumble dry-ers. This time, however, Dyson had his own resources to launch the product. He has also succeeded in penetrating the U.S. and Japanese markets with his dual cyclone cleaners; he had to design a small version with a digital motor for Japan.

Another Dyson product is his own design of wall mounted hand dryer – users don't hold their hands under a hot air outlet but place them between two flat plates. The machines are extremely powerful. More recently he has launched what he calls the "Air Multiplier" which is effectively a blade-free fan which blows cold air; a variant of this is his (warm air) room heater. Both look like rings – the secret lies in the way the air is circulated. Dyson controls 100 per cent of the shares in his business. He has learnt some painful lessons but is now

enjoying the rewards of his dogged determination. In recent years Dyson has transferred the majority of his manufacturing to lower cost plants in Malaysia and Singapore. Perhaps inevitably this was opposed by the U.K. workforce and it has brought him adverse publicity. Before the transfer there were 1800 employees in the U.K. This reduced to 1000, but has since been increased to between 1400 and 1500 none of them actually making any products. Several hundred people work in research and development and design.

Dyson himself has become a passionate spokesman for engineering and design and has funded the Dyson School of Design Innovation in Bath. He believes the U.K. must focus on what it can do well and accept that the actual manufacture should take place in lower-labour cost countries overseas.

Questions

1 Thinking about the issues of core competency and strategic capability, what is the "secret" of James Dyson's competitive advantage?

2 Has he been able to appropriate the rewards of the value he has added?

3 Dyson has moved the majority of his manufacturing to Malaysia and Singapore. In what ways will this affect the economy of this country and the economy in Britain?

CHAPTER REFERENCES

The 66Apps Web site at www.66apps.com (accessed January 11, 2012).

The Bureau of Economic Analysis Web site at www.bea.gov (accessed January 9 and 30, 2012).

The Bureau of Labor Statistics Web site at www.bls.gov (accessed January 8 and 12, 2012).

Dlabay, Les, "The Future of Global Business at 'Base of the Pyramid,'" *The Daily Herald Business Ledger,* November 29, 2011, p. 22.

The Environmental Protection Agency Web site at www.epa.gov (accessed January 9, 2012).

Fernandez, Idy, "Julie Stav," *Hispanic*, June–July 2005, 204.

The General Mills Web site at www.generalmills.com (accessed January 9, 2012).

The Investopedia Web site at www.investopedia.com (accessed January 9, 2012).

The Treasury Direct Web site at www.treasurydirect.gov (accessed January 9, 2012) and the U.S. Census Bureau Web site at www.census.gov (accessed January 9, 2012).

The Walmart stores Web site at www.walmartstores.com (accessed January 9, 2012).

Weir, Bill, "Made in China: Your Job, Your Future, Your Fortune," ABC News Web site at www.abcnews.com (accessed September 20, 2005).

2 RESPONSIBLE BUSINESS

LEARNING OBJECTIVES

Once you complete this chapter, you should be able to:

- Understand the concept of social responsibility and to consider the importance of businesses behaving responsibly
- Define and describe the importance of marketing ethics
- Become familiar with ways to improve ethical decisions in business and marketing
- Understand the role of social responsibility and ethics in improving marketing performance
- Explain the concept of social marketing and consider how it is used
- Appreciate how the marketing discipline is evolving

BUSINESS FOCUS

Kit Kat shifts to Fair Trade airtrade

Fair Trade promotes equal, fair and sustainable trade partnerships and aims to combat poverty by helping individuals in developing countries to compete in the global market. Many organisations support Fair Trade and certify Fair Trade products. The most well-known is the World Fair Trade Organisation (WFTO), which represents more than 350 organisations committed to Fair Trade. However, according to the WFTO, advocating Fair Trade is not enough; in order for it to succeed, there must be a demand for Fair Trade products. This is where mainstream brands can help.

Nestlé is one mainstream brand becoming more involved in Fair Trade. In the past, Nestlé faced criticism for its business practices in the developing world. In order to improve its reputation, Nestlé searched for ways to establish itself as a socially responsible company and decided to focus on its use of cocoa beans. The company announced its Cocoa Plan, an investment programme designed to address economic and social issues in cocoa farming communities. Through its Cocoa Plan, Nestlé provides cocoa farmers with fair compensation for their cocoa beans, additional training, and disease-resistant cocoa plants. The company uses only Fair Trade cocoa and sugar in its Kit Kat bars sold in the United Kingdom and Ireland. Nestlé also agreed to fight child labour and to provide better health care to cocoa suppliers.

Critics of Nestlé accuse the company of using Fair Trade merely to generate good publicity. Whether or not this is true, the company's Kit Kat bar is the second most popular chocolate bar in the U.K. Nestlé needs to purchase large amounts of Fair Trade cocoa, which will have a huge impact on the market. Nestlé's transition into Fair Trade may help motivate other companies to pursue Fair Trade – possibly supplying the demand that the WFTO says the Fair Trade movement so desperately needs.

There is a growing expectation among people and those who govern them that businesses will behave in a responsible manner. This expectation also extends to all areas of the business and the way in which they practise. Social responsibility and ethics are two issues that can have a profound impact on the success of a business.

This chapter gives an overview of how social responsibility and ethics must be considered in business, with particular emphasis on marketing decision-making. Most businesspeople operate responsibly and within the limits of the law. However, some companies engage in activities that customers, other businesses and society in general deem unacceptable. Such activities include questionable selling practices, bribery, price discrimination, deceptive advertising, misleading packaging and marketing defective products. For example, 37 per cent of the software programmes used by businesses worldwide are illegally pirated copies. Practices of this kind raise questions about obligations of business to society. Inherent in these questions are the issues of social responsibility and business ethics.

There is also growing interest in how marketing as a discipline can overtly contribute to the well-being of society and of individuals. One way in which this can be achieved is through social marketing activities, which use commercial marketing tools and techniques for the good of communities and those who live within them.

Businesspeople in all sectors are increasingly aware of expectations that companies will behave in a responsible and ethical manner. Having been previously criticised for some of its business activities, Nestlé has decided that turning to Fair Trade ingredients for its Kit Kat will help the company to be seen as more socially responsible and hopefully will also be well received by customers.

Nestlé also supports the values of the Fair Trade initiative. The implications of decisions such as this one are considered in more detail throughout this chapter.

This chapter begins by defining social responsibility and exploring its dimensions. Various social responsibility issues, such as the natural environment and the businessperson's role as a member of the community, are then discussed. Next, the definition and role of ethics in marketing decisions are explored. Ethical issues in marketing, the ethical decision-making process and ways to improve ethical conduct in business are all considered. Next, the ways in which social responsibility and ethics can be incorporated into marketing decisions are examined. Finally, the chapter explains the concept of social marketing and considers how marketing tools and techniques can be used to improve societal well-being.

SOCIAL RESPONSIBILITY

The nature of social responsibility

In business, **social responsibility** refers to an organisation's obligation to maximise its positive impact and minimise its negative impact on society. Social responsibility deals with the total effect of all business decisions on society. Ample evidence demonstrates that ignoring society's demands for responsible business can destroy customers' trust and even prompt government regulations.

> **social responsibility** an organisation's obligation to maximise its positive impact and minimise its negative impact on society

Irresponsible actions that anger customers, employees or competitors may not only jeopardise a business's financial standing but could have other repercussions as well. For example, following a report into misleading claims on food packaging, the U.K.'s Food Standards Agency (FSA) instigated a campaign to "name and shame" food manufacturers selling unhealthy products, including those with high sugar, salt or fat content.

In contrast, socially responsible activities can generate positive publicity and boost sales. In 2007, Marks & Spencer launched its sustainability programme Plan A, making 100 commitments on ethical, environmental and social issues facing the company. In 2010, the list of commitments grew to 180, divided between seven pillars of activity ranging from climate change and handling waste to the protection of natural resources and how the company does business (marksandspencer.com/plana). Cosmetics company Avon has become known for employing a large number of women and for promoting them to senior positions with the organisation. This commitment to the advancement of women has led to positive publicity for the business.

Socially responsible efforts have a positive impact on local communities; at the same time, they indirectly help the sponsoring organisation by attracting goodwill, publicity and potential customers and employees. Thus, while social responsibility is certainly a positive concept in itself, most organisations embrace it in the expectation of indirect long-term benefits. Procter & Gamble, Unilever, PepsiCo, Santander and McDonald's are just a few of the companies that have social responsibility commitments. Research suggests that an organisational culture that is conducive to social responsibility engenders greater employee commitment and improved business performance.

The dimensions of social responsibility

Socially responsible organisations strive for **citizenship marketing** by adopting a strategic focus for fulfilling the economic, legal, ethical and philanthropic social responsibilities that their stakeholders expect of them. **Stakeholders** include those constituents who have a "stake", or claim, in some aspect of the company's products, operations, markets, industry and outcomes; these include customers, employees, investors and shareholders, suppliers, governments, communities and many others. Companies that consider the diverse perspectives of stakeholders in their daily operations and strategic planning are said to have a "stakeholder orientation", an important element of social responsibility. For example, retailer B&Q secured stakeholder input on issues ranging from child labour, fair wages and equal opportunity to environmental impact. The company has a vision to the first choice for sustainable home improvement and has developed a series of principles to support this goal. These include achieving zero carbon stores, reducing transport emissions by 50 per cent and landfill waste by 98 per cent (socialresponsibility@b-and-q.co.uk). Social responsibility dimensions can be viewed as a pyramid, with philanthropic responsibilities at the peak, followed by ethical responsibilities on the next tier, followed by legal responsibilities on the next tier, and then finally economic responsibilities on the foundation tier. The economic and legal aspects have long been acknowledged, whereas philanthropic and ethical issues have gained recognition more recently.

citizenship marketing the adoption of a strategic focus for fulfilling the economic, legal, ethical and philanthropic social responsibilities expected by stakeholders

stakeholders constituents who have a "stake", or claim, in some aspect of a company's products, operations, markets, industry and outcomes

At the most basic level, all companies have an economic responsibility to be profitable so that they can provide a return on investment to their owners and investors, create jobs for the community, and contribute goods and services to the economy. How organisations relate to stockholders, employees, competitors, customers, the community and the natural environment affects the economy. When economic downturns or poor decisions lead companies to lay off employees, communities often suffer as they attempt to absorb the displaced employees. Customers may experience diminished levels of service as a result of fewer experienced employees. Share prices often decline when lay-offs are announced, affecting the value of stockholders' investment portfolios. Moreover, stressed-out employees facing demands to reduce expenses may make poor decisions that affect the natural environment, product quality, employee rights and customer service. An organisation's sense of economic responsibility is especially significant for employees, raising such issues as equal job opportunities, workplace diversity, job safety, health and employee privacy. Economic responsibilities require finding a balance between society's demand for social responsibility and investors' desire for profits.

Businesses also have an economic responsibility to compete fairly. Size frequently gives companies an advantage over rivals. Large companies can often generate economies of scale that allow them to put smaller companies out of business. Consequently, small companies and even whole communities may resist the efforts of businesses like Walmart, Tesco and McDonald's to open outlets in their neighbourhood. These companies are able to operate at such low costs that small, local businesses cannot compete. Though consumers appreciate lower prices, the failure of small businesses creates unemployment for some members of the community. Such issues create concerns about social responsibility for organisations, communities and consumers.

Businesses are also expected to obey laws and regulations. The efforts of elected representatives and special interest groups to promote responsible corporate behaviour have resulted in laws and regulations designed to keep European companies' actions within the range of acceptable conduct. When customers, interest groups or businesses become outraged over what they perceive as irresponsibility on the part of a business organisation, they may urge the government to draft new legislation to regulate the behaviour or engage in litigation. For example, following a record number of complaints about the practices of door-to-door sales people, the U.K. government looked at legislative action to control this kind of selling.

Economic and legal responsibilities are the most basic levels of social responsibility for a good reason: failure to consider them may mean that a business is not around long enough to engage in ethical or philanthropic activities. Beyond these dimensions is **marketing ethics** principles and standards that define acceptable conduct in marketing as determined by various stakeholders, including the public, government, regulators, private interest groups, consumers, industry and the organisation itself. Some companies, including the Body Shop and the Co-operative Bank, have built their businesses around ethical ideas. The Co-operative Group , in particular, is committed to joining up its business objectives and ethical principles. The most ethical principles have been codified as laws and regulations to encourage marketers to conform to society's expectations about conduct. However, business ethics goes beyond legal issues. Ethical business decisions foster trust, which helps build long-term business relationships. There is a more detailed look at the ethical dimension of social responsibility later in this chapter.

> **marketing ethics** principles and standards that define acceptable marketing conduct as determined by various stakeholders, including the public, government, regulators, private interest groups, consumers, industry and the organisation itself

Philanthropic responsibilities   At the top of the pyramid of corporate responsibility are philanthropic responsibilities. These responsibilities, which go beyond marketing ethics, are not required of a company, but they promote human welfare or goodwill, as do the economic, legal and ethical dimensions of social responsibility. The philanthropic responsibility that companies demonstrate is shown in the level of corporate support attracted by events such as LiveAid and Comic Relief. Even small companies participate in philanthropy through donations and volunteer support of local good causes and national charities, such as the NSPCC, Oxfam and the Red Cross.

More companies than ever are adopting a strategic approach to corporate philanthropy. Many businesses link their products to a particular social cause on an ongoing or medium-term basis, a practice known as **cause-related marketing**. For example, P&G baby brand Pampers supports UNICEF's programme to vaccinate mothers and babies against tetanus (http://www.pampers.co.uk/en_GB/ourPartners). For Pampers product carrying the '1 Pack = 1 Life-Saving Vaccine' logo, the

SUCCESS STORY

One Foundation

One Foundation was established for the purpose of generating revenue to support specific needy causes. It sources and markets a limited range of consumer products – each with its own related cause.

The founder, Duncan Goose, came up with the idea for the One Foundation when talking with friends about how roughly 1 billion people in the world do not have access to clean drinking water. Duncan Goose

© LEE KAREN STOW / ALAMY

believed they could – and should – do something about this.

One Water is bottled water from Powys in Wales, and the One Foundation has it bottled and branded and distributes it to earn money that is ploughed directly into building water pumps called Play Pumps, mainly in Africa. As is the case with all its products, the company has been able to secure distribution and make its products widely available – and the packaging makes clear how the surpluses generated will be used. One Water has been chosen by Virgin Atlantic for all of its flights.

As well as water, One Foundation also produces organic eggs to support community farming activities; hand-wash liquid soap to fund the sinking of pit latrines with

associated hand-washing facilities; toilet rolls to install proper toilets in developing countries with inadequate sanitation; plasters to fund bicycle-ambulances; and condoms to help with HIV/AIDS counselling. The One Foundation also works with a micro financing agency.

This is a different business and revenue model that changes perceptions on how aid might be brought to Africa and elsewhere and what can constitute the mission and purpose of an organisation. In one sense the One Foundation is clearly a charity; on the other hand it is developing and marketing products that compete directly with leading brands on the market – many of which are produced by some of the world's leading consumer goods companies.

company provides funding for a single dose of vaccine. Such cause-related programmes tend to appeal to consumers because they provide an additional reason to "feel good" about a particular purchase. Marketers like the programmes because well designed ones increase sales and create feelings of respect and admiration for the companies involved. Some companies are beginning to extend the concept of corporate philanthropy beyond financial contributions by adopting a **strategic philanthropy** approach, the synergistic use of organisational core competencies and resources to address key stakeholders' interests, and achieve both organisational and social benefits. Strategic philanthropy involves employees, organisational resources and expertise, and the ability to link these assets to the concerns of key stakeholders, including employees, customers, suppliers and social needs. Strategic philanthropy involves both financial and non-financial contributions to stakeholders (employee time, goods and services, and company technology and equipment, as well as facilities), but it also benefits the company.

> **cause-related marketing** the practice of linking products to a particular social cause on an ongoing or medium-term basis
>
> **strategic philanthropy** the synergistic use of organisational core competencies and resources to address key stakeholders' interests, and achieve both organisational and social benefits

Social responsibility issues

Although social responsibility may seem to be an abstract ideal, managers make decisions related to social responsibility every day. To be successful, a business must determine what customers, government regulators and competitors, as well as society in general, want or expect in terms of social responsibility. The success of international retailer the Body Shop has been attributed to the company's awareness of the Green movement and demonstration of social responsibility. Table 2.1 summarises three major categories of social responsibility issues: the natural environment, consumerism and community relations.

TABLE 2.1 Social responsibility issues

Issue	Description	Major social concerns
Natural environment	Consumers insisting not only on a good quality of life but on a healthful environment so they can maintain a high standard of living during their lifetimes	Conservation Water pollution Air pollution Land pollution
Consumerism	Activities undertaken by independent individuals, groups and organisations to protect their rights as consumers	The right to safety The right to be informed The right to choose The right to be heard
Community relations	Society eager to have marketers contribute to its well-being, wishing to know what marketers do to help solve social problems	Equality issues Disadvantaged members of society Safety and health Education and general welfare

Sustainability

One way in which businesses are increasingly demonstrating their social responsibility is through programmes designed to protect and preserve the natural environment. **Sustainability** is the potential for the long-term well-being of the natural environment, including all biological entities, as well as the interaction among nature and individuals, organisations and business strategies. Sustainability

In a bid to become "greener", more socially responsible, and to be considerate of future generations, many companies increasingly try to reduce or prevent pollution, through supporting clean-up events, promoting recycling and seeking to minimise waste in production processes.

includes the assessment and improvement of business strategies, economic sectors, work practices, technologies and lifestyles – all while maintaining the natural environment.

> **Sustainability** the potential for the long term well-being of the natural environment, including all biological entities, as well as the interaction among nature and individuals, organisations and business strategies

Many companies are making contributions to environmental protection organisations, supporting clean-up events, promoting recycling, re-tooling manufacturing processes to minimise waste and pollution, and generally re-evaluating the effects of their products on the natural environment. Many supermarkets, for example, provide on-site recycling for customers and encourage their suppliers to reduce wasteful packaging. Procter & Gamble uses recycled materials in some of its packaging and markets refills for some products, which reduces packaging waste. Such efforts generate positive publicity and often increase sales for the companies involved. The Food and Drink Federation (FDF) whose membership includes PepsiCo, Coca-Cola and Kraft, is encouraging sustainable practice by establishing strict environmental targets. These have included a reduction in road miles of 80 million by 2012 and cutting the carbon impact of packaging by 10 per cent.

Green marketing **Green marketing** is the specific development, pricing, promotion and distribution of products that do not harm the natural environment. Toyota and Nissan, for example, have succeeded in marketing "hybrid" cars that use electric motors to augment their internal-combustion engines, improving the vehicles' fuel economy without reducing their power. Ford introduced the first hybrid SUV in 2004. The U.K. government is now supporting these alternative fuel technologies by funding the installation of electric vehicle points in certain locations. Meanwhile Hewlett Packard (HP) has taken a leadership role in the recycling of electronic waste by creating drop-off locations for rechargeable batteries and recycling programmes for printer cartridges and other electronic items.

> **green marketing** the specific development, pricing, promotion and distribution of products that do not harm the natural environment

An independent coalition of environmentalists, scientists and marketers is one group involved in evaluating products to assess their environmental impact, determining marketers' commitment to the environment. Described as "The directory for planet-friendly living", *The Green Guide* which was first published in 1984, offers online and print guidance on green products and ethical living http://www.greenguide.co.uk/thegreenguide. Such information sources have an important role to play during what is a confusing time for many consumers, who are increasingly faced with an array of products making a variety of environmental claims. For example, most Chiquita bananas are

More and more companies are taking an increasing interest in producing successful "hybrid" and electric cars.

© CHRISTIAN DELBERT / SHUTTERSTOCK

certified through the Rainforest Alliance's Better Banana Project as having been grown using more environmentally and labour-friendly practices. In Europe, companies can apply for the EU Ecolabel to indicate that their products are less harmful to the environment than competing products, based on scientifically-determined criteria.

Although demand for economic, legal and ethical solutions to environmental problems is widespread, the environmental movement in business includes many different groups, whose values and goals often conflict. Some environmentalists and businesspeople believe companies should work to protect and preserve the natural environment by implementing the following goals:

1. *Eliminate the concept of waste.* Recognising that pollution and waste usually stem from inefficiency, the question is not what to do with waste but how to make things without waste.
2. *Reinvent the concept of a product.* Products should be reduced to only three types and eventually just two. The first type is consumables, which are eaten or, when placed in the ground, turn into soil with few harmful side-effects. The second type is durable goods – such as cars, televisions, computers and refrigerators – which should be made, used and returned to the manufacturer within a closed-loop system. Such products should be designed for disassembly and recycling. The third category is unsaleables and includes such products as radioactive materials, heavy metals and toxins. These products should always belong to the original makers, who should be responsible for the products and their full life-cycle effects. Reclassifying products in this way encourages manufacturers to design products more efficiently.
3. *Make prices reflect the cost.* Every product should reflect, or at least approximate, its actual cost – not only the direct cost of its effect on production but also the cost of its effect on air, water and soil.
4. *Make environmentalism profitable.* Consumers are beginning to recognise that competition in the marketplace should not occur between companies harming the environment and those trying to save it.

Consumerism Another significant issue in socially responsible business is consumerism, which is the efforts of independent individuals, groups and organisations to protect the rights of consumers. The underlying assumption is that consumers have a range of rights, including the right to safety, the right to choose, the right to be properly informed and the right to fair treatment when they complain. For example, the right to safety means that businesses are obligated not to market a product that they know could harm consumers. This right can be extended to imply that all products must be safe for their intended use, include thorough and explicit instructions for proper and safe use, and have been tested to ensure reliability and quality.

Interest groups play an important role in helping to protect consumers' rights by taking action against companies they consider irresponsible, by lobbying government officials and agencies, engaging in letter-writing campaigns and boycotts and making public service announcements. A number of high-profile consumer activists have also crusaded for consumer rights. Consumer activism has resulted in legislation requiring various safety features in cars: seat belts, padded dashboards, stronger door catches, headrests, shatterproof windscreens and collapsible steering columns. Activists' efforts have furthered the passage of several consumer protection laws, such as the Trade Descriptions Act 1968, the Consumer Protection Act 1987, the Fair Trading Act 1973, the Food Act 1984 and the Weights and Measures Act 1985 (in the U.K.).

The power of angry consumers should not be underestimated. Indeed, research suggests that such individuals not only fail to make repeat purchases but may retaliate against the source of their dissatisfaction.* Negative reaction from the public was partly the reason why News International took the decision to close the U.K.'s *News of the World* newspaper following damaging publicity that journalists working there had hacked the mobile phones of celebrities and members of the public involved in tragedies. The consumer movement has been helped by news format television programmes, such as the BBC's *Watchdog*. There has also been a growth of consumer sites on the Internet offering advice and reviews for consumers. For instance, tripadvisor.co.uk has thousands of customer reviews of hotels, flights and restaurants; and includes travel forums offering tips on travel in different locations.

Community relations   Social responsibility also extends to businesses' roles as community members. Individual communities expect businesses to make philanthropic contributions to civic projects and institutions, and to be "good corporate citizens". While most charitable donations come from individuals, corporate philanthropy is on the rise, with contributions of resources (money, product, time) to community causes such as education, the arts, recreation, disadvantaged members of the community and others. British Airways' "Change for Good"- partnership with UNICEF encourages donations of foreign currency from passengers, which can then be used to fund a range of health and educational projects aimed at children around the world. McDonald's, Shell, Ogilvy & Mather and Hewlett-Packard all have programmes that contribute funds, equipment and personnel to educational reform. Similarly, Sainsbury's has a scheme that allows shoppers to collect vouchers enabling their local schools to obtain sports equipment.

Actions such as these can significantly improve a community's quality of life through employment opportunities, economic development, and financial contributions to educational, health, cultural and recreational causes. These efforts also indirectly help the organisations in the form of goodwill, publicity and exposure to potential future customers. Thus, although social responsibility is certainly a positive concept, most organisations do not embrace it without the expectation of some indirect long-term benefit.

The manner in which organisations deal with equality is also a key social responsibility issue. Diversity in the work environment has focused attention on the need to integrate and utilise an increasingly diverse workforce. Companies that are successful in achieving this are finding increases in creativity and motivation, and reductions in staff turnover.

MARKETING ETHICS

Marketing ethics is a dimension of social responsibility involving principles and standards that define acceptable conduct in marketing. Acceptable standards of conduct in making individual and group decisions in marketing are determined by various stakeholders and by an organisation's ethical climate. Marketers should also use their own values and ethical standards to act responsibly and provide ethical leadership for others.

Marketers should be aware of ethical standards for acceptable conduct from several viewpoints: company, industry, government, customers, special interest groups and society at large. When marketing activities deviate from accepted standards, the exchange process can break down, resulting in customer dissatisfaction, lack of trust and legal action. In recent years, a number of ethical scandals have resulted in a massive loss of confidence in the integrity of businesses. The recent global financial crisis led to sharp criticism of the financial services sector and growing distrust among consumers. Once trust has been broken, it can take a considerable time to rebuild. In fact, some research suggests that 76 per cent of consumers would boycott the products of a socially irresponsible company, and 91 per cent would consider switching to a competitor's products.

For example, in the U.S., after 174 deaths and more than 700 injuries resulted from traffic accidents involving Ford Explorers equipped with Firestone tyres, Bridgestone/Firestone and Ford faced numerous lawsuits and much negative publicity. Ford claimed that defective Firestone tyres were to blame for the accidents, while Bridgestone/Firestone contended that design flaws in Ford's best-selling Explorer made it more likely to roll over than other sport-utility vehicles. Many consumers, concerned more for their own safety than with the corporate blame game, lost confidence in both companies and turned to competitors' products.

When managers engage in activities that deviate from accepted principles, continued marketing exchanges become difficult, if not impossible. The best time to deal with such problems is during the marketing strategy process, not after major problems have materialised.

Marketing ethics goes beyond legal issues. Marketing decisions based on ethical considerations foster mutual trust in marketing relationships. Although attempts are often made to draw a boundary between legal and ethical issues, the distinction between the two is frequently blurred in decision-making. Marketers operate in an environment in which overlapping legal and ethical issues often colour decisions. To separate legal and ethical decisions requires an assumption that marketing managers can instinctively differentiate legal and ethical issues. However, while the legal ramifications of some issues and problems may be obvious, others are not. Questionable decisions and actions often result in disputes that must be resolved through litigation. The legal system therefore provides a formal venue for marketers to resolve ethical disputes as well as legal ones.

Hasbro, for example, filed a lawsuit against a man who marketed a board game called Ghettopoly. Hasbro's suit accused David Chang's game of unlawfully copying the packaging and logo of Hasbro's long-selling Monopoly board game and causing "irreparable injury" to Hasbro's reputation and goodwill. After minority-rights groups complained that Ghettopoly promoted negative stereotypes of some minorities, some retailers stopped selling the game.

RESPONSIBLE PRACTICE   Can retailers be too powerful?

Is it possible for a retailer to become too large and powerful? This is a question some people have been asking about Walmart, the world's largest retail company, and about Tesco in the U.K. Walmart has aggressively pursued its low-price mantra, bringing better value to consumers and forcing suppliers to innovate. A possible concern is that Walmart has become so big that it can do virtually anything it wants in some areas. Obviously this kind of power has enormous ethical and social implications. Some suppliers suggest that Walmart is able to dictate every aspect of its operations, from product design to pricing, in its efforts to maximise savings for customers. Some suppliers claim they have been forced to reduce staff numbers and even locate to lower-cost regions, in order to meet the biggest retailer's margin demands. Their fear is that if they hesitate to comply, they risk losing their most lucrative outlet and will find their products quickly replaced by a competitor's on Walmart's shelves. For the customer, seeking keen prices and great choice, there are obvious benefits to Walmart's approach, but perhaps there is also a cost.

© JIM WILEMAN / ALAMY

What are some of the ethical and social implications of the power Walmart and other huge retailers are able to exert? What actions can these large companies take to manage these issues?

Indeed, most ethical disputes reported in the media involve the legal system at some level. In many cases, however, settlements are reached without requiring the decision of a judge or jury.

It is not the aim of this chapter to question individuals' ethical beliefs or personal convictions. Nor is it the purpose to examine the conduct of consumers, although some do behave unethically (engaging, for instance, in shoplifting, returning clothing after wearing it and other abuses). Instead, the goal here is to highlight the importance of understanding and resolving ethical issues in marketing and to help readers learn about marketing ethics.

Ethical issues in business

An **ethical issue** is an identifiable problem, situation or opportunity requiring an individual or organisation to choose between actions that must be evaluated as right or wrong, ethical or unethical. Any time an activity causes marketing managers or customers in their target market to feel manipulated or cheated, a marketing ethical issue exists, regardless of the legality of that activity.

> **ethical issue** an identifiable problem, situation or opportunity requiring a choice between several actions that must be evaluated as right or wrong, ethical or unethical

Regardless of the reasons behind specific ethical issues, businesspeople must be able to identify these issues and decide how to resolve them. To do so requires familiarity with the many kinds of ethical issue that may arise. Some examples of ethical issues related to product, people, promotion, price and place/distribution (the marketing mix) appear in Table 2.2.

TABLE 2.2 Typical ethical issues related to the marketing mix

Product issue Product information	Covering up defects in products that could cause harm to a consumer; withholding critical performance information that could affect a purchase decision
Place/distribution issue Counterfeiting	Counterfeit products are widespread, especially in the areas of computer software, clothing and audio and video products; the Internet has facilitated the distribution of counterfeit products
People issue Customer service	Promising or promoting aftermarket care with no intention of honouring the promise or warranty
Promotion issue Advertising	Deceptive advertising or withholding important product information in a personal selling situation
Pricing issue Pricing	Indicating that an advertised sale price is a reduction below the regular list price when, in fact, that is not the case

Product-related ethical issues generally arise when marketers fail to disclose the risks associated with a product, or information regarding the function, value or use of a product. Most car companies have experienced negative publicity associated with design or safety issues that resulted in a government-required recall of specific models. Pressures can build to substitute inferior materials or product components to reduce costs. Ethical issues also arise when marketers fail to inform customers about existing conditions or changes in product quality. Consider the introduction of a new size of confectionery bar, labelled with a banner touting its "new larger size". However, when placed in vending machines alongside older confectionery bars of the same brand, it became apparent that the product was actually slightly *smaller* than the bar it had replaced. Although this could have been a mistake, the company still has to defend and deal with the consequences of its actions.

Promotion can create ethical issues in a variety of ways, among them false or misleading advertising and manipulative or deceptive sales promotions, tactics and publicity. A major ethical issue in promotion pertains to the marketing of video games that allegedly promote violence and weapons to children. In the U.K., brand owners are being encouraged to sign a pledge to end promotional practices that exploit children. The pledge follows publication by Christian charity The Mother's Union of a U.K. report which states that 80 per cent of parents believe that marketing encourages the early sexualisation of children. One area of particular concern for parents has been the use of inappropriate images in music videos.

Many other ethical issues are linked to promotion, including the use of bribery in personal selling situations. Even bribes that might benefit the organisation can be unethical, because they jeopardise trust and fairness and can damage the organisation in the long run.

Several studies which examine the ethics of marketing vaccines against drug addiction and smoking show that many other ethical issues are linked to promotion and product attributes.

In pricing, common ethical issues are price fixing, predatory pricing and failure to disclose the full price of a purchase. The emotional and subjective nature of price creates many situations in which misunderstandings between the seller and buyer cause ethical problems. Businesses have the right to price their products to earn a reasonable profit, but ethical issues may crop up when a company seeks to earn high profits at the expense of its customers. Some pharmaceutical companies, for example, have been accused of pricing products at exorbitant levels and taking advantage of customers who must purchase the medicine to survive or to maintain their quality of life. Another issue relates to the quantity surcharges that occur when consumers are effectively overcharged for buying a larger package size of the same grocery product.

Ethical issues in distribution involve relationships among producers and marketing middlemen. Marketing middlemen, or intermediaries (wholesalers and retailers), facilitate the flow of products from the producer to the ultimate customer. Each intermediary performs a different role and agrees to certain rights, responsibilities and rewards associated with that role. For example, producers expect wholesalers and retailers to honour agreements and keep them informed of inventory needs. Serious ethical issues relating to distribution include manipulating a product's availability for purposes of exploitation and using coercion to force intermediaries to behave in a specific way. Some retailers have attracted criticism for driving down the price paid to producers of milk to an extent where many farmers have gone out of business. When companies outsource production and other functions, managing the supply chain become increasingly difficult. For instance, melamine-tainted milk founds its way into thousands of products around the world, making 300,000 people ill and killing six infants. The same issue resurfaced just over a year later. Companies that procured their milk from this source suffered reputational and financial damage as a result of these scandals.

The nature of marketing ethics

To grasp the significance of ethics in marketing decision-making, it is helpful to examine the factors that influence the ethical decision-making process. As Figure 2.1 shows, individual factors, organisational relationships and opportunity interact to determine ethical decisions in marketing.

Individual factors When people need to resolve ethical conflicts in their lives, they often base their decisions on their own values and principles of right or wrong. For example, a study by the Josephson Institute of Ethics reported that seven out of ten students admitted to cheating in a test at least once in the past year, and 92 per cent admitted to lying to their parents in the past year. One out of six students confessed to showing up for class drunk in the same period. People learn values and principles through socialisation by family members, social groups, religion and formal education. In the workplace, however, research has established that an organisation's values often have more influence on marketing decisions than do a person's own values.

Organisational relationships Although people can, and do, make ethical choices relating to marketing decisions, no one operates in a vacuum. Ethical choices in marketing are most often made jointly, in work groups and committees, or in conversations and discussions with colleagues. Marketing employees resolve ethical issues based not only on what they have learned from their own backgrounds but also on what they learn from others in the organisation. The outcome of this learning process depends on the strength of each individual's personal values, opportunities for unethical

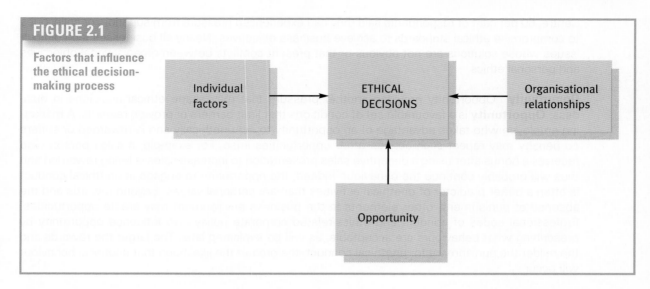

FIGURE 2.1

Factors that influence the ethical decision-making process

Individual factors → ETHICAL DECISIONS ← Organisational relationships

Opportunity ↑

behaviour, and exposure to others who behave ethically or unethically. Superiors, peers and subordinates in the organisation influence the ethical decision-making process. Although people outside the organisation, such as family members and friends, also influence decision-makers, organisational culture and structure operate through organisational relationships to influence ethical decisions.

Organisational (corporate) culture is a set of values, beliefs, goals, norms and rituals that members of an organisation share. These values also help shape employees' satisfaction with their employer, which may affect the quality of the service they provide to customers. At least 92 per cent of surveyed employees who see trust, respect and honesty applied frequently in their organisations express satisfaction with their employers. A company's culture may be expressed formally through codes of conduct, memos, manuals, dress codes and ceremonies, but it is also conveyed informally through work habits, extracurricular activities and anecdotes. An organisation's culture gives its members meaning, and suggests rules for how to behave and deal with problems within the organisation.

> **organisational (corporate) culture** a set of values, beliefs, goals, norms and rituals that members of an organisation share

Most experts agree that the chief executive, managing director or marketing director sets the ethical tone for the entire organisation. Lower level managers take their cue from top managers, but they too impose some of their personal values on the company. This interaction between corporate culture and executive leadership helps determine the company's ethical value system.

Colleagues' influence on an individual's ethical choices depends on the person's exposure to unethical behaviour. Especially in grey areas, the more a person is exposed to unethical activity by others in the organisational environment, the more likely he or she is to behave unethically. Most marketing employees take a lead from colleagues in learning how to solve problems, including ethical problems. Indeed, research suggests that marketing employees who perceive their work environment as ethical, experience less role conflict and ambiguity, are more satisfied with their jobs, and are more committed to their employer.

Organisational pressure plays a key role in creating ethical issues. For example, because of pressure to meet a deadline, a superior may ask a sales person to lie to a customer over the phone about a late product shipment. Similarly, pressure to meet a sales quota may result in overly aggressive sales tactics. Research in this area indicates that superiors and colleagues can generate organisational pressure, which plays a key role in creating ethical issues. In a study by the Ethics Resource

Centre, 60 per cent of respondents said they had experienced pressure from superiors or colleagues to compromise ethical standards to achieve business objectives. Nearly all businesses face difficult issues whose solutions are not obvious or that present conflicts between organisational objectives and personal ethics.

Opportunity Opportunity provides another pressure that may shape ethical decisions in business. **Opportunity** is a favourable set of conditions that limit barriers or provide rewards. A marketing employee who takes advantage of an opportunity to act unethically and is rewarded or suffers no penalty may repeat such acts as other opportunities arise. For example, a sales person who receives a bonus after using a deceptive sales presentation to increase sales is being rewarded and thus will probably continue the behaviour. Indeed, the opportunity to engage in unethical conduct is often a better predictor of unethical activities than are personal values. Beyond rewards and the absence of punishment, other elements in the business environment may create opportunities. Professional codes of conduct and ethics-related corporate policy also influence opportunity by prescribing what behaviours are acceptable, as will be explained later. The larger the rewards and the milder the punishment for unethical conduct, the greater the likelihood that unethical behaviour will occur.

 opportunity a favourable set of conditions that limit barriers or provide rewards

However, just as the majority of people who go into retail stores do not try to shoplift at each opportunity, most managers do not try to take advantage of every opportunity for unethical behaviour in their organisations. Although managers often perceive many opportunities to engage in unethical conduct in their companies and industries, research suggests that most refrain from taking advantage of such opportunities. Moreover, most managers do not believe unethical conduct in general results in success. Individual factors as well as organisational culture may influence whether an individual becomes opportunistic and tries to take advantage of situations unethically.

Improving ethical conduct in business

It is possible to improve ethical conduct in an organisation by taking on ethical employees and eliminating unethical ones, and by improving the organisation's ethical standards. One way to approach improvement of an organisation's ethical standards is to use a "bad apple/bad barrel" analogy. Some people always do things in their own self-interest, regardless of organisational goals or accepted moral standards; such people are sometimes referred to as "bad apples". To eliminate unethical conduct, an organisation must rid itself of bad apples through screening techniques and enforcement of the company's ethical standards. However, organisations sometimes become 'bad barrels' themselves, not because the individuals within them are unethical but because the pressures to survive and succeed create conditions (opportunities) that reward unethical behaviour. One way to resolve the problem of the bad barrel is to redesign the organisation's image and culture so that it conforms to industry and societal norms of ethical conduct.

If senior management develops and enforces ethics and legal compliance programmes to encourage ethical decision-making, it becomes a force to help individuals make better decisions. A recent National Business Ethics Survey in the U.S. found that ethics programmes that include written standards of conduct, ethics training, ethics advice lines or offices and systems for anonymous reporting increase the likelihood that employees will report misconduct observed in the workplace. Thus, a well implemented formal ethics and compliance programme and a strong corporate culture result in the greatest reduction of future misconduct. Companies that wish to improve their ethics, need to implement a strong ethics and compliance programme and encourage commitment to it. When marketers understand the policies and requirements for ethical conduct, they can more easily resolve ethical conflicts. However, marketers can never fully abdicate their personal ethical responsibility in making decisions. Claiming to be an agent of the business ("the company told me to do it") is unacceptable as a legal excuse and is even less defensible from an ethical perspective.

Codes of conduct Without compliance programmes, and uniform standards and policies regarding conduct, it is hard for employees to determine what conduct is acceptable within the company. In the absence of such programmes and standards, employees will generally make decisions based on their observations of how co-workers and superiors behave. To improve ethics, many organisations have developed **codes of conduct** (also called codes of ethics) consisting of formalised rules and standards that describe what the company expects of its employees. Most large businesses have formal codes of conduct. Codes of conduct promote ethical behaviour by reducing opportunities for unethical behaviour; employees know both what is expected of them and what kind of punishment they face if they violate the rules. Codes help marketers deal with ethical issues or dilemmas that develop in daily operations by prescribing or limiting specific activities. Codes of conduct have also made companies that subcontract manufacturing operations abroad more aware of the ethical issues associated with supporting facilities that underpay and even abuse their workforce.

codes of conduct formalised rules and standards that describe what the company expects of its employees

Codes of conduct do not have to take every situation into account, but they should provide guidelines that enable employees to achieve organisational objectives in an ethical, acceptable manner. The Ethical Trading Initiative (ETI) works in partnership with its membership of companies, trade unions and voluntary organisations to improve the quality of life of workers around the world. Among its members are Mothercare, Monsoon, Accessorize, Tesco, Premier Foods, The Body Shop International and Gap Inc. The alliance's vision is for people to work in freedom, equity and security and to be free from discrimination and exploitation. Table 2.3 summarises ETI's base ethical trade code.

 TABLE 2.3 The ethical trade initiative base code

The ethical trade initiative base code

1 Employment is freely chosen
   1.1 There is no forced, bonded or involuntary prison labour.
   1.2 Workers are not required to lodge 'deposits' or their identity papers with their employer and are free to leave their employer after reasonable notice.
2 Freedom of association and the right to collective bargaining are respected
   2.1 Workers, without distinction, have the right to join or form trade unions of their own choosing and to bargain collectively.
   2.2 The employer adopts an open attitude towards the activities of trade unions and their organisational activities.
   2.3 Workers' representatives are not discriminated against and have access to carry out their representative functions in the workplace.
   2.4 Where the right to freedom of association and collective bargaining is restricted under law, the employer facilitates, and does not hinder, the development of parallel means for independent and free association and bargaining.
3 Working conditions are safe and hygienic
   3.1 A safe and hygienic working environment shall be provided, bearing in mind the prevailing knowledge of the industry and of any specific hazards. Adequate steps shall be taken to prevent accidents and injury to health arising out of, associated with, or occurring in the course of work, by minimising, so far as is reasonably practicable, the causes of hazards inherent in the working environment.
   3.2 Workers shall receive regular and recorded health and safety training, and such training shall be repeated for new or reassigned workers.
   3.3 Access to clean toilet facilities and to potable water, and, if appropriate, sanitary facilities for food storage shall be provided.

   The ETI Base Code underpins all of ETI's work. It was negotiated and agreed by the founding trade union, NGO and corporate members of ETI and contains nine clauses which reflect the most relevant conventions of the International Labour Organisation with respect to labour practices.

Source: http://www.ethicaltrade.org/sites/default/files/resources/ETI%20Base%20Code%20%20English_0.pdf, accessed on 9th July, 2011.

Ethics officers   Organisational compliance programmes must be overseen by high-ranking members of the business, who are known to respect legal and ethical standards. Many companies including Starbucks and Walmart have ethics officers. Ethics officers are typically responsible for creating and distributing a code of conduct, enforcing the code, and meeting with organisational members to discuss or provide advice about ethical issues. They may also set up telephone "hotlines" to provide advice to employees faced with an ethical issue.

Implementing ethics and legal compliance programmes   To nurture ethical conduct in business, open communication and coaching on ethical issues are essential. This involves providing employees with ethics training, clear channels of communication and follow-up support throughout the organisation. Companies need to consistently enforce standards and impose penalties on those who violate codes of conduct. In addition, businesses must take reasonable steps in response to violations of standards and, as appropriate, revise their compliance programmes to diminish the likelihood of future misconduct.

To succeed, a compliance programme must be viewed as part of the overall marketing strategy implementation. If ethics officers and other executives are not committed to the principles and initiatives of marketing ethics and social responsibility, the programme's effectiveness will be compromised. Although the virtues of honesty, fairness and openness are often assumed to be self-evident and universally accepted, marketing strategy decisions involve complex and detailed matters in which correctness may not be so clear-cut. A high level of personal morality may not be sufficient to prevent an individual from violating the law in an organisational context in which even experienced lawyers debate the exact meaning of the law.

Because it is impossible to train all members of an organisation as lawyers, the identification of ethical issues and implementation of compliance programmes and codes of conduct that incorporate both legal and ethical concerns constitute the best approach to preventing violations and avoiding litigation. Codifying ethical standards into meaningful policies that spell out what is and is not acceptable gives marketers an opportunity to reduce the probability of behaviour that could create legal problems. Without proper ethical training and guidance, it is impossible for the average marketing manager to understand the exact boundaries of illegality in the areas of price fixing, copyright violations, fraud, export/import violations and so on. A corporate focus on ethics helps create a buffer zone around issues that could trigger serious legal considerations for a company.

INCORPORATING SOCIAL RESPONSIBILITY AND ETHICS INTO MARKETING DECISIONS

Although the concepts of marketing ethics and social responsibility are often used interchangeably, it is important to distinguish between them. *Ethics* relates to individual and group decisions: judgements about what is right or wrong in a particular decision-making situation. *Social responsibility*, on the other hand, deals with the total effect of marketing decisions on society. The two concepts are interrelated because a company that supports socially responsible decisions and adheres to a code of conduct is likely to have a positive effect on society. The Fair Trade Movement is dedicated to working with companies in the grocery industry to benefit supplying communities. Because ethics and social responsibility programmes can be profitable as well, an increasing number of companies are incorporating them into their overall marketing ethos. The Fair Trade movement is growing, but depends on the ethical behaviour of producers and marketers in order to ensure identified products conform to the movement's standards.

As has been emphasised throughout this chapter, ethics is just one dimension of social responsibility. Being socially responsible relates to doing what is economically sound, legal, ethical and socially conscious. One way to evaluate whether a specific activity is ethical and socially responsible is to ask other members of the organisation if they approve of it. Contact with concerned consumer groups and industry or government regulatory groups may be helpful. A check to see whether there is a specific company policy about an activity may help resolve ethical questions.

TABLE 2.4	Organisational audit of social responsibility and ethics control mechanisms

Answer 'True' (T) or 'False' (F) for each statement

1	No mechanism exists for top management to detect social responsibility and ethical issues relating to employees, customers, the community and society	T	F
2	There is no formal or informal communication within the organisation about procedures and activities that are considered acceptable behaviour	T	F
3	The organisation fails to communicate its ethical standards to suppliers, customers and groups that have a relationship with the organisation	T	F
4	There is an environment of deception, repression and cover-ups concerning events that could be embarrassing to the company	T	F
5	Reward systems are totally dependent on economic performance	T	F
6	The only concerns about environmental impact are those that are legally required	T	F
7	Concern for the ethical value systems of the community with regard to the company's activities is absent	T	F
8	Products are described in a misleading manner, with no information on negative impact or limitations communicated to customers	T	F

True answers indicate a lack of control mechanisms, which, if implemented, could improve ethics and social responsibility

If other organisation members approve of the activity and it is legal and customary within the industry, chances are the activity is acceptable from both an ethical and a social responsibility perspective. Table 2.4 provides an audit of mechanisms to help control ethics and social responsibility in marketing.

A rule of thumb for resolving ethical and social responsibility issues is that if an issue can withstand open discussion that results in agreement or limited debate, an acceptable solution may exist. Nevertheless, even after a final decision has been reached, different viewpoints on the issue may remain. Openness is not a complete solution to the ethics problem; however, it creates trust and facilitates learning relationships.

Being socially responsible and ethical is challenging

To promote socially responsible and ethical behaviour while achieving organisational goals, marketers must monitor changes and trends in society's values. In response to increasing concerns about sustainability, more firms are making commitments to behave responsibly in this regard. PepsiCo U.K. is one example, having committed to making all of its packaging renewable, biodegradable or recyclable by 2018. Although implementing the programme will not be without difficulty, the president of PepsiCo U.K. explains that, "The business case is clear. Building sustainability into our corporate DNA cuts costs, drives innovation, reduces risk and motivates employees".

Likewise, when consumers began to demand greater transparency, or openness, from companies in the wake of a number of ethics scandals, transparency became a factor in most marketing and management decisions.* An organisation's senior management must assume some responsibility for employees' conduct by establishing and enforcing policies that address society's desires.

After determining what society wants, managers try to predict the long-term effects of decisions relating to those wants. Specialists outside the company, such as doctors, lawyers and scientists, are often consulted, but sometimes there is a lack of agreement within a discipline as to what is an acceptable marketing decision. Today, not all scientists agree about the causes or likely impact of global warming. Forty years ago, tobacco marketers promoted cigarettes as being good for people's health, yet today it is recognised that cigarette smoking is linked to cancer and other medical problems. Consequently, society's attitude towards smoking has changed, and some governments have passed legislation banning smoking in public places. This has implications for marketers, such as those in hotels and leisure sites, who must implement this change and consider whether they wish to provide smoking areas away from the rest of their customers.

Many of society's demands impose costs. For example, society wants a cleaner environment and the preservation of wildlife and its habitats, but it also wants low priced products. This means that companies must carefully balance the costs of providing low priced products against the costs of manufacturing, packaging and distributing their products in an environmentally responsible manner.

In trying to satisfy the desires of one group, marketers may dissatisfy others. Regarding the smoking debate, for example, marketers must balance non-smokers' desire for a smoke-free environment against smokers' desire, or need, to continue to smoke. Some anti-smoking campaigners call for the complete elimination of tobacco products to ensure a smoke-free world. However, this attitude fails to consider the difficulty smokers have in quitting. Thus, this issue, like most ethical and social responsibility issues, cannot be viewed in black and white terms.

Satisfying the demands of all members of society is difficult, if not impossible. Marketers must evaluate the extent to which members of society are willing to pay for what they want. For instance, customers may want more information about a product but be unwilling to pay the costs the business incurs in providing the data. Marketers who want to make socially responsible decisions may find the task a challenge because, ultimately, they must ensure their economic survival.

Social responsibility and ethics improve marketing performance

Increasing evidence indicates that being socially responsible and ethical pays off. Research suggests that a relationship exists between a marketing orientation and an organisational climate that supports marketing ethics and social responsibility. This relationship implies that being ethically and socially concerned is consistent with meeting the demands of customers and other stakeholders. By encouraging employees to understand their markets, companies can help them respond to stakeholders' demands.

A survey of marketing managers found a direct association between corporate social responsibility and profits. In a survey of consumers, around three-quarters indicated that they would pay more for a product that came from a socially responsible company. Almost half of young adults aged 18 to 25 said they would take a pay cut to work for a socially responsible company.

Recognition is therefore growing that the long-term value of conducting business in a socially responsible manner far outweighs short-term costs. Companies that fail to develop strategies and programmes to incorporate ethics and social responsibility into their organisational culture may pay the price with poor marketing performance and the potential costs of legal violations, civil litigation and damaging publicity when questionable activities are made public.

Because marketing ethics and social responsibility are not always viewed as organisational performance issues, many managers do not believe they need to consider them in the strategic planning process. Individuals also have different ideas as to what is ethical or unethical, leading them to confuse the need for workplace ethics and the right to maintain their own personal values and ethics. While the concepts are undoubtedly controversial, it is possible, and desirable, to incorporate ethics and social responsibility into the planning process.

SOCIAL MARKETING

The use of marketing in commercial settings is well established. Social marketers use the same tools and techniques to achieve social, rather than commercial, objectives. **Social marketing** involves using commercial marketing ideas and tools to change behaviour in ways that will improve the well-being of individuals and society. For example, research evidence shows that images of smoking in movies can strongly influence young people to start smoking. The SmokeFree Liverpool youth group is using a campaign called "Toxic Movies" to put pressure on the film industry to remove images of smoking from movies which are rated as suitable for young people. The group is critical of what it describes as a "long history of close relationships between the studios and the tobacco industry ..."

TABLE 2.5	Difference in approach between commercial and social marketers

Commercial marketers	Social marketers
• Primary aim: Sales, profit and shareholder value	• Primary aim: Achieving a "social good"
• Privately accountable e.g.: Shareholders and directors	• Funded from public funds (taxes, donations)
• Funded from investments and sales	• Publicly accountable
• Performance measured in profits and market share	• Performance measured by actual behavioural goals
• Defined products or services driven by demand	• Products or services often focused on addressing complex, challenging or controversial behaviours
• Commercial culture – risk-taking culture often evident	• Public sector culture – risk averse culture often evident
• Relationships commonly competitive	• Relationships often based on building trust

Source: French, J. and Blair-Stevens, C. (2007), 'Social Marketing Big Pocket Guide', National Social Marketing Centre, (http://www.nsmcentre.org.uk/sites/default/files/NSMC_Big_Pocket_Guide_Aug_2007_2.pdf).

(www.liverpool.gov.uk/smokingfilms/; http://www.smokefreeliverpool.com/). Table 2.5 explains the differences in priorities and approach for commercial and social marketers.

> **social marketing** use of tools and techniques from commercial marketing to encourage positive behavioural changes, such as quitting smoking, reducing alcohol consumption, minimising anti-social behaviours or reducing carbon footprint.

Many social marketing programmes seek to achieve changes in health behaviour, such as encouraging individuals to quit smoking, exercise more often, eat more healthily or drink less alcohol. However, this is not always the case. Encouraging more sustainable behaviour by increasing recycling rates, getting drivers to reduce their speed or drive more safely, and even encouraging people to pay their taxes are some of the other situations in which social marketing has been applied. The common thread in all of these campaigns is the link between achieving behaviour change and enhancing social good.

The kinds of social marketing initiatives that target individuals whose behaviour needs to be changed are sometimes referred to as downstream social marketing. Often these downstream efforts need to be combined with upstream activities targeting influential stakeholders such as governments, regulators, health professionals and industries. For example, while health professionals in the U.K. have for many years targeted individual smokers with programmes designed to encourage them to quit (downstream initiatives), the introduction of legislation to ban smoking in public places (an upstream initiative) has had a profound effect on levels of quitting and smoking take-up.

Social marketers need to make sure that those who are targeted with social marketing programmes are actively involved in the process. The improvements to individual and social well-being at the heart of social marketing can only be achieved if voluntary behaviour change takes place. Just as in commercial marketing, social marketing involves an exchange between organisations or individuals responsible for a particular programme and the consumers who are on the receiving end. For example, the central exchange in a vaccination programme involves individuals who agree to be vaccinated being offered protection against future illness. Similarly, those who sign up to a programme to help them cut down on their calorie intake and increase their life expectancy as per the "Change4Life" campaign, are hoping to improve their health and reduce their financial outlay on drink in exchange for altering their behaviour.

One of the challenges faced by social marketing programmes is that the benefits on offer can be quite intangible. For instance, although the problems associated with global warming and sustainability are well recognised, many consumers struggle to change their behaviour in ways that will protect the environment. Cutting down on leisure travel, improving recycling behaviour and cutting energy use can seem like a major sacrifice for consumers. Sometimes people also find it difficult to accept that behaviour change made at the individual level can make a real difference to the global picture. For these reasons social marketers have to work hard to ensure that they are genuinely consumer orientated and must often use innovative approaches to encourage people to modify their behaviour. Nevertheless social marketing applications have broadened the scope for marketing practice.

SUMMARY

Social responsibility refers to an organisation's obligation to maximise its positive impact and minimise its negative impact on society. Although social responsibility is a positive concept, most organisations embrace it in the expectation of indirect long-term benefits.

Marketing citizenship involves adopting a strategic focus for fulfilling the economic, legal, ethical and philanthropic social responsibilities expected of organisations by their *stakeholders,* those constituents who have a stake, or claim, in some aspect of the company's products, operations, markets, industry and outcomes.

At the most basic level, companies have an economic responsibility to be profitable so that they can provide a return on investment to their stockholders, create jobs for the community and contribute goods and services to the economy. Businesses are also expected to obey laws and regulations. *Marketing ethics* refers to principles and standards that define acceptable conduct in marketing as determined by various stakeholders, including the public, government regulators, private interest groups, industry and the organisation itself. Philanthropic responsibilities, which encompass *cause-related marketing* go beyond marketing ethics; they are not required of a company, but they promote human welfare or goodwill, known as *strategic philanthropy.*

Three major categories of social responsibility issues are the natural environment, consumerism and community relations. A common way in which marketers demonstrate social responsibility is through programmes designed to protect and preserve the natural environment. *Green marketing* refers to the specific development, pricing, promotion and distribution of products that do not harm the environment. Consumerism consists of the efforts of independent individuals, groups and organisations to protect the rights of consumers.

Whereas social responsibility is achieved by balancing the interests of all stakeholders in the organisation, ethics relates to acceptable standards of conduct in making individual and group decisions. Marketing ethics goes beyond legal issues, fostering mutual trust in marketing relationships.

An *ethical issue* is an identifiable problem, situation or opportunity requiring an individual or organisation to choose between actions that must be evaluated as right or wrong, ethical or unethical. A number of ethical issues relate to the marketing mix (product, people, promotion, price and place/distribution).

Individual factors, organisational relationships and opportunity interact to determine ethical decisions in business. Individuals often base their decisions on their own values and principles of right or wrong. However, ethical choices in marketing are often made jointly, in work groups or with colleagues, and are shaped by *organisational (corporate) culture* and structure. The more someone is exposed to unethical activity in the organisational environment, the more likely he or she is to behave unethically. Organisational pressure and *opportunity* play a key role in creating ethical issues.

Improving ethical behaviour in an organisation can be achieved by developing and enforcing ethics and legal compliance programmes, establishing *codes of conduct,* formalised rules and standards that describe what the company expects of its employees, and having an ethics officer.

To nurture ethical conduct in business, open communication and coaching on ethical issues are essential. This requires providing employees with ethics training, clear channels of communication and follow-up support throughout the organisation. Companies must consistently enforce standards and impose penalties on those who violate codes of conduct.

Companies are increasingly incorporating ethics and social responsibility programmes into their marketing decisions. Increasing evidence indicates that being socially responsible and ethical results in valuable benefits: an enhanced public reputation, which can increase market share, costs savings and profits.

Social marketing uses tools and techniques from commercial marketing to encourage positive behavioural changes, such as quitting smoking, reducing alcohol consumption, minimising anti-social behaviours or reducing carbon footprint. The health and well-being of individuals, society and the planet are at the core of social marketing. Whereas the main aim of commercial marketing is to generate sales, profit and shareholder value, social marketers are concerned with achieving social good and behaviour change. Downstream social marketing activities targeting behaviour change often combined with upstream initiatives aimed at influential stakeholders such as governments, regulators, health professionals and industries.

EXERCISE QUESTIONS

1 What is social responsibility and why is it important?

2 What are some major social responsibility issues? Give an example of each.

3 What is the difference between ethics and social responsibility?

4 How can people with different personal values work together to make ethical decisions in organisations?

5 What evidence exists that being socially responsible and ethical is worthwhile?

CASE 2.1

Masdar

Masdar is a radical "project" in Abu Dhabi in the United Arab Emirates that raises interesting questions about how one might evaluate success.

The U.A.E. relies heavily on oil – Abu Dhabi has some 8 per cent of the known supplies in the world – which should last it for another 100 years. But it is a desert region with a hot and humid climate. Summer temperatures can easily exceed 50 degrees centigrade and sandstorms are normal. Air conditioning is ubiquitous. Research by the World Wildlife Fund and others (working together) has concluded that per capita it has the "world's worst environmental footprint".

Masdar is a planned city designed by U.K. architects Foster & Partners. It is being built by the Future Energy Company with seed capital from the government. Located next to the international airport, the new city will be entirely dependent on solar and other renewable energy and there will be a zero carbon and a zero waste ecology. In the first instance a solar energy plant is being constructed to (amongst other things) provide the energy for wind farms on the peripheries of the city, a hydrogen power plant and geothermal facilities. The intention is to attract "clean-tech" companies that both carry out research and design and manufacture environmentally friendly products.

The city project was started in 2006 with an intended timescale of 8 years to completion and with a first phase completion in 2009. But this was before the global financial crisis. Phase one is now scheduled to be finished in 2015 and with everything else some 5 to 10 years down the line. At the same time the budget has been reduced by between 10 and 15 per cent. The Masdar Institute of Science and Technology (with links to the Massachusetts Institute of Technology, MIT, in the U.S.) is already open and operating within the developing city. Large companies such as General Electric are "signed up", and it seems as if a solid cluster of related businesses will co-locate there.

When complete, Masdar will be a large block of around 6 square kilometres. There will be a perimeter wall to block out the hot desert winds but to also channel air movement in order to create an air flow down the carefully designed streets and reduce the need for extensive air conditioning. Between 45,000 and 50,000 people will live in the city and up to 60,000 will commute in to work. There will be no cars and instead a new rapid transit system. With around 100 stations and 3000 pods, people will be able to access transport within 150 metres of where they are anywhere inside the city boundary. This system will connect to the public transport outside the city. Water will come from a solar powered desalination plant and will be recycled as much as possible. Crops will be watered with grey water. Biological waste will be treated to make fertiliser. Plastics and metals will be recycled locally. Palmwood (taken from trees that no longer bear fruit) is being used extensively.

So how much is Masdar an exciting model for the future and how much is it an indulgence for the wealthy elite of Abu Dhabi?

The city is meant to be commercially viable. Revenues will be earned from its commercial and trading activities. There will be an income from selling and licensing its new technologies. Ideally there will be synergy from learning from doing and exploiting the new knowledge. There is the potential to learn lessons that are valuable for improving living conditions in desert countries everywhere.

A long-term sustainability perspective is being taken – given Abu Dhabi's oil reserves are thought to be finite. Throughout the world there is increasing interest in renewable energy sources not dependent on oil and other fossil fuels. There is perhaps an assumption that over time Abu Dhabi can become a knowledge economy and therefore more sustainable – at the same time, helping the rest of the world.

But there is perhaps one irony. The future energy company is a subsidiary of Mubadala – an organisation that is also committed to revenue generating from its attractions including the Formula 1 racetrack and a Ferrari-themed Amusement Park. Neither of these will be carbon neutral.

Question

1 Over time how do you think the relative success of Masdar will be evaluated?

2 Are you in favour of the "measures" you believe will be used? Are they sufficiently holistic?

Hence there is the potential for a cynical view that Masdar is largely a "balancing act". We must all decide for ourselves.

3 Use the Internet to research the latest developments with Masdar. How well have the original aims been met to date?

CHAPTER REFERENCES

Arnold, C., *Ethical Marketing and the New Consumer: Marketing in the New Ethical Economy* (Wiley, 2009).

Brenkert, G.G., *Marketing Ethics* (Wiley-Blackwell, 2008).

Crane, A. and Matten, B., *Business Ethics: Managing Corporate Citizenship and Sustainability in the Age of Globalisation* (Oxford University Press, 2010).

Eagle, L., Tapp, A., Dahl, S. and Bird, S., *Social Marketing* (FT/Prentice-Hall, 2012).

Ferrell, O.C., Fraedrich, J. and Ferrell, L., *Business Ethics: Ethical Decision Making and Cases,* 8th edn (Houghton Mifflin, 2010).

Grant, J., *The Green Marketing Manifesto* (Wiley, 2007).

Hastings, G., *Social Marketing: Why Should the Devil Have All the Best Tunes?* (Butterworth-Heinemann, 2007).

Hastings, G. and Domegan, C., *Social Marketing* (Routledge, 2012).

Kotler, P. and Lee, N.R., *Social Marketing: Influencing Behaviours for Good* (Sage, 2011).

Ottman, J.A., *The New Rules of Green Marketing: Strategies, Tools, and Inspiration for Sustainable Branding* (Greenleaf Publishing, 2010).

Paetzold, K., *Corporate Social Responsibility (CSR): An International Marketing Approach* (Diplomica Verlag, 2010).

Sage Publications, *Sage Brief Guide to Marketing Ethics* (Sage, 2011).

3 GLOBAL BUSINESS

BUSINESS FOCUS

Sole Rebels

Sole Rebels is a story about innovation and how an innovative young African company has found opportunities to reach international markets. The company is based in Addis Ababa, Ethiopia. Ethiopia is heavily dependent on foreign aid; and whilst micro businesses such as this are not at all unusual, successfully accessing foreign markets is.

Sole Rebels was founded in 2005 by a local entrepreneur, a young lady accountant, Bethlehem Alemu, who was in her mid-20s when she saw an opportunity to create jobs for local people. She saw a business opportunity in something people, particularly soldiers, had been doing for some time. She started making shoes from recycled materials. She cut up old truck tyres to make the soles and initially used old camouflage jackets and trousers for the tops. Because she wanted something more fashionable, she found some people who would use traditional spinning methods to produce hard-wearing cloth (in attractive designs) for the uppers. It so happened that these suppliers lived in a leprosy area, and so again there was a strong social element underlying the decision. Local strips of leather are also used.

Many of her shoes are causal – sandals, boat shoes, loafers and flip-flops. She is constantly trawling the Internet to find ideas for new designs and improving her range – which boasts names such as Night Rider, Pure Love, New Deal, Class Act, Gruuv Thong and Urban Runner.

The shoes can be bought online from Amazon, as well as direct from the business itself, and through physical outlets in the U.S., Canada and Australia as well as in Africa. Retailers include Whole Foods (because of the materials used) and Urban Outfitters. The African Growth and Opportunity Act (AGOA) is also useful as it allows businesses in certain African countries (Ethiopia is one) to import into the U.S. tariff-free. An Ethiopian government line of credit also helps with the cash flow for large orders.

Production is based in a local workshop but Sole Rebels remains in large part a family-run business. There are around 45 full-time staff and they produce some 500 pairs of shoes a day. Daily wages range from £1.50 for a trainee to £7.00 for a skilled worker. In a global context this is competitively low; in Ethiopian terms it is relatively generous. Customers can scan in the outline of their sole and have shoes hand cut to size. Retail prices range from £21.00 to £40.00. Bethlehem sees her shoes as the 'Timberland or Skechers of Africa' and always seeks to offer uniquely-designed products that have international appeal at affordable prices. She does not want Sole Rebels to look too African. She wants people to buy because they are good shoes that they will enjoy wearing and not because by buying from her they are helping Ethiopia's poor people.

Sole Rebels is just one of a growing number of companies, large and small, that are doing business in other countries across the world. Some companies, such as Coca-Cola, sell to firms in other countries; others, such as Pier 1 Imports, buy goods around the world to import into the United States. Whether they buy or sell products across national borders, these companies are all contributing to the volume of international trade that is fueling the global economy.

Theoretically, international trade is every bit as logical and worthwhile as national trade between, say, Cape Town and Pretoria in South Africa. Yet, nations tend to restrict the import of certain goods for a variety of reasons. For example, in the early 2000s, the United States restricted the import of Mexican fresh tomatoes because they were undercutting price levels of domestic fresh tomatoes.

Despite such restrictions, international trade has increased almost steadily since World War II. Many of the industrialised nations have signed trade agreements intended to eliminate problems in international business and to help less-developed nations, such as Ethiopia, participate in world trade. Individual firms around the world have seized the opportunity to compete in foreign markets by exporting products and increasing foreign production, as well as by other means.

In his bestselling book, *The World Is Flat*, the American author and newspaper columnist Thomas L. Friedman states, "The flattening of the world has presented us with new opportunities, new challenges, new partners but, also, alas new dangers, ... it is imperative that we be the best global citizens that we can be—because in a flat world, if you don't visit a bad neighbourhood, it might visit you."

We describe international trade in this chapter in terms of modern specialisation, whereby each country trades the surplus goods and services it produces most efficiently for products in short supply. We also explain the restrictions nations place on products and services from other countries and present some of the possible advantages and disadvantages of these restrictions. We then describe the extent of international trade and identify the organisations working to foster it. We describe several methods of entering international markets and the various sources of export assistance available from the federal government. Finally, we identify some of the institutions that provide the complex financing necessary for modern international trade.

THE BASIS FOR INTERNATIONAL BUSINESS

International business encompasses all business activities that involve exchanges across national boundaries. Thus, a firm is engaged in international business when it buys some portion of its input from, or sells some portion of its output to, an organisation located in a foreign country. (A small local shop may sell goods produced in some other country. However, because it purchases these goods from domestic distributors, it is not directly engaged in international trade.)

international business all business activities that involve exchanges across national boundaries

Absolute and comparative advantage

Some countries are better equipped than others to produce particular goods or services. The reason may be a country's natural resources, its labour supply, or even customs or a historical accident. Such a country would be best off if it could specialise in the production of such products so that it can produce them most efficiently. The country could use what it needed of these products and then trade the surplus for products it could not produce efficiently on its own.

Saudi Arabia thus has specialised in the production of crude oil and petroleum products; South Africa, in diamonds; and Australia, in wool. Each of these countries is said to have an absolute advantage with regard to a particular product. An **absolute advantage** is the ability to produce a specific product more efficiently than any other nation.

absolute advantage the ability to produce a specific product more efficiently than any other nation

One country may have an absolute advantage with regard to several products, whereas another country may have no absolute advantage at all. Yet it is still worthwhile for these two countries to specialise and trade with each other. To see why this is so, imagine that you are the president of a successful manufacturing firm and that you can accurately type 90 words per minute. Your assistant can type 80 words per minute but would run the business poorly. Thus, you have an absolute advantage over your assistant in both typing and managing. However, you cannot afford to type your own

Utilising an absolute advantage. For many years, Saudi Arabia has specialised in the production of crude oil. Because of its natural resource, Saudi Arabia and some other countries enjoy an absolute advantage—their ability to produce crude oil more efficiently than countries in other parts of the world.

letters because your time is better spent in managing the business. That is, you have a **comparative advantage** in managing. A comparative advantage is the ability to produce a specific product more efficiently than any other product.

comparative advantage the ability to produce a specific product more efficiently than any other product

Your assistant, on the other hand, has a comparative advantage in typing because he or she can do that better than managing the business. Thus, you spend your time managing, and you leave the typing to your assistant. Overall, the business is run as efficiently as possible because you are each working in accordance with your own comparative advantage.

The same is true for nations. Goods and services are produced more efficiently when each country specialises in the products for which it has a comparative advantage. Moreover, by definition, every country has a comparative advantage in some product. South Africa, for example, has comparative advantages in tourism, mining and mineral extraction, whereas the United States has comparative advantages in research and development, high-technology industries, and identifying new markets.

Exporting and Importing

Suppose that the United Kingdom specialises in producing cider. It then will produce a surplus of cider, but perhaps it will have a shortage of wine. France, on the other hand, specialises in producing wine but experiences a shortage of cider. To satisfy both needs—for cider and for wine—the two countries should trade with each other. The United Kingdom should export cider and import wine. France should export wine and import cider.

Exporting is selling and shipping raw materials or products to other nations. Anglo American Platinum based in South Africa, for example, exports its platinum and other metals to a number of countries for use in production of machinery and transport construction.

exporting selling and shipping raw materials or products to other nations

Importing is purchasing raw materials or products in other nations and bringing them into one's own country. Thus, buyers for a shopping mall department store in Dubai may purchase rugs in India or electronic goods in Germany and have them shipped back to the United Arab Emirates for resale.

importing purchasing raw materials or products in other nations and bringing them into one's own country

Importing and exporting are the principal activities in international trade. They give rise to an important concept called the *balance of trade*. A nation's **balance of trade** is the total value of its exports minus the total value of its imports over some period of time. If a country imports more than it exports, its balance of trade is negative and is said to be *unfavourable.* (A negative balance of trade is unfavourable because the country must export money to pay for its excess imports.)

balance of trade the total value of a nation's exports minus the total value of its imports over some period of time

In 2011, the United States imported $2,661 billion worth of goods and services and exported $2,103 billion worth. It thus had a trade deficit of $558 billion. A **trade deficit** is a negative balance of trade (see Figure 3.1). However, the United States has consistently enjoyed a large and rapidly growing surplus in services.

trade deficit a negative balance of trade

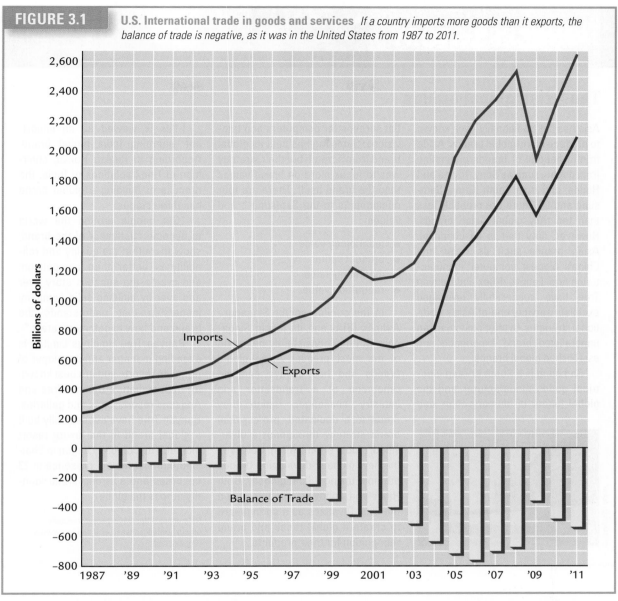

FIGURE 3.1 **U.S. International trade in goods and services** *If a country imports more goods than it exports, the balance of trade is negative, as it was in the United States from 1987 to 2011.*

Source: U.S. Department of Commerce, International Trade Administration, U.S. Bureau of Economic Analysis, www.census.gov/foreign-trade/Press-Release/curent_press_release/ft900.pdf (accessed March 8, 2012).

Question: *Are trade deficits bad?*

Answer: In testimony before the U.S. Senate Finance Committee, Daniel T. Griswold, associate director of the Center for Trade Policy at the Cato Institute, remarked, "The trade deficit is not a sign of economic distress, but of rising domestic demand and investment. Imposing new trade barriers will only make Americans worse off while leaving the trade deficit virtually unchanged."

On the other hand, when a country exports more than it imports, it is said to have a favourable balance of trade. This has consistently been the case for Japan over the last two decades or so.

A nation's **balance of payments** is the total flow of money into a country minus the total flow of money out of that country over some period of time. Balance of payments, therefore, is a much broader concept than balance of trade. It includes imports and exports, of course. However, it also includes investments, money spent by foreign tourists, payments by foreign governments, aid to foreign governments, and all other receipts and payments.

SUCCESS STORY

The Asian global brands

Asia has not traditionally been known to produce many global brands. Aside from a handful of brands originating from Japan, such as Sony, Toyota and Honda; and from South Korea, Samsung and LG, there are probably less than ten truly global Asian brands. However, now that is all changing, Asian brands such as Haier and China's biggest computer manufacturing firm, Lenovo, I-flex and Banyan Tree have successfully leveraged excellent service, one of Asia's traditional strengths, to offer customers an unparalleled brand experience and established global brands.

Samsung is a South Korean electrical goods manufacturer and the global leader in memory chips and

flat screens for computers and televisions. Samsung has built its global brand from scratch but their strategy was to focus more on brand values than the brand itself. There are four components to the Samsung brand values:

- technology value
- product value
- marketing value
- reputation value

In the service sector Singapore Airlines (SIA) and its iconic Singapore Girl has consistently been one of the most premier Asian global brands and has always had the reputation of a trendsetter and industry challenger, which they credit to a dedicated, professional brand strategy throughout a diversified, global organisation. However, the new globally-developing brands are now taking a hold globally. Both Haier and Lenovo companies used the 2008 Olympics as a springboard to create a global recall and brand recognition for their products.

I-flex is viewed as an important emerging India global brand. According to Rajesh Hukku, chairman of I-flex solutions of India, the process of building a global brand has three stages:

"Get people around the world to become customers of the brand; show them that the quality and reliability is better than competition; and create the success story over and over by building solid company leadership that understands the brand and how to communicate it."

Banyan Tree Holdings Limited is a leading manager and developer of premium resorts and are best known for their signature Banyan Tree and Angsana resorts, spas and galleries. Banyan Tree have successfully built a global brand in the luxury resort market. The company began in Thailand but now have a presence in 23 countries and a strong brand identity across the globe.

References: http://www.banyantree.com/ http://knowledge.insead.edu/ and http://www.reuters.com/.

---

balance of payments the total flow of money into a country minus the total flow of money out of that country over some period of time

A continual deficit in a nation's balance of payments (a negative balance) can cause other nations to lose confidence in that nation's economy. Alternatively, a continual surplus may indicate that the country encourages exports but limits imports by imposing trade restrictions.

RESTRICTIONS TO INTERNATIONAL BUSINESS

Specialisation and international trade can result in the efficient production of want-satisfying goods and services on a worldwide basis. As we have noted, international business generally is increasing. Yet the nations of the world continue to erect barriers to free trade. They do so for reasons ranging from internal political and economic pressures to simple mistrust of other nations. We examine first the types of restrictions that are applied and then the arguments for and against trade restrictions.

Types of trade restrictions

Nations generally are eager to export their products. They want to provide markets for their industries and to develop a favourable balance of trade. Hence, most trade restrictions are applied to imports from other nations.

Tariffs   Perhaps the most commonly applied trade restriction is the customs (or import) duty. An **import duty** (also called a **tariff**) is a tax levied on a particular foreign product entering a country. For example, the United States imposes a 2.2 per cent import duty on fresh Chilean tomatoes, an 8.7 per cent duty if tomatoes are dried and packaged, and nearly 12 per cent if tomatoes are made into ketchup or salsa. The two types of tariffs are revenue tariffs and protective tariffs; both have the effect of raising the price of the product in the importing nations, but for different reasons. *Revenue tariffs* are imposed solely to generate income for the government. For example, the United States imposes a duty on Scotch whiskey solely for revenue purposes. *Protective tariffs*, on the other hand, are imposed to protect a domestic industry from competition by keeping the price of competing imports level with or higher than the price of similar domestic products. Because fewer units of the product will be sold at the increased price, fewer units will be imported. The French and Japanese agricultural sectors would both shrink drastically if their nations abolished the protective tariffs that keep the price of imported farm products high. Today, U.S. tariffs are the lowest in history, with average tariff rates on all imports under 3 per cent.

> **import duty (tariff)** a tax levied on a particular foreign product entering a country

Some countries rationalise their protectionist policies as a way of offsetting an international trade practice called *dumping*. **Dumping** is the exportation of large quantities of a product at a price lower than that of the same product in the home market.

> **dumping** exportation of large quantities of a product at a price lower than that of the same product in the home market

Thus, dumping drives down the price of the domestic item. Recently, for example, the Pencil Makers Association, which represents eight U.S. pencil manufacturers, charged that low-priced pencils from Thailand and the People's Republic of China were being sold in the United States at less than fair value prices. Unable to compete with these inexpensive imports, several domestic manufacturers had to shut down. To protect themselves, domestic manufacturers can obtain an antidumping duty through the government to offset the advantage of the foreign product. Recently, for example, the U.S. Department of Commerce imposed antidumping duties of up to 99 per cent on a variety of steel products imported from China, following allegations by U.S. Steel Corp. and other producers that the products were being dumped at unfair prices.

Nontariff barriers   A **nontariff barrier** is a nontax measure imposed by a government to favour domestic over foreign suppliers. Nontariff barriers create obstacles to the marketing of foreign goods in a country and increase costs for exporters. The following are a few examples of government-imposed nontariff barriers:

> **nontariff barrier** a nontax measure imposed by a government to favour domestic over foreign suppliers

- An **import quota** is a limit on the amount of a particular good that may be imported into a country during a given period of time. The limit may be set in terms of either quantity (so many pounds of beef) or value (so many euros' or pounds' worth of shoes, for example). Quotas also may be set

What does the country of origin label say about the product? *A consumer might want fresh pasta, olive oil, or a coffee machine to be produce of Italy, but a reliable car to be made in Germany, for instance. Likewise, they might want ethically-sourced chocolate or coffee to be made in Africa where it originated.*

on individual products imported from specific countries. Once an import quota has been reached, imports are halted until the specified time has elapsed.

> **import quota** a limit on the amount of a particular good that may be imported into a country during a given period of time

- An **embargo** is a complete halt to trading with a particular nation or of a particular product. The embargo is used most often as a political weapon. At present, the United States has import embargoes against Iran and North Korea—both as a result of extremely poor political relations.

> **embargo** a complete halt to trading with a particular nation or in a particular product

- A **foreign-exchange control** is a restriction on the amount of a particular foreign currency that can be purchased or sold. By limiting the amount of foreign currency importers can obtain, a government limits the amount of goods importers can purchase with that currency. This has the effect of limiting imports from the country whose foreign exchange is being controlled.

> **foreign-exchange control** a restriction on the amount of a particular foreign currency that can be purchased or sold

- A nation can increase or decrease the value of its money relative to the currency of other nations. **Currency devaluation** is the reduction of the value of a nation's currency relative to the currencies of other countries.

> **currency devaluation** the reduction of the value of a nation's currency relative to the currencies of other countries

Devaluation increases the cost of foreign goods, whereas it decreases the cost of domestic goods to foreign firms. For example, suppose for the sake of illustrating the point that the British pound is worth €2. In this case, an Austrian-made €2,000 electronic appliance can be purchased for £1,000. However, if the United Kingdom devalues the pound so that it is worth only €1, that same appliance will cost £2,000. The increased cost, in pounds, will reduce the import of Austrian appliances—and all foreign goods—into England.

On the other hand, before devaluation, a £500 set of English bone china will cost an American $1,000. After the devaluation, the set of china will cost only $500. The decreased cost will make the china—and all English goods—much more attractive to U.S. purchasers. Bureaucratic red tape is more subtle than the other forms of nontariff barriers. Yet it can be the most frustrating trade barrier of all. A few examples are the restrictive application of standards and complex requirements related to product testing, labeling, and certification.

Cultural barriers Another type of nontariff barrier is related to cultural attitudes. Cultural barriers can impede acceptance of products in foreign countries. For example, illustrations of feet are regarded as despicable in Thailand. Even so simple a thing as the colour of a product or its package can present a problem. In Japan, black and white are the colours of mourning, so they should not be used in packaging. In Brazil, purple is the colour of death. And in Egypt, green is never used on a package because it is the national colour. When customers are unfamiliar with particular products from another country, their general perceptions of the country itself affect their attitude toward the product and help to determine whether they will buy it. Because Mexican cars have not been viewed by the world as being quality products, Volkswagen, for example, may not want to advertise that some of its models sold in the United States are made in Mexico. Many retailers on the Internet have yet to come to grips with the task of designing an online shopping site that is attractive and functional for all global customers.

Gifts to authorities—sometimes quite large ones—may be standard business procedure in some countries. In many others, including the United Kingdom, they are called bribes or payoffs and are strictly illegal.

Reasons for trade restrictions

Various reasons are given for trade restrictions either on the import of specific products or on trade with particular countries. We have noted that political considerations usually are involved in trade embargoes. Other frequently-cited reasons for restricting trade include the following:

- *To equalise a nation's balance of payments.* This may be considered necessary to restore confidence in the country's monetary system and in its ability to repay its debts.
- *To protect new or weak industries.* A new, or infant, industry may not be strong enough to withstand foreign competition. Temporary trade restrictions may be used to give it a chance to grow and become self-sufficient. The problem is that once an industry is protected from foreign competition, it may refuse to grow, and "temporary" trade restrictions will become permanent.
- *To protect national security.* Restrictions in this category generally apply to technological products that must be kept out of the hands of potential enemies. For example, strategic and defence-related goods cannot be exported to unfriendly nations.
- *To protect the health of citizens.* Products may be embargoed because they are dangerous or unhealthy (e.g., farm products contaminated with insecticides).
- *To retaliate for another nation's trade restrictions.* A country whose exports are taxed by another country may respond by imposing tariffs on imports from that country.
- *To protect domestic jobs.* By restricting imports, a nation can protect jobs in domestic industries. However, protecting these jobs can be expensive. For example, protecting 9,000 jobs in the U.S. carbon-steel industry costs $6.8 billion, or $750,000 per job.

Reasons against trade restrictions

Trade restrictions have immediate and long-term economic consequences—both within the restricting nation and in world trade patterns. These include the following:

- *Higher prices for consumers.* Higher prices may result from the imposition of tariffs or the elimination of foreign competition.
- *Restriction of consumers' choices.* Again, this is a direct result of the elimination of some foreign products from the marketplace and of the artificially high prices that importers must charge for products that are still imported.
- *Misallocation of international resources.* The protection of weak industries results in the inefficient use of limited resources. The economies of both the restricting nation and other nations eventually suffer because of this waste.
- *Loss of jobs.* The restriction of imports by one nation must lead to cutbacks—and the loss of jobs—in the export-oriented industries of other nations. Furthermore, trade protection has a significant effect on the composition of employment. Trade restrictions—whether on textiles, clothing, steel, or automobiles—benefit only a few industries while harming many others. The gains in employment accrue to the protected industries and their primary suppliers, and the losses are spread across all other industries.

THE EXTENT OF INTERNATIONAL BUSINESS

Restrictions or not, international business is growing. Although the worldwide recessions of 1991 and 2001–2002 slowed the rate of growth, and the 2008–2009 global economic crisis caused the sharpest decline in more than 75 years, globalisation is a reality of our time. In the United States, international trade now accounts for over one-fourth of GDP. As trade barriers decrease, new competitors enter the global marketplace, creating more choices for consumers and new opportunities for job seekers. International business will grow along with the expansion of commercial use of the Internet.

The world economic outlook for trade

Although the global economy continued to grow robustly until 2007 economic performance was not equal: growth in the advanced economies slowed and then stopped in 2009, whereas emerging and developing economies continued to grow. Looking ahead, the International Monetary Fund (IMF), an international bank with 187 member nations, expected a gradual global growth to continue in 2012 and 2013 in both advanced and emerging developing economies.*

Although the U.S. economy had been growing steadily since 2000 and recorded the longest peacetime expansion in the nation's history, the worldwide recession which began in December 2007 has slowed the rate of growth. The IMF estimated that the U.S. economy grew by less than half of 1 per cent in 2008 and, because of subprime mortgage lending and other global financial problems, declined 2.5 per cent in 2009. However, international experts expected global economic growth of

Caterpillar in Saudi Arabia. Restrictions or not, international business is booming. Globalisation is the reality of our time. As trade barriers decrease, ever increasing number of U.S. companies, such as Caterpillar, are selling in the global marketplace.

© COURTESY, CATERPILLAR CORPORATION

3.3 per cent in 2012 and 3.9 per cent in 2013, despite the high oil prices and financial crises in the euro area economies.

Canada and Western Europe   Canada, is projected to show a growth rate of 1.7 per cent in 2012 and 2.0 per cent in 2013. The euro area, which was projected to decline by 0.5 per cent in 2012 is expected to grow 0.8 per cent in 2013. The United Kingdom is expected to grow 0.6 per cent and 2.0 per cent in 2012 and 2013, respectively.

Mexico and Latin America   Mexico, suffered its sharpest recession ever in 1995, and experienced another major setback in 2009. However, its growth rate in 2012 and 2013 is expected to be 3.5 per cent. Brazil escaped the recent global economic crisis with only minor setbacks: Its growth in 2010 was more than 7.5 per cent, and in 2011 it declined to 2.9 per cent. Growth of about 3 per cent and 4 per cent is expected in 2012 and 2013, respectively. In general, the Latin American and the Caribbean economies are recovering at a robust pace.

Japan   Japan's economy is regaining some momentum after suffering from an earthquake, tsunami, and nuclear plant disaster in 2011. Stronger consumer demand and business investment make Japan less reliant on exports for growth. The IMF estimates the growth for Japan at 1.7 per cent in 2012 and 1.8 per cent in 2013.

Other Asian countries   The economic growth in Asia remained strong in 2010 and 2011 despite the global recession. Growth was led by China, where its economy expanded by 9.2 per cent in 2011, and is expected to grow at 8.2 per cent and 8.8 per cent in 2012 and 2013, respectively. Growth in India was 7.4 per cent in 2011, and is predicted to grow at 7 per cent and 7.3 per cent in 2012 and 2013, respectively. Growth in ASEAN-5 countries—Indonesia, Malaysia, the Philippines, Thailand, and Vietnam—is expected at 5.2 per cent and 5.6 per cent in 2012 and 2013, respectively. In short, the key emerging economies in Asia are leading the global recovery.

China's emergence as a global economic power has been among the most dramatic economic developments of recent decades. From 1980 to 2004, China's economy averaged a real GDP growth rate of 9.5 per cent and became the world's sixth-largest economy. By 2004, China had become the third-largest trading nation, behind the United States and Germany and just ahead of Japan. Today, China, the world's second-largest economy, generates 10 to 15 per cent of world GDP, and in 2011, accounted for about 25 per cent of world GDP growth. The United States now imports more goods from China than any other nation in the world. In fact, China, with almost €1.9 trillion in exports, is the world's number-one exporter. In 2012, China took steps to promote the international use of its currency, the renminbi.*

Commonwealth of Independent States   The growth in this region is expected to be 3.7 per cent in 2012 and 3.8 per cent in 2013. Strong growth is expected to continue in Azerbaijan and Armenia, whereas growth is projected to remain stable in Moldova, Tajikistan, and Uzbekistan.

After World War II, trade between the United States and the communist nations of Central and Eastern Europe was minimal. The United States maintained high tariff barriers on imports from most of these countries and also restricted their exports. However, since the disintegration of the Soviet Union and the collapse of communism, trade between the United States and Central and Eastern Europe has expanded substantially.

The countries that made the transition from communist to market economies quickly have recorded positive growth for several years—those that did not continue to struggle. Among the nations that have enjoyed several years of positive economic growth are the member countries of the Central European Free Trade Association: Hungary, the Czech Republic, Poland, Slovenia, and Slovakia.

Exports to Central and Eastern Europe and Russia will increase, as will foreign investment in these countries, as demand for capital goods and technology opens new markets for foreign products. Table 3.1 shows the growth rates from 2010 to 2013 for most regions of the world.

Even though the global economic crisis caused the number of jobs supported by exports to decline sharply in 2009, globalisation represents a huge opportunity for all countries—rich or poor. Indeed, in 2011, for the first time, the U.S. exports exceeded $2.1 trillion and supported 9.7 million jobs, an

TABLE 3.1	**Global growth is picking up gradually** *Growth has been led by developing countries and emerging markets.*			
		Annual per cent change		
	2010	2011	Projected 2012	Projected 2013
World	5.2	3.8	3.3	3.9
United States	3.0	1.8	1.8	2.2
Euro area	1.9	1.6	−0.5	0.8
United Kingdom	2.1	0.9	0.6	2.0
Japan	4.4	−0.9	1.7	1.8
Canada	3.2	2.3	1.7	2.0
Other advanced economies	5.8	3.3	2.6	3.4
Newly industrialised Asian economies	8.4	4.2	3.3	4.1
Developing countries and emerging markets	7.3	6.2	5.4	5.9
Developing Asia	9.5	7.9	7.3	7.8
Commonwealth of Independent States	4.6	4.5	3.7	3.8
Middle East and North Africa	4.3	3.1	3.2	3.6
Latin America and the Caribbean	6.1	4.6	3.6	3.9

Source: International Monetary Fund: World Economic Outlook by International Monetary Fund. Copyright 2012 by International Monetary Fund. Reproduced with permission of International Monetary Fund via Copyright Clearance Center. www.imf.org/external/pubs/ft/weo/2012/update/01/index.htm (accessed March 10, 2012).

increase of $1.2 million since 2009.* The 15-fold increase in trade volume over the past 60 years has been one of the most important factors in the rise of living standards around the world. During this time, exports have become increasingly important to the economy in many countries.

REGIONAL TRADE ALLIANCES AND MARKETS

While some businesses are beginning to view the world as one huge marketplace, opportunities for companies are affected by a range of regional trade alliances. This section examines several regional trade alliances and changing markets, including NAFTA, the European Union, the Pacific Rim markets, changing conditions in Central and Eastern Europe, GATT and the World Trade Organisation.

The North American Free Trade Agreement (NAFTA)

The **North American Free Trade Agreement (NAFTA)**, implemented in 1994, effectively merged Canada, Mexico and the United States into one market of more than 400 million consumers. NAFTA has eliminated virtually all tariffs on goods produced and traded between Canada, Mexico and the United States.

North American Free Trade Agreement (NAFTA) implemented in 1994, and designed to eliminate all tariffs on goods produced and traded between Canada, Mexico and the United States, providing for a totally free trade area by 2009

NAFTA makes it easier for businesses to invest in the participating countries; provides protection for intellectual property – of special interest to high-tech and entertainment industries; expands trade by requiring equal treatment of companies in all countries; and simplifies country-of-origin rules, hindering Japan's use of Mexico as a staging ground for further penetration into U.S. markets. NAFTA also links the United States with other Latin American countries, providing additional opportunities to integrate trade among all the nations in the western hemisphere. Although NAFTA has been controversial, it has become a positive factor for U.S. companies wishing to engage in international marketing. Because licensing requirements have been relaxed under the pact, smaller businesses that previously could not afford to invest in Mexico and Canada are able to do business in those markets without having to locate there.

The European Union (EU)

The **European Union (EU)** is one of three major market groups in Western Europe.* Formed by the Treaty of European Union, the EU has its origins in the European Common Market, set up in 1958, which later became known as the European Community (EC). Following the signing of the **Maastricht Treaty** in 1992 and the creation of the single European market in 1993, the group became known as the European Union. Today the EU has 27 members, including many Eastern European countries, such as the Czech Republic, Estonia, Hungary, Latvia, Lithuania, Poland, Slovakia and Slovenia, plus Mediterranean countries Cyprus, Greece and Malta. Bulgaria and Romania joined in 2007. Applicant countries include Turkey, Croatia, Serbia, Bosnia, Montenegro, Albania and Macedonia. The objectives of the Union are set out in the following extract from Article B of the Treaty on European Union.*

> **European Union (EU)** the major grouping in Western Europe, the EU has 27 members: Austria, Belgium, Denmark, Finland, France, Germany, Greece, Ireland, Italy, Luxembourg, the Netherlands, Portugal, Spain, Sweden and the United Kingdom have been joined by Bulgaria, Cyprus, the Czech Republic, Estonia, Hungary, Latvia, Lithuania, Malta, Poland, Romania, Slovakia and Slovenia
> **Maastricht Treaty** the treaty, signed in 1992, that established the European Union

- to promote economic and social progress which is balanced and sustainable, in particular through the creation of an area without internal frontiers, through the strengthening of economic and social cohesion and through the establishment of economic and monetary union, ultimately including a single currency in accordance with the provisions of this Treaty;
- to assert its identity on the international scene, in particular through the implementation of a common foreign and security policy including the eventual framing of a common defence policy, which might in time lead to a common defence;
- to strengthen the protection of the rights and interests of the nationals of its Member States through the introduction of a citizenship of the Union;
- to develop close co-operation on justice and home affairs.

On 1 January 1999 the European Union moved closer to economic and monetary union with the launch of the euro, the unit of European currency;* 11 of the then 15 European Union members became committed to the new currency. Only Sweden, Denmark and Britain postponed participation in the single currency, while Greece initially failed to meet the economic criteria; perhaps an omen of events that would follow. Greece's recent economic struggles and the ensuing strained relationships between some EU members have been well documented in the media internationally. Figure 3.2 shows the evolving European Union.

Although the 27 countries of the EU essentially function as one large market, and consumers in the EU are likely to become more homogeneous in their needs and wants, marketers know that cultural and social differences among the member states will require modifications in the marketing mix for consumers in many countries. Some researchers believe that eventually it will be possible to segment the European Union into six markets on the basis of cultural, geographic, demographic and economic variables. For example, the United Kingdom and Ireland would form one market, while Greece and Southern Italy would form another.* Differences in taste and preferences among these markets are significant for international marketers. For example, the British consume far more instant coffee than their European neighbours. Consumers in Spain eat far more poultry products than Germans do.* In some geographic regions, preferences even vary within the same country. Thus international marketing intelligence efforts remain very important in determining European consumers' needs and in developing marketing strategies that will satisfy those needs. It is also clear that EU organisations will have to face up to considerable changes in the way they operate and, for some, such as pharmaceutical companies, the prospects include harmonisation of prices and formulations and likely job losses.

Pacific Rim nations

Countries in the Pacific Rim represent an enormous part of the world market, with 60 per cent of the world's population living there. Although the region is characterised by considerable diversity, in

FIGURE 3.2 The evolving European Union *The European Union is now an economic force, with a collective economy larger than that of the United States or Japan.*

Source: http://europa.eu/abc/european_countries/index_en.htm (accessed March 14, 2012).

general companies of the Pacific Rim region – Japan, China, South Korea, Taiwan, Singapore, Hong Kong, the Philippines, Malaysia, Indonesia, Australia and Indochina – have become increasingly competitive and sophisticated in their marketing efforts in the last three decades. Throughout the early to mid-1990s the performances of Japan and the four so-called Tiger economies of the region – South Korea, Singapore, Taiwan and Hong Kong – were particularly impressive.* The Japanese, in particular, made considerable inroads into the world consumer markets for cars, motorcycles, watches, cameras and audio-visual equipment. Products made by Sony, Sanyo, Toyota, Honda, Canon, Suzuki and others are sold all over the world and have set quality standards by which other products are often judged. Through direct investment in Europe, the Japanese built strong distribution and developed a keen understanding of the market. However, Japan's marketing muscle attracted criticism in certain quarters, fuelled partly by fears that Japanese products might swamp the market. These concerns are compounded by Japan's reluctance to accept imports from other countries.*

South Korea also became very successful in world markets with familiar brands such as Samsung, Daewoo and Hyundai. South Korean companies even took market share away from Japanese companies in the world markets for VCRs, televisions and computers, despite the fact that the South Korean market for these products is limited. In Canada, the Hyundai Excel overtook Japan's Honda in just 18 months.* Towards the end of the 1990s many Far Eastern markets were substantially affected by economic recession. Currency markets in Japan, South Korea and Hong Kong were badly hit, affecting the economic strength of the Pacific Rim region. While the immense success of the 1980s and early 1990s may be difficult to replicate, many major Asia-Pacific corporations have divested unprofitable operations and are again performing very successfully in global markets.

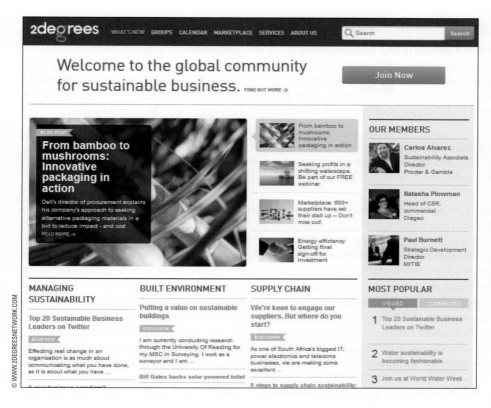

A new organisation called 2degrees is now the world's largest community for sustainable business with around 30,000 professional members from over 90 countries. The online platform helps members to improve their resource efficiency by sharing best practices and enabling them to solve common business problems together. 2degrees features webinars hosted by top experts; working groups on topics such as energy management, renewable power, greener health care and waste management; white papers; blogs; and the latest news on sustainability.

Less visible Pacific Rim regions, such as Singapore, Taiwan and Hong Kong, are major manufacturing and financial centres. Singapore also has large world markets for pharmaceutical and rubber goods. Taiwan may have the most promising future of all the Pacific Rim markets. It has a strong local economy and has lowered many import barriers, sending imports up. Taiwan has privatised state-run banks and is also opening its markets to foreign businesses. Some analysts believe that it may replace Hong Kong as a regional financial power centre.*

Much attention is now being given to the Pacific Rim nations that have reached the point of massive industrial growth. Thailand, Malaysia, Indonesia and of course China all offer considerable marketing potential.* For example, China has great market potential and opportunities for joint venture projects. Analysts are keeping a close watch on how these countries are affected by economic uncertainty in the region. The emergence of China presents marketers with considerable opportunities for exporting via joint ventures or trading alliances aided by China's "open door" policy. There is also a huge threat to Western companies, as Chinese enterprises strive to emulate Japan and enter global markets with their own products and services, and acquire Western businesses.

In general, attempts to form groups promoting trade and other links between Pacific Rim countries have not been particularly successful. Perhaps the best known is the **Association of South East Asian Nations (ASEAN)**, formed in 1967, which aims to build trade and other links between its six members: Brunei, Indonesia, Malaysia, the Philippines, Singapore and Thailand. More recently, the **Asia-Pacific Economic Cooperative (APEC)** has been set up to include the six ASEAN members, the United States, Australia, Canada, New Zealand, Japan, China, South Korea, Hong Kong and Taiwan.*

> **Association of South East Asian Nations (ASEAN)** formed in 1967 with the intention of building trade and other links among its six members: Brunei, Indonesia, Malaysia, the Philippines, Singapore and Thailand
> **Asia-Pacific Economic Cooperative (APEC)** aims to promote trade between its members: the six ASEAN members plus the United States, Australia, Canada, New Zealand, Japan, China, South Korea, Hong Kong and Taiwan

Central and Eastern Europe (CEE)

Central and Eastern Europe (CEE) encompasses the Commonwealth of Independent States (CIS, formerly the Soviet Union), the Czech and Slovak Republics, Hungary, Poland, Slovenia, Croatia, Bosnia and Herzegovina, Serbia and Montenegro, Bulgaria, FYR Macedonia and Albania. The decline of communism in Central and Eastern Europe, the fall of the Berlin Wall in 1989 and the break-up of the former Soviet Union in 1990 resulted in a host of new marketing opportunities in the region.

> **Central and Eastern Europe (CEE)** encompasses the Commonwealth of Independent States (formerly the Soviet Union), the Czech and Slovak Republics, Hungary, Poland, Slovenia, Croatia, Bosnia and Herzegovina, Serbia and Montenegro, Bulgaria, FYR Macedonia and Albania

Following a policy of *perestroika*, encompassing considerable political and economic change, the CEE countries replaced the Communist Party's centrally-planned economies with marketing-oriented democratic institutions. This process of market reforms, designed to lead to greater imports and exports, was not without difficulty. The challenge for many of the Eastern European countries has been to move forward from the inefficiencies of state-owned industry and to develop the marketing expertise, business culture, infrastructures and legal frameworks required to trade with capitalist countries.* For example, the poorly-developed distribution infrastructure in many parts of central and eastern Europe has restricted the outlets where Western products can be sold and limits the opportunities domestic companies can pursue.* However, the move towards market change has resulted in considerable social upheaval and, in some cases, unrest in countries going through this transition.

The **Commonwealth of Independent States (CIS)** emerged in 1996 as a loosely-connected group of former Soviet Union states. The CIS unites Azerbaijan, Armenia, Belarus, Georgia, Kazakhstan, Kyrgyzstan, Moldova, Russia, Tajikistan, Turkmenistan, Ukraine and Uzbekistan.* But key economic data show these countries to be relatively weak compared with Western EU states.

> **Commonwealth of Independent States (CIS)** the CIS unites Azerbaijan, Armenia, Belarus, Georgia, Kazakhstan, Kyrgyzstan, Moldova, Russia, Tajikistan, Turkmenistan, Ukraine and Uzbekistan in a trading bloc

Although after it was set up there were potential opportunities for the CIS to trade as a market group, in practice this idea has been severely restricted by the lack of cooperation between member states and, in particular, by economic and political problems in Russia.* The importance of Russia – the largest market – cannot be overlooked in the region's development.* For Western companies, the potential is considerable. Hewlett-Packard enjoyed a fourfold increase in sales in one year alone, and others – such as Coca-Cola and McDonald's – have also taken advantage of the new opportunities.

General Agreement on Tariffs and Trade (GATT) and the World Trade Organisation (WTO)

Like NAFTA and the EU, the **General Agreement on Tariffs and Trade (GATT)** was based on negotiations among member countries to reduce worldwide tariffs and increase international trade. Originally signed by 23 countries in 1947, GATT provided a forum for tariff negotiations, and a place where

Celebrating OPEC's 50th anniversary.
Secretary General of OPEC Abdalla Salem El-Badri and Iranian Oil Minister Masoud Mir Kazemi attend a ceremony to celebrate the 50th anniversary of the founding of OPEC, in Tehran, Iran, on April 19th, 2011.

international trade problems could be discussed and resolved. Eventually, GATT involved some 124 countries before giving way to the World Trade Organisation in the mid-90s. The Uruguay Round of negotiations reduced trade barriers for most products and provided new rules to prevent **dumping** – as noted earlier, the selling of products at unfairly low prices.

> **General Agreement on Tariffs and Trade (GATT)** an agreement between countries to reduce worldwide tariffs and increase international trade

The most significant outcome of the Uruguay Round was the establishment of the **World Trade Organisation (WTO)** to promote free trade among member countries. Fulfilling this purpose requires eliminating trade barriers; educating individuals, companies and governments about trade rules around the world; and assuring global markets that no sudden changes of policy will occur. The WTO also serves as a forum for trade negotiations and dispute resolution. At the heart of the WTO are agreements that provide legal ground rules for international commerce and trade policy. Figure 3.3 shows WTO members share in World Merchandise Trade, 2010.

> **Wold Trade Organisation (WTO)** an entity that promotes and facilitates free trade between member states

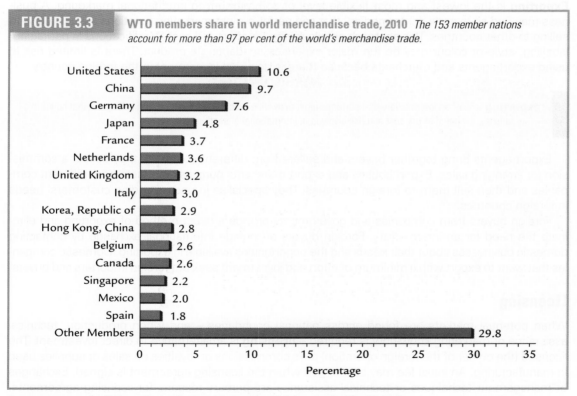

FIGURE 3.3 **WTO members share in world merchandise trade, 2010** *The 153 member nations account for more than 97 per cent of the world's merchandise trade.*

Source: www.wto.org/english/res_e/Statis_e/its2011_e/charts_e/chart07.xls (accessed on March 7, 2012).

ALTERNATIVE MARKET ENTRY STRATEGIES

The level of commitment to international business is a major variable in deciding what kind of involvement is appropriate. A company's market entry options range from occasional exporting to expanding overall operations (production and marketing) into other countries. This section examines exporting,

Exporting to international markets.
Companies may manufacture their products domestically and export them for sale in foreign markets. Exporting can be a relatively risk-free method of entering foreign markets.

© ALEXEY FUSOV/SHUTTERSTOCK

licensing, franchising, contract manufacturing, joint ventures, trading companies, foreign direct investment and other approaches to international involvement.*

Exporting

Exporting is the lowest and most flexible level of commitment to international marketing. A business may find an exporting intermediary that can perform most marketing functions associated with selling to other countries. This approach entails minimum effort and cost. Modifications in packaging, labelling, style or colour may be the major expenses in adapting a product. There is limited risk in using export agents and merchants because there is no direct investment in the foreign country.

> **exporting** use of an intermediary that performs most marketing functions associated with selling to other countries; entails the minimum effort, cost and risk involved in international marketing

Export agents bring together buyers and sellers from different countries; they collect a commission for arranging sales. Export houses and export merchants purchase products from different companies and then sell them to foreign countries. They specialise in understanding customers' needs in foreign countries.

Foreign buyers from companies and governments provide a direct method of exporting and eliminate the need for an intermediary. Foreign buyers encourage international exchange by contacting domestic businesses about their needs and the opportunities available in exporting. Domestic companies that want to export with a minimum of effort and investment seek out foreign importers and buyers.

Licensing

When potential markets are found across national boundaries – and when production, technical assistance or marketing know-how is required – **licensing** is an alternative to direct investment. The licensee (the owner of the foreign operation) pays commissions or royalties on sales or supplies used in manufacturing. An initial fee may be charged when the licensing agreement is signed. Exchanges of management techniques or technical assistance are primary reasons for licensing agreements. Yoplait is a French yoghurt that is licensed for production in the United States and numerous other countries; but the Yoplait brand tries to maintain a French image.

> **licensing** system in which a licensee pays commissions or royalties on sales or supplies used in manufacturing

Licensing is an attractive alternative to direct investment when the political stability of a foreign country is in doubt or when resources are unavailable for direct investment. This approach is especially advantageous for small manufacturers wanting to launch a well-known brand internationally. For example, Pierre Cardin has issued 500 licences and Yves St Laurent 200 to make their products.* Löwenbrau has used licensing agreements to increase sales worldwide without committing capital to build breweries.

Franchising

Another alternative to direct investment in non-domestic markets is **franchising**. This form of licensing, which grants the right to use certain intellectual property rights, such as trade names, brand names, designs, patents and copyrights, is becoming increasingly popular in Europe.* Under this arrangement the franchiser grants a licence to the franchisee, who pays to be allowed to carry out business under the name owned by the franchiser. The franchiser retains control over the manner in which the business is conducted and assists the franchisee in running the business. The franchisee retains ownership of his or her own business, which remains separate from that of the franchiser.*

> **franchising** a form of licensing granting the right to use certain intellectual property rights, such as trade names, brand names, designs, patents and copyrights

Franchising has recently experienced a period of rapid growth. Companies such as Benetton, Burger King, Holiday Inn and IKEA are particularly well-known for their commitment to growing global business in this way. There are various reasons why the popularity of franchising has increased so rapidly.* First, the general world decline in manufacturing and shift to service industries has increased the relevance of franchising. This is significant because franchising is a very common internationalisation process for service organisations. Second, franchising has been relatively free of restrictions from legislation, especially in the EU. Third, an increase in self-employment has provided a pool of individuals willing to become involved in franchising, and this activity has generally been supported by the major clearing banks.

Contract manufacturing

Contract manufacturing is the practice of hiring a foreign company to produce a designated volume of the domestic company's product to a set specification. The final product carries the domestic company's name. Gap, for example, relies on contract manufacturing for some of its clothing, and Reebok uses Korean contract manufacturers to produce many of its sports shoes. Marketing activity may be handled by the contract manufacturer or by the contracting company.

> **contract manufacturing** the practice of hiring a foreign company to produce a designated volume of product to a set specification

Joint ventures and strategic alliances

In international business, a **joint venture** is a partnership between a domestic company and a foreign company or government. Joint ventures are especially popular in industries that call for large investments, such as natural resources extraction or car manufacturing. Control of the joint venture can be split equally or can be retained by one party. Joint ventures are often a political necessity because of nationalism and governmental restrictions on foreign ownership. They also provide legitimacy in the eyes of the host country's people. Local partners have first-hand knowledge of the economic and socio-political environment, access to distribution networks or privileged access to local resources (raw material, labour management, contacts and so on). Moreover, entrepreneurs in many less-developed countries actively seek associations with an overseas partner as a ready means of implementing their own corporate strategy.*

> **joint venture** a partnership between a domestic company and a foreign company or government

Strategic alliance for mutual benefits.
Chairman and Managing Director of Air India, V. Thulasidas, and Chairman of Lufthansa AG, Wolfgang Mayrhuber, sign a strategic alliance agreement in Mumbai, India. The alliance improves their market leadership position on India–Europe–U.S. routes.

Joint ventures are assuming greater global importance because of cost advantages and the number of inexperienced businesses entering foreign markets. They may be the result of a trade-off between a company's desire for completely unambiguous control of an enterprise and its quest for additional resources. They may occur when internal development or acquisition is not feasible or unavailable, or when the risks and constraints leave no other alternative. As project sizes increase in the face of global competition, and businesses attempt to spread the huge costs of technological innovation, there is increased impetus to form joint ventures.* Several European truck makers used mergers and joint ventures with other European companies to consolidate their power after the unification of the EU in 1992 and the deregulation of the European haulage industry in 1993. Volvo and Renault developed such a partnership.* Of course, joint ventures are also possible between partners from different continents. The leading IT consultancies frequently form joint ventures or alliances with partners in order to exploit domestic and non-domestic opportunities.

Joint ventures are sometimes criticised as being inherently unstable,* or because they might result in a take-over attempt. For businesses trying to build longer-term joint ventures, there is also the danger that the relationship stifles flexibility. Of course, for many companies that become involved in joint ventures this may be their only feasible mode of entry at the time and may in any case be regarded purely as a transitional arrangement.* For example, European construction companies bidding for business in the Middle East found that joint ventures with Arab construction companies gain local support among the handful of people who make the contracting decisions.

Strategic alliances are partnerships formed to create a competitive advantage on a worldwide basis. They are very similar to joint ventures. Strategic alliances have been defined as "cooperation between two or more industrial corporations, belonging to different countries, whereby each partner seeks to add to its competencies by combining its resources with those of its partner".* The number of strategic alliances is growing at an estimated rate of about 20 per cent per year.* In fact, in some industries, such as cars and high technology, strategic alliances are becoming the predominant means of competing. International competition is so fierce and the costs of competing globally so high that few businesses have the required individual resources, and it makes sense to collaborate with other companies. Many car brands are co-created by apparently rival manufacturers acting in a strategic alliance.*

> **Strategic alliances** partnerships formed to create a competitive advantage on a worldwide basis

The partners forming international strategic alliances share common goals, yet often retain their distinct identities, each bringing a distinctive competence to the union. What distinguishes international strategic alliances from other business structures is that member companies in the alliance may have been traditional rivals competing for market share in the same product class.* This situation is common in the aerospace industry. Raytheon may partner certain companies in bidding for work from Boeing, while competing with the same suppliers when seeking work with Lockheed or Airbus.

Trading companies

A **trading company** provides a link between buyers and sellers in different countries. As its name implies, a trading company is not involved in manufacturing or owning assets related to manufacturing. The trading company buys in one country at the lowest price consistent with quality and sells to buyers in another country. An important function of trading companies is taking title to products and undertaking all the activities necessary to move the products from the domestic country to a foreign country. Large, grain trading companies, for example, control a major portion of the world's trade in basic food commodities. These trading companies sell agricultural commodities that are homogeneous, and can be stored and moved rapidly in response to market conditions.

> **trading company** a company that provides a link between buyers and sellers in different countries

Trading companies reduce risk for companies interested in becoming involved in international marketing, assisting producers with information about products that meet quality and price expectations in domestic or international markets. Additional services a trading company may provide include consulting, marketing research, advertising, insurance, research and development, legal assistance, warehousing and foreign exchange.

Foreign direct investment

Once a company makes a long-term commitment to foreign marketing, direct ownership of a foreign subsidiary or division is a possibility. **Foreign direct investment (FDI)** involves making a long-term commitment to business in a foreign nation through direct ownership of a foreign subsidiary or division. The expense of developing a separate foreign distribution system, in particular, can be tremendous. For example, as French hypermarket chain Carrefour discovered, the opening of retail stores in neighbouring countries can require a large financial investment in facilities, research and management.

> **Foreign direct investment (FDI)** a long-term commitment to marketing in a foreign nation through direct ownership of a foreign subsidiary or division

The term **multinational enterprise** refers to companies that have operations or subsidiaries located in many countries. Often the parent company is based in one country and cultivates production, management and marketing activities in other countries. The company's subsidiaries may be quite autonomous in order to respond to the needs of individual international markets. Companies such as Dell, Unilever and General Motors are multinational companies with worldwide operations.

> **multinational enterprise** a company with operations or subsidiaries in many countries

A wholly-owned foreign subsidiary may be allowed to operate independently of the parent company so that its management can have more freedom to adjust to the local environment. Cooperative arrangements are developed to assist in marketing efforts, production and management. A wholly-owned foreign subsidiary may export products to the home country. Some car manufacturers, such as Ford and General Motors, for example, import cars built by their foreign subsidiaries. A foreign subsidiary offers important tax, tariff and other operating advantages. The greatest advantages of direct foreign investment are greater strategy control and enhanced market capacity. To maximise these, a subsidiary may operate under foreign management, so that a genuinely local identity can be developed.

A company's success in achieving these advantages will tend to depend on whether the business has a competitive advantage allowing it to recover the costs of its investment.

Table 3.2 shows the ten largest public multinational companies; the ranking is based on a composite score reflecting each company's best three out of four rankings for sales, profits, assets, and market value. Table 3.3 describes steps in entering international markets.

TABLE 3.2 The ten largest multinational corporations

2011 Rank	Company	Business	Country	Revenue ($ millions)
1	Walmart Stores	General merchandiser	United States	421,849
2	Royal Dutch Shell	Energy	Netherlands/ United Kingdom	378,152
3	ExxonMobil	Energy	United States	354,674
4	BP	Energy	United Kingdom	308,928
5	Sinopec Group	Energy	China	273,422
6	China Natural Petroleum	Energy	China	240,192
7	State Grid	Power grids	China	226,294
8	Toyota Motor	Automobiles	Japan	221,760
9	Japan Post Holdings	Financial services	Japan	203,958
10	Chevron	Energy	United States	196,337

Source: From *Fortune Magazine*, "Global 500 Our Annual Ranking of the World's Largest Corporations," July 25, 2011, © 2011 Time Inc. Used under license. Fortune and Time Inc. are not affiliated with, and do not endorse products or services of, Licensee.

TABLE 3.3 Steps in entering international markets

Step	Activity	Marketing Tasks
1	Identify exportable products.	Identify key selling features. Identify needs that they satisfy. Identify the selling constraints that are imposed.
2	Identify key foreign markets for the products.	Determine who the customers are. Pinpoint what and when they will buy. Do market research. Establish priority, or "target," countries.
3	Analyse how to sell in each priority market (methods will be affected by product characteristics and unique features of country/market).	Locate available government and private-sector resources. Determine service and backup sales requirements.
4	Set export prices and payment terms, methods, and techniques.	Establish methods of export pricing. Establish sales terms, quotations, invoices, and conditions of sale. Determine methods of international payments, secured and unsecured.
5	Estimate resource requirements and returns.	Estimate financial requirements. Estimate human resources requirements (full- or part-time export department or operation?). Estimate plant production capacity. Determine necessary product adaptations.
6	Establish overseas distribution network.	Determine distribution agreement and other key marketing decisions (price, repair policies, returns, territory, performance, and termination). Know your customer.

(Continued)

| TABLE 3.3 | Steps in entering international markets *(Continued)* |

Step	Activity	Marketing Tasks
7	Determine shipping, traffic, and documentation procedures and requirements.	Determine methods of shipment (air or ocean freight, lorry, rail). Finalise containerisation. Obtain validated export license. Follow export-administration documentation procedures.
8	Promote, sell, and be paid.	Use international media, communications, advertising, trade shows, and exhibitions. Determine the need for overseas travel (when, where, and how often?). Initiate customer follow-up procedures.
9	Continuously analyse current marketing, economic, and political situations.	Recognise changing factors influencing marketing strategies. Constantly re-evaluate.

Source: U.S. Department of Commerce, International Trade Administration, Washington, DC.

According to the chairman of the board of Dow Chemical Company, a multinational firm, "The emergence of a world economy and of the multinational corporation has been accomplished hand in hand." He sees multinational enterprises moving toward what he calls the "anational company," a firm that has no nationality but belongs to all countries. In recognition of this movement, there already have been international conferences devoted to the question of how such enterprises would be controlled.

FINANCING INTERNATIONAL BUSINESS

International trade compounds the concerns of financial managers. Currency exchange rates, tariffs and foreign exchange controls, and the tax structures of host nations all affect international operations and the flow of cash. In addition, financial managers must be concerned both with the financing of their international operations and with the means available to their customers to finance purchases.

Fortunately, along with business in general, a number of large banks have become international in scope. Many have established branches in major cities around the world. Thus, like firms in other industries, they are able to provide their services where and when they are needed. In addition, financial assistance is available from government and international sources.

Several of today's international financial organisations were founded many years ago to facilitate free trade and the exchange of currencies among nations. Some, such as the Inter-American Development Bank, are supported internationally and focus on developing countries. Others, such as the Export-Import Bank, are operated by one country but provide international financing.

Multilateral development banks

A **multilateral development bank (MDB)** is an internationally-supported bank that provides loans to developing countries to help them grow. The most familiar is the World Bank, a cooperative of 187 member countries, which operates worldwide. Established in 1944 and headquartered in Washington, DC, the bank provides low-interest loans, interest-free credits, and grants to developing countries. The loans and grants help these countries to:

multilateral development bank (MDB) an internationally supported bank that provides loans to developing countries to help them grow

RESPONSIBLE PRACTICE   Ensuring ethical standards in international operations

© ZUMA PRESS, INC./ALAMY

A number of global brands have tried hard to ensure they avoid the sort of damaging scandals that have hit the reputation of Nike and Gap by introducing codes of practice with regard to the use of child labour. However, some have found even when trying to operate to high ethical standards there can be unintended consequences. Reebok inaugurated the Reebok Human Rights Production Standards, covering nine areas including "No Child Labour". They regularly monitor all suppliers to ensure that child labour is not used in stitching footballs so that their footballs can bear the label 'Guaranteed: Manufactured Without Child Labour'. They also built a centralised stitching factory to ensure better control, but then were criticised because a consequence of moving from home-working to a centralised workplace meant that the number of women in the workforce fell dramatically.

Levi Strauss used to manufacture its own products close to the places where they were sold. It has increasingly sub-contracted the work in low wage locations in Africa and Asia. They developed "Global Sourcing and Operating Guidelines", stipulating that workers must be at least 15 years of age to work for them or their suppliers. When they found that suppliers were using child labour in Bangladesh, Levi Strauss reportedly negotiated corrective action with their suppliers which involved removing the children from the factories, placing them in education and paying their wages until they reached an age at which they could return to work. The company also supports good causes, including AIDS charities, and (in South Africa) a home for children who have suffered serious physical or sexual abuse.

However market pressures took their toll on Levi Strauss. Sales of its main products, jeans and Dockers casual-wear, have consistently declined since the mid-1990s. The company cut 18,000 jobs in highwage locations, and has closed 30 factories in North America, and seven in Europe over the last five years. There is now the fear that cutting costs to the bone could damage the integrity of the brand if it is seen to be exploiting the workforce at home while supporting expensive good causes overseas.

Is it possible for a global brand to have a geocentric ethics strategy which meets the needs of all its operations around the globe? How should global companies resolve the ethical dilemmas identified above?

References: BBC World Service.com.Inside Global Giants: 'Levi's – Balancing ethics with profit', and http://www.unicef.org.uk/publications/all.

- supply safe drinking water
- build schools and train teachers
- increase agricultural productivity
- expand citizens' access to markets, jobs, and housing
- improve health care and access to water and sanitation
- manage forests and other natural resources
- build and maintain roads, railways, and ports, and
- reduce air pollution and protect the environment.*

Four other MDBs operate primarily in Central and South America, Asia, Africa, and Eastern and Central Europe. All five are supported by the industrialised nations, including the United States.

The Inter-American Development Bank   The Inter-American Development Bank (IDB), the oldest and largest regional bank, was created in 1959 by 19 Latin American countries and the United States.

The bank, which is headquartered in Washington, DC, makes loans and provides technical advice and assistance to countries. Today, the IDB is owned by 48 member states.

The Asian Development Bank With 67 member nations, the Asian Development Bank (ADB), created in 1966 and headquartered in the Philippines, promotes economic and social progress in Asian and Pacific regions. Noted contributors to the ADB's capital include Japan and the U.S.

The African Development Bank The African Development Bank (AFDB), also known as *Banque Africaines de Development*, was established in 1964 with headquarters in Abidjan, Ivory Coast. Its members include 53 African and 24 non-African countries from the Americas, Europe, and Asia. The AFDB's goal is to foster the economic and social development of its African members. The bank pursues this goal through loans, research, technical assistance, and the development of trade programmes.

European Bank for Reconstruction and Development Established in 1991 to encourage reconstruction and development in the Eastern and Central European countries, the London-based *European Bank for Reconstruction and Development* is owned by 61 countries and 2 intergovernmental institutions. Its loans are geared toward developing market-oriented economies and promoting private enterprise.

The International Monetary Fund

The **International Monetary Fund (IMF)** is an international bank with 188 member nations that makes short-term loans to developing countries experiencing balance-of-payment deficits. This financing is contributed by member nations, and it must be repaid with interest. Loans are provided primarily to fund international trade. Created in 1945 and headquartered in Washington, DC, the bank's main goals are to:

● promote international monetary cooperation,
● facilitate the expansion and balanced growth of international trade,
● promote exchange rate stability,
● assist in establishing a multilateral system of payments, and
● make resources available to members experiencing balance-of-payment difficulties.

> **International Monetary Fund (IMF)** an international bank with 188 member nations that makes short-term loans to developing countries experiencing balance-of-payment deficits

The challenges ahead

In a 2012 speech at Oxford University, Pascal Lamy, Director-General of the World Trade Organiztion stated, "We live in a world of ever-growing independence and interconnectedness. Our interdependence has grown beyond anyone's imagination. The world of today is virtually unrecognisable from the world in which we lived one generation ago." The most striking example of globalisation is Apple. Apple's iPod is designed in the United States, manufactured with components from Japan, Korea, and several other Asian countries, and assembled in China by a company from Chinese Taipei. Nowadays, most products are not "Made in the U.A.E." or "Made in France"; they are in fact "Made in the World." *

In 2012, the global economic recovery remained sluggish. Financial challenges in some euro-area economies slowed the economic growth. However, WTO rules and principles have assisted governments in keeping markets open and they now provide a platform for which the trade can grow as the global economy improves. According to Mr. Lamy, "We see the light at the end of the tunnel and trade promises to be an important part of the recovery. But we must avoid derailing any economic revival through protectionism."

SUMMARY

- Explain the economic basis for international business.

    International business encompasses all business activities that involve exchanges across national boundaries. International trade is based on specialisation, whereby each country produces the goods and services that it can produce more efficiently than any other goods and services. A nation is said to have a comparative advantage relative to these goods. International trade develops when each nation trades its surplus products for those in short supply.

    A nation's balance of trade is the difference between the value of its exports and the value of its imports. Its balance of payments is the difference between the flow of money into and out of the nation. Generally, a negative balance of trade is considered unfavourable.

- Discuss the restrictions nations place on international trade, the objectives of these restrictions, and their results.

    Despite the benefits of world trade, nations tend to use tariffs and nontariff barriers (import quotas, embargoes, and other restrictions) to limit trade. These restrictions typically are justified as being needed to protect a nation's economy, industries, citizens, or security. They can result in the loss of jobs, higher prices, fewer choices in the marketplace, and the misallocation of resources.

- Outline the extent of international business and the world economic outlook for trade.

    World trade is generally increasing. Trade between the United States and other nations is increasing in dollar value but decreasing in terms of share of the world market. Exports as a percentage of U.S. GDP have increased steadily since 1985, except in the 2001 and 2008 recessions.

- Discuss international trade agreements and international economic organisations working to foster trade.

    The General Agreement on Tariffs and Trade (GATT) was formed to dismantle trade barriers and provide an environment in which international business can grow. Today, the World Trade Organisation (WTO) and various economic communities carry on this mission. These world economic communities include the European Union, the NAFTA, the Association of Southeast Asian Nations, and the Pacific Rim.

- Define the methods by which a firm can organise for and enter into international markets.

    A firm can enter international markets in several ways. It may license a foreign firm to produce and market its products. It may export its products and sell them through foreign intermediaries or its own sales organisation abroad, or it may sell its exports outright to an export–import merchant. It may enter into a joint venture with a foreign firm. It may establish its own foreign subsidiaries, or it may develop into a multinational enterprise.

    Generally, each of these methods represents an increasingly deeper level of involvement in international business, with licensing being the simplest and the development of a multinational corporation the most involved.

- Identify the institutions that help firms and nations finance international business.

    The financing of international trade is more complex than that of domestic trade. Institutions such as the International Monetary Fund have been established to provide financing and ultimately to increase world trade for international firms.

EXERCISE QUESTIONS

1 What is the difference between absolute and comparative advantage? Give examples of both.

2 If the South African government places a trade restriction on a product exported by Japan, how might it affect both countries?

3 What are the main benefits of being part of the European Union for the purposes of trade? What negatives might be experienced?

4 Why might a company in one country choose to form a joint venture with another company? In what way is a joint venture different to a strategic alliance?

5 Unilever is an example of a multinational enterprise. Look on their website and find out the countries that they operate in and the differences in the products they offer to each country.

CASE 3.1

Islam, Ramadan and the tent business in the Middle East

Ramadan represents one of the five pillars of Islam, which all Muslims are expected to follow, the other four are "Faith" or Shahadah; "Prayer" or Salah, "Charitable Giving" or Zakah and the "Pilgrimage to Makkah" or Hajj. The month of Ramadan is a time for spiritual reflection and prayer. Ramadan is usually observed in the ninth month of the Islamic lunar calendar and is one of the most important months for Muslims as it is believed this is the month that the Quran was first revealed to the Prophet Mohammed. During this month all healthy Muslims fast from sunrise to sunset when they must refrain from all food, drink, gum chewing, any kind of tobacco use and any kind of sexual contact.

Muslims believe their good actions bring greater reward during these 30 days because the month has been blessed by Allah. "Fasting" reminds Muslims of the suffering of the poor who often don't get to eat well. During the "holy month" of Ramadan most Muslims will tend to wake up just before sunrise to have a meal or Suhoor. They will then not be able to eat or drink again until sunset when it is traditional to open the fast with a date and then eat and this meal is known as Iftar. People open their fasts with a "date" as it is believed that the Prophet Mohammed broke his fast with such a fruit.

Ramadan has both spiritual and physical significance. Certain individuals and/or groups hold Iftar parties (where they prepare lots of food and then invite people round to eat). Ramadan often lasts anything between 29 to 30 days, depending on the sighting of the new moon, which marks the celebration of Eid El Fitr. Prior to this final day of celebration, tents and/or marquees are traditionally put up by the privileged to cater for the less privileged in the spirit of charitable giving during this sombre and sober month.

Lavish tents and marquees have long been a mainstay of the corporate events industry during the holy month of Ramadan in the Middle East. However, recently due to the financial crisis the marquee business has suffered as big corporations cut spending and marquee companies began to "feel the pinch".

Depending on the quality and size of the structure, a complete tent costs a minimum of between Dh200,000 and Dh250,000 (£33,334 and £42,000) for the month of Ramadan alone. Even large businesses such as the likes of Tamani Hotel, Dubai Marina and the Hilton Hotel, Dubai Jumeirah, have moved their iftars and suhoors indoors after having previously had tents outdoors for the Ramadan period.

Two UAE-based companies, Al-Baddad International and Harlequin Marquees and Event Services both compete in this market so had to start looking further afield in order to maintain sales in the downturn. Al-Baddad International (henceforth Al-Baddad), a subsidiary of Al-Baddad Global, was established in the U.A.E capital, Abu Dhabi in 1971 (the same year the country attained independence from Great Britain) by the late Hajj Hassan Al-Baddad. The company is a leading provider of innovative mobile halls and prefabricated buildings in the Middle East and North Africa (MENA) region. The company provides outdoor solutions, exhibitions, conferences, weddings, special events, private occasions, festivals, camps, warehouses and temporary accommodations.

Since its founding, Al-Baddad has continually built a business across the Middle East and North African (MENA) region with Egypt and Libya being the latest markets it has entered (see Table 1). The company claims leadership in mobile halls and tents in the region – manufacturing large quantities of tents and pre-fabricated buildings all year round through a company known as "Al-Baddad Capital".

Al-Baddad's marketing strategy is to "explore, create, and always adopt new techniques and innovations to keep its solutions ahead of the curve", as it strives to guarantee its place among the top suppliers in its industry both regionally and internationally. As one of the major tents companies in the region, it now is facing the challenge of a downturn in business due to a decline in corporate sponsorship and so needs to think through how it might expand into new markets.

Table 1 *Al-Baddad Branches worldwide*

Year of entry	City/Country
1971	Abu Dhabi (U . A . E.)
1989	Al-Ain (U.A.E.)
1989	Sharjah (U.A.E.)
1992	Dubai (U.A.E.)
1996	Qatar
1996	California (U.S.)
1997	Jordan
2001	Riyadh (Saudi Arabia)
2002	Jeddah (Saudi Arabia)
2005	Ras Al-Khaimah (U.A.E.)
2005	Kuwait
2009	Damman (Saudi Arabia)
2010	Egypt
2010	Libya

Source: http://www.albaddadintl.com/aboutus.htm

Commenting on how they were now faring, Bilal Hamdan, the company's marketing manager remarked that "… this year we were more creative". This creativity underlined the company's marketing strategy including offering hotels price discounts in exchange for their branding to be displayed at the venues. They also looked at other cultural events and other opportunities across the MENA region having observed that some hotels had decided to use the structures they had set up for the recently concluded FIFA World Cup as Ramadan tents.

The second company Harlequin Marquees & Event Services (Harlequin henceforth), established in 1998, is a company that claims to be at the forefront of Gulf Hospitality, catering for all the usual events – from product launches to gala dinners and various other festivals. Harlequin also boasts Arabesque themed solutions in its opulent Ramadan Majlis (an Arabic term meaning 'a place of sitting' used to describe various types of special gatherings) tents.

Founder, Carmen Clews, a former employee of Britain's Royal Air Force air traffic control team, partnered with Charlie Wright to guide the full-service event design and rental company into a 45-employee operation that claims to have some of the world's biggest blue-chip companies as its clients. Indeed the creative enterprise of designing "modern Arabia" event environments, complete with frosted arabesque pattern tent windows and white LED-lit "star" fabrics, satisfies Harlequin's hunger for unique challenges. The company enjoys a dual advantage. First is the favourable climate – hot weather conditions and the second is the strategic location of the country. Indeed Dubai's location – almost midway between Europe and Asia – makes it both a hub for international commerce and a notable attraction for workers from around the world.

While this presents itself as an opportunity for Harlequin who consider themselves "… fortunate to have a fantastic team who all communicate, listen and talk very well together", it also poses a cultural challenge with ethnically diverse clientele (Arabic, Asian and/or Western). As part of its marketing strategy, the company considers itself a patient player, "we have to be extra careful, taking nothing for granted and never assuming anything". But while acknowledging the virtue of such patience, Clews was quick to point out that a bit of impulsiveness – "acting immediately on ideas that feel right", had got her and Harlequin where they are today.

Like the previous case, Harlequin has seen a downturn. According to Camilla Quinn, the client services manager of Harlequin, "we're finding that the main reason hotels have pulled out this year has been because they've not been able to get the sponsorship".

Another member of the company's management team stated, "We had four clients who were all quite far down the line with putting structures up, but they were all based on receiving corporate sponsorship. With all four of them it fell through at the last minute and they all completely pulled their Ramadan tents."

Source: Nnamdi O. Madichie, PhD

References: Bundhun, R. (2010) 'Now is the summer of our discount tent', Abu Dhabi: The National Newspaper, Business Section, 2 September; Daniyah Hafiz (2008) 'What is Ramadan?' BBC Lancashire, UK (5 September 2008). Online at: http://www.bbc.co.uk/lancashire/content/articles/2006/10/09/ramadan_feature.shtml [Accessed 3 September 2010]; Huda (about.com) Ramadan Information. Online at: http://islam.about.com/od/ramadan/tp/ramadan-hub.htm; Official website of Harlequin Marquees & Event Services, online at http://www.harlequinmarquees.com/

Questions

1 What are the advantages and disadvantages of Al-Baddad and Harlequin trading across different countries?

2 Visit the Al-Baddad International website. In what ways have they expanded out of just providing tents for Ramadan?

3 What challenges might Harlequin face trying to do business with both the East and the West?

CHAPTER REFERENCES

Adams, J. and Mendelsohn, M. (1986) 'Recent developments in franchising', Journal of Business Law, 206–19.

Ayling, D. (1987) 'Franchising has its dark side', Accountancy 99:113–17.

Bradley, F. (1995) International Marketing Strategy, London: Prentice-Hall, p. 393.

Cunningham, M. H. (1990) 'Marketing's new frontier: international strategic alliances', working paper, Queens University, Ontario.

Europe in Figures, 4th ed. (1995) Brussels: Eurostat.

Friberg, E. G. (1989) '1992: moves Europeans are making', Harvard Business Review, May–June, 89.

Gross, T. and Neuman, J. (1989) 'Strategic alliances vital in global marketing', Marketing News, June, 1–2.

Harrigan, K. R. (1988) 'Joint ventures and competitive advantage', Strategic Management Journal, May, 141–58.

Helm, L., Nakarmi, L., Soo, J. J., Holstein, W. J. and Terry, E. (1985) 'The Koreans are coming', Business Week, 25 December, 46–52.

Jain, S. C. (1987) 'Some perspectives on international strategic alliances', in Advances in International Marketing, New York: JAI Press, pp. 103–20.

Jeannet, J.-P. and Hennessey, H. D. (1995) Global Marketing Strategies, Boston, MA: Houghton Mifflin, pp. 170–173.

Keegan, W. J. (1995) Global Marketing Management, Englewood Cliffs, NJ: Prentice-Hall, pp. 285–86.

Killing, J. (1982) 'How to make a global joint venture work', Harvard Business Review 60: 120–27.

Kraar, L. (1989) 'Asia's rising export powers', *Fortune*, Special Pacific Rim issue, 43–50.

Kupfer, A. (1988) 'How to be a global manager', *Fortune*, 14 March, 52–58.

Lapidus, R. S. (1997) 'Global marketing strategies', *Journal of Global Marketing*.

Leeflang, P. S. H. and de Mortanges, C. P. (1993) 'The internal European market and strategic marketing planning: implications and expectations', *Journal of International Consumer Marketing* 6(2): 7–23.

Mazur, L. (1998) 'Failing the Euro test', *Marketing*, 3 December, 26–27.

'More companies prefer liaisons to marriage' (1988) *Wall Street Journal*, 12 April, 35.

O'Brien, Bob, "McDonald's Is Where the Beef Is," *Barron's*, April 21, 2010, http://online.barrons.com; Lindner, Melanie, "McDonald's Hits the Spot," *Forbes*, March 8, 2010, www.forbes.com; www.mcdonalds.com; www.aboutmcdonalds.com; "Jamie Oliver Praises McDonald's," *The Telegraph (UK)*, April 25, 2010, www.telegraph.co.uk.

Quelch, J. A. (1985) 'How to build a product licensing program', *Harvard Business Review*, May–June, 186–87.

Quelch, J. A., Joachimsthaler, E. and Nueno, J. L. (1991) 'After the wall: marketing guidelines for eastern Europe', *Sloan Management Review*, Winter, 90–91.

Rapaport, C. (1991) 'Why Japan keeps on winning', *Fortune*, 15 July, 76.

Reddy, A. C. (1991) 'The role of marketing in the economic development of eastern European countries', *Journal of Applied Business Research* 7(3):106–7.

'Rising in Russia' (1996) *Fortune*, 24 January, 93, 95.

Smith, D. (1989) 'Europe's truck-makers face survival of the biggest', *Business Week*, 6 November, 68.

Stern, P. and Stanworth, J. (1988) 'The development of franchising in Britain', *National Westminster Quarterly Review*, May, 38–48

The International Monetary Fund Web site at www.imf.org/external/pubs/ft/weo/2012/update/01/index.htm (accessed March 7, 2012).

The World Trade Organization at www.wto.org/english/news_e/sppl_e/spp1220_htm, (accessed March 12, 2012).

U.S. Department of Commerce, International Trade Administration, "Jobs Supported by Exports: An Update," March 12, 2012, www.trade.gov/mas/ian/index.asp (accessed March 13, 2012).

Vandermerwe, S. and L'Huillier, M.-A. (1989) 'Euroconsumers in 1992', *Business Horizons*, January–February, 34–40.

www.cisstat.com, August 2004.

World Economic Outlook Update, January 24, 2012, International Monetary Fund Web site at imf.org/external/pubs/ft/weo/2012/update/01/index.htm (accessed March 13, 2012).

Yang, D. J., Bennett, D. and Javerski, B. (1989) 'The other China is starting to soar', *Business Weekly*, 6 November, 60–62.

PART 2
BUSINESS OWNERSHIP AND ENTREPRENEURSHIP

In Part 2 of *Business*, we look at a very practical aspect of business: How businesses are owned. Issues related to ownership are particularly interesting in today's world, where large global businesses coexist with small businesses. In addition, because the majority of businesses are small, we look at specific issues related to small business.

4

TYPES OF BUSINESS OWNERSHIP

LEARNING OBJECTIVES

Once you complete this chapter, you should be able to:

- Describe the advantages and disadvantages for sole traders
- Describe the advantages and disadvantages of partnerships
- Summarise how a corporation is formed
- Describe the advantages and disadvantages of a corporation
- Discuss the purpose of a cooperative and joint venture
- Explain how growth from within and growth through mergers can enable a business to expand

BUSINESS FOCUS

Joint venture in Singapore

In November 2009, the Anglo-Dutch oil company, Royal Dutch Shell PLC, entered into an agreement with the state-owned Qatar Petroleum International (QPI) to create a joint venture whereby each own 50 per cent in the petrochemical industry in Singapore. The new joint venture company is called QPI & Shell Petrochemicals (Singapore). PetroChina is involved with gas and oil production and in a very short space of time has become the largest gas and oil producer in China. The deal with Shell and QPI is one of the ways in which a company like PetroChina is able to expand quickly and exploit the skills, knowledge, expertise and technology of other companies in its sector.

The deal in Singapore is an example of how joint ventures can be used to focus on developing business in different areas and how such deals can be relatively complex. Qatar wants to expand its operations into the potentially lucrative Asia-Pacific market and needs Shell's petrochemicals expertise to help it achieve its goal. Shell has its largest petrochemical production facility for the Asia-Pacific region in Singapore and it hopes that the joint venture will mean that Qatar will agree to supply raw materials including liquefied petroleum gas to Singapore.

This agreement is part of an on-going partnership between Shell and Qatar to develop and expand their operations. The agreements form part of a strategic cooperation which benefits both the state of Qatar and Shell. Both have been looking at ways that they can identify projects around the world which would benefit both and give them a competitive advantage over rivals in the energy supply chain. They are, for example, building massive production facilities in Qatar itself and also in China where they plan to build a large-scale refinery and petrochemical production complex. Singapore is recognised as a major hub in the supply of petrochemicals in the region and the joint venture with Shell gives Qatar a foothold in this area. Qatar sees the Far East as its "natural market" and a presence in Singapore allows it to monitor this market more effectively.

In establishing a joint venture, Qatar is not only able to gain access to an area where it might not have been able to easily without Shell's presence there, it enables it to share its expertise with Shell to produce new products and secure supplies which benefit both.

References: Variety of sources used including: Kelly & Ashwin, *The Business Environment* (2013, Cengage Learning); www.shell.com; http://www.petrochina.com.cn/ptr; http://www.qp.com.qa; 'Proposals for Singapore's next tranche of liquefied natural gas imports' http://news.xin.msn.com/en/singapore 31st October 2013

We opened with a *Business Focus* feature looking at a joint venture, one of many types of business discussed in this chapter. As you will see, we also look at sole traders, partnerships, limited liability partnerships, private limited companies, public limited companies amongst others.

TYPES OF FIRMS

Sole traders

A **sole trader** is the simplest and most common form of business organisation in existence in the world today. Millions of people set themselves up in business with little or no formal procedures being carried out. In some countries such business activity may be in the form of a painter and decorator, a corner shop newsagent, a window cleaner, chimney sweep, plumber, landscape garden designer, builder, farmer, musician and so on. In less-developed countries, individuals may "be in business" selling shells, trinkets and souvenirs, newspapers by the side of the road, a shoe-shine facility, making clay bricks, acting as a tourist guide or golf caddy and so on.

> **sole trader** a type of business entity which legally has no separate existence from its owner (the limitations of liability benefited from by a corporation, and limited liability partnerships, do not apply to sole traders) – the simplest form of business

Setting up as a sole trader is popular primarily because it is so simple. If an individual has a business idea that they think will work there is nothing to stop them from starting their business immediately and beginning to trade. As the name implies, a sole trader or sole proprietor is the owner of the business. Many sole traders employ other people but these people are not owners of the business. An important principle of a sole trader (or sole proprietorship) is the fact that there is no legal difference between the owner and the business. Dave Moss and his chimney sweep business, is one and the same thing as far as the law is concerned. What this means is that if any legal action was taken against the "business" then Dave, as the owner, would be responsible for answering that action. For example, if an accident occurred during the sweeping of a chimney which was the result of negligence on Dave's part, then the customer might choose to sue Dave for damages. Dave would be personally responsible for the payment of those damages if the action was upheld in court.

The principle of no legal separation between the owner and the business also has implications for taxation and where profit or loss is made. The sole trader is classed as being self-employed and is responsible for the payment of national taxes such as income tax and National Insurance Contributions (NICs) in the U.K., for example. For a sole trader it is important, therefore, that accurate records are kept of all income and payments in relation to the business to enable them to complete accurate tax returns. Failure to do so can result in the presentation of tax demands that can seriously affect the ability of the business to be able to continue.

Equally, if the business makes any profit (which for this type of business is classed as the same as the individual's income) then it is the owner who is able to benefit solely from those profits. He or she keeps all the profit as his or her own. However, the reverse is also the case. One of the main disadvantages of being a sole trader is that the owner has **unlimited liability**. This means that the owner is personally responsible and liable for all the debts of the business. If a sole trader had to cease trading then any debts owed to creditors, such as suppliers, landlords, the tax authorities and so on, are the personal responsibility of the owner. In some cases this can mean that a sole trader has to sell personal assets to raise the funds to settle these debts. If this means having to sell the house, car, prized antique or any other personal possession, then this has to be done.

 unlimited liability a situation where the owner of a business is legally responsible for all the debts of the business

Ultimately if the sole trader cannot settle these debts then they are declared bankrupt. Note that whilst the term "bankrupt" is often used in a generic way to describe any business failure, in legal terms it has a specific meaning. An individual can become bankrupt, a business becomes insolvent. The lack of legal separation between business and owner as a sole trader means that if the "business" fails the sole proprietor can declare bankruptcy.

Unlimited liability is the biggest risk facing a sole trader. It is important, however, to think about it in exactly this way – as a risk. Risk is defined as the chance or possibility of reward, loss, harm, or damage; it may have an upside (benefit to the organisation) or downside - negative occurrence. For a sole trader the risk is that if the business does not succeed (and many do not) then there is a chance that they could lose everything. However, the perception of this risk is important. For a chimney sweep like Dave Moss, the risk involved in setting up in that line of business might be small.

Do you dream of being your own boss? If you become a sole proprietor, you'll have all the flexibility that comes with making your own decisions. But remember: Although you'll have the final say, you'll also be responsible if something goes wrong.

The cost of setting up the business is limited – he does not need any expensive office space, the basic equipment needed – brushes, ladders and vacuum cleaner – are not expensive, a vehicle will be needed for transport and apart from fuel costs, insurance and depreciation, the set up and running costs are limited in comparison to an individual setting up a plant hire operation, for example. Assume Mike is setting up this type of business. In this case the set up costs are likely to be significant. The business will need extensive premises, the initial capital outlay on a wide range of equipment can be high, maintenance and insurance costs will be much higher than for Dave, several transport vehicles will be needed to transport hired equipment to customers, a number of employees might be needed to help run the business. The set up and running costs, therefore, are likely to be significantly higher. Assume that the set up costs for Dave were €8,000 whereas the set up costs for the plant hire business were €125,000. Both Dave and Mike might have borrowed the money from a bank to set themselves up however, if both businesses failed then Dave risks having to meet his liability to the bank to pay back the €8,000; for Mike the situation is much worse, he risks having to find a way of paying back €125,000, which may involve him having to sell his house in order to fund the debt. Dave may have to sell his van and personal car and whilst that is inconvenient it is not as serious a situation as that faced by Mike.

Any decision to set up as a sole trader, therefore, may have to balance out the likelihood of risk against the extent of the risk faced. For example, the risk of failure might be estimated by an individual at being 1 : 4 after 4 years. The potential loss incurred might total €100,000. The possible benefit might be estimated in terms of forecast profits of a total of €80,000 after 4 years. Given these "odds" should the sole trader go ahead? There is no right answer to this question. There is a 25% chance that the individual could lose €100,000 after 4 years but a 75% chance that profits of €80,000 could be realised after the same period of time. This risk-reward ratio has to be considered by the individual and a judgement made about whether the reward is worth the risk involved. Some individuals are risk averse and may feel that the prospect of the possible losses and the chance of it happening is too great, others may be more risk seeking and feel that the chance of success (as measured by the forecast profit) is worth taking since the prospect of loss is relatively small (at 25%). However, these same individuals' judgements might change if the odds of failure were higher (say 50%) or that the chance of generating €80,000 in profits was only estimated at 20%.

For many people considering setting up as a sole trader, the key issues to consider are the likelihood of the business not succeeding in relation to the extent of the loss that could be incurred as a result. The figures for survival rates of new businesses are notoriously difficult to identify with any certainty partly because many small businesses are sole traders and do not have to submit accounts. This means the data is not recorded and so it is often difficult to be precise. However, estimates put the failure rates for new businesses at between 75 and 90 per cent in the first ten years. In many cases the reasons for the failure of sole traders is not that the business itself is inherently "bad" but because of problems with cash flow.

Failure rates for businesses do depend to an extent on the type of business. The following represents an estimate of failure rates in different industries recorded in 2007. Whilst the precise proportions may have changed since then, the data does give an overall picture of variations in failure rates.

- Manufacturing - 11 per cent
- Marketing services - 8.9 per cent
- Personal services (includes hairdressers, beauticians) - 8.1 per cent
- Private hire transport - 7.5 per cent
- Retail - 6.9 per cent
- IT services - 6.3 per cent
- Financial services - 6.3 per cent
- Printing - 5.6 per cent
- Building & construction - 5 per cent
- Media & Entertainment - 2.5 per cent
- Recruitment and other professional services - 2.1 per cent*

(Source: With thanks to UHY Hacker Young LLP Charted Accountants)

SUCCESS STORY

Innocent Smoothies

Innocent Smoothies was started in the U.K. in 1998 by three friends: Richard Reed, Adam Balon and Jon Wright, who had known each other since their student days. They had identified a consumer need for readily-available fresh fruit smoothies to provide an easier means to a healthy life style. So they invested £500, bought lots of fresh fruit then sold it crushed into bottles from a stall at a music festival. They placed two large baskets on their stall

and erected a large sign – Should we *start this business*? The "yes" bucket was soon full!

After an initial struggle with sourcing start-up funds, they received an offer from an American serial entrepreneur of £235,000 for 18 per cent of the equity in the business. The three partners would retain 70 per cent with the remaining 12 per cent split amongst their colleagues in the business. Overcoming lots of legislation and distribution hurdles, they were soon on their way to success with a wide product range.

Within five years they had turned over £10 million and in 2007 (just under ten years) their turnover exceeded £100 million and Innocent had a 70 per cent share of the U.K. market for smoothies. In 2008 sales fell back with some concern expressed that smoothies as a discretionary consumer purchase might suffer in the anticipated eco-

nomic recession, combined with increased competition and rising fruit prices. But at the same time Innocent were keen to expand in selected overseas markets, especially Europe, and Coca-Cola bought a 20 per cent stake for £30 million. Innocent were careful to maintain their environmentally-aware image in all press reports, emphasising that the investment from Coca-Cola was simply to help secure new distribution opportunities.

Coca-Cola's stake has since been expanded to over 60%, and Innocent remains extremely successful, with the three partners emphasising that the secrets to success include: maintaining a clear purpose and set of values; being ethical; and listening to customers' needs.

References: A variety of sources used including Thompson, Scott & Martin, *Strategic Management: Awareness and Change*; www.innocentdrinks.co.uk and www.bbc.co.uk/news/business.

Sole traders are likely to be represented more in some of these sectors than others, for example, in personal services and building and construction, but they do highlight the potential risks in setting up different businesses.

One of the problems facing sole traders is that there are weaknesses in fundamental underlying business understanding. Planning, sources of finance, cash-flow forecasting and management and often simply the capacity to be able to manage time effectively, as well as many competing skills required are not given due weight and consideration. Setting up a restaurant because you are interested in and very good at cooking is one thing; managing and running a successful restaurant, which is about far more than simply food, is another matter. The pressure on sole traders to take full responsibility for every aspect of the business can be draining and whilst the promise of being able to enjoy all the profits will motivate many to continue to work hard at their business, many find the expected profits do not materialise in the way they expected.

Despite the potential risks involved, setting up as a sole trader is still extremely popular as a form of business organisation. One of the main reasons, as noted, is its simplicity. The individual has to register with tax authorities as being self employed and a self-assessment tax form completed each year for submission. The individual may have to gain various legal permissions to trade, depending on the type of business and of course has to adhere to the law of the land. Licenses may be required to set up as a care home, for example, if food and or alcohol is being produced and or sold and so on. Sole traders have a considerable degree of internal control over their business and can be flexible in response to changes. The business can also be "juggled" to balance out the competing demands facing the individual since all decision-making is in the hands of the owner.

Partnerships

A **partnership** is a business organisation that consists of two or more people. In many respects it has similarities with a sole proprietorship in that it is relatively simple to set up. A partnership has unlimited liability and so has no legal status separating the partners from the business. Individuals considering entering a partnership would normally draw up some sort of partnership agreement which clarified roles, responsibilities and liabilities. If, for example, five people entered a partnership but one put in 50 per cent of the capital of the business then the agreement might state that this individual would be entitled to 50 per cent of the profits generated by the business.

> **partnership** when you go into business with someone else (more commonly associated with professional services such as accountants, solicitors and doctors)

As is the case for a sole trader, partners have to register as self employed with the tax authorities but in addition to individual returns the partnership as a whole has to submit a self assessment form. Income tax and NICs will have to be paid on profits. Given that a partnership is not a legal entity, if one of the partners dies or wishes to leave then the partnership must be dissolved.

Limited Liability Partnerships

In recent years, changes to company law in the U.K. have permitted the setting up of **limited liability partnerships** (LLP). There are similarities to a traditional partnership but in addition similarities to the setting up of limited companies. However, non-profit making charities cannot form a LLP. The main reason for setting up a LLP is that the partners (of which there must be at least 2) can limit their liability to the debts of the business. In an LLP the business is responsible for the debts of the business rather than the individual partners. In the U.K. contact needs to be made with Companies House (a government body concerned with business) and an incorporation form completed. There is a small charge for this. The rights and responsibilities of each partner are laid out in a Deed of Partnership and one of the partners is identified as the contact with Companies House. This person would be responsible for the preparation of accounts and acting on behalf of the LLP in any legal negotiations.

> **Limited Liability Partnership (LLP)** a partnership in which some or all partners (depending on the jurisdiction) have limited liability

Sometimes it helps to have a famous partner with a proven track record. After leaving public office, former New York City Mayor Rudy Giuliani formed Giuliani Partners—a partnership with the accounting firm Ernst & Young. The objective of this partnership is to help business clients deal with the risks that stem from terrorism, crime, natural disasters, and other factors that threaten an organisation's ability to survive.

The Deed of Partnership is a legally-binding agreement which will include the personal details of the partners, how much capital each has put into the business, details of how the partnership would be terminated if one of the partners left or died as well as the roles and responsibilities of each partner. The designate partner must also contact the tax authorities to file a Partnership Statement along with the LLP tax return which provides details of how any profits made in the business have been divided up amongst the partners.

An LLP must have at least two designated members. A designated member has the same duties in an LLP as a member but in addition is responsible for appointing auditors, signing and delivering accounts, notifying the Registrar of Companies of changes to the business, such as change of address or name, preparing other documents that the Registrar of Companies may require and acting on behalf of the business if it is wound up.

An LLP can choose its own name but there are certain restrictions over this. Using the same name as a company already registered would not be allowed nor would a name which implies that the business is a government agency, is deemed offensive or where its use would constitute some sort of criminal offence. For example, names which use the words Authority, European, Charter, Registered, Association, Benevolent, Trade Union, Trust, Foundation, National and British might have to have approval from the Secretary of State. The reason being that the use of these and other words may mislead the public into thinking the business is something it is not.

There are also regulations relating to where the name of the LLP should appear. For example, the name must appear on all business letters sent by the LLP, all notices and official publications, invoices, receipts, credit notes, cheques or other documents that have come from the business.

Private limited companies

Private limited company status is an important and popular form of business organisation because it confers the benefits of **limited liability** on owners. A private limited company (abbreviated to Ltd) is a distinct legal entity. This means that the business is the entity that can sue or be sued rather than any of the individuals that may own the business. It is this legal status that makes a ltd company attractive. If the business fails then the owners risk losing the money they have invested into the company. However, creditors cannot seek to claim recovery of what they are owed by forcing owners to sell their personal possessions to settle these debts. This is an advantage to the company owner but not to the company who may be dealing with it. This is why some limited companies have greater problems accessing credit and supply agreements compared to non-limited companies.

> **limited liability** a situation where the liability (responsibility) of the owner/s of a business is limited to the amount that they have agreed to subscribe/invest

A limited company can issue shares as a means of raising capital, however, these shares cannot be sold to, or traded by, the public. There are normally 2 or more people involved as shareholders although there are cases of single member companies, limited by shares or guarantee, consisting of one member. Such cases usually arise when a limited company is reduced to one member due to the death of a shareholder or some other circumstance. Single member companies have to adhere to certain regulations given that the business could have some continuity, for example, it might be subject to acquisition by another business. As such it needs to have records of decisions taken and hold general meetings with notes made on any decisions taken even if the only person attending is the single member.

There are three types of private limited company:

● **Private company limited by shares**
  The business is owned by shareholders whose liability is limited to the amount they have agreed to invest in the business. Again using the U.K. as an example, if a member holds 10,000 shares

with a nominal value of £1 each then this is termed "unpaid share capital." If the business has to close then the shareholder risks losing all or part of this sum. If the business closed but was able to pay back £2,000 to the shareholder from the remaining assets of the business then the amount unpaid that the owner would be liable for would be £8,000. However, the shareholder would not be liable for any of the debts of the company in excess of the £10,000 they have originally invested.

- **Private company limited by guarantee**
  This type of company is used in cases such as social enterprises, sports associations and non-governmental organisations (NGOs) where the members, who are referred to as guarantors and not shareholders, wish to specify the liability they have to the business. In this case the business does not have share capital and so guarantors do not contribute to the capital of the business and do not, as a consequence, purchase shares. The members agree to a nominal sum, which may be £1, in the event of the business being wound up.

  It should be noted that there are in existence some companies limited by guarantee with share capital but these were formed prior to 1981. Legislation at that time prevented such companies from being formed.

- **Private unlimited company**
  A private unlimited company is one in which members may contribute share capital and be shareholders or be guarantors but the difference being that the liability of the members is unlimited. The trade-off for this lack of protection is that the amount of information that the members have to disclose is less than the other types of limited company.

  The rules surrounding Ltd companies in the U.K. have changed in recent years as a result of the Companies Act 2006. Much of the change relates to the documentation that has to be submitted and the way in which the company is organised and run. Two key documents are (1) the Memorandum of Association - a document which specifies basic details of the business and (2) the Articles of Association-that details the rules for the running and regulation of the company's internal affairs.

Public Limited Companies (PLCs)

Public Limited Company status tends to be associated with larger business organisations (although not exclusively). PLCs have to follow clear guidelines and regulations as well as the legislation. The main reason for this is the way that these organisations are financed. PLCs are able to sell shares to members of the general public and as such safeguards have to be put in place to protect members of the public who do choose to invest in these organisations.

> **Public Limited Company (PLC)** a limited company whose shares may be purchased by the public and traded freely on the open market and whose share capital is not less than a statutory minimum (for the U.K. – a company registered under the Companies Act (1980) as a public company)

In the U.K., PLCs cannot commence trading until they have fulfilled a number of requirements and received a Trading Certificate from the governing body, Companies House. To get this the company has to have a minimum allotted share capital of £50,000 or £65,000 in either pounds or euro but not a mixture. PLCs are subject to many of the same rules as private companies in respect of the number of members (at least two) and to have at least two company directors one of whom must be a human. In addition a PLC must have a company secretary who must meet certain qualifications and experience criteria, for example by having served as a secretary of a public company for three years out of five prior to appointment, be a member of a chartered accountant organisation or other similar recognised body, be a barrister, advocate or solicitor or deemed to have sufficient experience and qualities to be capable of carrying out the role.

There are a number of provisions in the 2006 Act outlined above that do not apply to PLCs. For example, these organisations have to submit accounts within 6 months of its accounting reference period to Companies House and failure to meet such a deadline incurs a penalty charge.

The major benefit of setting up a PLC is that the access to capital is much wider than in other forms of business organisation because a PLC can issue shares to the public. These shares can be freely traded through a stock exchange. If it needs additional capital, adverts can be placed inviting the public to take up more of its shares.

Flotation

It is possible for a private limited company by shares to be able to convert to PLC status. This is referred to as **flotation**. It has to go through a number of processes to do so including having members pass a special resolution, amending the memorandum and articles of association to suit, submitting up-to-date financial documents such as the balance sheet and a copy of a report and statement by the company's auditors and other documentation relating to the assets of the business and the valuation of its shares. If the company was a private unlimited company then it also has to state that a resolution has been passed confirming the fact that members will now have limited liability and the amount of share capital to be raised.

> **flotation** the process of offering a company's shares for sale on the stock market for the first time

A public limited company can also revert back to being a private limited company. Again there are statutory requirements to go through this procedure including passing of resolutions showing the agreement of members. A number of firms do this through management buyouts where the directors of the business, who may also be shareholders, buyout the remaining shareholders and re-register with Companies House as a private limited company. In some cases the managers concerned will raise the finance to buyout shareholders through borrowing funds and this is referred to as a "leveraged buyout."

Business organisation in European countries

In other countries, the principles of limited liability are similarly enshrined in law. In Germany, owners of a business are called Gesellschafter (members) and the acronym after a business name GmbH (Gesellschaft mit beschränkter Haftung) signifies that these members have limited liability. Such companies must have a minimum starting capital of €25,000 and are run by a managing director who acts on behalf of the company unless the business employs more than 500 workers. In this case the company has to be run by a supervisory board (Aufsichtsrat).

German company law has a number of features that increase bureaucracy. For example, stock issues, share transfer, any changes to articles of association have to involve the services of a specialist lawyer called a notary which can increase both the time taken and the cost. In addition, members can place significant limitations on the actions of directors through the issuance of bonding orders to which they must adhere.

The Table 4.1 shows the number of steps entrepreneurs have to go through to set up a business and the time taken in different European countries. Included are the number of steps entrepreneurs can expect to go through to launch, the time it takes on average, and the cost and minimum capital required as a percentage of gross national income (GNI) per capita.

TABLE 4.1	Indicator	Germany	Denmark	Spain	Iceland	UK	Oecd Average
	Procedures (number)	9	4	10	5	6	5.7
	Time (days)	18	6	47	5	13	13.0
	Cost (% of income per capita)	4.7	0.9	15.0	3.0	0.7	4.7

Source: http://www.doingbusiness.org

It can be seen that procedures in Germany can be more time consuming than in other European countries, with the exception of Spain where the procedures are clearly even more onerous.

Other forms of business organisation in Germany include the Aktiengesellschaft (AG). This used to be the more popular type of business organisation but was replaced by the GmbH primarily because of the complexity of the AG. The AG consists of a supervisory board controlled by shareholders and possibly employees, who provide the overall policy for the company which is managed on a day-to-day basis by a management board. The activities and remuneration of the management board is largely determined by the supervisory board that also have the power to remove members of the management board. This form of business organisation does have similarities with structures in other countries such as the Aktiebolag (AB) in Sweden, the Societate pe Actiuni (SA) in Romania and Aktieselskab (AS) in Denmark.

There are also a number of countries who use the suffix SA after the company name. These are similar to public limited companies in the U.K. The initials SA stand for Société Anonyme which translates in English to "anonymous society." The wide variation in the detail of company law throughout the European Union and the different regulatory structures under which countries operate can present problems to companies either operating in different European countries or who are seeking to consolidate through acquisition. As a result, Europe-wide legislation has been passed to help companies overcome some of these difficulties.

The Council Regulation on the Statute for a European Company of the EU became law in 2001 and applied to all EU states in 2004. It allows for companies to become a Societas Europaea (SE) and also enables the setting up of European Cooperative Societies. An SE can be set up in four main ways; through conversion from a national company, through the creation of a subsidiary to the main company, by acquisition of companies originating from different EU nations or through the creation of a joint-venture between companies from different European nations. The SE must have a minimum share capital to the value of €120,000 and have a registered office in a location where it carries out its main administration – its headquarters, in other words. The running of the SE combines elements of the single-tier administrative board system with the two-tier system outlined in the AG above. The management board are appointed by the supervisory board and carries out the day-to-day operations of the company. No member can be on the supervisory and management board. If running as a single-tier company, the administrative board runs the business.

Regardless of the system, each of these boards has responsibilities for authorising different actions including raising finance, acquisitions or disposal of assets, the signing of large scale contracts relating to supply or performance and certain investment projects. As with PLCs, an annual statement of accounts must be drawn up and made public. The SE is liable for tax in relation to wherever the administrative offices are located.

Cooperatives

The International Cooperative Alliance is an organisation that represents cooperative organisation around the world. It defines a cooperative as:

> "…an autonomous association of persons united voluntarily to meet their common economic, social, and cultural needs and aspirations through a jointly-owned and democratically-controlled enterprise" It adds: "Ranging from small-scale to multi-million dollar businesses across the globe, cooperatives employ more than 100 million women and men and have more than 800 million individual members".

(Source: With thanks to ICA http://www.2012.coop/en/what-co-op/co-operative-identity-values-principles)

From this definition and additional information, it is clear that cooperatives are a significant force in the way in which businesses are organised. The roots of this type of organisation go back to the North West of the U.K. in 1844 when workers in the cotton mills of Rochdale formed the Rochdale Equitable Pioneers Society. The basic idea was to try and find a way to gain some benefits of economies of scale by pooling their resources together to bulk purchase basic foodstuffs such as sugar, butter, flour and oatmeal. In so doing they aimed to get lower prices on these goods and then share the benefits between the members. Members had an equal say in the running of the cooperative and shared in any profits that were made. The success of the so-called Rochdale Pioneers has led to the expansion of the movement around the world. Whilst the modern cooperative movement has adapted to changing times the basic principles have been retained. Cooperatives have close philosophical ties with the social enterprise movement (see below).

There have been a number of different types of cooperative organisation relating to wholesale, retail, manufacturing, employee, banking and savings and agricultural and fishing activities amongst other things. Whilst these activities vary, the basis of the movement is similar.

A number of key principles underpin every cooperative movement. These include:

- Equality of opportunity for anyone to be a member of the organisation regardless of gender, race, religion etc.
- Cooperatives are voluntary organisations
- Most organisations are democratic with all members having the right to vote on policy and decisions. Elected representatives are responsible to the membership
- Members mostly pay a nominal sum to become a member and receive a share in the organisation. No one member is able to build up share allocations. The share capital invariably becomes the common property of all the members who have control over this capital
- In some cases, any profits (regarded as "surpluses") are either divided equally amongst all members or are allocated to specific purposes such as re-investment into the organisation or a nominated non-governmental organisation (NGO) agreed by the members
- The early forms of retail cooperative distributed profits in the form of a "dividend" which was based on the amount of purchases made by each member. At certain periods of the year, members were advised of the dividend they would receive. Each purchase recorded the share number of the member to help calculate the dividend received
- Cooperatives are independent and autonomous. Any agreement with external organisations has to be made with the agreement of the membership
- In keeping with the cooperative and self-help ideal, organisations promote the benefits of education and training as means to improve the welfare of all
- Active cooperation between cooperative movements is encouraged as a means of strengthening the organisation as a whole
- Cooperatives have a concern for sustainable development of communities at a local, national and international level
- Cooperatives emphasise a concern for ethical trading and business operation.

The importance of cooperatives varies in different countries. In a number of countries around 10 per cent of the population are members of some sort of cooperative in other countries such as Germany, Argentina, Japan, Kenya, Iran, U.S. and Malaysia the proportion ranges from a quarter of the population to around a third. In New Zealand up to 40 per cent of the population belong to either a cooperative or a mutual society (organised very similarly to a cooperative) and in Singapore around a half of the population are involved.

The sectors of the economy represented by cooperatives are similarly varied. As noted, as well as the cooperative retail outlets the organisation is involved in pharmacies, sugar, wheat, potato, coffee, dairy and meat production, forestry and fishing, schools and road building and services such as funerals, travel agents, banking and savings and credit. Millions of people around the world rely on cooperatives for their employment and their livelihoods.

Charities and social enterprises

Charities have existed since the middle ages. Up to the development of welfare states in most European countries in the 20th century, many charities fulfilled the function of caring for those who could not access the normal expected provision of society. Charities were often set up as a result of bequests in wills with a number of schools, hospitals and houses being set up as a result of some sort of charitable bequest. As governments absorbed the provision of the basic essentials of life into the welfare state, charities have taken on a different but related function. Many charities are now global organisations which also act as pressure groups for a particular cause such as poverty, the environment, animal welfare and disease. In addition, however, each country may have smaller charitable organisations focused on particular issues relevant to the local area.

The basis of any charitable organisation is that it operates as a normal business organisation but its aims are to serve the needs of the cause/charitable activity. Its income comes, primarily, from donations from the general public although there are now charities such as Oxfam and Help the Aged which run shops selling second hand and donated items. The main emphasis of the organisation is on maximising the funds they can make available to the cause they are associated with, whilst minimising the administration costs of running the organisation.

In most countries, charities are regulated to ensure that they meet appropriate standards of accounting and administration. This is designed to prevent fraud and misuse of funds. In operating like any business organisation, a charity will have income (revenue) and costs. If revenue exceeds income then the charity will make a profit which is referred to as a surplus. This surplus can be used to improve the operational efficiency of the charity but is mostly used to fund the cause which the charity was set up for. In different countries the word "charities" may not be used or familiar to the population. In India, for example, charities are more likely to be known as NGOs or non-profit organisations (NPOs).

Social enterprises

One major development in the type of business organisation in this field has been the growth of social enterprises. **Social enterprises** are a mix of business activity and charity. The idea of social enterprises originated in Italy in the early 1980s. The primary objective of a social enterprise is to focus on investing any surpluses (profits) into some community, social objective or business activity or issue rather than dividing the profit up between the owners of the business. As such they have been described as a "third sector" – the private not-for-profit sector. As these enterprises have developed, there has been increasing interest from government in how social enterprises can be utilised to provide products and services that might have traditionally been seen as being within the remit of the public sector. Governments may be prepared to provide some financial support and assistance to such enterprises (for example by speeding up planning applications) as a means of providing public sector services more efficiently.

> **social enterprise** an enterprise which lies somewhere between the for-profit and not-for-profit organisation, aiming to make money, but using it mainly for social causes

Examples of such enterprises in the U.K. include the provision of sports and leisure facilities in Birmingham, childcare, such as the TLC Neighbourhood Nursery in Wolverhampton in the West Midlands, People to Places, an enterprise providing accessible transport for people with disabilities and mobility problems in Berkshire, the Dead Earnest Theatre group and Fresh Pastures, a company providing milk to schools, both based in Yorkshire.

© MANGOSTOCK/SHUTTERSTOCK

Two entrepreneurs with one goal. There is a special pride of ownership that takes place when two people are solving problems and working together for the same purpose. Being responsible for what happens to the company— as well as your business partner—can be a motivating force for working that much harder to be successful.

Community Interest Companies

Companies set up with the specific intention of providing community benefits in the U.K. are called **Community Interest Companies** and have the initials CIC after their names. Such organisations are set up as companies limited by share or guarantee as described above. In registering, however, the company has to provide a community interest statement which outlines the specific social purpose of the business. This is scrutinised via a community interest test and if the company passes this test then they can trade. There are a number of specific requirements of CICs. These include:

- An asset lock whereby in the event of the company folding, community assets are protected and the business cannot transfer or sell assets or profits for less than the full market value
- CICs set up as a company limited by shares have the option of setting a cap on the dividend paid to investors
- CICs must provide an annual statement of accounts and also an annual community interest company report which outlines what the company has done in relation to the community interest project it was set up to help
- Specific rules on voting rights of the chair and directors. A CIC chairperson, for example, does not have the right to a casting vote in the event of a divided vote at a board meeting.

> **Community Interest Company (CIC)** a limited company set to function as a social enterprise, which adheres to strict statutory requirements for adhering to social purposes

Whilst many social enterprises have a philanthropic objective, they do operate ostensibly as any ordinary business. The main objectives of the business tend to be social and environmental and whilst they may have the objective of maximising profit; that profit maximisation goal is there to enable the organisation to be able to fund or promote the cause they are working for. The cause may be helping those who are homeless, providing facilities to help local communities access water, promoting fair trade or recycling, providing affordable homes, insulation, sustainable energy projects, services for young people and so on.

Social enterprises are becoming an increasingly important sector. In the U.K., it has been estimated that there are over 60,000 social enterprises with a combined turnover of £27 billion accounting for some 5 per cent of businesses with employees*. In other countries social enterprises have developed in different ways. The following is a short summary of social enterprise activity in other European states.

Belgium   There are only a small number of social enterprise organisations in Belgium. In 1996 the legal framework was amended to include the concept of a "social purpose company." The administration associated with setting up a social enterprise in Belgium is more onerous than in other countries and may explain the limited development of this form of organisation.

Denmark   The concept is beginning to take hold in Denmark; there are four key areas of activity seeing a rise in social enterprise which include voluntary support groups such as self-help groups for those who have contemplated suicide, going through divorce, suffering from domestic abuse etc., cooperatives in retail, insurance and farming, education and training groups such as the "work-integration social enterprises" (WISE) and various urban development projects.

Finland   The Finnish Act on Social Enterprises came into force in January 2004. The Act does not provide any restrictions on the use of surpluses or profits but at the same time there is little government support available for setting up enterprises. As a result there are only a handful of such enterprises at the time of writing.

France   In 2002 French law was amended to allow for the creation of a "collective interest cooperative society" – SCIC (société coopérative d'intérêt collectif). This type of organisation allows a wide range of stakeholders such as voluntary workers, local government and other partners to develop local projects. As in other European countries the idea of social enterprises is gathering momentum and moving on from projects designed to support greater integration of disadvantaged persons into the labour force which had been the primary focus of WISE organisation in the 1990s.

Germany   Given the country's political background, the idea of a social enterprise is not seen as being distinct from the idea of a social market economy which dominates German political thinking. There are what might be recognised as social enterprises in other countries in Germany, but many of these do not see themselves as being distinct in the same way that may be the case in the U.K., for example. Such organisations include welfare organisations, volunteer services, cooperatives, local community and trading groups and women's movements. There are not, however, separate legal structures for these types of organisations as yet.

Italy   Italy is the home of social enterprise primarily in the form of social cooperatives. However, the concept has expanded beyond these types of organisation and legislation passed in 2005 has now clarified the legal and organisational structures of social enterprises. There are a number of key areas where social enterprises can develop including education and training, social tourism, culture and heritage, welfare, health and environment.

Sweden   The development of the social enterprise concept in Sweden is closely linked with the provision of public sector services which have increased in demand since the 1980s. Government has been unable to keep up with the demand and social enterprise has filled some of the gap. Child care services are a good example of this; some 10 per cent of provision is through social cooperatives.

Joint ventures

Joint ventures (touched upon in the previous chapter, from an international perspective) refer to the formal links made between businesses to carry out some economic activity or business enterprise. The formal links may involve all parties contributing capital and subsequently agreeing to some form of sharing of cost, revenues and profits. Joint ventures can be beneficial to all parties without the formal expense of undergoing acquisition. There may be a number of reasons why businesses might want to form a joint venture. These include:

> **Joint venture**   cooperating firms create a legally independent firm in which they invest and from which they share any profits that are created

- Risk bearing economies of scale – all parties can share the risk which can be spread across a greater range of output and thus reduce unit costs
- Synergies – uniting the different strengths of each partner to create a venture in which the whole is greater than the sum of its parts
- Financial economies of scale – the joint venture may be in a stronger position to negotiate favourable rates of finance and improve their access to such sources
- Technology – all parties may be in a better position to share technology and to benefit from the economies of scale that result
- Markets – expertise and involvement in different markets can be shared leading to greater penetration of the key target market/s for all parties to the joint venture
- Parties may see the joint venture as being a way to strategically position themselves in a growing or mature market to protect or develop competitive advantage or to mount a defensive strategy against competitor threats
- Securing the supply chain – parties may join together to ensure stability of supplies for production or access to supplies which had previously not existed

Multinational Corporations (MNCs)

MNCs represent businesses operating on a larger scale where the headquarters are in one country but where the firm has operations in a number of other countries. MNCs will typically do this to be able to access different markets (especially where the market may be restricted due to the existence of trade barriers), to better meet production needs for that local market, expand the brand, exploit the availability of resources such as labour and raw materials, benefit from tax or investment allowances and reduce transport and distribution costs.

> **Multinational Corporations (MNC)** Companies who own and control operations in more than one country

Whilst MNCs offer extended opportunities to the countries in which they base their operations in terms of inward investment, employment and benefits to local communities, they have come in for some criticism that they seek to exploit host countries. There have been some high profile examples of firms who have appeared to have acted in a manner which has not put the interests of wider stake-holders at the heart of their operations and instead have allegedly generated negative externalities such as pollution, environmental degradation and illness. Whilst it seems clear that these sorts of issues can arise, the growing concern with reputation and realisation that firms have some corporate social responsibility would indicate that the benefits that such firms provide may outweigh the costs which some impose.

In today's competitive environment, it's common to hear of large companies that are profitable. It is less common to hear of profitable companies that are held in high regard because they are good corporate citizens.

While not all sole proprietorships and partnerships become corporations, there are reasons why business owners choose the corporate form of ownership. Let's begin with a definition of a corporation. Perhaps the best definition of a corporation was given by Chief Justice John Marshall in a famous Supreme Court decision in 1819. A corporation, he said, "is an artificial person, invisible, intangible, and existing only in contemplation of the law." In other words, a **corporation** (sometimes referred to as a *regular* or *C-corporation*) is an artificial person created by law, with most of the legal rights of a real person. These include:

- The right to start and operate a business
- The right to buy or sell property
- The right to borrow money
- The right to sue or be sued
- The right to enter into binding contracts

> **corporation** an artificial person created by law with most of the legal rights of a real person, including the rights to start and operate a business, to buy or sell property, to borrow money, to sue or be sued, and to enter into binding contracts

Unlike a real person, however, a corporation exists only on paper. There are approximately 6 million corporations in the United States. They comprise about 19 per cent of all businesses, but they account for 81 per cent of sales revenues.

Procter & Gamble: Once a sole proprietorship, then a partnership, and now a very large corporation.
Although one of the largest corporations in the world, P&G was started when two sole traders formed a partnership to sell soap and candles. Today the corporation's product line has expanded and it now operates in 180 different countries around the globe.

© AP PHOTO/AL BEHRMAN

Corporate ownership

The shares of ownership of a corporation are called **stock**. The people who own a corporation's stock—and thus own part of the corporation—are called **stockholders**. Once a corporation has been formed, it may sell its stock to individuals or other companies that want to invest in the corporation. It also may issue stock as a reward to key employees in return for certain services or as a return to investors in place of cash payments.

> **stock** the shares of ownership of a corporation
> **stockholder** a person who owns a corporation's stock

A **closed corporation** is a corporation whose stock is owned by relatively few people and is not sold to the general public. As an example, Mars—the company famous for M&Ms, Snickers, Milky Way, Twix, and other chocolate bars—is a privately held, family-owned, closed corporation. Although many people think that a closed corporation is a small company, there are exceptions. Mars, for example, has annual sales of more than $30 billion, employs more than 65,000 associates worldwide, and operates in 70 different countries.*

> **closed corporation** a corporation whose stock is owned by relatively few people and is not sold to the general public

An **open corporation** is one whose stock can be bought and sold by any individual. Examples of open corporations include Microsoft, Apple, and Sony.

> **open corporation** a corporation whose stock can be bought and sold by any individual

Forming a corporation

Although you may think that incorporating a business guarantees success, it does not. There is no special magic about placing the word *Incorporated* or the abbreviation *Inc.* after the name of a business. Unfortunately, like sole proprietorships or partnerships, corporations can go broke. The decision to incorporate a business therefore should be made only after carefully considering whether the corporate form of ownership suits your needs better than the sole proprietorship or partnership forms.

If you decide that the corporate form is the best form of organisation for you, most experts recommend that you begin the incorporation process by consulting a solicitor to be sure that all legal requirements are met. While it may be possible to incorporate a business without legal help, this is certainly not advised. Table 4.2 lists some aspects of starting and running a business that may require legal help.

Where to incorporate Most small- and medium-sized businesses are incorporated in the region or country where they do the most business. The founders of larger corporations or of those that will do business nationwide often compare the benefits that various regions provide to corporations. The decision on where to incorporate usually is based on two factors: (1) the cost of incorporating in one region compared with the cost in another region and (2) the advantages and disadvantages of each region's corporate laws and tax structure. Some countries or regions are more hospitable than others, and some offer fewer restrictions, lower taxes, and other benefits to attract new firms.

Stockholders' rights There are two basic types of stock. Owners of **ordinary share** may vote on corporate matters. Generally, an owner of ordinary share has one vote for each share owned. However, any claims of ordinary share owners on profits, dividends, and assets of the corporation are paid after the claims of others. The owners of **preferred stock** usually have no voting rights, but

TABLE 4.2	**Ten aspects of business that may require legal help**

1. Choosing either the sole proprietorship, partnership, corporate, or some special form of ownership
2. Constructing a partnership agreement
3. Incorporating a business
4. Registering a corporation's stock
5. Obtaining a trademark, patent, or copyright
6. Filing for licenses or permits at the local, state, and federal levels
7. Purchasing an existing business or real estate
8. Creating valid contracts
9. Hiring employees and independent contractors
10. Extending credit and collecting debts

© Cengage Learning 2014

their claims on dividends are paid before those of ordinary share owners. Although large corporations may issue both common and preferred stock, generally small corporations issue only ordinary share.

ordinary share stock owned by individuals or firms who may vote on corporate matters but whose claims on profits and assets are subordinate to the claims of others

preferred stock stock owned by individuals or firms who usually do not have voting rights but whose claims on dividends are paid before those of ordinary share owners

Perhaps the most important right of owners of both common and preferred stock is to share in the profit earned by the corporation through the payment of dividends. A **dividend** is a distribution of earnings to the stockholders of a corporation. Other rights include receiving information about the corporation, voting on changes to the corporate charter, and attending the corporation's annual stockholders' meeting, where they may exercise their right to vote.

dividend a distribution of earnings to the stockholders of a corporation

Because ordinary shareholders are usually scattered across a large geographical area, very few actually may attend a corporation's annual meeting. Instead, they vote by proxy. A **proxy** is a legal form listing issues to be decided at a stockholders' meeting and enabling stockholders to transfer their voting rights to some other individual or individuals. The stockholder can register a vote and transfer voting rights simply by signing and returning the form. Today, most corporations also allow stockholders to exercise their right to vote by proxy by accessing the Internet or using a toll-free phone number.

proxy a legal form listing issues to be decided at a stockholders' meeting and enabling stockholders to transfer their voting rights to some other individual or individuals

Organisational meeting As the last step in forming a corporation, the incorporators and original stockholders meet to adopt corporate by-laws and elect their first board of directors. (Later, directors will be elected or reelected at the corporation's annual meetings by the firm's stockholders.) The board members are directly responsible to the stockholders for the way they operate the firm.

Corporate structure

The organisational structure of most corporations is more complicated than that of a sole proprietorship or partnership. In a corporation, both the board of directors and the corporate officers are involved in management.

© AP PHOTO/KEVIN P. CASEY

Even if you own a single share of ordinary share, you're legally a part-owner of the corporation. You're entitled to receive any dividends paid to shareholders and you can vote on important matters such as electing the board of directors. Your vote is counted—and it counts.

Board of directors As an artificial person, a corporation can act only through its directors, who represent the corporation's stockholders. The **board of directors** is the top governing body of a corporation and is elected by the stockholders. In theory, then, the stockholders are able to control the activities of the entire corporation through its directors because they are the group that elects the board of directors (see Figure 4.1).

board of directors the top governing body of a corporation, the members of which are elected by the stockholders

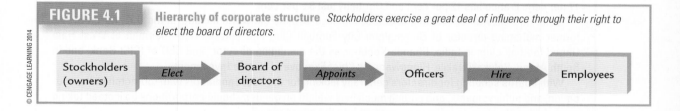

© CENGAGE LEARNING 2014

FIGURE 4.1 **Hierarchy of corporate structure** *Stockholders exercise a great deal of influence through their right to elect the board of directors.*

Stockholders (owners) → *Elect* → Board of directors → *Appoints* → Officers → *Hire* → Employees

Board members can be chosen from within the corporation or from outside it. *Note:* For a small corporation, often only one director is required although you can choose to have more. Directors who are elected from within the corporation are usually its top managers—the president and executive vice presidents, for example. Those elected from outside the corporation generally are experienced managers or entrepreneurs with proven leadership ability and/or specific talents the organisation seems to need. In smaller corporations, majority stockholders usually serve as board members.

The major responsibilities of the board of directors are to set company goals and develop general plans (or strategies) for meeting those goals. The board also is responsible for the firm's overall operation and appointing corporate officers.

Corporate officers **Corporate officers** are appointed by the board of directors. Although a small corporation may not have all of the following officers, the chairman of the board, president, executive vice presidents, corporate secretary, and treasurer are all corporate officers. They help the board to make plans, carry out strategies established by the board, hire employees, and manage day-to-day business activities. Periodically (usually each month), they report to the board of directors. And at the annual meeting, the directors report to the stockholders.

RESPONSIBLE PRACTICE Do we need more women in the board room?

Half of the world is female, yet women remain significantly under-represented at boardroom and director level.

In the U.K., nearly half of all FTSE 350 companies do not have a woman in the boardroom. In February 2011, the former U.K. trade minister and chairman of the Women in the Boardroom Review, Lord Davies, urged FTSE 350 companies to boost the percentage of women at the boardroom table to 25 per cent by 2015, declaring that "radical change is needed in the mindset of the business community if we are to implement the scale of change that is needed".

This is disappointing news from a business perspective, as women directors tend to be in tune with the views of female customers, employees, and managers. In many cases, women handle negotiations differently than men do, their careers follow slightly different paths, and their leadership styles may differ, as well. Not only do board members with different perspectives challenge the status quo, they also introduce multiple views on the risks, consequences and possible implications of any board decision. In short, board diversity is integral to building a successful long term business.

International Business School INSEAD's Professor of Strategy Annet Aris sits on six corporate boards. She was first invited to a media company board in 2004 because of her reputation as a media specialist, particularly in digital media. "I was brought in not because I was a woman but because I had the knowledge that the companies didn't have," Aris says. "That helped to establish my credibility." Other companies heard about her and she soon started receiving offers to sit on other boards as digitalisation began to take place in insurance and other industries. Aris' story of being a woman in demand on company boards is not a common one. Scandinavian countries lead the way with the highest representation of women on boards - about 17 per cent. France has 12 per cent and Germany just 8.5 per cent.

Other notable women working at boardroom level around the world include: in the U.K., Karen Brady, former managing director of Birmingham City Football Club and current vice-chairman of West Ham United football club; in India, Chanda Kochhar as the managing director and CEO of ICICI Bank; and in South Africa, Salukazi Dakile-Hlongwane as Chief Exective of Nozala Investments.

With boards scouting for directors generally looking for the best candidates with top-notch skills, education, and achievements, and putting much less weight on gender, should corporations be instead taking more deliberate steps to bring more women into the board room?

References: 'Still too few women in boardroom, warns ABI' Jamie Dunkley, *The Independent*, December 11th, 2012; 'Too few good women: Why are boards still male domains?' http://knowledge.insead.edu; Grace Segran, June 27, 2011; http://www.icicibank.co.uk/; http://whoswho.co.za; http://www.karrenbrady.com; http://www.forbes.com/power-women/

corporate officers the chairman of the board, president, executive vice presidents, corporate secretary, treasurer, and any other top executive appointed by the board of directors

ADVANTAGES AND DISADVANTAGES OF CORPORATIONS

Back in October 2000, Manny Ruiz decided that it was time to start his own company. With the help of a team of media specialists, he founded Hispanic PR Wire. Hispanic PR Wire has established itself as a premier news distribution service reaching U.S. Hispanic media and opinion leaders. Today, the business continues to build on its early success.* Mr. Ruiz chose to incorporate this business because it provided a number of advantages that other forms of business ownership did not offer. Typical advantages include limited liability, ease of raising capital, ease of transfer of ownership, perpetual life, and specialised management.

Advantages of corporations

Limited liability   One of the most attractive features of corporate ownership is limited liability, as discussed earlier in the chapter. With few exceptions, each owner's financial liability is limited to the amount of money he or she has paid for the corporation's stock. This feature arises from the fact that the corporation is itself a legal person, separate from its owners. If a corporation fails or is involved in a lawsuit and loses, creditors have a claim only on the corporation's assets, not on the stockholders' (owners') personal assets. Because it overcomes the problem of unlimited liability connected with sole proprietorships and general partnerships, limited liability is one of the chief reasons why entrepreneurs often choose the corporate form of organisation.

Ease of raising capital   The corporation is one of the most effective forms of business ownership for raising capital. Like sole proprietorships and partnerships, corporations can borrow from lending institutions. However, they also can raise additional sums of money by selling stock. Individuals are more willing to invest in corporations than in other forms of business because of limited liability, and they can generally sell their stock easily—hopefully for a profit.

Ease of transfer of ownership   Accessing a brokerage firm Web site or a telephone call to a stockbroker is all that is required to put most stock up for sale. Willing buyers are available for most stocks at the market price. Ownership is transferred when the sale is made, and practically no restrictions apply to the sale and purchase of stock issued by an open corporation.

Perpetual life   Since it is essentially a legal "person," a corporation exists independently of its owners and survives them. The withdrawal, death, or incompetence of a key executive or owner does not automatically cause the corporation to be terminated. Sears, Roebuck and Co. incorporated in 1893 and is one of America's largest retailing corporations, even though its original co-founders, Richard Sears and Alvah Roebuck, have been dead for decades.

Specialised management   Typically, corporations are able to recruit more skilled, knowledgeable, and talented managers than proprietorships and partnerships. This is so because they pay bigger salaries, offer excellent employee benefits, and are large enough to offer considerable opportunity for advancement. Within the corporate structure, administration, human resources, finance, marketing, and operations are placed in the charge of experts in these fields.

© AP PHOTO/PAUL SAKUMA

Would you buy stock in Facebook?
Facebook—the company that started in a Harvard University dorm room back in 2004—finally sold stock to the general public in 2012. The money raised from the public stock offering can be used to "grow" the company. For investors, it was a chance to "cash in" on the phenomenal success of the world's most recognised social media company.

Disadvantages of corporations

Like its advantages, many of a corporation's disadvantages stem from its legal definition as an artificial person or legal entity. The most serious disadvantages are described in the following text. (See Table 4.3 for a comparison of some of the advantages and disadvantages of a sole proprietorship, general partnership, and corporation.)

TABLE 4.3　Some advantages and disadvantages of a sole proprietorship, partnership, and corporation

	Sole proprietorship	General partnership	Regular C-Corporaton
Protecting against liability for debts	Difficult	Difficult	Easy
Raising money	Difficult	Difficult	Easy
Ownership transfer	Difficult	Difficult	Easy
Preserving continuity	Difficult	Difficult	Easy
Government regulations	Few	Few	Many
Formation	Easy	Easy	Difficult
Income taxation	Once	Once	Twice

© CENGAGE LEARNING 2014

Difficulty and expense of formation　Forming a corporation can be a relatively complex and costly process. The use of legal representatives is usually necessary to complete the legal forms that are submitted to the secretary of state. Application fees, legal fees, registration costs associated with selling stock, and other organisational costs can amount to thousands of euros for even a medium-sized corporation. The costs of incorporating, in terms of both time and money, discourage many owners of smaller businesses from forming corporations.

Government regulation and increased paperwork　A corporation must meet various government standards before it can sell its stock to the public. Then it must file many reports on its business operations and finances with local, regional and national governments. In addition, the corporation must make periodic reports to its stockholders about various aspects of the business. To prepare all the necessary reports, even small corporations often need the help of a legal adviser, an accountant, and other professionals on a regular basis. In addition, a corporation's activities are restricted by law to those spelled out in its charter.

Conflict within the corporation　Because a large corporation may employ thousands of employees, some conflict is inevitable. For example, the pressure to increase sales revenue, reduce expenses, and increase profits often leads to increased stress and tension for both managers and employees. This is especially true when a corporation operates in a competitive industry, attempts to develop and market new products, or must downsize the workforce to reduce employee salary expense during an economic crisis.

Double taxation　Corporations must pay a tax on their profits. In addition, stockholders must pay a personal income tax on profits received as dividends. Corporate profits thus are taxed twice—once as corporate income and a second time as the personal income of stockholders.

Lack of secrecy　Because open corporations are required to submit detailed reports to government agencies and to stockholders, they cannot keep their operations confidential. Competitors can study these corporate reports and then use the information to compete more effectively. In effect, every public corporation has to share some of its secrets with its competitors.

CORPORATE GROWTH

Growth seems to be a basic characteristic of business. One reason for seeking growth has to do with profit: A larger firm generally has greater sales revenue and thus greater profit. Another reason is that in a growing economy, a business that does not grow is actually shrinking relative to the economy.

A third reason is that business growth is a means by which some executives boost their power, prestige, and reputation.

Growth poses new problems and requires additional resources that first must be available and then must be used effectively. The main ingredient in growth is capital—and as we have noted, capital is most readily available to corporations.

Growth from within

Most corporations grow by expanding their present operations. Some introduce and sell new but related products. Others expand the sale of present products to new geographic markets or to new groups of consumers in geographic markets already served. Although Walmart was started by Sam Walton in 1962 with one discount store, today Walmart has over 10,000 stores in 28 countries across the world and has long-range plans for expanding into additional international markets.*

Growth from within, especially when carefully planned and controlled, can have relatively little adverse effect on a firm. For the most part, the firm continues to do what it has been doing, but on a larger scale.

Growth through mergers and acquisitions

Another way a firm can grow is by purchasing another company. The purchase of one corporation by another is called a **merger**. An *acquisition* is essentially the same thing as a merger, but the term usually is used in reference to a large corporation's purchases of other corporations. Although most mergers and acquisitions are friendly, hostile takeovers also occur. A **hostile takeover** is a situation in which the management and board of directors of a firm targeted for acquisition disapprove of the merger.

> **merger** the purchase of one corporation by another
> **hostile takeover** a situation in which the management and board of directors of a firm targeted for acquisition
> disapprove of the merger

When a merger or acquisition becomes hostile, a corporate raider—another company or a wealthy investor—may make a tender offer or start a proxy fight to gain control of the target company. A **tender offer** is an offer to purchase the stock of a firm targeted for acquisition at a price just high enough to tempt stockholders to sell their shares. Corporate raiders also may initiate a proxy fight. A **proxy fight** is a technique used to gather enough stockholder votes to control a targeted company.

> **tender offer** an offer to purchase the stock of a firm targeted for acquisition at a price just high enough to tempt
> stockholders to sell their shares
> **proxy fight** a technique used to gather enough stockholder votes to control a targeted company

Growth through global joint ventures.
General Electric, which owns many businesses that fortify the world's infrastructure, recently formed two joint ventures in Russia. Here is Russian president Vladimir Putin meeting with GE executives.

© AFP/GETTY IMAGES

If the corporate raider is successful and takes over the targeted company, existing management usually is replaced. Faced with this probability, existing management may take specific actions, sometimes referred to as "poison pills," "shark repellents," or "porcupine provisions," to maintain control of the firm and avoid the hostile takeover. Whether mergers are friendly or hostile, they are generally classified as *horizontal, vertical,* or *conglomerate* (see Figure 4.2).

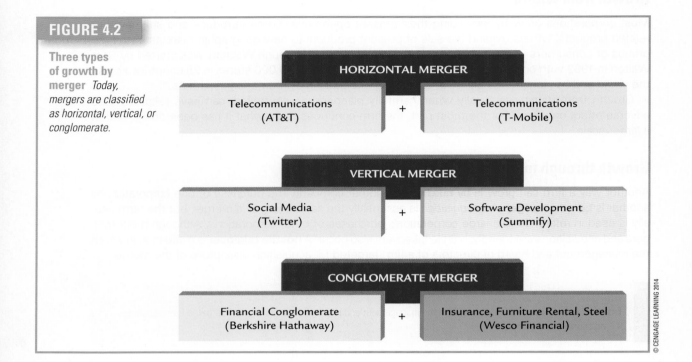

FIGURE 4.2

Three types of growth by merger *Today, mergers are classified as horizontal, vertical, or conglomerate.*

© CENGAGE LEARNING 2014

Horizontal mergers A *horizontal merger* is a merger between firms that make and sell similar products or services in similar markets. The proposed merger between AT&T and T-Mobile was an example of a horizontal merger because both firms provide mobile phone service to their customers. This type of merger tends to reduce the number of firms in an industry—and thus may reduce competition. As a result most horizontal mergers are reviewed carefully by regulatory bodies before they are approved in order to protect competition in the marketplace. In fact, the AT&T merger with T-Mobile was effectively blocked when the U.S. Department of Justice filed a law suit to block the merger. According to the Department of Justice, the main reason behind the government's legal action was to protect the competitive environment and the consumers' right to choose. Rather than fight the government's attempt to block the merger, AT&T withdrew its offer to acquire T-Mobile.

Vertical mergers A *vertical merger* is a merger between firms that operate at different but related levels in the production and marketing of a product. Generally, one of the merging firms is either a supplier or a customer of the other. A vertical merger occurred when social media giant Twitter acquired Summify. At the time of the 2012 merger, Summify, based in Vancouver, was a startup technology company in the process of building the next generation of news-reader software that had a unique approach to summarising the most important information from social media feeds from Google, Facebook, and Twitter. Rather than develop its own software to summarise the most important information, Twitter simply purchased the Summify company.*

Conglomerate mergers A *conglomerate* merger takes place between firms in completely different industries. A conglomerate merger occurred when financial conglomerate Berkshire Hathaway acquired Wesco Financial Corporation. While both companies were recognised as successful companies that have a history of increasing sales revenues and profits, they operate in different industries. Berkshire Hathaway, led by its CEO Warren Buffett, has a long history of acquiring firms that have great financial potential. Wesco, on the other hand, is a smaller company with its main business interests in insurance, furniture rental, and steel.* The Berkshire Hathaway–Wesco merger was friendly because it was beneficial for both firms.

Merger and acquisition trends for the future

While there have always been mergers and acquisitions, the recent economic crisis has changed the dynamics of how and why firms merge. Recently, mergers and acquisitions have been fueled by the desire of financially secure firms to take over firms in financial trouble. For a firm experiencing financial difficulties, a merger or acquisition is often a better option than bankruptcy. During the recent economic crisis, this trend was especially evident in the financial services and banking industry. In other situations, a financially secure firm will purchase a company experiencing financial problems because it is a good investment.

Economists, financial analysts, corporate managers, and stockholders still hotly debate whether mergers and acquisitions are good for the economy—or for individual companies—in the long run. Takeover advocates argue that for companies that have been taken over, the purchasers have been able to make the company more profitable and productive by installing a new top-management team, by reducing expenses, and by forcing the company to concentrate on one main business.

Takeover opponents argue that takeovers do nothing to enhance corporate profitability or productivity. These critics argue that the only people who benefit from takeovers are investment bankers, brokerage firms, and takeover "artists," who receive financial rewards by manipulating corporations rather than by producing tangible products or services.

Most experts now predict that mergers and acquisitions after the economic crisis will be the result of cash-rich companies looking to acquire businesses that will enhance their position in the marketplace. Analysts also anticipate more mergers that involve companies or investors from other countries. Regardless of the companies involved or where the companies are from, future mergers and acquisitions will be driven by solid business logic and the desire to compete in the international marketplace.

Whether they are sole proprietorships, partnerships, corporations, or some other form of business ownership, most businesses are small. In the next chapter, we focus on these small businesses. We examine, among other things, the meaning of the word *small* as it applies to business and the place of small business in the economy.

SUMMARY

● Describe the advantages and disadvantages for sole traders.

In a sole proprietorship, all business profits become the property of the owner, but the owner is also personally responsible for all business debts. A successful sole proprietorship can be a great source of pride for the owner. When comparing different types of business ownership, the sole proprietorship is the simplest form of business to enter, control, and leave. It also pays no special taxes. Perhaps for these reasons, a large percentage of business firms are sole proprietorships. Sole proprietorships nevertheless have disadvantages, such as unlimited liability and limits on one person's ability to borrow or to be an expert in all fields. As a result, this form of ownership accounts for only 4 per cent of total revenues when compared with partnerships and corporations.

- Describe the advantages and disadvantages of partnerships.

  Although partnership eliminates some of the disadvantages of sole proprietorship, it is the least popular of the major forms of business ownership. The major advantages of a partnership include ease of start-up, availability of capital and credit, personal interest, combined skills and knowledge, retention of profits, and possible tax advantages. The effects of management disagreements are one of the major disadvantages of a partnership. Other disadvantages include unlimited liability (in a general partnership), lack of continuity, and frozen investment. By forming a limited partnership, the disadvantage of unlimited liability may be eliminated for the limited partner(s). This same disadvantage may be eliminated for partners that form a limited-liability partnership (LLP). Of course, special requirements must be met if partners form either the limited partnership or the limited-liability partnership.

- Summarise how a corporation is formed.

  A corporation is an artificial person created by law, with most of the legal rights of a real person, including the right to start and operate a business, to buy or sell property, to borrow money, to be sued or sue, and to enter into contracts. With the corporate form of ownership, stock can be sold to individuals to raise capital. The people who own a corporation's common or preferred stock are called stockholders. Stockholders are entitled to receive any dividends paid by the corporation, and ordinary shareholders can vote either in person or by proxy. Generally, corporations are classified as closed corporations (few stockholders) or open corporations (many stockholders).

  The process of forming a corporation is called incorporation. Most experts believe that the services of a solicitor are necessary when making decisions about where to incorporate and about obtaining a corporate charter, issuing stock, holding an organisational meeting, and all other legal details involved in incorporation. In theory, stockholders are able to control the activities of the corporation because they elect the board of directors who appoint the corporate officers.

- Describe the advantages and disadvantages of a corporation.

  Perhaps the major advantage of the corporate form is limited liability—stockholders are not liable for the corporation's debts beyond the amount they paid for its stock. Other important advantages include ease of raising capital, ease of transfer of ownership, perpetual life, and specialised management. A major disadvantage of a large corporation is double taxation: All profits are taxed once as corporate income and again as personal income because stockholders must pay a personal income tax on the profits they receive as dividends. Other disadvantages include difficulty and expense of formation, government regulation, conflict within the corporation, and lack of secrecy.

- Discuss the purpose of a cooperative and joint venture.

  Additional forms of business ownership—the cooperative and joint venture—are used by their owners to meet special needs. A cooperative is an association of individuals or firms whose purpose is to perform some business function for its members. A joint venture is formed when two or more groups form a business entity in order to achieve a specific goal or to operate for a specific period of time. Once the goal is reached, the period of time elapses, or the project is completed, the joint venture is dissolved.

- Explain how growth from within and growth through mergers can enable a business to expand.

  A corporation may grow by expanding its present operations or through a merger or an acquisition. Although most mergers are friendly, hostile takeovers also occur. A hostile takeover is a situation in which the management and board of directors of a firm targeted for acquisition disapprove of the merger. Mergers generally are classified as horizontal, vertical, or conglomerate.

  During the recent economic crisis, mergers and acquisitions have been fueled by the desire of financially secure firms to take over firms in financial trouble. For a firm experiencing financial trouble, a merger or acquisition is often a better option than bankruptcy. In other situations, a financially secure firm will purchase a company experiencing financial problems because it is a good investment.

  While economists, financial analysts, corporate managers, and stockholders debate the merits of mergers, some trends should be noted. First, experts predict that future mergers will be the result of cash-rich companies looking to acquire businesses that will enhance their position in the marketplace. Second, more mergers are likely to involve foreign companies or investors. Third, mergers will be driven by business logic and the desire to compete in the international marketplace.

EXERCISE QUESTIONS

1 Explain the difference between common stock and preferred stock

2 List some of the advantages and disadvantages of corporations

3 Explain what is meant by a horizontal merger, a vertical merger and a conglomerate merger

4 How has the recent financial crisis impacted upon merger and acquisition trends

5 Define corporate ownership and list some of the different types of it

CASE 4.1

Tata and the Acquisition of Jaguar

Tata is India's largest conglomerate, with interests spanning tea, motors, steel and software consultancy. It is over 140 years old. It is controlled by three family-run trusts and the CEO is Ranan Tata, who took over from an uncle in 1991. He set about "modernising" the conglomerate to "make it ready for international expansion". Ranan Tata initially made the group more centralised to bring cohesion to the 90 operating companies around the world. There have since been selective investments – but also disposals – with a general drive to become more international. IT has been developed and used to drive control systems which allow for increasingly decentralised authority. The international strategy began to really gather pace in 2000.

Tetley Tea, bought in 2001, is part of Tata, as are Daewoo Trucks, NatSteel of Singapore (2004) and Teleglobe, the Bermuda-based wholesale telecoms group it bought in 2005. In 2007 Tata paid US$13 billion to acquire the U.K.'s largest steelmaker, Corus. Linked to Corus, Tata was keen to develop iron ore mining in South Africa and Canada in order to extend its control of the supply chain. Steel, of course, is a key material for car manufacture.

In 2007 Tata bought Jaguar and Land Rover from Ford of America. This was an interesting move, given Tata's parallel strategy of developing the so-called People's Car, the Tata Nano, the truly low price car (see Case 12.1). Tata really had no previous experience of luxury brands. There

were commentators who expressed the view that they could not understand this move. After all, Tata was more used to building rudimentary trucks for relatively poor roads across India.

Jaguar was thought to be in need of repositioning – it had lost some of its edge through association with the broader range of less exclusive Ford models. There was a stated belief that Tata would be able to offer Jaguar greater access to investment funding and greater independence than it enjoyed at Ford.

But would it? When the credit crunch and recession began to bite car sales fell. But so did steel demand and Tata found itself needing to make major savings at Corus. The conglomerate in the ex-colony that had become a coloniser itself was enquiring about foreign government subsidies to preserve jobs. However there was a parallel view that the recession would provide a good opportunity for Tata to cut waste and build the core strengths of its businesses.

Another problem was that Ranan Tata was past normal retirement age and "there was no obvious successor". Despite questions and concerns on the part of some commentators Jaguar has thrived under Tata's ownership. Moreover, in 2012, Tata announced a new joint venture with a Chinese manufacturer – Land Rovers and Range Rovers are to be manufactured in China specifically for the local market.

Questions

1 Acquisitions of this nature should add value to the parent organisation. At the same time the parent should add value to the new acquisition. Why do you think this acquisition has turned out to be a "win-win"?

2 Why do companies sometimes choose to branch out into new territory during the acquisitions process, with Tata branching out into luxury car brands?

3 Would you describe this merger as a vertical or a horizontal merger?

CHAPTER REFERENCES

Aspen, Maria, "Berkshire Hathaway to Buy Rest of Wesco," The Thomson Reuters Web site at www.reuters.com (accessed February 4, 2012).

"Facebook, Banks Sued Over Pre-IPO Analyst Calls," The Reuters Web site at www.reuters.com (accessed May 23, 2012).

http://www.smallbusiness.co.uk/homepage/news/254967/failure-rates-for-uk-business.thtml

The Hispanic PR Wire Web site at www.hispanicprwire.com (accessed February 3, 2012).

The Mars Corporate Web site at www.mars.com (accessed February 5, 2012).

The Walmart Corporate Web site at www.walmartstores.com (accessed February 4, 2012).

This information was reproduced with the permission of Social Enterprise UK, the U.K. membership organisation for social enterprises from http://www.socialenterprise.org.uk/pages/about-social-enterprise.html

"Twitter Acquires Social Media Feed Condenser Summify," The Tech World Web site at www.techworld.com (accessed February 4, 2012).

5 SMALL BUSINESS, ENTREPRENEURSHIP, AND FRANCHISES

BUSINESS FOCUS

William Chase and Tyrrell Crisps

At the ripe old age of 20, William Chase purchased the Tyrrell Court Farm in the U.K. from his father in 1984. Poor sales and a recession saw his investment turn sour with Chase being made bankrupt. However, not to be put off, William Chase fought back. He leased his farm back from the lenders and eventually bought the farm back and moved on to become a successful potato farmer in his own right.

However, Chase believed that the only people making any money out of farming were the supermarkets who were forever forcing down the prices they gave to the farmer. On this basis Chase felt that his business of supplying potatoes would not be profitable for much longer. As with many examples of business change the new direction for William Chase came about through circumstance. A

batch of his potatoes scheduled to be turned into oven ready chips (fries) by frozen food manufacturers McCain were rejected. Chase quickly found an alternative customer for the potatoes and sold them to a crisp maker. Upon tasting the final product Chase thought he could do better.

Showing entrepreneurial flair, in 2002 he decided to do market research by going to America to taste as many handmade crisps as he could. Upon returning he set about making his own crisps. He knew that success had to be based upon selling them as a new innovative product. He invested a great deal of money in marketing and packaging to put across the quality handmade image Chase felt was crucial to the success of his venture.

Over the next few years Chase built up his handmade crisp business

by selling firstly to independent retail stores, farm shops and to delicatessens rather than to the big supermarkets, who he would not let dictate to him. In September 2006, Chase won a legal battle against the large supermarket chain Tesco, preventing them from stocking his products without his permission. By 2007 the turnover of the business had reached £8.5 million, now selling a range of flavours such as strawberry sweet chilli and white wine. His next great product idea was to launch in 2008 the first British pure potato vodka.

Chase personified the business. Whilst very ambitious, he was very keen on keeping the business based around the Tyrrell Farm and he is a firm believer in the happy personalised team approach to doing business. Would this approach be appropriate into the future?

As with the case of William Chase and Tyrrell potato chips, most businesses start small, however those that survive usually stay small. They provide a solid foundation for the economy—as employers, as suppliers and purchasers of goods and services, and as taxpayers.

In this chapter, we do not take small businesses for granted. Instead, we look closely at this important business sector—beginning with a definition of small business, a description of industries that often attract small businesses, and a profile of some of the people who start small businesses. Next, we consider the importance of small businesses in an economy. We also present the advantages and disadvantages of smallness in business. We then look at the importance of developing a business plan, before describing some of the services provided internationally for small businesses. We conclude the chapter with a discussion of the pros and cons of franchising, an approach to small-business ownership that has become very popular in the last 50 years.

SMALL BUSINESS: A PROFILE

The Small Business Administration (SBA), a U.S.-based institution, defines a **small business** as "one which is independently owned and operated for profit and is not dominant in its field." How small must a firm be not to dominate its field? That depends on the particular industry it is in. The SBA has developed the following specific "smallness" guidelines for the various

TABLE 5.1	**Industry group-size standards** *Small-business size standards are usually stated in number of employees or average annual sales. In the United States, 99.7 per cent of all businesses are considered small.*

Industry group	Size standard
Manufacturing, mining industries	500 employees
Wholesale trade	100 employees
Agriculture	$750,000
Retail trade	$7 million
General and heavy construction (except dredging)	$33.5 million
Dredging	$20 million
Special trade contractors	$14 million
Travel agencies	$3.5 million (commissions and other income)
Business and personal services except	$7 million
• Architectural, engineering, surveying, and mapping services	$4.5 million
• Dry cleaning and carpet cleaning services	$4.5 million

Source: www.sba.gov/content/summary-size-standards-industry (accessed March 19, 2012).

industries, as shown in Table 5.1.* The SBA periodically revises and simplifies its small-business size regulations.

small business one that is independently owned and operated for profit and is not dominant in its field

Annual sales in millions of dollars may not seem very small. However, for many firms, profit is only a small percentage of total sales. Thus, a firm may earn only $40,000 or $50,000 on yearly sales of $1 million—and that is small in comparison with the profits earned by most medium-sized and large firms. In many countries, small businesses play a very important part in the economy. Often they represent a majority percentage of employer firms and create many new jobs. For instance, according to *Small Business South Africa*, "Small, Medium and Mirco Enterprises (SMMEs) contribute around 40% of South Africa's gross domestic profit and employ more than half of the private sector work-force".*

Small businesses can also produce many times more patents per employee than large patenting firms. In the U.S., for example, small businesses produced 16.5 times more patents than large patenting firms. Whilst this last point may be skewed to some extent by the amount of employees per company, it may also be indicative of a greater level of entrepreneurial and creative spirit fostered in smaller businesses.

The small-business sector

The exact legal and financial requirements of setting up a small business vary from country to country, depending on various factors, not least local laws and legislation. In the United States, it typically takes less than a week and $500 to establish a business as a legal entity. The steps include registering the name of the business, applying for tax IDs, and setting up unemployment and workers' compensation insurance. In South Africa, no specific permits are required for residents to begin trading, and this can be done in a relatively low time scale and at minimal expense. Non-residents must apply for a business permit, which is typically valid for 2 years. Successful applicants are likely to need a comprehensive business plan, funding of 2.5 million Rand, must agree to employ at least five South African residents and register with the South African Revenue Service. In Japan, however, a typical entrepreneur spends more than $3,500 and 31 days to follow 11 different procedures.

Interest in owning or starting a small business has never been greater than it is today. During the last decade, the number of small businesses in many countries has increased dramatically. Furthermore, part-time entrepreneurs have increased fivefold in recent years; they now account for one-third of all small businesses.*

Sometime in your career, you're likely to have a job in a small business. You might work in a shop, in a service business, or in production. If you're thinking of starting your own business, be sure to watch how these entrepreneurs manage their companies.

© KZENON/SHUTTERSTOCK

According to a recent American study, 69 per cent of new businesses survive at least two years, about 50 per cent survive at least five years, and 31 per cent survive at least ten years.* The primary reason for these failures is mismanagement resulting from a lack of business know-how. The makeup of the small-business sector thus is constantly changing. Despite the high failure rate, many small businesses succeed modestly. Some, like Apple Computer, Inc., are extremely successful—to the point where they can no longer be considered small. Taken together, small businesses are responsible for providing a high percentage of jobs.

Industries that attract small businesses

Some industries, such as auto manufacturing, require huge investments in machinery and equipment. Businesses in such industries are big from the day they are started—if an entrepreneur or group of entrepreneurs can gather the capital required to start one.

By contrast, a number of other industries require only a low initial investment and some special skills or knowledge. It is these industries that tend to attract new businesses. Growing industries, such as outpatient-care facilities, are attractive because of their profit potential. However, knowledgeable entrepreneurs choose areas with which they are familiar, and these are most often the more established industries.

Small enterprise spans the gamut from corner newspaper selling to the development of optical fibres. The owners of small businesses sell petrol, flowers, and coffee to go. They publish magazines, haul freight, teach languages, and programme computers. They make wines, movies, and high-fashion clothes. They build new homes and restore old ones. They fix appliances, recycle metals, and sell used cars. They drive taxis and fly planes. They sell us the products of corporate giants. In the U.S., for example, 74 per cent of property, rental, and leasing industries; 61 per cent of the businesses in the leisure and hospitality services; and 86 per cent of the construction industries are dominated by small businesses. While the exact figures will vary from country to country, these high percentages are certainly reflective of the importance of small businesses throughout the world. The various kinds of businesses generally fall into three broad categories of industry: distribution, service, and production.

Distribution industries This category includes retailing, wholesaling, transportation, and communications—industries concerned with the movement of goods from producers to consumers. Distribution industries account for approximately 33 per cent of all small businesses. Of these, almost three-quarters are involved in retailing, that is, the sale of goods directly to consumers. Clothing and jewellery stores, pet shops, bookstores, and grocery stores, for example, are all retailing firms. Slightly less than one-quarter of the small distribution firms are wholesalers. Wholesalers purchase products in quantity from manufacturers and then resell them to retailers.

Service industries This category accounts for more than 48 per cent of all small businesses. Of these, about three-quarters provide such nonfinancial services as medical and dental care; watch, shoe, and TV repairs; haircutting and styling; restaurant meals; and dry cleaning. About 8 per cent of the small service firms offer financial services, such as accounting, insurance, real estate, and investment counselling. An increasing number of self-employed people are running service businesses from home.

Production industries This last category includes the construction, mining, and manufacturing industries. Only about 19 per cent of all small businesses are in this group, mainly because these industries require relatively large initial investments. Small firms that do venture into production generally make parts and subassemblies for larger manufacturing firms or supply special skills to larger construction firms.

THE PEOPLE IN SMALL BUSINESSES: THE ENTREPRENEURS

The entrepreneurial spirit is alive and well in many countries throughout the world, although in some regions it is particularly prevalent. More than 70 per cent of Americans would prefer being an entrepreneur to working for someone else. This compares with 46 per cent of adults in Western Europe and 58 per cent of adults in Canada. The popularity of TV shows such as the BBC's "Dragons' Den", in which budding entrepreneurs pitch their ideas to a panel of successful businesspeople in hope of gaining investment, is testament to the growing trend for people to set up their own businesses and build a future on their own terms.

Small businesses typically are managed by the people who started and own them. Most of these people have held jobs with other firms and still could be so employed if they wanted. Yet owners of small businesses would rather take the risk of starting and operating their own firms, even if the money they make is less than the salaries they otherwise might earn.

Researchers have suggested a variety of personal factors as reasons why people go into business for themselves. These are discussed next.

Characteristics of entrepreneurs

Entrepreneurial spirit is the desire to create a new business. For example, Nikki Olyai always knew that she wanted to create and develop her own business. Her father, a successful businessman in Iran, was her role model. She came to the United States at the age of 17 and lived with a host family in Salem, Oregon, attending high school there. Undergraduate and graduate degrees in computer

Meet Sam Altman, co-founder and CEO of Loopt.
In 2004, Altman co-founded a location-based social networking mobile application when he was a sophomore majoring in computer science at Stanford University. BusinessWeek *named him one of the "Best Young Entrepreneurs in Technology" and Inc. magazine ranked him number 4 among the top 30 entrepreneurs under the age of 30. In 2012, prepaid money card issuer Green Dot Corp. agreed to acquire Loopt Inc. for $43.4 million.*

science led her to start Innovision Technologies while she held two other jobs to keep the business going and took care of her four-year-old son. Recently, Nikki Olyai's business was honoured by the Women's Business Enterprise National Council's "Salute to Women's Business Enterprises" as one of 11 top successful firms. For three consecutive years, her firm was selected as a "Future 50 of Greater Detroit Company."

Other personal factors

Other personal factors in small-business success include:

- independence;
- a desire to determine one's own destiny;
- a willingness to find and accept a challenge;
- family background (in particular, researchers think that people whose families have been in business, successfully or not, are most apt to start and run their own businesses); and
- age (those who start their own businesses also tend to cluster around certain ages—more than 70 per cent are between 24 and 44 years of age; see Figure 5.1).

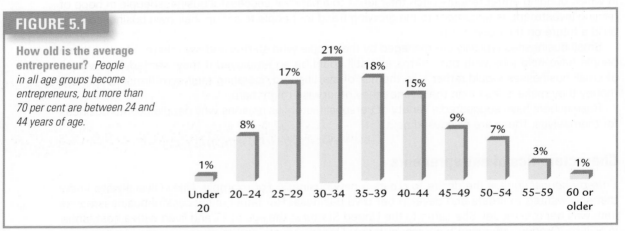

FIGURE 5.1

How old is the average entrepreneur? *People in all age groups become entrepreneurs, but more than 70 per cent are between 24 and 44 years of age.*

1% Under 20
8% 20–24
17% 25–29
21% 30–34
18% 35–39
15% 40–44
9% 45–49
7% 50–54
3% 55–59
1% 60 or older

Source: Data developed and provided by the National Federation of Independent Business Foundation and sponsored by the American Express Travel Related Services Company, Inc.

Motivation

There must be some motivation to start a business. A person may decide that he or she simply has "had enough" of working and earning a profit for someone else. Another may lose his or her job for some reason and decide to start the business he or she has always wanted rather than to seek another job. Still another person may have an idea for a new product or a new way to sell an existing product. Or the opportunity to go into business may arise suddenly, perhaps as a result of a hobby.

Teenagers as small-business owners

High-tech teen entrepreneurship is definitely exploding. "There's not a period in history where we've seen such a plethora of young entrepreneurs," comments Nancy F. Koehn, associate professor of business administration at Harvard Business School. Still, teen entrepreneurs face unique pressures in juggling their schoolwork, their social life, and their high-tech workload. Some ultimately drop out of education, whereas others quit or cut back on their business activities. Consider Brian Hendricks at Winston Churchill High School in Maryland, U.S. He is the founder of StartUpPc and VB Solutions, Inc. StartUpPc, founded in 2001, sells custom-built computers and computer services for home users, home offices, small businesses, and students. Brian's services include design, installation of systems, training, networking, and on-site technical support. In October 2002, Brian founded VB Solutions, Inc.,

Mary Rodas, a child entrepreneur. *At age 13, Mary scored an instant success with the 'Balzac,' a ball made by blowing up a balloon inside a fabric sack, jazzed up with vivid colours and designs. At Catco, Inc., she became vice president of marketing at age 14, earning €200,000 a year. Balzac Balloon Ball sales have exceeded €100 million per year.*

© AP PHOTO/ED BAILEY

which develops and customises Web sites and message boards. The firm sets up advertising contracts and counsels Web site owners on site improvements. The company has designed corporate ID kits, logos, and Web sites for clients from all over the world. Brian learned at a very young age that working for yourself is one of the best jobs available. According to Brian, a young entrepreneur must possess "the five *P*s of entrepreneurship"—planning, persistence, patience, people, and profit. Brian knows what it takes to be a successful entrepreneur. His accolades include Junior Achievement's "National Youth Entrepreneur of the Year" and SBA's 2005 "Young Entrepreneur of the Year" awards.*

In some people, the motivation to start a business develops slowly as they gain the knowledge and ability required for success as a business owner. Knowledge and ability—especially, management ability—are probably the most important factors involved. A new firm is very much built around the entrepreneur. The owner must be able to manage the firm's finances, its personnel (if there are any employees), and its day-to-day operations. He or she must handle sales, advertising, purchasing, pricing, and a variety of other business functions. The knowledge and ability to do so are acquired most often through experience working for other firms in the same area of business.

Why some entrepreneurs and small businesses fail

Small businesses are prone to failure. Capital, management, and planning are the key ingredients in the survival of a small business, as well as the most common reasons for failure. Businesses can experience a number of money-related problems. It may take several years before a business begins to show a profit. Entrepreneurs need to have not only the capital to open a business but also the money to operate it in its possibly lengthy start-up phase. One cash flow obstacle often leads to others. Moreover, a series of cash flow predicaments usually ends in a business failure. This scenario is played out all too often by small and not-so-small start-up Internet firms that fail to meet their financial backers' expectations and so are denied a second wave of investment to continue their drive to establish a profitable online firm. According to Maureen Borzacchiello, co-owner of Creative Display Solutions, a trade show products company, "Big businesses… can get bailouts, but small-business owners are on their own when times are tough and credit is tight."

Many entrepreneurs lack the management skills required to run a business. Money, time, personnel, and inventory all need to be managed effectively if a small business is to succeed. Starting a small business requires much more than optimism and a good idea.

Success and expansion sometimes lead to problems. Frequently, entrepreneurs with successful small businesses make the mistake of overexpansion. Fast growth often results in dramatic changes in a business. Thus, the entrepreneur must plan carefully and adjust competently to new and potentially disruptive situations.

Every day, new businesses are being opened all across the world. However, for every new venture that is starting up, there is likely to be another somewhere else closing down. Although many fail, others represent well-conceived ideas developed by entrepreneurs who have the expertise, resources, and determination to make their businesses succeed. As these well-prepared entrepreneurs pursue their individual goals, our society benefits in many ways from their work and creativity. Billion-pound companies such as Apple Computer, the supermarket chain Tesco, and Procter & Gamble are all examples of small businesses that expanded into industry giants.

THE IMPORTANCE OF SMALL BUSINESSES IN AN ECONOMY

History abounds with stories of ambitious men and women who turned their ideas into business dynasties. The Ford Motor Company started as a one-man operation with an innovative method for industrial production. As seen in the opening chapter's case, Dyson, the U.K.-based home appliances company that introduced bagless vacuum cleaners, super-efficient hand dryers, and fans and heaters without external propeller blades, began in the very humble surroundings of James Dyson's garden shed. After several serious setbacks, opposition from industry, patent disputes and countless proto-types, Dyson has gone onto to become a hugely successful billion-pound revenue company, winning design awards and employing thousands, in the U.K. office and overseas.

Providing technical innovation

Invention and innovation are part of the foundations of the economy. The increases in productivity that have characterised the past 200 years of history are largely rooted in one principal source: new ways to do a job with less effort for less money. Studies show that the incidence of innovation among small-business workers is significantly higher than among workers in large businesses. Small firms produce two-and-a-half times as many innovations as large firms relative to the number of persons employed. In fact, small firms employ 40 per cent of all high-tech workers such as scientists, engineers, and computer specialists. No wonder small firms produce 13 to 14 times more patents per employee than large patenting firms.

Consider Waymon Armstrong, the owner of a small business that uses computer simulations to help government and other clients prepare for and respond to natural disasters, medical emergencies, and combat. In presenting the 2010 National Small Business Person of the Year award, Karen Mills, Administrator of the U.S. Small Business Administration, said, "Waymon Armstrong is a perfect example of the innovation, inspiration, and determination that exemplify America's most successful entrepreneurs. He believed in his brainchild to the point where he deferred his own salary for three years to keep it afloat. When layoffs loomed for his staff after 9/11, their loyalty and belief in the company was so great that they were willing to work without pay for four months."

More than half the major technological advances of the 20th century originated with individual inventors and small companies. Even just a sampling of those innovations is remarkable:

- Air conditioning
- Aeroplane
- Automatic transmission
- FM radio
- Heart valve
- Helicopter
- Instant camera
- Insulin
- Jet engine

Providing technical innovation. Meet Time magazine's 2010 Person of the Year, entrepreneur Mark Zuckerberg, who founded Facebook while still a student at Harvard. In 2008, Zuckerberg became the world's youngest billionaire at age 25.

©WIREIMAGE/GETTY IMAGES

Sustainability isn't just about big business! Green Plus is an organisation that works with smaller businesses in their efforts towards becoming more sustainable through certification, education, networking, and recognition. Explore their Web site and learn more about how the organisation is helping small businesses reduce their environmental impact.

- Penicillin
- Personal computer
- Power steering

Perhaps even more remarkable—and important—is that many of these inventions sparked major new industries or contributed to an established industry by adding some valuable service.

Providing employment

Small firms traditionally have added more than their proportional share of new jobs to the economy. Seven out of the ten industries that added the most new jobs were small-business-dominated industries. Small businesses creating the most new jobs recently included business services, leisure and hospitality services, and special trade contractors. Small firms hire a larger proportion of employees who are younger workers, older workers, women, or workers who prefer to work part time.

Furthermore, in the U.S. small businesses provide 67 per cent of workers with their first jobs and initial on-the-job training in basic skills. According to the SBA, small businesses represent 99.7 per cent of all employers, employ more than 50 per cent of the private workforce, and provide about two-thirds of the net new jobs added to the economy.* Small businesses thus contribute significantly to solving unemployment problems.

The business cycle, as discussed in Chapter 1, is an important factor in the net creation or loss of jobs. During the 2008–2009 recession, businesses with fewer than 20 employees began losing jobs as early as mid-2007. From 2008 to mid-2009, these smallest businesses accounted for 24 per cent of the net job losses, while those with 20–499 employees accounted for 36 per cent; the remaining 40 per cent of job losses were in larger firms with more than 500 employees.*

Providing competition

Small businesses challenge larger, established firms in many ways, causing them to become more efficient and more responsive to consumer needs. A small business cannot, of course, compete with a large firm in all respects. However, a number of small firms, each competing in its own particular area and its own particular way, together have the desired competitive effect. Thus, several small companies together add up to reasonable competition for the larger corporations.

Filling needs of society and other businesses

Small firms also provide a variety of goods and services to each other and to much larger firms. Sears, Roebuck & Co. purchases merchandise from approximately 12,000 suppliers—and most of them are small businesses. General Motors relies on more than 32,000 companies for parts and supplies and depends on more than 11,000 independent dealers to sell its automobiles and lorries. Large firms generally buy parts and assemblies from smaller firms for one very good reason: It is less expensive than manufacturing the parts in their own factories. This lower cost eventually is reflected in the price that consumers pay for their products.

It is clear that small businesses are a vital part of most typical economies and that consumers and members of the labour force all benefit enormously from their existence. Now let us look at the situation from the viewpoint of the owners of small businesses.

THE PROS AND CONS OF SMALLNESS

Do most owners of small businesses dream that their firms will grow into giant corporations—managed by professionals—while they serve only on the board of directors? Or would they rather stay small, in a firm where they have the opportunity (and the responsibility) to do everything that needs to be done? The answers depend on the personal characteristics and motivations of the individual owners. For many, the advantages of remaining small far outweigh the disadvantages.

Advantages of small business

Small-business owners with limited resources often must struggle to enter competitive new markets. They also have to deal with increasing international competition. However, they enjoy several unique advantages.

Personal relationships with customers and employees For those who like dealing with people, small business is the place to be. The owners of retail shops get to know many of their customers by name and deal with them on a personal basis. Through such relationships, small-business owners often become involved in the social, cultural, and political life of the community.

Relationships between owner-managers and employees also tend to be closer in smaller businesses. In many cases, the owner is a friend and counsellor as well as the boss.

These personal relationships provide an important business advantage. The personal service small businesses offer to customers is a major competitive weapon—one that larger firms try to match but often cannot. In addition, close relationships with employees often help the small-business owner to keep effective workers who might earn more with a larger firm.

Ability to adapt to change Being his or her own boss, the owner-manager of a small business does not need anyone's permission to adapt to change. An owner may add or discontinue merchandise or services, change opening hours, and experiment with various pricing strategies in response to changes in market conditions. And through personal relationships with customers, the owners of small businesses quickly become aware of changes in people's needs and interests, as well as in the activities of competing firms.

Simplified record keeping Many small firms need only a simple set of records. Record keeping might consist of an accounts book, a cash-receipts book in which to record all sales, and a cash-disbursements book in which to record all amounts paid out. Obviously, enough records must be kept to allow for producing and filing accurate tax returns.

Getting personal. For those who like dealing with people, small business is the place to be. Here a business owner provides personalised service to a happy customer.

© TYLER OLSON/SHUTTERSTOCK

Independence   Small-business owners do not have to punch in and out, bid for holiday times, take orders from superiors, or worry about being fired or laid off. They are the masters of their own destinies—at least with regard to employment. For many people, this is the prime advantage of owning a small business.

Other advantages   According to the SBA, the most profitable companies in the United States are small firms that have been in business for more than ten years and employ fewer than 20 people. Small-business owners also enjoy all the advantages of sole proprietorships. These include being able to keep all profits, the ease and low cost of going into business and (if necessary) going out of business, and being able to keep business information secret.

Disadvantages of small business

Personal contacts with customers, closer relationships with employees, being one's own boss, less cumbersome record-keeping chores, and independence are the bright side of small business. In contrast, the dark side reflects problems unique to these firms.

Risk of failure   As we have noted, small businesses (especially new ones) run a heavy risk of going out of business—about 50 per cent survive at least five years. Older, well-established small firms can be hit hard by a business recession mainly because they do not have the financial resources to weather an extended difficult period.

Limited potential   Small businesses that survive do so with varying degrees of success. Many are simply the means of making a living for the owner and his or her family. The owner may have some technical skill—as a hair stylist or electrician, for example—and may have started a business to put this skill to work. Such a business is unlikely to grow into big business. In addition, employees' potential for advancement is limited.

Limited ability to raise capital   Small businesses typically have a limited ability to obtain capital. Figure 5.2 shows that most small-business financing comes out of the owner's pocket. Personal

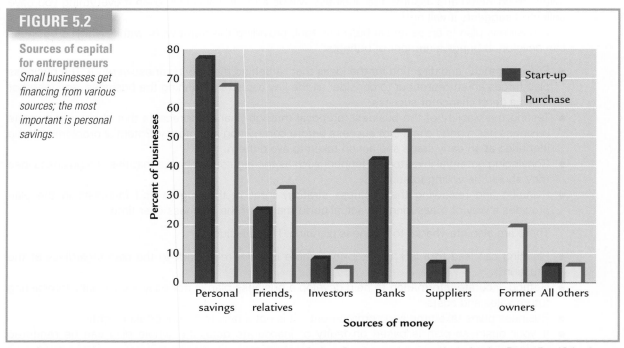

FIGURE 5.2

Sources of capital for entrepreneurs
Small businesses get financing from various sources; the most important is personal savings.

Source: Data developed and provided by the National Federation of Independent Business Foundation and sponsored by the American Express Travel Related Services Company, Inc.

loans from lending institutions provide only about one-fourth of the capital required by small businesses.

Although every person who considers starting a small business should be aware of the hazards and pitfalls we have noted, a well-conceived business plan may help to avoid the risk of failure. Many governments are committed to supporting and advancing small businesses, offering schemes, incentives and advice to those wishing to branch out on their own.

DEVELOPING A BUSINESS PLAN

In this next section we will consider the importance of planning for a new business start-up. You will learn that careful thought and effective planning at the early stage in the life of a business will help to identify potential problems and prepare the business for these, and will also tell an individual whether a business is likely to be viable.

The purpose and contents of a business plan

However good the business idea and however skilled the entrepreneur, without effective business planning a new business will quickly lose its way. A **business plan** is designed to help an entrepreneur in setting objectives, researching the market, planning strategy, and monitoring and evaluating finance and progress. A well-researched business plan that is regularly reviewed and updated can make the difference between success and failure.

business plan a carefully constructed guide for the person starting a business

A business plan is a document that sets out how the business will operate and what it hopes to achieve. One of the important points about such a business plan is that it serves to help the prospective business identify whether it will be viable or not. There is always a tendency to ignore the evidence collected and assume the business will be a roaring success, even if everything you have collected suggests it will not!

A business plan is an essential business tool, providing the framework within which a business can develop. It brings a number of benefits:

- Providing focus and direction for the ideas that lie behind the new business venture. The business plan forces an entrepreneur to consider all the key aspects of running the business, and whether it has a good chance of success.
- Testing the viability of the business proposal through financial forecasts that show whether the business has a good chance of success before committing any money. Potential problems can be identified at an early stage and action taken to avoid them.
- Convincing potential investors or lenders such as the high street banks that this is a business idea they should be willing to support.
- Planning and reviewing the business strategy through the targets and forecasts in the plan provides a way of measuring the actual performance of the business over time.

There are also drawbacks to business planning. These include:

- Planning can lead to a lack of flexibility – there is a desire to stick to the plan regardless of the situation.
- Getting accurate information to help develop a business plan is not easy – especially forecasting future sales and costs.
- Business plans take time and commitment – it is not a task to be undertaken lightly.
- If your business plan is based on faulty or inaccurate data, the whole plan can be rendered useless.

SUCCESS STORY

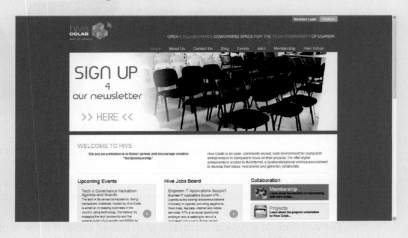

Tech-savvy entrepreneurs from Kampala lead the way

Young technologists from the Ugandan capital are taking centre-stage in the pan-African tech scene: Kampalans have won an Apps for Africa contest with a mobile app that measures foetal heart rates. They have established tech incubators like Hive Colab and set up computer coding lessons for girls.

"With over half the population in Uganda under 15, there is a great deal of youthful energy." The laying of undersea fibre-optic cables in neighbouring Kenya from 2009 which brought Internet access to the region even in remote villages via the use of dongles and 3G has made a huge difference.

So what comes next? "Kampala is relatively naïve in its tech awakening – only now is it riding the wave of African urban development," says Solomon King, founder of robotics startup Fundi Bots. "The raw energy is tangible."

Coding for girls

Maureen Agena, 28, has been a champion of citizen journalism and is the cofounder of the Ugandan chapter of global women's technology network Girl Geeks. The group is to provide support and career advice for women with a background in technology subjects but who have been unable to turn it into a career.

Medical apps

WinSenga is a low-cost app that analyses foetal heart rates, built by physician Davis Musinguzi and programmers Joshua Okello and Aaron Tushabe from Kampala. They were among the winners of Microsoft's Imagine Cup for 2012.

Tech incubators

A pioneer of Africa's nascent tech community, TMS Ruge helped found the Hive Colab incubator. Ruge, 37, has built a digital platform for engaging African diaspora with Ugandan development issues and been named a Champion of Change by the White House.

References: Variety of sources used including: http://www.wired.co.uk/magazine/archive/2013/09/start/ugandas-tech-pioneers; The Uganda National Council for Science and Technology (UNCST) www.uncst.go.ug; http://www.howwemadeitinafrica.com; girlgeeks.org; winsenga.wordpress.com; and tmsruge.com

---

- The planner might not have the skills or expertise to analyse and report on every aspect of a business plan.
- Unrealistic financial projections can lead to misplaced confidence in the likely success of a business venture.

The plan

In the early stages a business idea may only be fairly sketchy without much detail. For example, if you were considering setting yourself up in business as a window cleaner, you might be able to identify a local need and be thinking of targeting home owners. You might also have worked out what you need to run the business – a van, ladders, bucket, squeegee, and so on – but do not have much in the way

Although writing a business plan won't guarantee your success, it will help you think through many of the issues that can trip up entrepreneurs. And if you work for a big company, you may find yourself writing a kind of business plan for a product or project.

©MAST3R/SHUTTERSTOCK

of details about how much these things cost or the precise nature of the local market. The next stage, therefore, is to try to get more detail.

Business plans can be difficult to draw up because getting accurate information about the range of things that are included in the plan might not be easy, but it can also be due to a lack of care in the gathering of information.

We will look at a typical business plan based around a decision by an individual to set up as a window cleaner. The case will go through the main sections of a business plan and briefly outline what the individual in this example might include.

1 Introduction   This section will contain the basic business details – name and address, what the business function will be, the type of legal ownership and the goals of the business. In the case of a window cleaner, the business function will be to provide high quality window-cleaning services. The legal ownership is likely to be a partnership, sole trader or private limited company (see Chapter 4). The goals of the business might include some comment on the business philosophy – to provide high quality window-cleaning services, and about the expectation about the returns for the entrepreneur. This area of the plan might also consider the following areas: legal requirements of the business (health and safety, employment legislation, and so on) and tax liabilities – in the U.K., for instance, Value Added Tax (VAT), Income Tax and National Insurance Contributions (NICs).

2 The business idea   This section will provide more details about the nature of the business and the product or service to be provided. This might include more details on exactly what the business proposition is going to be. This might detail whether the service will cover residential accommodation, shops and offices, skyscrapers, city centre buildings, rural areas, and so on. If the aim is to provide window-cleaning services for businesses in city centres, then that might well be a different proposition from someone planning to offer window-cleaning services to a new residential development on the outskirts of a town.

This section will also include some details about the key selling points – what will this business offer that is different from any other window-cleaning service that already exists? This is where the entrepreneur has to think about the market they are targeting and what its needs might be and how they might add value. In addition, this is where the entrepreneur will have to think carefully about what it is about this business that offers competitive advantage.

3 Management and personnel   This section will outline the role of management and personnel in the organisation. A sole trader may only have themselves to worry about, but many sole traders employ other people and it needs to be clear what the relationship is between the people in the business and what their roles and responsibilities will be.

As a means of giving further information to prospective lenders, as well as identifying constraints for the business, the experience and skills of the workforce will be included. This helps the business to identify areas where they may have skill deficiencies, for example, in accounting or in administration. This section might also include information about the insurance that is required.

4 The marketing plan Marketing is about identifying consumer needs, seeking to satisfy those needs profitably and gaining a competitive advantage over rivals. In a window-cleaning business, you might want to specify a particular unique selling point (USP), such as time of day or special kind of service which might persuade customers to use your service. You will also need to identify the level of demand for such a service and the type of market you will be targeting. If you plan to focus on a new housing estate, you will need to think about how many potential customers there are, how often they might want your service – every week, every month? – what the level of competition is, what the opportunity for market expansion is, and so on.

This section might also include some detail on networking. This involves the contacts that businesses might need to help develop, and may include building relationships with local trade associations, such as the local Chambers of Commerce (in the U.K.) and trade associations. Networking is becoming increasingly important for many small businesses as a means of building contacts that help to develop the business, and can be a key part of the marketing process.

5 The production plan Because the example we are using is a service, the details of the production plan might be different from when a business is manufacturing a product. This is concerned with the day-to-day activities of the business referred to as operational planning. If you are considering a business that is actually making something, you will need to consider how this will work in practice and what you will need to be able to produce effectively and efficiently.

Some of the issues to think about in this section will be:

- Where will you get your supplies/raw materials?
- How reliable and secure are these supplies? (You do not want to let customers down!)
- Will you need to have a Web site? Will you need to sell online?
- What security arrangements might you need to make with regard to your business?
- How might you expand the business in the future?

The window-cleaning business, for example, might involve consideration about where the equipment will be stored when not in use to prevent theft or vandalism, and whether an online presence is really required for this type of business. How many employees do you need now, and, if the business is a success, in the next 12 months? Where will you get these employees from and what will you require of them in terms of qualifications, training, personality, and so on?

Details of the production process, in this case, might involve the equipment needed to make production levels efficient. In the case of a window cleaner, thought needs to be given to the equipment needed. In addition, the business might think about how to actually go about the job of cleaning windows – is there a routine, a way of cleaning the windows on a house that maximises productivity (number of windows cleaned per hour)? The business will also need to consider how it is going to provide and maintain quality and what it will do if it receives complaints about quality.

6 The financial plan The financial planning section requires you to consider the following issues:

- costs and prices
- cash flow monitoring
- record-keeping
- setting up financial reserves and contingency plans
- availability of long-term or emergency finance.

In the case of a window cleaner, the production plan will have identified the equipment needed to be able to run the business. Checking on the costs involved, therefore, needs some further research. Examples are given below:

- Transport – what type is appropriate, how much will it cost, what are the insurance and tax costs? How much will the petrol costs be?
- Ladders – how many and what type? If the round is likely to be residential properties only (as opposed to high-rise office blocks, for example) then a ladder that can reach relevant heights is essential. Also needed is a ladder that is able to reach lower levels but that is not so bulky to carry around.
- Basic equipment – cloths, leathers, buckets, squeegees, and so on.
- Business cards to advertise the service.
- Invoices to record payments and money owing for services carried out.

Having detailed the costs, some consideration will need to be given about how the finance to pay for the start-up will be raised. There will need to be detail of prices. This, along with the market information from the section above, helps the business to be able to produce a forecast profit and loss account, a break-even forecast and a cash flow forecast.

The Table 5.2 provides a business plan checklist for potential new business owners to follow.

TABLE 5.2	Business plan checklist

1. Does the executive summary grab the reader's attention and highlight the major points of the business plan?
2. Does the business-concept section clearly describe the purpose of the business, the customers, the value proposition, and the distribution channel and convey a compelling story?
3. Do the industry and market analyses support acceptance and demand for the business concept in the marketplace and define a first customer in depth?
4. Does the management team plan persuade the reader that the team could implement the business concept successfully? Does it assure the reader that an effective infrastructure is in place to facilitate the goals and operations of the company?
5. Does the product/service plan clearly provide details on the status of the product, the time line for completion, and the intellectual property that will be acquired?
6. Does the operations plan prove that the product or service could be produced and distributed efficiently and effectively?
7. Does the marketing plan successfully demonstrate how the company will create customer awareness in the target market and deliver the benefit to the customer?
8. Does the financial plan convince the reader that the business model is sustainable—that it will provide a superior return on investment for the investor and sufficient cash flow to repay loans to potential lenders?
9. Does the growth plan convince the reader that the company has long-term growth potential and spin-off products and services?
10. Does the contingency and exit-strategy plan convince the reader that the risk associated with this venture can be mediated? Is there an exit strategy in place for investors?

Source: From ALLEN, *Launching New Ventures,* 6E. © 2012 Cengage Learning.

Sources of information and guidance

The business plan is going to be an important source of information about the business and is often used as the basis for advice. It helps pinpoint particular areas of concern. New businesses can get advice from a range of different sources. Increasingly more free advice services are available online, with relevant information targeted at businesses operating in specific countries and regions. If the new business itself has international elements, for example, an online retail business, it is all the more important to be aware of trading regulations and legislation in the countries in which you wish to trade.

Some of the main sources of help are detailed below.

Banks   Many businesses will use a high-street bank as a source of funds for their business, as well as holding a business account with them. For the bank, it is important that the business flourishes, so it is in their interest to provide support services and advice for small businesses.

Accountants   Most small businesses will employ an accountant to prepare and check their accounts each year. Many accountants will also offer the benefit of their experience and expertise to the business. They might be able to see particular problems or potential problems facing the business, and as a result, be able to offer valuable advice to the business.

The Small Business Advice Service   This is a U.K.-centred body managed by the National Federation for Enterprise Agencies (NFEA) and is funded by sponsors who offer free and independent information for small businesses. It has a Web site with a series of frequently asked questions and will also provide individual advice to particular questions. It also has a number of resources available from the site to help those thinking of starting up or who have just started up their business.

www.smallbusiness.co.uk   This Web site www.smallbusiness.co.uk is a source of online-only advice which covers all the main areas of advice for start-ups and new businesses including finance, market research, business formation, sales and marketing, legal advice, business technology and operating overseas.

Small Business South Africa   This is one of many independent online services dedicated to assisting the South African small business entrepreneur. The Web site contains advice on budgeting, the business plan, insurance, investments and security amongst the other components required to set-up and maintain a healthy business.

Other small business advisors   There are a host of small business advisors providing advice and consultancy services to small businesses. They are represented in the U.K. by the Institute of Consulting (IC), formerly the Institute of Business Consulting. The IC is dedicated to increasing the standard of advice provided by its members in helping improve the performance and standards of new and small businesses. There is a directory to find a local business advisor but the business will have to pay for the advice received.

Government agencies   One of the main sources of government-sponsored help in the U.K. is GOV.UK, which replaces the former services Business Link and DirectGov. The Web site https://www.gov.uk/business contains large amounts of information for small businesses and those thinking of starting up a business. It also has affiliated organisations elsewhere in the United Kingdom (as a result of devolution) which include Business Wales, Invest NI for Northern Ireland, The Highlands and Islands Enterprise in Scotland and Business Gateway which is based in Glasgow.

In addition to this, various government departments will provide some form of advice and Her Majesty's Revenue and Customs will also offer advice to small businesses in relation to tax and National Insurance matters.

The South African Revenue Service (SARS) has a section of its Web site dedicated to small businesses, with links to registering for tax as well as other useful information.

Start-ups in the U.S. are aided by the Small Business Administration (SBA), a governmental agency created by Congress in 1953 to assist, counsel, and protects the interests of small businesses. It helps people get into business and stay in business. The agency provides assistance to owners and managers of prospective, new, and established small businesses. Through more than 1,000 offices and resource centres throughout the nation, the SBA provides both financial assistance and management counselling. Recently, the SBA provided training, technical assistance, and education to more than 3 million small businesses. It helps small firms to bid for and obtain government contracts, and it helps them to prepare to enter foreign markets.

Franchises and large corporations encroaching on local businesses and culture?

Multinational grocery giants like Tesco in the U.K. are regularly criticised for being the cause of numerous small businesses closing, as high street stores find it impossible to compete with supermarket low prices and dominant brand franchising. In 2013, the British Independent Retailers Association said 98% of the U.K.'s £150bn grocery industry was controlled by just nine stores.

In February 2013 Sir Terry Leahy the former boss of Tesco was asked if he thought it was "tough" that a family butcher had to close because they couldn't compete with the "three-quid chicken" sold at the supermarket. Sir Terry Leahy explained that the benefits for thousands of families can be a big loss for the family of the butcher and the boarding up of local shops was sad, but this was simply because consumers were choosing to shop at the bigger supermarkets.

Cultural insensitivity has also been an issue with global franchises, including American global coffee giant Starbucks. For example, in 2007 Beijing's Forbidden City palace closed down a branch of Starbucks on its grounds, following protests led by a state TV personality Rui Chenggang, who said the presence of the American coffeehouse was eroding Chinese culture.

In Rui Chenggang's January 2007 online blog campaign against Starbucks he said, "The Forbidden City is a symbol of China's cultural heritage. Starbucks is a symbol of lower middle class culture in the West. We need to embrace the world, but we also need to preserve our cultural identity. There is a fine line between globalisation and contamination."

References: Variety of sources used including Kelly & Ashwin, *The Business Environment*, Cengage Learning EMEA 2013; http://www.bbc.co.uk/news/uk-21310808; http://www.nytimes.com ;http://www.smallbusiness.co.uk;

We have discussed the importance of the small-business segment of the economy. We have weighed the advantages and drawbacks of operating a small business as compared with a large one. But is there a way to achieve the best of both worlds? Can one preserve one's independence as a business owner and still enjoy some of the benefits of "bigness"? Let's take a close look at franchising.

FRANCHISING

A **franchise** is a license to operate an individually owned business as if it were part of a chain of outlets or stores. Often, the business itself is also called a *franchise*. Some of the more familiar franchises include McDonald's, Toni & Guy hair salons originating in the U.K., and Nando's (in South Africa, New Zealand and Australia). Many other franchises carry familiar names; this method of doing business has become very popular in the last 30 years or so. It is an attractive means of starting and operating a small business.

franchise a license to operate an individually owned business as though it were part of a chain of outlets or stores

What is franchising?

Franchising is the actual granting of a franchise. A **franchisor** is an individual or organisation granting a franchise. A **franchisee** is a person or organisation purchasing a franchise. The franchisor supplies a known and advertised business name, management skills, the required training and materials, and a method of doing business. The franchisee supplies labour and capital, operates the franchised business, and agrees to abide by the provisions of the franchise agreement. Table 5.3 lists the basic franchisee rights and obligations that would be covered in a typical franchise agreement.

> **franchising** the actual granting of a franchise
> **franchisor** an individual or organisation granting a franchise
> **franchisee** a person or organisation purchasing a franchise

TABLE 5.3 Basic rights and obligations delineated in a franchise agreement

Franchisee rights include:

1. use of trademarks, trade names, and patents of the franchisor;
2. use of the brand image and the design and decor of the premises developed by the franchisor;
3. use of the franchisor's secret methods;
4. use of the franchisor's copyrighted materials;
5. use of recipes, formulae, specifications, processes, and methods of manufacture developed by the franchisor;
6. conducting the franchised business upon or from the agreed premises strictly in accordance with the franchisor's methods and subject to the franchisor's directions;
7. guidelines established by the franchisor regarding exclusive territorial rights; and
8. rights to obtain supplies from nominated suppliers at special prices.

Franchisee obligations include:

1. to carry on the business franchised and no other business upon the approved and nominated premises;
2. to observe certain minimum operating hours;
3. to pay a franchise fee;
4. to follow the accounting system laid down by the franchisor;
5. not to advertise without prior approval of the advertisements by the franchisor;
6. to use and display such point-of-sale advertising materials as the franchisor stipulates;
7. to maintain the premises in good, clean, and sanitary condition and to redecorate when required to do so by the franchisor;
8. to maintain the widest possible insurance coverage;
9. to permit the franchisor's staff to enter the premises to inspect and see if the franchisor's standards are being maintained;
10. to purchase goods or products from the franchisor or his designated suppliers;
11. to train the staff in the franchisor's methods to ensure that they are neatly and appropriately clothed; and
12. not to assign the franchise contract without the franchisor's consent.

Source: Excerpted from the SBA's "Is Franchising for Me?" www.sba.gov (accessed March 12, 2012).

Types of franchising

Franchising arrangements fall into three general categories. In the first approach, a manufacturer authorises a number of retail stores to sell a certain brand-name item. This type of franchising arrangement, one of the oldest, is prevalent in sales of passenger cars and lorries farm equipment, shoes, paint, earth-moving equipment, and petroleum. About 90 per cent of all petrol is sold through franchised, independent retail service stations, and franchised dealers handle virtually all sales of new cars and lorries. In the second type of franchising arrangement, a producer licenses distributors to sell a given product to retailers. This arrangement is common in the soft drink industry. Most national manufacturers of soft drink syrups—The Coca-Cola Company, Dr. Pepper/Seven-Up Companies, PepsiCo, Royal Crown Companies, Inc.—franchise independent bottlers who then serve retailers. In a third form of franchising, a franchisor supplies brand names, techniques, or other services instead of a complete product. Although the franchisor may provide certain production and distribution services, its primary role is the careful development and control of marketing strategies. This approach to franchising, which is the most typical today, is used by Holiday Inns, Howard Johnson Company, McDonald's, Dairy Queen, Avis, Hertz Corporation, KFC (Kentucky Fried Chicken), and SUBWAY, to name but a few.

THE GROWTH OF FRANCHISING

Franchising, which, in the form that we understand it today, began in the United States around the time of the Civil War, was used originally by large firms, such as the Singer Sewing Company, to distribute their products. Franchising has been increasing steadily in popularity since the early 1900s, primarily for filling stations and car dealerships; however, this retailing strategy has experienced enormous growth since the mid-1970s. The franchise proliferation generally has paralleled the expansion of the fast-food industry.

Of course, franchising is not limited to fast foods. Hair salons, tanning parlours, and dentists and solicitors are expected to participate in franchising arrangements in growing numbers. Franchised health clubs, pest exterminators, and campgrounds are already widespread, as are franchised tax preparers and travel agencies. The property industry also has experienced a rapid increase in franchising.

Also, franchising is attracting more women and minority business owners than ever before. Franchisors such as Wendy's, McDonald's, Burger King, and Church's Chicken all have special corporate programmes to attract minority and women franchisees. Just as important, successful women and minority franchisees are willing to get involved by offering advice and guidance to new franchisees.

Herman Petty, the first African-American McDonald's franchisee, remembers that the company provided a great deal of help while he worked to establish his first units. In turn, Petty travelled to help other black franchisees, and he invited new franchisees to gain hands-on experience in his Chicago restaurants before starting their own establishments. In 1972, Petty also organised a support group, the National Black McDonald's Operators Association, to help black franchisees in other areas. Today, members of this association own nearly 1,400 McDonald's restaurants throughout the United States, South Africa, and the Caribbean with annual sales of more than $3.2 billion. "We are really concentrating on helping our operators to be successful both operationally and financially," says Craig Welburn, the McDonald's franchisee who leads the group.

Dual-branded franchises, in which two franchisors offer their products together, are a new small-business trend. For example, in 1993, pleased with the success of its first cobranded restaurant with Texaco in Beebe, Arkansas, McDonald's now has more than 400 cobranded restaurants in the United States. Also, an agreement between franchisors Doctor's Associates, Inc., and TCBY Enterprises, Inc., now allows franchisees to sell SUBWAY sandwiches and TCBY yoghurt in the same establishment.

Are franchises successful?

Franchising is designed to provide a tested formula for success, along with ongoing advice and training. The success rate for businesses owned and operated by franchisees is significantly higher than the success rate for other independently owned small businesses. In a recent nationwide Gallup poll of 944 franchise owners, 94 per cent of franchisees indicated that they were very or somewhat successful, only 5 per cent believed that they were very unsuccessful or somewhat unsuccessful, and 1 per cent did not know. Despite these impressive statistics, franchising is not a guarantee of success for either franchisees or franchisors. Too rapid expansion, inadequate capital or management skills, and a host of other problems can cause failure for both franchisee and franchisor. Thus, for example, the Dizzy Dean's Beef and Burger franchise is no longer in business. Timothy Bates, a Wayne State University economist, warns, "Despite the hype that franchising is the safest way to go when starting a new business, the research just doesn't bear that out." Just consider Boston Chicken, which once had more than 1,200 restaurants before declaring bankruptcy in 1998.

Advantages of franchising

Franchising plays a vital role in our economy and soon may become the dominant form of retailing. Why? Because franchising offers advantages to both the franchisor and the franchisee.

To the franchisor The franchisor gains fast and well-controlled distribution of its products without incurring the high cost of constructing and operating its own outlets. The franchisor thus has more capital available to expand production and to use for advertising. At the same time, it can ensure, through the franchise agreement, that outlets are maintained and operated according to its own standards.

The franchisor also benefits from the fact that the franchisee—a sole proprietor in most cases—is likely to be very highly motivated to succeed. The success of the franchise means more sales, which translate into higher royalties for the franchisor.

To the franchisee The franchisee gets the opportunity to start a business with limited capital and to make use of the business experience of others. Moreover, an outlet with a widely advertised name, such as RadioShack, McDonald's, or Century 21, has guaranteed customers as soon as it opens.

If business problems arise, the franchisor gives the franchisee guidance and advice. This counselling is primarily responsible for the very high degree of success enjoyed by franchises. In most cases, the franchisee does not pay for such help.

The franchisee also receives materials to use in local advertising and can take part in national promotional campaigns sponsored by the franchisor. McDonald's and its franchisees, for example, constitute one of the nation's top 20 purchasers of advertising. Finally, the franchisee may be able to minimise the cost of advertising, supplies, and various business necessities by purchasing them in cooperation with other franchisees.

Disadvantages of franchising

The main disadvantage of franchising affects the franchisee, and it arises because the franchisor retains a great deal of control. The franchisor's contract can dictate every aspect of the business: decor, design of employee uniforms, types of signs, and all the details of business operations. All Burger King French fries taste the same because all Burger King franchisees have to make them the same way.

The growth of franchising. Franchising is designed to provide a tested formula for success, along with ongoing advice and training. The franchisor supplies a known and advertised business name, management skills, the required training and materials, and a method of doing business. Franchising, however, is not a guarantee of success for either franchisees or franchisors.

©SUSAN VAN ETTEN

Contract disputes are the cause of many lawsuits. For example, Rekha Gabhawala, a Dunkin' Donuts franchisee in Milwaukee (U.S.), alleged that the franchisor was forcing her out of business so that the company could profit by reselling the downtown franchise to someone else; the company, on the other hand, alleged that Gabhawala breached the contract by not running the business according to company standards. In another case, Dunkin' Donuts sued Chris Romanias, its franchisee in Pennsylvania, alleging that Romanias intentionally underreported gross sales to the company. Romanias, on the other hand, alleged that Dunkin' Donuts, Inc., breached the contract because it failed to provide assistance in operating the franchise. Other franchisees claim that contracts are unfairly tilted toward the franchisors. Yet others have charged that they lost their franchise and investment because their franchisor would not approve the sale of the business when they found a buyer.

Because disagreements between franchisors and franchisees have increased in recent years, many franchisees have been demanding government regulation of franchising.

Franchise holders pay for their security, usually with a one-time franchise fee and continuing royalty and advertising fees, collected as a percentage of sales. A SUBWAY franchisee, for instance, pays an initial franchise fee of around €15,000 and an annual fee of 8 per cent of gross sales. In some fields, franchise agreements are not uniform. One franchisee may pay more than another for the same services.

Even success can cause problems. Sometimes a franchise is so successful that the franchisor opens its own outlet nearby, in direct competition—although franchisees may fight back. For example, a court recently ruled that Burger King could not enter into direct competition with the franchisee because the contract was not specific on the issue. A spokesperson for one franchisor contends that the company "gives no geographical protection" to its franchise holders and thus is free to move in on them. Franchise operators work hard. They often put in 10- and 12-hour days, six days a week. The International Franchise Association advises prospective franchise purchasers to investigate before investing and to approach buying a franchise cautiously. Franchises vary widely in approach as well as in products. Some, such as Dunkin' Donuts and Baskin-Robbins, demand long hours. Others, such as Great Clips hair salons and Albert's Family Restaurants, are more appropriate for those who do not want to spend many hours at their stores.

GLOBAL PERSPECTIVES IN SMALL BUSINESS

For small businesses, the world is becoming smaller. National and international economies are growing more and more interdependent as political leadership and national economic directions change and trade barriers diminish or disappear. Globalisation and instant worldwide communications are rapidly shrinking distances at the same time that they are expanding business opportunities. According to a recent study, the Internet is increasingly important to small-business strategic thinking, with more than 50 per cent of those surveyed indicating that the Internet represented their most favoured strategy for growth. This was more than double the next-favoured choice, strategic alliances reflecting the opportunity to reach both global and domestic customers. The Internet and online payment systems enable even very small businesses to serve international customers. In fact, technology now gives small businesses the gearing and power to reach markets that were once limited solely to large corporations. No wonder the number of businesses exporting their goods and services has tripled since 1990, with two-thirds of that boom coming from companies with fewer than 20 employees.*

International trade will become more important to small-business owners as they face unique challenges in the new century. Small businesses, which are expected to remain the dominant form of organisation in this country, must be prepared to adapt to significant demographic and economic changes in the world marketplace.

From here on, we shall be looking closely at various aspects of business operations. This will include a discussion of management—what management is, what managers do, and how they work to coordinate the basic economic resources within a business organisation.

SUMMARY

- Define what a small business is and recognise the fields in which small businesses are concentrated.

  A small business is one that is independently owned and operated for profit and is not dominant in its field. In many countries, small businesses employ more than half the nation's workforce. About 69 per cent of small businesses survive at least two years and about 50 per cent survive at least five years. More than half of all small businesses are in retailing and services.

- Identify the people who start small businesses and the reasons why some succeed and many fail.

  Such personal characteristics as independence, desire to create a new enterprise, and willingness to accept a challenge may encourage individuals to start small businesses. Various external circumstances, such as special expertise or even the loss of a job, also can supply the motivation to strike out on one's own. Poor planning and lack of capital and management experience are the major causes of small-business failures.

- Assess the contributions of small businesses to the economy.

  Small businesses have been responsible for a wide variety of inventions and innovations, some of which have given rise to new industries. Historically, small businesses have created the bulk of new jobs in many nations. Further, they have mounted effective competition to larger firms. They provide things that society needs, act as suppliers to larger firms, and serve as customers of other businesses, both large and small.

- Describe the advantages and disadvantages of operating a small business.

  The advantages of smallness in business include the opportunity to establish personal relationships with customers and employees, the ability to adapt to changes quickly, independence, and simplified record keeping. The major disadvantages are the high risk of failure, the limited potential for growth, and the limited ability to raise capital.

- Explain the concept and types of franchising.

  A franchise is a license to operate an individually owned business as though it were part of a chain. The franchisor provides a known business name, management skills, a method of doing business, and the training and required materials. The franchisee contributes labour and capital, operates the franchised business, and agrees to abide by the provisions of the franchise agreement. There are three major categories of franchise agreements.

- Analyse the growth of franchising and its advantages and disadvantages.

  Franchising has grown tremendously since the mid-1970s. The franchisor's major advantage in franchising is fast and well-controlled distribution of products with minimal capital outlay. In return, the franchisee has the opportunity to open a business with limited capital, to make use of the business experience of others, and to sell to an existing clientele. For this, the franchisee usually must pay both an initial franchise fee and a continuing royalty based on sales. He or she also must follow the dictates of the franchise with regard to operation of the business.

  Worldwide business opportunities are expanding for small businesses. Many agencies exist to assist small-business owners in penetrating foreign markets. The next century will present unique challenges and opportunities for small-business owners.

EXERCISE QUESTIONS

1 Explain what is meant by a "distribution industry" and provide some examples

2 What are some of the personal factors which determine peoples' decision to start up their own small businesses?

3 Give some of the typical reasons why small businesses can fail.

4 Explain what is meant by a "franchise" and give three different categories of it.

5 Give some examples of early franchise successes and explain why those industries were suited to the franchise concept.

CASE 5.1

Glasses Direct

Glasses Direct is a story of entrepreneurship in action. It illustrates how someone with entrepreneurial potential, a keen motivation and a simple but winning idea can quickly become established with a widely recognised brand. It is also the story of a business and an entrepreneur that have won multiple awards.

Jamie Murray Wells comes from something of a business background – his father is an investment analyst and his maternal grandfather was involved when both Chrysler and Ford established plants in the U.K. – but he chose to read English at University in Bristol. He confesses he had been searching for business ideas when, and whilst studying for his final exams, he was told he needed glasses. He was surprised at the prices of around £150 that opticians were charging for glasses and thought there must be a lower cost alternative. When he checked he discovered professional labs can make glasses with quality prescription lenses at relatively low cost. He had his idea – glasses supplied through online ordering – which he then researched thoroughly before taking the metaphorical plunge. Customers with a prescription from an optician could log on, choose a frame (or frames) and provide details of the lenses they needed. A trial pair (or pairs) would be sent out – which the customer would return and which would then be sent to another prospective customer. New glasses would be produced and posted out with little delay. The prices they would pay for good quality products have always been substantially lower than the traditional high street. With up-front payments from their customers and trade credit for their laboratory suppliers the business had a sound cash flow. The business model also passes the test advocated by the founders of Innocent Smoothies – a simple idea that anyone could understand quickly.

Jamie used his own funds to pay a fellow student to produce the Web site and his early marketing involved him distributing flyers to rail commuters and passengers in the West Country. His simple viral marketing approach worked. Reflecting current trends, Glasses Direct now makes extensive use of online social networks but Jamie Murray Wells has always looked for valuable publicity opportunities and relevant stories for the press. Although there are aspects of creative irreverence such as fun cleaning sprays, Murray Wells acknowledges that glasses are a serious purchase for most people and is careful to preserve the right image for the business.

The first base for Glasses Direct (in 2004) was his parents' home in Wiltshire but as others started to join the business it became necessary to decamp to a nearby converted barn. As the business grew he expanded in the same area but now the head office and marketing are based in London with manufacturing – Glasses Direct originally relied on laboratories but switched to producing their own – and distribution in Swindon. Qualified opticians were recruited to the business to support the business experts. As time has gone on varifocal lenses have been added to the range – supported by opticians who will travel to people's homes – as have designer frames and a wide range of prescription and non-prescription sunglasses. Innovation is taken seriously, but Glasses Direct has so far chosen not to supply non-prescription reading and distance glasses with "standard" lenses. Venture Capital funding (from Index Ventures and Highland Capital Partners) supplemented business angel funding which itself had helped the business move on from a personal and family funding dependency. Straightforward prescription glasses can be bought for £39 but there are more expensive alternatives. The leading designer frames are, not unexpectedly, the most expensive with typical prices of £159 (glasses) and £220 (sunglasses).

With annual sales revenue now in the millions of pounds, Glasses Direct has become the leading online supplier in the industry sector it created. He reckons he has saved customers in the U.K. over £50 million in 6 years. Again not unexpectedly Murray Wells' success provoked a reaction from high street opticians, most noticeably the high-advertising Specsavers – but threatened legal actions have led to nothing of consequence. Invoking reminders of how the then small Ben & Jerry's saw off competition from the owners of Häagen-Dazs (Pillsbury Corporation) in the U.S., Murray Wells published letters from Specsavers' lawyers on the Glasses Direct Web site.

A more recent diversification (2010) is Hearing Direct, a separate company based in Andover. Murray Wells supplies, again online, digital hearing aids with prices ranging from £99 to £299, depending on looks and specification. Prospective customers can take a simple hearing test online and again be supplied with a trial hearing aid (which they return) before they make a final choice. Industry experts have been recruited to ensure the products are reliable and appropriate.

Going forward, Murray Wells appreciates that businesses have to develop and move on if they are to preserve their existing markets and open new opportunities. He knows he must explore the potential of the "higher end" of the market for glasses where margins will be higher but not threaten his volume sales of lower price glasses by doing this. He also appreciates there are strategic opportunities overseas.

The main lessons

Jamie Murray Wells believes he has learnt a number of simple but important lessons:

- First, all staff in the business should engage with customers on a regular basis.
- Second, it can pay off to stir things up occasionally if it brings valuable publicity. The provocative and charismatic CEO of Ryanair Michael O'Leary would undoubtedly agree with this.

- Third, it is important to build the right team and to exploit people's talents.
- Fourth, in the end the product is going to be more important than the marketing, but marketing, especially social marketing, does matter – as does customer service.
- Fifth, a business evolves and revolves around its culture. A set of understood and practiced guiding principles can really help.

Questions

1 Why do you think this is a successful business?

2 How different and distinctive is it?

3 Is Hearing Direct a logical extension? Why? Why not?

CHAPTER REFERENCES

Hatten, Timothy S., *Small Business Management: Entrepreneurship and Beyond*, 4th ed., Copyright © 2009 by Houghton Mifflin Company, 238. Reprinted with permission.

SBA Press Release, *Fact Sheet*, September 11, 2008, 2.

SBA Press Release, "Computer Simulation Company from Florida Is National Small Business of the Year," May 25, 2010, www.sba.gov/news (accessed March 15, 2012).

SBA Press Release, "President Obama Proclaims National Small Business Week," May 21, 2010, www.sba.gov/news (accessed March 7, 2012).

SBA Press Release 12-12, "SBA Announces a New Partnership to Connect Small Businesses With Corporate Supply Chains," March 22, 2012, www.sba.gov/news (accessed March 23, 2012); and International Trade Web site at www.trade.gov/CS/ (accessed March 23, 2012).

SBA Press Release Number 10–414, *News Release*, May 14, 2010, www.sba.gov/news (accessed March 12, 2012).

SBIC Program Overview, Web site at http://archive.sba.gov/idc/groups/public/documents/sba_program_office/inv_sbic; and Small Business Investor Alliance Web site at www.nabic.org (accessed March 23, 2012).

SCORE Web site at www.score.org/about-score (accessed March 19, 2012).

Small Business South Africa, http://www.sabusinesswarrior.com/article3.html, accessed 25 October 2013

http://southafrica.angloinfo.com/working/starting-a-business/ (accessed 25 October 2013.)

U.S. Small Business Administration, *News Release*, Number 05–53, September 13, 2005, www.sba.gov/teens/brian_hendricks.html (accessed March 19, 2012).

U.S. Small Business Administration, *News Release*, Release Number 10–33, May 26, 2010, www.sba.gov/news (accessed March 18, 2012).

U.S. Small Business Administration, Office of Advocacy, *Frequently Asked Questions*, September 2009, www.sba.gov/advo (accessed March 15, 2011).

U.S. Small Business Administration, Office of Advocacy, *Frequently Asked Questions*, updated January 2011, www.sba.gov/advo (accessed March 15, 2012).

U.S. Small Business Administration, Office of Advocacy, *News Release*, Number 10-03 ADVO, March 3, 2010, www.sba.gov/advo/press/10-03.html (accessed March 15, 2011).

U.S. Small Business Administration, www.sba.gov/managing/marketing/intlsales.html (accessed October 4, 2008).

U.S. Small Business Administration Web site at www.sba.gov/content/summary-size-standards-industry (accessed March 18, 2012).

© DIEGO CERVO / SHUTTERSTOCK

PART 3
MANAGEMENT AND ORGANISATION

This Part of the book deals with the organisation—the "thing" that is a business. We begin with a discussion of the management functions involved in developing and operating a business. Next, we analyse the organisation's elements and structure. Then we consider a firm's operations that are related to the production of goods and services.

6   **Leadership and Managing a Business**

7   **Flexibility Within the Organisation**

8   **Products and Services**

6

LEADERSHIP AND MANAGING A BUSINESS

BUSINESS FOCUS

The visionary leadership of Jochen Zeitz

The "image" of some companies is projected largely by the products they sell. Others are led by a talismanic, charismatic leader; a figurehead who embodies the spirit of the company. Virgin has the adventurer Sir Richard Branson, Apple had the visionary late Steve Jobs, Ryanair has the brash, controversy-courting but plain-talking Michael O'Leary. Each in their own individual way, and through a larger-than-life personality, has brought great international success to the organisation they run. To this list can be added Jochen Zeizt, who at only 30 years old became the youngest ever Chief Executive Office of a listed company in Germany, when he was elected into the top job at Puma in 1993.

Zeitz is responsible for turning Puma – then a once successful but increasingly tired, receding brand – into one of the world's most profitable and desirable sportswear labels, only surpassed by the twin giants, Nike and Adidas. He did this, in large part,

by playing to Puma's legacy and vintage appeal, recruiting respected and on-trend designers such as Alexander McQueen and aligning the brand with aspirational figures in sports and music, like the tennis champion Serena Williams and Madonna. Zeitz recognised the commercial value in pursuing a strategy and image that was equally at home in the fashion markets, as well as the traditional sportswear trade. Of his revival of Puma's fortunes, Zeitz has noted, "There are 100,000 brands with heritage and history that never come back. It was a wonderful brand for a long period of time. It just needed to be re-awoken".

His success at Puma led to a position on the board of Harley Davison, the renowned producers of motorcycles, in 2007. Zeitz has been CEO of Kering, the holdcompany that holds Puma. Zeitz has won multiple awards for his business acumen and commitment to sustainability, including several stints as *The Financial Times'* "Strategist

of the Year" and "Honorary Warden of Kenya" in 2009. Zeizt is now the Director and Chairman of the sustainable development committee at Kering, the holding company which incorporates Puma. In 2013, Zeitz teamed up with the aforementioned Richard Branson, to launch The B Team, an initiative aimed at promoting "sustainable business models for people and planet". Like Branson, his impressive business resume is matched only by his colourful pursuits out of the office. The multi-lingual Zeitz's interests over the years, when not partying with Brad Pitt, have included wild boar hunting, running marathons and flying planes.

Despite his young age, or perhaps in part because of it, Zeitz was able to inject new life into a fading brand, through his strength of character and visionary leadership.

References: 'New tack that got the sporty cat back on track', D. Teather, *The Guardian* (20th June, 2008); 'Richard Branson and Jochen Zeitz', J. Confino, *The Guardian* (13th June 2013); 'Jochen Zetiz announced as FT Boldness in Business keynote speaker', *Financial Times*

As the example of Jochen Zeitz and Puma illustrates, management can be one of the most exciting and rewarding professions available today. Depending on its size, a firm may employ a number of specialised managers who are responsible for particular areas of management, such as marketing, finance, and operations. That same organisation also includes managers at several levels within the firm. In this chapter, we define *management* and describe the four basic management functions of planning, organising, leading and motivating, and controlling. Then we focus on the types of managers with respect to levels of responsibility and areas of expertise. Next, we focus on the skills of effective managers and the different roles managers must play. We examine several styles of leadership and explore the process by which managers make decisions. We also describe how total quality management can improve customer satisfaction.

WHAT IS MANAGEMENT?

Management is the process of coordinating people and other resources to achieve the goals of an organisation. Most organisations make use of four kinds of resources: material, human, financial, and informational (see Figure 6.1).

> **management** the process of coordinating people and other resources to achieve the goals of an organisation

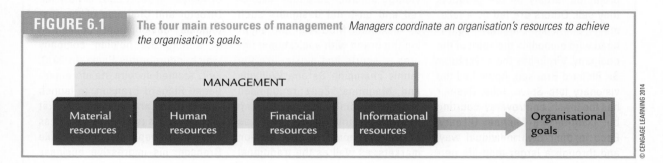

FIGURE 6.1 **The four main resources of management** *Managers coordinate an organisation's resources to achieve the organisation's goals.*

© CENGAGE LEARNING 2014

Material resources are the tangible, physical resources an organisation uses. For example, Volkswagen uses steel, glass, and fibreglass to produce cars and lorries on complex machine-driven assembly lines. A university uses books, classroom buildings, desks, and computers to educate students. And hospitals and health clinics use operating room equipment, diagnostic machines, and laboratory tests to provide health care.

Perhaps the most important resources of any organisation are its *human resources*—people. In fact, some firms live by the philosophy that their employees are their most important assets. Some managers believe that the way employees are developed and managed may have more impact on an organisation than other vital components such as marketing, sound financial decisions about large expenditures, production, or use of technology. While all firms should – and most do – recognise the potential of their employees, some companies actively pursue employee satisfaction as a specific and targetted core strategy for their success. The John Lewis Partnership, for example, who run 39 department stores and 300 Waitrose supermarkets across the U.K., pride themselves on placing the value of their employees at the heart of their business. In fact the workers are technically not employees at all, but partners, as each of 85,500 individuals working for the company in permanent positions actually own a stake in the business. Hence they have a vested interest in the company's success and are rewarded accordingly.

In South Africa, the annual "Deloitte Best Company To Work For Survey" is rising in prominence as a gauge of employee satisfaction. The results for 2013 were announced in October of that year in Johannesburg. Old Mutual, which deals in investments, insurance, asset management and other financial solution services, was deemed the best employer out of businesses with over 2500 staff; Flight Centre (South Africa) won the accolade in the medium-sized category of between 301-2500 people; and The Unlimited, another financial services provider, came out on top in the category for small businesses employing 300 employees or less.

Maybe you've never thought of yourself as a manager. But if you've ever headed a committee or organised a new school club, you've actually been involved in management. Understanding more about the way management works can make you more successful in the daily business of your life.

© AISPIX BY IMAGE SOURCE/SHUTTERSTOCK

Financial resources are the funds an organisation uses to meet its obligations to investors and creditors. A convenience store obtains money from customers at the checkout counter and uses a portion of that money to pay its suppliers. Your university or institution may obtain money in the form of tuition, income from its endowments, and governmental grants. It uses the money to pay utility bills, insurance premiums, and lecturers' salaries.

Finally, many organisations increasingly find that they cannot afford to ignore *information*. External environmental conditions—including the economy, consumer markets, technology, politics, and cultural forces—are all changing so rapidly that a business that does not adapt probably will not survive. To adapt to change, the business must know what is changing and how it is changing. Most companies gather information about their competitors to increase their knowledge about changes in their industry and to learn from other companies' failures and successes.

It is important to realise that the four types of resources described earlier are only general categories of resources. Within each category are hundreds or thousands of more specific resources. It is this complex mix of specific resources—and not simply "some of each" of the four general categories—that managers must coordinate to produce goods and services.

Another interesting way to look at management is in terms of the different functions managers perform. These functions have been identified as planning, organising, leading and motivating employees, and controlling. We look at each of these management functions in the next section.

BASIC MANAGEMENT FUNCTIONS

When pharmaceutical company Eli Lilly decided to focus on the emerging market of China, the company reorganised its structure so that one of its six units would handle emerging markets, doubled its employee count from 1,100 to 2,200, and began construction on a second manufacturing plant in Suzhou, China. The company also implemented a partnering strategy in China to handle research and development. Eli Lilly's key strategies include maximising their core assets, accelerating new product launches, capitalising on longer product life-cycles in areas like China, and establishing local alliances to access fast-growing market segments.*

Management functions such as those just described do not occur according to some rigid, preset timetable. Managers do not plan in January, organise in February, lead and motivate in March, and control in April. At any given time, managers may engage in a number of functions simultaneously. However, each function tends to lead naturally to others. Figure 6.2 provides a visual framework for a more detailed discussion of the four basic management functions. How well managers perform these key functions determines whether a business is successful.

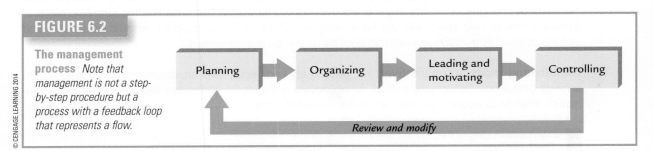

FIGURE 6.2

The management process *Note that management is not a step-by-step procedure but a process with a feedback loop that represents a flow.*

Planning → Organizing → Leading and motivating → Controlling

Review and modify

© CENGAGE LEARNING 2014

Planning

Planning, in its simplest form, is establishing organisational goals and deciding how to accomplish them. It is often referred to as the "first" management function because all other management functions depend on planning. Organisations such as Starbucks, Alibaba Group (which is featured in the end of chapter case section) and Facebook begin the planning process by developing a mission statement.

Superior human resources management can set a firm apart. Do you have a great business plan or product? A competitor can easily copy both. Great employees, however, are much harder to duplicate. That's why being able to attract, train, and retain talented workers can give a firm a competitive advantage over its rivals.

© KURHAN/SHUTTERSTOCK

planning establishing organisational goals and deciding how to accomplish them

An organisation's **mission** is a statement of the basic purpose that makes that organisation different from others. Starbucks' mission statement, for example, is "to inspire and nurture the human spirit—one person, one cup, and one neighbourhood at a time." Alibaba Group's mission is "to make it easy to do business anywhere"* Facebook's mission statement is "to give people the power to share and make the world more open and connected."* Once an organisation's mission has been described in a mission statement, the next step is to engage in strategic planning.

mission a statement of the basic purpose that makes an organisation different from others

Strategic planning process The **strategic planning process** involves establishing an organisation's major goals and objectives and allocating resources to achieve them. Top management is responsible for strategic planning, although customers, products, competitors, and company resources are some of the factors that are analysed in the strategic planning process.

strategic planning process the establishment of an organisation's major goals and objectives and the allocation of resources to achieve them

In today's rapidly changing business environment, constant internal or external changes may necessitate changes in a company's goals, mission, or strategy. The time line for strategic plans is generally one to two years and can be as long as ten years. Strategic plans should be flexible and include action items, such as outlining how plans will be implemented.

Establishing goals and objectives A **goal** is an end result that an organisation is expected to achieve over a one- to ten-year period. An **objective** is a specific statement detailing what the organisation intends to accomplish over a shorter period of time.

goal an end result that an organisation is expected to achieve over a one- to ten-year period
objective a specific statement detailing what an organisation intends to accomplish over a shorter period of time

Goals and objectives can deal with a variety of factors, such as sales, company growth, costs, customer satisfaction, and employee morale. Whereas a small manufacturer may focus primarily on sales objectives for the next six months, a large firm may be more interested in goals that impact several years in the future. Starbucks, for example, has established several goals under its "Shared Planet" programme to be completed in the next few years, specifically in the areas of ethical sourcing, environmental stewardship, and community involvement. By 2015, Starbucks hopes to purchase 100 per cent

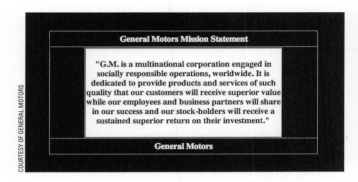

General Motors Mission Statement

"G.M. is a multinational corporation engaged in socially responsible operations, worldwide. It is dedicated to provide products and services of such quality that our customers will receive superior value while our employees and business partners will share in our success and our stock-holders will receive a sustained superior return on their investment."

General Motors

What is your organisation's purpose? How is it different than other organisations? *Those are the questions a firm's mission statement like the one shown here should answer. Mission statements are meant for multiple audiences, including a company's customers, investors, the general public, and employees. Most firms familiarise their personnel with their mission statements so they know what's expected of them and what they should strive for.*

of its coffee from ethical sources or farmers who grow their coffee responsibly without permanently harming the environment. The company also hopes to combat climate change by encouraging farmers to prevent deforestation through the use of incentive programmes. Starbucks hopes to make 100% of its cups reusable or recyclable by 2015. Also, the company hopes to use their stores to lead volunteer programmes in each store's community.* Finally, goals are set at every level of an organisation. Every member of an organisation—the president of the company, the head of a department, and an operating employee at the lowest level—has a set of goals that he or she hopes to achieve.

The goals developed for these different levels must be consistent. However, it is likely that some conflict will arise. A production department, for example, may have a goal of minimising costs. One way to do this is to produce only one type of product and offer "no frills." Marketing may have a goal of maximising sales. One way to implement this goal is to offer customers a wide range of products and options. As part of goal setting, the manager who is responsible for *both* departments must achieve some sort of balance between conflicting goals. This balancing process is called *optimisation.*

The optimisation of conflicting goals requires insight and ability. Faced with the marketing-versus-production conflict just described, most managers probably would not adopt either viewpoint completely. Instead, they might decide on a reasonably diverse product line offering only the most widely sought-after options. Such a compromise would seem to be best for the whole organisation.

SWOT analysis **SWOT analysis** is the identification and evaluation of a firm's strengths, weaknesses, opportunities, and threats. Strengths and weaknesses are internal factors that affect a company's capabilities. Strengths refer to a firm's favourable characteristics and core competencies. **Core competencies** are approaches and processes that a company performs well that may give it an advantage over its competitors. These core competencies may help the firm attract financial and human resources and be more capable of producing products that better satisfy customers. Weaknesses refer to any internal limitations a company faces in developing or implementing plans. At times, managers have difficulty identifying and understanding the negative effects of weaknesses in their organisations.

> **SWOT analysis** the identification and evaluation of a firm's strengths, weaknesses, opportunities, and threats
> **core competencies** approaches and processes that a company performs well that may give it an advantage over its competitors

External opportunities and threats exist independently of the firm. Opportunities refer to favourable conditions in the environment that could produce rewards for the organisation. That is, opportunities are situations that exist but must be exploited for the firm to benefit from them. Threats, on the other hand, are conditions or barriers that may prevent the firm from reaching its objectives. Opportunities and threats can stem from many sources within the business environment. For example, a competitor's actions, new laws, economic changes, or new technology can be threats. Threats for some firms may be opportunities for others. Examples of strengths, weaknesses, opportunities, and threats are shown in Figure 6.3.

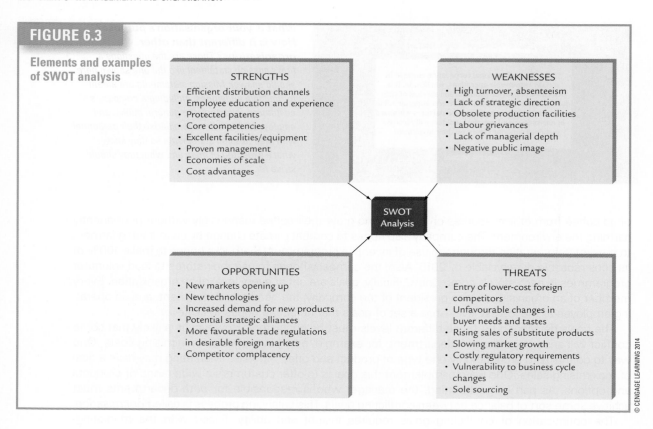

FIGURE 6.3

Elements and examples of SWOT analysis

STRENGTHS
- Efficient distribution channels
- Employee education and experience
- Protected patents
- Core competencies
- Excellent facilities/equipment
- Proven management
- Economies of scale
- Cost advantages

WEAKNESSES
- High turnover, absenteeism
- Lack of strategic direction
- Obsolete production facilities
- Labour grievances
- Lack of managerial depth
- Negative public image

SWOT Analysis

OPPORTUNITIES
- New markets opening up
- New technologies
- Increased demand for new products
- Potential strategic alliances
- More favourable trade regulations in desirable foreign markets
- Competitor complacency

THREATS
- Entry of lower-cost foreign competitors
- Unfavourable changes in buyer needs and tastes
- Rising sales of substitute products
- Slowing market growth
- Costly regulatory requirements
- Vulnerability to business cycle changes
- Sole sourcing

© CENGAGE LEARNING 2014

Types of plans Once goals and objectives have been set for the organisation, managers must develop plans for achieving them. A **plan** is an outline of the actions by which an organisation intends to accomplish its goals and objectives. Just as it has different goals and objectives, the organisation also develops several types of plans, as shown in Figure 6.4.

plan an outline of the actions by which an organisation intends to accomplish its goals and objectives

Resulting from the strategic planning process, an organisation's **strategic plan** is its broadest plan, developed as a guide for major policy setting and decision making. Strategic plans are set by the board of directors and top management and are generally designed to achieve the organisation's long-term goals. Thus, a firm's strategic plan defines what business the company is in or wants to be in and the kind of company it is or wants to be. Gannett, a major publisher of 82 different newspapers, revamped its strategic plan in the face of a prolonged advertising slump. The firm's plan involved increasing sports coverage and revamping its subscriber model in an effort to boost revenues. The new strategic plan recognises that subscribers increasingly obtain their news online in a digital format and implemented an online subscriber system. Customers can read between 5 and 15 articles per month for free, after which they have to pay.*

strategic plan an organisation's broadest plan, developed as a guide for major policy setting and decision making

In addition to strategic plans, most organisations also employ several narrower kinds of plans. A **tactical plan** is a smaller scale plan developed to implement a strategy. Most tactical plans cover a one- to three-year period. If a strategic plan will take five years to complete, the firm may

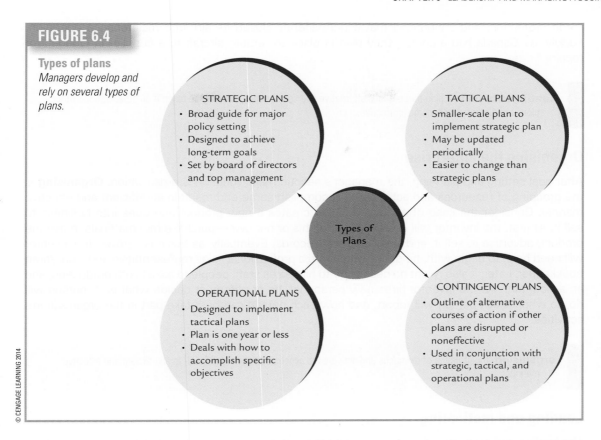

FIGURE 6.4

Types of plans
Managers develop and rely on several types of plans.

Types of Plans

STRATEGIC PLANS
- Broad guide for major policy setting
- Designed to achieve long-term goals
- Set by board of directors and top management

TACTICAL PLANS
- Smaller-scale plan to implement strategic plan
- May be updated periodically
- Easier to change than strategic plans

OPERATIONAL PLANS
- Designed to implement tactical plans
- Plan is one year or less
- Deals with how to accomplish specific objectives

CONTINGENCY PLANS
- Outline of alternative courses of action if other plans are disrupted or noneffective
- Used in conjunction with strategic, tactical, and operational plans

develop five tactical plans, one covering each year. Tactical plans may be updated periodically as dictated by conditions and experience. Their more limited scope permits them to be changed more easily than strategies. IKEA has a tactical plan that involves opening three stores per year in China through 2016. These stores must be located in urban areas near transit, such as train or light rail. Because Chinese infrastructure, income levels, lifestyles, and living spaces all differ from those of its customers in the west, IKEA must utilise a different tactical plan for its Chinese expansion.*

tactical plan a smaller scale plan developed to implement a strategy

An **operational plan** is a type of plan designed to implement tactical plans. Operational plans are usually established for one year or less and deal with how to accomplish the organisation's specific objectives.

operational plan a type of plan designed to implement tactical plans

Regardless of how hard managers try, sometimes business activities do not go as planned. Today, most corporations also develop contingency plans along with strategies, tactical plans, and operational plans. A **contingency plan** is a plan that outlines alternative courses of action that may be taken if an organisation's other plans are disrupted or become ineffective. For instance, Air Canada was forced to enact its contingency plan for servicing aircraft after its normal supplier, Aveos Fleet Performance, suspended operations. Without warning, Aveos locked out 2,300 workers, filed for credit protection, and announced that it permanently closed its airframe maintenance operation. Luckily, Air Canada had a contingency plan in place to reroute aircraft to a supplier in Quebec for repairs.*

> **contingency plan** a plan that outlines alternative courses of action that may be taken if an organisation's other plans are disrupted or become ineffective

Organising the enterprise

After goal setting and planning, the manager's second major function is organisation. **Organising** is the grouping of resources and activities to accomplish some end result in an efficient and effective manner. Consider the case of an inventor who creates a new product and goes into business to sell it. At first, the inventor will do everything on his or her own—purchase raw materials, make the product, advertise it, sell it, and keep business records. Eventually, as business grows, the inventor will need help. To begin with, he or she might hire a professional sales representative and a part-time bookkeeper. Later, it also might be necessary to hire sales staff, people to assist with production, and an accountant. As the inventor hires new personnel, he or she must decide what each person will do, to whom each person will report, and how each person can best take part in the organisation's activities.

> **organising** the grouping of resources and activities to accomplish some end result in an efficient and effective manner

Leading and motivating

The leading and motivating function is concerned with the human resources within an organisation. Specifically, **leading** is the process of influencing people to work toward a common goal. **Motivating** is the process of providing reasons for people to work in the best interests of an organisation. Together, leading and motivating are often referred to as **directing**.

> **leading** the process of influencing people to work toward a common goal
> **motivating** the process of providing reasons for people to work in the best interests of an organisation
> **directing** the combined processes of leading and motivating

We have already noted the importance of an organisation's human resources. Because of this importance, leading and motivating are critical activities. Obviously, different people do things for different reasons—that is, they have different *motivations*. Some are interested primarily in earning as much money as they can. Others may be spurred on by opportunities to get promoted. Part of a manager's job, then, is to determine what factors motivate workers and to try to provide those incentives to encourage effective performance. Jeffrey R. Immelt, GE's chairperson and CEO, has worked to transform GE into a leader in essential themes tied to world development, such as emerging markets, environmental solutions, demographics, and digital connections. He believes in giving freedom to his teams and wants them to come up with their own solutions. However, he does not hesitate to intervene if the situation demands. He believes that a leader's primary role is to teach, and he makes people feel that he is willing to share what he has learned. Immelt also laid the vision for GE's ambitious "ecomagination initiative" and has been named one of the "World's Best CEOs" three times by *Barron's*.* A lot of research has been done on both motivation and leadership. Research on motivation has yielded very useful information. However, research on leadership has been less successful. Despite decades of study, no one has discovered a general set of personal traits or characteristics that makes a good leader. Later in this chapter, we discuss leadership in more detail.

Controlling ongoing activities

Controlling is the process of evaluating and regulating ongoing activities to ensure that goals are achieved. To see how controlling works, consider a rocket launched by NASA to place a satellite in orbit. Do NASA personnel simply fire the rocket and then check back in a few days to find out whether the satellite is in place? Of course not. The rocket is monitored constantly, and its course is regulated and adjusted as needed to get the satellite to its destination.

controlling the process of evaluating and regulating ongoing activities to ensure that goals are achieved

The control function includes three steps (see Figure 6.5). The first is *setting standards* with which performance can be compared. The second is *measuring actual performance* and comparing it with the standard. The third is *taking corrective action* as necessary. Notice that the control function is circular in nature. The steps in the control function must be repeated periodically until the goal is achieved. For example, suppose that Southwest Airlines establishes a goal of increasing profits by 12 per cent. To ensure that this goal is reached, Southwest's management might monitor its profit on a monthly basis. After three months, if profit has increased by 3 per cent, management might be able to assume that plans are going according to schedule. In this case, it is likely that no action will be taken. However, if profit has increased by only 1 per cent after three months, some corrective action is needed to get the firm on track. The particular action that is required depends on the reason for the small increase in profit.

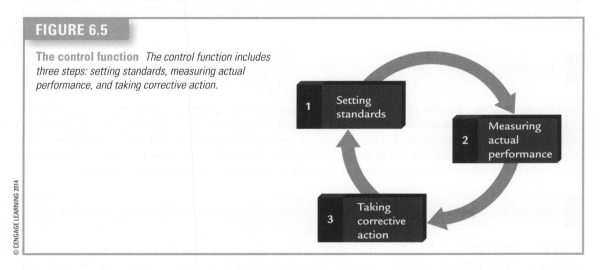

FIGURE 6.5

The control function *The control function includes three steps: setting standards, measuring actual performance, and taking corrective action.*

© CENGAGE LEARNING 2014

KINDS OF MANAGERS

Managers can be classified in two ways: according to their level within an organisation and according to their area of management. In this section, we use both perspectives to explore the various types of managers.

Levels of management

For the moment, think of an organisation as a three-story structure (as illustrated in Figure 6.6). Each story corresponds to one of the three general levels of management: top managers, middle managers, and first-line managers.

Top managers A **top manager** is an upper-level executive who guides and controls an organisation's overall fortunes. Top managers constitute a small group. In terms of planning, they are generally

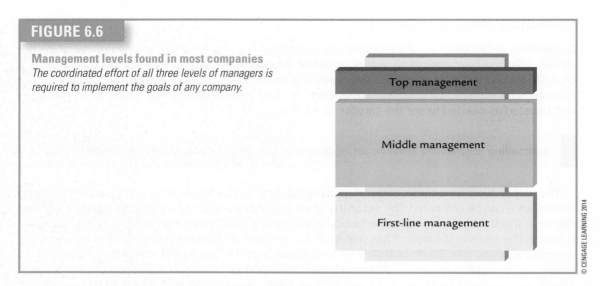

FIGURE 6.6

Management levels found in most companies
The coordinated effort of all three levels of managers is required to implement the goals of any company.

Top management

Middle management

First-line management

© CENGAGE LEARNING 2014

responsible for developing the organisation's mission. They also determine the firm's strategy. It takes years of hard work, long hours, and perseverance, as well as talent and no small share of good luck, to reach the ranks of top management in large companies. Common job titles associated with top managers are president, vice president, chief executive officer (CEO), and chief operating officer (COO).

 top manager an upper-level executive who guides and controls the overall fortunes of an organisation

Middle managers Middle managers probably make up the largest group of managers in most organisations. A **middle manager** is a manager who implements the strategy and major policies developed by top management. Middle managers develop tactical plans and operational plans, and they coordinate and supervise the activities of first-line managers. Titles at the middle-management level include division manager, department head, plant manager, and operations manager.

 middle manager a manager who implements the strategy and major policies developed by top management

First-Line managers A **first-line manager** is a manager who coordinates and supervises the activities of operating employees. First-line managers spend most of their time working with and motivating their employees, answering questions, and solving day-to-day problems. Most first-line managers are former operating employees who, owing to their hard work and potential, were promoted into management. Many of today's middle and top managers began their careers on this first management level. Common titles for first-line managers include office manager, supervisor, and foreman.

 first-line manager a manager who coordinates and supervises the activities of operating employees

Areas of management specialisation

Organisational structure can also be divided into areas of management specialisation (see Figure 6.7). The most common areas are finance, operations, marketing, human resources, and administration. Depending on its mission, goals, and objectives, an organisation may include other areas as well—research and development (R&D), for example.

SUCCESS STORY

Tony Elumelu

Tony Elumelu is regarded by many to be one of the most influential and successful living African businesspeople. In fact, his name often crops up on lists such *Forbes*' "Africa's 20 Most Powerful People in 2012", amongst others. Africa Investor magazine named Elumelu as its "African Business Leader of the Year 2006" and he has received many national honours in recognition of his achievements from his native Nigerian government, including Member of the Order of the Federal Republic, then later Commander of the Order of the Niger, in 2012.

It was Elumelu's successes in the banking industry which arguably brought him to attention on the global stage, first with Nigeria's Standard Trust Bank, which Elumelu transformed, then later, between 2005-2010, with the United Bank for Africa which now services over 7.2 million customers across Africa. Elumelu has long been an ardent supporter of social justice, using his influence to champion and bring attention to many causes, particularly related to Africa's development.

Speaking at a conference in 2011, Elumelu coined the phrase "Africapitalism" in response to the need, in his view, for a long-term financial commitment from the private sector to actively develop and improve the socioeconomic infrastructure of Africa. In other words, private companies have a wider social responsibility beyond generating profits for the owners' and shareholders' financial gain, through contributing to the society in which they operate. He continues to pursue this aim through his Tony Elumelu Foundation, a non-profit organisation.

A keen user of social media, realising its potential as a tool to connect with a wider audience, at time of writing he has over 43,000 followers on Twitter, which he uses as a forum for dialogue on current affairs in the business world.

References: '100 Most Influential People in Africa', *New African*, June 2011; 'Nigeria: Africapitalism', *All Africa*, December 2011; '10 African business leaders to follow on Twitter', *IT News Africa*, October 2013; www.ubagroup.com/group/history, accessed 13th November 2013.

FIGURE 6.7 Areas of management specialisation *Other areas may have to be added, depending on the nature of the firm and the industry.*

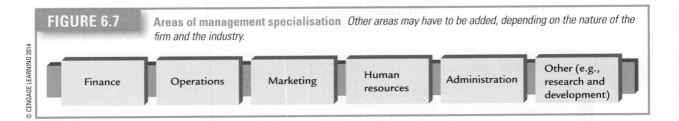

Financial managers A **financial manager** is primarily responsible for an organisation's financial resources. Accounting and investment are specialised areas within financial management. Because financing affects the operation of the entire firm, many of the CEOs and presidents of this country's largest companies are people who got their "basic training" as financial managers.

> **financial manager** a manager who is primarily responsible for an organisation's financial resources

Operations managers An **operations manager** manages the systems that convert resources into goods and services. Traditionally, operations management has been equated with manufacturing—the production of goods. However, in recent years, many of the techniques and procedures of operations management have been applied to the production of services and to a variety of nonbusiness

Harnessing the cooperation of an organisation's specialised managers. Imagine the managers of different departments as a team of horses. If they—and their employees—don't all work together and pull in the same direction, the organisation won't get to the destination it's trying to reach.

© AUREMAR/SHUTTERSTOCK

activities. As with financial management, operations management has produced a large percentage of today's company CEOs and presidents.

 operations manager a manager who manages the systems that convert resources into goods and services

Marketing managers A **marketing manager** is responsible for facilitating the exchange of products between an organisation and its customers or clients. Specific areas within marketing are marketing research, product management, advertising, promotion, sales, and distribution. A sizable number of today's company presidents have risen from the ranks of marketing management.

marketing manager a manager who is responsible for facilitating the exchange of products between an organisation and its customers or clients

Human resources managers A **human resources manager** is charged with managing an organisation's human resources programmes. He or she engages in human resources planning; designs systems for hiring, training, and evaluating the performance of employees; and ensures that the organisation follows government regulations concerning employment practices. Some human resources managers make effective use of technology. For example, more than 1 million job openings are posted on Monster.com, which attracts about 23 million visitors monthly.*

human resources manager a person charged with managing an organisation's human resources programmes

Administrative managers An **administrative manager** (also called a *general manager*) is not associated with any specific functional area but provides overall administrative guidance and leadership. A hospital administrator is an example of an administrative manager. He or she does not specialise in operations, finance, marketing, or human resources management but instead coordinates the activities of specialised managers in all these areas. In many respects, most top managers are really administrative managers.

 administrative manager a manager who is not associated with any specific functional area but who provides overall administrative guidance and leadership

Whatever their level in the organisation and whatever area they specialise in, successful managers generally exhibit certain key skills and are able to play certain managerial roles. However, as we shall see, some skills are likely to be more critical at one level of management than at another.

KEY SKILLS OF SUCCESSFUL MANAGERS

As shown in Figure 6.8, managers need a variety of skills, including conceptual, analytic, interpersonal, technical, and communication skills.

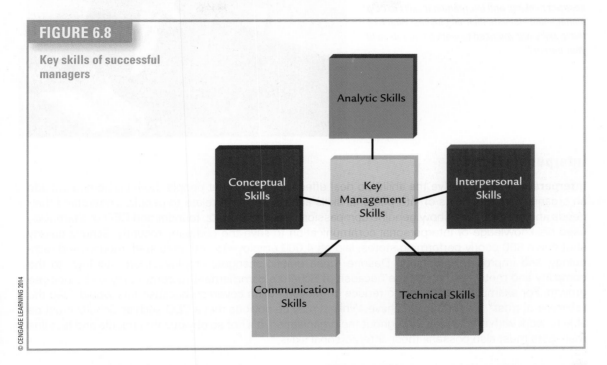

FIGURE 6.8

Key skills of successful managers

© CENGAGE LEARNING 2014

Conceptual skills

Conceptual skills involve the ability to think in abstract terms. Conceptual skills allow a manager to see the "big picture" and understand how the various parts of an organisation or idea can fit together. For example, Jim Whitehurst of Red Hat, an open-source technology company, strongly believes in the advantage offered by conceptual thinkers. He believes that managers should solicit creative ideas from all levels of the organisation in order to help them see the big picture better and to obtain a wide variety of creative viewpoints.* These skills are useful in a wide range of situations, including the optimisation of goals described earlier.

> **conceptual skills** the ability to think in abstract terms

Analytic skills

Employers expect managers to use **analytic skills** to identify problems correctly, generate reasonable alternatives, and select the "best" alternatives to solve problems. Top-level managers especially need these skills because they need to discern the important issues from the less important ones, as well as recognise the underlying reasons for different situations. Managers who use these skills not only address a situation but also correct the initial event or problem that caused it to occur. Thus, these skills are vital to run a business efficiently and logically.

> **analytic skills** the ability to identify problems correctly, generate reasonable alternatives, and select the "best" alternatives to solve problems

How good are your managerial skills?
To be successful, managers must master and simultaneously utilise a number of skills, including: technical skills that aid with specialised work; conceptual skills that foster abstract thinking; and interpersonal skills to help manage and motivate their employees. Which of these skills will you need to work on as you build your career?

Interpersonal skills

Interpersonal skills involve the ability to deal effectively with other people, both inside and outside an organisation. Examples of interpersonal skills are the ability to relate to people, understand their needs and motives, and show genuine compassion. Howard Schultz, founder and CEO of Starbucks, used his knowledge of interpersonal communication to save the company recently. Schultz quickly shut down 800 poorly performing stores, laid off 4,000 employees, retrained staff, modernised technology, and improved operations. Despite these drastic changes, employees are still loyal to the company and motivated for change because of Schultz's commitment to community and employee growth. For example, he refused to reduce employee health coverage because this would "sap the reservoir of trust" that employees have. While it may be obvious that a CEO such as Schultz must be able to work with employees throughout the organisation, it's not so obvious that middle and first-line managers must also possess these interpersonal skills.*

 interpersonal skills the ability to deal effectively with other people

Technical skills

Technical skills involve specific skills needed to accomplish a specialised activity. For example, the skills engineers and machinists need to do their jobs are technical skills. First-line managers (and, to a lesser extent, middle managers) need the technical skills relevant to the activities they manage. Although these managers may not perform the technical tasks themselves, they must be able to train subordinates, answer questions, and otherwise provide guidance and direction. A first-line manager in the accounting department of the Hyatt Corporation, for example, must be able to perform computerised accounting transactions and help employees complete the same accounting task. In general, top managers do not rely on technical skills as heavily as managers at other levels. Still, understanding the technical side of a business is an aid to effective management at every level.

 technical skills specific skills needed to accomplish a specialised activity

Communication skills

Communication skills, both oral and written, involve the ability to speak, listen, and write effectively. Managers need both oral and written communication skills. Because a large part of a manager's day is spent conversing with others, the ability to speak *and* listen is critical. Oral communication skills are used when a manager makes sales presentations, conducts interviews, and holds press conferences.

Written communication skills are important because a manager's ability to prepare letters, e-mails, memos, sales reports, and other written documents may spell the difference between success and failure. Computers, smartphones, and other high-tech devices make communication in today's business world both easier and more complex. To effectively manage an organisation and to stay adequately informed, it is very important that managers understand how to use and maximise the potential of digital communication devices.

communication skills the ability to speak, listen, and write effectively

LEADERSHIP

Leadership has been defined broadly as the ability to influence others. A leader can use his or her power to affect the behaviour of others. Leadership is different from management in that a leader strives for voluntary cooperation, whereas a manager may have to depend on coercion to change employee behaviour.

leadership the ability to influence others

Leaders

The prime responsibility for strategic management and making sure that it works lies at the top of the organisation. The executive and other senior managers must lead the organisation so it will achieve its purpose. Effective strategic leadership is the foundation for successfully using the strategic management process.

Consistency and constancy of purpose, objectives and strategies, at every level and part of the organisation, require forms of strategic leadership that will build and sustain a team effort across the whole organisation. Leadership is the ability of an individual or a group of individuals to influence others to achieve an organisation's purpose and objectives. The nature of leadership varies for different stages of an organisation's development, especially its size, when senior levels of management become more distant from daily management. Also, leadership styles vary according to the personalities and group dynamics of senior managers, and the importance they place on their

Think of a leader you admire—someone in the business world or an entertainer raising awareness for a social cause, for example. Why does this person inspire you or make you want to take action? What can you learn from his or her leadership that will help you become a leader in your life?

A CEO who leads by example. *Bill Gates's leadership style and technological know-how have helped him foster an environment at Microsoft in which top-notch products can be created. Gates's leadership style includes dimensions of both autocratic and participative leadership.*

own personal goals and motivations; this is especially true of chief executives. However, whatever the form and style, strategic leadership should work to promote organisation-wide synergy and harmony.

The popular notion of a leader is of a person who is followed by others. There may be any number of reasons for following, but it is usually because they exercise a power to influence events. In the context of strategic management, a **leader** is one who by influencing others has an ability to take the organisation forward to a common purpose. The most powerful people in an organisation in this sense are, of course, the executives and other senior managers, who make the most important decisions for moving an organisation towards its goals. While the basis for such decisions may emerge and be worked out involving many people throughout the organisation, perhaps after conflict and many compromises, it is only the top managers that, in the end, make the decisions for the organisation as a whole.

> **leader** a person, who by influencing others, has an ability to take the organisation forward to serve a common purpose

Strategic leadership

Strategic leadership is the style and general approach used by a senior management to articulate purpose, objectives and strategy, to influence implementation and execution of these through the organisation. However, at every organisational level there are people with leadership qualities and abilities: for example, individuals who lead units, sections, teams, and those who are specialists in important areas of knowledge and competency. Many of these are **strategic leaders** in the sense that they are located in different parts of the organisation but they use the strategic management process to help achieve the organisation's purpose by influencing and empowering others to create strategic change as necessary. The ability to manage people is central, especially to develop core competences.

> **strategic leadership** the style and general approach used by a senior management to articulate purpose, objectives and strategy, to influence implementation and execution of these through the organisation
> **strategic leaders** leaders who are dispersed across the organisation, who influence and empower others to participate in strategic management

Peter Senge, in an influential book about the learning organisation, argues for dispersed leadership; this is when it is important to enhance the strategic skills and decision-making for managers and employees generally.* The word, leader, in Senge's view is not a synonym for senior management, but a more complex concept that applies to anybody in an organisation who is able to carry out three roles. The first is as a designer of living systems, or in other words, how a leader conditions working behaviour so people will say, 'We did it ourselves?' The second is a teacher role, when the leader enables people to self-develop within a space that is a priority for the organisation. The third role is to be a steward for the larger purpose of the organisation, which a leader uses to bring a depth of meaning to an individual's aspirations. The required skills for strategic leadership involve building shared visions for everybody; this is an ability to bring to the surface and test the mental models people have, or, in other words, the beliefs that people have which underlie their work. Finally, it is also an ability to use systems thinking to see and understand the important organisational inter-dependencies that condition action and relations.

Senge places an emphasis on the reflective nature of good enabling leadership to enhance inter-personal relations. This is present in the work of Goleman and others; they argue that an effective leader must skilfully switch between different leadership styles depending upon the situation they are faced with.* This ability is (at least in part) dependent upon a leader's **emotional intelligence**, the ability to recognise and understand their own emotions and the emotions of others. The attributes that comprise this quality are:

> **emotional intelligence** an individual's ability to recognise their own emotions and those of others, and act to take these into account in relationships

- self-awareness (the ability to articulate openly about feelings);
- self-management (the ability to control and use emotions to good effect);
- social awareness (the ability to empathise with others).

Executive leadership, however, is by its nature remote in the sense that only a small part of a large organisation's staff will have regular contact with top managers. In this case, the appearance of leadership is also important. The political philosopher, Niccolo Machiavelli, writing in the early 16th century, observed that "men in general judge by their eyes rather than by their hands; because everyone is in a position to watch, few are in a position to come in close touch with you. Everyone sees what you appear to be, few experience what you really are".*

The representation of what leaders do, especially in the symbols and artefacts that are associated with them, such as strategic plans, reports, purpose statements, public relations, and so on, can be as important in themselves as signifiers of credibility and legitimacy, as much as they are in practical terms to help a strategic decision or action.

The four competences of leadership

Warren Bennis maintains that leaders display **four competences of leadership**.* The first is management of attention: this is the ability to attract and draw people to them, and hold their attention and inspire them. This is typically associated with charismatic leadership (see below), but in fact the leader can be ordinary and the attraction of the intensity arises from the vision of the leader itself. There is a sense of conviction about what should happen next and that it will happen.

> **four competences of leadership** management of attention; management of meaning; management of trust and management of self

The second is the management of meaning: this is the sense of understanding the underlying patterns that make apparently unrelated elements form a coherent and understandable whole. Followers see the way forward and respond with organised energy and focus. It is not enough to be informed, but it is necessary to use language and visual slogans that communicate clarity. In other words, keep it simple and abstract simply from a complex and messy reality.

The third competency is the management of trust: it means that a leader can be trusted to keep to a constant theme or motif. Leaders, while periodically changing direction as events unfold, must be true to their underlying principles. These may not be articulated, but perhaps conveyed in similar phrases and slogans over again. A constancy of purpose must be felt by others if loyalty is to be maintained over time, or else they will feel betrayed.

The fourth competency is the management of self: leaders know what their abilities are and will not worry about taking decisions and agonising over progress and results. They will reflect just long enough on mistakes to learn from experience, but will move ahead again quickly. This gives confidence to others – it is not the confidence of leaders as such, but the sureness of their bearing and actions.

Transformational and transactional leadership

James McGregor Burns, a political scientist, in his book, *Leadership*, distinguishes between **transformational leadership** and **transactional leadership**.* Transformational leadership is charismatic and inspirational in a way that exploits the motives and higher needs of the follower, so that the 'full person of the follower is engaged'. He suggests that the relations between most leaders and followers are transactional, when leaders approach followers to exchange one thing for another, such as jobs for votes, and bargaining is central to most of the relationships between leaders and the groups and parties that follow them.

> **transformational leadership** charismatic leadership which works to associate individual self-interest with the larger vision of the organisation by inspiring people with a sense of collective vision
> **transactional leadership** centred on mission and explicit management systems, which clarify expectations, agreements, and utilise constructive feedback about performance

Burns' ideas have been used to explain the role of leadership in organisation management in general (notably in Bass*). Transformational leadership is charismatic, and aims to associate individual self-interest with the larger vision of the organisation, by inspiring people with a sense of collective vision. Good transformational leadership creates excitement, raises enthusiasm for challenges that bring about change. Transactional leaders, on the other hand, is more centred on mission and explicit management systems that clarify expectations, agreements, and which provide constructive feedback about performance. Burns was active in American politics and argued for strong leadership, and he favoured a visionary style of leadership.

Charismatic or visionary Leadership

Charismatic or **visionary leadership** is a personalised form of strategic leadership based on a leader's vision about purpose and behaviour of the organisation that helps condition an organisation's culture and strategic management. One of the most renowned examples is that of Henry Ford, who had a clear idea about why he founded his car company. In 1907, two years after the Ford Motor Company was incorporated, he wrote in the company prospectus:

> **charismatic or visionary leadership** a personalised form of strategic leadership based on a leader's vision about purpose and behaviour of the organisation that helps condition an organisation's culture and strategic management

I will build a car for the great multitude. It will be large enough for the family but small enough for the individual to run and care for. It will be constructed of the best materials, by the best men to be hired, after the simplest designs that modern engineering can devise. But it will be low in price so that no man making a good salary will be unable to own one and enjoy with his family the blessing of hours of pleasure in God's great open spaces. *

It would be a few years before this vision produced the Model-T car, and the development of a modern mass production assembly line that made Ford's vision possible.

Sometimes a leader's vision has more to do with values. Richard Branson is never seen wearing a tie and his hair is long; he embodies an unconventionality that is used to colour the Virgin Group's identity. Many of the industries that Virgin has invested in are long-established and the aim of Virgin has been to do things differently, or to challenge the existing rules, to give customers a choice, to be entertaining and "put a thumb in the eye of complacent incumbents". The culture is one of "why not" rather than "why" – an essence that Branson himself seems to personify and which suggests that Virgin competes very differently from its competitors. For example, when the Virgin record label was competing with EMI:

Virgin's studios were more than twice as profitable as those of EMI's, and the reason was not hard to see. At EMI, there was an elaborate system of incentives, with managers setting targets and receiving salaries at the end of the year that reflected how well they had performed against these. At Virgin there was no formal system at all. Yet Virgin was managed more aggressively, and with more concern for the pennies, while at EMI the managers had simply set themselves targets that were low enough to be easily beaten. *

A similar form of leadership is **entrepreneurial leadership**, a style that is associated with small- and medium-sized businesses. This is characterised by the personality, usually of a single owner-manager, or sometimes of a few collaborating individuals, who impose their view on the business in ways that are characteristically innovative. However, it can also be used to describe an innovative leader, often a visionary one, in a large organisation. Both entrepreneurial and visionary leadership have been cited as examples of transformational leadership. Over recent years, these types of leadership have been popularly favoured as the sort of leadership that reflects the pace of change a modern economy requires. However, these styles can encourage a dominating form of managing. This is classically so with smaller enterprises: as businesses grow entrepreneurs need to recruit specialist managers as their lieutenants, but it is often hard for the chief executive to let them get on and do their jobs. A natural entrepreneur typically wants to do everything.

> **entrepreneurial leadership** is characterised by the personality, usually of a single owner-manager, or sometimes of a few collaborating individuals, who impose their view on the business in ways that are characteristically innovative.

The Hopper brothers lament the passing of what they call the "Golden Age of American management", when the chief executive had been a thoughtful listener, who had shared responsibility with the members of his or her team, and was paid only moderately more than them.21 Now, they argue, this collegiate style of leadership has given way to the imperial chief executive. Michael O'Leary, the charismatic chief executive of Ryanair, thinks he can spot the trappings of empire:

The more successful you are, the more likely you are to lose sight of the things that made you successful … Someone wrote a book in the States twenty years ago and said the three things you can always use to tell the time when a company turns from being a success to a failure are when they build a headquarters – the glass palace headquarters office – helicopter outside of it, and the chief executive writes a book. So I think as long as we stay away from all those things, we're fine. *

History is full of examples where belief appears to have achieved the impossible. However, there are also (probably many more) examples to show that the power of will and optimism may be less important than the reality of the adequacy of resources for the task envisaged. All leaders require good subordinates and it seems wise to involve them as much as possible.

Participative or backroom leadership

Participative or backroom leadership is low profile and self-effacing, and aims to involve colleagues in taking and forming decisions on purpose, objectives and strategy; they lead quietly from the backroom, rather than publicly and loudly from the front. In research that paired above and average performing companies, Bill Collins found that the above average performer was associated with leaders who do not force change nor try to directly motivate people, but that instead they stress the importance of understanding an organisation's core values. In this they work to build up a disciplined culture that sustains results over the long term. This does not mean command and control, but it does require people to adhere to a consistent working system:

> **participative or backroom leadership** low profile, self-effacing, and aims to involve colleagues in taking and forming decisions on purpose, objectives and strategy; they lead quietly from the backroom to build up a disciplined sense of core values

... it gives people freedom and responsibility within the framework of that system ... [a disciplined culture] is not just about action. It is about getting disciplined people who engage in disciplined thought and who then take disciplined action.*

This kind of leadership style is low key and does not require great efforts to raise motivation and commitment, particularly if the right thinking people have been put in place.

Clearly, the good-to-great companies did get incredible commitment and alignment – they artfully managed change – but they never really spend much time thinking about it. It was utterly transparent to them. We learned that under the right conditions, the problems of commitment, alignment, motivation, and change just melt away. They largely take care of themselves ... CEOs who personally discipline through sheer force of personality usually fail to produce sustained results ... [leadership is a] quiet, deliberate process of figuring out what needs to be done and simply doing it.*

Table 6.1 summarises the four main leadership styles.

TABLE 6.1	Leadership styles and their characteristics
Transformational leadership	Leaders have a clear view of purpose as a desired future state. They are more concerned with objectives that indicate a broad direction rather than its detail, which is left to others to determine.
Transactional leadership	Leaders have a view of purpose as mission. They are more concerned with objectives linked to a clear programme of change that ensures staff know what is expected of them.
Charismatic or visionary leadership	Leaders embody a strong (often personalised brand) image that is distinctive. They scan opportunities in the external environment and sense purpose, sometimes as entrepreneurial action.
Participative or backroom leadership	Leaders involve others in understanding purpose as core values to share common ways of working (core competences) and participate in setting objectives so that they are more committed to executing them.

Many of the more innovative companies in business today boast a decentralised organisational structure, in which members of staff are awarded a huge degree of autonomy in their day-to-day practices. This can be a very powerful motivating factor, promoting independence and personal responsibility, enhancing sense of self-worth, and fostering a creative environment for developing novel ideas, products or processes. However, this does beg the question of how such a system can be effectively regulated.

What happens if trust is abused as a result of this freedom and who is ultimately accountable when things go wrong or if moral codes are broken? Can the senior management team justifiably claim ignorance of what goes on in the company that they lead? Some recent events that have shocked the world have brought these questions to the fore.

The U.K., for example, has been plagued by a phone-hacking scandal centred around the now defunct *News of the World*, bringing the entire newspaper industry into disrepute. The tabloid newspaper owned by media tycoon Rupert Murdoch's global News Corporation was charged with tapping into the private phone calls of celebrities, politicians and even members of the British royal family. Under pressure to be the first to break stories and "scoop" world exclusives, the paper resorted to illegal security breaches and morally-dubious practices to obtain information. Murdoch argued that, as head of a huge multinational enterprise, he couldn't be held accountable for actions much further down the chain of command. Similarly, the paper chiefs initially used a "rogue reporter" defence, which appeared increasingly disingenuous as the full scale of the operation came to light. Several journalists themselves, no doubt fearing being made into scapegoats, responded that hacking was widespread throughout the paper and the broader industry and that "everyone was doing it". As one reporter put it, "Everyone knew. The office cat knew". At time of writing, court cases are ongoing.

The defences of this scandal are eerily reminiscent of those adopted following the recent economic crisis, when arguably irresponsible trading and reckless investing in the city led to billions of euros being dwindled. Again the blame was placed on junior traders acting alone and going against established practices.

Whatever the truth, in both examples, many critics will reason that there are only two conceivable scenarios, neither of which can be presented in a positive light. Either leaders at a higher level were implicit in these practices (whether through active endorsement or wilful ignorance), or they were dangerously negligent and incompetent of taking close charge of the organisation they were employed to lead.

References: *Strategic Management: Principles and Practice*, 2nd ed., Witcher and Chau (2014); *Organization Theory and Design: An International Perspective*, 2nd ed., Daft, Murphy and Willmott (2014); 'Phone-hacking: how the 'rogue reporter' defence slowly crumbled', *The Guardian*, D. Sabbagh, March 13th, 2012

MANAGERIAL DECISION MAKING

Decision making is the act of choosing one alternative from a set of alternatives.* In ordinary situations, decisions are made casually and informally. We encounter a problem, mull it over, settle on a solution, and go on. Managers, however, require a more systematic method for solving complex problems. As shown in Figure 6.9, managerial decision making involves four steps: (1) identifying the

FIGURE 6.9

Major steps in the managerial decision-making process *Managers require a systematic method for solving problems in a variety of situations.*

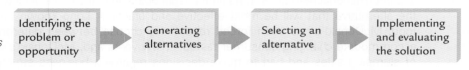

Identifying the problem or opportunity → Generating alternatives → Selecting an alternative → Implementing and evaluating the solution

problem or opportunity, (2) generating alternatives, (3) selecting an alternative, and (4) implementing and evaluating the solution.

 decision making the act of choosing one alternative from a set of alternatives

Identifying the problem or opportunity

A **problem** is the discrepancy between an actual condition and a desired condition—the difference between what is occurring and what one wishes would occur. For example, a marketing manager at an outdoor activities and sports outlet has a problem if sales revenues for its camping equipment are declining (the actual condition). To solve this problem, the marketing manager must take steps to increase sales revenues (desired condition). Most people consider a problem to be "negative"; however, a problem also can be "positive." A positive problem should be viewed as an "opportunity."

 problem the discrepancy between an actual condition and a desired condition

Although accurate identification of a problem is essential before it can be solved or turned into an opportunity, this stage of decision making creates many difficulties for managers. Sometimes managers' preconceptions of the problem prevent them from seeing the actual situation. They produce an answer before the proper question has been asked. In other cases, managers overlook truly significant issues by focusing on unimportant matters. Also, managers may mistakenly analyse problems in terms of symptoms rather than underlying causes.

Effective managers learn to look ahead so that they are prepared when decisions must be made. They clarify situations and examine the causes of problems, asking whether the presence or absence of certain variables alters a situation. Finally, they consider how individual behaviours and values affect the way problems or opportunities are defined.

Generating alternatives

After a problem has been defined, the next task is to generate alternatives. The more important the decision, the more attention must be devoted to this stage. Managers should be open to fresh, innovative ideas as well as obvious answers.

Certain techniques can aid in the generation of creative alternatives. Mind mapping, commonly used in group discussions, encourages participants to produce many new ideas. During mind mapping, other group members are not permitted to criticise or ridicule. Another approach is called "Blast! Then Refine." Group members tackle a recurring problem by erasing all previous solutions and procedures. The group then re-evaluates its original objectives, modifies them if necessary, and devises new solutions. Other techniques—including trial and error—are also useful in this stage of decision making.

Selecting an alternative

Final decisions are influenced by a number of considerations, including financial constraints, human and informational resources, time limits, legal obstacles, and political factors. Managers must select the alternative that will be most effective and practical. Long known for its simple menu of fast food, McDonald's has been forced recently to choose between different alternatives in order to accommodate changing consumer tastes. A few years ago, McDonald's was faced with a problem of slumping sales and had to make decisions regarding business structure and the type of food offerings that would attract customers. Management outlined its alternatives selection in the "Plan to Win," which involved changing the fast food chain's menu to include more salads, smoothies, and other healthier items; as well as acquiring other companies, such as Chipotle, which offers healthy Mexican fast food. Management also implemented a careful leadership succession plan in order to make leadership transfers as smooth as possible.*

At times, two or more alternatives or some combination of alternatives will be equally appropriate. Managers may choose solutions to problems on several levels. The coined word *satisfice* describes solutions that are only adequate and not ideal. When lacking time or information, managers often make decisions that "satisfice." Whenever possible, managers should try to investigate alternatives carefully and select the ideal solution.

Implementing and evaluating the solution

Implementation of a decision requires time, planning, preparation of personnel, and evaluation of results. Managers usually deal with unforeseen consequences even when they have carefully considered the alternatives.

The final step in managerial decision making entails evaluating a decision's effectiveness. If the alternative that was chosen removes the difference between the actual condition and the desired condition, the decision is considered effective. If the problem still exists, managers may select one of the following choices:

- Decide to give the chosen alternative more time to work.
- Adopt a different alternative.
- Start the problem identification process all over again.

Failure to evaluate decisions adequately may have negative consequences. After the recent global financial crisis, stakeholders and regulators spent years debating what happened and how to prevent a similar financial system breakdown in the future. Derivatives were largely blamed for the meltdown. At the time, organisational management, gatekeepers, and regulators all failed to adequately assess the risks of using derivatives. Recently, regulators came together to approve new rules that they hope will reduce the likelihood of widespread derivatives problems in the future.*

MANAGING TOTAL QUALITY

The management of quality is a high priority in some organisations today. Major reasons for a greater focus on quality include foreign competition, more demanding customers, and poor financial performance resulting from reduced market shares and higher costs. Over the last few years, several firms have lost the dominant competitive positions they had held for decades.

Total quality management is a much broader concept than just controlling the quality of the product itself. **Total quality management (TQM)** is the coordination of efforts directed at improving customer satisfaction, increasing employee participation, strengthening supplier partnerships, and facilitating an organisational atmosphere of continuous quality improvement. For TQM programmes to be effective, management must address each of the following components:

> **total quality management (TQM)** the coordination of efforts directed at improving customer satisfaction, increasing employee participation, strengthening supplier partnerships, and facilitating an organisational atmosphere of continuous quality improvement

- *Customer satisfaction.* Ways to improve include producing higher-quality products, providing better customer service, and showing customers that the company cares.
- *Employee participation.* This can be increased by allowing employees to contribute to decisions, develop self-managed work teams, and assume responsibility for improving the quality of their work.

Total quality management accelerates Toyota's competitiveness. Toyota Motor Company worked hard on its image by pioneering the use of total quality management practices. As a part of these practices, Toyota meticulously inspects its products and continuously strives to improve them.

- *Strengthening supplier partnerships.* Developing good working relationships with suppliers can ensure that the right supplies and materials will be delivered on time at lower costs.
- *Continuous quality improvement.* A programme based on continuous improvement has proven to be the most effective long-term approach.

One tool that is used for TQM is called benchmarking. **Benchmarking** is the process of evaluating the products, processes, or management practices of another organisation for the purpose of improving quality. Xerox, for example, "used a study of the London ambulance service to improve its emergency call-out service for its engineers to visit customers."* The focal organisation may be superior in safety, customer service, productivity, innovativeness, or in some other way.

> **benchmarking** a process used to evaluate the products, processes, or management practices of another organisation that is superior in some way in order to improve quality

For example, competitors' products might be disassembled and evaluated, or wage and benefit plans might be surveyed to measure compensation packages against the labour market. The four basic steps of benchmarking are identifying objectives, forming a benchmarking team, collecting data, analysing data, and acting on the results. Best practices may be discovered in any industry or organisation.

Although many factors influence the effectiveness of a TQM programme, two issues are crucial. First, top management must make a strong commitment to a TQM programme by treating quality improvement as a top priority and giving it frequent attention. Firms that establish a TQM programme but then focus on other priorities will find that their quality-improvement initiatives will fail. Second, management must coordinate the specific elements of a TQM programme so that they work in harmony with each other.

Although not all companies have TQM programmes, these programmes provide many benefits. Overall financial benefits include lower operating costs, higher return on sales and on investments, and an improved ability to use premium pricing rather than competitive pricing. Firms that do not implement TQM are sometimes afraid that the costs of doing so will be prohibitive. While implementing TQM can be high initially, the savings from preventing future problems and integrating systems usually make up for the expense. The long-term costs of not implementing TQM can involve damage to a company's reputation and lost productivity and time from fixing mistakes after they have happened.*

SUMMARY

- Define what management is.

Management is the process of coordinating people and other resources to achieve an organisation's goals. Managers are concerned with four types of resources—material, human, financial, and informational.

- Describe the four basic management functions: planning, organising, leading and motivating, and controlling.

Managers perform four basic functions. Management functions do not occur according to some rigid, preset timetable, though. At any time, managers may engage in a number of functions simultaneously. However, each function tends to lead naturally to others. First, managers engage in planning—determining where the firm should be going and how best to get there. One method of planning that can be used is SWOT analysis, which identifies and evaluates a firm's strengths, weaknesses, opportunities, and threats. Three types of plans, from the broadest to the most specific, are strategic plans, tactical plans, and operational plans. Managers also organise resources and activities to accomplish results in an efficient and effective manner, and they lead and motivate others to work in the best interests of the organisation. In addition, managers control ongoing activities to keep the organisation on course. There are three steps in the control function: setting standards, measuring actual performance, and taking corrective action.

- Distinguish among the various kinds of managers in terms of both level and area of management.

Managers—or management positions—may be classified from two different perspectives. From the perspective of level within the organisation, there are top managers, who control the fortunes of the organisation; middle managers, who implement strategies and major policies; and first-line managers, who supervise the activities of operating employees. From the viewpoint of area of management, managers most often deal with the areas of finance, operations, marketing, human resources, and administration.

- Identify the key management skills of successful managers.

Managers need a variety of skills in order to run a successful and efficient business. Conceptual skills are used to think in abstract terms or see the "big picture." Analytic skills are used to identify problems correctly, generate reasonable alternatives, and select the "best" alternatives to solve problems. Interpersonal skills are used to deal effectively with other people, both inside and outside an organisation. Technical skills are needed to accomplish a specialised activity, whether they are used to actually do the task or used to train and assist employees. Communication skills are used to speak, listen, and write effectively.

- Explain the different types of leadership.

Managers' effectiveness often depends on their styles of leadership—that is, their ability to influence others, either formally or informally. Autocratic leaders are very task oriented; they tell their employees exactly what is expected from them and give them specific instructions on how to do their assigned tasks. Participative leaders consult their employees before making decisions and can be classified into three groups: consultative, consensus, and democratic. Entrepreneurial leaders are different depending on their personalities, but they are generally enthusiastic and passionate about their work and tend to take initiative.

- Discuss the steps in the managerial decision-making process.

Decision making, an integral part of a manager's work, is the process of developing a set of possible alternative solutions to a problem and choosing one alternative from among the set. Managerial decision making involves four steps: Managers must accurately identify problems, generate several possible solutions, choose the solution that will be most effective under the circumstances, and implement and evaluate the chosen course of action.

- Describe how organisations benefit from total quality management.

Total quality management (TQM) is the coordination of efforts directed at improving customer satisfaction, increasing employee participation, strengthening supplier partnerships, and facilitating an organisational atmosphere of continuous quality improvement. Another tool used for TQM is benchmarking, which is used to evaluate the products, processes, or management practices of another organisation that is superior in some way in order to improve quality. The five basic steps in benchmarking are identifying objectives, forming a benchmarking team, collecting data, analysing data, and acting on the results. To have an effective TQM programme, top management must make a strong, sustained commitment to the effort and must be able to coordinate all the programme's elements so that they work in harmony. Overall financial benefits of TQM include lower operating costs, higher return on sales and on investment, and an improved ability to use premium pricing rather than competitive pricing.

EXERCISE QUESTIONS

1 Explain how managers coordinate an organisation's resources to achieve the organisation's goals

2 Why is clearly establishing goals and objectives so important to an organization? What are some of the typical factors they take into account?

3 List some of the key skills of a successful manager

4 Define what is meant by "leadership" and explain some of its different types

5 What is "benchmarking" and how is it used as a tool in Total Quality Management?

CASE 6.1

Jack Ma and Alibaba.com

Jack Ma is now the Chairman and CEO of the Alibaba Group of companies with a personal wealth estimated in 2011 to be over $1.5 billion dollars. In the world of business Jack Ma is the epitome of the successful Chinese businessman who has, from nothing, created a major Chinese company. What lies behind his success and what, if anything, can be learned from and applied to other businesses, especially those based in Asia?

Ma was born in Hangzhou, Zhejiang Province, China. He graduated in 1988 with a Bachelor's degree in English having initially failed the entrance exam for the Hangzhou Teachers College on two occasions. From his graduation he followed what could be anticipated as the expected or traditional route and became a lecturer in English and International Trade at the Hangzhou Dianzi University. In 1995 Jack Ma visited the U.S. for the first time. He was able to go on this trip, on behalf of a public body in his province, through his superior skills in English – and it was then that he saw the Internet in operation.

Following on from his trip to the U.S. Ma, in 1995, was behind an Internet business-to-business (B2B) start-up that had to be effectively shut down through the lack of businesses wishing to trade online. The main product of this web business set up by Ma was Haibao.net, which had, as its b2b platform, a product called China Page. This was one of the earliest Internet companies in China – and Jack Ma had invested 20,000 Yuan of his own money in it. At this time Ma experienced very heavy competition for the local B2B market from Hangzhou Telecom and he was eventually forced to co-operate with this local Telecom company and in order to survive he sold different equity stakes in China Page. Subsequently Ma became the minority shareholder in his own business and as a result he decided to withdraw dividing his 21 per cent of shares in China Page amongst the staff who had helped him to start up China Page.

Closely following this Ma was given the opportunity, in 1997, to join the Ministry of Foreign Trade and Economic Cooperation, where he was given responsibility to develop the Ministry's official site for the online trading of Chinese products. Ma was however not willing to settle for the Ministry position and resigned his post in 1999. What the post had given him, though, was further experience in the needs of Chinese businesses wanting to sell their products on the Internet. Ma became convinced that the answer to his need for revenue development was based on helping small-to-medium Chinese businesses get online and trading both with each other and with other businesses outside China.

With a start-up fund of 500,000 Yuan Ma bought the domain name of Alibaba.com and other related domain names e.g. Alibaby.com. To get the site up and running the staff recruited by Ma all worked 16 hours a day sleeping on the floor of Jack Ma's house. The site was in operation by March 1999 and almost immediately started to attract venture capital offers. The key to success for Ma was that he believed that China must have its own mode of Internet and that if Alibaba stuck to providing services for small and medium enterprises then the business would grow as these enterprises grew.

"Those who need our help are not nationally owned business firms – while international corporates don't need us either. We should always help those who need our help," said Jack Ma in 2001. He realised he must "put the customer first".

This focus on the needs of the Chinese business or consumer has seen the Alibaba group of companies grow rapidly since 2001. Alibaba China is now the world's largest online business-to-business marketplace with over 500,000 people visiting the site everyday. Alternatively eBay, Google and Amazon have struggled in the Chinese market through not being able to adjust their U.S. business practices to the needs of a Chinese SME wanting to sell in the world market whether that be in New York or not.

In 2003, Jack Ma, through Alibaba.com, started an auction website, Taobao.com, which made use of an escrow payment system called Alipay which was needed at the time to work with the cash based payment system that was the norm for transactions in China. In 2011 Taobao was ranked the 21st most popular global Web site in terms of traffic by Alexa.com, a subsidiary of Amazon.com, that measures global Internet traffic. Taobao now has a 67 per cent share of the Chinese auction online market and the value of the transactions on the site has reached $1billion.

In recent years Alibaba.com has opened a European office and in Spring 2009 it opened its U.K. office. Ma has not stopped at this and has in 2011 added Alibaba Cloud to the stable of businesses within the Alibaba group. In a shareholders meeting in May 2009 Ma urged those attending to take matters into their own hands. He reminded everyone there that the great fortunes of the world were made by people who saw opportunities that others missed and that the present global recession provided the opportunity for people to take matters into their own hands in the form of starting businesses to cope with the economic downturn rather than waiting for government or businesses to help them.

Questions

1   Do you agree that Jack Ma is a typical entrepreneur?

2   What actions has he done that represent the blend of entrepreneurial characteristics found in the literature profiling entrepreneurs?

3   What is the basic business model of Alibaba.com?

CHAPTER REFERENCES

http://news.alibaba.com/specials/aboutalibaba/aligroup/index.html, accessed October 28, 2013.

Bass, B. M. (1985), *Leadership and Performance Beyond Expectations*, London: Collier Macmillan.

Bennis, W. (1993), *An Invented Life: Reflections on Leadership and Change*, Reading MA: Addison-Wesley.

Bryant, Adam, "The Memo List: Where Everyone Has an Opinion," New York Times, March 10, 2012, www.nytimes.com/2012/03/11/business/jim-whitehurst-of-red-hat-on-merits-of-an-open-culture.html

Burns, J. M. (1978), *Leadership*, New York: Harper & Row.

Chozick, Amy, "Gannet Pushes its Pay Wall Plan to Investors," *New York Times,* February 22, 2012, http://mediadecoder.blogs.nytimes.com/2012/02/22/gannett-pushes-its-pay-wall-plan-to-investors.

Collins, J. (2001), *Good to Great: Why Some Companies Make the Leap ... and Others Don't*, London: Harper-Collins, p. 146, p. 178.

Dubrin, Andrew J., *Leadership: Research Findings, Practice and Skills*, 7th ed. (Mason, OH: South-Western/Cengage Learning, 2013).

"Eli Lilly Made China Pharma Market a Top Priority," *Transmedia.com*, January 1, 2010, http://transmedia-china.com/default.aspx?portalid5442&tabid50&mid55606&ctl5news&iid53561.

Ford, H. (1922), *My Life and Work*, Chapter IV.

http://fastcompany.com/tag/Ecomagination (accessed February 15, 2012); http://ge.com/company/leadership/ceo.html (accessed February 15, 2012).

www.flatworldknowledge.com/pub/1.0/principles-management/32395;www.google.com/intl/en/corporate/culture.html (accessed January 5, 2012).

Goleman, D., Boyatzis, R. and McKee, A. (2002), *Primal Leadership: Realising the Power of Emotional Intelligence*, London.

Griffin, Ricky, *Management*, 11th ed. (Mason, OH: South-Western Cengage, 2012), 7.

Hansegard, Jens, "IKEA Taking China by Storm," *The Wall Street Journal,* March 20, 2012, http://online.wsj.com/article/SB10001424052702304636404577293083481821536.html.

Hopper, K. and Hopper, W. (2009), *The Puritan Gift; Reclaiming the American Dream Amidst Global Financial Chaos*, London: I. B. Tauris & Co.

Isaacson, Walter, "The Real Leadership Lessons of Steve Jobs," *Harvard Business Review,* April 2012, http://hbr.org/2012/04/the-real-leadership-lessons-of-steve-jobs/ar/1.

Jackson, T. (1995), *Virgin King: Inside Richard Branson's Business Empire*, paperback edn, London: Harper-Collins Publishers, p. 295.

Jacobs, Deborah L., "McDonald's Recipe for Success Brought New CEO to the Table," *Forbes,* March 22, 2012, www.forbes.com/sites/deborahljacobs/2012/03/22/mcdonalds-recipe-for-success-brought-new-ceo-to-the-table/.

Kaplan, David A., "The 2011 Business Person of the Year: Howard Schultz, Strong Coffee," *Fortune*, December 12, 2011, pp. 101–116.

http://kwikiblog.blogspot.com/2008/03/korean-management-practices-at-hyundai.html (accessed February 5, 2012).

Machiavelli, N. (1950), *The Price and the Discourses*, New York: Random House, p. 165.

Murray, Martin, "Total Quality Management (TQM)," http://logistics.about.com/od/qualityinthesupplychain/a/TQM.htm (accessed March 23, 2012).

Protess, Ben, "Regulators Approve New Derivatives Rules," *New York Times Dealbook*, March 20, 2012, http://dealbook.nytimes.com/2012/03/20/regulators-approve-new-derivatives-rule.

http://quantcast.com/monster.com (accessed February 14, 2012).

Ruddock, A. (2007), *Michael O'Leary: A Life in Full Flight*, Dublin: Penguin, p. 267.

Senge, P. (1990) (2006: revised edn), *The Fifth Discipline: The Art and Practice of the Learning Organization*, New York: Doubleday.

Staff reporter, "Air Canada Uses Contingency Plan to Service Planes," Reuters, March 21, 2012, www.reuters.com/article/2012/03/21/aircanada-idUSL1E8ELL3F20120321.

Starbucks, http://starbucks.com/about-us/company-information/mission-statement (accessed February 15, 2012); Facebook, http://facebook.com/facebook#!/facebook?v=info (accessed February 15, 2012).

Starbucks, http://starbucks.com/responsibility (accessed February 15, 2012).

Witcher & Chau, *Strategic Management: Principles and Practice*, 2nd edition (2014, Cengage Learning).

7 FLEXIBILITY WITHIN THE ORGANISATION

LEARNING OBJECTIVES

Once you complete this chapter, you should be able to:

- Understand what an organisation is and identify its characteristics
- Explain why job specialisation is important
- Identify the various bases for departmentalisation
- Explain how decentralisation follows from delegation
- Understand how the span of management describes an organisation
- Describe the four basic forms of organisational structure
- Describe the effects of corporate culture
- Understand how committees and task forces are used
- Explain the functions of the informal organisation and the grapevine in a business

BUSINESS FOCUS

Oxfam – a structure for emergent strategy

Oxfam is a well-known international charity engaged in "doing good" around the world, both through routine operations (such as improving fresh-water availability in developing countries) and responding to emergencies such as the Indian Ocean tsunami a few years ago with both physical goods and people; campaigning and lobbying; fundraising and promotion; and running a chain of charity shops and warehouses.

These activities might be (and clearly are) related, but they are different in respect of key success factors, competencies and culture. The challenge is compounded by the fact that Oxfam operates globally – but it is not one single operation. The charity was started in the U.K., in Oxford, in 1942; and whilst the U.K. operation remains substantially the largest, there are now 12 Oxfams around the world. There are national operations in Spain, Germany, Holland, Hong Kong, Australia and the U.S., for example – all "working together" and coordinated from Oxford.

Each national operation has something of a distinctive and preferred modus operandi, or 'way of operating'. For example, the Dutch Oxfam prefers to ally with local partners whilst the U.K. is big enough to deploy its own field workers.

When some new disaster or emergency arises and Oxfam's help is needed, there are a number of things to co-ordinate. The delivery of actual aid to various points of need must be overseen. Staff need to be deployed to those areas where they can be of most help – some quite senior staff have to be available on a flexible basis to travel at short notice. Oxfam's efforts overall must link with parallel work by the United Nations and other aid agencies.

Decision-making must be speedy and to a genuine degree devolved. Moreover it is important that Oxfam is genuinely responsive – its efforts should be targeted at the needs its clients have, rather than in the pursuit of a provider's agenda.

It was clear not very long ago that sometimes the different national operations were working "side-by-side" at least as much as they were behaving as a single operation with joined-up thinking and effort. As a consequence Oxford took on a stronger centralised co-ordination role – helped by (subsidised) investment in new IT systems.

Given the nature of the needs and challenges outlined, to what extent do you think Oxfam should be centralised and to what extent decentralised?

To survive and to grow, all organisations, whether nonprofits such as Oxfam or large multinationals, must constantly look for ways to improve their methods of doing business. Managers at many organisations often have to deliberately reorganise the company to achieve its goals and to create satisfying products that foster long-term customer relationships.

When firms are organised, or reorganised, the focus is sometimes on achieving low operating costs. Other firms, such as audio-visual specialists Bang & Olufsen, emphasise providing high-quality products to ensure customer satisfaction. A firm's organisation influences its performance. Thus, the issue of organisation is important.

We begin this chapter by examining the business organisation—what it is and how it functions in today's business environment. Next, we focus one by one on five characteristics that shape an organisation's structure. We discuss job specialisation within a company, the grouping of jobs into manageable units or departments, the delegation of power from management to workers, the span of management, and establishment of a chain of command. Then we step back for an overall view of organisational structure, describe the effects of corporate culture, and focus in on how committees and task forces are used. Finally, we look at the network of social interactions—the informal organisation—that operates within the formal business structure.

WHAT IS AN ORGANISATION?

We used the term *organisation* throughout the previous chapter without really defining it mainly because its everyday meaning is close to its business meaning. Here, however, let us agree that an **organisation** is a group of two or more people working together to achieve a common set of goals. A neighbourhood dry cleaner owned and operated by a husband-and-wife team is an organisation. Fashion retailer H&M and multinational energy company BP, which employ thousands of workers worldwide, are also organisations in the same sense. Although each corporation's organisational structure is more complex than the dry-cleaning establishment, all must be organised to achieve their goals.

organisation a group of two or more people working together to achieve a common set of goals

An inventor who goes into business to produce and market a new invention hires people, decides what each will do, determines who will report to whom, and so on. These activities are the essence of organising, or creating, the organisation. One way to create this "picture" is to create an organisation chart.

Developing organisation charts

An **organisation chart** is a diagram that represents the positions and relationships within an organisation. An example of an organisation chart is shown in Figure 7.1. Each rectangle represents a particular position or person in the organisation. At the top is the president, at the next level are the vice presidents. The solid vertical lines connecting the vice presidents to the president indicate that the vice presidents are in the chain of command. The **chain of command** is the line of authority that extends from the highest to the lowest levels of the organisation. Moreover, each vice president reports directly to the president. Similarly, the plant managers, regional sales managers, and accounting department manager report to the vice presidents. The chain of command can be short or long. A small local restaurant may have a very short chain of command consisting of the owner at the top and employees below. Large multinational corporations, on the other hand, may have very long chains of command. No matter what the length of the chain of command, organisations must make certain that communication along the chain is clear. In the chart, the connections to the directors of legal services, public affairs, and human resources are shown as broken lines; these people are not part of the direct chain of command. Instead, they hold *advisory,* or *staff,* positions. This difference will be examined later in this chapter when we discuss line-and-staff positions.

organisation chart a diagram that represents the positions and relationships within an organisation
chain of command the line of authority that extends from the highest to the lowest levels of an organisation

Most smaller organisations find organisation charts useful. They clarify positions and report relationships for everyone in the organisation, and they help managers to track growth and change in the organisational structure. However, many large organisations, such as Kellogg's and Procter & Gamble, do not maintain complete, detailed charts. There are two reasons for this. First, it is difficult to chart even a few dozen positions accurately, much less the thousands that characterise larger firms. Second, larger organisations are almost always changing parts of their structure. An organisation chart would be outdated before it was completed. However, organisations must exist without a chart in order for the business to be successful. Technology is helping large companies implement up-to-date organisation charts.

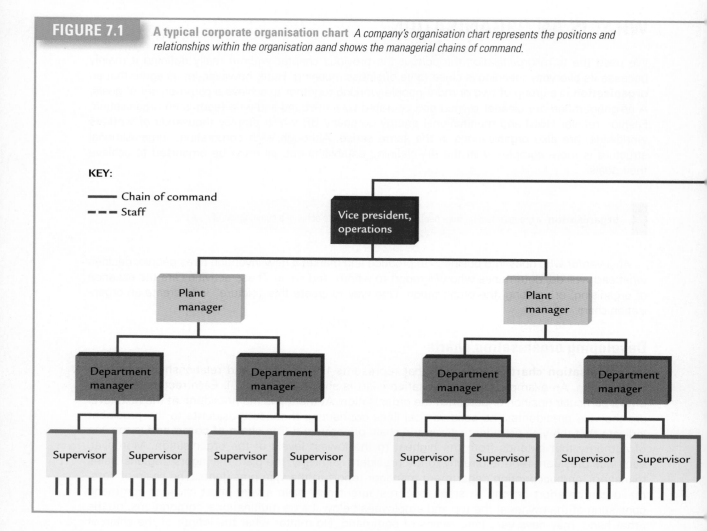

FIGURE 7.1 **A typical corporate organisation chart** *A company's organisation chart represents the positions and relationships within the organisation aand shows the managerial chains of command.*

Major considerations for organising a business

When a firm is started, management must decide how to organise the firm. These decisions focus on job design, departmentalisation, delegation, span of management, and chain of command. In the next several sections, we discuss major issues associated with these dimensions.

JOB DESIGN

In the opening chapter, we defined *specialisation* as the separation of a manufacturing process into distinct tasks and the assignment of different tasks to different people. Here we are extending that concept to *all* the activities performed within an organisation.

Job specialisation

Job specialisation is the separation of all organisational activities into distinct tasks and the assignment of different tasks to different people. Adam Smith, the 18th-century Scottish economist whose theories gave rise to capitalism, was the first to emphasise the power of specialisation in his book, *The Wealth of Nations*. According to Smith, the various tasks in a particular pin factory were arranged so that one worker drew the wire for the pins, another straightened the wire, a third cut it, a fourth

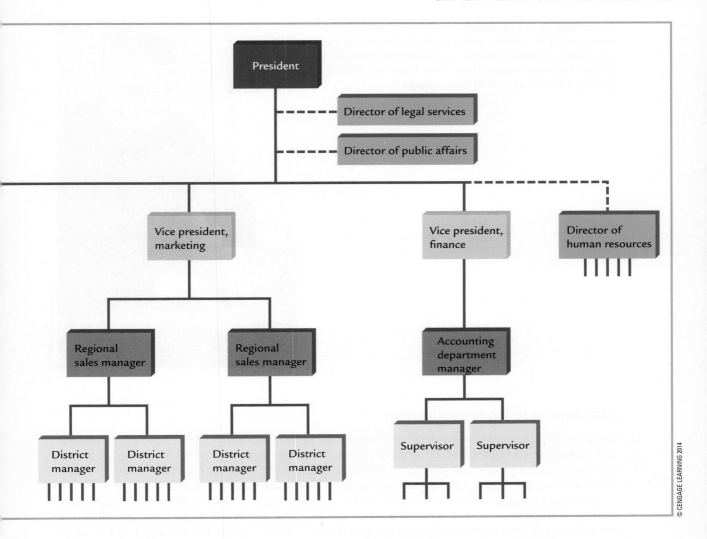

ground the point, and a fifth attached the head. Smith claimed that 10 men were able to produce 48,000 pins per day. Before specialisation, they could produce only 200 pins per day because each worker had to perform all five tasks!

> **job specialisation** the separation of all organisational activities into distinct tasks and the assignment of different tasks to different people

The rationale for specialisation

For a number of reasons, some job specialisation is necessary in every organisation because the "job" of most organisations is too large for one person to handle. In a firm such as Renault or Fiat, thousands of people are needed to manufacture automobiles. Others are needed to sell the cars, control the firm's finances, and so on.

Second, when a worker has to learn one specific, highly specialised task, that individual should be able to learn it very efficiently. Third, a worker repeating the same job does not lose time changing from operations, as the pin workers did when producing complete pins. Fourth, the more specialised the job, the easier it is to design specialised equipment. And finally, the more specialised the job, the easier the job training.

Specialisation has its drawbacks. This employee has a specialised job that includes cutting out leather components that will be used to produce handbags. Specialisation is efficient for the firm, but it can leave employees bored and dissatisfied. What do you think a firm can do to offset these problems?

© OLAF SPELER/SHUTTERSTOCK

Alternatives to job specialisation

Unfortunately, specialisation can have negative consequences as well. The most significant drawback is the boredom and dissatisfaction employees may feel when repeating the same job. Devalued and demotivated employees may be absent from work frequently, may not put much effort into their work, and may even sabotage the company's efforts to produce quality products.

To combat these problems, managers often turn to job rotation. **Job rotation** is the systematic shifting of employees from one job to another. For example, a worker may be assigned a different job every week for a four-week period and then return to the first job in the fifth week. Job rotation provides a variety of tasks so that workers are less likely to become bored and dissatisfied. Intel, for instance, offers an internal database of short-term assignments for employees. Job rotation helps workers stay interested in their jobs, develop new skills, and identify new roles where they may like to focus their energies in the future. According to a Society for Human Resource Management survey, 43 per cent of firms offer some sort of cross-training for workers.*

job rotation the systematic shifting of employees from one job to another

Two other approaches—job enlargement and job enrichment—also can provide solutions to the problems caused by job specialisation.

DEPARTMENTALISATION

After jobs are designed, they must be grouped together into "working units," or departments. This process is called *departmentalisation*. More specifically, **departmentalisation** is the process of grouping jobs into manageable units. Several departmentalisation bases are used commonly. In fact, most firms use more than one. Today, the most common bases for organising business into effective departments are by function, by product, by location, and by customer.

departmentalisation the process of grouping jobs into manageable units

By function

Departmentalisation by function groups jobs that relate to the same organisational activity. Under this scheme, all marketing personnel are grouped together in the marketing department, all production personnel in the production department, and so on.

departmentalisation by function grouping jobs that relate to the same organisational activity

Most smaller and newer organisations departmentalise by function. Supervision is simplified because everyone is involved in the same activities, and coordination is easy. The disadvantages of this method of grouping jobs are that it can lead to slow decision making and that it tends to emphasise the department over the whole organisation, potentially leading to fragmentation and ill feeling between departments.

By product

Departmentalisation by product groups activities related to a particular good or service. This approach is used often by older and larger firms that produce and sell a variety of products. Each department handles its own marketing, production, financial management, and human resources activities.

departmentalisation by product grouping activities related to a particular product or service

Departmentalisation by product makes decision making easier and provides for the integration of all activities associated with each product. However, it causes some duplication of specialised activities—such as finance—from department to department. Moreover, the emphasis is placed on the product rather than on the whole organisation.

How is your institution organised? Call centre employees are organised by their function. Some businesses are organised by more than their functions, though. For example, if your university has more than one campus, they are organised by location but also by function such as by their business, social sciences, and maths departments. Your school also might be organised by customer such as by undergraduate, graduate, and continuing education students.

© ANTONIO GUILLEM / SHUTTERSTOCK

By location

Departmentalisation by location groups activities according to the defined geographic area in which they are performed. Departmental areas may range from whole countries (for international firms) to regions within countries (for national firms) to areas of several city blocks (for police departments organised into precincts), or counties and boroughs for local governments. Departmentalisation by location allows the organisation to respond readily to the unique demands or requirements of different locations. Nevertheless, a large administrative staff and an elaborate control system may be needed to coordinate operations in many locations.

departmentalisation by location grouping activities according to the defined geographic area in which they are performed

By customer

Departmentalisation by customer groups activities according to the needs of various customer populations. A local Toyota dealership, for example, may have one sales staff to deal with individual consumers and a different sales staff to work with corporate fleet buyers. The obvious advantage of this approach is that it allows the firm to deal efficiently with unique customers or customer groups. The biggest drawback is that a larger-than-usual administrative staff is needed.

departmentalisation by customer grouping activities according to the needs of various customer populations

Combinations of bases

Many organisations use more than one of these departmentalisation bases. PepsiCo, for instance, is divided by product and location. It has product divisions such as Beverages, Frito-Lay, Quaker, and Latin American Foods, as well as divisions based on location such as Asia, Europe, the Middle East, and Africa.*

Take a moment to examine Figure 7.2. Notice that departmentalisation by customer is used to organise Bushveld Fashions, Inc., into three major divisions: men's, women's, and children's clothing.

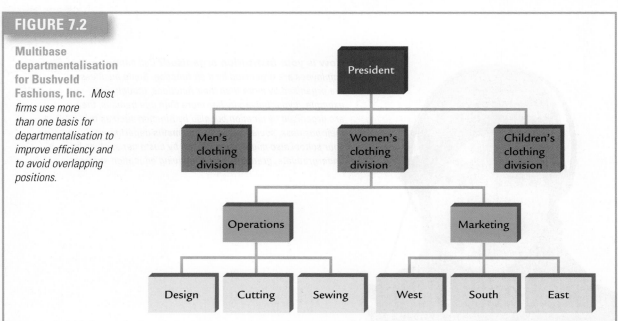

FIGURE 7.2

Multibase departmentalisation for Bushveld Fashions, Inc. *Most firms use more than one basis for departmentalisation to improve efficiency and to avoid overlapping positions.*

© CENGAGE LEARNING 2014

Then functional departmentalisation is used to distinguish the firm's production and marketing activities. Finally, location is used to organise the firm's marketing efforts.

DELEGATION, DECENTRALISATION, AND CENTRALISATION

The third major step in the organising process is to distribute power in the organisation. **Delegation** assigns part of a manager's work and power to other workers. The degree of centralisation or decentralisation of authority is determined by the overall pattern of delegation within the organisation.

> **delegation** assigning part of a manager's work and power to other workers

Delegation of authority

Because no manager can do everything, delegation is vital to completion of a manager's work. Delegation is also important in developing the skills and abilities of subordinates. It allows those who are being groomed for higher-level positions to play increasingly important roles in decision making.

SUCCESS STORY

W. L. Gore & Associates

W.L. Gore & Associates, Inc. is still run in the same way as its founder, Bill Gore (who died in 1986), intended. Employees are called associates, and one of the key tenets of the business is that associates decided what they want to do and where they can contribute. Bosses are not appointed or promoted specifically, but associates work with "leaders" who emerge organically.

What is most surprising is that this successful business strategy works with such a large company – over 9,000 associates in 45 worldwide locations. This is because the plants area purposefully kept small (with a maximum of 200 people) to keep a familial atmosphere.

One of the best examples of the successes of this system is Jack Dougherty, who started his career at W.L. Gore & Associates five years before becoming responsible for the marketing and advertising in the fabrics group. When Dougherty began, he reported to Bill Gore, who told him, "Why don't you find something you'd like to do". After talking to various managers, Dougherty became attracted to a new product called Gore-Tex, a membrane that was waterproof but breathable when bonded to fabric. His career at W.L Gore & Associates had begun.

The success of this company has been recognised. It was named several times as one of Fortune magazine's "100 Best Companies to Work For in America". In 2009 it was listed twelfth on the "50 Best Large Workplaces in Europe" list, and in 2012, in the top ten workplaces in the world named by the Great Place to Work Institute. The company was featured in Malcolm Gladwell's famous book *The Tipping Point*, to illustrate how small sized plants and mutual familiarity make for positive and efficient working teams. Gore continues to grow and prosper.

References: Daft, Murphy, Willmott (2014), *Organization Theory and Design* (2nd ed.); Malcolm Gladwell (2000), *The Tipping Point: How Little Things Can Make a Big Difference*, New York, Little Brown. Press Association, 14 November, 2012, 'Great Place to Work Unveils World's Best Multinational Workplaces', Gary Hamel; March 18, 2010, 'W.L. Gore: Lessons from a Management Revolutionary', *Wall Street Journal*.

© COSMIN MUNTEANU / SHUTTERSTOCK

Delegate, delegate, delegate. *The industrialist Andrew Carnegie once said, "No person will make a great business who wants to do it all himself or get all the credit." Delegating gives employees different tasks to do, which can enrich and enlarge their jobs. It also enables both employees and their superiors to learn new skills required for higher-level positions.*

Steps in delegation The delegation process generally involves three steps (see Figure 7.3). First, the manager must *assign responsibility*. **Responsibility** is the duty to do a job or perform a task. In most job settings, a manager simply gives the worker a job to do. Typical job assignments might range from having a worker prepare a report on the status of a new quality control programme to placing the person in charge of a task force. Second, the manager must *grant authority*. **Authority** is the power, within the organisation, to accomplish an assigned job or task. This might include the power to obtain specific information, order supplies, authorise relevant expenditures, or make certain decisions. Finally, the manager must *create accountability*. **Accountability** is the obligation of a worker to accomplish an assigned job or task.

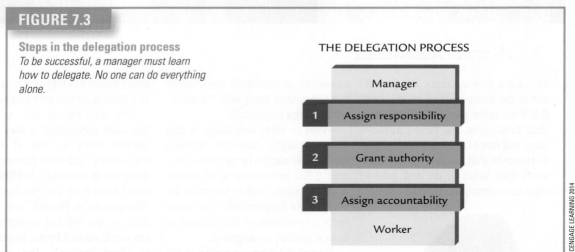

FIGURE 7.3

Steps in the delegation process
To be successful, a manager must learn how to delegate. No one can do everything alone.

THE DELEGATION PROCESS

Manager

1 Assign responsibility

2 Grant authority

3 Assign accountability

Worker

responsibility the duty to do a job or perform a task
authority the power, within an organisation, to accomplish an assigned job or task
accountability the obligation of a worker to accomplish an assigned job or task

Note that accountability is created, but it cannot be delegated. Suppose that you are an operations manager for Target and are responsible for performing a specific task. You, in turn, delegate this task to someone else. You nonetheless remain accountable to your immediate supervisor for getting the task done properly. If the other person fails to complete the assignment, you—not the person to whom you delegated the task—will be held accountable.

Barriers to delegation For several reasons, managers may be unwilling to delegate work. Many managers are reluctant to delegate because they want to be sure that the work gets done. Another reason for reluctance stems from the opposite situation. The manager fears that the worker will do the work well and attract the approving notice of higher-level managers. Finally, some managers do not delegate because they are so disorganised that they simply are not able to plan and assign work effectively.

Decentralisation of authority

The pattern of delegation throughout an organisation determines the extent to which that organisation is decentralised or centralised. In a **decentralised organisation**, management consciously attempts to spread authority widely across various organisation levels. A **centralised organisation**, on the other hand, systematically works to concentrate authority at the upper levels. For example, many publishers of university textbooks are centralised organisations, with authority concentrated at the top. Large organisations may have characteristics of both decentralised and centralised organisations.

> **decentralised organisation** an organisation in which management consciously attempts to spread authority widely in the lower levels of the organisation
>
> **centralised organisation** an organisation that systematically works to concentrate authority at the upper levels of the organisation

A number of factors can influence the extent to which a firm is decentralised. One is the external environment in which the firm operates. The more complex and unpredictable this environment, the more likely it is that top management will let lower-level managers make important decisions. After all, lower-level managers are closer to the problems. Another factor is the nature of the decision itself. The riskier or more important the decision, the greater is the tendency to centralise decision making. A third factor is the abilities of lower-level managers. If these managers do not have strong decision-making skills, top managers will be reluctant to decentralise. And, in contrast, strong lower-level decision-making skills encourage decentralisation. Finally, a firm that traditionally has practiced centralisation or decentralisation is likely to maintain that posture in the future.

In principle, neither decentralisation nor centralisation is right or wrong. What works for one organisation may or may not work for another. The U.K. National Health Service needs decentralisation because of its sheer size; charity Oxfam, meanwhile, needed centralisation to achieve a co-ordinated effort.* Every organisation must assess its own situation and then choose the level of centralisation or decentralisation that will work best.

THE SPAN OF MANAGEMENT

The fourth major step in organising business is establishing the **span of management** (or **span of control**), which is the number of workers who report directly to one manager. For hundreds of years, theorists have searched for an ideal span of management. When it became apparent that there is no perfect number of subordinates for a manager to supervise, they turned their attention to the general issue of whether the span should be wide or narrow. This issue is complicated because the span of management may change by department within the same organisation. A highly mechanised factory where all operations are standardised may allow for a fairly wide span of management. An advertising agency, where new problems and opportunities arise every day and where teamwork is a constant necessity, will have a much narrower span of management.

> **span of management** (or **span of control**) the number of workers who report directly to one manager

Wide and narrow spans of management

A *wide* span of management exists when a manager has a larger number of subordinates. A *narrow* span exists when the manager has only a few subordinates. Several factors determine the span that is better for a particular manager (see Figure 7.4). Generally, the span of control may be wide when (1) the manager and the subordinates are very competent, (2) the organisation has a well-established set of standard operating procedures, and (3) few new problems are expected to arise. The span should be narrow when (1) workers are physically located far from one another, (2) the manager has much work to do in addition to supervising workers, (3) a great deal of interaction is required between supervisor and workers, and (4) new problems arise frequently.

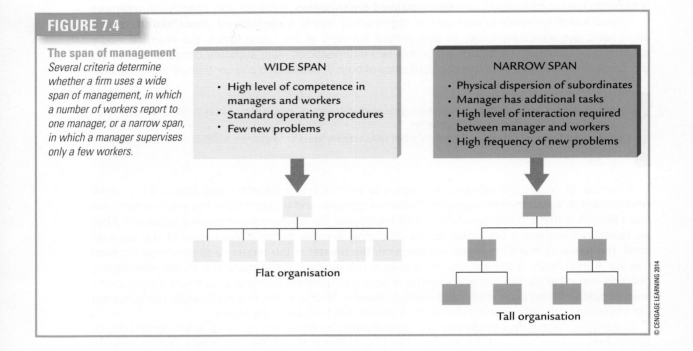

FIGURE 7.4

The span of management
Several criteria determine whether a firm uses a wide span of management, in which a number of workers report to one manager, or a narrow span, in which a manager supervises only a few workers.

WIDE SPAN
- High level of competence in managers and workers
- Standard operating procedures
- Few new problems

Flat organisation

NARROW SPAN
- Physical dispersion of subordinates
- Manager has additional tasks
- High level of interaction required between manager and workers
- High frequency of new problems

Tall organisation

© CENGAGE LEARNING 2014

Organisational height

The span of management has an obvious impact on relations between managers and workers. It has a more subtle but equally important impact on the height of the organisation. **Organisational height** is the number of layers, or levels, of management in a firm. The span of management plays a direct role in determining the height of the organisation (see Figure 7.4). If spans of management are wider, fewer levels are needed, and the organisation is *flat*. If spans of management generally are narrow, more levels are needed, and the resulting organisation is *tall*.

 organisational height the number of layers, or levels, of management in a firm

In a taller organisation, administrative costs are higher because more managers are needed. Communication among levels may become distorted because information has to pass up and down through more people. When companies are cutting costs, one option is to decrease organisational height in order to reduce related administrative expenses. For example, when cosmetics provider Avon experienced declining sales, the company began a series of long and extensive restructuring programmes. The programmes focused on increasing efficiency and organisational effectiveness. The restructuring programme is expected to save the company an estimated $200 million per year upon full implementation.* Although flat organisations avoid these problems, their managers may perform more administrative duties simply because there are fewer managers. Wide spans of management also may require managers to spend considerably more time supervising and working with subordinates.

FORMS OF ORGANISATIONAL STRUCTURE

Up to this point, we have focused our attention on the major characteristics of organisational structure. In many ways, this is like discussing the parts of a jigsaw puzzle one by one. It is now time to put the puzzle together. In particular, we discuss four basic forms of organisational structure: line, line-and-staff, matrix, and network.

The line structure

The simplest and oldest form of organisational structure is the **line structure**, in which the chain of command goes directly from person to person throughout the organisation. Thus, a straight line could be drawn down through the levels of management, from the chief executive down to the lowest level in the organisation. In a small retail store, for example, an hourly employee might report to an assistant manager, who reports to a store manager, who reports to the owner.

line structure an organisational structure in which the chain of command goes directly from person to person throughout the organisation

Managers within a line structure, called **line managers**, make decisions and give orders to subordinates to achieve the organisation's goals. A line structure's simplicity and clear chain of command allow line managers to make decisions quickly with direct accountability because the decision-maker only has one supervisor to report to.

line manager a position in which a person makes decisions and gives orders to subordinates to achieve the organisation's goals

The downside of a line structure, however, is that line managers are responsible for many activities, and therefore must have a wide range of knowledge about all of them. While this may not be a problem for small organisations with a lower volume of activities, in a larger organisation, activities become more numerous and complex, thus making it more difficult for line managers to fully understand what they are in charge of. Therefore, line managers in a larger organisation would have a hard time making an educated decision without expert advice from outside sources. As a result, line structures are not very effective in medium- or large-sized organisations, but are very popular in small organisations.

The line-and-staff structure

A **line-and-staff structure** not only utilises the chain of command from a line structure but also provides line managers with specialists, called staff managers. Therefore, this structure works much better for medium- and large-sized organisations than line management alone. **Staff managers** provide support, advice, and expertise to line managers, thus eliminating the previous drawback of line structures. Staff managers are not part of the chain of command like line managers are, but they do have authority over their assistants (see Figure 7.5).

line-and-staff structure an organisational structure that utilises the chain of command from a line structure in combination with the assistance of staff managers
staff manager a position created to provide support, advice, and expertise within an organisation

Both line and staff managers are needed for effective management, but the two positions differ in important ways. The basic difference is in terms of authority. Line managers have *line authority*, which means that they can make decisions and issue directives relating to the organisation's goals. Staff

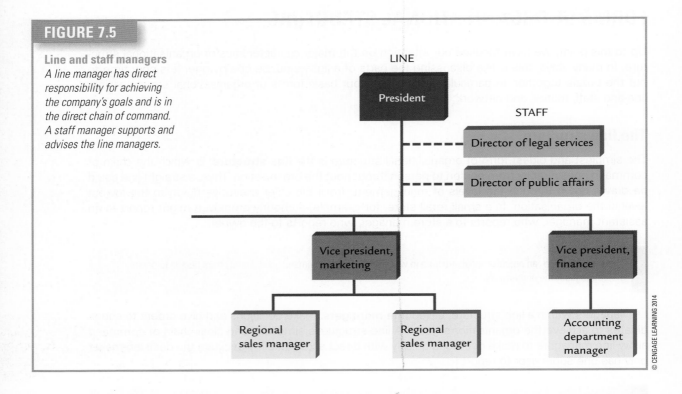

FIGURE 7.5

Line and staff managers
A line manager has direct responsibility for achieving the company's goals and is in the direct chain of command. A staff manager supports and advises the line managers.

© CENGAGE LEARNING 2014

managers seldom have this kind of authority. Instead, they usually have either advisory authority or functional authority. *Advisory authority* is the expectation that line managers will consult the appropriate staff manager when making decisions. Functional authority is stronger. *Functional authority* is the authority of staff managers to make decisions and issue directives about their areas of expertise. For example, a legal adviser for Adidas can decide whether to retain a particular clause in a contract but not product pricing.

Staff managers in a line-and-staff structure tend to have more access to information than line managers. This means that line managers must rely on the staff managers for information. This is usually not an issue, unless the staff manager makes a wrong decision and there is no one else to catch his or her mistake.* For a variety of reasons, conflict between line managers and staff managers is fairly common in business. Staff managers often have more formal education and sometimes are younger (and perhaps more ambitious) than line managers. Line managers may perceive staff managers as a threat to their own authority and thus may resent them. For their part, staff managers may become annoyed or angry if their expert recommendations—for example, in public relations or human resources management—are not adopted by line management.

Fortunately, there are several ways to minimise the likelihood of such conflict. One way is to integrate line and staff managers into one team. Another is to ensure that the areas of responsibility of line and staff managers are clearly defined. Finally, line and staff managers both can be held accountable for the results of their activities.

Line-and-staff organisation structure.
Ronald McDonald occupies a staff position and does not have direct authority over other employees at McDonald's. The other individuals shown here occupy line positions and do have direct authority over some of the other McDonald's employees.

© AP PHOTO

The matrix structure

When the matrix structure is used, individuals report to more than one superior at the same time. The **matrix structure** combines vertical and horizontal lines of authority, which is why it is called a matrix structure. The matrix structure occurs when product departmentalisation is superimposed on a functionally departmentalised organisation. In a matrix organisation, authority flows both down and across.

> **matrix structure** an organisational structure that combines vertical and horizontal lines of authority, usually by superimposing product departmentalisation on a functionally departmentalised organisation

Since information flows are more complicated in a matrix structure, many organisations choose to utilise software and technologies to help them manage information. For instance, Aqayo, a leading producer of recruiting and talent management software and programs, offers features especially for organisations utilising a matrix structure.

Another example of a matrix organisation could be an automobile manufacturer whose company is divided into functional departments, such as production, sales, marketing, distribution, and accounting, which co-manage with product departments (the vehicle models).

To understand the structure of a matrix organisation, consider the usual functional arrangement, with people working in departments such as engineering, finance, and marketing. Now suppose that we assign people from these departments to a special group that is working on a new project as a team—a cross-functional team. A **cross-functional team** consists of individuals with varying specialties, expertise, and skills that are brought together to achieve a common task. Frequently, cross-functional teams are charged with the responsibility of developing new products. The manager in charge of a team is usually called a *project manager.* Any individual who is working with the team reports to *both* the project manager and the individual's superior in the functional department (see Figure 7.6).

FIGURE 7.6

A matrix structure
A matrix is usually the result of combining product departmentalisation with function departmentalisation. It is a complex structure in which employees have more than one supervisor.

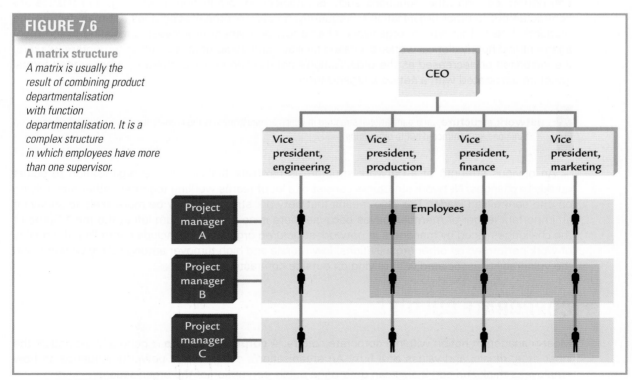

Source: Ricky W. Griffin, *Management,* 11th ed. Copyright © 2012 by South-Western/Cengage Learning, Mason, OH. Adapted with permission.

> **cross-functional team** a team of individuals with varying specialtiaes, expertise, and skills that are brought together to achieve a common task

Cross-functional team projects may be temporary, in which case the team is disbanded once the mission is accomplished, or they may be permanent. GE employs a permanent cross-functional team within its Appliances division, called the Lean Big Room, which works to identify and remove wastefulness from its production processes, while developing exciting new products for the market.*

These teams often are empowered to make major decisions. When a cross-functional team is employed, prospective team members may receive special training because effective teamwork can require different skills. For cross-functional teams to be successful, team members must be given specific information on the job each performs. The team also must develop a sense of cohesiveness and maintain good communications among its members.

Matrix structures offer advantages over other organisational forms. Added flexibility is probably the most obvious advantage. The matrix structure also can increase productivity, raise morale, and nurture creativity and innovation. In addition, employees experience personal development through doing a variety of jobs.

The matrix structure also has disadvantages. Having employees report to more than one supervisor can cause confusion about who is in charge. Like committees, teams may take longer to resolve problems and issues than individuals working alone. Other difficulties include personality clashes, poor communication, undefined individual roles, unclear responsibilities, and finding ways to reward individual and team performance simultaneously. Because more managers and support staff may be needed, a matrix structure may be more expensive to maintain.

The network structure

In a **network structure** (sometimes called a *virtual organisation*), administration is the primary function performed, and other functions such as engineering, production, marketing, and finance are contracted out to other organisations. Frequently, a network organisation does not manufacture the products it sells. This type of organisation has a few permanent employees consisting of top management and hourly clerical workers. Leased facilities and equipment, as well as temporary workers, are increased or decreased as the organisation's needs change. Thus, there is rather limited formal structure associated with a network organisation.

> **network structure** an organisational structure in which administration is the primary function, and most other functions are contracted out to other firms

An obvious strength of a network structure is flexibility that allows the organisation to adjust quickly to changes. Network structures consist of a lot of teams working together, rather than relying on one centralised leader. This also means that network structures may be more likely to survive if an important leader or member leaves because there is no power vacuum left at the top.* Some of the challenges faced by managers in network-structured organisations include controlling the quality of work performed by other organisations, low morale and high turnover among hourly workers, and the vulnerability associated with relying on outside contractors.

CORPORATE CULTURE

Most managers function within a corporate culture. A **corporate culture** is generally defined as the inner rites, rituals, and values of a firm. An organisation's culture has a powerful influence on how employees think and act. It also can determine public perception of the organisation.

> **corporate culture** the inner rites, rituals, heroes, and values of a firm

Corporate culture generally is thought to have a very strong influence on a firm's performance over time. Hence, it is useful to be able to assess a firm's corporate culture. Common indicators include the physical setting (building or office layouts), what the company says about its corporate culture (in advertising or press releases), how the company greets guests (formal or informal reception areas), and how employees spend their time (working alone in an office or working with others).

Goffee and Jones have identified four distinct types of corporate cultures (see Figure 7.7). One is called the *networked culture,* characterised by a base of trust and friendship among employees, a strong commitment to the organisation, and an informal environment. A small nonprofit organisation may seek to build a networked culture where employees look out for each other and believe strongly in the organisational mission. Building a networked culture in such an organisation is important because employees may have to work long hours for little pay, and a strong sense of community and commitment helps to keep productivity high and turnover low.

FIGURE 7.7 **Types of corporate cultures** *Which corporate culture would you choose?*

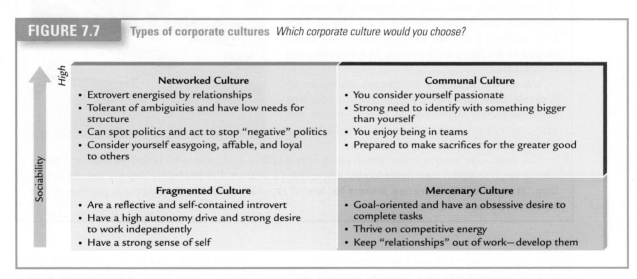

Networked Culture
- Extrovert energised by relationships
- Tolerant of ambiguities and have low needs for structure
- Can spot politics and act to stop "negative" politics
- Consider yourself easygoing, affable, and loyal to others

Communal Culture
- You consider yourself passionate
- Strong need to identify with something bigger than yourself
- You enjoy being in teams
- Prepared to make sacrifices for the greater good

Fragmented Culture
- Are a reflective and self-contained introvert
- Have a high autonomy drive and strong desire to work independently
- Have a strong sense of self

Mercenary Culture
- Goal-oriented and have an obsessive desire to complete tasks
- Thrive on competitive energy
- Keep "relationships" out of work—develop them

Sociability (vertical axis, High)

Source: "Types of Corporate Culture," in Rob Goffee and Gareth Jones, *The Character of a Corporation* (New York: HarperCollins, 1998). Copyright © 1998 by Rob Goffee and Gareth Jones. Permission granted by Rob Goffee and Gareth Jones.

The *mercenary culture* embodies the feelings of passion, energy, sense of purpose, and excitement for one's work. Large banks and investment firms often have mercenary cultures because the environment is fast-paced, the stakes are high, and winning is important. Ever since the global financial crisis set in, many stakeholders internal and external to firms have been calling on the major players of the financial industry to change their excessively mercenary corporate cultures. This kind of culture can be very stressful for an employee with an incompatible personality.* The term *mercenary*

© AP PHOTO/TED S. WARREN

Food and fun are a part of the corporate culture at Google. *This company believes satisfied employees produce the best and most innovative ideas. How would you describe Google's corporate culture in Goffee and Jones's terms—as networked, mercenary, fragmented, or communal? Why?*

RESPONSIBLE PRACTICE Internships—Who benefits?

For many young people, internships are a great way to get work experience. The vast majority of internships are a valuable and helpful method to get training, experience different sectors and departments, and even make useful contacts. But it is important to be aware that internships are supposed to be an education: the company teaching and giving experience in return for the intern's services.

However, there are also concerns that some companies see interns as a source of cheap labour. In the U.K., there is a growing importance placed on interns knowing their rights. Cases such as that of Chris Jarvis, who took an unpaid internship at Sony and who later argued that he should have been paid as a worker, are becoming more widespread in the news as the focus on employee laws is intensified.

The answer to what a prospective intern can do is simple: know their rights. If you have any concerns about an unpaid internship, do some research into your country's employment laws, for example, https://www.gov.uk/employment-rights-for-interns.

© GOLDEN PIXELS LLC / SHUTTERSTOCK

This does raise another issue, which could have negative implications for would-be interns: if savvy interns begin to assert their rights too vocally, is there a chance that employers might in turn be put off from taking on work experience seekers for fear of reprisals, or due to the additional paperwork and bureacracy it will cause them?

does not imply that employees are motivated to work only for the money, but this is part of it. In this culture, employees are very intense, focused, and determined to win. In the *fragmented culture,* employees do not become friends, and they work "at" the organisation, not "for" it. Employees have a high degree of autonomy, flexibility, and equality. The *communal culture* combines the positive traits of the networked culture and the mercenary culture—those of friendship, commitment, high focus on performance, and high energy. People's lives revolve around the product in this culture, and success by anyone in the organisation is celebrated by all.*

Some experts believe that cultural change is needed when a company's environment changes, when the industry becomes more competitive, the company's performance is mediocre, and when the company is growing or is about to become a truly large organisation. An example of a company that some believe is due for a culture change is the investment giant Goldman Sachs. The organisation was placed under scrutiny when a manager at its London office wrote a scathing op-ed piece for *The New York Times,* calling out its highly negative corporate culture.*

Organisations in the future will look quite different. Experts predict that tomorrow's businesses will comprise small, task-oriented work groups, each with control over its own activities. These small groups will be coordinated through an elaborate computer network and held together by a strong corporate culture. Businesses operating in fast-changing industries will require leadership that supports trust and risk taking. Creating a culture of trust in an organisation can lead to increases in growth, profit, productivity, and job satisfaction. A culture of trust can retain the best people, inspire customer loyalty, develop new markets, and increase creativity.

Another area where corporate culture plays a vital role is the integration of two or more companies. Business leaders often cite the role of corporate cultures in the integration process as one

Take the "R" For Tomorrow: *P&G clearly communicates sustainability as part of its corporate culture. The company vision includes goals for packaging, eliminating consumer and manufacturing waste, and resource conservation by 2020.*

of the primary factors affecting the success of a merger or acquisition. Experts note that corporate culture is a way of conducting business both within the company and externally. If two merging companies do not address differences in corporate culture, they are setting themselves up for missed expectations and possibly failure.

COMMITTEES AND TASK FORCES

Today, business firms use several types of committees that affect organisational structure. An **ad hoc committee** is created for a specific short-term purpose, such as reviewing the firm's employee benefits plan. Once its work is finished, the ad hoc committee disbands. A **standing committee** is a relatively permanent committee charged with performing a recurring task. A firm might establish a budget review committee, for example, to review departmental budget requests on an ongoing basis. Finally, a **task force** is a committee established to investigate a major problem or pending decision. A firm contemplating a merger with another company might form a task force to assess the pros and cons of the merger.

> **ad hoc committee** a committee created for a specific short-term purpose
> **standing committee** a relatively permanent committee charged with performing some recurring task
> **task force** a committee established to investigate a major problem or pending decision

Committees offer some advantages over individual action. Their several members are able to bring information and knowledge to the task at hand. Furthermore, committees tend to make more accurate decisions and to transmit their results through the organisation more effectively. However, committee deliberations take longer than individual actions. In addition, unnecessary compromise may take place within the committee, or the opposite may occur, as one person dominates (and thus negates) the committee process.

THE INFORMAL ORGANISATION AND THE GRAPEVINE

So far, we have discussed the organisation as a formal structure consisting of interrelated positions. This is the organisation that is shown on an organisation chart. There is another kind of organisation, however, that does not show up on any chart. We define this **informal organisation** as the pattern of behaviour and interaction that stems from personal rather than official relationships. Firmly embedded within every informal organisation are informal groups and the notorious grapevine.

When you are searching for a new job, look for clues that reveal the inner workings of the firm's corporate culture. You'll want to be in step with the culture, understand what the organisation values, and if those values fit your own.

©.SHOCK/SHUTTERSTOCK

> **informal organisation** the pattern of behaviour and interaction that stems from personal rather than official relationships

An **informal group** is created by the group members themselves to accomplish goals that may or may not be relevant to the organisation. Workers may create an informal group to go bowling, form a union, get a particular manager fired or transferred, or meet for lunch. The group may last for several years or a few hours.

> **informal group** a group created by the members themselves to accomplish goals that may or may not be relevant to an organisation

Informal groups can be powerful forces in organisations. They can restrict output, or they can help managers through tight spots. They can cause disagreement and conflict, or they can help to boost morale and job satisfaction. They can show new people how to contribute to the organisation, or they can help people to get away with substandard performance. Clearly, managers should be aware of these informal groups. Those who make the mistake of fighting the informal organisation have a major obstacle to overcome.

The **grapevine** is the informal communications network within an organisation. It is completely separate from—and sometimes much faster than—the organisation's formal channels of communication. Formal communications usually follow a path that parallels the organisational chain of command. Information can be transmitted through the grapevine in any direction—up, down, diagonally, or horizontally across the organisational structure. Subordinates may pass information to their bosses, an executive may relay something to a maintenance worker, or there may be an exchange of information between people who work in totally unrelated departments. Grapevine information may be concerned with topics ranging from the latest management decisions to gossip.

> **grapevine** the informal communications network within an organisation

How should managers treat the grapevine? Certainly, it would be a mistake to try to eliminate it. People working together, day in and day out, are going to communicate. A more rational approach is to recognise its existence. For example, managers should respond promptly and actively to inaccurate grapevine information to minimise the damage that such misinformation might do. Moreover, the grapevine can come in handy when managers are on the receiving end of important communications from the informal organisation.

SUMMARY

- Understand what an organisation is and identify its characteristics.

An organisation is a group of two or more people working together to achieve a common set of goals. The relationships among positions within an organisation can be illustrated by means of an organisation chart. Five specific characteristics—job design, departmentalisation, delegation, span of management, and chain of command—help to determine what an organisation chart and the organisation itself look like.

- Explain why job specialisation is important.

Job specialisation is the separation of all the activities within an organisation into smaller components and the assignment of those different components to different people. Several factors combine to make specialisation a useful technique for designing jobs, but high levels of specialisation may cause employee dissatisfaction and boredom. One technique for overcoming these problems is job rotation.

- Identify the various bases for departmentalisation.

Departmentalisation is the grouping of jobs into manageable units. Typical bases for departmentalisation are by function, product, location, or customer. Because each of these bases provides particular advantages, most firms—especially larger ones—use a combination of different bases in different organisational situations.

- Explain how decentralisation follows from delegation.

Delegation is the assigning of part of a manager's work to other workers. It involves the following three steps: (1) assigning responsibility, (2) granting authority, and (3) creating accountability. A decentralised firm is one that delegates as much power as possible to people in the lower management levels. In a centralised firm, on the other hand, power is systematically retained at the upper levels.

- Understand how the span of management describes an organisation.

The span of management is the number of workers who report directly to a manager. Spans generally are characterised as wide (many workers per manager) or narrow (few workers per manager). Wide spans generally result in flat organisations (few layers of management); narrow spans generally result in tall organisations (many layers of management).

- Describe the four basic forms of organisational structure.

There are four basic forms of organisational structure. The line structure is the oldest and most simple structure, in which the chain of command goes in a straight line from person to person down through the levels of management. The line-and-staff structure is similar to the line structure, but adds specialists called staff managers to assist the line managers in decision making. The line structure works most efficiently for smaller organisations, whereas the line-and-staff structure is used by medium- and large-sised organisations. The matrix structure may be visualised as product departmentalisation superimposed on functional departmentalisation. With the matrix structure, an employee on a cross-functional team reports to both the project manager and the individual's supervisor in a functional department. In an organisation with a network structure, the primary function performed internally is administration, and other functions are contracted out to other firms.

- Describe the effects of corporate culture.

Corporate culture has both internal and external effects on an organisation. An organisation's culture can influence the way employees think and act, and it can also determine the public's perception of the organisation. Corporate culture can affect a firm's performance over time, either negatively or positively. Creating a culture of trust, for example, can lead to increased growth, profits, productivity, and job satisfaction, while retaining the best employees, inspiring customer loyalty, developing new markets, and increasing creativity. In addition, when two or more companies undergo the integration process, their different or similar corporate cultures can affect the success of a merger or acquisition.

- Understand how committees and task forces are used.

Committees and task forces are used to develop organisational structure within an organisation. An ad hoc committee is created for a specific short-term purpose, whereas a standing committee is relatively permanent. A task force is created to investigate a major problem or pending decision.

- Explain the functions of the informal organisation and the grapevine in a business.

Informal groups are created by group members to accomplish goals that may or may not be relevant to the organisation, and they can be very powerful forces. The grapevine—the informal communications network within an organisation—can be used to transmit information (important or gossip) through an organisation much faster than through the formal communication network. Information transmitted through the grapevine can go in any direction across the organisational structure, skipping up or down levels of management and even across departments.

EXERCISE QUESTIONS

1 Pick a business you are familiar with (for example, your university department) and draw an organisation chart for it.

2 Give definitions and examples of wide and narrow spans of management.

3 Pick a well-known business. Imagine you are the new CEO and are looking to make structural changes. Pick three ways it could be departmentalised, with reasons as to how and why you would do this; and decide which would be the most effective.

4 Use the same business as you did for Question 3. Imagine you are hiring a new employee to work there. This employee seems passionate, team-orientated and loyal. Would this employee fit in well with the corporate culture of your business? Why/ why not?

5 Imagine you are a recently appointed manager. How would you respond to the following pieces on information you hear on the grapevine?

a. The CEO's assistant tells you that over the next few months you and another colleague may be up for the same promotion.

b. In the canteen at lunch, you overhear an employee telling their table that they saw two members of your department arguing outside a restaurant that weekend.

c. One of your employees has been told that she may lose her job soon. You know that this is true, but you also know that this is confidential information.

CASE 7.1

ABB (Asea Brown Boveri)
Barnevik's matrix structure

ABB was formed in 1988 when the Swedish company ASEA merged with Brown Boveri of Switzerland to create a global electrical engineering giant. At the time this was the largest cross-border merger in modern history.

The chief executive who masterminded the merger and consequent restructuring was Percy Barnevik (of ASEA), who realised that he had a major challenge if he was to maintain both drive and dynamism during the integration. He became committed to an individualised matrix structure and his aim was to make ABB the global low-cost competitor. His creation has been declared "the ultimate global organisation" – a decentralised structure with centralised control over information and knowledge development.

Under Barnevik ABB was divided up into 1,300 identifiable companies and 5,000 profit centres. These were aggregated into eight business segments and 59 business areas. There were over 200,000 employees worldwide. The basic structure, therefore, was based on small units (of 50 people each on average) supported by good communications and IT.

Under Barnevik, every employee had a country manager and a business sector manager. Dual responsibilities such as this have often been key issues in matrix structures which failed. However, Barnevik insisted that ABB's version was "loose and decentralised" and that it was easily recognised that the two bosses are rarely of equal status.

The front-line managers, the heads of the 1,300 businesses, were no longer implementers of decisions from the strategic leader; instead they were initiators of entrepreneurial action, creating and chasing new opportunities. The role of middle managers – in this flatter structure – concerned coaching and technology and skill transfer. Strategic leadership was about creating purpose, challenging the status quo and setting stretching, demanding targets for front-line managers; it was not simply, as historically it was, to allocate corporate resources and resolve internal conflicts.

Life – and structure – after Barnevik

In 1997 Barnevik gave up the chief executive role and became non-executive Chairman of ABB. His successor was Göran Lindahl, perceived as more of a detail and less a concept person. Under Lindahl the process of transferring manufacturing to Asia and Eastern Europe from America and Western Europe accelerated. He initially reduced the importance of those executives with geographical responsibilities to focus more emphasis on manufacturing and to iron out some of the complex, dual-reporting issues. But he waited eighteen months before dismantling the matrix structure of his predecessor. He was, however, anxious to retain the learning style and the concentration on small units.

Lindahl decided to take ABB out of capital-intensive and low margin activities, here targeting transportation and power generation. He wanted to focus more on automation businesses. In three years the number of employees would fall from 215,000 to 160,000.

Lindahl resigned in 2000 after initiating these changes of strategic direction. When he left the share price was half the value when he took over. At this time there were four industrial divisions – power transmission; power distribution; building technologies; and automation.

In fairness to Lindahl, some of ABB's markets had been declining and many agreed the company had diversified too quickly and too far. Adverse interest rate movements affected pre-tax profits and an ill-judged acquisition in America left ABB saddled with asbestos liabilities.

Lindahl's successor, Jörgen Centerman opted to restructure ABB again, this time around four consumer segments – utilities; process industries; manufacturing and consumer industries; oil, gas and petrochemicals – and two product segments – power technology and automation technology. It took him just one month to instigate this change. In recent years, sales growth had fallen back and Centerman believed ABB had to focus more on its customers. However he also created a stronger central executive team. The general assumption was that he would focus even more on automation and exit power transmission and distribution.

In November 2001 Barnevik resigned as Chairman, "accepting responsibility for the collapse of the business". The share price was now back to the 1988 merger value. Barnevik was replaced by Jurgen Doorman. He was a "hard-headed numbers man".

When Centerman also left in September 2002, Doorman took over his role as well.

Questions

1 While the idea of a matrix structure is very attractive, it is inherently complex. Why do you think Barnevik's structure was at one time described as the "ultimate global organisation"?

Almost immediately, ABB's financial services business was sold to General Electric and oil and petrochemicals were put up for sale. ABB was to be structured around two core activities: automation technologies and power technologies. There would be twelve business areas. Current staff levels of 150,000 would shrink further. ABB was now a "mid-size engineering group with a lot of debt and a list of disposable assets".

ABB began its recovery in 2003, but it was a dramatically different company from when Asea and Brown Boveri were merged. Fred Kindle (from Sulzer) was appointed in 2004 to succeed Doorman as CEO from 1 January 2005. Doorman would progressively reduce his commitment to the business. There were 115,000 employees and the 2003/4 financial year showed a profit after three consecutive trading losses.

In 2004 ABB announced it was to build the world's largest underwater HVSC power cable link, joining Norway and Holland. The asbestos liabilities were finally settled in 2006. At this time a HVSC link between Finland and Estonia was completed. When the final oil and gas interests were sold in 2008, ABB was "free to focus on power and automation".

Profits exceeded $1 billion in 2007 – although the global economic downturn would follow, ABB appeared to be once more a robust – if different – organisation. But in February 2008 Fred Kindle announced he was leaving – because of "irreconcilable differences about how to lead the company". It was announced that these differences did not relate to strategy or to acquisitions, and they did not imply "problems lurking in the bushes".

2 What is the situation today? Have further strategic changes required more structural changes?

3 How do you think it would feel to work within a structure such as this?

CHAPTER REFERENCES

"Avon Expects Savings and Benefits Approaching $900 Million From Original Restructuring, Product Line Simplification and Strategic Sourcing Programs—Higher Than Anticipated," Avon, news release, February 19, 2009, http://media.avoncompany.com/index.php?s=10922&item=22955.

Craig, Susan and Thomas Jr, Landon, "Public Rebuke of Goldman Culture Opens Debate," *New York Times*, March 14, 2012, http://dealbook.nytimes.com/2012/03/14/public-rebuke-of-culture-at-goldman-opens-debate.

Goffee, Rob and Jones, Gareth, "The Character of a Corporation: How Your Company's Culture Can Make or Break Your Business," *Jones Harper Business*, December 2003, 182.

Griffin, Dana, "Disadvantages of a Line & Staff Organization Structure," *Small Business*, http://smallbusiness.chron.com/disadvantages-line-staff-organization-structure-2762.html (accessed March 21, 2012).

Kotter, John, "Can Your Organization Handle Losing a Leader?" *Forbes*, March 21, 2012, www.forbes.com/sites/johnkotter/2012/03/21/can-your-organization-handle-losing-a-leader/.

PepsiCo Corporate Profile, www.pepsico.com/Investors/Corporate-Profile.html (accessed March 21, 2012).

Schwartz, Nelson D., "Public Exit from Goldman Raises Doubt Over a New Ethic," *New York Times*, March 15, 2012, www.nytimes.com/2012/03/15/business/a-public-exit-from-goldman-sachs-hits-a-wounded-wall-street.html

Thompson, Scott, Martin, *Strategic Management: Awareness and Change*, seventh edition (2014, Cengage Learning), pp. 495-6

Weber, Lauren and Kwoh, Leslie, "Co-Workers Change Places," *Wall Street Journal*, February 21, 2012, http://online.wsj.com/article/SB10001424052970204059804577229123891255472.html.

"Working Together as One," *GE Works*, www.ge-works.com/profile/working-together-as-one/ (accessed March 21, 2012).

8 PRODUCTS AND SERVICES

BUSINESS FOCUS

We're committed to helping you: banks remember customer service

A trend for close to 20 years has been for banks to close rural branches and reduce the number of town-centre branches. Many Victorian banks, with their large chambers, grand facades and prime locations, have been turned into bars or restaurants. TV viewers in the U.K. will have seen a well-known retail bank advertising the last of its branches being turned into wine bars: instead it was decided that branches were to be kept open. A separate advertisement revealed that customers would once again be able to talk directly to staff in their local branch, rather than only to anonymous personnel in a far-flung faceless call centre. In 2010, NatWest went even further, announcing its *Customer Charter* and stating that it intended to be the U.K.'s most helpful bank by 2011, to be verified via independent research, with a focus on in-branch customer service. So, why the about-turn in these policies?

For some time pundits had forecast the demise of the bank branch, as first telephone banking and then the Internet enabled customers to conduct their transactions and make enquiries via telecommunications. The era of the call centre permitted banks to make further cost savings by directing apparently local calls to regional call centres rather than into branches. This also reduced the number of personnel in branches and often removed mortgage, investment and insurance specialists

altogether. In effect, for many customers, this had the impact of further reducing or downgrading the appeal of visiting branches. Mergers and acquisitions in the banking sector have also encouraged a reduction in branch numbers, as newly merged chains close and relocate branches in order to reduce duplication and operating costs. From 1999 to 2003, over 1,700 U.K. bank branches closed.

There is little doubt that telephone, e-banking and now mobile apps have become increasingly popular. Nevertheless, there is talk of an end to the culling of bank branches. This is because marketing research reveals that not all customers wish to deal with call centres or to conduct their business via a PC or smartphone. Many customers find face-to-face contact reassuring, and only the bank branch environment provides this direct interaction.

The role of the branch may be rejuvenated even further. Leading consultants Booz Allen Hamilton produced a report pointedly entitled "Implementing the Customer-centric Bank – the Rebirth of the Forgotten Branch". The report concluded that 90 per cent of customer relationships are made – and lost – in branches. Even customers utilising e-banking often need to visit branches, and the vast majority of customers still believe that complex enquiries or topics perceived as risky by the

consumer are better handled face to face, inside a bank branch. Unfortunately, the removal of specialist staff from many branches and the downgrading of the majority of branches to simple transaction-processing points, have led to a growing level of customer dissatisfaction with bank branches.

Now, in a strategy shift, the leading high-street banking brands are acknowledging that they must reinvest in their bank branches: more and better trained staff, improved IT enabling speedy processing of enquiries and creating more opportunities for the cross-selling of products, plus enhanced interior designs. As part of this shift in emphasis, different staff – with a greater customer orientation – are required. NatWest announced that it planned to invest in additional members of branch staff. Barclays, Santander and the other leading brands quickly followed suit.

While efficiency and reducing operating costs are still important to the boards of these companies, there is an acceptance that customers expect improved service and that many prefer the bank branch as the setting for interactions with, it is hoped, more customer-oriented personnel.

References: NatWest 2003–11; Barclays, 2004–11; 'Back to the branch', *Marketing*, 26 May 2004, pp. 30–2; Fujitsu Services, 2003–8; Box Technologies, 2007; http://www.natwest.com/personal.ashx, 8 March 2011; http://www.natwest.com/global/customer-charter.ashx, March 2011.

We begin this chapter with an overview of operations management—the activities required to produce goods and services that meet the needs of customers. In this section, we also discuss the role of manufacturing in the economy, competition in the global marketplace, and careers in operations management. Next, we describe the conversion process that makes production possible and also note the growing role of services in our economy. Then we examine more closely three important aspects of operations management: developing ideas for new products, planning for production, and effectively controlling operations after production has begun. We close the chapter with a look at the productivity trends and the ways that manufacturing can be improved through the use of technology.

WHAT IS PRODUCTION?

Have you ever wondered where a new pair of Levi's jeans comes from? Or an Apple iPhone, or a Uniroyal tyre for your car? Even factory service on a Hewlett-Packard computer or a Maytag clothes dryer would be impossible if it weren't for the activities described in this chapter. In fact, these products and services and millions of others like them would not exist if it weren't for production activities.

Let's begin this chapter by reviewing what an operating manager does. In the previous chapter, we described an *operations manager* as a person who manages the systems that convert resources into goods and services. This area of management is usually referred to as **operations management,** which consists of all the activities required to produce goods and services.

 operations management all the activities required to produce goods and services

To produce a product or service successfully, a business must perform a number of specific activities. For example, suppose that Audi has an idea for a new, sport version of the A6 that will cost approximately $50,000. Marketing research must determine not only if customers are willing to pay the price for this product but also what special features they want. Then Audi's operations managers must turn the idea into reality.

Audi's managers cannot just push the "start button" and immediately begin producing the new automobile. Production must be planned. As you will see, planning takes place both *before* anything is produced and *during* the production process.

Managers also must concern themselves with the control of operations to ensure that the organisation's goals are achieved. For a product such as the A6, control of operations involves a number of important issues, including product quality, performance standards, the amount of inventory of both raw materials and finished products, and production costs.

We discuss each of the major activities of operations management later in this chapter. First, however, let's take a closer look at manufacturers and how they compete in the global marketplace.

How manufacturers compete in the global marketplace

Whilst U.S. manufacturers largely tended to dominate in terms of productivity in the decades that immediately followed the end of World War II, the playing field has levelled out considerably since the late 1970s. Today's global marketplace is abundant with quality products coming from all reaches of the globe, including Japan, Germany, Korea, Singapore, and the U.K. to name but a few. Increasingly China is at the forefront of several industries, manufacturing everything from sophisticated electronic equipment and automobiles to less expensive everyday items, often at a lower cost than the same goods can be manufactured elsewhere.

The bad news for traditional manufacturers   In recent years, the number of workers employed in the manufacturing sector has decreased in countries that have historically been recognised for their

Why is the product in this photo important? While it may be hard to tell at this stage of production, the product at this work station is one of the most successful products in recent history—the Apple iPhone. On the left, the man in the yellow coat is Apple CEO Tim Cook who is talking with lab technicians that produce the product in this Chinese factory.

manufacturing output. While there are many factors responsible, three major factors explain why employment in this economic sector has declined.

● Many of the manufacturing jobs that were lost were outsourced to low-wage workers in nations where there are few labour and environmental regulations.
● It can cost up to 20% more to manufacture goods in Western countries compared to other regions in the world.
● The number of unemployed factory workers increased during the recent economic crisis because of decreased consumer demand for manufactured goods.

The good news for traditional manufacturers   Nevertheless, the manufacturing sector is still a very important part of many established countries' economies. Although the number of manufacturing jobs has declined, often productivity has increased. At least two very important factors account for increases in productivity: First, innovation—finding a better way to produce products—is the key factor that has enabled domestic manufacturers to compete in the global marketplace. Often, innovation is the result of manufacturers investing money to purchase new, state-of-the-art equipment that helps employees improve productivity. Second, today's workers in the manufacturing sector are highly skilled in order to operate sophisticated equipment. In essence, many manufacturers are making more goods, but with fewer employees.

Even more good news is that many traditional manufacturers that outsourced work to factories in foreign nations are once again beginning to manufacture goods domestically. For our purposes, the term **reshoring** (sometimes referred to as onshoring or insourcing) describes a situation where domestic manufacturers, which had previously decided to move their production to cheaper plants overseas, bring manufacturing jobs back to "home soil". For example, General Electric (GE) opened a new plant in Louisville, Kentucky, to manufacture hybrid electric water heaters in 2012.* Before the Kentucky plant was built, the water heaters were manufactured in China.* Ford, Procter & Gamble, Honda and many other firms are involved in reshoring. The primary reasons why firms are "coming back home" include increasing labour costs in foreign nations, higher shipping costs, significant quality and safety issues, faster product development when goods are produced domestically, and government subsidies to encourage manufactures to produce products at home.

 reshoring a situation in which manufacturers bring manufacturing jobs back to domestic soil

Although there are many challenges facing manufacturers, experts predict that there could be a significant resurgence for manufacturers that can meet current and future challenges. The bottom line: The global marketplace has never been more competitive and successful international firms will focus on the following:

1. Meeting the needs of customers and improving product quality.
2. Motivating employees to cooperate with management and improve productivity.

3. Reducing costs by selecting suppliers that offer higher quality raw materials and components at reasonable prices.
4. Using computer-aided and flexible manufacturing systems that allow a higher degree of customisation.
5. Improving control procedures to help ensure lower manufacturing costs.
6. Using green manufacturing to conserve natural resources and sustain the planet.

For most firms, competing in the global marketplace is not only profitable but also an essential activity that requires the cooperation of everyone within the organisation.

Careers in operations management

Although it is hard to provide information about specific career opportunities in operations management, some generalisations do apply to this management area. First, you must appreciate the manufacturing process and the steps required to produce a product or service. A basic understanding of mass production and the difference between an analytical process and a synthetic process is essential. **Mass production** is a manufacturing process that lowers the cost required to produce a large number of identical or similar products over a long period of time. An **analytical process** breaks raw materials into different component parts. For example, a barrel of crude oil refined by Saudi Aramco (the Saudi Arabian Oil Company) can be broken down into petrol, oil, lubricants, and many other petroleum by-products. A **synthetic process** is just the opposite of the analytical one; it combines raw materials or components to create a finished product. Dyson uses a synthetic process when it combines plastic, steel, and other components to produce a cyclone vacuum cleaner.

> **mass production** a manufacturing process that lowers the cost required to produce a large number of identical or similar products over a long period of time
> **analytical process** a process in operations management in which raw materials are broken into different component parts
> **synthetic process** a process in operations management in which raw materials or components are combined to create a finished product

Once you understand that operations managers are responsible for producing tangible products or services that customers want, you must determine how you fit into the production process. Today's successful operations managers must:

1. Be able to motivate and lead people.
2. Understand how technology can make a manufacturer more productive and efficient.
3. Appreciate the control processes that help lower production costs and improve product quality.
4. Understand the relationship between the customer, the marketing of a product, and the production of a product.

If operations management seems like an area you might be interested in, why not do more career exploration?

THE CONVERSION PROCESS

The purpose of manufacturing or a service business is to provide utility to customers. **Utility** is the ability of a good or service to satisfy a human need. Although there are four types of utilities—form, place, time, and possession—operations management focuses primarily on form utility. **Form utility** is created by people converting raw materials, finances, and information into finished products.

> **utility** the ability of a good or service to satisfy a human need
> **form utility** utility created by people converting raw materials, finances, and information into finished products

But how does the conversion take place? How does a cereal manufacturer convert grain, sugar, salt, and other ingredients; money from previous sales and stockholders' investments; production workers and managers; and economic and marketing forecasts into Frosted Flakes cereal products? How does a financial services provider employ more than 100,000 tax preparers and convert retail locations, computers and software, and advertising and promotion into tax services for its clients. They do so through the use of a conversion process like the one illustrated in Figure 8.1. As indicated by our financial services example, the conversion process can be used to produce services.

FIGURE 8.1

The conversion process *The conversion process converts ideas and resources into useful goods and services. The ability to create ideas and to produce goods and services is a crucial step in the economic development of any nation.*

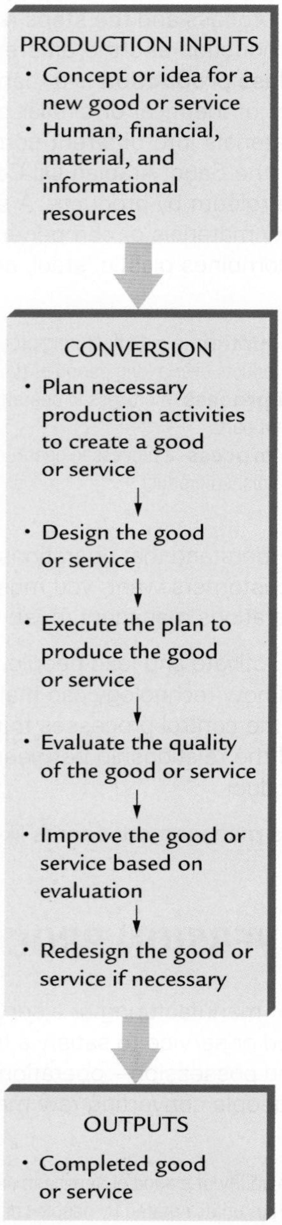

PRODUCTION INPUTS
- Concept or idea for a new good or service
- Human, financial, material, and informational resources

CONVERSION
- Plan necessary production activities to create a good or service
- Design the good or service
- Execute the plan to produce the good or service
- Evaluate the quality of the good or service
- Improve the good or service based on evaluation
- Redesign the good or service if necessary

OUTPUTS
- Completed good or service

Pretty expensive product! *The worker in this photo is creating gold bars. Although the original resource comes from the ground, the final product—100 gram gold bars—is often used by some people as a means of retaining and accumulating wealth—especially when they are concerned about a downturn in the economy or a decline in the value of other investments.*

Factors that affect a conversion process

The conversion of resources into products and services can be described in several ways. We limit our discussion here to three: the focus or major resource used in the conversion process, its magnitude of change, and the number of production processes employed.

Focus   By the *focus* of a conversion process, we mean the resource or resources that make up the major or most important *input*. The resources are financial, material, information, and people. For an institution such as the Central Bank of Kuwait, for example, financial resources are the major resource. A chemical or energy company such as Saudi Basic Industries Corporation concentrates on material resources. Your college or university is concerned primarily with information. And temporary employment services, such as Manpower, focus on the use of human resources.

Magnitude of change   The *magnitude* of a conversion process is the degree to which the resources are physically changed. At one extreme lie such processes as the one by which the Glad Products Company produces Glad® Cling Wrap. Various chemicals in liquid or powder form are combined to produce long, thin sheets of plastic Glad Cling Wrap. Here, the original resources are totally unrecognizable in the finished product. At the other extreme, Ryanair or EasyJet produce no physical change in original resources. The airlines simply provide a service and transport people from one place to another.

Number of production processes   A single firm may employ one production process or many. In general, larger firms that make a variety of products use multiple production processes. For example, GE manufactures some of its own products, buys other merchandise from suppliers, and operates multiple divisions including a finance division, a lighting division, an appliance division, a healthcare division, and other divisions responsible for the products and services that customers associate with the GE name. Smaller firms, by contrast, may use one production process. For example, a manufacturer of one basic product: building materials made from concrete, for instance.

THE INCREASING IMPORTANCE OF SERVICES

The application of the basic principles of operations management to the production of services has coincided with a dramatic growth in the number and diversity of service businesses. In many countries, there has been a shift over the last century as increasingly more workers have been employed in service industries. The economy in countries such as the U.S. and the U.K are characterised as a service economy. A **service economy** is one in which more effort is devoted to the production of services than to the production of goods.

service economy an economy in which more effort is devoted to the production of services than to the production of goods

Planning quality services

Today, the managers of restaurants, laundries, estate agencies, banks, cinemas, airlines, travel agencies, and other service firms have realised that they can benefit from the experience of manufacturers. And while service firms are different from manufacturing firms, both types of businesses must complete many of the same activities in order to be successful. For example, as illustrated in the middle section of Figure 8.1, service businesses must plan, design, execute, evaluate, improve, and redesign their services in order to provide the services that their customers want.

For a service firm, planning often begins with determining who the customer is and what needs the customer has. After customer needs are identified, the next step for successful service firms is to develop a plan that will enable the firm to deliver the services that their customers want or need. For example, a swimming pool repair business must develop a business plan that includes a process for hiring and training qualified employees, obtaining necessary parts and supplies, marketing the firm's services, and creating management and accounting systems to control the firm's activities. Once the firm provides a service to a customer, successful firms evaluate their operating systems and measure customer satisfaction. And if necessary, redesign their operating systems and their services to improve the customer's experience.

Evaluating the quality of a firm's services

The production of services is very different from the production of manufactured goods in the following five ways:

1. When compared to manufactured goods, customers are much more involved in obtaining the service they want or need.
2. Services are consumed immediately and, unalike manufactured goods, cannot be stored. For example, a hair stylist cannot store completed haircuts.
3. Services are provided when and where the customer desires the service. In many cases, customers will not travel as far to obtain a service.
4. Services are usually labour-intensive because the human resource is often the most important resource used in the production of services.
5. Services are intangible, and it is therefore more difficult to evaluate customer satisfaction.*

Although it is often more difficult to measure the customer's level of satisfaction, today's successful service firms work hard to exceed the customer's expectations. To make their guests feel at home, Affinia Hotels has developed a revolutionary new customer service programme that allows guests to customise every aspect of their stay. Using the new online service, guests of this upscale hotel chain can pre-select not only the type of pillow they want, but also amenities including a guitar, golf ball and putter, a fitness kit, or even a rubber ducky to help make their stay perfect and at the same time build repeat business.*

Compared with manufacturers, service firms often listen more carefully to customers and respond more quickly to the market's changing needs. For example, Maggiano's Little Italy restaurant is a chain of eating establishments owned by Brinker International. In order to continuously improve customer service, the restaurant encourages diners to complete online surveys that prompt diners to evaluate the food, atmosphere, service, and other variables. The information from the surveys is then used to fine-tune the way Maggiano's meets its customers' needs.

In addition, many service firms are now using social media to build relationships with their customers. Coldwell Banker, one of the largest real estate companies in the United States sponsors an Internet blog that can be used not only to provide information about the current housing market, but also as a method to encourage comments and questions from customers. And Olive Garden, the restaurant chain owned by the Darden family of restaurants, uses the Internet to provide recipes for many of its menu items so customers can try their hand at creating the "perfect" Italian meal in their own kitchens.

Now that we understand something about the production process that is used to transform resources into goods and services, we can consider three major activities involved in operations management: research and development, planning for production, and operations control.

WHERE DO NEW PRODUCTS AND SERVICES COME FROM?

No firm can produce a product or service until it has an idea. Both Apple's iPad and Ford's Electric Focus automobile began as an idea. Although no one can predict with 100 per cent accuracy what types of products and services will be available in the next five years, it is safe to say that companies will continue to introduce new products and services that will change our everyday lives.

Research and development

How did we get the Apple iPad or the Tesla Roadster electric sportscar? We got them as a result of people working with new ideas that developed into useful products. These activities generally are referred to as research and development. For our purposes, **research and development (R&D)** involves a set of activities intended to identify new ideas that have the potential to result in new goods and services.

> **research and development (R&D)** a set of activities intended to identify new ideas that have the potential to result in new goods and services

Today, business firms use three general types of R&D activities. *Basic research* consists of activities aimed at uncovering new knowledge. The goal of basic research is scientific advancement, without regard for its potential use in the development of goods and services. *Applied research*, in contrast, consists of activities geared toward discovering new knowledge with some potential use. *Development and implementation* involves research activities undertaken specifically to put new or existing knowledge to use in producing goods and services. For many companies, R&D is a very important part of their business operations. The Dyson consumer household appliances company, for example, is known for its development and implementation research activities. The Dyson headquarters in Malmesbury, U.K., is home to a large and dedicated R&D team. In addition, founder James Dyson has also set up a design award across 18 countries and a charitable foundation encouraging and sponsoring young students to study engineering.

Product extension and refinement

When a brand-new product is first marketed, its sales start at zero and slowly increase from that point. If the product is successful, annual sales increase more and more rapidly until they reach some peak. Then, as time passes, annual sales begin to decline, and they continue to decline until it is no longer profitable to manufacture the product. (This rise-and-decline pattern, called the *product life-cycle*, is discussed in more detail later in the text.)

Your idea for a new good or service may be your ticket to a small business of your own, if you have entrepreneurial spirit. But don't forget that big corporations also value people with new product ideas.

Schering GmbH and Company, a subsidiary of Bayer Schering Pharmaceutical, produces over 7 billion tablets and pills each year. While the company already produces over 40 different drug products sold in over 100 countries, research and development is constantly working to identify new products to treat illness and disease.

©MARTIN SCHUTT/DPA/LANDOV

If a firm sells only one product, when that product reaches the end of its life-cycle, the firm will die, too. To stay in business, the firm must, at the very least, find ways to refine or extend the want-satisfying capability of its product. Consider television sets. Since they were introduced in the late 1930s, television sets have been constantly *refined* so that they now provide clearer, sharper pictures with less dial adjusting. During the same time, television sets also were *extended*. There are basic flat-screen televisions without added features, and many others that include DVD or Blu-Ray players and Internet streaming options. The latest development—high-definition television—has already become the standard.

For most firms, extension and refinement are expected results of their research, development, and implementation activities. Each refinement or extension results in an essentially "new" product whose sales make up for the declining sales of a product that was introduced earlier. When consumers were introduced to the original five varieties of Campbell's Soup, they discovered that these soups were of the highest quality, as well as inexpensive, and the soups were an instant success. Although one of the most successful companies at the beginning of the 1900s, Campbell's had to

SUCCESS STORY

Elon Musk

Elon Musk is a classic example of a driven entrepreneur. As a young boy he taught himself computer programming and sold the computer code for a video game at the age of 12. After moving from South Africa to Canada, he received degrees in business and physics.

Musk was aware that he wanted to pursue the Internet, renewable energy and outer space, and so this is exactly what he did. Some of Musk's companies include PayPal, SpaceX, Tesla Motors and SolarCity.

Musk has described himself as a workaholic and admits to putting in huge amounts of hours into running his company. He has made his long-term goal of creating a space-faring civilisation well known; as is his desire to promote renewable energy technologies (he pioneers products such as the electric car, and is rumoured to be working on an electric plane). His "technology billionaire" image may be most familiar as that of the *Iron Man* character Tony Stark, who is said to have been based on Musk.

© TESLA MOTORS

continue to innovate, refine, and extend its product line. For example, many consumers live in what is called an "on-the-go" society. To meet this need, Campbell's Soup has developed ready-to-serve products that can be popped into a microwave at work or school.

HOW DO MANAGERS PLAN PRODUCTION?

Only a few of the many ideas for new products, refinements, and extensions ever reach the production stage. For those ideas that do, however, the next step is planning for production. Once a new idea for a product or service has been identified, planning for production involves three different phases: design planning, facilities planning, and operational planning (see Figure 8.2).

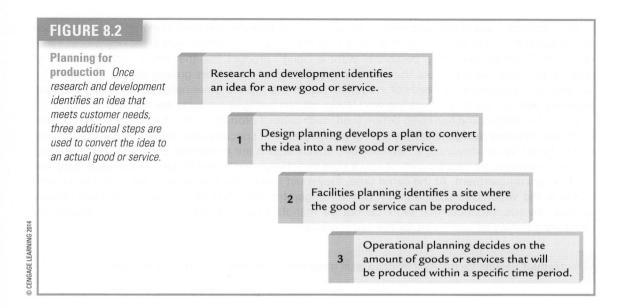

FIGURE 8.2

Planning for production *Once research and development identifies an idea that meets customer needs, three additional steps are used to convert the idea to an actual good or service.*

Research and development identifies an idea for a new good or service.

1   Design planning develops a plan to convert the idea into a new good or service.

2   Facilities planning identifies a site where the good or service can be produced.

3   Operational planning decides on the amount of goods or services that will be produced within a specific time period.

© CENGAGE LEARNING 2014

Design planning

When the R&D staff at Samsung recommended to top management that the firm manufacture and market a "Smart Fridge" with an LCD screen, Wi-Fi connectivity, and apps that allow consumers to update their calendars, leave notes to family members, or listen to music, the company could not simply swing into production the next day. Instead, a great deal of time and energy had to be invested in determining what the new refrigerator would look like, where and how it would be produced, and what options would be included. These decisions are a part of design planning. **Design planning** is the development of a plan for converting an idea into an actual product or service. The major decisions involved in design planning deal with product line, required capacity, and use of technology.

> **design planning** the development of a plan for converting an idea into an actual product or service

Product line   A **product line** is a group of similar products that differ only in relatively minor characteristics. During the design-planning stage, a manufacturer like Samsung must determine how many different models to produce and what major options to offer. Likewise, a restaurant chain such as Italian-themed Zizzi's must decide how many menu items to offer.

> **product line** a group of similar products that differ only in relatively minor characteristics

A product that has been around for a long time. *Building on a rich (and profitable) history, Campbell's Soup continues to listen to customers to develop new products and to adapt and to refine existing products to meet customer needs.*

An important issue in deciding on the product line is to balance customer preferences and production requirements. For this reason, marketing managers play an important role in making product-line decisions. Typically, marketing personnel want a "long" product line that offers customers many options. Because a long product line with more options gives customers greater choice, it is easier to sell products that meet the needs of individual customers. On the other hand, production personnel generally want a "short" product line with fewer options because products are easier to produce.

Once the product line has been determined, each distinct product within the product line must be designed. **Product design** is the process of creating a set of specifications from which a product can be produced. When designing a new product, specifications are extremely important. For example, product engineers for Samsung must make sure that their new "Smart Fridge" keeps food frozen in the freezer compartment. At the same time, they must make sure that lettuce and tomatoes do not freeze in the vegetables compartment of the refrigerator. The need for a complete product design is fairly obvious; products that work cannot be manufactured without it. But services should be designed carefully as well—and *for the same reason*.

 product design the process of creating a set of specifications from which a product can be produced

Required production capacity **Capacity** is the amount of products or services that an organisation can produce in a given period of time. (For example, the capacity of a Panasonic assembly plant might be 1.3 million high-definition televisions per year.) Operations managers—again working with the firm's marketing managers—must determine the required capacity. This, in turn, determines the size of the production facility. If the facility is built with too much capacity, valuable resources (plant, equipment, and money) will lie idle. If the facility offers insufficient capacity, additional capacity may have to be added later when it is much more expensive than in the initial building stage.

 capacity the amount of products or services that an organisation can produce in a given time

Capacity means about the same thing to service businesses. For example, the capacity of a restaurant such Le Meurice in Paris, is the number of customers it can serve at one time. As with the Panasonic manufacturing facility described earlier, if the restaurant is built with too much capacity—too many tables and chairs—valuable resources will be wasted. If the restaurant is too small, customers may have to wait for service; if the wait is too long, they may leave and choose another restaurant.

Use of technology During the design-planning stage, management must determine the degree to which *automation* and *technology* will be used to produce a product or service. Here, there is a trade-off between high initial costs and low operating costs (for automation) and low initial costs and high operating costs (for human labour). Ultimately, management must choose between a labour-intensive technology and a capital-intensive technology. A **labour-intensive technology** is a process in which people must do most of the work. Housecleaning services and the Manchester United football team, for example, are labour-intensive. A **capital-intensive technology** is a process in which machines and equipment do most of the work. A Sony automated assembly plant is capital intensive.

> **labour-intensive technology** a process in which people must do most of the work
> **capital-intensive technology** a process in which machines and equipment do most of the work

Site selection and facilities planning

Generally, a business will choose to produce a new product in an existing factory as long as (1) the existing factory has enough capacity to handle customer demand for both the new product and established products and (2) the cost of refurbishing an existing factory is less than the cost of building a new one.

After exploring the capacity of existing factories, management may decide to build a new production facility. In determining where to locate production facilities, management must consider a number of variables, including the following:

- Locations of major customers and suppliers.
- Availability and cost of skilled and unskilled labour.
- Quality of life for employees and management in the proposed location.
- The cost of land and construction to build a new facility.
- Local and regional taxes, environmental regulations, and zoning laws.
- The amount of financial support and subsidies, if any, offered by local and national governments.
- Special requirements, such as great amounts of energy or water used in the production process.

Before making a final decision about where a proposed plant will be located and how it will be organised, two other factors—human resources and plant layout—should be examined.

Human resources Several issues involved in site selection and facilities planning fall within the province of human resources managers. When Nestlé built its new 900,000-square-foot production facility to make liquid Nesquik® and Coffee-Mate® products in Anderson, Indiana, human resources managers were involved to make sure the necessary managers and employees needed to staff the plant were available. And when a company decides to build a new facility in a foreign country, again human resources managers are involved. For example, suppose that a U.K. firm like construction and agricultural machinery manufacturer JCB wants to lower labour costs by importing products from China. It has two choices. It can build its own manufacturing facility in a foreign country or it can outsource production to local firms. In either case, human resources become involved in the decision. If the decision is made to build its own plant, human resources managers will have to recruit managers and employees with the appropriate skills who are willing to relocate to a foreign country, develop training programmes for local Chinese workers, or both. On the other hand, if the decision is made to outsource production to local suppliers, human resources managers must make sure that

©AP PHOTO/MARK HERTZBERG

Ice cream that tastes as good as homemade. *The goal for Roundy's Supermarkets is to make their ice cream taste just like Mum's—but production is on a much larger scale. To accomplish the task, the company uses a stainless steel assembly line that snakes through the company's food manufacturing and processing plant.*

local suppliers are complying with the U.K. company's human rights policies and with all applicable national and local wage and hour laws.

Plant layout **Plant layout** is the arrangement of machinery, equipment, and personnel within a production facility. Three general types of plant layout are used (see Figure 8.3).

plant layout the arrangement of machinery, equipment, and personnel within a production facility

FIGURE 8.3

Facilities planning
The process layout is used when small batches of different products are created or when working on different parts of a product. The product layout (assembly line) is used when all products undergo the same operations in the same sequence. The fixed-position layout is used in producing a product too large to move.

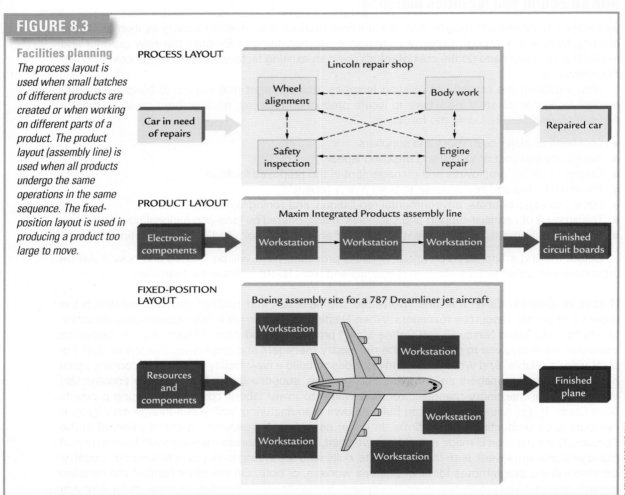

© CENGAGE LEARNING 2014

The *process layout* is used when different operations are required for creating small batches of different products or working on different parts of a product. The plant is arranged so that each operation is performed in its own particular area. An auto repair facility at a local automobile dealership provides an example of a process layout. The various operations may be engine repair, bodywork, wheel alignment, and safety inspection. If you take your Nissan Micra for a wheel alignment, your car "visits" only the area where alignments are performed.

A *product layout* (sometimes referred to as an *assembly line*) is used when all products undergo the same operations in the same sequence. Workstations are arranged to match the sequence of operations, and work flows from station to station. An assembly line is the best example of a product layout. For example, Maxim Integrated Products, Inc., uses a product layout to manufacture components for consumer and business electronic products. A *fixed-position layout* is used when a very large product is produced. Aircraft manufacturers and shipbuilders apply this method because of the difficulty of moving a large product such as an airliner or a ship. The product remains stationary, and people and machines are moved as needed to assemble the product. Boeing, for example, uses the fixed-position layout to build 787 Dreamliner jet aircraft.

Operational planning

The objective of operational planning is to decide on the amount of products or services each facility will produce during a specific period of time. Four steps are required.

Step 1: Selecting a planning horizon   A **planning horizon** is simply the time period during which an operational plan will be in effect. A common planning horizon for production plans is one year. Then, before each year is up, management must plan for the next. A planning horizon of one year generally is long enough to average out seasonal increases and decreases in sales. At the same time, it is short enough for planners to adjust production to accommodate long-range sales trends.

  planning horizon the period during which an operational plan will be in effect

Step 2: Estimating market demand   The *market demand* for a product is the quantity that customers will purchase at the going price. This quantity must be estimated for the time period covered by the planning horizon. Sales projections developed by marketing managers are the basis for market-demand estimates.

Step 3: Comparing market demand with capacity   The third step in operational planning is to compare the estimated market demand with the facility's capacity to satisfy that demand. (Remember that capacity is the amount of products or services that an organisation can produce in a given time period.) One of three outcomes may result: Demand may exceed capacity, capacity may exceed demand, or capacity and demand may be equal. If they are equal, the facility should be operated at full capacity. However, if market demand and capacity are not equal, adjustments may be necessary.

Step 4: Adjusting products or services to meet demand   The biggest reason for changes to a firm's production schedule is changes in the amount of products or services that a company sells to its customers. For example, Indiana-based Berry Plastics produces all kinds of plastic products. One particularly successful product line for Berry Plastics is drink cups that can be screen-printed to promote a company or its products or services.* If Berry Plastics obtains a large contract to provide promotional cups to a large fast-food chain such as Subway or McDonald's, the company may need to work three shifts a day, seven days a week, until the contract is fulfilled. Unfortunately, the reverse is also true. If the company's sales force does not generate new sales, there may be only enough work for the employees on one shift.

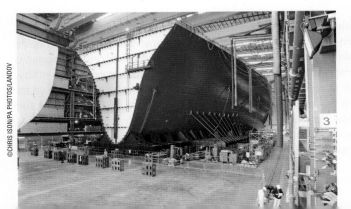

A big product! The British Royal Navy's aircraft carrier HMS Queen Elizabeth was constructed using a fixed-position layout. To see how large the ship is, compare its size with the people at the bottom of this photo. When a product is this large, it is easier to move people, machinery, and parts to where they are needed instead of moving the ship.

©CHRIS ISON/PA PHOTOS/LANDOV

When market demand exceeds capacity, several options are available to a firm. Production of products or services may be increased by operating the facility overtime with existing personnel or by starting a second or third work shift. For manufacturers, another response is to subcontract or outsource a portion of the work to other manufacturers. If the excess demand is likely to be permanent, the firm may expand the current facility or build another facility.

What happens when capacity exceeds market demand? Again, there are several options. To reduce output temporarily, workers may be laid off and part of the facility shut down, or the facility may be operated on a shorter-than-normal workweek for as long as the excess capacity persists. To adjust to a permanently decreased demand, management may shift the excess capacity of a manufacturing facility to the production of other goods or services. The most radical adjustment is to eliminate the excess capacity by selling unused manufacturing facilities.

OPERATIONS CONTROL

We have discussed the development of an idea for a product or service and the planning that translates that idea into the reality. Now we are ready to begin the actual production process. In this section, we examine four important areas of operations control: purchasing, inventory control, scheduling, and quality control (see Figure 8.4).

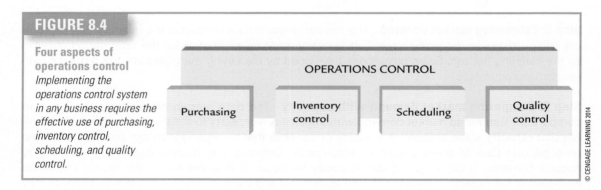

FIGURE 8.4

Four aspects of operations control
Implementing the operations control system in any business requires the effective use of purchasing, inventory control, scheduling, and quality control.

© CENGAGE LEARNING 2014

Purchasing

Purchasing consists of all the activities involved in obtaining required materials, supplies, components (or subassemblies), and parts from other firms. Levi Strauss, for example, must purchase denim cloth, thread, and zips before it can produce a single pair of jeans. For all firms, the purchasing function is far from routine, and its importance should not be underestimated. For some products, purchased materials make up more than 50 per cent of their wholesale costs.

purchasing all the activities involved in obtaining required materials, supplies, components, and parts from other firms

The objective of purchasing is to ensure that required materials are available when they are needed, in the proper amounts, and at minimum cost. Generally, the company with purchasing needs and suppliers must develop a working relationship built on trust. In addition to a working relationship built on trust, many companies believe that purchasing is one area where they can promote diversity. For example, AT&T developed a Supplier Diversity Programme in 1968. Today, more than 40 years later, goals for the AT&T programme include purchasing a total of 21.5 per cent of all products and services from minorities, women, and disabled veteran business enterprises.*

Purchasing personnel should constantly be on the lookout for new or backup suppliers, even when their needs are being met by their present suppliers, because problems such as strikes

RESPONSIBLE PRACTICE   Africa's new role in socially-responsible production

From boots to chocolate bars, Africa is attracting socially-responsible manufacturing firms that want to make good use of the continent's abundance of raw materials. Tal Dehtiar started Oliberte with the goal of bringing good-paying jobs to Africa while selling high-quality fashion shoes in the world marketplace. Rather than build facilities from scratch, he partnered with local leather suppliers and small factories in Ethiopia, Liberia, and Kenya. Although output is relatively low—the company makes and sells about 18,000 pairs of shoes per year—it is steadily increasing production capacity and expanding distribution as the Oliberte brand becomes better known.

© JOSHUA RAINEY PHOTOGRAPHY / SHUTTERSTOCK

Madecasse Chocolate, founded by former Peace Corps volunteers Tim McCollum and Brett Beach, transforms locally-grown cocoa beans into premium chocolate bars for export from the company's base in Madagascar. The entrepreneurs began by contracting with farming cooperatives that grow top-quality cocoa. Next, they figured out how to transport a ton of cocoa beans to a contract manufacturing plant downriver, where the beans are roasted and turned into chocolate bars. Finally, they arranged for stores like Whole Foods Market to sell the chocolate bars. With annual sales topping $2 million, Madecasse Chocolate is about to expand its storage facilities to prepare for future growth.

References: Peter Wonacott, "Small Factories Take Root in Africa," *Wall Street Journal*, September 24, 2011, www.wsj.com; Lisa Desai and Sarah Gross, "Shoe Company Hopes to Kick-Start Manufacturing in Africa," *CNN*, February 1, 2011, www.cnn.com; Barry Silverstein, "Madecasse, Rich," *Brand Channel*, March 17, 2010, www.brandchannel.com; and telephone interview with Tim McCollum, Madecasse Chocolate, May 4, 2012.

and equipment breakdowns can cut off the flow of purchased materials from a primary supplier at any time.

The choice of suppliers should result from careful analysis of a number of factors. The following are especially critical:

- *Price*. Comparing prices offered by different suppliers is always an essential part of selecting a supplier.
- *Quality*. Purchasing specialists always try to buy materials at a level of quality in keeping with the type of product being manufactured. The lowest acceptable quality is usually specified by product designers.
- *Reliability*. An agreement to purchase high-quality materials at a low price is the purchaser's dream. However, the dream becomes a nightmare if the supplier does not deliver.
- *Credit terms*. Purchasing specialists should determine if the supplier demands immediate payment or will extend credit.
- *Shipping costs*. The question of who pays the shipping costs should be answered before any supplier is chosen.

Inventory control

Can you imagine what would happen if a manufacturing plant for the Swiss chocolatier Lindt ran out of foil, wrappers and labels for packaging their luxury chocolates? It would be impossible to complete the manufacturing process and ship the boxes of chocolate bars to retailers. Management would be forced to shut the assembly line down until the next shipment of packaging arrived from a supplier.

Tracking inventory can be a tedious, but necessary chore. For a wholesaler or retailer, running out of inventory means a business has nothing to sell. For a manufacturer, no inventory can lead to shutting down a production facility and no finished products. In either case, no inventory equals no sales and can lead to no profits.

© NDOELJINDOEL / SHUTTERSTOCK

The simple fact is that shutdowns are expensive because costs such as wages, rent, utilities, insurance, and other expenses still must be covered.

Operations managers are concerned with three types of inventories. A *raw-materials inventory* consists of materials that will become part of the product during the production process. The *work-in-process inventory* consists of partially completed products. The *finished-goods inventory* consists of completed goods. Each type of inventory also has a *holding cost,* or storage cost, and a *stock-out cost,* the cost of running out of inventory. **Inventory control** is the process of managing inventories in such a way as to minimise inventory costs, including both holding costs and potential stock-out costs.

> **inventory control** the process of managing inventories in such a way as to minimise inventory costs, including both holding costs and potential stock-out costs

Today, computer systems are being used to keep track of inventories and alert managers to impending stock-outs. One of the most sophisticated methods of inventory control used today is materials requirements planning. **Materials requirements planning (MRP)** is a computerised system that integrates production planning and inventory control. One of the great advantages of an MRP system is its ability to juggle delivery schedules and lead times effectively. For a complex product such as an automobile with 4,000 or more individual parts, it is virtually impossible for individual managers to oversee the hundreds of parts that go into the finished product. However, a manager using an MRP system can arrange both order and delivery schedules so that materials, parts, and supplies arrive when they are needed.

> **materials requirements planning (MRP)** a computerised system that integrates production planning and inventory control

Today a popular extension of MRP is known as *enterprise resource planning (ERP).* The primary difference between ERP and MRP is that ERP software is more sophisticated and can monitor not only inventory and production processes but also quality, sales, and even such variables as inventory at a supplier's location.

Because large firms can incur huge inventory costs, much attention has been devoted to inventory control. The just-in-time system being used by some businesses is one result of all this attention. A **just-in-time inventory system** is designed to ensure that materials or supplies arrive at a facility just when they are needed so that storage and holding costs are minimised. The customer must specify what will be needed, when, and in what amounts. The supplier must be sure that the right supplies arrive at the agreed-upon time and location. For example, managers using a just-in-time inventory system at a Toyota assembly plant determine the number of automobiles that will be assembled in a specified time period. Then Toyota purchasing personnel order just the parts needed to produce those automobiles. In turn, suppliers deliver the parts in time or when they are needed on the assembly line.

just-in-time inventory system a system designed to ensure that materials or supplies arrive at a facility just when they are needed so that storage and holding costs are minimised

Without proper inventory control, it is impossible for operations managers to schedule the work required to produce goods that can be sold to customers.

Scheduling

Scheduling is the process of ensuring that materials and other resources are at the right place at the right time. The materials and resources may be moved from a warehouse to the workstations, they may move from station to station along an assembly line, or they may arrive at workstations "just in time" to be made part of the work-in-process there.

scheduling the process of ensuring that materials and other resources are at the right place at the right time

As our definition implies, both place and time are important to scheduling. The *routing* of materials is the sequence of workstations that the materials will follow. Assume that Delonghi—the Italian home and kitchen appliance manufacturer—is scheduling production of a deluxe coffee machine finished with brushed chrome and glass. Operations managers route the needed materials (glass, metal, electronic components, packaging materials, etc.) through a series of individual workstations along an assembly line. At each workstation, a specific task is performed, and then the partially finished coffee machine moves to the next workstation. When routing materials, operations managers are especially concerned with the sequence of each step of the production process. For the coffee machine, the electronics must be fitted and tested before the base unit is assembled and finished, to prevent repetition of processes and damage being caused to the finish at a later stage.

When scheduling production, managers also are concerned with timing. The *timing* function specifies when the materials will arrive at each station and how long they will remain there. For the deluxe coffee machine, it may take workers 20 minutes to solder the electronic components together and another 40 minutes to assemble and finish the base section.

Regardless of whether the finished product requires a simple or complex production process, operations managers are responsible for monitoring schedules—called *follow-up*—to ensure that the work flows according to a timetable. For some products, operations managers often prefer to use Gantt charts or the PERT technique to schedule production activities.

Scheduling through gantt charts   Developed by Henry L. Gantt, a **Gantt chart** is a graphic scheduling device that displays the tasks to be performed on the vertical axis and the time required for each task on the horizontal axis. Gantt charts do the following:

Gantt chart a graphic scheduling device that displays the tasks to be performed on the vertical axis and the time required for each task on the horizontal axis

- Allow you to determine how long a project should take.
- Lay out the order in which tasks need to be completed.
- Determine the resources needed.
- Monitor progress of different activities required to complete the project.

A Gantt chart that describes the activities required to build three dozen golf buggies is illustrated in Figure 8.5. Gantt charts usually are not suitable for scheduling extremely complex situations.

FIGURE 8.5   **A gantt chart** *This chart details the job of building three dozen electric golf buggies.*

	Week 1	Week 2	Week 3	Week 4
■ Completed ■ Planned				
1. Design on computer				
2. Purchase parts				
3. Fabricate fibreglass bodies				
4. Fabricate frames				
5. Build drive trains				
6. Assemble carts				
7. Test carts				

Source: From Kreitner/Cassidy, *Management,* 12th ed. © 2013 Cengage Learning.

Nevertheless, using them forces a manager to plan the steps required to get a job done and to specify time requirements for each part of the job.

Scheduling via PERT   A technique for scheduling a complex project and maintaining control of the schedule is **PERT (Programme Evaluation and Review Technique).** To use PERT, you begin by identifying all the major *activities* involved in the project. For example, the activities involved in producing a typical textbook are illustrated in Figure 8.6.

FIGURE 8.6   **Simplified PERT diagram for producing a typical book** *A PERT diagram identifies the activities necessary to complete a given project and arranges the activities based on the total time required for each to become an event. The activities on the critical path determine the minimum time required.job of building three dozen electric golf buggies.*

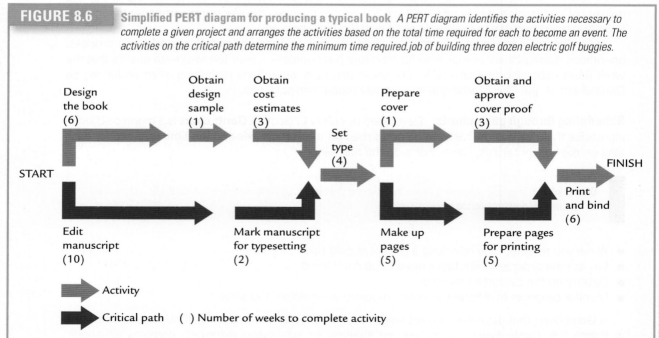

> **PERT (Programme Evaluation and Review Technique)** a scheduling technique that identifies the major activities necessary to complete a project and sequences them based on the time required to perform each one

All events are arranged in a sequence. In doing so, we must be sure that an event that must occur before another event in the actual process also occurs before that event on the PERT chart. The manuscript, for example, must be edited before the type is set. Next, we use arrows to connect events that must occur in sequence. We then estimate the time required for each activity and mark it near the corresponding arrow. The sequence of production activities that take the longest time from start to finish is called the *critical path*. The activities on this path determine the minimum time in which the process can be completed. These activities are the ones that must be scheduled and controlled carefully. A delay in any one of them will cause a delay in completion of the project as a whole.

Quality control

Over the years, more and more managers have realised that quality is an essential "ingredient" of the good or service being produced. This view of quality provides several benefits. The number of defects decreases, which causes profits to increase. Furthermore, making products or completing services right the first time reduces many of the rejects and much of the rework.

A large proportion of business firms that compete in the very competitive global marketplace have taken another look at the importance of improving quality. Many countries have even created national quality awards to incentivise organisations to incorporate improvements in quality more comprehensively into their culture and general day-to-day business practices. The benefits are multiple, and addressing this issue head on can often result in:

- better employee relations,
- higher productivity,
- greater customer satisfaction,
- increased market share, and
- improved profitability.*

Quality control is the process of ensuring that goods and services are produced in accordance with design specifications. The major objective of quality control is to see that the organisation lives up to the standards it has set for itself on quality. Some firms, such as Mercedes-Benz, have built their reputations on quality. Other firms adopt a strategy of emphasising lower prices along with reasonable (but not particularly high) quality. Today, many firms use the techniques described in Table 8.1 to gather information and statistics that can be used to improve the quality of a firm's products or services.

> **quality control** the process of ensuring that goods and services are produced in accordance with design specifications

Quality matters! In this photo, an employee inspects a custom-made shoe to make sure small details like the quality of leather and stitching meet the company's design specifications. Products that are not within design specifications and don't pass inspection are removed from production.

©TORANICO/SHUTTERSTOCK

TABLE 8.1 Four widely used techniques to improve the quality of a firm's products.

Technique	Description
Benchmarking	A process of comparing the way a firm produces products or services to the methods used by organisations known to be leaders in an industry in order to determine the "best practices" that can be used to improve quality.
Continuous Improvement	Continuous improvement is a never-ending effort to eliminate problems and improve quality. Often this method involves many small changes or steps designed to improve the production process on an ongoing basis.
Statistical Process Control (SPC)	Sampling to obtain data that are plotted on control charts and graphs to see if the production process is operating as it should and to pinpoint problem areas.
Statistical Quality Control (SQC)	A detailed set of specific statistical techniques used to monitor all aspects of the production process to ensure that both work-in-process and finished products meet the firm's quality standards.

Although the techniques described in Table 8.1 can provide information and statistics, it is people who must act on the information and make changes to improve the production process. And the firm's employees are often the most important component needed to improve quality.

Improving quality through employee participation One of the first steps needed to improve quality is employee participation. Simply put: Successful firms encourage employees to accept full responsibility for the quality of their work. When Toyota, once the role model for world-class manufacturing, faced a quality crisis, the company announced a quality-improvement plan based on its famous "Toyota Way." One tenet of the Toyota Way is the need to solve problems at their source, which allows factory workers to stop the production line if necessary to address a problem. Another tenet that enabled Toyota to resolve quality problems was the use of quality circles designated to deal with difficulties as they arise. A **quality circle** is a team of employees who meet on company time to solve problems of product quality. This level of employee participation allowed Toyota to correct the problems and improve the firm's motorcars. Today, Toyota is once again recognised as one of the most reliable motorcar brands. Quality circles have also been used successfully in companies such as IBM, Northrop Grumman Corporation, Lockheed Martin, and GE.

 quality circle a team of employees who meet on company time to solve problems of product quality

Increased effort is also being devoted to **inspection**, which is the examination of the quality of work-in-process. Employees perform inspections at various times during production. Purchased materials may be inspected when they arrive at the production facility. Subassemblies and manufactured parts may be inspected before they become part of a finished product. In addition, finished goods may be inspected before they are shipped to customers. Items that are within design specifications continue on their way. Those that are not within design specifications are removed from production.

 inspection the examination of the quality of work-in-process

Total quality management (TQM) can also be used to improve quality of a firm's products or services. As noted earlier in the book, a TQM programme coordinates the efforts directed at improving customer satisfaction, increasing employee participation, strengthening supplier partnerships, and facilitating an organisational atmosphere of continuous quality improvement. Firms such as AT&T,

Motorola, and Hewlett-Packard all have used TQM to improve product quality and, ultimately, customer satisfaction.

Another technique that businesses may use to improve not only quality but also overall performance is Six Sigma. **Six Sigma** is a disciplined approach that relies on statistical data and improved methods to eliminate defects for a firm's products and services. Although many experts agree that Six Sigma is similar to TQM, Six Sigma often has more top-level support, much more teamwork, and a new corporate attitude or culture. The companies that developed, refined, and have the most experience with Six Sigma are Motorola, GE, and Honeywell. Although each of these companies is a corporate giant, the underlying principles of Six Sigma can be used by any firm, regardless of size.*

> **Six Sigma** a disciplined approach that relies on statistical data and improved methods to eliminate defects for a firm's products and services

World quality standards: ISO 9000 and ISO 14000 Without a common standard of quality, customers may be at the mercy of manufacturers and vendors. As the number of companies competing in the global marketplace has increased, so has the seriousness of this problem. To deal with the problem of standardisation, the International Organisation for Standardisation, a nongovernmental organisation with headquarters in Geneva, Switzerland, was created. The **International Organisation for Standardisation (ISO)** is a network of national standards institutes and similar organisations from over 160 different countries that is charged with developing standards for quality products and services that are traded throughout the globe. According to the organisation,

> **International Organisation for Standardisation (ISO)** a network of national standards institutes and similar organisations from over 160 different countries that is charged with developing standards for quality products and services that are traded throughout the globe

ISO's work makes a positive difference to the world we live in. ISO standards add value to all types of business operations. They contribute to making the development, manufacturing and supply of products and services more efficient, safer and cleaner. They make trade between countries easier and fairer. ISO standards also serve to safeguard consumers and users of products and services in general, as well as making their lives simpler. *

Standardisation is achieved through consensus agreements between national delegations representing all the economic stakeholders—suppliers, customers, and often governments. Member organisations, amongst many others, include the South African Bureau of Standards (SABS), the BSI Group of the U.K., and the Emirates Authority of Standardization & Metrology (ESMA) based in the United Arab Emirates.

In 1987, the panel published ISO 9000 (*iso* is Greek for "equal"), which sets the guidelines for quality management procedures that manufacturers and service providers must use to receive certification. Certification by independent auditors and laboratory testing services serves as evidence that a company meets the standards for quality control procedures in design, production processes, and product testing.

Although certification is not a legal requirement to conduct business globally, the organisation's member countries have approved the ISO standards. In fact, ISO standards are so prevalent around the globe that many customers refuse to do business with noncertified companies. As an added bonus, companies completing the certification process often discover new, cost-efficient ways to improve their existing quality-control programmes.

As a continuation of this standardisation process, the International Organisation for Standardisation has developed ISO 14000. ISO 14000 is a family of international standards for incorporating environmental concerns into operations and product standards. Both the ISO 9000 and ISO 14000 family of standards are updated periodically. For example, ISO 9001:2008 includes important clarifications and addresses issues of compatibility with ISO's other quality standards.

IMPROVING PRODUCTIVITY WITH TECHNOLOGY

No coverage of operations management would be complete without a discussion of productivity and technology. Productivity concerns all managers, but it is especially important to operations managers, the people who must oversee the creation of a firm's goods or services. In the opening chapter, *productivity* was defined as the average level of output per worker per hour. Hence, if each worker at plant A produces 75 units per day and each worker at plant B produces only 70 units per day, the workers at plant A are more productive. If one bank teller serves 25 customers per hour and another serves 28 per hour, the second teller is more productive.

Improving productivity growth

Figure 8.7 shows productivity growth from across the globe. In an effort to improve productivity, an increasingly large number of business firms are adopting the concept of lean manufacturing. **Lean manufacturing** is a concept built on the idea of eliminating waste from all of the activities required to produce a product or service. Benefits of lean manufacturing include a reduction in the amount of resources required to produce a product or service, more efficient use of employee time, improved quality, and increased profits. In addition to lean manufacturing, several other factors must be considered if firms are going to increase productivity *and* their ability to compete in the global marketplace. For example:

> **lean manufacturing**   a concept built on the idea of eliminating waste from all of the activities required to produce a product or service

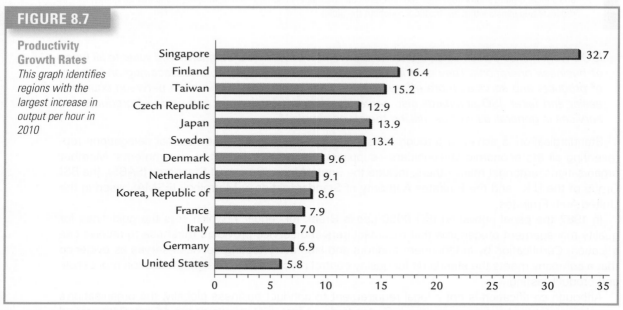

FIGURE 8.7

Productivity Growth Rates
This graph identifies regions with the largest increase in output per hour in 2010

Singapore	32.7
Finland	16.4
Taiwan	15.2
Czech Republic	12.9
Japan	13.9
Sweden	13.4
Denmark	9.6
Netherlands	9.1
Korea, Republic of	8.6
France	7.9
Italy	7.0
Germany	6.9
United States	5.8

Source: Based on information in "International Comparisons of Manufacturing Productivity and Unit Labor Cost Trends News Release," The Bureau of Labor Statistics Web site at www.bls.gov (accessed October 13, 2011).

- The economy must be stabilised so that firms will invest more money in new facilities, equipment, technology and employee training.
- Business firms must cooperate with employees to increase employee motivation and participation in the workplace.
- All government policies must be examined to ensure that unreasonable regulations that may be hindering productivity growth are eliminated.

- Successful techniques that have been used in manufacturing firms must be used to increase productivity in the service industry.
- Increased use of automation, robotics, and computer manufacturing systems must be used to lower production costs.
- There must be more emphasis on satisfying the customer's needs with quality goods and services.

Finally, innovation and research and development efforts to create new products and services must be increased in order for any firm to compete effectively in the global marketplace.

The impact of automation, robotics, and computers on productivity

Automation is the total or near-total use of machines to do work. The rapid increase in automated procedures has been made possible by the microprocessor, a silicon chip that led to the production of desktop computers for businesses, homes, and schools. In factories, microprocessors are used in robotics and in computer manufacturing systems.

 automation the total or near-total use of machines to do work

Robotics   **Robotics** is the use of programmable machines to perform a variety of tasks by manipulating materials and tools. Robots work quickly, accurately, and steadily. For example, Illumina, Inc., an American company, sells robotic equipment that performs medical laboratory tests. Available information then is sold to some of the world's largest pharmaceutical companies where it is used to alter existing prescription drugs, develop new drug therapies, and customise treatments for all kinds of serious diseases. As an added bonus, Illumina's robotic equipment can work 24 hours a day at much lower costs than if human lab workers performed the same tests.*

 robotics the use of programmable machines to perform a variety of tasks by manipulating materials and tools

Robots are especially effective in tedious, repetitive assembly-line jobs, as well as in handling hazardous materials. Robotic arc welders, for example, eliminate the hot, dirty job of welding, which is key to many manufacturing tasks. As an added bonus, robotic arc welders are often quicker and are more precise than old-fashioned welding machines. Robots are also useful as artificial "eyes" that can check the quality of products as they are being processed on assembly lines. To date, the automotive industry has made the most extensive use of robotics, but robots also have been used to mine coal, inspect the inner surfaces of pipes, assemble computer components, provide certain kinds of patient care in hospitals, and clean and guard buildings at night.

Computer manufacturing systems   People are quick to point out how computers have changed their everyday lives, but most people do not realise the impact computers have had on manufacturing. In simple terms, the factory of the future has already arrived. For most manufacturers, the changeover began with the use of computer-aided design and computer-aided manufacturing.

Robotics can be a manufacturer's best friend. One of the first industries to use robotics to increase the number of products produced and improve employee productivity was the automobile industry. In this photo, robotics are used to move the right side of a motorcar from one workstation on an assembly line to the next station.

©NATALIYA HORA/SHUTTERSTOCK

Computer-aided design (CAD) is the use of computers to aid in the development of products. Ford speeds up car design, Canon designs new photocopiers, and Funky Pigeon, a U.K.-based online novelty card and stationary producer, creates new personalised birthday cards by using CAD.

 computer-aided design (CAD) the use of computers to aid in the development of products

Computer-aided manufacturing (CAM) is the use of computers to plan and control manufacturing processes. A well-designed CAM system allows manufacturers to become much more productive. Not only are a greater number of products produced, but speed and quality also increase. Using CAM systems, Toyota produces automobiles, Hasbro manufactures toys, and Apple Computer creates electronic products.

 computer-aided manufacturing (CAM) the use of computers to plan and control manufacturing processes

If you are thinking that the next logical step is to combine the CAD and CAM computer systems, you are right. Today, the most successful manufacturers use CAD and CAM together to form a computer-integrated manufacturing system. Specifically, **computer-integrated manufacturing (CIM)** is a computer system that not only helps to design products but also controls the machinery needed to produce the finished product. For example, Fifth & Pacific Companies (formerly Liz Claiborne), uses CIM to design clothing, to establish patterns for new fashions, and then to cut the cloth needed to produce the finished product. Other advantages of using CIM include improved flexibility, more efficient scheduling, and higher product quality—all factors that make a production facility more competitive in today's global economy.

 computer-integrated manufacturing (CIM) a computer system that not only helps to design products but also controls the machinery needed to produce the finished product

Flexible manufacturing systems   Manufacturers have known for a number of years that the mass-production and traditional assembly lines used to manufacture products present a number of problems. For example, although traditional assembly lines turn out extremely large numbers of identical products economically, the system requires expensive, time-consuming retooling of equipment whenever a new product is to be manufactured. This type of manufacturing is often referred to as a continuous process. **Continuous process** is a manufacturing process in which a firm produces the same product(s) over a long period of time. Now it is possible to use flexible manufacturing systems to solve such problems. A **flexible manufacturing system (FMS)** combines electronic machines and computer-integrated manufacturing in a single production system. Instead of having to spend large amounts of time and effort to retool the traditional mechanical equipment on an assembly line for each new product, an FMS is rearranged simply by reprogramming electronic machines. Because FMSs require less time and expense to reprogramme than traditional systems, manufacturers can produce smaller batches of a variety of products without raising the production cost. Flexible manufacturing is sometimes referred to as an intermittent process. An **intermittent process** is a manufacturing process in which a firm's manufacturing machines and equipment are changed to produce different products.

continuous process a manufacturing process in which a firm produces the same product(s) over a long period of time
flexible manufacturing system (FMS) a single production system that combines electronic machines and computer-integrated manufacturing
intermittent process a manufacturing process in which a firm's manufacturing machines and equipment are changed to produce different products

For most manufacturers, the driving force behind FMSs is the customer. In fact, the term *customer-driven production* is often used to describe a manufacturing system that is driven by customer needs and what customers want to buy. For example, advanced software and a flexible manufacturing system have enabled Dell Computer to change to a more customer-driven manufacturing process. The process starts when a customer phones a sales representative on a toll-free line or accesses Dell's Web site. Then the representative or the customer enters the specifications for the new product directly into a computer. The order then is sent to a nearby plant. Once the order is received, a team of employees, with the help of a reprogrammable assembly line, can build the product just the way the customer wants it. Products include desktop computers, notebook computers, and other Dell equipment.* Although the costs of designing and installing an FMS such as this are high, the electronic equipment is used more frequently and efficiently than the machinery on a traditional assembly line.

Sustainability and technological displacement

Earlier in the book, *sustainability* was defined as meeting the needs of the present without compromising the ability of future generations to meet their own needs. While sustainability affects all aspects of a nation, its people, and the economy, the concept is especially important for manufacturers and service providers. Because of the amount of resources required to produce goods and services, these businesses must conserve resources whenever possible. As an added bonus, efforts to reduce waste and sustain the planet can often improve a firm's bottom-line profit amount.

In the future, most experts agree that, because manufacturers will continue to innovate, workers who have manufacturing jobs will be highly skilled and can work with the automated and computer-assisted manufacturing systems. Those that don't possess high-tech skills will be dispensable and unemployed. Many workers will be faced with the choice of retraining for new jobs or seeking jobs in other sectors of the economy. Government, business, and education will have to cooperate to prepare workers for new roles in an automated workplace.

SUMMARY

- Explain the nature of production.

  Operations management consists of all the activities that managers engage in to create goods and services. Operations are as relevant to service organisations as to manufacturing firms. Today, companies are forced to compete in an ever-smaller world to meet the needs of more-demanding customers. As a result, manufacturers have used innovation to improve productivity. Because of innovation, fewer workers are needed, but those workers who are needed possess the skills to use automation and technology. In an attempt to regain a competitive edge, manufacturers have taken another look at the importance of improving quality and meeting the needs of their customers. They also have used new techniques to motivate employees, reduced costs, used computer-aided and flexible manufacturing systems, improved control procedures, and used green manufacturing. Competing in the global economy is not only profitable but also an essential activity that requires the cooperation of everyone within an organisation. A number of career

  options are available for employees in operations management.

- Outline how the conversion process transforms raw materials, labour, and other resources into finished goods or services.

  A business transforms resources into goods and services in order to provide utility to customers. Utility is the ability of a good or service to satisfy a human need. Form utility is created by people converting raw materials, finances, and information into finished products. Conversion processes vary in terms of the major resources used to produce goods and services (focus), the degree to which resources are changed (magnitude of change), and the number of production processes that a business uses.

- Understand the importance of service businesses to consumers, other business firms, and the nation's economy.

  The application of the basic principles of operations management to the production of services has coincided with the growth and importance of service businesses. For a service firm, planning often begins with determining who the customer is and what needs the customer has. After customer needs are identified the next step is to develop a plan that will enable the firm to deliver the services that their customers want or need. Although it is often more difficult to measure customer satisfaction, today's successful service firms work hard at providing the services customers want. For example, compared with manufacturers, service firms often listen more carefully to customers and respond more quickly to the market's changing needs.

- Describe how research and development lead to new products and services.

  Operations management often begins with product research and development and often referred to as R&D. The results of R&D may be entirely new products or services or extensions and refinements of existing products or services. R&D activities are classified as basic research (aimed at uncovering new knowledge), applied research (discovering new knowledge with some potential use), and development and implementation (using new or existing knowledge to produce goods and services). If a firm sells only one product or provides only one service, when that product or service reaches the end of its life-cycle, the firm will die, too. To stay in business, the firm must, at the very least, find ways to refine or extend the want-satisfying capability of its product or service.

- Discuss the components involved in planning the production process.

  Planning for production involves three major phases: design planning, site selection and facilities planning, and operational planning. First, design planning is undertaken to address questions related to the product line, required production capacity, and the use of technology. Then production facilities, human resources, and plant layout must be considered. Operational planning focuses on the use of production facilities and resources. The steps for operational planning include (1) selecting a planning horizon, (2) estimating market demand, (3) comparing market demand with capacity, and (4) adjusting production of products or services to meet demand.

- Explain how purchasing, inventory control, scheduling, and quality control affect production.

  The major areas of operations control are purchasing, inventory control, scheduling, and quality control. Purchasing involves selecting suppliers. The choice of suppliers should result from careful analysis of a number of factors, including price, quality, reliability, credit terms, and shipping costs. Inventory control is the management of stocks of raw materials, work-in-process, and finished goods to minimise the total inventory cost. Scheduling ensures that materials and other resources are at the right place at the right time. Both Gantt charts and PERT can be used to improve a firm's ability to schedule the production of products. Quality control guarantees that products and services are produced in accordance with design specifications. The major objective of quality control is to see that the organisation lives up to the standards it has set for itself on quality. A number of different activities can be used to improve quality.

- Summarise how technology can make firms more productive and competitive in the global marketplace.

  Productivity is the average level of output per worker per hour. Several factors must be considered if firms are going to increase productivity and their ability to compete in the global marketplace.

  Automation, the total or near-total use of machines to do work, has for some years been changing the way work is done in factories. A growing number of industries are using programmable machines called robots. Computer-aided design, computer-aided manufacturing, and computer-integrated manufacturing use computers to help design and manufacture products. FMS combines electronic machines and computer-integrated manufacturing to produce smaller batches of products more efficiently than on the traditional assembly line. Instead of having to spend vast amounts of time and effort to retool the traditional mechanical equipment on an assembly line for each new product, an FMS is rearranged simply by reprogramming electronic machines.

EXERCISE QUESTIONS

1 Describe and give examples of a synthetic and an analytical process.

2 Chose a business you are familiar with. Give a broad outline of one of its product lines.

3 Think about the same business you chose for Question 3. Do some research into their conversation process.

How do they turn their concepts into completed goods or services?

4 Using the same business, create a schedule via PERT for one of their products.

5 Explain the four important areas of operations control listed in this chapter.

CASE 8.1

Reverse innovation from emerging markets

For decades, global companies have flourished by making relatively high-priced products for prosperous consumers in the West. Meanwhile, these multinationals often off-loaded their production surpluses – typically outdated stock from the previous season – in developing economies at discounted prices, instead of also developing entry-level products to cater for the needs of low-income buyers. Thus, innovation used to trickle down from rich nations to emerging markets.

But the flow of new products can also go the other way. Today, corporations such as Nestlé, Nokia and Philips realise that it may be more profitable to create cheap products specifically for the developing world. Then, after successfully penetrating these mass markets, they can make additional profit by offering virtually the same items – as bargains – to price-sensitive buyers in richer nations. This new strategy – called trickle-up or reverse innovation – transforms the traditional product develop-ment method: instead of innovation coming from Europe or the United States and then descending to emerging mar-kets, the process is reversed. To successfully shift their resources to emerging markets and sell products in devel-oping as well as developed nations, marketers must get out of their comfort zone and come up with strategies for largely identical products tailored to buyers – consumers or companies – with different levels of purchasing power.

In business-to-business marketing, one reason why companies in the West are purchasing simplified products that suppliers originally designed for the developing world is that – with recession-era budgets – they are more cost-conscious than ever. General Electric's management identified this marketing opportunity when it began selling a lightweight, battery-powered model of an electrocardi-ograph (ECG) machine – initially developed for healthcare providers in China and India – in the U.S. With a retail price of $500 – a fraction of the price of much larger machines with similar high-tech features – this field model turned out to be perfect to meet the needs of first responders in industrialised countries. The smaller and cheaper machine will be pitched to a new target market of medical professionals – primary-care doctors, rural clinics and visiting nurses – who need an affordable device they can easily carry around.

In addition to gaining market share worldwide, GE Healthcare also benefits from lower product development costs. Instead of spending millions of dollars and taking several years to develop a new portable ECG device, the company managed to cut its investment by 90 per cent and launch the machine in industrialised nations within months. It simply enhanced the Chinese model by adding some accessories, such as USB ports and Ethernet (a type of local area network) to upload and transfer patients' medical data. For GE, this reverse innovation approach rapidly reduced the cost of doing business. Managers looking for reverse innovation opportunities in consumer markets should not waste any time either. By successfully developing inexpensive products for emerging markets and then quickly repackaging them (with or without adapt-ations) for more advanced markets, they may stop local startups that are trying to create a 'first mover' advant-age in developing countries and then compete with them head-on after entering the European or U.S. market. More and more companies in the West are relying on trickle-up innovation, motivated by the effective introduction of developing-world products in African and Asian markets as well as the changing purchasing behaviour of buyers in industrialised countries. Nokia, for instance, conducted extensive marketing research to find out how consumers in Morocco and Ghana share their mobile phones so others can listen in on interesting phone conversations. This enabled the Finnish corporation to not only create an improved handset for the African market, but also to install better speakers in smart phones targeted at European consumers who like to share their favourite songs and videos with friends.

There are numerous other examples of companies that are now marketing innovations intended for emer-ging markets to price-conscious consumers in advanced economies. Swiss multinational Nestlé gained so many new customers in India and Pakistan for its Maggi dried noodles – priced at 15 eurocents per single-serve package – that it repositioned this low-fat product as an inexpens-ive health food in the New Zealand and Australian market. Levi's success with its inexpensive Denizen brand in India and China prompted the company to start selling the same jeans in its home market. Denizen jeans now sell for $18 to $30 in the U.S., about one-third to one-half the price of a pair of Levi's in that country. And Procter & Gamble suc-cessfully offered its Vick's honey cough syrup, made for the Mexican market, as a basic cold-remedy product to American and European consumers.

So what's the downside of reverse innovation for firms pursuing this strategy? The greatest risk is cannibalisa-tion: customers buying the new, lower-priced product as a substitute for the company's more expensive brand (with a higher profit margin) that they used to buy. This fear of a cheap new product "stealing" sales of an established one was the main reason for Philips Electronics, after installing inexpensive, solar-powered LED lighting centres in African countries (South Africa, Egypt, Kenya, Ghana and Morocco), to not launch this product in the West. A second risk is that potential buyers in advanced markets may worry that cheap products designed for emerging markets could lack the quality and features they need, which, to them, is even more crucial than a decent price. Therefore, marketers should make sure that new products, no matter at what price they are offered, meet the needs and wants of the target market.

Most firms that systematically develop innovations for emerging markets are still at the beginning of the cycle. Economists predict that over the next two decades, 75 per cent of the world's economic growth will be generated by the more than 130 developing countries. Without doubt, this high level of economic growth will create huge marketing opportunities for companies with reverse innovation strategies across the globe.

References: Reena Jana, 'Inspiration from Emerging Economies', Business-week, March 23 & 30, 2009, pp. 38–41; Natalie Zmuda, 'P&G, Levi's, GE innovate by thinking in reverse', Advertising Age, June 12, 2011; 'Philips to install 100 solar-powered lighting centres across Africa', ledsmagazine.com, August 20, 2012.

Questions

1 Do some research and find three examples of other firms that pursue this strategy. What kind of products do they sell?

2 Can you think of examples of companies which have been forced to offer products at a lower price for all markets?

3 Pick a global company you are familiar with. What products do they offer in some countries that they don't in others?

CHAPTER REFERENCES

Buczynski, Beth, The Earth Techling Web site at www.earthtechling.com (accessed February 20, 2012).

Kreitner, Robert and Cassidy, Carlene, *Management*, 12th ed. (Mason, OH: Cengage Learning, 2013).

Kuczmarski, Thomas D., "Remanufacturing America's Factory Sector," *BusinessWeek*, September 9, 2009, Web site at www.businessweek.com.

The Affinia Hotel Web site at www.affinia.com (accessed February 15, 2012).

The AT&T Supplier Web site at www.attsuppliers.com (accessed February 13, 2012).

The Berry Plastics Corporation Web site at www.berry-plastics.com (accessed February 13, 2012).

The Bureau of Labor Statistics Web site at www.bls.gov (accessed February 13, 2012).

The Dell Computer Corporation Web site at www.dell.com (accessed February 19, 2012).

The Illumina, Inc., Web site at www.illumina.com (accessed February 15, 2012).

The International Organization of Standardization (ISO) Web site at www.iso.org (accessed February 19, 2012).

The iSixSigma Web site at www.isixsigma.com (accessed February 13, 2012).

The National Institute for Standards and Technology *Web* site at www.nist.gov (accessed February 16, 2012).

PART 4
HUMAN RESOURCES

This part of the book is concerned with the most important and least predictable of all resources—people. We begin by examining the human resources efforts that organisations use to hire, develop, and retain their best employees. Then we discuss employee motivation and satisfaction.

9   **Recruitment and Retaining the Best Employees**

10 **Employee Motivation and Team Building**

9 RECRUITMENT AND RETAINING THE BEST EMPLOYEES

LEARNING OBJECTIVES

Once you complete this chapter, you should be able to:

- Describe the major components of human resources management
- Identify the steps in human resources planning
- Describe cultural diversity and understand some of the challenges and opportunities associated with it
- Explain the objectives and uses of job analysis
- Describe the processes of recruiting, employee selection, and orientation
- Discuss the primary elements of employee compensation and benefits
- Explain the purposes and techniques of employee training and development
- Discuss performance appraisal techniques and performance feedback

BUSINESS FOCUS

Companies and job candidates get LinkedIn

Are you LinkedIn? LinkedIn (www. linkedin.com) is a professionals' social media site, an online place where businesspeople in nearly every industry can network with their peers, showcase their credentials, research potential employers, and explore career possibilities. In today's wired world, companies are increasingly reaching out to job-seekers through technology. Because LinkedIn has more than 150 million members in 200 nations, it has become a key hub for many firms' online recruitment activities.

For example, member companies pay to search for job candidates through LinkedIn's listings and post open positions. FedEx created a Careers Connections group on LinkedIn to network with experienced professionals seeking to change jobs and with college students interested in learning about career opportunities. FedEx also pays to advertise jobs so that

LinkedIn members with the right qualifications see the ads when they visit the site. LinkedIn itself maintains a careers page on the site, filled with information about the benefits of working for LinkedIn, job postings, testimonials from people who were recently hired, and direct links to the company's recruiters.

Multinational corporations find LinkedIn an efficient way to recruit in multiple regions. Invensys, a London-based company that makes electronic controls for factories, power plants, and transit systems, has used LinkedIn to attract applicants for jobs in Kazakhstan, Slovakia, and Nigeria. Even for companies that hire locally, LinkedIn is supplementing traditional recruiting methods. When the biochemicals firm AMRESCO schedules a job fair in its home state of Ohio, its 250 employees post the place, date, and time to alert their LinkedIn member networks. Now one-third

of AMRESCO's new hires come through referrals from employees who are LinkedIn members.

When the software developer Softchoice wants to hire professionals for its Toronto office, its recruiters sift through LinkedIn membership profiles to identify individuals with the relevant skills and experience. Then the recruiters contact these people, often via a LinkedIn message, to initiate a conversation about open positions. This allows Softchoice to expand its pool of candidates by reaching out to people who are not actively seeking to change jobs—yet.

References: Josh Bersin, "LinkedIn Is Disrupting the Corporate Recruiting Market," *Forbes. com*, February 12, 2012, http://forbes.com/sites/joshbersin/2012/02/12/linkedin-is-disrupting-the-corporate-recruiting-market/; Wallace Immen, "Making the Social-Media Link to a New Job," *Globe & Mail (Toronto)*, December 2, 2011, p. B16; Elisabeth Geisse, "The In Crowd," *Inside Business*, September–October 2011, p. NC52; "The Challenge: A Joined-Up Hiring Solution," *Recruiter*, March 23, 2011, p. 20.

L inkedIn has become an important tool for job seekers and professionals alike, as it allows firms to recruit and individuals to post and share their résumés and professional experiences online. We begin our study of human resources management (HRM) with an overview of how businesses acquire, maintain, and develop their human resources. After listing the steps by which firms match their human resources needs with the supply available, we explore several dimensions of cultural diversity. Then we examine the concept of job analysis. Next, we focus on a firm's recruiting, selection, and orientation procedures as the means of acquiring employees. We also describe forms of employee compensation that motivate employees to remain with a firm and to work effectively. Then we discuss methods of employee training, management development, and performance appraisal. Finally, we consider legislation that affects HRM practices.

HUMAN RESOURCES MANAGEMENT: AN OVERVIEW

The human resource is not only unique and valuable but also an organisation's most important resource. It seems logical that an organisation would expend a great deal of effort to acquire and make full use of such a resource. This effort is known as *human resources management*. It also has been called *staffing* and *personnel management*.

Human resources management (HRM) consists of all the activities involved in acquiring, maintaining, and developing an organisation's human resources. As the definition implies, HRM begins with acquisition—getting people to work for the organisation. The acquisition process can be quite competitive for certain types of qualified employees. Next, steps must be taken to keep these valuable resources. (After all, they are the only business resources that can leave an organisation.) Finally, the human resources should be developed to their full capacity.

> **human resources management (HRM)** all the activities involved in acquiring, maintaining, and developing an organisation's human resources

HRM activities

Each of the three phases of HRM—acquiring, maintaining, and developing human resources—consists of a number of related activities. Acquisition, for example, includes planning, as well as the various activities that lead to hiring new personnel. Altogether this phase of HRM includes five separate activities:

- *Human resources planning*—determining the firm's future human resources needs
- *Job analysis*—determining the exact nature of the positions
- *Recruiting*—attracting people to apply for positions
- *Selection*—choosing and hiring the most qualified applicants
- *Orientation*—acquainting new employees with the firm

Maintaining human resources consists primarily of encouraging employees to remain with the firm and to work effectively by using a variety of HRM programmes, including the following:

- *Employee relations*—increasing employee job satisfaction through satisfaction surveys, employee communication programmes, exit interviews, and fair treatment
- *Compensation*—rewarding employee effort through monetary payments
- *Benefits*—providing rewards to ensure employee well-being

The development phase of HRM is concerned with improving employees' skills and expanding their capabilities. The two important activities within this phase are:

- *Training and development*—teaching employees new skills, new jobs, and more effective ways of doing their present jobs
- *Performance appraisal*—assessing employees' current and potential performance levels

These activities are discussed in more detail shortly, when we have completed this overview of HRM.

Responsibility for HRM

In general, HRM is a shared responsibility of line managers and staff HRM specialists. In very small organisations, the owner handles all or most HRM activities. As a firm grows in size, a human resources manager is hired to take over staff responsibilities. In large organisations, HRM activities tend to be very highly specialised. There are separate groups to deal with compensation, benefits,

The power of people. Many firms believe their employees are their most important assets. However, unalike other assets such as machinery, capital, and products, employees can pick up and leave an organisation. Carefully designing compensation and reward packages can help a firm attract and retain valuable employees.

The more skills you develop, the more valuable you are to any employer. Do your own personal skills inventory before you write a résumé or interview for a job. Then you'll be prepared to explain the special skills you can bring to an employer.

training and development, and other staff activities. GE, for example, has many divisions and offices all over the world. Because of the size and complexity of the organisation, GE has hundreds of different HR managers to cover different geographic areas and departments within the firm.*

Specific HRM activities are assigned to those who are in the best position to perform them. Human resources planning and job analysis usually are done by staff specialists, with input from line managers. Similarly, recruiting and selection are handled by staff experts, although line managers are involved in hiring decisions. Orientation programmes are devised by staff specialists and carried out by both staff specialists and line managers. Compensation systems (including benefits) most often are developed and administered by the HRM staff. However, line managers recommend pay increases and promotions. Training and development activities are the joint responsibility of staff and line managers. Performance appraisal is the job of the line manager, although HRM personnel design the firm's appraisal system in many organisations.

HUMAN RESOURCES PLANNING

Human resources planning is the development of strategies to meet a firm's future human resources needs. The starting point is the organisation's overall strategic plan. From this, human resources planners can forecast future demand for human resources. Next, the planners must determine whether the needed human resources will be available. Finally, they have to take steps to match supply with demand.

> **human resources planning** the development of strategies to meet a firm's future human resources needs

Forecasting human resources demand

Planners should base forecasts of the demand for human resources on as much relevant information as available. The firm's overall strategic plan will provide information about future business ventures, new products, and projected expansions or contractions of specific product lines. Information on past staffing levels, evolving technologies, industry staffing practices, and projected economic trends also can be helpful. Technological advances are creating new opportunities in forecasting and planning for human resources demand. A survey released by Deloitte Consulting found that new technologies such as social media, cloud computing, and analytics have increased the speed of doing business, which increases the importance of international growth and strong leadership in organisations. Firms must hire HR talent that is fluent in using these new technologies in order to take advantage of opportunities and be aware of threats.*

HRM managers use this information to determine both the number of employees required and their qualifications. Planners use a wide range of methods to forecast specific personnel needs.

For example, with one simple method, personnel requirements are projected to increase or decrease in the same proportion as sales revenue. Thus, if a 30 per cent increase in sales volume is projected over the next two years, then up to a 30 per cent increase in personnel requirements may be expected for the same period. (This method can be applied to specific positions as well as to the workforce in general. It is not, however, a very precise forecasting method.) At the other extreme are elaborate, computer-based personnel planning models used by some large firms such as ExxonMobil Corporation.

Forecasting human resources supply

The forecast of the supply of human resources must take into account both the present workforce and any changes that may occur within it. For example, suppose that planners project that in five years a firm that currently employs 100 engineers will need to employ a total of 200 engineers. Planners simply cannot assume that they will have to hire 100 engineers; during that period, some of the firm's present engineers are likely to be promoted, leave the firm, or move to other jobs within the firm. Thus, planners may project the supply of engineers in five years at 87, which means that the firm will have to hire a total of 113 new engineers. When forecasting supply, planners should analyse the organisation's existing employees to determine who can be retrained to perform the required tasks.

Two useful techniques for forecasting human resources supply are the replacement chart and the skills inventory. A **replacement chart** is a list of key personnel and their possible replacements within a firm. The chart is maintained to ensure that top-management positions can be filled fairly quickly in the event of an unexpected death, resignation, or retirement. Some firms also provide additional training for employees who might eventually replace top managers.

replacement chart a list of key personnel and their possible replacements within a firm

A **skills inventory** is a computerised data bank containing information on the skills and experience of all present employees. It is used to search for candidates to fill available positions. For a special project, a manager may be seeking a current employee with specific information technology skills, at least six years of experience, and fluency in French. The skills inventory can quickly identify employees who possess such qualifications. Skill-assessment tests can be administered inside an organisation, or they can be provided by outside vendors. Some companies, such as eSkill, offer customizable skills assessment and training software that allows firms to more expertly examine skills without contracting with an outside provider.*

skills inventory a computerised data bank containing information on the skills and experience of all present employees

Matching supply with demand

Once they have forecasted the supply and demand for personnel, planners can devise a course of action for matching the two. When demand is predicted to be greater than supply, they must make plans to recruit new employees. The timing of these actions depends on the types of positions to be filled. Suppose that we expect to open another plant in five years that will need, along with other employees, a plant manager and 25 maintenance workers. We probably can wait quite a while before we begin to recruit maintenance personnel. However, because the job of a plant manager is so critical, we may start searching for the right person for that position immediately.

When supply is predicted to be greater than demand, the firm must take steps to reduce the size of its workforce. When the oversupply is expected to be temporary, some employees may be *laid off*—dismissed from the workforce until they are needed again.

Perhaps the most humane method for making personnel cutbacks is through attrition. *Attrition* is the normal reduction in the workforce that occurs when employees leave a firm.

The demand for labour versus its supply: A balancing act. The supply and demand for employees with different skills is constantly shifting. In some industries, qualified workers are plentiful. In others, they are hard to find, even when the unemployment rate is high.

©IOFOTO/SHUTTERSTOCK

Early retirement is another option. Under early retirement, people who are within a few years of retirement are permitted to retire early with full benefits. Depending on the age makeup of the workforce, this may or may not reduce the staff enough.

As a last resort, unnecessary employees are sometimes simply *fired*. However, because of its negative impact, this method generally is used only when absolutely necessary.

CULTURAL DIVERSITY IN HUMAN RESOURCES

Today's workforce is made up of many types of people. Firms can no longer assume that every employee has similar beliefs or expectations. Whereas people from some cultural backgrounds may see it as a perfectly acceptable practice to challenge authority, others may have been brought up to respect and defer to it. A job applicant who will not make eye contact during an interview may be rejected for being unapproachable, when, according to his or her culture, he or she was just being polite.

In many countries, the workforce is becoming increasingly more diverse, due to a variety of reasons including the gradual erosion of traditional gender roles and rising immigration. The last decade, for instance, has witnessed a huge rise in immigrants from EU member countries in Eastern Europe entering Western European countries such as France and the U.K. to find work. Immigration is often a key topic in national debates. Critics complain that it puts an additional strain on the economy and takes jobs away from domestic workers, whereas others will argue that it strengthens the economy through a greater diversity of workers and that immigrants are often willing to work harder whilst accepting a lower wage.

Cultural (or workplace) diversity refers to the differences among people in a workforce owing to race, ethnicity, and gender. Increasing cultural diversity is forcing managers to learn to supervise and motivate people with a broader range of value systems. The high proportion of women in the workforce, combined with a new emphasis on participative parenting by men, has brought many family-related issues to the workplace. Today's more educated employees also want greater independence and flexibility. In return for their efforts, they want both compensation and a better quality of life.

cultural (workplace) diversity differences among people in a workforce owing to race, ethnicity, and gender

Although cultural diversity presents a challenge, managers should view it as an opportunity rather than a limitation. When managed properly, cultural diversity can provide advantages for an organisation. Table 9.1 shows several benefits that creative management of cultural diversity can offer. A firm that manages diversity properly can develop cost advantages over other firms. Moreover, organisations that manage diversity creatively are in a much better position to attract the best personnel.

TABLE 9.1	Advantages of cultural diversity	
	Economic measure	**Description**
	Cost	As organisations become more diverse, the cost of doing a poor job of integrating workers will increase. Companies that handle this well thus can create cost advantages over those that do a poor job. In addition, companies also experience cost savings by hiring people with knowledge of various cultures as opposed to having to train domestic workers about how business is carried out in other countries.
	Resource acquisition	Companies develop reputations as being favourable or unfavourable prospective employers for women and ethnic minorities. Those with the best reputations for managing diversity will win the competition for the best personnel.
	Marketing edge	For multinational organisations, the insight and cultural sensitivity that members with roots in other countries bring to marketing efforts should improve these efforts in important ways. The same rationale applies to marketing subpopulations domestically.
	Flexibility	Culturally diverse employees often are open to a wider array of positions within a company and are more likely to move up the corporate ladder more rapidly, given excellent performance.
	Creativity	Diversity of perspectives and less emphasis on conformity to norms of the past should improve the level of creativity.
	Problem solving	Differences within decision-making and problem-solving groups potentially produce better decisions through a wider range of perspectives and more thorough critical analysis of issues.
	Bilingual skills	Cultural diversity in the workplace brings with it bilingual and bicultural skills, which are very advantageous to the ever-growing global marketplace. Employees with knowledge about how other cultures work not only can speak to them in their language but also can prevent their company from making embarrassing moves owing to a lack of cultural sophistication. Thus, companies may seek job applicants with a background in cultures in which the company does business.

Sources: Taylor H. Cox and Stacy Blake, "Managing Cultural Diversity: Implications for Organisational Competitiveness," *Academy of Management Executive* 5(3):46, 1991; Ricky Griffin and Gregory Moorhead, *Organisational Behavior* (Mason, OH: South-Western/Cengage Learning, 2010), 40; and Richard L. Daft, *Management* (Mason, OH: South-Western/Cengage Learning, 2010), 348–349.

A culturally diverse organisation may gain a marketing edge because it understands different cultural groups. Proper guidance and management of diversity in an organisation also can improve the level of creativity. People who embrace cultural diversity frequently are more flexible in the types of positions they will accept and are more comfortable working with culturally diverse co-workers.

Because cultural diversity creates challenges along with advantages, it is important for an organisation's employees to understand it. To accomplish this goal, numerous firms have trained their managers to respect and manage diversity. Diversity training programmes may include recruiting minorities, training minorities to be managers, training managers to view diversity positively, teaching English as a second language, and facilitating support groups for immigrants. Many companies

Why hiring a diverse group of employees can benefit your business. *Organisations that hire diverse types of employees benefit from their different skills and life experiences. The different points of view of these workers can help a firm find new opportunities and ways of doing things. In addition, diverse employees often have a greater understanding of diverse customers and the goods and services they prefer.*

© YURI ARCUR/SHUTTERSTOCK

SUCCESS STORY

Good firms to work for

Strong employee development goals and a clear commitment to personal growth are one of the characteristics common to organisations that regularly show up on lists of the best companies to work for.

Spansion, a joint chip-making venture between Japan's Fujitsu and the U.S.-based AMD, has been voted best employer in Asia. Its employees, mainly based in Thailand and China, appreciate the company's commitment to employee development, even though it doesn't necessarily pay the highest wages.

Its Singaporean CEO, Loh Poh Chye, says, "We are always willing to offer training to someone who's motivated, or move someone to a new department, laterally, to work across and up in a new area".

Likewise, in 2012 Google was ranked No.1 in Fortune's latest annual list of "100 Best Companies to Work For." Google's creative and innovative corporate culture helps its employees to thrive Google co-founder Larry Page described it as,"my job as a leader is to make sure everybody in the company has

great opportunities and that they feel they're having a meaningful impact and are contributing to the good of society".

Vodacom in South Africa (a division of Vodafone) are well known for their youthful, inspired and high-tech workforce and their commitment to diversity.

Innocent Drinks has won several awards, including the Times 100 Best Companies to work for award and again, they place a heavy emphasis on the importance of developing their employees and helping them learn.

are realising the necessity of having diversity training span beyond just racial issues. For example, companies such as PricewaterhouseCoopers require annual diversity training and use company-sanctioned global employee-resource groups.* Companies such as these are continuously expanding their business worldwide and therefore need to meld a cohesive workforce from a labour pool whose demographics are constantly becoming more diverse.

A diversity programme will be successful only if it is systematic, is ongoing, and has a strong, sustained commitment from top leadership. Cultural diversity is here to stay. Its impact on organisations is widespread and will continue to grow within corporations. Management must learn to overcome the obstacles and capitalise on the advantages associated with culturally diverse human resources.

JOB ANALYSIS

There is no sense in hiring people unless we know what we are hiring them for. In other words, we need to know the nature of a job before we can find the right person to do it.

Job analysis is a systematic procedure for studying jobs to determine their various elements and requirements. Consider the position of an administration assistant, for example. In a large corporation, there may be 50 kinds of administration assistant positions. They all may be called "administration assistants," but each position may differ from the others in the activities performed, the level of proficiency required for each activity, and the particular set of qualifications that the position demands. These distinctions are the focus of job analysis.

job analysis a systematic procedure for studying jobs to determine their various elements and requirements

The job analysis for a particular position typically consists of two parts—a job description and a job specification. A **job description** is a list of the elements that make up a particular job. It includes

FIGURE 9.1

Job description and job specification *This job description explains the job of sales coordinator and lists the responsibilities of the position. The job specification is contained in the last paragraph.*

JOB DESCRIPTION

TITLE:	Cairo Sales Coordinator	**DATE:**	4th February 2014
DEPARTMENT:	University, Sales	**GRADE:**	12
REPORTS TO:	Regional Manager	**EXEMPT/NONEXEMPT:**	Exempt

BRIEF SUMMARY:
Supervise one other Cairo-based sales representative to gain supervisory experience. Lead the four members of the outside sales rep team that are assigned to territories consisting of colleges and universities in Egypt. Oversee, coordinate, advise, and make decisions regarding Egyptian sales activities. Based upon broad contact with customers across the region and communication with administrators of schools, the person will make recommendations regarding issues specific to the needs of higher education, both in Cairo and wider Egypt, such as distance learning, conversion to the semester system, potential adoptions, and faculty training.

PRINCIPAL ACCOUNTABILITIES:
1. Supervises/manages/trains one other Cairo-based sales rep.
2. Advises two other sales reps regarding the Egyptian institutions in their territories.
3. Increases overall sales in Egypt as well as his or her individual sales territory.
4. Assists regional manager in planning and coordinating regional meetings and Cairo conferences.
5. Initiates a dialogue with campus administrators, particularly in the areas of the semester conversion, distance learning, and faculty development.

DIMENSIONS:
This position will have one direct report in addition to the leadership role played within the region. Revenue most directly impacted will be within the individually assigned territory, the supervised territory, and the overall sales for Egypt.

KNOWLEDGE AND SKILLS:
Must have displayed a history of consistently outstanding sales in personal territory. Must demonstrate clear teamwork and leadership skills and be willing to extend beyond the individual territory goals. Should have a clear understanding of the company's systems and product offerings in order to train and lead other sales representatives. Must have the communication skills and presence to communicate articulately with higher education administrators and to serve as a bridge between the company and higher education in the state.

the duties to be performed, the working conditions, the responsibilities, and the tools and equipment that must be used on the job (see Figure 9.1).

> **job description** a list of the elements that make up a particular job

A **job specification** is a list of the qualifications required to perform a particular job, such as certain skills, abilities, education, and experience. When attempting to hire a financial analyst, the United Bank for Africa might use the following job specification: "Requires eight to ten years of financial experience, a broad-based financial background, strong customer focus, the ability to work confidently with the client's management team, strong analytical skills. Must have strong Excel and Word skills. Personal characteristics should include strong desire to succeed, impact performer (individually and as a member of a team), positive attitude, high energy level and ability to influence others."

 job specification a list of the qualifications required to perform a particular job

The job analysis is not only the basis for recruiting and selecting new employees; it is also used in other areas of HRM, including evaluation and the determination of equitable compensation levels.

RECRUITING, SELECTION, AND ORIENTATION

In an organisation with jobs waiting to be filled, HRM personnel need to (1) find candidates for the jobs and (2) match the right candidate with each job. Three activities are involved: recruiting, selection, and new employee orientation.

Recruiting

Recruiting is the process of attracting qualified job applicants. Because it is a vital link in a costly process (the cost of hiring an employee can be several thousand euros), recruiting needs to be a systematic process. One goal of recruiters is to attract the "right number" of applicants. The right number is enough to allow a good match between applicants and open positions but not so many that matching them requires too much time and effort. For example, if there are five open positions and five applicants, the firm essentially has no choice. It must hire those five applicants (qualified or not), or the positions will remain open. At the other extreme, if several hundred job seekers apply for the five positions, HRM personnel will have to spend weeks processing their applications.

 recruiting the process of attracting qualified job applicants

Recruiters may seek applicants outside the firm, within the firm, or both. The source used depends on the nature of the position, the situation within the firm, and sometimes the firm's established or traditional recruitment policies.

External recruiting **External recruiting** is the attempt to attract job applicants from outside an organisation. External recruiting may include recruiting via newspaper advertising, employment agencies, and online employment organisations; recruiting on college campuses; soliciting recommendations from present employees; and conducting "open houses." Increasingly, people utilise the Internet to conduct their job searches. Social networking sites like LinkedIn or TweetMyJobs help match employers with interested potential employees. Online job search sites, like Monster.com or Indeed, help job seekers search for jobs by a variety of criteria like location and industry.*

 external recruiting the attempt to attract job applicants from outside an organisation

Clearly, it is best to match the recruiting means with the kind of applicant being sought. Technology is helping organisations with this matching process. TweetMyJobs, a more recent addition to the social networking HRM arsenal, is a new means of matching job seekers with available positions. It is a service that alerts people via Twitter when a job opens up for which they are qualified. Web sites like LinkedIn allow employees to post their résumés, skills, and experiences; and employers can search for qualified employees. Technologies like these allow employers and employees to more easily locate positions that are a good fit.*

External recruiting has both advantages and disadvantages. A primary advantage of external recruiting is that it brings in people with new perspectives and varied business backgrounds. Some

Don't just search the classified ads to find a job. *Potential employees are being recruited in increasingly different ways today. Companies often keep statistics on their recruiting sources so they can determine which methods are the best for finding good employees.*

©FENG YU/SHUTTERSTOCK

firms prefer to hire recruits directly out of university because they believe that graduates will be more trainable to fit with the corporate culture and the needs of the company. An additional benefit of hiring younger talent is that they tend to be more technologically savvy than their older counterparts, a characteristic that is highly desirable in today's fast-moving workplace. A disadvantage of external recruiting is that it is often expensive, especially if private employment agencies must be used. External recruiting also may provoke resentment among present employees.

Internal recruiting **Internal recruiting** means considering present employees as applicants for available positions. Generally, current employees are considered for *promotion* to higher-level positions. However, employees may be considered for *transfer* from one position to another at the same level. Among leading companies, 85 per cent of CEOs are promoted from within. In the companies that hire CEOs from outside, 60 to 80 per cent of the CEOs are gone after 18 months.*

> **internal recruiting** considering present employees as applicants for available positions

Promoting from within provides strong motivation for current employees and helps the firm to retain quality personnel. The practice of *job posting*, or informing current employees of upcoming openings, may be a company policy or required by union contract. The primary disadvantage of internal recruiting is that promoting a current employee leaves another position to be filled. Not only does the firm still incur recruiting and selection costs, but it also must train two employees instead of one.

In many situations it may be impossible to recruit internally. For example, a new position may be such that no current employee is qualified, or the firm may be growing so rapidly that there is no time to reassign positions that promotion or transfer requires.

Selection

Selection is the process of gathering information about applicants for a position and then using that information to choose the most appropriate applicant. Note the use of the word *appropriate*. In selection, the idea is not to hire the person with the *most* qualifications but rather the applicant who is *most appropriate*. The selection of an applicant is made by line managers responsible for the position. However, HRM personnel usually help by developing a pool of applicants and by expediting the assessment of these applicants. Common means of obtaining information about applicants' qualifications are employment applications, interviews, references, and assessment centres.

> **selection** the process of gathering information about applicants for a position and then using that information to choose the most appropriate applicant

Employment applications   An employment application is useful in collecting factual information on a candidate's education, work experience, and personal history. The data obtained from applications usually are used for two purposes: to identify applicants who are worthy of further scrutiny and to familiarise interviewers with their backgrounds. Many firms offer online applications, which help to streamline the process and improve data gathering capabilities for the firm. In fact, paper applications are becoming increasingly rare.

Many job candidates submit résumés, and some firms require them. A *résumé*, or curriculum vitae (CV), is a one- or two-page summary of the candidate's background and qualifications. It may include a description of the type of job the applicant is seeking. A résumé may be sent to a firm to request consideration for available jobs, or it may be submitted along with an employment application.

To improve the usefulness of information, HRM specialists ask current employees about factors in their backgrounds most related to their current jobs. Then these factors are included on the applications and may be weighted more heavily when evaluating new applicants' qualifications.

Employment tests   Tests administered to job candidates usually focus on aptitudes, skills, abilities, or knowledge relevant to the job. Such tests (basic computer skills tests, for example) indicate how well the applicant will do the job. Occasionally, companies use general intelligence or personality tests, but these are seldom helpful in predicting specific job performance. Many organisations, from the very small up to *Fortune* 500 companies, use predictive behaviour tests. Improved technology has brought down substantially the costs of administering such tests.

Interviews   The interview is perhaps the most widely used selection technique. Job candidates are interviewed by at least one member of the HRM staff and by the person for whom they will be working. Candidates for higher-level jobs may meet with a department head or vice president over several interviews.

Interviews provide an opportunity for applicants and the firm to learn more about each other. Interviewers can pose problems to test the candidate's abilities, probe employment history, and learn something about the candidate's attitudes and motivation. The candidate has a chance to find out more about the job and potential co-workers. In some instances, companies are able to use video conferencing software like Skype. This has made the interviewing process easier for companies. Some companies have been able to reduce the number of applicants being flown in for interviews.*

Unfortunately, interviewing may be the stage at which discrimination begins. For example, suppose that a female applicant mentions that she is the mother of small children. Her interviewer may assume that she would not be available for job-related travel. In addition, interviewers may be unduly influenced by such factors as appearance, or they may ask different questions of different applicants so that it becomes impossible to compare candidates' qualifications. Table 9.2 contains interview questions that are difficult to answer.

Some of these problems can be solved through better interviewer training and use of structured interviews. In a *structured interview,* the interviewer asks only a prepared set of job-related questions. The firm also may consider using several different interviewers for each applicant, but this is likely to be costly.

References   A job candidate generally is asked to furnish the names of references—people who can verify background information and provide personal evaluations. Naturally, applicants tend to list only references who are likely to say good things. Thus, personal evaluations obtained from references may not be of much value. However, references are often contacted to verify such information as previous job responsibilities and the reason an applicant left a former job. In some instances, online social networking has changed the order in which employers receive information. Usually, references come after interviews. However, applicants may have former employers and colleagues post recommendations to their LinkedIn accounts so that potential employers see positive reviews about their work even before interviewing them.

Assessment centres   An assessment centre is used primarily to select current employees for promotion to higher-level positions. Typically, a group of employees is sent to the centre for a few days.

TABLE 9.2	Interview questions that may be difficult to answer

1. Tell me about yourself.
2. What do you know about our organisation?
3. What can you do for us? Why should we hire you?
4. What qualifications do you have that make you feel that you will be successful in your field?
5. What have you learned from the jobs that you have held?
6. Where do you see yourself in five years?
7. What are your special skills, and how did you acquire them?
8. Have you had any special accomplishments in your lifetime that you are particularly proud of?
9. Why did you leave your most recent job?
10. How do you spend your spare time? What are your hobbies?
11. What are your strengths and weaknesses?
12. Discuss five major accomplishments.
13. What kind of boss would you like? Why?
14. If you could spend a day with someone you have known or known of, who would it be?
15. What personality characteristics rub you the wrong way?
16. How do you show your anger? What type of things make you angry?
17. With what type of person do you spend the majority of your time?
18. What activities have you ever quit?
19. Define cooperation.
20. Do you have any questions for me?

Sources: From GREENE/MARTEL, *The Ultimate Job Hunter's Guidebook,* 6E. © 2012 Cengage Learning.

While there, they participate in activities designed to simulate the management environment and to predict managerial effectiveness. Trained observers make recommendations regarding promotion possibilities. Although this technique is gaining popularity, the expense involved limits its use.

Orientation

Once all information about job candidates has been collected and analysed, the company extends a job offer. If it is accepted, the candidate becomes an employee.

Soon after a candidate joins a firm, he or she goes through the firm's orientation programme. **Orientation** is the process of acquainting new employees with an organisation. Orientation topics range from the location of the company cafeteria to career paths within the firm. The orientation itself may consist of a half-hour informal presentation by a human resources manager, or it may be an elaborate programme involving dozens of people and lasting several days or weeks.

 orientation the process of acquainting new employees with an organisation

COMPENSATION AND BENEFITS

An effective employee reward system must (1) enable employees to satisfy basic needs, (2) provide rewards comparable with those offered by other firms, (3) be distributed fairly within the organisation, and (4) recognise that different people have different needs.

A firm's compensation system can be structured to meet the first three of these requirements. The fourth is more difficult because it must account for many variables. Most firms offer a number of benefits that, taken together, generally help to provide for employees' varying needs.

Compensation decisions

Compensation is the payment employees receive in return for their labour. Its importance to employees is obvious. Because compensation can account for a significant percentage of a firm's operating costs, it is equally important to the management. Therefore, the firm's **compensation system**, the policies and strategies that determine employee compensation, must be designed carefully to provide for employees' needs while keeping labour costs within reasonable limits. For most firms, designing an effective compensation system requires three separate management decisions—wage level, wage structure, and individual wages.

> **compensation** the payment employees receive in return for their labour
> **compensation system** the policies and strategies that determine employee compensation

Wage level   Management first must position the firm's general pay level relative to pay levels of comparable firms. Most firms choose a pay level near the industry average. However, a firm that is not in good financial shape may pay less than average, and large, prosperous organisations may pay more than average.

To determine the average pay for a job, the firm may use wage surveys. A **wage survey** is a collection of data on prevailing wage rates within an industry or a geographic area. Such surveys are compiled by industry associations, local governments, personnel associations, and (occasionally) individual firms.

> **wage survey** a collection of data on prevailing wage rates within an industry or a geographic area

Wage structure   Next, management must decide on relative pay levels for all the positions within the firm. Will managers be paid more than secretaries? Will secretaries be paid more than custodians? The result of this set of decisions is often called the firm's *wage structure*.

The wage structure almost always is developed on the basis of a job evaluation. **Job evaluation** is the process of determining the relative worth of the various jobs within a firm. Most observers probably would agree that a secretary should make more money than a custodian, but how much more? Job evaluation should provide the answer to this question.

> **job evaluation** the process of determining the relative worth of the various jobs within a firm

A number of techniques may be used to evaluate jobs. The simplest is to rank all the jobs within the firm according to value. A more frequently used method is based on the job analysis. Points are allocated to each job for each of its elements and requirements. For example, "university degree required" might be worth 50 points, whereas the need for a secondary school education might count for only 25 points. The more points a job is allocated, the more important it is presumed to be (and the higher its level in the firm's wage structure).

Individual wages   Finally, the company must determine the specific payments individual employees will receive. Consider the case of two secretaries working side by side. Job evaluation has been used to determine the relative level of secretarial pay within the firm's wage structure. However, suppose that one secretary has 15 years of experience and can type 80 words per minute accurately and the other has two years of experience and can type only 55 words per minute; in most firms, these two people would not receive the same pay. Instead, a wage range would be established for the secretarial position. In this case, the range might be €8.50 to €12.50 per hour. The more experienced and proficient secretary then would be paid an amount near the top of the range (say, €12.25 per hour); the less experienced secretary would receive an amount that is lower but still within the range (say, €8.75 per hour).

Two wage decisions come into play here. First, the employee's initial rate must be established. It is based on experience, other qualifications, and expected performance. Later, the employee may be given pay increases based on seniority and performance.

Comparable worth

Consider some jobs—nurses, secretaries, and medical records analysts, for example—that require education, skills, and training equal to higher-paid positions but are undervalued. **Comparable worth** is a concept that seeks equal compensation for jobs that require about the same level of education, training, and skill. In recent decades, many governments have taken steps to ensure that all workers have equal pay for comparable worth, but the issue remains contentious. Critics of comparable worth believe that the market should determine the worth of jobs and laws should not tamper with the market's pricing mechanisms.*

 comparable worth a concept that seeks equal compensation for jobs requiring about the same level of education, training, and skills

Types of compensation

Compensation can be paid in a variety of forms. Most forms of compensation fall into the following categories: hourly wage, weekly or monthly salary, commissions, incentive payments, lump-sum salary increases, and profit sharing.

Hourly wage An **hourly wage** is a specific amount of money paid for each hour of work. Often, depending on the laws specific to that country, region or state, or the employer's policy on wages, an increased rate will be paid for "overtime", that is any additional hours the employee works over their contracted hours. For example, in some countries, where the full-time working week is considered to be 40 hours, the employee will earn "time and a half" for every additional hour worked that week. Workers in retail and fast-food chains, on assembly lines, and in clerical positions usually are paid an hourly wage.

 hourly wage a specific amount of money paid for each hour of work

Weekly or monthly salary A **salary** is a specific amount of money paid for an employee's work during a set calendar period, regardless of the actual number of hours worked. Salaried employees receive no overtime pay, but they do not typically lose pay when they are absent from work. Most professional and managerial positions are salaried.

 salary a specific amount of money paid for an employee's work during a set calendar period, regardless of the actual number of hours worked

Commissions A **commission** is a payment that is a percentage of sales revenue. Sales representatives and sales managers often are paid entirely through commissions or through a combination of commissions and salary.

 commission a payment that is a percentage of sales revenue

Incentive payments An **incentive payment** is a payment in addition to wages, salary, or commissions. Incentive payments are really extra rewards for outstanding job performance. They may be distributed to all employees or only to certain employees. Some firms distribute incentive payments to all employees annually. The size of the payment depends on the firm's earnings and, at times, on the particular employee's length of service with the firm. Firms sometimes offer incentives to employees who exceed specific sales or production goals, a practice called *gain sharing*.

incentive payment a payment in addition to wages, salary, or commissions

To avoid yearly across-the-board salary increases, some organisations reward outstanding workers individually through *merit pay*. This pay-for-performance approach allows management to control labour costs while encouraging employees to work more efficiently. An employee's merit pay depends on his or her achievements relative to those of others.

Lump-sum salary increases   In traditional reward systems, an employee who receives an annual pay increase is given part of the increase in each pay period. For example, suppose that an employee on a monthly salary gets a 10 per cent annual pay hike. He or she actually receives 10 per cent of the former monthly salary added to each month's paycheck for a year. Companies that offer a **lump-sum salary increase** give the employee the option of taking the entire pay raise in one lump sum. The employee then draws his or her "regular" pay for the rest of the year. The lump-sum payment typically is treated as an interest-free loan that must be repaid if the employee leaves the firm during the year.

> **lump-sum salary increase** an entire pay raise taken in one lump sum

Profit-sharing   **Profit-sharing** is the distribution of a percentage of a firm's profit among its employees. The idea is to motivate employees to work effectively by giving them a stake in the company's financial success. General Motors employees participate in employee profit-sharing plans. Employees at the John Lewis Partnership based in the U.K. are referred to as "partners" as each owns a stake in the company and thus benefits from profits.

> **profit-sharing** the distribution of a percentage of a firm's profit among its employees

Employee benefits

An **employee benefit** is a reward in addition to regular compensation that is provided indirectly to employees. Employee benefits consist mainly of services (such as insurance) that are paid for partially or totally by employers and employee expenses (such as college or university tuition) that are reimbursed by employers. Currently, the average cost of these benefits is nearly 30 per cent of an employee's total compensation, which includes wages plus benefits.* Thus, a person who received total compensation (including benefits) of €50,000 a year earned €35,300 in wages and received an additional €14,700 in benefits.

> **employee benefit** a reward in addition to regular compensation that is provided indirectly to employees

Types of benefits   Employee benefits take a variety of forms. *Pay for time not worked* covers such absences as holiday time, holidays, and sick leave. *Insurance packages* may include health, life, and dental insurance for employees and their families. Some firms pay the entire cost of the insurance

When you're applying for a new job, wait to ask about benefits until you've been offered the position. During your first interview, stay focused on the company and how you can be an asset in this position, not on the benefits or compensation.

What job benefits are crucial to you? The benefits companies provide vary widely. Large companies are often able to offer employees more benefits than small ones. However, in small firms, employees are more likely to do a broader range of tasks and advance to higher positions more quickly.

© CARRITEATER/SHUTTERSTOCK

package, and others share the cost with the employee. The costs of *pension and retirement programmes* also may be borne entirely by the firm or shared with the employee.

Depending on the country in question, some benefits are required by law. For example, employers working in countries such as the U.S., which does not have a national health service, must maintain *workers' compensation insurance,* which pays medical bills for injuries that occur on the job and provides income for employees who are disabled by job-related injuries. Workers in the U.K. must pay National Insurance contributions to pay for state benefits and services, which are usually automatically deducted from their monthly wage through the PAYE (pay as you earn) system, if they are not self-employed.

Other benefits provided by employers include tuition-reimbursement plans, credit unions, child-care services, company cafeterias, exercise rooms, and broad share option plans available to all employees.

Some companies offer unusual benefits to attract and retain employees. Google is known for its unusual perks and fun activities, which include bocce courts, a bowling alley, eyebrow shaping, and free food in companywide cafes. Employees at Autodesk can bring their dogs to work and can take a six-week paid sabbatical every four years. Many larger companies offer use of an onsite gym for use by staff.*

Flexible benefit plans Through a **flexible benefit plan**, an employee receives a predetermined amount of benefit dollars and may allocate those dollars to various categories of benefits in the mix that best fits his or her needs. Some flexible benefit plans offer a broad array of benefit options, including health care, dental care, life insurance, accidental death and dismemberment coverage for both the worker and dependents, long-term disability coverage, holiday benefits, retirement savings, and dependent-care benefits. Other firms offer limited options, primarily in health and life insurance and retirement plans.

> **flexible benefit plan** compensation plan whereby an employee receives a predetermined amount of benefit money to spend on a package of benefits he or she has selected to meet individual needs

Although the cost of administering flexible plans is high, a number of organisations, including Quaker Oats and Coca-Cola, have implemented this option for several reasons. Because employees' needs are so diverse, flexible plans help firms to offer benefit packages that more specifically meet their employees' needs. Flexible plans can, in the long run, help a company to contain costs because a specified amount is allocated to cover the benefits of each employee. Furthermore, organisations that offer flexible plans with many choices may be perceived as being employee-friendly. Thus, they are in a better position to attract and retain qualified employees.

The following chapter revisits the theme of compensation, and the impact that its various forms play in motivating employees.

TRAINING AND DEVELOPMENT

Training and development are extremely important at the Container Store. Because great customer service is so important, every first-year full-time salesperson receives about 185 hours of formal training as opposed to the industry standard, which is approximately seven hours. Training and development continue throughout a person's career. Each store has a full-time trainer called the *super sales trainer*. This trainer provides product training, sales training, and employee-development training. A number of top managers believe that the financial and human resources invested in training and development are well worth it.

Both training and development are aimed at improving employees' skills and abilities. However, the two are usually differentiated as either employee training or management development. **Employee training** is the process of teaching operations and technical employees how to do their present jobs more effectively and efficiently. **Management development** is the process of preparing managers and other professionals to assume increased responsibility in both present and future positions. Thus, training and development differ in who is being taught and the purpose of the teaching. However, both are necessary for personal and organisational growth. Companies that hope to stay competitive typically make huge commitments to employee training and development. Internet-based e-learning is growing. Driven by cost, travel, and time savings, online learning alone (and in conjunction with face-to-face situations) is a strong alternative strategy. Development of a training programme usually has three components: analysis of needs, determination of training and development methods, and creation of an evaluation system to assess the programme's effectiveness.

> **employee training** the process of teaching operations and technical employees how to do their present jobs more effectively and efficiently
>
> **management development** the process of preparing managers and other professionals to assume increased responsibility in both present and future positions

Some employers are using new approaches to train and certify workers. They have found that having a good education may not provide an employee with necessary skills to do a job well, so some organisations have developed a system that works similarly to the Boy Scouts merit badge. A potential employee completes a certification course geared toward a certain line of work and receives a "badge" upon successful completion. Programmes like this cut down on the additional on-the-job training required after being hired because they are geared toward training in a specific field. Having such certification provides an employer with a better idea of the exact skill set of a potential employee. Once hired, employees undergo additional training, which varies a great deal from firm to firm and between industries.*

Analysis of training needs

When thinking about developing a training programme, managers first must determine if training is needed and, if so, what types of training needs exist. At times, what at first appears to be a need for training is actually, on assessment, a need for motivation. Training needs can vary considerably.

© ADAM GREGOR/SHUTTERSTOCK

What job training methods have you experienced, and how effective were they? *Organisations train employees using a variety of methods and locations. Depending on the type of business, the training may take just a few hours or more than a year.*

For example, some employees may need training to improve their technical skills, or they may need training about organisational procedures. Training also may focus on business ethics, product information, or customer service. Because training is expensive, it is critical that the correct training needs be identified.

Training and development methods

A number of methods are available for employee training and management development. Some of these methods may be more suitable for one or the other, but most can be applied to both training and management development.

- *On-the-job methods.* The trainee learns by doing the work under the supervision of an experienced employee.
- *Simulations.* The work situation is simulated in a separate area so that learning takes place away from the day-to-day pressures of work.
- *Classroom teaching and lectures.* You probably already know these methods quite well.
- *Conferences and seminars.* Experts and learners meet to discuss problems and exchange ideas.
- *Role-playing.* Participants act out the roles of others in the organisation for better understanding of those roles (primarily a management development tool).

Evaluation of training and development

Training and development are very expensive. The training itself costs quite a bit, and employees are usually not working—or are working at a reduced load and pace—during training sessions. To ensure that training and development are cost-effective, the managers responsible should evaluate the company's efforts periodically.

The starting point for this evaluation is a set of verifiable objectives that are developed before the training is undertaken. Suppose that a training programme is expected to improve the skills of machinists. The objective of the programme might be stated as follows: "At the end of the training period, each machinist should be able to process 30 parts per hour with no more than one defective part per 90 parts completed." This objective clearly specifies what is expected and how training results may be measured or verified. Evaluation then consists of measuring machinists' output and the ratio of defective parts produced after the training.

The results of training evaluations should be made known to all those involved in the programme—including trainees and upper management. For trainees, the results of evaluations can enhance motivation and learning. For upper management, the results may be the basis for making decisions about the training programme itself.

PERFORMANCE APPRAISAL

Performance appraisal is the evaluation of employees' current and potential levels of performance to allow managers to make objective human resources decisions. The process has three main objectives. First, managers use performance appraisals to let workers know how well they are doing and how they can do better in the future. Second, a performance appraisal provides an effective basis for distributing rewards, such as pay raises and promotions. Third, performance appraisal helps the organisation monitor its employee selection, training, and development activities. If large numbers of employees continually perform below expectations, the firm may need to revise its selection process or strengthen its training and development activities. Most performance appraisal processes include a written document. An example appears in Figure 9.2.

performance appraisal the evaluation of employees' current and potential levels of performance to allow managers to make objective human resources decisions

Performance appraisal

Common evaluation techniques

The various techniques and methods for appraising employee performance are either objective or judgmental in nature.

Objective methods   Objective appraisal methods use some measurable quantity as the basis for assessing performance. Units of output, euro volume of sales, number of defective products, and number of insurance claims processed are all objective, measurable quantities. Thus, an employee who processes an average of 26 insurance claims per week is given a higher evaluation than one whose average is 19 claims per week.

Such objective measures may require some adjustment for the work environment. Suppose that the first of our insurance claims processors works in Paris and the second works in rural Provence. Both must visit each client because they are processing homeowners' insurance claims. The difference in their average weekly output may be entirely because of the long distances the worker based in Provence must travel to visit clients. In this case, the two workers may very well be equally competent and motivated. Thus, a manager must take into account circumstances that may be hidden by a purely statistical measurement.

Judgmental methods   Judgmental appraisal methods are used much more frequently than objective methods. They require that the manager judge or estimate the employee's performance level. However, judgmental methods are not capricious. These methods are based on employee ranking or rating scales. When ranking is used, the manager ranks subordinates from best to worst. This approach has a number of drawbacks, including the lack of any absolute standard. Use of rating scales is the most popular judgmental appraisal technique. A *rating scale* consists of a number of statements; each employee is rated on the degree to which the statement applies. For example, one statement might be, "This employee always does high-quality work." The supervisor would give the employee a rating, from 5 down to 1, corresponding to gradations ranging from "strongly agree" to "strongly disagree." The ratings on all the statements are added to obtain the employee's total evaluation.

Avoiding appraisal errors   Managers must be cautious if they are to avoid making mistakes when appraising employees. It is common to overuse one portion of an evaluation instrument, thus

---

RESPONSIBLE PRACTICE   Investigating workplace bullying – what if there aren't any witnesses?

What happens if an issue over bullying or harassment is reported to you and there are no witnesses? How can you take one person's word that they are being bullied or harassed?

There are in fact a number of ways in which this can be done. Firstly, the alleged incident may not be an isolated event. If an employee is being targeted, try and find colleagues, customers or clients who may have noticed something previously: for example, back-handed compliments; unnecessary criticism or shouting.

What about witnesses to the aftereffects of the alleged incident? Was the employee seen crying in the toilets and did they confide in others? Ask the alleged victim if they told anyone else about the issues for if anyone saw them upset after an incident.

Don't forget the alleged bully. They could respond to the investigation in a way that allows the investigator to become a witness to their behaviour.

Look at electronic records for "digital witnesses" sent around the time of the alleged incident. Ask for any emails, text messages or voicemails sent around the time the alleged incident took place. Are there any from the alleged bully to the alleged victim? Or from the alleged victim to friends or colleagues?

Look for a paper trail showing previous grievances made against the alleged bully; accident reports; excessive sick leave requests made by the alleged victim or others working with or for the alleged bully; exit interviews; records from an employee assistance programme; and finally, any statistics or surveys that might show data or names of potential witnesses originally reluctant to come forward.

overemphasising some issues and underemphasising others. A manager must guard against allowing an employee's poor performance on one activity to influence his or her judgment of that subordinate's work on other activities. Similarly, putting too much weight on recent performance distorts an employee's evaluation. For example, if the employee is being rated on performance over the last year, a manager should not permit last month's disappointing performance to overshadow the quality of the work done in the first 11 months of the year. Finally, a manager must guard against discrimination on the basis of race, age, gender, religion, national origin, or sexual orientation.

Performance feedback

No matter which appraisal technique is used, the results should be discussed with the employee soon after the evaluation is completed. The manager should explain the basis for present rewards and should let the employee know what he or she can do to be recognised as a better performer in the future. The information provided to an employee in such discussions is called *performance feedback,* and the process is known as a *performance feedback interview.*

There are three major approaches to performance feedback interviews: tell-and-sell, tell-and-listen, and problem solving. In a *tell-and-sell* feedback interview, the superior tells the employee how good or bad the employee's performance has been and then attempts to persuade the employee to accept the evaluation. Because the employee has no input into the evaluation, the tell-and-sell interview can lead to defensiveness, resentment, and frustration on the part of the subordinate. The employee may not accept the results of the interview and may not be committed to achieving the goals that are set.

With the *tell-and-listen* approach, the supervisor tells the employee what has been right and wrong with the employee's performance and then gives the employee a chance to respond. The subordinate may simply be given an opportunity to react to the supervisor's statements or may be permitted to offer a full self-appraisal, challenging the supervisor's assessment.

In the *problem-solving* approach, employees evaluate their own performance and set their own goals for future performance. The supervisor is more a colleague than a judge and offers comments and advice in a noncritical manner. An active and open dialogue ensues in which goals for improvement are mutually established. The problem-solving interview is most likely to result in the employee's commitment to the established goals.

To avoid some of the problems associated with the tell-and-sell interview, supervisors sometimes use a mixed approach. The mixed interview uses the tell-and-sell approach to communicate administrative decisions and the problem-solving approach to discuss employee-development issues and future performance goals.

An appraisal approach that has become popular is called a *360-degree evaluation.* A 360-degree evaluation collects anonymous reviews about an employee from his or her peers, subordinates, and supervisors and then compiles these reviews into a feedback report that is given to the employee. Companies that invest significant resources in employee-development efforts are especially likely to use 360-degree evaluations. An employee should not be given a feedback report without first having a one-on-one meeting with his or her supervisor. The most appropriate way to introduce a 360-degree evaluation system in a company is to begin with upper-level management. Then managers should be trained on how to interpret feedback reports so that they can coach their employees on how to use the feedback to achieve higher-level job-related skills and behaviours.

© WILLIAM CASEY / SHUTTERSTOCK

Performance feedback can help employees progress within an organisation. *A business usually evaluates its employees on an annual basis, but sometimes it does so quarterly and even monthly, especially when they are newly hired. Performance reviews that gather feedback about an employee from his or her peers, subordinates, and supervisors can help the person get a realistic view of his or her strengths and weaknesses.*

Finally, we should note that many managers find it difficult to discuss the negative aspects of an appraisal. Unfortunately, they may ignore performance feedback altogether or provide it in a very weak and ineffectual manner. In truth, though, most employees have strengths that can be emphasised to soften the discussion of their weaknesses. An employee may not even be aware of the weaknesses and their consequences. If such weaknesses are not pointed out through performance feedback, they cannot possibly be eliminated. Only through tactful, honest communication can the results of an appraisal be fully used.

Legislation regarding HRM practices has been passed in many countries across the world, mainly to protect the rights of employees, to promote job safety, and to eliminate discrimination in the workplace. This regulation differs – sometimes greatly – from country to country.

SUMMARY

- Describe the major components of human resources management.

  Human resources management (HRM) is the set of activities involved in acquiring, maintaining, and developing an organisation's human resources. Responsibility for HRM is shared by specialised staff and line managers. HRM activities include human resources planning, job analysis, recruitment, selection, orientation, compensation, benefits, training and development, and performance appraisal.

- Identify the steps in human resources planning.

  Human resources planning consists of forecasting the human resources that a firm will need and those that it will have available and then planning a course of action to match supply with demand. Layoffs, attrition, early retirement, and (as a last resort) firing are ways to reduce the size of the workforce. Supply is increased through hiring.

- Describe cultural diversity and understand some of the challenges and opportunities associated with it.

  Cultural diversity refers to the differences among people in a workforce owing to race, ethnicity, and gender. With an increasing number of women, minorities, and immigrants entering the U.S. workforce, management is faced with both challenges and competitive advantages. Some organisations are implementing diversity-related training programmes and working to make the most of cultural diversity. With proper guidance and management, a culturally diverse organisation can prove beneficial to all involved.

- Explain the objectives and uses of job analysis.

  Job analysis provides a job description and a job specification for each position within a firm. A job description is a list of the elements that make up a particular job. A job specification is a list of qualifications required to perform a particular job. Job analysis is used in evaluation and

  in the determination of compensation levels and serves as the basis for recruiting and selecting new employees.

- Describe the processes of recruiting, employee selection, and orientation.

  Recruiting is the process of attracting qualified job applicants. Candidates for open positions may be recruited from within or outside a firm. In the selection process, information about candidates is obtained from applications, résumés, tests, interviews, references, or assessment centres. This information then is used to select the most appropriate candidate for the job. Newly hired employees will then go through a formal or an informal orientation programme to acquaint themselves with the firm.

- Discuss the primary elements of employee compensation and benefits.

  Compensation is the payment employees receive in return for their labour. In developing a system for paying employees, management must decide on the firm's general wage level (relative to other firms), the wage structure within the firm, and individual wages. Wage surveys and job analyses are useful in making these decisions. Employees may be paid hourly wages, salaries, or commissions. They also may receive incentive payments, lump-sum salary increases, and profit-sharing payments. Employee benefits, which are nonmonetary rewards to employees, add about 28 per cent to the cost of compensation.

- Explain the purposes and techniques of employee training and development.

  Employee-training and management-development programmes enhance the ability of employees to contribute to a firm. When developing a training programme, the company should analyse training needs and then select training methods. Because training is expensive, an organisation should periodically evaluate the effectiveness of its training programmes.

- Discuss performance appraisal techniques and performance feedback.

 Performance appraisal, or evaluation, is used to provide employees with performance feedback, to serve as a basis for distributing rewards, and to monitor selection and training activities. Both objective and judgmental appraisal techniques are used. Their results are communicated to employees through three performance feedback approaches: tell-and-sell, tell-and-listen, and problem solving.

EXERCISE QUESTIONS

1 Explain the key elements of the acquisitions process
2 Give some examples of employee benefits that might be offered in a company.
3 Describe the common evaluation techniques.
4 Why is training staff important for a company?
5 Explain the process of orientation.

CASE 9.1

Tranquillity Resorts

NB: This fictional case uses a recruitment scenario to address issues of diversity and discrimination in the workplace

Tranquillity Resorts consists of a game lodge and two luxury boutique hotels in Mpumalanga, South Africa. They currently employee 46 full time employees ranging from the Managing Director, Sam Petersen, three operational managers (one for each of the venues) Johan Liebenberg, Heinrich Rossouw and Christo van Zyl, an HR manager Patricia Mohale, receptionists, administrative personnel, game rangers, spa therapists and gardeners who are also responsible for general maintenance. The managers and administrative personnel in the three locations deal with day-to-day HR matters that are coordinated by a single HR manager located at the Sabi Lodge. They do not appoint catering and cleaning staff but enter into contracts with labour brokers, who render specialised services, to fill these positions. The resorts are well known for their superior facilities and exceptional service. They cater for overseas visitors and the upper income class and have an annual turnover of well beyond R10 million. They wish to maintain their high standards which have been the secret of their success and therefore employ only the best people. They are currently in the process of filling a receptionist position at one of the hotels. They have interviewed a number of people and have compiled a list of three possible candidates. However, they do not see eye to eye on the matter. During a heated management meeting the following conversation takes place:

Patricia: We currently have three candidates with the required qualifications and experience. As far as we could determine they are all equally competent to fill the position. The only difference is their race and gender: one white woman (Megan Smith), one black woman (Liz Hlongwane) and a black man (Lucas Sadiki). For me it is quite clear. In terms of legal requirements, the black women should get the job.

Sam: Hold on Patricia. I don't agree with you. What legal requirements are you referring to? We are not bound by the Employment Equity Act. We only employ 46 people. Why do you think we have opted to use labour brokers to keep our numbers down? We don't want to be bothered with all that affirmative action nonsense. We want to employ the best person for the job.

Johan: I only agree with Patricia on one thing. We should not even consider appointing a man as a receptionist. We all know women are better at that job even if this guy seemed to be quite in touch with his feminine side. What self-respecting man would want to be a receptionist anyway?

Heinrich: Maybe it would be a good thing to bring a man into the mix. We already have too many women. They drive me crazy. They either socialise all the time or they have cat fights. Not to mention the fact that I have to make a plan each time one of them has a sick child that needs to be taken care of. It's just so much simpler to appoint a man. They don't come with all the additional baggage.

Christo: Speaking of baggage. Did you notice that Liz seemed to stutter during the interview? She did not say anything about it but surely we cannot appoint someone as a receptionist that cannot speak properly?

Patricia: Maybe she was just nervous. I would have been if I had to face the four of you in an interview. I think you were insensitive blabbering on in Afrikaans as it was quite clear that she did not understand a word of it. Afrikaans is not my first language either but don't think I did not follow your insensitive comments about her appearance when she left the room.

Sam: Come on Patricia. Don't take everything so seriously. We were just joking around. But don't you think a receptionists' appearance is an important matter? This is the face of our business.

Patricia: I sometimes wonder why you appointed me. I certainly don't fit your white male preference. It's clear to me that you do not yet appreciate the diversity of people in this beautiful country of ours and see advantages that a variety of people can bring to this business. Gentlemen, we still have a long way to go.

Questions

1   Which dimensions of diversity can you identify from the above scenario? Identify them and explain how each dimensions identified can potentially lead to discrimination.

2   Identify examples of stereotypes and prejudices from the conversation. What actions can Patricia, as HR manager, take to overcome these stereotypes and prejudices?

3   Patricia refers to the advantages of a diverse workforce. Identify potential advantages of a more diverse workforce for Tranquillity Resorts and explain how she should go about building a culture where diversity is valued.

CHAPTER REFERENCES

Bergen, Jennifer, "The 10 Best Job Search Websites," *PC Mag*, February 24, 2012, www.pcmag.com/slideshow/story/294523/the-10-best-job-search-websites/.

Byrnes, Nanette, "Star Search," *BusinessWeek*, October 10, 2005, http://businessweek.com/mediacenter/podcasts/cover_stories/covercast_09_29_05.htm.

"Employment Cost Index News Release," U.S. Department of Labor, Bureau of Labor Statistics, *Economic News Release*, October 28, 2011, http://bls.gov/news.release/archives/eci_10282011.htm.

eSkill, www.eskill.com/, accessed March 16, 2012.

Fish, Jeff, "Yes, Social Media Helps you in Real Life!," The New Great Generation, March 24, 2012, www.boston.com/lifestyle/blogs/thenextgreatgeneration/2012/03/yes_social_media_helps_you_in.html.

Frankel, Barbara, "The DiversityInc Top 10 Companies for Global Diversity," *DiversityInc Magazine*, May 18, 2009, http://diversityinc.com/diversity-management/the-diversityinc-top-10-companies-for-global-diversity-2/.

Greengard, Samuel, "Technology Drives Major Changes to HR," *Baseline*, March 14, 2012, www.baselinemag.com/c/a/IT-Management/Technology-Drives-Major-Changes-to-HR-771760/; "Human Capital Trends 2012: Leap Ahead," Deloitte, www.deloitte.com/view/en_US/us/Services/consulting/human-capital/human-capital-trends-2012/index.htm?id=us_furl_cons_general_hct12_main_022812, accessed March 16, 2012.

"Human Resources Jobs at GE," http://jobs.gecareers.com/go/Human-Resources-Jobs/236325/, accessed March 23, 2012.

Moskowitz, Milton and Levering, Robert, "100 Top Companies to Work For," *Fortune*, February 8, 2012, http://money.cnn.com/magazines/fortune/best-companies/2012/full_list/.

Tweet My Jobs, http://TweetMyJobs.com; "On the Job Hunt: Job Seekers Leverage Social Media," My Fox DC, March 9, 2012, www.myfoxdc.com/dpp/news/national/foxnews/On-the-Job-Hunt-Job-seekers-leverage-social-media_81538431.

Young, Jeffery R., "Merit Badges for the Job Market," *The Wall Street Journal,* January 21, 2012, http://online.wsj.com/article/SB10001424052970204301404577170912221516638.html, accessed March 25, 2012.

10 EMPLOYEE MOTIVATION AND TEAM BUILDING

BUSINESS FOCUS

Business transformation at Birmingham City Council

Business transformation involves major changes to the way in which business is conducted so that it can more effectively deal with shifts in the market environment. There are many reasons why a business transformation may take place, for example funding or income streams being changed or new regulations coming in to force. However, they must also consider the effects that these changes may have on the motivation of employees. Due to a need to make savings and cut costs, many local government councils across the U.K. are undertaking business transformation exercises, the biggest of which is being conducted by Birmingham City Council.

Birmingham City Council (BCC) is one of the largest councils in Europe, employing 50,000 people. In April 2006, BCC embarked on the largest business transformation programme in U.K. local government, which aims to change the way in which the council provides services to people who live in and visit Birmingham and to deliver £1 billion of savings over ten years.

There are eight strands to the business transformation programme including Corporate Services, Working for the Future and Housing Transformation. The CIPD has conducted research which focused on the Excellence in People Management strand. This strand of the programme is designed to help the council make the best use of its employees and improve performance through live management information and corporate behaviour standards. A new workforce scorecard and performance development review process was implemented to make it possible to compare people performance across the authority as well as predict future workforce trends.

When undertaking a business transformation, it is very important to have metrics in place to help inform how work is done and to enable planning processes. At BCC, one of their priorities is to increase the workforce information that is available to managers through performance development plans and tools and support from HR. As a result of having appropriate metrics, BCC have improved the way in which information is collected and fed back in to the organisation and workforce and financial information are being tied together. This should help to maintain cohesion within the organisation and lead to a more informed, and hence more satisfied workforce.

The research conducted by CIPD has concluded that the improved flow of information means that managers are more accountable for what they and their team do and are more aware of the skills and resources they need to do it. They are also more responsible for making sure that they act on the information they receive efficiently and appropriately.

BCC have further plans to improve performance and make significant savings including further enhancements to their Web site and more savings through better procurement and contract management. To date, they are on course to meet their target of saving £1 billion by 2016.

References: http://www.westmidlandsiep.gov.uk/index.php?page=829 (Accessed 4th November 2013); http://www.birmingham.gov.uk/btsp (Accessed 4th November 2013); http://www.cipd.co.uk/binaries/5728%20StF%20Metrics%20PT.pdf (Accessed 4th November 2013); http://www.cio.co.uk/insight/strategy/cios-role-in-business-transformation-five-key-steps/ (Accessed 4th November 2013)

To achieve its goals, any organisation—whether it is Birmingham City Council, Google or the local newsagents—must be sure that its employees have more than the right raw materials, adequate facilities, and equipment that works. The organisation also must ensure that its employees are *motivated*. To some extent, a high level of employee motivation derives from effective management practices.

WHAT IS MOTIVATION?

A *motive* is something that causes a person to act. A successful athlete is said to be "highly motivated." A student who avoids work is said to be "unmotivated." We define **motivation** as the individual internal process that energises, directs, and sustains behaviour. It is the personal "force" that causes you or me to act in a particular way. For example, although job rotation may increase your job satisfaction and your enthusiasm for your work so that you devote more energy to it, job rotation may not have the same impact on me.

> **motivation** the individual internal process that energises, directs, and sustains behaviour; the personal "force" that causes you or me to behave in a particular way

Morale is an employee's attitude or feelings about the job, about superiors, and about the firm itself. To achieve organisational goals effectively, employees need more than the right raw materials, adequate facilities, and efficient equipment. High morale results mainly from the satisfaction of needs on the job or as a result of the job. One need that might be satisfied on the job is the need *to be recognised* as an important contributor to the organisation. A need satisfied as a result of the job is the need for *financial security*. High morale, in turn, leads to dedication and loyalty, as well as to the desire to do the job well. Low morale, however, can lead to shoddy work, absenteeism, and high turnover rates as employees leave to seek more satisfying jobs with other firms. After the most recent recession, job turnover rates lowered as many people considered themselves lucky to have work. As the economy continues to recover, job turnover is again rising.* To offset this turnover trend, companies are creating work environments focused on increasing employee satisfaction. One obvious indicator of satisfaction at a specific organisation is whether employees like working there and whether other people want to work there. In a recent list of *Fortune* magazine's "Top 100 Companies to Work For," the top ten best companies to work for were Google, Boston Consulting Group, SAS, Wegmans Food Markets, Edward Jones, Netapp, Camden Property Trust, REI Recreational Equipment, CHG Healthcare Services, and Quicken Loans.* Motivation, morale, and the satisfaction of employees' needs are thus intertwined. Along with productivity, they have been the subject of much study since the end of the 19th century. We continue our discussion of motivation by outlining some landmarks of the early research.

> **morale** an employee's feelings about his or her job and superiors and about the firm itself

Motivated employees perform better, benefiting not only the individuals concerned but the company as a whole. By the end of this chapter you should understand the different approaches businesses adopt to try and motivate their staff.

WHY MOTIVATE EMPLOYEES?

Businesses need to ensure that their employees are motivated or they can potentially suffer from poor performance and high staff turnover rates. Poor performance can lose business through poor quality goods or service, for example, and staff replacement is extremely costly.

If employees are unhappy in their work they are unlikely to perform as well as they might, and they are more likely to want to leave. The goal for businesses is to find ways of motivating their staff to stay in the business – **staff retention** – and to perform to the best of their ability. Employees' **motivation** can be affected by many different factors, from pay levels to the way they are managed and the environment they work in.

> **staff retention** this measures a business's ability to keep its employees
> **motivation** the desire, interest or drive to want to work

It is therefore important to offer the right pay, incentives and working conditions package to the right level of employee; employees at different levels within a business's hierarchy will want and desire different things. For example, a £1,000 pay rise to a junior employee may prove quite an effective incentive, but for the Finance Director such an increase may not provide any extra incentive.

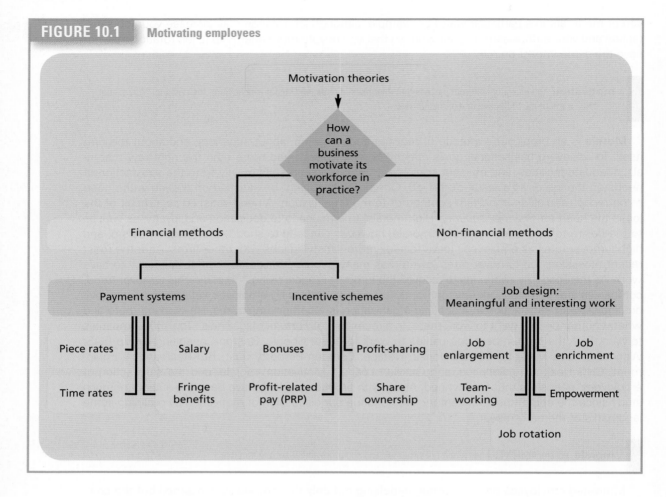

FIGURE 10.1 Motivating employees

A motivated workforce is important because it can help a business to boost its profitability, through both increased revenues and reduced costs.

- Increased effort results in higher productivity.
- Pride in the work leads to improved quality.
- Loyalty to the business reduces labour turnover.
- Commitment to the business reduces absenteeism and the likelihood of industrial conflict.
- Personal development can allow the business to get the very best from its workers' skills.

Table 10.1 lists some of the key motivators in fostering job satisfaction in the workplace, in addition to factors which can have the adverse effect. A key underlying theme in all of these is the idea of *value*, both perceived and actual; an employee who feels valued in their role is more likely to want to please employers and achieve their full potential, for the advancement of themselves and that of the company.

Businesses use a variety of financial and non-financial motivators to create a reward package suitable for their employees. But the "package" of rewards offered to employees must achieve certain objectives:

- a motivated and productive workforce
- a workforce that is flexible in meeting the organisation's needs
- the recruitment and retention of the best workers
- value for money in ensuring the reward is cost-effective in what it achieves.

To start with we will examine the variety of financial motivators businesses can offer, instead of just a basic pay.

TABLE 10.1	Typical motivators and demotivators in the workplace

Motivating factors	Demotivating factors
Leading by example: Employees can be inspired and motivated by a manager who is willing to get actively involved rather than simply delegating.	**Abusing power:** This can come in many forms, from the very blatant, to the understated. Either way, it indicates a lack of mutual respect and even seemingly minor instances might grow into major concerns if not checked.
Being approachable and available: Listening is just as important as being able to give orders; make communication a free, two-way process where grievances, concerns and ideas can be expressed openly and without repercussions, showing that employees' views are valued.	**Distancing oneself from employees:** Putting up barriers and being unapproachable can lead to a feeling "us versus them", detachment from managers and, ultimately, resentment amongst employees. Being inaccessible may also lead to any grievances being voiced elsewhere.
Encouraging work-life balance: Offering flexibility and being understanding of family commitments will nurture a positive atmosphere where employees feel respected.	**Off-loading duties:** Closely related to the other demotivating factors, this discourages a positive work-life balance in employees through unfair and uneven distribution of work-load.
Offering employee incentives: Financial benefits such as a performance-related bonus schemes and additional holidays can show that positive efforts will be recognized and rewarded.	**Claiming the credit:** Also an opposite of leading by example, this can seriously hinder an employee's career prospects and their progression in the company, leading to discontent and showing that good work goes unrewarded.
Nurturing career development: Giving advice and providing opportunities for the employee to advance their career, such as training days and autonomous projects, gives a sense of self-worth and boosts confidence and experience.	**Scape-goating:** Much like claiming the credit, failing to stand up for an employee, using them to "take a fall" on another's behalf, or shouting at them for company failures, can have a hugely adverse effect on their career prospects and the level respect they have for their manager.

USING FINANCIAL METHODS TO MOTIVATE EMPLOYEES

No theory of motivation ignores the relevance of money. Some theorists see it as a factor of primary importance; others see money as important in preventing employee dissatisfaction but not a motivator in itself.

Financial rewards can be divided into two types:

- payment systems – methods of calculating and providing the basic pay for a job
- incentive schemes – rewards to recruit, retain and motivate workers.

Payment systems

In the previous chapter, we looked at types of compensation and benefits offered to employees. We now return briefly to this theme, focusing more specifically on the various motivational aspects of each.

Piece rates   A **piece rate** system pays workers for each unit of output that they produce. The main problem with this method is that there is no guaranteed level of basic pay, and no sickness or holiday pay. Piece rates are most commonly used in manufacturing industries, such as clothing. Piece rates are thought to motivate employees because they directly reward those who work harder, that is, the more an individual produces, the more they themselves get paid. The theory is then that this should encourage employees to work as hard as they can as they will directly benefit from it. However, piece rates have been criticised for:

- producing low pay and insecurity, even for those who work hard
- encouraging workers to sacrifice quality in the search for a greater quantity of output
- making the workforce resistant to change, for fear that it will harm their rate of earnings.

 piece rate a method of paying employees for each unit of output they produce

Time rates   With **time rates**, employees are paid for the length of time that they work. This may be an hourly rate, common in the retail sector, or a weekly wage for completing a set number of hours or shifts. Overtime, possibly at a higher rate, may be paid for working longer than the agreed number of hours. Time rates encourage workers to produce a higher quality of work than do piece rates, as there is no focus on the quantity produced. Time rates are also commonly used in the service sector where there is no measurable unit of output.

 time rates employees are paid a set rate for a specific length of time, for example, per hour or per shift

However, their power to motivate is questionable, in that:

- there is no reward for those who work the hardest or achieve the most within the time
- there is still little security of income, leaving pay a potential source of anxiety and dissatisfaction
- workers on a weekly wage have no encouragement to be flexible in how or when they work, leaving businesses overstaffed at times and understaffed at others.

Salary   As noted earlier, employees on a salary system are paid an agreed sum for a year's work. This is beneficial for the business in that there is much greater flexibility in terms of when and how long an employee may work in a day, week or month. A fixed salary encourages workers to be flexible and open to change, knowing that their financial rewards will be unaffected.

However, a salary system provides no incentive to work hard, as employees know that their financial reward will be the same regardless of effort.

Fringe benefits   In addition to money payments, many organisations offer other forms of reward as part of a worker's basic pay. These are called **fringe benefits** and can include:

 fringe benefits payments to workers in a non-monetary form, such as company cars or private health care

- company cars
- private medical insurance
- discounts on company products
- leisure and social facilities.

Fringe benefits have become increasingly important as part of the total payment package given to employees – particularly for management and executive positions. They offer employees a feeling of status that can prove to be a motivating factor, but fringe benefits can swiftly become an expected "right" and thus lose any motivational effect. They could equally become a cause of status envy and dissatisfaction between employees.

Incentive schemes

Businesses have available a number of other ways to improve an employee's pay package. These usually try to motivate employees to work harder by offering them a chance at increased personal rewards in return for meeting specific objectives or targets. The most common of these is the idea of offering an employee a bonus.

Bonuses   To recap, a bonus is the general term for an additional financial reward given to a worker in recognition of the contribution that he or she has made. Bonuses, such as **commission**, can act as an incentive because they offer the prospect of additional reward for increased effort or for achieving a certain target. On the other hand, bonuses may come to be expected as part of the overall payment package, breaking the link between effort and reward. In addition, bonuses can cause conflict due to jealousy between workers. In this instance employees may actively work against each other trying to ensure that they are the employee or branch, for example, that earns the bonus.

> **commission** employees (usually salespeople) are paid a percentage of the value of what they have sold by way of reward

Performance-related pay (PRP)   Another type of bonus scheme is **performance-related pay (PRP)**. This provides a financial reward to an employee for meeting agreed, individual targets. Employees will agree performance targets with a line manager and then their individual performance is measured against the targets set. The size of the reward payment they then receive will reflect their degree of achievement.

> **performance-related pay** an incentive scheme that is used to motivate employees by linking their pay to the achievement of pre-agreed performance targets

PRP is now commonly used for executives in both the private and the public sectors. It represents a management equivalent to piece rate, in the sense that it provides a financial reward for the "output" of managers. However, some companies have become sceptical of its benefits, because:

- the potential exists for conflict between employees and their line managers over the targets that are set, achievement and the level of reward they should receive;
- PRP is individual and so fails to promote teamwork and a spirit of unity;
- the business needs to keep financial rewards to an affordable level, so frequently PRP payments are too small to make any great motivational impact.

Profit-sharing   As we have seen, under this system employees are offered a share of the annual profits made by the business. In contrast to the individual approach of PRP, **profit-sharing** encourages employees to work collectively to the benefit of the whole organisation. How far this is a motivator to employees depends on the proportion of the organisation's profit that will be shared out to them, and whether worker commitment is sufficient to make that business sufficient profit to begin with.

> **profit-sharing** a scheme which involves distributing a share of the profits made by the company to its workforce

Share ownership   Incentive schemes that provide company shares to employees as the reward produce similar benefits to profit-sharing schemes. As shareowners, employees will benefit financially from the success of the business through the issuing of dividends and growth in the business's share price.

At the heart of most **share ownership** schemes is the concept of a share option. A share option is the right to buy a share at an agreed price at a given future date. The agreed price is likely to be the share's market price at the beginning of the scheme, or even a discounted rate below this.

If the share price rises over the period of the scheme, the employee will gain significantly. On the agreed date, the employee will be able to "exercise" the option and then sell the shares at a much higher price.

> **share ownership** this is similar to a profit-share scheme except that employees gain shares in the company and then receive a share of profits via dividend distribution

Share ownership schemes are, typically, of two types:

- Savings-related schemes, which allow staff to save a set amount from their pay each month over a period of time and then exchange these savings for share options
- Incentives for executives, which often link the number of share options offered to status or performance.

Share options should encourage employees to work towards achieving the business's objectives as they will directly benefit from any increases in profits or the company's value.

THEORIES OF MOTIVATION

F W Taylor

The work of Frederick Winslow Taylor (1856 –1917) shaped the views of managers on motivation for most of the twentieth century and remains influential today.

Taylor studied the movements and working practices of workers in the U.S. at the turn of the 20th century – most famously, those involved in pig-iron production at the Bethlehem Steel Works in Bethlehem, Pennsylvania. These "time and motion studies" found that workers took their own decisions about the methods and speed required to do a job, and that many of their ways of working were inefficient.

Theory of scientific management Taylor's ideas to improve efficiency became known as scientific management. He believed managers could find the "best way" to complete a job through a scientific procedure of observation, experiment and calculations. Based on these ideas, he set out a number of recommendations:

- Managers should study the tasks being carried out by workers and identify the quickest way of doing each one. Any unnecessary movement or tasks should be eliminated.
- The skills of each employee should be matched to the tasks that need to be carried out, and each given specific instructions on what to do and how to do it.
- All workers should be supervised and controlled, and those who do not work efficiently should be punished – the "stick".
- Workers should be rewarded financially for being efficient, and pay schemes designed to pay more to those who produce more – the "carrot". Taylor believed that money motivates – "a fair day's pay for a fair day's work". Workers seek to maximise their pay, he said, and want managers to design a system that will allow them to do this.

Theory into practice Taylor's ideas formed the basis for the mass production assembly lines that dominated manufacturing in the twentieth century. To put "scientific management" into practice involves:

- eliminating wasted time and resources in production
- closely supervising workers, controlling their methods and speed of work, possibly through the use of a conveyor-belt system, which dictates the speed they must work at
- introducing either a piece rate system of payment – where workers are paid so much for each unit ("piece") of output they produce – or a financial incentive system based on meeting output targets.

Problems   A number of objections have been raised to Taylor's theory:

- The theory assumes there is a scientific "best way" to organise production, but this ignores differences between workers, which may affect the success of any one method.
- The approach treats workers as machines to be used and controlled, creating an atmosphere of conflict between workers and managers.
- Money is not the only motivator, nor is it the most important one for some people. Taylor's ideas ignore the personal and social needs of individuals at work.

Elton Mayo

Elton Mayo lectured on psychology in Australia in the early 20th century and from 1922 in the U.S. Following F W Taylor's work-study research, Mayo studied the impact of rest breaks on workers' productivity. Just as Taylor had found that the right type of work methods and payment systems could improve productivity, Mayo was investigating whether there was a similarly ideal length or frequency of rest break. Initial experiments suggested regular breaks boosted productivity, and led Mayo to call for the more humane treatment of employees at work.

Mayo's most famous studies took his ideas a stage further. Experiments between 1927 and 1932 at the Hawthorne Plant of the Western Electric Company in Chicago became the foundation for the "human relations school" of management theory. The Hawthorne studies involved varying working conditions, such as lighting, heating and hours of work, and measuring the impact on the productivity of small groups of workers. A change in conditions was made every 12 weeks, but beforehand researchers would discuss the change fully with the workers. The results surprised everyone.

Every change that was introduced brought higher productivity. Productivity went up even when no changes were made. The final change was to go back to the original working conditions – with the effect of achieving the highest productivity of all.

Theory of human relations   Mayo drew two different but equally important conclusions from the surprising results of his workplace experiments:

1. The importance of teamwork. The experiments had led to groups of individuals becoming a team, whose members worked closely in cooperation with each other. A sense of team spirit, and doing what the group expected, motivated employees to work harder.
2. The need for managers to take an interest in their workers. Workers responded well to being observed and to the feeling of importance that this produced. The morale-boosting effect of the experiments suggested that managers who communicated closely with workers and showed an interest in them would be rewarded with an increase in productivity – the so-called Hawthorne effect.

Theory into practice   Mayo's findings led to a number of practical conclusions for motivating workers:

- Getting the physical conditions of work and the financial rewards right are less important than getting right the social conditions – teamwork and good communication are essential.
- Giving workers the opportunity to be involved in making decisions and to be creative is more likely to motivate them than Taylor's assembly-line approach.
- Personnel departments that focus on the wellbeing of workers are central to business success.

Problems   Mayo's theory has been criticised on at least two grounds:

- The experiments themselves were far from scientific – only small groups of workers were observed, and subsequent experiments have failed to confirm the findings.
- Workers will not always share the goals of managers, despite their best efforts. Trade unions may see these efforts as management attempts to fool workers into boosting productivity when there is little gain for workers in doing so.

Abraham Maslow

In 1954 the American psychologist Abraham Maslow put forward his theory of what motivates human beings. His ideas did not apply solely to the workplace but nevertheless had an important message for business.

Theory of the hierarchy of needs   Maslow suggested that all human beings have the same types of needs and that these could be organised as a hierarchy of needs. The five levels of needs he referred to are shown in Figure 10.2.

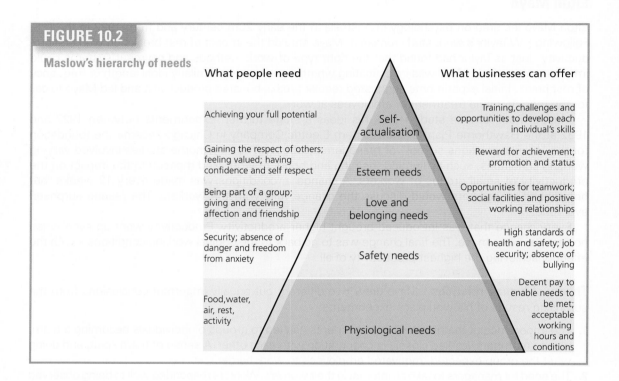

FIGURE 10.2

Maslow's hierarchy of needs

What people need — What businesses can offer

What people need		What businesses can offer
Achieving your full potential	Self-actualisation	Training, challenges and opportunities to develop each individual's skills
Gaining the respect of others; feeling valued; having confidence and self respect	Esteem needs	Reward for achievement; promotion and status
Being part of a group; giving and receiving affection and friendship	Love and belonging needs	Opportunities for teamwork; social facilities and positive working relationships
Security; absence of danger and freedom from anxiety	Safety needs	High standards of health and safety; job security; absence of bullying
Food, water, air, rest, activity	Physiological needs	Decent pay to enable needs to be met; acceptable working hours and conditions

At the base of the hierarchy lie "physiological needs" – the essentials for human survival, such as food and rest. Maslow placed this type of need at the bottom of the hierarchy because such needs are the most fundamental set of needs for any human being. They will always be the first type of need that must be satisfied.

Once this level of needs is met, it no longer remains a focus or a motivation. Instead, it is the next level of needs in the hierarchy that an individual seeks to satisfy. So, once their physiological needs have been met, people seek the "safety" needs of security and freedom from anxiety. Motivation stems from each individual's desire to have their next level of needs met. The final level of needs, "self-actualisation", refers to the need to fulfil one's potential. Once all other levels of need are met, it is this need that can continue to motivate.

Theory into practice   Maslow's theory has important practical implications for businesses:

● To motivate a workforce requires an approach that will identify the level of need of each individual.
● Each worker will first need sufficient pay to provide for his or her basic physiological needs, then will seek job security and a safe working environment. Figure 10.2 shows how businesses might seek to meet each level of needs in the hierarchy.
● Financial rewards alone will not motivate. Boosting workers' esteem and developing their talents will be crucial. But, without decent pay and job security, these are worthless.

Problems   Opponents of Maslow have found his theory unconvincing on several grounds:

- Any generalisation about "levels" of human needs is bound to have exceptions – businesses may find they have workers who place little value on gaining praise or developing their potential. Some workers – such as artists or musicians – may even seek creativity needs before financial reward.
- Even if Maslow's theory holds good, workers may not seek all levels of need within the workplace. They may be satisfied with pay alone from their job, meeting other needs through their leisure time.
- Matching rewards to needs for each and every worker is a well-nigh impossible task in practice.

Frederick Herzberg

Frederick Herzberg, an American psychologist, conducted research in the 1950s that directly addressed the question of motivation. He asked 200 engineers and accountants which factors in their work created job satisfaction and which caused dissatisfaction. His results are presented in a simplified form in Figure 10.3.

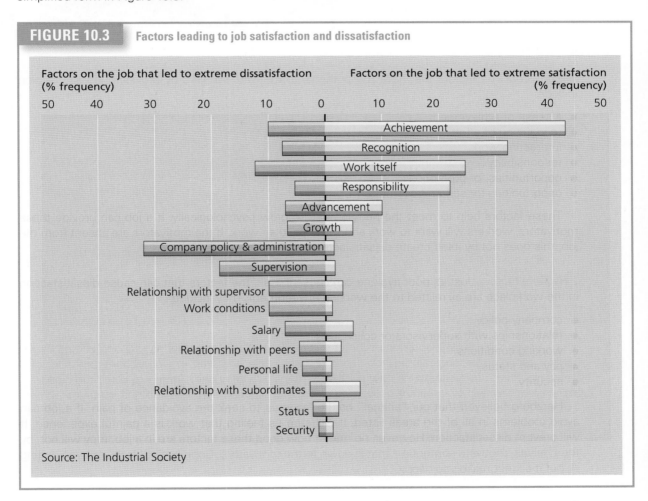

FIGURE 10.3   Factors leading to job satisfaction and dissatisfaction

Source: The Industrial Society

The results showed that six factors, including achievement and recognition, were frequently mentioned as causing satisfaction at work. On the other hand, ten factors, such as company policy and working conditions, were often mentioned as causes of dissatisfaction, but rarely as a source of pleasure!

"Two-factor theory"   Herzberg used this research to develop his "two-factor theory" of motivation. This states that there are two sets of factors – motivators and hygiene factors – that are both important in motivating workers, but for very different reasons.

What satisfies employees? Companies sometimes use travel awards as incentives for better employee performance. According to the motivation–hygiene theory, when an incentive for higher performance is not provided, is that a dissatisfier?

© MAUGLI/SHUTTERSTOCK

1 Motivators The factors that have the potential to motivate workers by providing job satisfaction include:

- a sense of achievement
- recognition of effort
- interesting work
- responsibility
- opportunities for promotion
- opportunities for self-improvement.

These factors help to meet the human need to grow psychologically. If a job can provide these motivators, workers will want to work and will enjoy their work. If the motivators are absent from the job, this does not by itself create dissatisfaction – only a lack of motivation.

2 Hygiene factors Just as poor hygiene can cause illness, the factors that can cause dissatisfaction in the workplace are all related to the working environment. They include:

- company policy
- relationships with supervisors or colleagues
- working conditions
- pay and status
- security.

Herzberg believed that our "animal" nature leads us to seek the avoidance of pain. If a job can avoid problems in all of the areas listed, it will stop us feeling that work is a painful experience. It will prevent dissatisfaction. However, no matter how good these factors are in a job, they will not, by themselves, motivate someone – that is down to the motivators. Good hygiene can stop you getting ill, but it cannot make you happy.

Theory into practice   Several practical conclusions can be drawn from the two-factor theory:

- To motivate a workforce, a business must first make sure that all of the hygiene factors are being met – a decent salary, fair rules and policies and pleasant working conditions.
- The motivators must be there – ensuring that the job itself is meaningful and interesting, that workers are trained to do their jobs well and that they have the opportunity to develop their skills. Specifically, Herzberg advocated "job enrichment" – building a variety of tasks, skills and responsibilities into each job.

Problems   Herzberg's theory has encountered major criticisms.

● Subsequent research around the world has failed to confirm that Herzberg's theory can generally be applied to workers in every business.
● Some jobs, especially low-skilled ones, cannot be easily "enriched", and many workers may not seek responsibility or advancement.

Theory X and Theory Y

The concepts of Theory X and Theory Y were advanced by Douglas McGregor in his book *The Human Side of Enterprise*. They are, in essence, sets of assumptions that underlie management's attitudes and beliefs regarding workers' behaviour.

Theory X is a concept of employee motivation generally consistent with Taylor's scientific management. Theory X assumes that employees dislike work and will function effectively only in a highly controlled work environment.

> **Theory X** a concept of employee motivation generally consistent with Taylor's scientific management; assumes that employees dislike work and will function only in a highly controlled work environment

Theory X is based on the following assumptions:

1. People dislike work and try to avoid it.
2. Because people dislike work, managers must coerce, control, and frequently threaten employees to achieve organisational goals.
3. People generally must be led because they have little ambition and will not seek responsibility; they are concerned mainly about security.

The logical outcome of such assumptions will be a highly controlled work environment—one in which managers make all the decisions and employees take all the orders.

On the other hand, **Theory Y** is a concept of employee motivation generally consistent with the ideas of the human relations movement. Theory Y assumes that employees accept responsibility and work toward organisational goals, and by doing so they also achieve personal rewards. Theory Y is based on the following assumptions:

> **Theory Y** a concept of employee motivation generally consistent with the ideas of the human relations movement; assumes responsibility and work toward organisational goals, and by doing so they also achieve personal rewards

1. People do not naturally dislike work; in fact, work is an important part of their lives.
2. People will work toward goals to which they are committed.
3. People become committed to goals when it is clear that accomplishing the goals will bring personal rewards.
4. People often seek out and willingly accept responsibility.
5. Employees have the potential to help accomplish organisational goals.
6. Organisations generally do not make full use of their human resources.

Obviously, this view is quite different from—and much more positive than—that of Theory X. McGregor argued that most managers behave in accordance with Theory X, but he maintained that Theory Y is more appropriate and effective as a guide for managerial action (see Table 10.2).

The human relations movement and Theories X and Y increased managers' awareness of the importance of social factors in the workplace. However, human motivation is a complex and dynamic process to which there is no simple key. Neither money nor social factors alone can provide the answer. Rather, a number of factors must be considered in any attempt to increase motivation.

TABLE 10.2	Theory X and Theory Y contrasted		
Area		**Theory X**	**Theory Y**
Attitude toward work		Dislike	Involvement
Control systems		External	Internal
Supervision		Direct	Indirect
Level of commitment		Low	High
Employee potential		Ignored	Identified
Use of human resources		Limited	Not limited

© CENGAGE LEARNING 2014

Theory Z

William Ouchi, a management professor at UCLA, studied business practices in American and Japanese firms. He concluded that different types of management systems dominate in these two countries.* In Japan, Ouchi found what he calls *type J* firms. They are characterised by lifetime employment for employees, collective (or group) decision making, collective responsibility for the outcomes of decisions, slow evaluation and promotion, implied control mechanisms, nonspecialised career paths, and a holistic concern for employees as people.

American industry is dominated by what Ouchi calls *type A* firms, which follow a different pattern. They emphasise short-term employment, individual decision making, individual responsibility for the outcomes of decisions, rapid evaluation and promotion, explicit control mechanisms, specialised career paths, and a segmented concern for employees only as employees.

A few very successful American firms represent a blend of the type J and type A patterns. These firms, called *type Z* organisations, emphasise long-term employment, collective decision making, individual responsibility for the outcomes of decisions, slow evaluation and promotion, informal control along with some formalised measures, moderately specialised career paths, and a holistic concern for employees.

Ouchi's **Theory Z** is the belief that some middle ground between his type A and type J practices is best for American business (see Figure 10.4). A major part of Theory Z is the emphasis on participative decision making. The focus is on "we" rather than on "us versus them." Theory Z employees and managers view the organisation as a family. This participative spirit fosters cooperation and the dissemination of information and organisational values.

Theory Z the belief that some middle ground between type A and type J practices is best for American business

---

FIGURE 10.4	**The features of theory Z** *The best aspects of Japanese and American management theories combine to form the nucleus of Theory Z.*

TYPE J FIRMS
(Japanese)
- Lifetime employment
- Collective decision making
- Collective responsibility
- Slow promotion
- Implied control mechanisms
- Nonspecialised career paths
- Holistic concern for employees

TYPE Z FIRMS
(Best choice for American firms)
- Long-term employment
- Collective decision making
- Individual responsibility
- Slow promotion
- Informal control
- Moderately specialised career paths
- Holistic concern for employees

TYPE A FIRMS
(American)
- Short-term employment
- Individual decision making
- Individual responsibility
- Rapid promotion
- Explicit control mechanisms
- Specialised career paths
- Segmented concern for employees

© CENGAGE LEARNING 2014

Reinforcement theory

Reinforcement theory is based on the premise that behaviour that is rewarded is likely to be repeated, whereas behaviour that is punished is less likely to recur. A *reinforcement* is an action that follows directly from a particular behaviour. It may be a pay raise after a particularly large sale to a new customer or a reprimand for coming to work late.

> **reinforcement theory** a theory of motivation based on the premise that rewarded behaviour is likely to be repeated, whereas punished behaviour is less likely to recur

Reinforcements can take a variety of forms and can be used in a number of ways. A *positive reinforcement* is one that strengthens desired behaviour by providing a reward. For example, many employees respond well to praise; recognition from their supervisors for a job done well increases (strengthens) their willingness to perform well in the future. A *negative reinforcement* strengthens desired behaviour by eliminating an undesirable task or situation. Suppose that a machine factory must be cleaned thoroughly every month—a dirty, miserable task. During one particular month when the workers do a less-than-satisfactory job at their normal work assignments, the boss requires the workers to clean the factory rather than bringing in the usual private maintenance service. The employees will be motivated to work harder the next month to avoid the unpleasant cleanup duty again.

Punishment is an undesired consequence of undesirable behaviour. Common forms of punishment used in organisations include reprimands, reduced pay, disciplinary layoffs, and termination (firing). Punishment often does more harm than good. It tends to create an unpleasant environment, fosters hostility and resentment, and suppresses undesirable behaviour only until the supervisor's back is turned.

Managers who rely on *extinction* hope to eliminate undesirable behaviour by not responding to it. The idea is that the behaviour eventually will become "extinct." Suppose, for example, that an employee writes memo after memo to his or her manager about insignificant events. If the manager does not respond to any of these memos, the employee probably will stop writing them, and the behaviour will be squelched.

The effectiveness of reinforcement depends on which type is used and how it is timed. One approach may work best under certain conditions, although some situations lend themselves to the use of more than one approach. Generally, positive reinforcement is considered the most effective, and it is recommended when the manager has a choice.

Continual reinforcement can become tedious for both managers and employees, especially when the same behaviour is being reinforced over and over again in the same way. At the start, it may be necessary to reinforce a desired behaviour every time it occurs. However, once a desired behaviour has become more or less established, occasional reinforcement seems to be most effective.

CONTEMPORARY VIEWS ON MOTIVATION

Maslow's hierarchy of needs and Herzberg's motivation–hygiene theory are popular and widely known theories of motivation. Each is also a significant step up from the relatively narrow views of scientific management and Theories X and Y. However, they do have one weakness: each attempts to specify *what* motivates people, but neither explains *why* or *how* motivation develops or is sustained over time. In recent years, managers have begun to explore three other models that take a more dynamic view of motivation. These are equity theory, expectancy theory, and goal-setting theory.

Equity theory

The **equity theory** of motivation is based on the premise that people are motivated to obtain and preserve equitable treatment for themselves. As used here, *equity* is the distribution of rewards in

SUCCESS STORY

Motivation breeds innovation at Google

Much of Google's success is perhaps down to the creation of a working environment in which employees feel satisfied and are free to innovate. Google is frequently used an example of a company that has dared to be different, with a creative and pioneering outlook woven into its very fabric.

Google spearheaded the concept of 80/20 time – the simple but revolutionary idea that 20 per cent of the time of all employees can be spent on "creative side projects" of their own choosing. Historically this culture appears to have paid dividends, with 20 per cent time oft cited as being responsible for innovations including

AdSense, Gmail, Google Talk and Google News. In a talk at Stanford University, Marissa Mayer, then Google's Vice President of Search Products and User Experience, stated that her analysis showed that half of the new product launches originated from the 20 per cent time.

Other perks for employees have included the "Kinderplex" day care programme, providing nursery and children's activities for employees who are also parents; free on site haircuts, gymnasiums and swimming pools; table tennis, pool and table football; massages; laundry facilities; and a healthcare plan with onsite staff. When combined, these

various incentives foster a friendly, informal atmosphere, happy employees, and ultimately a more productive workforce.

However, with recent reports suggesting that 80/20 time is being squeezed out of the company's corporate culture – with all 20 per cent now having to be pre-approved, and some reports claiming that managers are discouraged from approving it – time will tell whether this will have an adverse effect on Google's success.

References: J. Strickland, 'How the Googleplex Works', *How Stuff Works*; C. Townsend, '"Innovate or die": Why Google's 80/20 Rule is a Red Herring', *Wired*, August 28th, 2013.

direct proportion to each employee's contribution to the organisation. Everyone need not receive the same rewards, but the rewards should be in accordance with individual contributions.

equity theory a theory of motivation based on the premise that people are motivated to obtain and preserve equitable treatment for themselves

According to this theory, we tend to implement the idea of equity in the following way. First, we develop our own input-to-outcome ratio. *Inputs* are the time, effort, skills, education, experience, and so on, that we contribute to the organisation. *Outcomes* are the rewards we get from the organisation, such as pay, benefits, recognition, and promotions. Next, we compare this ratio with what we perceive as the input-to-outcome ratio for some other person. It might be a co-worker, a friend who works for another firm, or even an average of all the people in our organisation. This person is called the *comparison other*. Note that our perception of this person's input-to-outcome ratio may be absolutely correct or completely wrong. However, we believe that it is correct.

If the two ratios are roughly the same, we feel that the organisation is treating us equitably. In this case, we are motivated to leave things as they are. However, if our ratio is the higher of the two, we feel under-rewarded and are motivated to make changes. We may (1) decrease our own inputs by not working so hard, (2) try to increase our total outcome by asking for a raise in pay, (3) try to get the comparison other to increase some inputs or receive decreased outcomes, (4) leave the work situation, or (5) do a new comparison with a different comparison other.

Equity theory is most relevant to pay as an outcome. Because pay is a very real measure of a person's worth to an organisation, comparisons involving pay are a natural part of organisational life. Managers can try to avoid problems arising from inequity by making sure that rewards are distributed on the basis of performance and that everyone clearly understands the basis for his or her own pay.

Employees want to be treated fairly. *Employees compare the amount of effort they put into their jobs and the outcomes they get to that of their coworkers. This is the idea behind equity theory. At sweatshops, though, all employees are treated unfairly. Does equity theory come into play in this instance?*

Expectancy theory

Expectancy theory, developed by Victor Vroom, is a very complex model of motivation based on a deceptively simple assumption. According to expectancy theory, motivation depends on how much we want something and on how likely we think we are to get it (see Figure 10.5). Consider, for example, the case of three sales representatives who are candidates for promotion to one sales manager's job. Johan has had a very good sales year and always gets good performance evaluations. However, he is not sure that he wants the job because it involves a great deal of travel, long working hours, and much stress and pressure. Paul wants the job badly, but does not think he has much chance of getting it. He has had a terrible sales year and gets only mediocre performance evaluations from his present boss. Gita wants the job as much as Paul, and she thinks that she has a pretty good chance of getting it. Her sales have improved significantly this past year, and her evaluations are the best in the company.

> **expectancy theory** a model of motivation based on the assumption that motivation depends on how much we want something and on how likely we think we are to get it

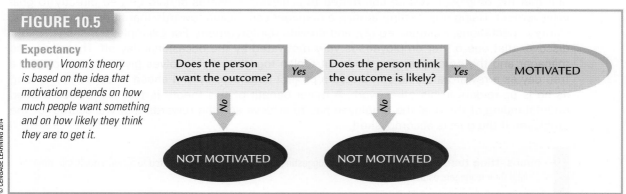

FIGURE 10.5

Expectancy theory *Vroom's theory is based on the idea that motivation depends on how much people want something and on how likely they think they are to get it.*

Does the person want the outcome? — *Yes* → Does the person think the outcome is likely? — *Yes* → MOTIVATED

No ↓ NOT MOTIVATED

No ↓ NOT MOTIVATED

What do employees want? *That's what their managers need to determine. Different employees are motivated by different rewards. Figuring out which rewards motivate each is key step in goal setting.*

© YURI ARCURS/SHUTTERSTOCK

Expectancy theory would predict that Johan and Paul are not very motivated to seek the promotion. Johan does not really want it, and Paul does not think that he has much of a chance of getting it. Gita, however, is very motivated to seek the promotion because she wants it and thinks that she can get it.

Expectancy theory is complex because each action we take is likely to lead to several different outcomes; some we may want, and others we may not want. For example, a person who works hard and puts in many extra hours may get a pay raise, be promoted, and gain valuable new job skills. However, that person also may be forced to spend less time with his or her family and be forced to cut back on his or her social life.

For one person, the promotion may be paramount, the pay raise and new skills fairly important, and the loss of family and social life of negligible importance. For someone else, the family and social life may be most important, the pay raise of moderate importance, the new skills unimportant, and the promotion undesirable because of the additional hours it would require. The first person would be motivated to work hard and put in the extra hours, whereas the second person would not be motivated at all to do so. In other words, it is the entire bundle of outcomes—and the individual's evaluation of the importance of each outcome—that determines motivation.

Expectancy theory is difficult to apply, but it does provide several useful guidelines for managers. It suggests that managers must recognise that (1) employees work for a variety of reasons; (2) these reasons, or expected outcomes, may change over time; and (3) it is necessary to clearly show employees how they can attain the outcomes they desire.

Goal-setting theory

Goal-setting theory suggests that employees are motivated to achieve goals that they and their managers establish together. The goal should be very specific, moderately difficult, and one that the employee will be committed to achieve.* Rewards should be tied directly to goal achievement. Using goal-setting theory, a manager can design rewards that fit employee needs, clarify expectations, maintain equity, and provide reinforcement. For example, a manager might discover that one of her employees is very motivated by the occasional day off. Therefore, the manager and the employee may work out a plan together that involves giving the employee a free day as a reward after he completes a project satisfactorily and ahead of schedule, as long as he is up-to-date in his other work. A major benefit of this theory is that it provides a good understanding of the goal the employee has to achieve and the rewards that will accrue for the employee if the goal is accomplished.

> **goal-setting theory** a theory of motivation suggesting that employees are motivated to achieve goals that they and their managers establish together

KEY MOTIVATION TECHNIQUES

As discussed earlier, and shown in Table 10.1, it takes more than a generous salary to motivate employees. Increasingly, companies are trying to provide motivation by satisfying employees' less-tangible needs. At times, businesses use simple, low- or no-cost approaches such as those listed in Table 10.3 to motivate workers. Organisations also use more complex approaches. In this section, we discuss this further, addressing several specific techniques that help managers to boost employee motivation and job satisfaction.

TABLE 10.3 No-cost/low-cost motivation techniques

1. Acknowledge and celebrate birthdays and other important events.
2. Allow an employee to choose his or her next assignment.
3. Call an employee to your office to thank him or her (do not discuss any other issue).
4. In the department newsletter, publish a "kudos" column and ask for nominations throughout the department.
5. Nominate the employee for a formal award programme.
6. Plan a surprise achievement celebration for an employee or group of employees.
7. Pop in at the first meeting of a special project team and express your appreciation for their involvement.
8. Send a letter to all team members at the conclusion of a project, thanking them for their participation.
9. When you hear a positive remark about someone, repeat it to that person as soon as possible in person or electronically.
10. Widely publicise suggestions used and their positive impact on your department.
11. Support flexible work schedules.
12. Ask the employee to be a mentor to a new recruit.
13. Put up a bulletin board in your department and post letters of thanks from customers.
14. Take the opportunity to learn what your people are working on and recognise their efforts.
15. Interview your people and capture their wisdom. Compile the quotes and stories in a booklet and hand it out to employees.
16. Send a letter of praise to the employee's spouse or family.
17. Honour employee subgroups in your department with their own day or week (e.g., Administrative Staff Week, Custodian Week) and present them with flowers, sweets, breakfast, and so on.
18. Recognise highly skilled employees with increased responsibility that will develop new skills that may be helpful for advancement.
19. Pass around an office trophy to the employee of the week or other travelling awards.
20. Volunteer to do an employee's least favourite task.
21. Wash the employee's car.
22. Give the person tickets to a football match, golf lessons, cinema tickets, a book by his or her favourite author, "Lunch on me" coupons, and so on.
23. Reserve the best parking spot for employees who have done something truly worthwhile.
24. Send a handwritten note or praise about a specific action, not "thanks for all you do."
25. Create a yearbook for your team with pictures and stories of accomplishments during the year.
26. Copy senior management on your thank-you note to the employee, to advise them of an employee's efforts or accomplishments.
27. Introduce employees to key suppliers, customers, or someone in senior management.
28. Reward good ideas even if they fail.
29. Set aside a public space inside your firm as a "wall of fame" and place photos of employees who have accomplished something truly special along with the details of what they did to earn that space.
30. Say, "Thank you."

Sources: Texas A&M University Human Resources Department, http://employees.tamu.edu/docs/employment/classComp/
614recognitionIdeas.pdf; HRWorld, www.hrworld.com/features/25-employee-rewards/; Michigan Office of Great Workplace Development,
www.michigan.gov/documents/firstgentleman/50_242400_7.pdf.

Management by objectives

Management by objectives (MBO) is a motivation technique in which managers and employees collaborate in setting goals. The primary purpose of MBO is to clarify the roles employees are expected to play in reaching the organisation's goals.

> **management by objectives (MBO)** a motivation technique in which managers and employees collaborate in setting goals

By allowing individuals to participate in goal setting and performance evaluation, MBO increases their motivation. Most MBO programmes consist of a series of five steps. The first step in setting up an MBO programme is to secure the acceptance of top management. It is essential that top managers endorse and participate in the programme if others in the firm are to accept it. The commitment of top management also provides a natural starting point for educating employees about the purposes and mechanics of MBO.

Next, preliminary goals must be established. Top management also plays a major role in this activity because the preliminary goals reflect the firm's mission and strategy. The intent of an MBO programme is to have these goals filter down through the organisation.

The third step, which actually consists of several smaller steps, is the heart of MBO:

1. The manager explains to each employee that he or she has accepted certain goals for the group (the manager as well as the employees) and asks the individual to think about how he or she can help to achieve these goals.
2. The manager later meets with each employee individually. Together they establish goals for the employee. Whenever possible, the goals should be measurable and should specify the time frame for completion (usually one year).
3. The manager and the employee decide what resources the employee will need to accomplish his or her goals.

As the fourth step, the manager and each employee meet periodically to review the employee's progress. They may agree to modify certain goals during these meetings if circumstances have changed. For example, a sales representative may have accepted a goal of increasing sales by 20 per cent. However, an aggressive competitor may have entered the marketplace, making this goal unattainable. In light of this circumstance, the goal may be revised downward to 10 or 15 per cent.

The fifth step in the MBO process is evaluation. At the end of the designated time period, the manager and each employee meet again to determine which of the individual's goals were met and which were not met, and why. The employee's reward (in the form of a pay raise, praise, or promotion) is based primarily on the degree of goal attainment.

As with every other management method, MBO has advantages and disadvantages. MBO can motivate employees by involving them actively in the life of the firm. The collaboration on goal setting and performance appraisal improves communication and makes employees feel that they are an important part of the organisation. Periodic review of progress also enhances control within an organisation. A major problem with MBO is that it does not work unless the process begins at the top of an organisation. In some cases, MBO results in excessive paperwork. Also, a manager may not like sitting down and working out goals with subordinates and may instead just assign them goals. Finally, MBO programmes prove difficult to implement unless goals are quantifiable.

Job enrichment

Job enrichment is a method of motivating employees by providing them with variety in their tasks while giving them some responsibility for, and control over, their jobs. At the same time, employees gain new skills and acquire a broader perspective about how their individual work contributes to the goals of the organisation. Herzberg's motivation–hygiene theory is one rationale for the use of job enrichment; that is, the added responsibility and control that job enrichment confers on employees

Job enlargement versus job enrichment.
It's no secret. Doing the same task over and over at your job is boring. Being able to do a variety of tasks helps. Having more responsibility over how you do your job is even better.

increases their satisfaction and motivation. For example, engineers at Google get to spend 20 per cent of their time at work on projects of their choosing.* This type of enrichment can motivate employees and create a variety of benefits for the company. At times, **job enlargement**, expanding a worker's assignments to include additional but similar tasks, can lead to job enrichment. Job enlargement might mean that a worker on an assembly line who used to connect three wires to components moving down the line now connects five wires. Unfortunately, the added tasks often are just as routine as those the worker performed before the change. In such cases, enlargement may not be effective.

> **job enrichment** a motivation technique that provides employees with more variety and responsibility in their jobs
> **job enlargement** expanding a worker's assignments to include additional but similar tasks

Whereas job enlargement does not really change the routine and monotonous nature of jobs, job enrichment does. Job enrichment requires that added tasks give an employee more responsibility for what he or she does. It provides workers with both more tasks to do and more control over how they perform them. In particular, job enrichment removes many controls from jobs, gives workers more authority, and assigns work in complete, natural units. Moreover, employees frequently are given fresh and challenging job assignments. By blending more planning and decision making into jobs, job enrichment gives work more depth and complexity.

Job redesign is a type of job enrichment in which work is restructured in ways that cultivate the worker–job match. Job redesign can be achieved by combining tasks, forming work groups, or establishing closer customer relationships. Employees often are more motivated when jobs are combined because the increased variety of tasks presents more challenge and therefore more reward. Work groups motivate employees by showing them how their jobs fit within the organisation as a whole and how they contribute to its success. Establishing client relationships allows employees to interact directly with customers. This type of redesign adds a personal dimension to employment. Another motivation for job redesign is to reduce employees' stress at work. A job redesign that carefully matches worker to job can prevent stress-related injuries. Employees can sometimes play an active role in redesigning their jobs more to their liking. If an employee recognises an opportunity at work to rework his or her job in such a way as to improve efficiency or productivity, he or she may want to approach a superior with the idea. Redesigning a position based around organisational needs may help improve employee satisfaction and reduce employee turnover—all while improving efficiency at the firm.*

> **job redesign** a type of job enrichment in which work is restructured to cultivate the worker–job match

Job enrichment works best when employees seek more challenging work. Of course, not all workers respond positively to job-enrichment programmes. Employees must desire personal growth and have the skills and knowledge to perform enriched jobs. Lack of self-confidence, fear of failure, and distrust of management's intentions are likely to lead to ineffective performance on enriched jobs. In addition, some workers do not view their jobs as routine and boring, and others even prefer routine jobs because they find them satisfying. Companies that use job enrichment as an alternative to specialisation also face extra expenses, such as the cost of retraining.

Behaviour modification

Behaviour modification is a systematic programme of reinforcement to encourage desirable behaviour. Behaviour modification involves both rewards to encourage desirable actions and punishments to discourage undesirable actions. However, studies have shown that rewards, such as compliments and expressions of appreciation, are much more effective behaviour modifiers than punishments, such as reprimands and scorn.

 behaviour modification a systematic programme of reinforcement to encourage desirable behaviour

When applied to management, behaviour modification strives to encourage desirable organisational behaviour. Use of this technique begins with identification of a *target behaviour*—the behaviour that is to be changed. (It might be low production levels or a high rate of absenteeism, for example.) Existing levels of this behaviour are then measured. Next, managers provide positive reinforcement in the form of a reward when employees exhibit the *desired behaviour* (such as increased production or less absenteeism). The reward might be praise or a more tangible form of recognition, such as a gift, meal, or trip. Apple created the Corporate Gifting and Rewards Programme in order to give companies the ability to reward their staff with iPods, iPhones, iPads, Mac computers, or iTunes gift cards.* Finally, the levels of the target behaviour are measured again to determine whether the desired changes have been achieved. If they have been achieved, the reinforcement is maintained. However, if the target behaviour has not changed significantly in the desired direction, the reward system must be changed to one that is likely to be more effective. The key is to devise effective rewards that will not only modify employees' behaviour in desired ways but also motivate them. To this end, experts suggest that management should reward quality, loyalty, and productivity.

Flexitime

Flexitime is a system in which employees set their own work hours within certain limits determined by employers. Typically, the firm establishes two bands of time: the *core time*, when all employees must be at work, and the *flexible time,* when employees may choose whether to be at work. The only condition is that every employee must work a total of eight hours each day. For example, the hours between 9 and 11 a.m. and 1 and 3 p.m. might be core times, and the hours between 6 and 9 a.m., 11 a.m. and 1 p.m., and 3 and 6 p.m. might be flexible times. This would give employees the option of coming in early and getting off early, coming in later and leaving later, or taking a long lunch break. But flexitime also ensures that everyone is present at certain times, when conferences with supervisors and department meetings can be scheduled. Another type of flexitime allows employees to work a 40-hour work week in four days instead of five. Workers who put in ten hours a day instead of eight get an extra day off each week. Offering flexitime can be a low-cost way for a firm to show an employee that it cares about his or her well-being through offering a better work–life balance.* The needs and lifestyles of today's workforce are changing. Dual-income families make up a much larger share of the workforce than ever before, and women are one of its fastest-growing sectors. In addition, more employees are responsible for the care of elderly relatives. Recognising that these changes increase the demand for family time, many employers are offering flexible work schedules that not only help employees to manage their time better but also increase employee motivation and job satisfaction. The sense of independence and autonomy employees gain from having a say in what hours they work can be a motivating factor. In addition, employees who have enough time to deal with non-work issues often work more productively and with greater satisfaction when they are on the job. Two common problems associated with using flexitime are (1) supervisors sometimes find

Part-time pay, full-time benefits. *Many employees want to work part-time but can't afford not to have benefits such as health insurance. Companies known for hiring part-time employees with full benefits include UPS, REI, Land's End, and Starbucks.*

their jobs complicated by having employees who come and go at different times and (2) employees without flexitime sometimes resent co-workers who have it.

flexitime a system in which employees set their own work hours within employer-determined limits

To most people, a work schedule means the standard nine-to-five, 40-hour work week. In reality, though, some people have work schedules that are quite different from this. Flexible schedules are becoming much more common as improvements in technology allow people to stay connected, no matter where they are or what time it is. However, some industries are more likely to offer their workers flexible schedules than others. Medical and health, education and training, administrative jobs, and accounting are all likely to offer flexible schedule options. For example, many high-pressure accounting firms, such as Ernst & Young, have implemented flexitime as a reward for working in an intense industry that requires some long hours during busy times. In order to offset the 60- or 70-hour work weeks during tax season, some accounting firms allow their employees to work 3-day weeks or take extended breaks during the summer. Flex policies like this help to reduce employee burnout and keep turnover low in what can be a stressful industry.*

Part-time work and job sharing

Part-time work is permanent employment in which individuals work less than a standard work week. The specific number of hours worked varies, but part-time jobs are structured so that all responsibilities can be completed in the number of hours an employee works. Part-time work is of special interest to parents who want more time with their children and people who simply desire more leisure time. One disadvantage of part-time work is that it often does not provide the benefits that come with a full-time position. However, working without benefits is not always the case. A few large retailers do offer good benefit packages to part-time employees. Among the best firms for part-timers are REI, Land's End, and Starbucks. All of these organisations offer insurance packages to nearly all of their employees. Outfitter chain REI even offers its part-time employees incentive pay and the option to participate in a retirement and profit-sharing plan.*

part-time work permanent employment in which individuals work less than a standard work week

Job sharing (sometimes referred to as *work sharing*) is an arrangement whereby two people share one full-time position. One job sharer may work from 8 a.m. to noon, and the other may work from 1 to 5 p.m., or they may alternate workdays. Job sharing is different than part-time work because two people share one single position, which is generally more skilled than a part-time position would

Cash for conservation?

Is money a motivator? If you work at Genentech, you might just be able to earn cash rewards for "going green." In an effort to help preserve the environment, Genentech's employee commuter programme helps its employees save time and money by sharing rides to work and using carpool lanes while they earn cash rewards. The programme pays employees $4 per day for not driving to work alone or $4 per passenger per day for the drivers of carpools and vanpools. The company also offers free bus service, pre-tax transportation payroll deductions, and a company subsidy for commuting expenses, all designed to help employees avoid stress and traffic and protect the environment.

References: www.gene.com/gene/careers/gride.html

be. Job sharing can be difficult to orchestrate at the beginning, but may contribute to greater job satisfaction and ease in creating work–life balance. Job sharing can actually lead people to be more productive, as they know that their time at work is limited and that someone else is directly depending on the quality of their work. This arrangement may be especially appealing to parents who wish to maintain a professional position while also making time for children.* Job sharing combines the security of a full-time position with the flexibility of a part-time job. For firms, job sharing provides a unique opportunity to attract highly skilled employees who might not be available on a full-time basis. In addition, companies can save on expenses by reducing the cost of benefits and avoiding the disruptions of employee turnover. For employees, opting for the flexibility of job sharing may mean giving up some of the benefits received for full-time work. In addition, job sharing is difficult if tasks are not easily divisible or if two people do not work or communicate well with one another.

 job sharing an arrangement whereby two people share one full-time position

Telecommuting

A growing number of companies allow **telecommuting**, working at home all the time or for a portion of the work week. E-mail, cloud computing; smart phones, laptops, and tablets; video conferencing, and overnight couriers all facilitate the work-at-home trend. Working at home means that individuals can set their own hours and have more time with their families. Nevertheless, workers who do telecommute remain concerned that lack of in-person time with their superiors will hurt their careers.*

 telecommuting working at home all the time or for a portion of the work week

Technological advances have been so great that even CEOs are spending more time telecommuting. CEOs have found that they can be more effective and save time by occasionally touching base with staff virtually, via e-mail, text message, or video chats, rather than having long face-to-face meetings. Increasingly, CEOs spend time on social media and other digital sites, monitoring competition and getting ideas.*

Office space—at home. *More companies are finding it cost-effective to allow employees to work at home. Working at home means that this mother can spend more time with her daughter. Telecommuting arrangements such as this can be a win-win situation for both employees and their firms.*

Companies that allow telecommuting experience several benefits, including increased productivity, lower real estate and travel costs, reduced employee absenteeism and turnover, increased work–life balance, improved morale, and access to additional labour pools. Telecommuting also helps improve the community by decreasing air pollutants, reducing traffic congestion, and lowering consumption of fossil fuels, which can give a company a green factor.

Among the disadvantages of telecommuting are feelings of isolation, putting in longer hours, and being distracted by family or household responsibilities. Although most bosses say that they trust their staff to work from home, many think that home workers are work-shy and less productive than office-based staff. In addition, some supervisors have difficulty monitoring productivity.

Cisco, for example, is an industry leader at providing a virtual work environment. Cisco's employees use many of the company's own products, including WebEx and TelePresence, which allow employees to attend meetings, do training, and hold video conferences online. Cisco's telecommuting programme has boosted employee satisfaction, reduced turnover, and earned the company numerous sustainability awards. Telecommuting has saved the company millions and lowers employees' annual fuel costs considerably.*

Employee empowerment

Many companies are increasing employee motivation and satisfaction through the use of empowerment. **Empowerment** means making employees more involved in their jobs and in the operations of the organisation by increasing their participation in decision making. With empowerment, control no longer flows exclusively from the top level of the organisation downward. Empowered employees have a voice in what they do and how and when they do it. In some organisations, employees' input is restricted to individual choices, such as when to take breaks. In other companies, their responsibilities may encompass more far-reaching issues. Successful companies tend to treat their employees like assets. Rather than forcing everyone to conform to an assigned role, empowered employees feel fully utilised and their responsibilities shift with the firm's needs. Technology clearly plays a role in empowering employees, but so does creating an open and safe workplace where employees feel like they can speak up and be heard. Allowing employees access to information can empower them and make them feel more satisfied with their jobs.

> **empowerment** giving employees greater control by providing them with decision-making powers that have an effect on their working lives.

For empowerment to work effectively, management must be involved. Managers should set expectations, communicate standards, institute periodic evaluations, and guarantee follow-up. If effectively implemented, empowerment can lead to increased job satisfaction, improved job

Using technology to close time and space and get more done. *Skype, e-mail, and other electronic methods are allowing employees continents away from one another to work together effectively. Being able to hire the best employees from all around the globe to work virtually with one another can give a firm a competitive advantage. Virtual teams located in different time zones and on different continents can also enable a company to work on important projects 24-7.*

performance, higher self-esteem, and increased organisational commitment. Obstacles to empowerment include resistance on the part of management, distrust of management on the part of workers, insufficient training, and poor communication between management and employees.

Employee ownership

Some organisations are discovering that a highly effective technique for motivating employees is **employee ownership**—that is, employees own the company they work for by virtue of being stockholders. Employee-owned businesses directly reward employees for success. When the company enjoys increased sales or lower costs, employees benefit directly. As a means to motivate top executives and, frequently, middle-ranking managers who are working long days for what are generally considered poor salaries, some firms provide share options as part of the employee compensation package. The option is simply the right to buy shares of the firm within a prescribed time at a set price. If the firm does well and its stock price rises past the set price (presumably because of all the work being done by the employee), the employee can exercise the option and immediately sell the stock and cash in on the company's success.

> **employee ownership** a situation in which employees own the company they work for by virtue of being stockholders

TEAMS AND TEAMWORK

The concepts of teams and teamwork may be most commonly associated with sports, but they are also integral parts of business organisations. This organisational structure is popular because it encourages employees to participate more fully in business decisions. The growing number of companies organising their workforces into teams reflects an effort to increase employee productivity and creativity because team members are working on specific goals and are given greater autonomy. This leads to greater job satisfaction as employees feel more involved in the management process.*

What is a team?

In a business organisation, a **team** is two or more workers operating as a coordinated unit to accomplish a specific task or goal.* A team may be assigned any number of tasks or goals, from development of a new product to selling that product. A team can also be created to identify or solve a problem that an organisation is experiencing. Kotter International, an organisation that specialises in helping other firms implement their strategic initiatives, believes in utilising teams of volunteers from within an organisation to assist in implementing change and problem solving. John Kotter recommends assembling a diverse team, with different viewpoints, skills, and experience-levels represented. Members need to be good at working with others and open to others' ideas.* Although teamwork may seem like a simple concept, teams function as a microcosm of the larger organisation. Therefore, it is important to understand the types, development, and general nature of teams.

 team two or more workers operating as a coordinated unit to accomplish a specific task or goal

Types of teams

There are several types of teams within businesses that function in specific ways to achieve different purposes, including problem-solving teams, self-managed teams, cross-functional teams, and virtual teams.

Problem-solving teams The most common type of team in business organisations is the **problem-solving team**. It is generally used temporarily in order to bring knowledgeable employees together to tackle a specific problem. Once the problem is solved, the team typically is disbanded.

 problem-solving team a team of knowledgeable employees brought together to tackle a specific problem

Self-managed work teams **Self-managed teams** are groups of employees with the authority and skills to manage themselves. Experts suggest that workers on self-managed teams are more motivated and satisfied because they have more task variety and job control. On many work teams, members rotate through all the jobs for which the team is responsible. Some organisations cross-train the entire team so that everyone can perform everyone else's job. In a traditional business structure, management is responsible for hiring and firing employees, establishing budgets, purchasing supplies, conducting performance reviews, and taking corrective action. When self-managed teams are in place, they take over some or all of these management functions. Xerox, Procter & Gamble, Ferrari, and numerous other companies have used self-managed teams successfully. The major advantages and disadvantages of self-managed teams are mentioned in Figure 10.6.

 self-managed teams groups of employees with the authority and skills to manage themselves

FIGURE 10.6

Advantages and disadvantages of self-managed teams
While self-managed teams provide advantages, managers must recognise their disadvantages.

ADVANTAGES	DISADVANTAGES
• Boosts employee morale	• Additional training costs
• Increases productivity	• Teams may be disorganised
• Aids innovation	• Conflicts may arise
• Reduces employee boredom	• Leadership role may be unclear

© CENGAGE LEARNING 2014

Cross-functional teams Traditionally, businesses have organised employees into departments based on a common function or specialty. However, increasingly, business organisations are faced with projects that require a diversity of skills not available within a single department. A **cross-functional team** consists of individuals with varying specialties, expertise, and skills that are brought together to achieve a common task. For example, a purchasing agent might create a cross-functional team with representatives from various departments to gain insight into useful purchases for the

Go team, go! *More companies today are using team-building exercises to help their employees figure out how to work better with another.*

company. This structure avoids departmental separation and allows greater efficiency when there is a single goal. Although cross-functional teams are not necessarily self-managed, most self-managed teams are cross-functional. Cross-functional teams can also be cross-divisional. By 2008, Ford Motor Company, along with other major automakers and their suppliers, were struggling. Making sure the company had parts to build vehicles was a critical component of rebounding from disaster, but their supply chain was on the verge of failing. In order to rethink its supply chain and improve efficiency, Ford VP of Global Purchasing Tony Brown set up a cross-functional team, which included representatives from all business units and all departments. These individuals were put in charge of monitoring parts manufacturers, preventing supply chain disruptions, and helping in efforts to shrink Ford's supply base. This team got together every day and worked long into the night, but they were able to address many of Ford's problems and helped to speed the automaker's recovery.*

> **cross-functional team** a team of individuals with varying specialties, expertise, and skills that are brought together to achieve a common task

Virtual teams With the advent of sophisticated communications technology, it is no longer necessary for teams to be geographically close. A **virtual team** consists of members who are geographically dispersed but communicate electronically. In fact, team members may never meet in person but rely solely on e-mail, teleconferences, faxes, voice mail, and other technological interactions. In the modern global environment, virtual teams connect employees on a common task across continents, oceans, time zones, and organisations. For example, Mozilla, the software provider responsible for Firefox, regularly requests the help of volunteers to test and improve their products virtually. Some of these volunteers become employees of the organisation based on their performance in the project they did.* In some cases, the physical distances between participants and the lack of face-to-face interaction can be difficult when deadlines approach or communication is not clear.

> **virtual team** a team consisting of members who are geographically dispersed but communicate electronically

Developing and using effective teams

When a team is first developed, it takes time for the members to establish roles, relationships, **delegation** of duties, and other attributes of an effective team. As a team matures, it passes through five stages of development, as shown in Figure 10.7.

> **delegation** giving authority to lower levels of management so they have the power to use the business's resources to produce and deliver goods and services

FIGURE 10.7

Stages of team development *When attempting to develop teams, managers must understand that multiple stages are generally required.*

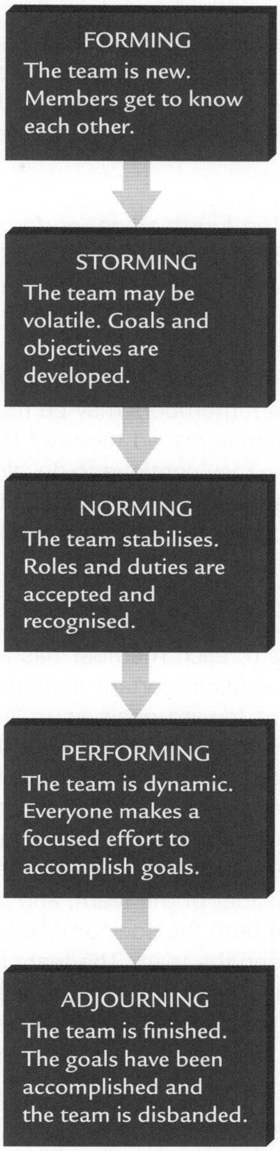

FORMING
The team is new. Members get to know each other.

STORMING
The team may be volatile. Goals and objectives are developed.

NORMING
The team stabilises. Roles and duties are accepted and recognised.

PERFORMING
The team is dynamic. Everyone makes a focused effort to accomplish goals.

ADJOURNING
The team is finished. The goals have been accomplished and the team is disbanded.

Forming In the first stage, *forming*, team members are introduced to one another and begin to develop a social dynamic. The members of the team are still unsure about how to relate to one another, what behaviours are considered acceptable, and what the ground rules are for the team. Through group member interaction over time, team members become more comfortable and a group dynamic begins to emerge.

Storming During the storming stage, the interaction may be volatile and the team may lack unity. Because the team is still relatively new, this is the stage at which goals and objectives begin to develop. Team members will use mind maps to develop ideas and plans and establish a broad-ranging agenda. It is important at this stage for team members to grow more comfortable around the others so that they can contribute openly. At this time, the leadership role likely will be formally undefined.

A team member may emerge as the informal leader. The success or failure of the ideas in storming determines how long the team will take to reach the next stage.

Norming   After storming and the first large burst of activity, the team begins to stabilise during the *norming* stage. During this process, each person's role within the group starts to become apparent, and members begin to recognise the roles of others. A sense of unity will become stronger. If it has not occurred already, an identified leader will emerge. The group still may be somewhat volatile at this point and may regress back to the second stage if any conflict, especially over the leadership role, occurs.

Performing   The fourth stage, *performing*, is when the team achieves its full potential. It is usually slow to develop and occurs when the team begins to focus strongly on the assigned task and away from team-development issues. The members of the team work in harmony under the established roles to accomplish the necessary goals.

Adjourning   In the final stage, *adjourning*, the team is disbanded because the project has been completed. Team members may be reassigned to other teams or tasks. This stage does not always occur if the team is placed together for a task with no specific date of completion. For example, a marketing team may continue to develop promotional efforts for a store even after a specific promotional task has been accomplished. This stage is especially common in problem-solving teams that are dismantled after the assigned problem has been resolved.

Roles within a team

Within any team, each member has a role to play in helping the team attain its objectives. Each of these roles adds important dimensions to team member interactions. The group member who pushes forward toward goals and places the objective first plays the *task-specialist role* by concentrating fully on the assigned task. In a cross-functional team, this might be the person with the most expertise relating to the current task. The *socioemotional* role is played by the individual who supports and encourages the emotional needs of the other members. This person places the team members' personal needs over the task of the team. Although this may sound unimportant, the socioemotional member's dedication to team cohesiveness will lead to greater unity and higher productivity. The leader of the team, and possibly others as well, will play a *dual role*. This dual role is a combination of both the socioemotional and task-specialist roles because this individual focuses on both the task and the team. The team leader might not always play a dual role, but the team is likely to be most successful when he or she does. Sometimes an individual assumes the *nonparticipant role*. This role behaviour is characterised by a person who does not contribute to accomplishing the task and does not provide favourable input with respect to team members' socioemotional needs.

Team cohesiveness

Developing a unit from a diverse group of personalities, specialties, backgrounds, and work styles can be challenging and complicated. In a cohesive team, the members get along and are able to

Thanks to all the technology in your pocket and on your desk, it's a small world after all. Friends, family, and coworkers are never more than a text message, e-mail, or Skype conversation away. Virtual teams also rely on these and other technologies to stay in touch.

© EDBOCHSTUDIO/SHUTTERSTOCK

accomplish their tasks effectively. There are factors that affect cohesiveness within a team. Teams generally are ideal when they contain five to 12 people. Teams with fewer than five people often fail to accomplish tasks and generate a variety of ideas. Teams with more than 12 are too large because members do not develop relationships, may feel intimidated to speak, or may disconnect. It also may be beneficial to have team members introduce themselves and describe their past work experiences. This activity will foster familiarity and shared experiences. One of the most reliable ways to build cohesiveness within a team is through competition with other teams. When two teams are competing for a single prise or recognition, they are forced to put aside conflict and accomplish their goal. By adding an incentive to finishing the task, the team automatically becomes more goal oriented. Also, a favourable appraisal from an outsider may strengthen team cohesiveness. Because the team is being praised as a group, team members recognise their contribution as a unit. Teams are also more successful when goals have been agreed upon. A team that is clear about its objective will focus more on accomplishing it. Frequent interaction also builds cohesiveness as relationships strengthen and familiarity increases.

Team conflict and how to resolve it

Conflict occurs when a disagreement arises between two or more team members. Conflict traditionally has been viewed as negative; however, if handled properly, conflict can work to improve a team. For example, if two team members disagree about a certain decision, both may analyse the situation more closely to determine the best choice. As long as conflict is handled in a respectful and professional manner, it can improve the quality of work produced. However, if conflict turns hostile and affects the work environment, then steps must be taken to arrive at a suitable compromise. Compromises can be difficult in a business organisation because neither party ends up getting everything he or she wants. The best solution is a middle-ground alternative in which each party is satisfied to some degree. It is best to avoid attempting to minimise or ignore conflicts within a group because this may cause the conflict to grow as members concentrate on the problem instead of the task. However the conflict is resolved, it is important to remember that conflict must be acknowledged if it is to either be resolved or serve a constructive purpose.

Benefits and limitations of teams

Teamwork within a company has been credited as a key to reducing turnover and costs and increasing production, quality, and customer service. There is also evidence that working in teams leads to higher levels of job satisfaction among employees and a harmonious work environment. Thus, an increasingly large number of companies are considering teams as a viable organisational structure. However, the process of reorganising into teams can be stressful and time consuming with no guarantee that the team will develop effectively. If a team lacks cohesiveness and is unable to resolve conflict, the company may experience lower productivity.

SUMMARY

- Explain what motivation is.

   Motivation is the individual internal process that energises, directs, and sustains behaviour. Motivation is affected by employee morale—that is, the employee's feelings about the job, superiors, and the firm itself. Motivation, morale, and job satisfaction are closely related.

- Understand some major historical perspectives on motivation.

One of the first approaches to employee motivation was Frederick Taylor's scientific management, the application of scientific principles to the management of work and workers. Taylor believed that employees work only for money and that they must be closely supervised and managed. This thinking led to the piece-rate system, under which employees are paid a certain amount for each unit they produce. The Hawthorne Studies attempted to determine the effects of the work environment on productivity. Results of these studies indicated that human factors affect productivity more than do physical aspects of the workplace.

Maslow's hierarchy of needs suggests that people are motivated by five sets of needs. In ascending order of importance, these motivators are physiological, safety, social, esteem, and self-actualisation needs. People are motivated by the lowest set of needs that remains unfulfilled. As needs at one level are satisfied, people try to satisfy needs at the next level.

Frederick Herzberg found that job satisfaction and dissatisfaction are influenced by two distinct sets of factors. Motivation factors, including recognition and responsibility, affect an employee's degree of satisfaction, but their absence does not necessarily cause dissatisfaction. Hygiene factors, including pay and working conditions, affect an employee's degree of dissatisfaction but do not affect satisfaction.

Theory X is a concept of motivation that assumes that employees dislike work and will function effectively only in a highly controlled work environment. Thus, to achieve an organisation's goals, managers must coerce, control, and threaten employees. This theory generally is consistent with Taylor's ideas of scientific management. Theory Y is more in keeping with the results of the Hawthorne Studies and the human relations movement. It suggests that employees can be motivated to behave as responsible members of the organisation. Theory Z emphasises long-term employment, collective decision making, individual responsibility for the outcomes of decisions, informal control, and a holistic concern for employees. Reinforcement theory is based on the idea that people will repeat behaviour that is rewarded and will avoid behaviour that is punished.

- Describe three contemporary views of motivation: equity theory, expectancy theory, and goal-setting theory.

Equity theory maintains that people are motivated to obtain and preserve equitable treatment for themselves. Expectancy theory suggests that our motivation depends on how much we want something and how likely we think we are to get it. Goal-setting theory suggests that employees are motivated to achieve a goal that they and their managers establish together.

- Explain several techniques for increasing employee motivation.

Management by objectives (MBO) is a motivation technique in which managers and employees collaborate in setting goals. MBO motivates employees by getting them more involved in their jobs and in the organisation as a whole. Job enrichment seeks to motivate employees by varying their tasks and giving them more responsibility for and control over their jobs. Job enlargement, expanding a worker's assignments to include additional tasks, is one aspect of job enrichment. Job redesign is a type of job enrichment in which work is restructured to improve the worker–job match.

Behaviour modification uses reinforcement to encourage desirable behaviour. Rewards for productivity, quality, and loyalty change employees' behaviour in desired ways and also increase motivation.

Allowing employees to work more flexible hours is another way to build motivation and job satisfaction. Flexitime is a system of work scheduling that allows workers to set their own hours as long as they fall within the limits established by employers. Part-time work is permanent employment in which individuals work less than a standard work week. Job sharing is an arrangement whereby two people share one full-time position. Telecommuting allows employees to work at home all or part of the work week. All of these types of work arrangements give employees more time outside the workplace to deal with family responsibilities or to enjoy free time.

Employee empowerment, self-managed work teams, and employee ownership are also techniques that boost employee motivation. Empowerment increases employees' involvement in their jobs by increasing their decision-making authority. Self-managed work teams are groups of employees with the authority and skills to manage themselves. When employees participate in ownership programmes, such as employee stock ownership plans (ESOPs), they have more incentive to make the company succeed and therefore work more effectively.

- Understand the types, development, and uses of teams.

A large number of companies use teams to increase their employees' productivity. In a business organisation, a team is a group of workers functioning together as a unit to complete a common goal or purpose.

There are several types of teams within businesses that function in specific ways to achieve different purposes. A problem-solving team is a team of knowledgeable employees brought together to tackle a specific problem. A virtual team is a team consisting of members who are geographically dispersed but communicate electronically. A cross-functional team is a team of individuals with varying specialties, expertise, and skills.

The five stages of team development are forming, storming, norming, performing, and adjourning. As a team develops, it should become more productive and unified. The four roles within teams are task specialist, socioemotional, dual, and nonparticipative. Each of these roles plays a specific part in the team's interaction. For a team to be successful, members must learn how to resolve and manage conflict so that the team can work cohesively to accomplish goals.

EXERCISE QUESTIONS

1 Give three reasons why a business might want to motivate its employees.

2 Explain the benefits and problems of PRP.

3 List and explain some of the main advantages and disadvantages – to both employers and employees – of telecommuting.

4 List and explain the four main types of teams.

5 What are the potential benefits of team working? Why might they not be achieved?

CASE 10.1

PGT Motor Company – the place to work...

PGT Motor Company manufactures passenger vehicles in East-London, South Africa. They manufacture various models of light passenger vehicles of which the Coru model is the most popular. The office hours for admin and managerial staff are from 08:00-17:00 Mondays to Fridays, and the manufacturing staff work three eight-hour shifts on weekdays.

The motor manufacturing plant mainly consists of three assembly lines of which some have sub-cells. The three assembly lines are: the bodyshop, the paint-shop and the trim line. Michael and Peter are both an assembly line workers on one of the trimline sub-cells responsible for fitting the dashboards and doing the wiring of the Coru passenger vehicles. Michael has been working at PGT for three days, he is still learning; and Peter has been working at the company for nearly seven years and he is extremely talented.

The organisational structure of the Production division appears in the exhibit.

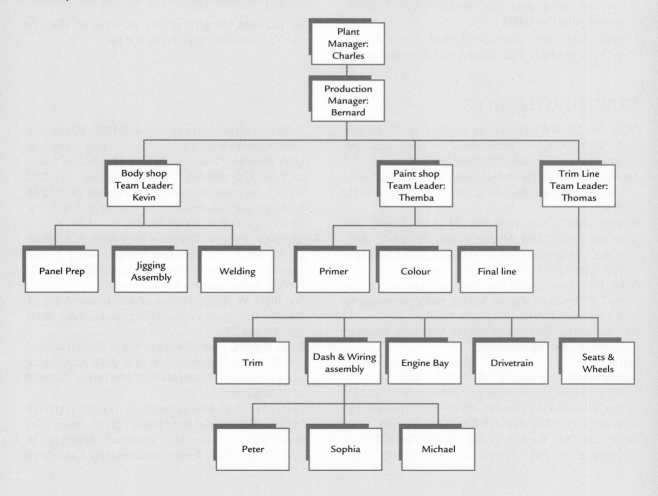

The company has a Plant Manager, Charles, and the Production Manager, Bernard, reports to him. As mentioned earlier three main assembly lines can be distinguished and each assembly line is managed by a team leader. The team leader reports directly to Bernard.

The team leader on the Trimline assembly line, Thomas, will become a father in the next week or two and according to company policy he is entitled to five working days, paternity leave. The Manager has called Thomas to his office to enquire how he plans to deal with ensuring that the operations are not disrupted during his absence and also how he plans to reach the production targets and standards. Thomas informs the Manager that he already has a contingency plan in place and he tells the Manager the following:

Peter is a very capable assembly line worker on the trim line. He has more than seven years' experience in the dashboard and wiring sub-cell and he also has extensive experience on the trim, engine bay, drivetrain, seats

and wheels. Peter is very responsible and has excellent communication skills. His colleagues respect him and he has shown potential to manage people, would like to give Peter the opportunity to act as team leader during my absence. We need a person that will be able to do this whenever I am on leave and I think he will be the perfect person. I am afraid that if we do not give him an opportunity like this, he might get frustrated and become demotivated. We cannot afford to lose him. Michael has recently joined the company and he needs training to be able to work efficiently but we cannot afford to not have him work on the assembly line to go for training.

The Plant Manager is very impressed with what he has read about Thomas. He wishes him well with the birth of his daughter. After speaking to the Plant Manager, Thomas calls Peter and discusses the plans with him. Peter is very excited and promises not to disappoint Thomas.

Questions

1 If Peter temporarily takes over Thomas's job in his absence, what does this move represent? Briefly explain what this entails.

2 What motivation intensive method can they use to train Michael and make him understand what

the job is all about? Provide a motivation for your answer.

3 Do you think this arrangement will have an effect on Peter's motivation? Explain you answer.

CHAPTER REFERENCES

"2012 Top 100 Best Companies to Work For," February 6, 2012, Fortune, http://money.cnn.com/magazines/fortune/best-companies/2012/full_list/.

Apple, http://store.apple.com/us_smb_78313/browse/home/campaigns/corporate_gifting, accessed February 16, 2012.

Baldoni, John, "Your Next Job May Be Staring You in the Face," CBS Money Watch, March 6, 2012, www.cbsnews.com/8301-500395_162-57390281/your-next-job-may-be-staring-you-in-the-face/.

Birkin, Emily Guy, "The 16 Best Part-Time Jobs with Benefits," PT Money, February 1, 2012, http://ptmoney.com/the-ten-best-part-time-jobs-with-benefits/.

Daft, Richard L., *Management* (Mason, OH: South-Western/Cengage Learning, 2012), 510.

Dell'Antonia, K.J., "Flexible Work Schedules Mean Employees Stay Longer," *New York Times*, March 1, 2012, http://parenting.blogs.nytimes.com/2012/03/01/flexible-work-schedules-mean-employees-stay-longer/?scp=4&sq=flexible%20schedule&st=cse.

Gates, Lisa, "Yes, You Can Negotiate a Job Share Without Taking a Pay Cut," *Forbes*, January 24, 2012, www.

forbes.com/sites/shenegotiates/2012/01/24/yes-you-can-negotiate-a-job-share-without-taking-a-pay-cut/; Ellen Weinreb, "How Job Sharing May be the Secret to Work-Life Balance," *Forbes*, October 24, 2012, www.forbes.com/sites/work-in-progress/2011/10/24/how-job-sharing-may-be-the-secret-to-work-life-balance/, accessed March 25, 2012.

Greenhouse, Stephen, "Flexitime Flourishes in Accounting Industry," *The New York Times*, January 7, 2011, www.nytimes.com/2011/01/08/business/08perks.html?_r=1&ref=kpmg, accessed March 25, 2012.

Griffin, Ricky W., *Fundamentals of Management*, 6th ed. (Mason, OH: South-Western/Cengage Learning, 2012), 303–305 and 396.

Hoffman, Bryce G., "Inside Ford's Fight to Avoid Disaster," *The Wall Street Journal*, March 8, 2012, http://online.wsj.com/article/SB10001424052970204781804577269410217101038.html.

http://money.cnn.com/magazines/fortune/bestcompanies/2011/benefits/telecommuting.html; Cisco, cisco.com/en/US/products/index.html, accessed February 16, 2012; "Cisco Study Finds Telecommuting Significantly

Increases Employee Productivity, Work-Life Flexibility and Job Satisfaction," *Cisco, News Release*, June 25, 2009, http://newsroom.cisco.com/dlls/2009/prod_062609.html.

Kotter, John, "Guiding Coalition: A Dream Team to Help You Implement Strategy Quickly," *Forbes,* February 2, 2012, www.forbes.com/sites/johnkotter/2012/02/08/guiding-coalition-a-dream-team-to-help-you-implement-strategy-quickly/.

Matuson, Robert, "Low-Cost Ways to Show Employees They're Highly Valued," *Fast Company*, March 7, 2012, www.fastcompany.com/1822943/low-cost-ways-to-show-your-employees-they-are-highly-valued?partner=gnews.

Mozilla, www.mozilla.org/about/governance.html, accessed February 16, 2012.

Ouchi, William, *Theory Z* (Reading, MA: Addison-Wesley, 1981).

PR Newswire, "Job Absence Rates Down Over Year-Ago Levels," March 14, 2012, MarketWatch, www.marketwatch.com/story/job-absence-rates-down-over-year-ago-levels-yearly-turnover-in-2011-stable-with-2010-rates-bloomberg-bna-survey-of-employers-2012-03-14.

Pynchon, Victoria, "Working Mothers, CEOs, and the Death of Face Time," *Forbes,* February 19, 2012, www.forbes.com/sites/shenegotiates/2012/02/19/working-mothers-ceos-and-the-death-of-facetime/.

Schawbel, Dan, "The Rise of the Remote Worker, or How o Work from Home Without Getting Fired," *Time,* March 13, 2012, http://moneyland.time.com/2012/03/13/the-rise-of-the-remote-worker-or-how-to-work-from-home-without-getting-fired/.

"The Engineer's Life at Google," Google Jobs, www.google.com/jobs/lifeatgoogle/englife/index.html, accessed March 16, 2012.

PART 5
MARKETING, SOCIAL MEDIA, AND E-BUSINESS

The business activities that make up a firm's marketing efforts are those most directly concerned with satisfying customers' needs. In this part, we explore these activities in some detail. Initially, we discuss markets, marketing mixes, marketing environment forces, marketing plans, and buying behaviour. Then, we discuss the four elements that together make up a marketing mix: product, price, distribution, and promotion. This is followed by a look at how business firms use social media to build relationships with customers and promote their products and services. We also investigate how companies use e-business to reduce expenses and increase sales and profits.

11 THE MARKETING CONCEPT

BUSINESS FOCUS

Ireland: marketing a country

How do you develop a marketing strategy for a country? This was a question faced by the Irish government during difficult times in the 1960s and 1970s. The challenge was to build the Irish economy to match the affluence enjoyed by some of its European neighbours. At the time, Ireland was viewed as being backward and unattractive for investment by international corporations. The Industrial Development Authority (IDA) played an important role in developing the country's economy, moving it away from its traditional over-reliance on agriculture. Today, with well over a third of the country's GDP coming from industry, and services also accounting for approaching a third, agriculture's contribution has fallen to just 10 per cent.

Marketing and good promotion alone were not responsible for this turnaround. The Irish government realised that to attract investment from overseas it had to provide a stable economy, desirable residential suburbs, modern road and air infrastructure, state-of-the-art telecommunications and, crucially, a well-qualified, dynamic and motivated workforce. These improvements took some time to achieve, but today the companies located in Dublin and around Ireland's airports testify readily to the excellent infrastructure, communications, workforce and tax breaks. The Irish workforce is one of the best educated and most highly prized in Europe.

Having improved the amenities, infrastructure and the workforce, the perceptions of investors overseas had to be addressed. In order to instigate this change, the IDA established a clear strategy by pinpointing attractive sectors for growth and actively encouraging growth businesses in those areas. Consumer products, electronics, healthcare and financial services were some of the key targets. Once decisions about growth priorities had been made, the aim was to develop a marketing programme based around the particular assets that Ireland was able to offer. For example, promotional material focused on – among other things – the young, highly educated workforce, the low rates of corporate taxation, excellent digital and satellite telecommunications systems and a stable currency with low inflation. The attractive countryside and vibrant cultural scene also featured prominently in the IDA's branding of Ireland.

Considerable care was taken to ensure that the propositions developed matched the requirements of the businesses targeted. This provided many overseas businesses with substantial, tangible reasons for establishing a base in Ireland, bringing with them the investment the country so badly craved. Leading computer manufacturers, pharmaceutical businesses, financial corporations and telecommunications businesses are just some of those who have located facilities in the country: over 1000 well-known organisations have chosen Ireland ahead of other locations for their European operations.

After the recent meltdown of the Irish economy following the global financial crisis, there is once more the need to develop a marketing strategy for Ireland. Most of the work of the past 20 years must be repeated and reinforced, in order to ensure continued inward investment. The marketing toolkit will play a significant part in the overhaul of Ireland's target market strategy, positioning and new-look measures to attract global businesses to locate in the country.

References: Irish Embassy, London; Industrial Development Authority (IDA); 'Facts about Ireland', IDA, 1995, 1996, 1999, 2003, 2008, 2011; http://www.idaireland.com, 2 February 2011.

Marketing's primary aim is the identification of target markets and the satisfaction of these customers, now and in the future. In most organisations, marketing fulfils an analytical function, provides strategic direction and executes a set of tactical activities designed to attract and retain the targeted customers to the organisation's products or services. Marketers should strive to be the "radar" or "eyes and ears" for their organisations in terms of assessing opportunities, identifying threats and preparing their colleagues for the evolving challenges in the marketplace. There is much more to marketing than creating an advertisement, producing an eye-catching price promotion, "jazzing up" a Web site or developing a brand.

Organisations with a marketing orientation have more than a few staff engaged in marketing activities. Such organisations have a sound awareness of customers' needs and buying behaviour, of competitors' offerings and strategies, and of market trends. They take steps to ensure they know how these market conditions will evolve. In addition, they orientate their operational practices and coordinate their inter-functional thinking around these market conditions.

Effective marketing involves an analytical process combining marketing analysis, strategising and the creation of marketing programmes designed to implement a designated marketing strategy. Marketing opportunity analysis is a pivotal part of marketing, involving the determination of emerging and existing market opportunities and the choice of which to address. At the heart of a marketing strategy is the formation of a target market strategy and a basis for competing in order to focus on the opportunities prioritised by the organisation.

Most members of the general public think of "advertising", "marketing research" or "sales persuasion" when the term "marketing" is mentioned. These brief introductory comments explain that there is in fact much more to marketing. This chapter is designed to define marketing and explain its role.

This chapter first overviews the concept of marketing orientation before developing a definition of marketing. The focus then moves on to consider why people should study marketing and why marketing is important. The chapter proceeds to explore the marketing concept and examines several issues associated with successful implementation. The chapter explains the importance of an analytical process to effective marketing, from analysis to strategy formulation to the creation of marketing programmes. How the marketing concept has evolved and topical themes are highlighted.

The concepts and strategies discussed throughout this chapter are applicable to consumer goods and services, business-to-business products and services, public sector organisations, as well as to not-for-profit and many social sector organisations. The term "customer" in the definitions of marketing should be treated somewhat loosely. While in commercial settings, it means consumers in consumer markets, or business customers in business marketing, the themes explored here extend beyond such parameters. The understanding and satisfying of audiences served or represented is just as important in the public and voluntary sectors. Such organisations benefit from adopting the marketing concept and process, as they also must strive to stay ahead of changing environmental conditions, maximise use of their resources to deliver their aims, compete for attention, and seek to understand and satisfy their audiences and stakeholders.

MARKETING EXPLAINED AND DEFINED

Marketing orientation

An organisation exhibiting a **marketing orientation** is said to have a sound understanding of customer needs, buying behaviour and the issues influencing the purchasing choices of customers. A marketing-oriented organisation also has a shrewd appreciation of competitors and external marketing environment forces and trends.* In addition to comprehending these customer, competitor and marketing environment issues, a marketing-oriented organisation ensures its operations, personnel and capabilities are aligned to reflect these external drivers. A truly marketing-oriented organisation understands these current issues, but is also focused on identifying how they will evolve, so ensuring that the organisation's strategy and capabilities are modified to reflect not just current market requirements but also future market conditions.

> **marketing orientation**   a marketing-oriented organisation devotes resources to understanding the needs and buying behaviour of customers, competitors' activities and strategies, and of market trends and external forces – now and as they may shape up in the future; inter-functional coordination ensures that the organisation's activities and capabilities are aligned to this marketing intelligence

A marketing-oriented organisation, therefore, devotes resources to understanding the needs and buying behaviour of customers, competitors' activities and strategies and market trends and external forces (now and as they may shape up in the future). Inter-functional coordination ensures that the organisation's activities and capabilities are aligned to this marketing intelligence.

Not all organisations can claim to have a marketing orientation. For example, some are purely sales led, concentrating on short-term sales targets, whereas other organisations are production oriented, choosing to emphasise product development and production efficiency in their business strategy. Few experts would argue against maximising sales or seeking leading-edge production practices, or indeed the adoption of best-practice financial and human resource approaches. Similarly, the adoption of a marketing orientation is highly desirable. A marketing orientation is of significant benefit to an organisation, as it facilitates a better understanding of customers and helps a business to prepare for external market developments, threats and opportunities. It is difficult to contemplate a scenario where a marketing orientation would not be beneficial to an organisation.

An organisation practising the concepts explained here is well on the way to having a marketing orientation; but it is important that inter-functional coordination aligns the activities within the organisation and also the leadership team to the marketplace, and specifically to customer buying behaviour, competitive pressures and marketing environment forces, and to the evolving nature of these market conditions. The use of some of marketing's concepts and an understanding of the role of marketing in attracting and satisfying customers, are not enough on their own to establish a marketing orientation. However, failure to comprehend the core concepts of marketing will make a marketing orientation impossible to achieve. The focus of this chapter, therefore, is on explaining the core concepts of marketing which are the entry point requirements for going on to establish a marketing orientation.

It is possible for an organisation lacking a full marketing orientation to nevertheless deploy and benefit from aspects of the marketing toolkit as described in the following chapters. For instance, many businesses have an adequate understanding of their customers, but not all have fully grasped their competitors' strategies or the forces present in the external marketing environment. Obviously, it is better not to operate in ignorance of these external pressures, which may create threats or opportunities. The definition of marketing *per se* is not, therefore, the same as the definition of marketing orientation.

Marketing defined

Asking members of the public to define marketing is an illuminating experience. They will respond with a variety of descriptions, including "advertising", "selling", "hype", "conning people", "targeting" and "packaging". In reality, marketing encompasses many more activities than most people realise and depends on a wealth of formal concepts, processes and models beyond the soundbites just listed. Since it is practised and studied for many different reasons, marketing has been, and continues to be, defined in many different ways, whether for academic, research or applied business purposes. This chapter examines what is meant by the term **marketing**.

> **marketing**   individual and organisational activities that facilitate and expedite satisfying exchange relationships in a dynamic environment through the creation, distribution, promotion and pricing of goods, services and ideas

"Marketing consists of individual and organisational activities that facilitate and expedite satisfying exchange relationships in a dynamic environment through the creation, distribution, promotion and pricing of goods, services and ideas."

Dibb, Simkin, Pride and Ferrell in Marketing: Concepts and Strategies

The basic rationale of marketing is that a successful organisation requires satisfied and happy customers who return to the organisation to provide additional custom. In exchange for something of value, typically payment or a donation, the customers receive a product or service that satisfies their needs. Such a product has an acceptable level of quality, reliability, customer service and support, is available at places convenient for the customer at the "right" price and is promoted effectively by means of a clear message that is readily comprehended by the customers in question. For example, in return for quenching thirst at affordable prices with a reliable product that is widely available in easy-to-use containers, Coca-Cola receives a great deal of money from customers. Unfortunately for companies and their marketers, customers' requirements change as their needs alter, marketing messages infiltrate their thinking, friends and colleagues discuss purchases, and competing products are pushed by rival organisations. In the dynamic world of marketing, an effective solution to satisfying customer needs rarely has longevity. High-specification cassette decks no longer satisfy the majority of music lovers' needs, nor for many consumers do compact disc players, so MP3 players and music downloads now dominate the product ranges of firms like Sony. Marketers must constantly assess their customers' requirements and competitors' propositions, being prepared to modify their marketing activity accordingly. An assessment of marketing opportunities is an ever evolving process requiring regular revision and updating.

"Marketing is the management process responsible for identifying, anticipating and satisfying customer requirements profitably."

Chartered Institute of Marketing

Understanding customers and anticipating their requirements is a core theme of effective marketing.* So, too, is understanding general market trends and developments that may affect both customers' views and the activities of organisations operating in a particular market. These factors may include social trends, technological enhancements, economic patterns and changes in the legal and regulatory arena, as well as political influences. These are often termed the forces of the **marketing environment**. Compared with five years ago, for example, look at how many companies now produce products in "environmentally friendly" packaging in line with the social trend of the "green consumer". Or, owing to recession, consider how many brands now have value versions. An organisation does not have a marketplace to itself. There are direct competitors, new entrant rivals, substitute products offering alternative solutions to a customer's specific need. Construction-equipment giant JCB markets trench-digging equipment to utilities and local authorities. The growth of subterranean tunnelling robotic "moles" for pipe laying, requiring no trench digging, is a substitute for the traditional JCB backhoe loader and a major competitive threat. The competitive context is of fundamental importance to marketers of any good or service. The internal resource base of the business which drives its strengths and weaknesses will determine which market opportunities are viable for the organisation to pursue. Marketing, therefore, depends on the successful analysis of customers, the marketing environment, competition and internal capabilities.

> **marketing environment** external changing forces within the trading environment: laws, regulations, political activities, societal pressures, economic conditions and technological advances

"The aim of marketing is to make selling superfluous. The aim is to know and to understand the customer so well that the product or service fits him/her and sells itself!"

US management guru Peter Drucker

With an understanding of these aspects of the marketplace, an organisation must then develop a marketing strategy. Even the mighty global organisations such as GM/Vauxhall, DuPont or Unilever choose not to offer a product for every type of consumer or customer need. Instead, they attempt to identify groups of customers where each separate group, or "market segment", has "similar" needs. Each group of customers may then be offered a specifically tailored product or service proposition and a "marketing mix" programme. The Ford Kuga off-roader appeals to a separate group of customers than does the Ford Focus town car, and it is marketed totally differently. In developing unique marketing programmes for individual market segments – groups of customers – an organisation must prioritise which particular groups of customers it has the ability to serve and which will provide satisfactory returns. Organisations have limited resources, which restricts the number of segments in a market which can be targeted. In deciding which segments to target, an organisation must be clear about the image – or brand *positioning* – it intends to offer to each group of customers. The organisation should endeavour to serve those customers it targets in a manner that gives it an edge over its competitors. Knowing how to group customers sensibly into homogeneous market segments; determining which to target; selecting a suitable positioning; and seeking superiority over rivals, are some of the core elements of marketing strategy.

"The marketing concept holds that the key to achieving organisational goals lies in determining the needs and wants of target markets and delivering the desired satisfaction more efficiently and effectively than the competition."

U.S. marketer Philip Kotler

Once a company has devised a marketing strategy, its attention must switch to marketing mix programmes.* As consumers of food brands, audio products or banking services, all readers of this text will have experienced the marketing mix programmes of major companies such as Cadbury's, Apple or Barclays. These are the tactical actions of marketing departments, which are designed to implement the desired marketing strategy by attracting, engaging and continuing to serve targeted customers. The product or offer must be clearly defined in line with target customer needs; service levels and guarantees must be determined; pricing and payment issues decided; channels of distribution established to make the product or service available; and promotional strategies devised and executed to communicate with the targeted customers. These tactical aspects of marketing programmes – often referred to as *the marketing mix* – must be supported with carefully managed controls in an organisation to ensure their successful execution and the monitoring of their effectiveness.

Marketers must understand their markets – customers, competitors, market trends – and their own capabilities before developing marketing programmes. A marketing strategy must be determined that reflects the analyses, before the marketing programmes that will be used to action the recommended strategy are specified. **A**nalysis first, then **S**trategy decisions with, finally, the formulation of marketing **P**rogrammes: the *ASP* of the marketing process. The focus must be on providing customer satisfaction, but in a manner that leads to the organisation's successful performance. For example, by addressing customers' needs and adopting a marketing culture incorporating clear controls, construction equipment manufacturer JCB has enjoyed the most successful financial returns in the company's history.

The intention of this introductory marketing text is to comprehensively explore these facets of marketing and thus provide a sound conceptual basis for understanding the nature and activities of marketing. There are many definitions of marketing, since it is not a pure science. However, certain core ingredients of the various definitions collectively indicate the basic priorities of marketing:

- satisfying customers
- identifying/maximising marketing opportunities
- targeting the "right" customers
- facilitating exchange relationships
- staying ahead in dynamic environments
- endeavouring to beat and pre-empt competitors
- utilising resources/assets effectively
- increasing market share
- enhancing profitability or income
- satisfying the organisation's stakeholders.

These aims form the objectives for many marketing directors and marketing departments. This chapter formally adopts two definitions of marketing by the American Marketing Association. As already stated, *Marketing consists of individual and organisational activities that facilitate and expedite satisfying exchange relationships in a dynamic environment through the creation, distribution, promotion and pricing of goods, services and ideas.* Along with the Association's more recent explanation;

Marketing. Noun. An organisational function and a set of processes for creating, communicating and delivering value to customers and for managing customer relationships in ways that benefit the organisation and its stakeholders.

SUCCESS STORY

Manchester United's global appeal

© JEREMY SUTTON-HIBBERT / ALAMY

Manchester United, the British Premier League football team, was the first club in football to fully realise the importance of marketing itself. Fans across Europe, Asia, and Latin America grew familiar with the team via televised matches, and this led to huge sales of the club's merchandise.

Manchester United conducts an aggressive marketing style and offers a vast range of products and services to its global market: from football strips to a television channel, themed restaurants and financial services. Visits by the team to its overseas fan bases serve to fuel the club's popularity.

United also has sponsorships with firms that have influence in emerging markets (for example Concha y Toro in Chile, Telekom Malaysia in Kuala Lumpar, and MTN Group in South Africa).

The club is also helped by the diversity of its players. Manchester United signs local players from all over the world; and then ensures that these players stay in touch with their fans. In this way, the players bring the brand alive and personalise it. Manchester United is a team made up of international players, and a brand supported by international fans.

References: Ogden, M. 'United target expansion on new frontier in India', *Daily Telegraph*, 18 March 2010.

Marketing indeed must be viewed as a process… of analysis to gain market insights, strategy decisions to make choices, and the management of marketing programmes in order to implement the desired marketing strategy. A definition of marketing must acknowledge that it relates to more than just tangible goods, that marketing activities occur in a dynamic environment and that such activities are performed by individuals as well as organisations.* The ultimate goal is to satisfy targeted customers and stakeholders, seeking their loyalty and consumption, in a way that adds value for the organisation and its stakeholders. This should be achieved in a manner that is differentiated in the view of customers and stakeholders vis-à-vis competitors' marketing, that provides an organisation with a competitive edge over rivals and that is updated regularly to reflect market forces and developments. To be in a position to satisfy targeted customers or stakeholders, much work is required by those tasked within the organisation and their external partners to conduct the required marketing analyses, develop sensible marketing strategies and create appropriate marketing programmes to take to market… repeatedly and regularly.

THE DEFINITIONS OF MARKETING EXPLORED

Marketing consists of individual and organisational activities that facilitate and expedite satisfying exchange relationships in a dynamic environment through the creation, distribution, promotion and pricing of goods, services and ideas.

Marketing consists of activities

The marketing of products or services effectively requires many activities. Some are performed by producers; some are accomplished by intermediaries, who purchase products from producers or from other intermediaries and resell them; and some are even performed by purchasers. Marketing does not include all human and organisational activities, only those aimed at facilitating and expediting exchanges. Table 11.1 lists several major categories and examples of marketing activities, as

| TABLE 11.1 | Possible decisions and activities associated with marketing mix variables |

Marketing mix variables	Possible decisions and activities
Product	Develop and test market new products; modify existing products; eliminate products that do not satisfy customers' desires; formulate brand names and branding policies; create product guarantees and establish procedures for fulfilling guarantees; provide customer service; plan packaging, including materials, sizes, shapes, colours and designs
Place/distribution	Analyse various types of distribution channels; design appropriate distribution channels; select appropriate channel members and partners; design an effective programme for dealer relations; establish distribution centres; formulate and implement procedures for efficient product handling; set up inventory controls; analyse transportation methods; minimise total distribution costs; analyse possible locations for plants and wholesale or retail outlets; manage multiple channels to market
Promotion (marketing communications)	Set promotional objectives; determine major types of promotion to be used; select and schedule advertising media; develop advertising messages; measure the effectiveness of advertisements; recruit and train salespeople; formulate payment programmes for sales personnel; establish sales territories; plan and implement sales promotion efforts such as free samples, coupons, displays, competitions, sales contests and cooperative advertising programmes; prepare and disseminate publicity releases; evaluate sponsorships; provide direct mail; and establish Web sites and a digital presence
Price	Analyse competitors' prices; formulate pricing policies; determine method(s) used to set prices; set prices; determine discounts for various types of buyer; establish conditions and terms of sales; determine credit and payment terms; understand the consumers' notion of value
People	Manipulate the marketing mix and establish service levels, guarantees, warranties, expertise, sales support, after sales back-up, customer handling requirements, personnel skills training and motivation (people as marketers); make products and services available (people as intermediaries); provide a market for products (people as consumers); manage customer retention

ultimately encountered by the consumer or business customer, who remains at the "sharp end" of such decisions and marketing programmes. Note that this list is not all-inclusive. Each activity could be sub-divided into more specific activities.

Marketing is performed by individuals and organisations

All organisations perform marketing activities to facilitate exchanges. Businesses as well as not-for-profit and public-sector organisations, such as colleges and universities, charitable organisations, community theatres and hospitals, perform marketing activities. For example, colleges and universities and their students engage in exchanges. To receive instruction, knowledge, entertainment, a degree, the use of facilities and sometimes room and board, students give up time, money and perhaps services in the form of labour; they may also give up opportunities to do other things! Many organisations engage in marketing activities. Various police forces have surveyed their communities in order to prioritise services and reassure the general public that people's concerns will be addressed. Politicians now conduct analyses before determining strategies; they think of target markets rather than just the electorate. Even the sole owner of, and worker in, a small corner shop decides which products will sell, arranges deliveries to the shop, prices and displays products, advertises and serves customers.

Marketing facilitates satisfying exchange relationships

For an **exchange** to take place, four conditions must exist.

 exchange the provision or transfer of goods, services and ideas in return for something of value

1. Two or more individuals, groups or organisations must participate.
2. Each party must possess something of value that the other party desires (for example, cash for a product or a donation for a charitable cause).
3. Each party must be willing to give up its "something of value" to receive the "something of value" held by the other party. The objective of a marketing exchange is to receive something that is desired more than that which is given up to get it – that is, a reward in excess of costs.
4. The parties to the exchange must be able to communicate with each other to make their "something of value" available.*

Figure 11.1 illustrates the process of exchange. The arrows indicate that the parties communicate and that each has something of value available to exchange. Note, though, that an exchange will not necessarily take place just because these four conditions exist. Nevertheless, even if there is no exchange, marketing activities have still occurred. The "somethings of value" held by the two parties are most often products and/or financial resources, such as money or credit. When an exchange occurs, products are traded for other products or for financial resources.

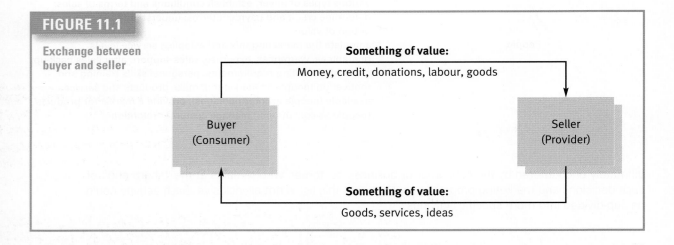

FIGURE 11.1

Exchange between buyer and seller

An exchange should be *satisfying* to both the buyer and the seller. In fact, in a study of marketing managers, 32 per cent indicated that creating **customer satisfaction** was the most important concept in a definition of marketing.* Marketing activities should be oriented towards creating and maintaining satisfying exchange relationships. To maintain an exchange relationship, the buyer must be satisfied with the goods, service or idea obtained in the exchange; the seller must be satisfied with the financial reward or something else of value received in the exchange.

customer satisfaction a state that results when an exchange meets the needs and expectations of the buyer

Maintaining a positive relationship with buyers is an important goal for a seller, regardless of whether the seller is marketing cereal, financial services or construction plant. Through buyer–seller interaction, the buyer develops expectations about the seller's future behaviour. To fulfil these expectations, the seller must deliver on promises made. Over time, a healthy buyer–seller relationship results in interdependencies between the two parties. The buyer depends on the seller to furnish information, parts and service; to be available; and to provide satisfying products in the future.

Marketing occurs in a dynamic environment

The marketing environment consists of many external changing forces within the trading environment: laws, regulations, political activities, societal pressures, changing economic conditions and technological advances. Each of these dynamic forces has an impact on how effectively marketing activities can facilitate and expedite exchanges. For example, the development and acceptance of the Internet in home or mobile PCs has given organisations another vehicle through which to promote and distribute their products. Another example is the impact EU regulations have had on reducing distribution headaches within much of Europe.

Marketing involves products, distribution, promotion, pricing and people

Marketing means more than simply advertising or selling a product; it involves developing and managing a product that will satisfy certain needs. It focuses on making the product available at the right place, at the right time, at a price that is acceptable to customers and with appropriate people and service support. It also requires transmitting through marketing communications the kind of promotional information that will help customers determine whether the product will in fact be able to satisfy their needs.

Marketing focuses on goods, services and ideas

The word "product" has been used a number of times in this chapter. For purposes of discussion in this text, a **product** is viewed as being a good, a service or an idea. A **good** is a physical entity that can be touched. A Ford Focus, a Sony MP3 player, Kellogg's Cornflakes, a bar of Lux soap and a kitten in a pet shop are examples of goods. A **service** is the application of human and mechanical efforts to people or objects in order to provide intangible benefits to customers. Services such as air travel, dry cleaning, hairdressing, banking, medical care and childcare are just as real as goods, but an individual cannot actually touch or stockpile them. Marketing is utilised for services but requires certain enhancements in order to be effective. **Ideas** include concepts, philosophies, images and issues. For instance, a marriage counsellor gives couples ideas and advice to help improve their relationships. Other marketers of ideas include political parties, charities, religious groups, schools and marketing lecturers.

> **product** a good, service or idea
> **good** a physical entity that can be touched
> **service** the application of human and mechanical efforts to people or objects in order to provide intangible benefits to customers
> **Ideas** a concept, philosophy, image or issue

An organisational function and a set of processes for creating, communicating and delivering value to customers and for managing customer relationships in ways that benefit the organisation and its stakeholders

The more recent definition suggested by the American Marketing Association came as a welcome addition, as for over two decades we have presented marketing to our students as an analytical process of analysis, strategising and then programmes for implementation in our *marketing process*. This process is relevant to not only those organisations with consumers or business customers.

Given that all organisations have stakeholders which must be influenced and satisfied, this process is suitable for any organisation, including those in the third sector.

THE MARKETING PROCESS

Marketers spend much of their time managing existing products, target markets and marketing programmes. Even with such so-called "steady-state" operations, the dynamic nature of marketing leads to continual changes in the marketing environment, competitors and their activities, as well as in customers' needs, expectations, perceptions and buying behaviour. Without a sound understanding of these issues, marketing strategies and their associated marketing programmes cannot be truly effective. Marketers must, therefore, undertake analyses of these market conditions. As changes in the marketplace occur, marketers should revise their marketing strategies accordingly. Any strategy modifications will necessitate changes to the organisation's marketing programmes.

This analytical process of marketing analyses, strategy formulation and the creation or modification of marketing programmes is necessary for existing activities and target markets. This marketing process is also required when an organisation contemplates entering new markets, launching new or replacement products, modifying the brand strategy, changing customer service practices, rethinking advertising and promotional plans, altering pricing or evaluating distribution policies. Unexpected sales patterns also require such a process of understanding, thinking and action. This is the **marketing process**: the analysis of market conditions, the creation of an appropriate marketing strategy and the development of marketing programmes designed to execute the agreed strategy, as depicted in Figure 11.2. Finally, as part of this process, the implementation of the marketing strategy and its associated marketing programmes must be managed and controlled.

> **marketing process** analysis of market conditions, creation of strategy, development of marketing programmes to
> action the strategy, and the implementation and control of the marketing strategy and programmes

With an understanding of customers' needs, buying behaviour, expectations and product or brand perceptions, marketers are able to create marketing programmes likely to attract, satisfy and retain customers. With an appreciation of competitors' activities and plans, the marketing programmes are more likely to combat rivals' marketing programmes and to differentiate an organisation's product. Without an awareness of changes in the marketing environment, it is unlikely that the specified marketing programme will be sustainable in the longer term. As trading environment changes occur, it is important that an organisation's capabilities are modified in order to reflect market conditions and likely demands. The marketing analysis stage of the marketing process is, therefore, of fundamental importance.

Equipped with an awareness of the marketplace made possible through marketing analyses, a marketing strategy may be derived. This involves selecting the opportunities to be pursued and devising an associated target market strategy. Few organisations have adequate financial, managerial and employee resources to address all of the possible marketing opportunities that exist: there must be some trade-offs. This generally involves selecting only some of the opportunities to pursue and focusing on specific target markets. Having made these decisions, marketers must ensure that they develop a compelling brand positioning and that they create a strong basis for competing versus their rivals, aimed specifically at attracting customers in the prioritised target markets. These strategic recommendations should then translate into specific marketing objectives, designed to hone the creation of marketing programmes.

In most organisations the majority of the budget, time and effort within the marketing function is devoted to creating and managing marketing programmes. These programmes revolve around specifying product, people, promotion (communication), pricing and place (distribution channel) attributes and policies, designed to appeal to and serve those customers identified as being in the priority target market(s). In addition to these ingredients of the marketing mix, marketers of services include other ingredients. Finally, the marketing programmes must be rolled out and controlled.

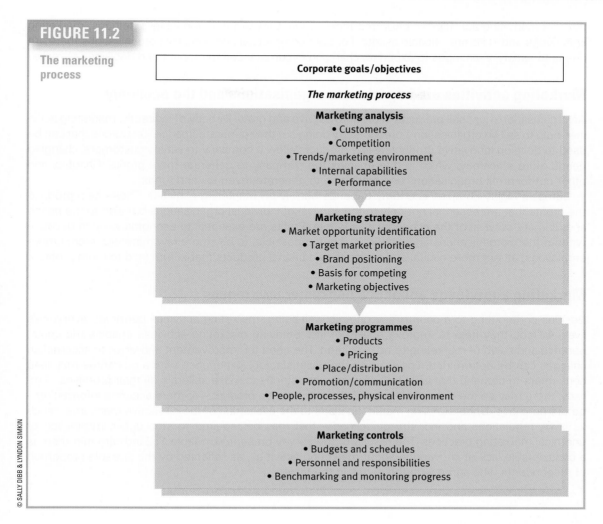

FIGURE 11.2

The marketing process

THE IMPORTANCE OF MARKETING

Marketing activities are carried out in many organisations

The commercial importance of marketing and its relevance as a topic worth studying are apparent from the definitions of marketing just presented. The use of marketing techniques and the development of a marketing orientation should enable an organisation to understand its customers and stakeholders better, address competitors' activities and market developments, and effectively harness its capabilities. The results should be enhanced customer satisfaction and retention, improved market share in key target markets and stronger financial performance. This section discusses several less obvious reasons why marketing should be studied.

In Europe and the U.S. between 25 per cent and 33 per cent of all civilian workers perform marketing activities. The marketing field offers a variety of interesting and challenging career opportunities, such as strategic planning, personal selling, advertising, packaging, transport, storage, marketing research, product development, creative design, wholesaling, retailing, marketing planning and consultancy. In addition, many individuals who work for not-for-profit organisations – such as charities or health agencies – engage in marketing activities. Marketing skills are used to promote political, cultural, religious, civic and charitable activities. Whether a person earns a living through marketing activities or performs them without reward in non-business settings, marketing knowledge and skills are valuable assets. For both commercial and non-profit organisations there are needs to satisfy, exchanges to expedite, changing circumstances to monitor and decisions to make.

Marketing activities are important to organisations and the economy

An organisation must sell products in order to survive and grow. Directly or indirectly, marketing activities help to sell an organisation's products. By doing so, they generate financial resources that can be used to develop innovative products. New products allow a company to satisfy customers' changing needs more efficiently, which in turn enables the company to generate more profits. Charities and other not-for-profit organisations use marketing to generate revenues and funds.

Europe's highly complex economy depends heavily on marketing activities. These help produce the profits that are essential not only to the survival of individual organisations but also to the health and ultimate survival of the economy as a whole. Profits are essential to economic growth because without them organisations find it difficult, if not impossible, to buy more raw materials, recruit more employees, attract more capital and create the additional products that in turn lead to more profits.

Marketing knowledge enhances consumer awareness

Besides contributing to a country's economic well-being, marketing activities permeate everyone's lives. In fact, they help to improve quality of life. Studying marketing activities enables the costs, benefits and flaws of marketing to be evaluated. The need for improvement and ways to accomplish changes can be determined. For example, an unsatisfactory experience with a guarantee may lead consumers to demand that laws be enforced more strictly to make sellers fulfil their promises. Similarly, there may be the desire for more information about a product – or more accurate information – before purchase. Understanding marketing leads to the evaluation of the corrective measures – such as laws, regulations and industry guidelines – that may be required to stop unfair, misleading or unethical marketing practices. The results of the survey presented in Table 11.2 indicate that there is a considerable lack of knowledge about marketing activities, as reflected by the sizeable proportion of respondents who agree with the myths in the table.

TABLE 11.2   Popular marketing myths

Myths	Strongly agree	Somewhat agree	Neither agree nor disagree	Somewhat disagree	Strongly disagree
Marketing is selling	34%	14%	26%	18%	8%
Marketers persuade	21%	25%	20%	11%	23%
Dealers' profits significantly increase prices consumers pay	21%	32%	12%	8%	27%
Marketing depends on advertising	44%	17%	12%	9%	18%
Strategic planning has nothing to do with marketing	19%	19%	21%	17%	24%

Marketing costs consume a sizeable proportion of buyers' incomes

The study of the marketing discipline emphasises that many marketing activities are necessary to provide people with satisfying goods and services. Obviously, these marketing activities cost money. A family with a monthly income of £2000, of which £600 goes towards taxes and savings, spends about £1400 on goods and services. Of this amount, typically £700 goes towards marketing activities. Clearly, if marketing expenses consume that much income, it is necessary to know how this money is used.

RESPONSIBLE PRACTICE Emerging markets improving energy efficiency

The emerging markets are expected to make an increasingly significant contribution to energy efficiency. There are extremes with highly publicised, old, very energy-inefficient factories but also, due to their fast growth, many new facilities that tend to be built with energy efficiency in mind. By contrast firms in the developed countries largely put efficient technology in old infrastructure. The economies, climate and topographies also affect the focus of work, so China's contribution is improving the energy efficiency of factories, whereas in Latin America it is reducing emissions from deforestation and land degradation.

Brazil is forging ahead with sugar cane based ethanol production. Most of its new cars can switch between ethanol and petrol and it launched its first electricity generating plant from ethanol. Suzlon Energy, a former textile business in India, is the third largest wind turbine supplier. South Africa plans to build the world's largest solar energy park in the Northern Cape. Abu Dhabi is using oil wealth to invest in sustainable energy development and aims to create Masdar in the desert as a zero-carbon city (see the case in Chapter 2). Small scale initiatives are important too. In Ghana and Kenya the World Bank is funding a programme to replace polluting kerosene lamps with LED lanterns.

How can firms make sense of the many technology-based initiatives that might affect their international markets and their potential impact on the firm?

References: S. Murray, 'Emerging markets: Developing nations count up the opportunities', *Financial Times*, 3 June 2010.

Business performance

Marketing puts an emphasis on satisfying customers. Marketing analyses should lead an organisation to develop a marketing strategy that takes account of market trends, aims to satisfy customers, is aware of competitive activity and targets the right customers with a clear positioning message. In so doing, an organisation should benefit from customer loyalty and advantages over its rivals, while making the most efficient use of resources to effectively address the specific requirements of those markets it chooses to target. Hence, marketing should provide both a financial benefit and a greater sense of well-being for the organisation.

THE MARKETING CONCEPT AND ITS EVOLUTION

Some organisations have tried to be successful by buying land, building a factory, equipping it with people and machines, and then making a product that they believe consumers need. However, these organisations frequently fail to attract buyers with what they have to offer because they defined their business as "making a product" rather than as "helping potential customers satisfy their needs and wants". Such organisations have failed to implement the marketing concept. It is not enough to be product-led, no matter how good the product. An organisation must be in tune with consumer or business customer requirements.

According to the **marketing concept**, an organisation should try to provide products that satisfy customers' needs through a coordinated set of activities that also allows the organisation to achieve its goals. Customer satisfaction is the major aim of the marketing concept. First, an organisation must find out what will satisfy customers. With this information, it then attempts to create satisfying products. But the process does not end there. The organisation must continue to alter, adapt and develop products to keep pace with customers' changing desires and preferences. The marketing concept stresses the importance of customers, and emphasises that marketing activities begin and end with them.*

> **marketing concept** the philosophy that an organisation should try to provide products that satisfy customers' needs through a coordinated set of activities that also allows the organisation to achieve its goals

In attempting to satisfy customers, organisations must consider not only short-term, immediate needs but also broad, long-term desires. Trying to satisfy customers' current needs by sacrificing their long-term desires will only create future dissatisfaction. For instance, people want efficient, low-cost energy to power their homes and cars, yet they react adversely to energy producers that pollute the air and water, kill wildlife or cause disease or birth defects. To meet these short- and long-term needs and desires, a company must coordinate all its activities. Production, finance, accounting, personnel and marketing departments must work together.

The marketing concept is not another definition of marketing. It is a way of thinking: a management philosophy guiding an organisation's overall activities. This philosophy affects all the efforts of the organisation, not just marketing activities, and is strongly linked to the notion of marketing orientation. However, the marketing concept is by no means a philanthropic philosophy aimed at helping customers at the expense of the organisation. A company that adopts the marketing concept must not only satisfy its customers' objectives but also achieve its own goals, or it will not stay in business long. The overall goals of an organisation may be directed towards increasing profits, market share, sales or a combination of all three. The marketing concept stresses that an organisation can best achieve its goals by providing customer satisfaction. Thus, implementing the marketing concept should benefit the organisation as well as its customers.

The evolution of the marketing concept

The marketing concept may seem an obvious and sensible approach to running a business. However, business people have not always believed that the best way to make sales and profits is to satisfy customers. A famous example is the marketing philosophy for cars widely attributed to Henry Ford in the early 1900s: "The customers can have any colour car they want as long as it's black". The philosophy of the marketing concept emerged in the third major era in the history of business, preceded by the **production era** and the **sales era.** Surprisingly, it took nearly 40 years after the **marketing era** began before many organisations started to adopt the marketing concept. The more advanced marketing-led companies have now entered a spin-off from the marketing era: the **relationship**. More recently, there have been several significant developments for marketers, most notable of which are value-based marketing, digital marketing and the associated surge in consumer-to-consumer communication, the growth of social marketing applications, and the emergence of so-called critical marketing.

> **production era** the period of mass production following industrialisation
> **sales era** the period from the mid-1920s to the early 1950s when competitive forces and the desire for high sales volume led a company to emphasise selling and the sales person in its business strategy
> **marketing era** the period in which product and aggressive selling were no longer seen to suffice if customers either did not desire a product or preferred a rival brand, and in which customer needs were identified and satisfied
> **relationship marketing era** in which the focus is not only on expediting the single transaction but on developing ongoing relationships with customers to maintain lifetime share of wallet

The production era During the second half of the nineteenth century, the Industrial Revolution was in full swing in Europe and the United States. Electricity, railways, the division of labour, the assembly line and mass production made it possible to manufacture products more efficiently. With new technology and new ways of using labour, products poured into the marketplace, where consumer demand for manufactured goods was strong. This production orientation continued into the early part of the last century, encouraged by the scientific management movement that championed rigidly structured jobs and pay based on output.

The sales era   In the 1920s, the strong consumer demand for products subsided. Companies realised that products, which by this time could be made quite efficiently, would have to be "sold" to consumers. From the mid-1920s to the early 1950s, companies viewed sales as the major means of increasing profits. As a result, this period came to have a sales orientation. Business people believed that the most important marketing activities were personal selling and advertising.

The marketing era   By the early 1950s, some business people began to recognise that efficient production and extensive promotion of products did not guarantee that customers would buy them. Companies found that they first had to determine what customers wanted and then produce it, rather than simply making products first and then trying to change customers' needs to correspond to what was being produced. As organisations realised the importance of knowing customers' needs, companies entered into the marketing era – the era of customer orientation.*

The relationship marketing era   By the 1990s, many organisations had grasped the basics of the marketing concept and had created marketing functions. However, their view of marketing was often largely transaction based. The priority for marketing was to identify customer needs, determine priority target markets and achieve sales through marketing programmes. The focus was on the individual transaction or exchange. It should be recognised that long-term success and market share gains depend on such transactions, but also on maintaining a customer's loyalty and on repeatedly gaining sales from existing customers. This requires ongoing, committed, reassuring and tailored relationship-building marketing programmes.

Relationship marketing refers to "long-term, mutually beneficial arrangements in which both the buyer and seller focus on value enhancement through the creation of more satisfying exchanges".* Relationship marketing continually deepens the buyer's trust in the company and, as the customer's confidence grows, this in turn increases the company's understanding of the customer's needs. Successful marketers respond to customers' needs and strive to increase value to buyers over time. Eventually this interaction becomes a solid relationship that allows for cooperation and mutual dependency.

As the era of relationship orientation developed, it became clear that it is not only relationships with customers that are important. Suppliers, agents, distributors, recruiters, referral bodies (such as independent financial advisers recommending financial services companies' products), influencers (such as government departments, national banks or the EU), all should be 'marketed to' in order to ensure their support, understanding and resources. The internal workforce must be motivated and provided with a clear understanding of a company's target market strategy, marketing mix activities and, indeed, of the corporate strategy and planned direction. Hence, the current era is moving away from transaction-based marketing and towards nurturing ongoing relationships.*

From the 1990s, lifetime value (of the customer) became a buzz term for marketers. This concept is linked to relationship marketing, said by many observers to be the new paradigm for marketing. This evolution of marketing, from focusing on individual transactions with customers to building ongoing relationships and repeat business, has been very important for the success of many organisations. Until relatively recently, relationship marketing was the main significant change in how the discipline has been perceived. In the last few years, however, there have been several new trends for marketing, each of which has stretched the bounds for the discipline, adding complex new dimensions and further shaping the marketing paradigm.

Focus on value-based marketing   Since the late 1990s, marketing has been through a period of reflection, amidst demands that the discipline demonstrates its credibility and proves its contribution to organisational goals. **Value-based marketing** recognises that marketing must prove its long-term financial worth and be accountable to organisations. This involves showing that marketing enables both the creation of short-term customer value and longer-term value for shareholders.

> **value-based marketing** value-based marketing recognises that marketing must prove its long term financial worth and be accountable to organisations, which involves showing that marketing enables both the creation of short-term customer value and longer-term value for shareholders

The growth of consumer-to-consumer (C2C) communications in the digital era This has significant consequences for brands and marketers, for consumers and for society in general. Previously, brand managers largely controlled what information was available to consumers and business customers. These customers based their decisions about brands and products on the marketing and sales information communicated to them by brand managers. Today, **consumer-to-consumer (C2C) communication** is routine, enabled by the digital era generally and social media in particular. Consumers readily and rapidly share views, experiences and information with one another. A positive or negative customer experience is tweeted instantly, blogged or shared on Facebook with many potential fellow consumers. Such messaging, whether positive or negative, has moved beyond the control of marketers. Many consumers trust and value the views of their peers far more than the views of brand managers, advertising messages or media reviews. The surge of C2C communication has redefined the boundaries and created huge new challenges for marketers.

> **consumer-to-consumer (C2C) communication** consumer-to-consumer (C2C) communication is now routine, enabled by the digital era and social media in particular. Consumers readily and rapidly share views, experiences and information with each other. A positive or negative customer experience is tweeted instantly, blogged or shared on Facebook with potentially very many fellow consumers

Digital media, the surge in Internet usage and the uptake of personal mobile communications and information provision, have fostered changing consumer behaviours, greater consumer-to-consumer influence on brands and purchasing decisions, and business-to-business interaction. These developments have created an entirely new domain for marketers, known as **digital marketing**. This domain encompasses the use of the Web and mobile phones, as well as radio, TV and other forms of digital media, to attract, engage and build relationships with customers and other target audiences. The immediacy, intimacy and customisation of many Internet and mobile digital communications and customer interactions have transformed the ability of marketers to target customer groups and individuals with bespoke propositions and nurture an ongoing relationship. While the digital era poses significant challenges to marketers, most marketers recognise its exciting potential. The implications of digital are explored throughout this text.

> **digital marketing** the use of particularly the Web and mobile phones, as well as radio, TV and any other form of digital media to attract, engage and build relationships with customers and other target audiences

Social marketing's adoption of marketing's toolkit in non-commercial settings **Social marketing** uses tools and techniques from commercial marketing to encourage positive behavioural changes, such as quitting smoking, reducing alcohol consumption, minimising anti-social behaviours or reducing carbon footprint. The health and well-being of individuals, society and the planet are at the core of social marketing. The social marketing field now provides interesting career opportunities for marketing professionals interested in applying marketing analyses, notably in terms of understanding behaviours of a particular audience or social group, developing targeting strategies and in creating programmes to communicate with such audiences. Rising interest in these applications reflects the increasing importance of the strategic marketing process to a growing set of audiences and stakeholders beyond those from traditional commercial markets.

> **social marketing** use of tools and techniques from commercial marketing to encourage positive behavioural changes, such as quitting smoking, reducing alcohol consumption, minimising anti-social behaviours or reducing carbon footprint. The health and well-being of individuals, society and the planet are at the core of social marketing.

The emergence of critical marketing Although this cannot really be described as a paradigm shift in the sense of relationship marketing, critical marketing nevertheless warrants consideration. Those interested in this field agree that critical marketing is difficult to define. **Critical marketing** is espoused by individuals who challenge orthodox views that are central to the core principles of the discipline. Sometimes this involves promoting radical philosophies and theories in relation to the understanding of economies, society, markets and consumers, which may have implications for the practice of marketing. In some instances, the assumptions at the heart of many of the core principles of the discipline are challenged. Critical marketing is connected with the growing area of critical management.

> **critical marketing** critical marketing involves challenging orthodox views that are central to the core principles of the discipline. Sometimes this involves promoting radical philosophies and theories in relation to the understanding of economies, society, markets and consumers, which may have implications for the practice of marketing. Critical marketing is connected with the growing area of critical management

While a detailed exploration of critical marketing is beyond the scope of this text, it is right to highlight the alternative views that exist about the domain and the activities associated with it. Once readers are familiar with the core concepts associated with effective marketing, they might also wish to explore the views of critical marketers.* This group is interested in issues such as postmodernism; the biological base for consumer behaviour; the connections between marketing activities and society (including social marketing), such as sustainable marketing; anti-globalisation challenges to marketing; ecofeminism; and the inter-connection of cultural studies and consumer research. Although many of these themes are not explored in detail here, a more detailed examination of aspects of social marketing is included. In addition, reflections on marketing in practice are incorporated throughout this book, contributing to the critical marketing debate around the distinction between theory and practice.

A further aspect of critical marketing that warrants consideration relates to concerns that marketing sometimes has damaging consequences and that marketers are not always aware of these outcomes.* For example, some critics argue that marketing is responsible for heightening consumerism and generating 'must have' attitudes amongst consumers. This has resulted in negative consequences for society in relation to carbon footprint, the use of scarce resources, landfill, state spending priorities and even on changing societal values. Although there are divergent opinions on these matters, there can be little doubt that marketing influences consumption and that these patterns have significant impacts for the environment, for society and for consumers.

Implementing the marketing concept A philosophy may sound reasonable and look good on paper, but that does not mean it can be put into practice easily. The marketing concept is a case in point. To implement it, an organisation must focus on some general conditions and recognise several problems. Because of these conditions and problems, the marketing concept has yet to be fully accepted by some organisations.

Because the marketing concept affects all types of business activities, not just marketing activities, the top management of an organisation must adopt it wholeheartedly. High-level executives must incorporate the marketing concept into their philosophies of business management so completely that it becomes the basis for all the goals and decisions that they set for their companies. They should also convince other members of the organisation to accept the changes in policies and operations that flow from their acceptance of the marketing concept. Costs and budgetary controls are important, products and manufacturing essential, and personnel management necessary; but all are to no avail if the organisation's products or services are not desired by the targeted customers.

As a first step, management must set up a system for capturing information that enables it to discover customers' real needs and to use the information to create satisfying products. Because such a system is usually expensive, management must be willing to commit money and time for development and maintenance. Without an adequate information system, an organisation cannot be customer oriented.

Management's second major task is to structure the organisation appropriately. If a company is to satisfy its customers' objectives as well as its own, it must coordinate all its activities. To achieve this, the internal operations and the overall objectives of one or more departments may need restructuring. If the head of the marketing unit is not a member of the organisation's top-level management, he or she should be. Some departments may have to be abolished and new ones created. Implementing the marketing concept demands the support not only of top management but also of managers and staff at all levels within the organisation.

Even when the basic conditions of establishing an information system and reorganising the organisation are met, the organisation's new marketing approach may not work perfectly, for the following reasons:

- There is a limit to a company's ability to satisfy customers' needs for a particular product. In a mass-production economy, most business organisations cannot tailor products to fit the exact needs of each customer.
- Although a company may attempt to learn what customers want, it may be unable to do so, and when the organisation does identify customers' needs correctly, it often has a difficult time developing a product that satisfies those needs. Many companies spend considerable time and money researching customers' needs and yet still create some products that do not sell well.
- By striving to satisfy one particular segment of society, a company sometimes dissatisfies other segments. Certainly, government and non-business organisations also experience this problem.
- An organisation may have difficulty maintaining employee morale, particularly if restructuring is needed to coordinate the activities of various departments. Management must clearly explain the reasons for the various changes and communicate its own enthusiasm for the marketing concept. Adoption of the marketing philosophy takes time, resources, endurance and commitment.

THE ESSENTIALS OF MARKETING

Marketing analyses

From these brief introductory comments, it should be evident that marketing can enhance an organisation's understanding of its customers, competitors, market trends, threats and opportunities. Marketing should direct an organisation's target market strategy, product development and communication with its distribution channels and customers. In order to carry out these activities, marketing personnel need access to good quality marketing intelligence about the following issues:

- customers
- competitors
- marketing environment forces
- the organisation's capabilities, marketing assets and performance.

There are other marketing analyses which can be carried out, but these just mentioned are the essential building blocks for the development of marketing strategies and the creation of marketing programmes.

Marketing strategy

To achieve the broad goal of expediting desirable exchanges, an organisation's marketing managers are responsible for developing and managing marketing strategies. A **marketing strategy** involves selecting the best opportunities to pursue, identify an appropriate target market (the group of people the organisation wants to reach), develop a competitive edge, and create and maintain a suitable **marketing mix** (the product, place [distribution], promotion, price and people) that will satisfy those customers in the target market. A marketing strategy articulates a plan for the best use of the organisation's resources and directs the required tactics to meet its objectives.

> **marketing strategy** the selection of which marketing opportunities to pursue, identification of associated target market(s), creation of a basis for competing and 'wow' positioning, and the development and maintenance of an appropriate marketing mix to satisfy those in the target market(s)
>
> **marketing mix** the tactical 'toolkit' of the marketing programme; product, place/distribution, promotion, price and people variables that an organisation can control in order to appeal to the target market and facilitate satisfying exchange

When marketing managers attempt to develop and manage marketing activities, they must deal with three broad sets of variables:

1. those relating to the marketing mix
2. those inherent in the accompanying target market strategy
3. those that make up the marketing environment.

The marketing mix decision variables – product, place/distribution, promotion, price and people – and the target market strategy variables are factors over which an organisation has control. As Figure 11.3 shows, these variables are constructed around the buyer or consumer. The marketing environment variables are political, legal, regulatory, societal, technological and economic and competitive forces.

| FIGURE 11.3 | *The marketing environment, marketing strategy, the marketing mix and customer satisfaction; consumers and organisations are affected by the forces of the marketing environment; organisations must determine a marketing strategy, implemented through the ingredients of the marketing mix, which aims to satisfy targeted customers* |

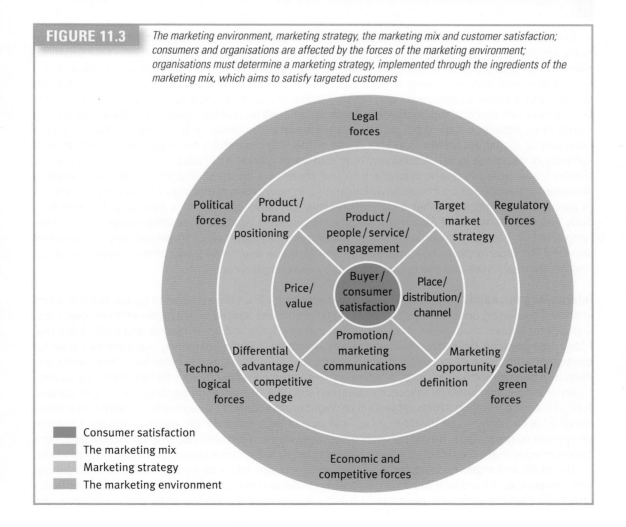

These factors are subject to less control by an organisation, but they affect buyers' needs as well as marketing managers' decisions regarding marketing mix variables.

To develop and manage marketing strategies, marketers must focus on several marketing tasks: marketing opportunity analysis and marketing analyses, the determination of a marketing strategy and target market selection, marketing mix development and management of the programmes that facilitate implementation of the marketing strategy. Figure 11.4 lists these tasks, along with the chapters of this book in which they are discussed.

Marketing opportunity analysis A **marketing opportunity** exists when circumstances allow an organisation to take action towards reaching a particular group of customers. An opportunity provides a favourable chance or opening for a company to generate sales from identifiable markets for specific products or services. For example, during a heatwave, marketers of electric fans have a marketing opportunity – an opportunity to reach customers who need electric fans. Various "no frills" airlines have entered the rapidly growing market for low-priced scheduled air travel, as consumers have demonstrated their liking for this alternative to high-priced full-service airlines or charters. Bluetooth and wireless connectivity are creating numerous opportunities for computer manufacturers and online service providers, as wireless access to the Internet offers users greater flexibility. Most new products or services reflect the identification by marketers of a marketing opportunity.

> **marketing opportunity** one that exists when circumstances allow an organisation to take action towards reaching a particular group of consumer or business customers

Marketers should be capable of recognising and analysing marketing opportunities. An organisation's long-term survival depends on developing products that satisfy its customers. Few organisations can assume that products popular today will interest buyers ten years from now. A marketing-led organisation can choose among several alternatives for continued product development through which it can achieve its objectives and satisfy buyers. It can modify existing products (for example, by reducing salt content and additives in foods to address increasing health consciousness among customers), introduce new products (such as e-readers like Kindle, pay-as-you-talk mobile phone packages or digital flat-screen TVs) and delete some that customers no longer want (such as disc cameras or cassette decks). A company may also try to market its products to a greater number of customers, persuade current customers to use more of a product, or perhaps expand marketing activities into additional countries. Diversification into new product offerings through internal efforts or through acquisitions of other organisations may be viable options for a company. For example, Sony has established itself as a major supplier of business laptop and desktop computers, diversifying from its base of consumer home entertainment products; while Virgin has entered financial services. An organisation's ability to pursue any of these alternatives successfully depends on its internal characteristics and the forces within the marketing environment.

Internal organisational factors The primary factors inside an organisation to be considered when analysing marketing opportunities and devising target market strategies are organisational objectives, financial resources, managerial skills, organisational strengths and weaknesses, and cost structures. Most organisations have overall organisational objectives. Some marketing opportunities may be consistent with these objectives; others may not, and to pursue them is hazardous. Frequently, the pursuit of such opportunities ends in failure, or forces the company to alter its long-term objectives.

An organisation's financial resources constrain the type of marketing opportunities it can pursue. Typically, an organisation avoids projects that might bring economic catastrophe. In some situations, however, a company must invest in a high-risk opportunity, because the costs of not pursuing the project are so great. Thus, despite an economic recession and reduced house and road building, construction equipment manufacturer JCB has continued to launch new ranges and enter new markets.

The skills and experience of management also limit the types of opportunity that an organisation can pursue. A company must be particularly cautious when exploring the possibility of entering unfamiliar markets with new products. If it lacks appropriate managerial skills and experience, the

FIGURE 11.4

Marketing tasks, analysis, strategy and programmes for implementation and control

Marketing opportunity analysis	Chapters
• Marketing strategy and competitors	2
• The marketing environment	3/4
• Marketing in international markets	4
• Consumer buying behaviour	5
• Business markets	6
• Marketing research	9

Target market strategy	Chapters
• Marketing strategy	2
• Market segmentation and prioritization	7/8
• Product and brand positioning	8
• Competitive advantage	2, 8

Marketing mix development	Chapters
• Product, branding, packaging and service decisions	10–13
• Place (distribution and marketing channel) decisions	14/15
• Promotion (marketing communications) decisions	16–18
• Pricing decisions	19
• Manipulating the marketing mix	20

Marketing management	Chapters
• Marketing planning and forecasting sales potential	21
• Implementing strategies, internal marketing relationships and measuring performance	22
• Responsible marketing	23

business can sometimes acquire them by recruiting additional managerial personnel. Most organisations at some time are limited in their growth plans by a lack of sufficient managers with suitable skills and market insights.

Like people, most organisations have strengths and weaknesses. Because of the types of operation in which a company is engaged, it will normally have employees with specialist skills and technological information. Such characteristics are a strength when launching marketing strategies that require them. However, lack of them may be a weakness if the company tries to compete in new, unrelated product areas. A major IT services company altered its strategy to focus on winning more business for IT infrastructure management from existing clients rather than from attracting new clients. This required a different set of selling skills, and managers with the ability to nurture relationships and exploit emerging sales opportunities within a client company. The revised target market strategy resulted in redundancies among the existing salesforce, and the recruitment of account managers with the necessary skills and interpersonal abilities.

An organisation's cost structure may be an advantage if the company pursues certain marketing opportunities, and a disadvantage if it pursues others. Such factors as geographic location, employee skills, access to raw materials and type of equipment and facilities can all affect cost structure. Previous investment levels and priorities will have ramifications for the current cost structure. The cost structure of an organisation may provide a competitive advantage over rivals, or may place a business at a competitive disadvantage.

Marketing environment forces The marketing environment, which consists of political, legal, regulatory, societal, technological and economic/competitive forces, surrounds the buyer (consumer) and the organisation's marketing mix (see Figure 11.3), impacting on both. Marketers know that they cannot predict changes in the marketing environment with certainty. Even so, over the years marketers have become more systematic in taking these forces into account when planning their competitive actions.* An organisation that fails to monitor the forces of the marketing environment is likely to miss out on emerging opportunities at the expense of rivals with the foresight to examine these market drivers.

Marketing environment forces affect a marketer's ability to facilitate and expedite exchanges, in four general ways:

1. They influence customers by affecting or regulating their lifestyles, standards of living, preferences and needs for products. Because a marketing manager tries to develop and adjust the marketing mix to satisfy consumers or business customers, the effects of environmental forces on customers also have an indirect impact on the marketing mix components.
2. Marketing environment forces help determine whether and how a marketing manager can perform certain marketing activities. They may force marketers to cease certain practices or to adopt new strategies.
3. Environmental forces may affect a marketing manager's decisions and actions by influencing buyers' reactions to the company's marketing mix.
4. Marketing environment forces may provide an organisation with a window of opportunity over rivals that fail to notice the market development or that take no action themselves.

Equally, market drivers may provide competitors with such an opportunity ahead of a marketer's own organisation.

Although forces in the marketing environment are sometimes viewed as "uncontrollables", a marketing manager may be able to influence one or more of them. However, marketing environment forces fluctuate quickly and dramatically, which is one reason why marketing is so interesting and challenging. Because these forces are highly interrelated, a change in one may cause others to change. For example, from Freons in fridges to additives in foods, most consumers have become increasingly aware of health and environmental issues. Manufacturers have altered product specifications and production methods to reflect this awareness. Legislators and regulatory bodies have also responded to expert and consumer opinions with new regulations and informal agreements, forcing companies to rethink their manufacturing and marketing policies.

Even though changes in the marketing environment produce uncertainty for marketers and at times impede marketing efforts, they can also create opportunities. After the 1989 oil spills, for example, more companies began developing and marketing products designed to contain or dissipate spilled oil. The BSE beef crisis gave producers of other meats significant opportunities. Environmental concerns have encouraged car manufacturers to develop emission-free engines. Rising mobile phone usage and improvements to network technologies have enabled various information providers to tailor their services for sports fans or stock-market investors. Recession has led to a growth in demand for domestic vacations, at the expense of more expensive flight-based holidays. Thus, a marketer must be aware of changes in environmental forces so that they can capitalise on the opportunities they provide.

Target market selection   A **target market** is a group of people for whom a company creates and maintains a marketing mix that specifically fits the needs and preferences of that group.* When choosing a target market, marketing managers try to evaluate possible markets to see how entering them would affect the company's sales, costs and profits. Marketers also attempt to determine whether the organisation has the resources to produce a marketing mix that meets the needs of a particular target market, and whether satisfying those needs is consistent with the company's overall objectives and mission. The size and number of competitors already marketing products in possible target markets are also of concern.

> **marketing environment** external changing forces within the trading environment: laws, regulations, political activities, societal pressures, economic conditions and technological advances

   Marketing managers may define a target market as a vast number of people or as a relatively small group. For example, Ford produces cars suitable for much of the population – although specific models are quite narrowly targeted, such as the family runaround Focus or the executive Mondeo. Porsche focuses its marketing effort on a small proportion of the population, believing that it can compete more effectively by concentrating on an affluent target market desiring sports coupés. Although a business may concentrate its efforts on one target market through a single marketing mix, organisations often focus on several target markets by developing and deploying multiple marketing mixes. Reebok, for example, markets different types of shoes to meet the specific needs of joggers, walkers, aerobics enthusiasts and other groups.

   Target market selection is crucial to generating productive marketing efforts. At times, products and organisations fail because marketers do not identify the appropriate customer groups at which to aim their efforts. Organisations that try to be all things to all people typically end up not satisfying the needs of any customer group very well. It is important for an organisation's management to designate which customer groups the company is trying to serve and to have adequate information about these customers. The identification and analysis of a target market provide a foundation on which a marketing mix can be developed. It is important to strive to develop an advantage over competitors in the markets targeted.

Marketing programmes

In order to make the devised marketing strategy become a reality, marketers must specify the set of marketing mix ingredients forming the marketing programme for implementing the agreed marketing strategy. These marketing mix decisions occupy the majority of marketers' time and account for the bulk of a marketing department's budget. However, as previously explained, before the marketing mix is specified, marketers should undertake sufficient marketing analyses and reflect the findings of these analyses in their marketing strategy.

Marketing mix development   Traditionally, the marketing mix was deemed to consist of four major components: product, place (distribution), promotion and price. Increasingly, a fifth component is viewed as "people", who provide customer service and interact with customers and organisations within the supply chain. These components are called "marketing mix decision variables" because a marketing manager decides which type of each component to use and in what amounts. A primary goal of a marketing manager is to create and maintain a marketing mix that satisfies consumers' needs for a general product type. Note that in Figure 11.3, the marketing mix is built around the buyer – as is stressed by the marketing concept and definition of marketing. Bear in mind, too, that the forces of the marketing environment affect the marketing mix variables in many ways.

Marketing mix variables are often viewed as controllable variables because they can be changed. However, there are limits to how much these variables can be altered. For example, because of economic conditions or government regulations, a manager may not be free to adjust prices daily. Changes in sizes, colours, shapes and designs of most tangible goods are expensive; therefore such product features cannot be altered very often. In addition, promotional campaigns and the methods used to distribute products ordinarily cannot be changed overnight. People, too, require training and motivating, and cannot be recruited or sacked overnight, so customer service is not always flexible.

Marketing managers must develop a marketing mix that precisely matches the needs of the people – or organisations in business-to-business marketing – in the target market. Before they can do so, they have to collect in-depth, up-to-date information about those needs. The information might include data about the age, income, ethnic origin, sex and educational level of people in the target market; their preferences for product features; their attitudes towards competitors' products; and the frequency and intensity with which they use the product. Armed with these kinds of data, marketing managers are better able to develop a product, service package, distribution system, promotion programme and price that will satisfy the people in the target market.

This section looks more closely at the decisions and activities related to each marketing mix variable (product, place/distribution, promotion, price and people – the "5Ps" of the marketing mix).

The product variable   A product can be a good, a service or an idea. The **product variable** is the aspect of the marketing mix that deals with researching consumers' product wants and designing a product with the desired characteristics. It also involves the creation or alteration of packaging and brand names, and may include decisions about guarantees, repair services and customer support. The actual manufacturing of products is not a marketing activity, but marketing-oriented businesses look to marketers to specify product development requirements that reflect customer needs and evolving expectations.

Product-variable decisions and related activities are important because they directly involve creating products and services that satisfy consumers' needs and wants. To maintain a satisfying set of products that will help an organisation achieve its goals, a marketer must be able to develop new products, modify existing ones and eliminate those that no longer satisfy buyers or yield acceptable profits. For example, after realising that competitors were capturing large shares of the low-calorie market, Heinz introduced new product items under its Weight Watchers name. To reflect greater use of microwave ovens, rice company Tilda introduced its steam-in-a-pouch range of quick-cook microwavable sachets.

> **product variable** the aspect of the marketing mix that deals with researching consumers' product wants and designing a product with the desired characteristics

The place/distribution variable   To satisfy consumers, products must be available at the right time and in a convenient location. In dealing with the **Place/distribution variable**, a marketing manager seeks to make products available in the quantities desired to as many intended customers as possible, and to keep the total inventory, transport and storage costs as low as possible. A marketing manager may become involved in selecting and motivating intermediaries (wholesalers, retailers and dealers), establishing and maintaining inventory control procedures, and developing and managing transport and storage systems. Many organisations distribute their products through multiple channels, now typically including the Web, adding to the complexity of marketing management but providing exciting opportunities.

> **place/distribution variable** the aspect of the marketing mix that deals with making products available in the quantities desired to as many customers as possible and keeping the total inventory, transport and storage costs as low as possible

The promotion variable   The **Promotion variable** relates to communication activities that are used to inform one or more groups of people about an organisation and its products. Promotion can be aimed at increasing public awareness of an organisation and of new or existing products. In addition, promotion can serve to educate consumers about product features or to urge people to take a particular stance on a political or social issue. It may also be used to keep interest strong in an established product that has been available for decades. Marketers increasingly refer to the promotion variable in the marketing mix as "marketing communications". Recently, this has become even more important for marketers, as they struggle to understand the power of growing consumer-to-consumer communications about their brands, made possible by social media and the Web.

> **promotion variable** the aspect of the marketing mix that relates to marketing communications used to inform one or more groups of people about an organisation and its products

The price variable   The **price variable** relates to activities associated with establishing pricing policies and determining product prices. Price is a critical component of the marketing mix because consumers and business customers are concerned about the value obtained in an exchange. Price is often used as a competitive tool; in fact, extremely intense price competition sometimes leads to price wars. For example, airlines like Aer Lingus, British Airways and Virgin Atlantic are engaged in ruthless price cutting in the battle for transatlantic routes. Price can also help to establish a product's image. For instance, if Chanel tried to sell Chanel No. 5 in a two-litre bottle for £3 or €4, consumers would probably not buy it because the low price would destroy the prestigious image of this deluxe brand. Linked to the notion of perceived value, recent recession has placed even greater emphasis on the pricing ingredient of many organisations' marketing programmes.

> **price variable** the aspect of the marketing mix that relates to activities associated with establishing pricing policies and determining product prices

The people variable   Product, place/distribution, promotion and price are traditionally the principal elements of the marketing mix: the "4Ps". Marketers of services include people as a core element, along with other ingredients. Whether part of the product element or a separate element of the marketing mix, there is no doubt that people are important, and are integral to providing customer service. As marketers, they manipulate the rest of the marketing mix. As intermediaries in the marketing channel, they help make products and services available to the marketplace. As consumers or organisational purchasers, they create the need for the field of marketing. In the marketing mix, the **people variable** reflects the level of customer service, advice, sales support and after-sales back-up required, involving recruitment policies, training, retention and motivation of key personnel. For many products and most services, personnel interface directly with the intended purchaser and are often perceived by such consumers as being part and parcel of the product offering.

> **people variable** the aspect of the marketing mix that reflects the level of customer service, advice, sales support and after-sales back-up required, involving recruitment policies, training, retention and motivation of key personnel

It is the marketing mix that readers, as consumers, will most frequently have experienced for products and services purchased. It is important to remember, however, that analysis must precede the development of a marketing strategy, which in turn must be formulated before the marketing mix is determined for a product or a service.

Marketing management

Marketing management is the process of planning, organising, implementing and controlling marketing activities to facilitate and expedite exchanges effectively and efficiently. Effectiveness and efficiency are important dimensions of this definition. *Effectiveness* is the degree to which an exchange helps achieve an organisation's objectives. *Efficiency* is the minimisation of resources an organisation must spend to achieve a specific level of desired exchanges. Thus, the overall goal of marketing management is to facilitate highly desirable exchanges and to minimise as much as possible the costs of doing so.

> **marketing management** a process of planning, organising, implementing and controlling marketing activities to facilitate and expedite exchanges effectively and efficiently

Marketing planning is a systematic process of assessing opportunities and resources, determining marketing objectives, developing a marketing strategy and constructing plans for implementation and control. Planning determines when and how marketing activities will be performed and who is to perform them. It forces marketing managers to think ahead, to establish objectives and to consider future marketing activities. Effective marketing planning also reduces or eliminates daily crises. Marketing planning and the management of the execution of the resulting marketing plan are intrinsic aspects of marketing management.

Organising marketing activities refers to developing the internal structure of the marketing unit. The structure is the key to directing marketing activities. The marketing unit can be organised by function, product, region, type of customer or a combination of all four.

Proper implementation of marketing plans hinges on the coordination of marketing activities, motivation of marketing personnel and effective communication within the unit. Marketing managers must motivate marketing personnel, coordinate their activities and integrate their activities, both with those in other areas of the company and with the marketing efforts of personnel in external organisations, such as advertising agencies and marketing research businesses. An organisation's communication system must allow the marketing manager to stay in contact with high-level management, with managers of other functional areas within the company and with personnel involved in marketing activities both inside and outside the organisation.

The marketing control process consists of establishing performance standards, evaluating actual performance by comparing it with established standards and reducing the difference between desired and actual performance. An effective control process has the following four requirements:

1. The control process should ensure a rate of information flow that allows the marketing manager to quickly detect differences between actual and planned levels of performance.
2. The control process must accurately monitor different kinds of activities and be flexible enough to accommodate changes.
3. The control process must be economical so that its costs are low, relative to the costs that would arise if there were no controls.
4. Finally, the control process should be designed so that both managers and subordinates can understand it. To maintain effective marketing control, an organisation needs to develop a comprehensive control process that evaluates marketing operations at regular intervals.

SUMMARY

Organisations that practise marketing do not necessarily have a *marketing orientation*. Organisations with a marketing orientation have a sound awareness of customers' needs and buying behaviour, of competitors' offerings and strategies, and of market trends. They also take steps to ensure they know how these market conditions will evolve. Crucially, they orientate their operational practices and coordinate their inter-functional thinking around these market conditions. In order to have a marketing orientation, it is necessary to adopt a range of marketing concepts and techniques. To practise marketing and to benefit from the activities of marketing, however, it is not necessary for an organisation to have a fully developed marketing orientation. A few managers, whether or not in an organisation's marketing function, utilising the concepts described in this chapter, will make a significant contribution to the organisation's fortunes and its understanding of its marketplace.

Marketing consists of individual and organisational activities that facilitate and expedite satisfying exchange relationships in a dynamic environment through the creation, distribution, promotion and pricing of goods, services and ideas. Marketing is an organisational function and a set of processes for creating, communicating and delivering value to customers and for managing customer relationships in ways that benefit the organisation and its stakeholders.

Marketing opportunity analysis involves reviewing both internal factors (organisational objectives and mission, financial resources, managerial skills, organisational strengths, organisational weaknesses and cost structures) and external ones in the *marketing environment* (the political, legal, regulatory, societal, technological and economic/competitive forces).

An *exchange* is the provision or transfer of goods, services and ideas in return for something of value. Four conditions must exist for an exchange to occur: (1) two or more individuals, groups or organisations must participate; (2) each party must have something of value desired by the other; (3) each party must be willing to give up what it has in order to receive the value held by the other; and (4) the parties to the exchange must be able to communicate with each other to make their 'somethings of value' available. In an exchange, products are traded either for other products or for financial resources, such as cash or credit. Through the exchange, the recipient (the customer) and the provider (the organisation) must be satisfied (leading to *customer satisfaction*). *Products* can be *goods, services or ideas*.

The *marketing process* is the analysis of market conditions, the creation of an appropriate marketing strategy, the development of marketing programmes designed to action the agreed strategy and, finally, the implementation and control of the marketing strategy and its associated marketing programme(s). Organisations contemplating entering new markets or territories, launching new products or brands, modifying their strategies or manipulating their marketing programmes, should use this sequential analytical process. Even steady-state markets and products encounter changing market conditions, and marketers should continually analyse and then modify their marketing strategies and marketing programmes accordingly.

It is important to study marketing because it permeates society. Marketing activities are performed in both business and non-business organisations. Moreover, marketing activities help business organisations generate profits and income, the life-blood of an economy. Even organisations without "customers" have to maximise the deployment of their resources, address trends, identify stakeholders and develop compelling propositions to satisfy these stakeholders. The study of marketing enhances consumer awareness. Marketing costs absorb about half of what the consumer spends. Marketing, practised well, improves business performance.

The *marketing concept* is a management philosophy that prompts an organisation to try to satisfy customers' needs through a coordinated set of activities that also allows the organisation to achieve its goals. Customer satisfaction is the major objective of the marketing concept. The philosophy of the marketing concept emerged during the 1950s, as the *marketing era* succeeded the *production era* and the *sales era*. As the 1990s progressed into the *relationship marketing era*, a focus on transaction-based marketing was replaced by relationship marketing. Recent significant advances in the field of marketing relate to demands for *value-based marketing*, growing *consumer-to-consumer communication* and *digital marketing*, the growth of *social marketing* applications, and the challenges posed to the discipline by critical management scholars theorists in the form of *critical marketing*. To make the marketing concept work, top management must accept it as an overall management philosophy. Implementing the marketing concept requires an efficient information system and sometimes the restructuring of the organisation.

The essentials of marketing are that there are marketing analyses, a marketing strategy, marketing programmes centred around well-specified marketing mixes, plus marketing management controls and implementation practices. *Marketing strategy* involves selecting which marketing opportunities to pursue, analysing a target market (the group of people the organisation wants to reach), and creating and maintaining an appropriate *marketing mix* (product, place/distribution, promotion, price and people) to satisfy this target market. Effective marketing requires that managers focus on four tasks to achieve set objectives: (1) marketing opportunity analysis, (2) target market selection, (3) marketing mix development and (4) marketing management.

Marketers should be able to recognise and analyse *marketing opportunities*, which are circumstances that allow an organisation to take action towards reaching a particular group of customers.

A *target market* is a group of people or organisations for whom a company creates and maintains a marketing mix that specifically fits the needs and preferences of that group. It is important for an organisation's management to designate which customer groups the company is trying to serve and to have some information about these customers. The identification and analysis of a target market provide a foundation on which a marketing mix can be developed.

The five principal variables that make up the marketing mix are product, place/distribution, promotion, price and people: the "5Ps". The *product variable* is the aspect of the marketing mix that deals with researching consumers' or business customers' wants and designing a product with the desired characteristics. A marketing manager tries to make products available in the quantities desired to as many customers as possible, and to keep the total inventory, transport and storage costs as low as possible – the *place/distribution variable*. The *promotion variable* relates to marketing communications used to inform one or more groups of people about an organisation and its products. The *price variable* refers to establishing pricing policies and determining product prices. The *people variable* controls the marketing mix; provides customer service and often the interface with customers, facilitates the product's distribution, sale and service; and – as consumers or buyers – gives marketing its rationale. Marketing exists to encourage consumer satisfaction.

Marketing management is a process of planning, organising, implementing and controlling marketing activities to facilitate and expedite exchanges effectively and efficiently. Marketing planning is a systematic process of assessing opportunities and resources, developing a marketing strategy, determining marketing objectives and developing plans for implementation and control. The operationalisation of the marketing plan is a core element of marketing management. Organising marketing activities refers to developing the internal structure of the marketing unit. Properly implementing marketing plans depends on coordinating marketing activities, motivating marketing personnel and communicating effectively within the unit. The marketing control process consists of establishing performance standards, evaluating actual performance by comparing it with established standards, and reducing the difference between desired and actual performance.

EXERCISE QUESTIONS

1 Discuss the basic elements of the marketing concept. Which organisations use this concept? Have these organisations adopted the marketing concept? Explain your views.

2 What is consumer-to-consumer communication and why is it now so important to marketers?

3 Describe the major components of a marketing strategy. How are these major components related?

4 Why is the selection of a target market such an important issue?

5 What type of management activities are involved in marketing management?

CASE 11.1

Reaching global markets

For some people the encroachment of western ideas, philosophy and goods into the Middle East represents a pernicious erosion of standards and culture. Perhaps one of the icons of such an encroachment is the pair of denim jeans. Jeans are very much associated with the United States although Levi Strauss and Jacob Davis, who are credited with developing the style we now recognise as jeans, were immigrants to the U.S. from Germany and Latvia respectively. It was in 1873 that Davis and Strauss gained a patent on the riveted pockets that made the jeans strong. Originally jeans were used by manual labourers but by the 1960s attitudes changed and jeans became a fashion item.

The very nature and association of jeans does not make them the first item of clothing that you might expect to succeed in the Middle East. Styles of dress for men and women are different and the hotter temperatures that are experienced in many countries that form part of the Gulf Cooperation Council (GCC) mean that jeans can be uncomfortably hot and heavy. The very fact that jeans have become an accepted and popular style of clothing in the Middle East as elsewhere in the world may be a testament to the skills of marketers who have managed to extend sales of jeans into just about every market on the planet.

Over the years clothing manufacturers and retailers have produced a wide range of different style jeans – tight-fit, baggy, prison style, drainpipe fit, boot-cut, flared, stressed denim, dyed, bleached, low-rise, hipster, straight leg, cut-off jeans, ripped jeans, harem jeans, jeans skirts – all have taken their turns to parade in the fashion limelight. The popularity of jeans has been matched by the ability of marketers to keep reinventing the product in different guises to suit the changing fashions.

For retailers and distributors the opening up of markets in the Middle East, which has accompanied the rise in average incomes in many of the countries of the GCC, has afforded them the opportunity of breaking into new markets where jeans may not be seen as a traditional item of clothing. The marketing imperatives are, therefore, different.

One important factor for marketers to understand, therefore, is the customer relationship with the product. If this can be understood then the chance of success of breaking into or expanding in new markets is greater. There is no shortage of retailers and distributors looking to do just this. One such example is the fashion chain *New Look*.

It developed a new range of jeans called "Yes Yes". *New Look* originated in the U.K. in 1969 and did not open its first franchise in the Middle East until 2006 when a store opened in Dubai. It now has 1 store in Kuwait, 9 in the UAE, 1 in Bahrain, 1 in Egypt and 17 in Saudi Arabia. In 2008 distribution centres opened in Singapore and Istanbul to help serve its Middle East and Asian markets.

Before the release of the "Yes Yes" brand of jeans in the GCC region the company carried out a survey of customer buying habits in the area. The survey covered around 2 000 customers from across the Middle East. What they found is helping the company to understand the way in which the market for jeans might differ in the Middle East compared with other parts of the globe – or not as they case may be!

The survey found that over 33 per cent of fashion conscious individuals in the GCC population represented by the survey owned in excess of 15 pairs of jeans! 84 per cent of those who owned jeans said that they were reluctant to part company with a pair of jeans that they regarded as 'good'. Peter Whittle, New Look's Middle East chief, was quoted as saying "It is fascinating to see how attached people get to their collection of jeans and that, despite the array of colourful, decorative designer pairs in the shops today, comfortable, well styled high street denim is still the most popular choice for even the most discerning denim enthusiast. New Look has positioned itself as the leading high street denim retailer and the launch of the 'Yes Yes' collection is sure to be extremely popular with our shoppers."

The survey also told *New Look* that customers who buy jeans feel that the high street is the best place to purchase the product; around a third of the respondents to the survey said they liked to go to a store to buy their jeans. When they buy jeans, customers are looking for the quality of the fit as being the most important factor in their purchasing decision. Around four-fifths of respondents said that a perfect fit was crucial. Another important decision affecting purchases is value for money with around 50 per cent of those surveyed saying that it was a high priority in their decision-making.

In terms of style, the attachment people feel to their jeans was interpreted as being relevant to the fact that fashions with regard to jeans tends to be cyclical with a particular style re-appearing after a period of years. If customers keep jeans over a long period of time but are not put off making repeat purchases as new styles come out (as evidenced by the number who have in excess of 15 pairs) the jeans in their collection can be brought out as a style comes back into fashion. 10 per cent of those surveyed said that they keep their jeans for as long as ten years before discarding them. The most popular style of the time as revealed by the survey was the skinny jean.

The information gathered by *New Look* allows them to plan the launch of the Yes Yes brand in the Middle East to better meet customer needs. This highlights the importance of accurate and detailed market research as well as the role of customer relationship management in successful marketing. The Yes Yes brand was launched in Dubai in Deira City Centre, Ibn Battuta and Dubai Mall and was then rolled out to other outlets in the U.A.E. The range not only included new styles and colours but also came in a wide size range to cater for women of all different sizes.

New Look is not the only jeans seller looking to break into the Middle East. Pepe Jeans not only sells denim jeans but also a range of ladies and gentlemen's clothing, shoes and fashion accessories. In 2008, *Pepe jeans* opened a new store in Kuwait. Building relationships with a business with knowledge of the local market is important in accessing and understanding global markets. *Pepe jeans* partnered with *Liwa Trading Enterprises LLC*, a company set up to establish the retail presence of *Al Nasser Holding*, based in Abu Dhabi. As a licensee for *Pepe jeans*, Liwa is helping the company to access markets in the Middle East. The store in Kuwait's "The Avenues" was part of a series of expansions into the region with stores planned in Marina Mall Extension in Abu Dhabi and Jumeirah Beach Residence, Dubai Mall and Mall of the Arabia in Dubai. Liwa had already opened Pepe Jeans stores at Deira City Centre and the Mall of the Emirates in Dubai and the Abu Dhabi Mall in Dubai's neighboring emirate.

Aniss Baobied, the General Manager of Liwa, said "*Pepe jeans* is known to be trendy, fashionable and high quality brand. The brand is modern, sophisticated, youthful and aspirational, primarily targeting students and young professionals who are opinion leaders, in the forefront of their generation. These uber-trendy people are interested in fashion, music, arts and new trends in design culture. I am very Confident about the brand. It has been very successful in the Middle East and I think in this market exists for high quality aspirational lifestyle collections. *Pepe jeans* fills this gap and we look forward to accelerated organic growth in the Kuwaiti market?" Similar business relationships exist with other distributors who help businesses; side the area to gain access to new markets. *True Religion*, founded in 2002 by Jeffrey Lubell, is another retailer of jeans who is expanding into the Middle East. It has partnered with the *Aishti Group* that started in 1989 in Lebanon and grew from a single store selling clothes to the top end of the market to a chain of stores that now sells luxury brands. *Aishti* will handle the distribution of *True Religion* products in Lebanon, the UAE, Qatar and Bahrain.

What this case study shows is that whilst a product might not have a natural home in some parts of the world, an understanding of the market and making the right links with those that know the market from the inside is an important way of breaking into a market, reducing risk and improving the chance of success.

Questions

1 What could *New Look* do to further infiltrate the Middle Eastern and Asian markets?

2 Does this type of marketing only work within the fashion markets? Discuss other sectors it may be successful in.

3 What could *New Look* do to keep customers loyal?

CHAPTER REFERENCES

Baker, M., *Marketing:An Introductory Text* (Westburn, 2007).

Baker, M. and Saren, M., *Marketing Theory: a Student Text* (Sage, 2010).

Boone, L. and Kurtz, D., *Contemporary Marketing* (Cengage, 2011).

Day, G.S., *The Market Driven Organisation: Attracting and Keeping Valuable Customers* (Free Press, 1999).

Dibb, S., Simkin, L., Pride, W.M and Ferrell, O.C., *Marketing: Concepts & Strategies* 6th ed. (Cengage Learning, 2012)

Hart, S., *Marketing Changes* (Thomson Learning/Cengage, 2003).

Jobber, D., *Principles and Practice of Marketing* (McGraw-Hill, 2009).

Kotler, P. and Armstrong, G., *Principles of Marketing* (Pearson, 2010).

12 PRODUCT DEVELOPMENT AND PRICING STRATEGIES

BUSINESS FOCUS

Unilever's cupboard of billion-euro brands

From Ben & Jerry's and Lipton to Dove and Rexona, Unilever's cupboard is bulging with billion-euro brands as the multinational consumer goods company launches innovative new products and sets different strategies for products purchased by new types of consumers. With over €40 billion in annual sales, Unilever invests considerable sums in product innovation, aiming to create products that will both keep pace with changes in consumer lifestyles and appeal to people from all income levels. For example, the company targets a new brand of health-conscious consumers by constantly developing new products that are deemed to have a new health benefit, like Lifebuoy's new soap with 10 times better germ protection.

Unilever constantly seeks to re-invent itself in a healthy and sustainable new light. Targeting consumers who crave ice cream, but who are progressively becoming more health and weight conscious, they have developed a new "ice structuring protein" which allegedly allows them to make ice cream which is lower in fat, sugar and calories and at the same time includes more fruit. Meanwhile its Flora/Becel business will benefit from their new development of a Cool Blending technology which changes the way fats are processed and will allow Unilever to reduce its environmental impact along with its use of saturated fats. This reduction in the use of saturated fats is particularly important for Unilever since it will tie in with its Heart Health campaign and will coincide with the re-launch of Flora spreads.

The company's knowledge of consumer behaviour is especially vital for its marketing strategies and product development. Unilever has an extremely wide variety of brands and products, however, it has realised that the image of a company who cares is becoming increasingly important for consumers and all of its product innovation focus seems to be on increasing sustainability and promoting a healthier lifestyle. Most recent product developments across Unilever's brands have focused on developing new technologies which will in some way improve consumers' wellbeing. Unilever combines this with clever marketing campaigns which raise media brand awareness while linking it closely with movements for social change; for example Dove's well known campaign for "Real Beauty", which intends to challenge stereotypical beauty norms in the media. Looking ahead how will the company manage its profits while developing new products which correspond with the growing demand for ethical consumerism?

A **product**, like a Ben & Jerry's ice cream, is everything one receives in an exchange, including all tangible and intangible attributes and expected benefits. An Apple iPod purchase, for example, includes not only the iPod itself but also earbuds, a power adapter, instructions, and a warranty. A new car includes a warranty, an owner's manual, and perhaps free emergency road service for a year. Some of the intangibles that may go with an automobile include the status associated with ownership and the memories generated from past rides. Developing and managing products effectively are crucial to an organisation's ability to maintain successful marketing mixes.

> **product** everything one receives in an exchange, including all tangible and intangible attributes and expected benefits; it may be a good, a service, or an idea

A product may be a good, a service, or an idea. A *good* is a real, physical thing that we can touch, such as an Electrolux washing machine. A *service* is the result of applying human or mechanical effort to a person or thing. Basically, a *service* is a change we pay others to make for us. An estate agent's services result in a change in the ownership of property. A barber's services result in a change in your appearance. An *idea* may take the form of philosophies, lessons, concepts, or advice. Often ideas are included with a good or service. Thus, we might buy a book (a good) that provides ideas on how to lose weight. Alternatively, we might join Weight Watchers for ideas on how to lose weight and for help (services) in doing so.

We look at products first in this chapter. We examine product classifications and describe the four stages, or life-cycles, through which every product moves. Next, we illustrate how firms manage products effectively by modifying or deleting existing products and by developing new products. We also discuss branding, packaging, and labelling of products. Then our focus shifts to pricing. We explain competitive factors that influence sellers' pricing decisions and also explore buyers' perceptions of prices. After considering organisational objectives that can be accomplished through pricing, we outline several methods for setting prices. Finally, we describe pricing strategies by which sellers can reach target markets successfully.

CLASSIFYING PRODUCTS

Products fall into one of two general categories. **Consumer products** are purchased to satisfy personal and family needs. **Industrial** or **business products** are bought for use in a company's operations or to make other products. The same item can be both a consumer product and an industrial product. For example, when consumers purchase light bulbs for their homes, they are classified as consumer products. However, when a large company purchases light bulbs to provide lighting in a factory or office the same goods are considered industrial products. Thus the buyer's intent, or the ultimate use of the product, determines whether an item is classified as a consumer or an industrial/ business-to-business product. It is common for more people to be involved in buying an industrial product than in a consumer purchase.

> **consumer products** items purchased to satisfy personal or family needs
> **industrial or business products** items bought for use in a company's operations or to make other products

It is important to know about product classifications because different classes of product are aimed at particular target markets, and classification affects distribution, promotion and pricing decisions. Furthermore, the types of marketing activity and effort needed – in short, the entire marketing mix – differ according to how a product is classified. This section examines the characteristics of consumer and industrial products and explores the marketing activities associated with some of them.

Consumer products

The most widely accepted approach to classifying consumer products relies on the common characteristics of consumer buying behaviour. It divides products into four categories: convenience, shopping, speciality and unsought products. However, not all buyers behave in the same way when purchasing a specific type of product. Thus, a single product can fit into more than one category. To minimise this problem, marketers think in terms of how buyers *generally* behave when purchasing a specific item. In addition, they recognise that the "correct" classification can be determined only by considering a particular company's intended target market.

Convenience products   Relatively inexpensive, frequently purchased and rapidly consumed items on which buyers exert only minimal purchasing effort are called **convenience products**. They range from chocolate, magazines and chewing gum to petrol and soft drinks. The buyer spends little time planning the purchase or comparing available brands or sellers. Even a buyer who prefers a specific brand will readily choose a substitute if the preferred brand is not conveniently available.

> **convenience products** inexpensive, frequently purchased and rapidly consumed items that demand only minimal
> purchasing effort

Convenience product or shopping product? Dreyer's ice cream is a convenience product. It's an item you are likely to grab off the shelf without much thought as you walk through the frozen-food aisle of a store. By contrast, people may spend considerable amount of time and effort when buying a shopping product, like furniture.

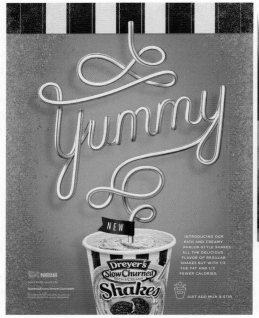

Classifying a product as a convenience product has several implications for a company's marketing strategy. A convenience product is normally marketed through many retail outlets. Because sellers experience high inventory turnover, the per unit gross margins can be relatively low. Producers of convenience products such as PG Tips tea and Domestos bleach expect little promotional effort at the retail level and so must provide their own through advertising, sales promotion and the item's packaging. The package may have an especially important role to play, because many convenience items are available only on a self-service basis at the retail level. The use of on-pack sales promotion and point-of-sale displays are ways to maximise the impact of the package. Such products are known as low-involvement products because consumers spend very little time considering their purchase and there is little opportunity for marketers to persuade consumers to examine alternatives … except for price discounting and prominent point of sale offers.

Shopping products   Items that are chosen more carefully than convenience products are called **shopping products**. They are purchased infrequently and are expected to last a long time. Buyers are willing to expend effort in planning and purchasing these items. They allocate time for comparing stores and brands with respect to prices, credit, product features, qualities, services and perhaps guarantees. Appliances, furniture, bicycles, stereos, jewellery and cameras are examples of shopping products. Even though shopping products are more expensive than convenience products, few buyers of shopping products are particularly brand loyal. If they were, they would be unwilling to shop and compare brands.

shopping products items chosen more carefully than convenience products; consumers will expend effort in planning and purchasing these items

Marketers seeking to market shopping products effectively must consider that they require fewer retail outlets than convenience products. Because they are purchased less frequently, inventory (stock) turnover is lower and middlemen (retailers) expect to receive higher gross margins. Although large sums of money may be required to advertise shopping products, an even larger proportion of resources is likely to be used for personal selling. Indeed, the quality of the service may be a factor in the consumer's choice of outlet. Thus, a couple that buys a new dishwasher might expect sales personnel in the chosen retail outlet to explain the advantages and features of competing brands. In many cases, the producer and the middlemen also expect some cooperation from one another with respect to providing parts and repair services, and performing promotional activities.

Speciality products   Products that possess one or more unique characteristics and which a significant group of buyers is willing to expend considerable effort to obtain are called **speciality products**. Buyers plan the purchase of a speciality product carefully; they know exactly what they want and will not accept a substitute. An example of a speciality product is a painting by L.S. Lowry or a Cartier watch. When searching for speciality products, buyers do not compare alternatives; they are concerned primarily with finding an outlet that has a pre-selected product available.

speciality products   items that possess one or more unique characteristics; consumers of speciality products plan their purchases and will expend considerable effort to obtain them

The marketing of a speciality product is very distinctive. The exclusivity of the product is accentuated by the fact that speciality products are often distributed through a limited number of retail outlets. Some companies go to considerable lengths to control this aspect of their distribution. Like shopping goods, speciality products are purchased infrequently, causing lower inventory turnover and thus requiring relatively high gross margins.

Unsought products   Products that are purchased when a sudden problem arises, or when aggressive selling obtains a sale that otherwise would not take place, are called **unsought products**. The consumer does not usually expect to buy these products regularly. Emergency windscreen replacement services and graveyard headstones are examples of unsought products. Life insurance is an example of an unsought product that often needs aggressive personal selling.

unsought products   items that are purchased when a sudden problem arises or when aggressive selling is used to obtain a sale that would not otherwise take place

Business products

Business products are usually purchased on the basis of a company's goals and objectives. The functional aspects of these products are usually more important than the psychological rewards sometimes associated with consumer products. Business products can be classified into seven categories according to their characteristics and intended uses:

1. raw materials
2. major equipment
3. accessory equipment
4. component parts
5. process materials
6. consumable supplies
7. industrial/business services.

Raw materials   The basic materials that become part of physical products are **raw materials**. These include minerals, chemicals, agricultural products, and materials from forests and oceans. They are usually bought and sold in relatively large quantities according to grades and specifications.

raw materials   the basic materials that become part of physical products

Major equipment   Large tools and machines used for production purposes, such as cranes and spray painting machinery, are types of **major equipment**. Major equipment is often expensive, may be used in a production process for a considerable length of time and is often custom-made to perform specific functions. For example, Alsthom manufactures purpose-built large gears and turbines. Other items are more standardised, performing similar tasks for many types of company. Because major equipment is so expensive, purchase decisions are often long and complex and may be made by senior management. Marketers of major equipment are frequently called upon to provide a variety of services, including installation, training, repair, maintenance assistance and financing. This may lead to long-term relationships being developed between suppliers of major equipment and their customers.

major equipment large tools and machines used for production purposes

Accessory equipment
Equipment that does not become a part of the final physical product, but is used in production or office activities is referred to as **accessory equipment**. Examples include telephone systems, stationery supplies, fractional horsepower motors and tools. Compared with major equipment, accessory items are usually much cheaper, are purchased routinely with less negotiation and are treated as expenditure items rather than capital items because they are not expected to last long. More outlets are required for distributing accessory equipment than for major equipment, but sellers do not have to provide the multitude of services expected of major equipment marketers.

accessory equipment tools and equipment used in production or office activities that do not become part of the final physical product

Component parts
Parts that become part of the physical product and are either finished items ready for assembly or products that need little processing before assembly are called **component parts**. Although they become part of a larger product, component parts can often be easily identified and distinguished. Tyres, spark plugs, gears, lighting units, screws and wires are all component parts of a delivery van. Buyers purchase such items according to their own specifications or industry standards. They expect the parts to be of specified quality and delivered on time so that production is not slowed or stopped. Producers that are primarily assemblers, such as most washing machine or lawnmower manufacturers, depend heavily on suppliers of component parts.

component parts parts that become a part of the physical product and are either finished items ready for assembly or products that need little processing before assembly

Process materials
Materials that are used directly in the production of other products are called **process materials**. Unlike component parts, however, process materials are not readily identifiable. For example, Reichhold Chemicals markets a treated fibre product: a phenolicresin, sheet-moulding compound used in the production of flight deck instrument panels and aircraft cabin interiors. Although the material is not identifiable in the finished aircraft, it retards burning, smoke and formation of toxic gas when subjected to fire or high temperatures.

process materials materials used directly in the production of other products, but not readily identifiable

Consumable supplies
Supplies that facilitate production and operations but do not become part of the finished product are referred to as **consumable supplies**. Paper, print cartridges, pencils, oils, cleaning agents and paints are in this category. They are purchased by many different types of business. Consumable supplies are purchased routinely and sold through numerous outlets. To ensure that supplies are available when needed, buyers often deal with more than one seller. Consumable supplies can be

divided into three subcategories – maintenance, repair and operating (or overhaul) supplies – and are sometimes called **MRO items**.

> **consumable supplies** supplies that facilitate production and operations but do not become part of the finished product
> **MRO items** consumable supplies in the subcategories of maintenance, repair and operating (or overhaul) supplies

Industrial/business services **Industrial/business services** are the intangible products that many organisations use in their operations. They include financial, legal, marketing research, computer programming and operation, caretaking and printing services for business. Some companies decide to provide their own services internally, while others outsource them. This decision depends largely on the costs associated with each alternative and the frequency with which the services are needed.

> **industrial/business services** the intangible products that many organisations use in their operations, including financial, legal, marketing research, computer programming and operation, caretaking and printing services

THE THREE LEVELS OF PRODUCT

The product may appear obvious – a carton of fresh orange juice or a designer handbag – but generally the purchaser is buying much more than a drink or a means of carrying personal items. To be motivated to make the purchase, the product must have a perceived or real core benefit or service. This level of product, termed the **core product**, is illustrated in Figure 12.1. The **actual product** is a composite of several factors: the features and capabilities offered, quality and durability, design and product styling, packaging and, often of great importance, the brand name.

> **core product** the level of a product that provides the perceived or real core benefit or service
> **actual product** a composite of the features and capabilities offered in a product, quality and durability, design and product styling, packaging and brand name

In order to make the purchase, the consumer often needs the assistance of sales personnel; there may be delivery and payment credit requirements and, for bulky or very technical products, advice regarding installation. The level of warranty back-up and after-sales support, particularly for innovative, highly technical or high value goods, will be of concern to most consumers. Increasingly, the overall level of customer service constitutes part of the purchase criteria, and in many markets it is deemed integral to the product on offer. These "support" issues form what is termed the **augmented product** (see Figure 12.1).

> **augmented product** support aspects of a product, including customer service, warranty, delivery and credit, personnel, installation and after-sales support

When a £35,000 BMW 3 Series executive car is purchased, the vehicle's performance specification and design may have encouraged the sale. Speed of delivery and credit payment terms may have been essential to the conclusion of the deal. The brand's image, particularly in the case of a car costing £35,000, will also have influenced the sale. Once behind the wheel of the BMW, its new owner will expect reliability and efficient, friendly, convenient service in the course of maintenance being required. The purchase might have been lost at the outset had the salesperson mishandled the initial enquiry. Repeat servicing business and the subsequent sale of another new car may be ruled out if the owner encounters incompetent, unhelpful service engineers. The core benefit may have been

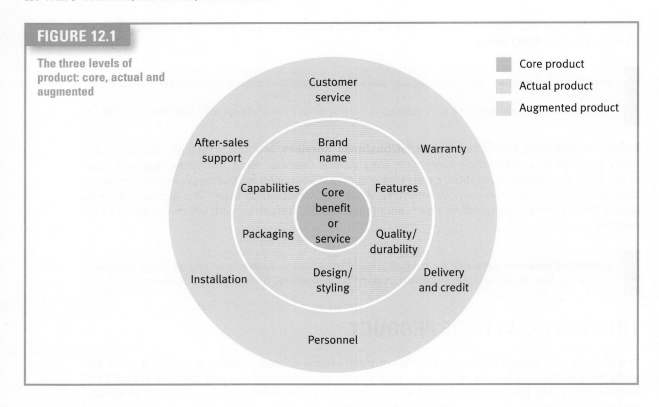

FIGURE 12.1

The three levels of product: core, actual and augmented

Core product
Actual product
Augmented product

Customer service
After-sales support
Brand name
Warranty
Capabilities
Core benefit or service
Features
Packaging
Quality/durability
Installation
Design/styling
Delivery and credit
Personnel

a car to facilitate journeys to work, transport for the family or the acquisition of a recognised status symbol. Customer satisfaction will depend on the product's actual performance and also on service aspects of the augmented product. This example is not unusual. For most consumer or business products and services, the consumer is influenced by the three levels of the product: core, actual and augmented. Marketers need to take this into consideration when developing product offers. Careful consideration of all levels of the product can provide the basis for a competitive edge. Indeed, often it is aspects of the augmented product which make or break the relationship with the customer and can create differentiation vis-à-vis competing propositions.

Many marketers now recognise the important role that personnel play in product exchanges. People are responsible for the design, production, marketing, sale and distribution of products. Personnel are especially important in the sale and delivery of services. Thus, a financial services adviser must have considerable expertise in the sector to give good advice. Similarly, a good-quality haircut can only be delivered by a skilled hairdresser. As consumers, people make decisions and ultimately adopt products for use and consumption. When deciding which products to adopt and use, people now pay considerable attention to the skills, attitudes and motivations of personnel involved in the marketing channel. Personnel also constitute an essential ingredient of the marketing mix for consumer and business goods.

PRODUCT LINE AND PRODUCT MIX

Marketers must understand the relationships between all their organisation's products if they are to coordinate their marketing. The following concepts describe the relationships between an organisation's products. A **product item** is a specific version of a product that can be designated as a distinct offering among a business's products – for example, Procter & Gamble's Pantene shampoo. A **product line** includes a group of closely related product items that are considered a unit because of marketing, technical or end-use considerations. All the shampoos manufactured by Procter & Gamble constitute one of its product lines. To come up with the optimum product line, marketers must understand buyers' goals. Specific items in a product line reflect the desires of different target markets or the different needs of consumers.

> **product item** a specific version of a product that can be designated as a distinct offering among a business's products
>
> **product line** a group of closely related product items that are considered a unit because of marketing, technical or end-use considerations

A **product mix** is the composite, or total, group of products that a company makes available to customers. For example, all the personal care products, laundry detergent products and other products that Procter & Gamble manufactures constitute its product mix. **Depth (of product mix)** of a product mix is measured by the number of different products offered in each product line.

> **product mix** the composite group of products that a company makes available to customers
>
> **depth (of product mix)** the number of different products offered in each product line

The **width** of a product mix is measured by the number of product lines a company offers. For example, Procter & Gamble's product mix width includes laundry detergents; toothpastes and dental care products; bar soaps; deodorants; shampoos; tissue/towel products. Procter & Gamble is known for using distinctive technology, branding, packaging and consumer advertising to promote individual items in its detergent product line. Tide, Bold and Cheer – all Procter & Gamble detergents – share similar distribution channels and manufacturing facilities. Yet due to variations in product formula and attributes, each is promoted as being distinct, adding depth to the product line.

> **width (of product mix)** the number of product lines a company offers

PRODUCT LIFE CYCLES

Just as biological cycles progress through growth and decline, so too do **product life cycles**. A new product is introduced into the marketplace; it grows; it matures; and when it loses appeal and sales decline, it is terminated. Different marketing strategies are appropriate at different stages in the product life cycle. Thus, packaging, branding and labelling techniques can be used to help create or modify products that have reached different points in their life.

> **product life cycles** the four major stages through which products move: introduction, growth, maturity and decline

As Figure 12.2 shows, a product life cycle has four major stages:

1. introduction
2. growth
3. maturity
4. decline

When a product moves through its cycle, the strategies relating to competition, promotion, place/distribution, pricing and market information must be evaluated periodically and possibly changed. Astute marketing managers use the life-cycle concept to make sure that the introduction, alteration and termination of a product are timed and executed properly. By understanding the typical life-cycle pattern, marketers are better able to maintain profitable products and drop unprofitable ones.

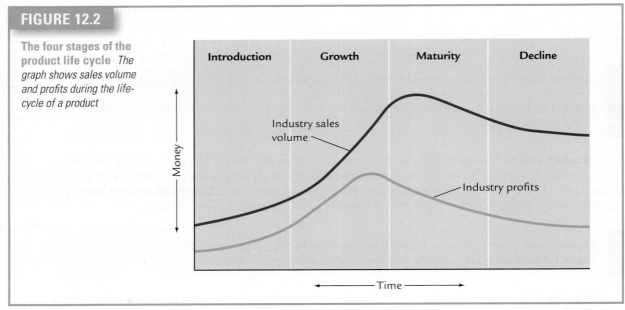

FIGURE 12.2

The four stages of the product life cycle *The graph shows sales volume and profits during the life-cycle of a product*

Source: William M. Pride and O. C. Ferrell, *Marketing: Concepts and Strategies*, 17th ed. (Mason, OH: South-Western/Cengage Learning, 2014). Adapted with permission.

Introduction

The **introduction stage** of the life cycle begins at a product's first appearance in the marketplace, when sales are zero and profits are negative. Profits are below zero because a new product incurs development costs, initial revenues are low, and at the same time a company must generally incur the significant expenses incurred during promotion and distribution. As time passes, sales should move upwards from zero and profits should build up from the negative position (see Figure 12.2).

 introduction stage a product's first appearance in the marketplace, before any sales or profits have been made

Because of cost, very few product introductions represent major inventions. Developing and introducing a new product can mean an outlay of many millions of pounds. The failure rate for new products is quite high, ranging from 60 to 90 per cent depending on the industry and on how product failure is defined. For example, in the food and drinks industry, 80 per cent of all new products fail. Typically, product introductions involve a new style of deodorant, a new type of vacuum cleaner or a new leisure concept rather than a major product innovation. In general, the more marketing-oriented the company, the more likely it will be to launch innovative products that are new to the market.

New product ideas are more likely to be successful when senior management is involved in product development and launch. In addition, research shows that a clear, stable vision, flexibility and improvisation, information exchange and collaboration are also key ingredients in new product success.

Potential buyers must be made aware of the new product's features, uses and advantages. Two difficulties may arise at this point. Only a few sellers may have the resources, technological knowledge and marketing know-how to launch the product successfully; and the initial product price may have to be high in order to recoup expensive marketing research or development costs. Given these difficulties, it is not surprising that many products never get beyond the introduction stage; indeed many are never launched commercially at all.

Growth

During the **growth stage**, sales rise rapidly, and profits reach a peak and then start to decline (see Figure 12.2). The growth stage is critical to a product's survival because competitive reactions to its success during this period will affect the product's life expectancy. For example, Mars successfully launched Ice Cream Mars, the first ice-cream version of an established confectionery product. Today the product competes with more than a dozen other brands. Some of the competing brands failed quickly and others followed. Profits decline late in the growth stage as more competitors enter the market, driving prices down and creating the need for heavy promotional expenses. At this point a typical marketing strategy encourages strong brand loyalty, perhaps using sales promotion, and competes with aggressive emulators of the product. During the growth stage, a company tries to strengthen its market share and develop a competitive position by emphasising the product's benefits. This is what the various smartphone providers are currently striving to achieve.

> **growth stage** the stage at which a product's sales rise rapidly and profits reach a peak, before levelling off into maturity

Aggressive promotional pricing, including price cuts, is typical during the growth stage. The smartphone industry is now well into its growth stage, and many competitors have entered the market. Companies like Samsung and Blackberry must battle hard to maintain their existing positions in this competitive arena.

Maturity

During the **maturity stage**, the sales curve peaks and starts to decline, and profits continue to decline (see Figure 12.2). This stage is characterised by severe competition, with many brands in the

Think back to toys that were wildly popular when you were younger. How many do you still see in shops? This shows how quickly some products can pass through the stages of the product life-cycle.

Saying "goodbye" to the pay telephone.
With mobile phones and smartphones becoming increasingly popular amongst the general public, whether out and about or travelling abroad, the traditional pay telephone is in the decline stage of the product life cycle. Do you recall when you last actually had to use one? If so, when and where? You might have a hard time remembering.

© SAMOT / SHUTTERSTOCK

market. Competitors emphasise improvements and differences in their versions of the product. Inevitably, during the maturity stage, some weaker competitors are squeezed out or switch their attention to other products. For example, some Internet service providers are perishing or being acquired by rivals now that the product is in its maturity stage.

> **maturity stage** the stage during which a product's sales curve peaks and starts to decline, and profits continue to decline

During the maturity stage, the producers who remain in the market must make fresh promotional and distribution efforts. These efforts must focus on dealers as much as on consumers to ensure that brand visibility is maintained at the point of sale. Advertising and dealer-oriented promotions are typical during this stage of the product life cycle. The promoters must also take into account the fact that, as the product reaches maturity, buyers' knowledge of it attains a high level. Consumers of the product are no longer inexperienced generalists, but rather experienced specialists.

Decline

During the **decline stage**, sales fall rapidly (see Figure 12.2). New technology or a new social trend may cause product sales to take a sharp downturn. For example, iPods have reduced CD sales and green concerns have damaged the sales volumes of certain models of vehicles. When this happens, the marketer must consider pruning items from the product line to eliminate those not earning a profit. Sony surprised the market by announcing it would be pulling out of selling PDAs. The decision came because Sony believed that technology changes are signalling a move away from handheld organisers towards multifunctional mobile phones. At this time, too, the marketer may cut promotion efforts, eliminate marginal distributors and, finally, plan to phase out the product.

> **decline stage** the last stage of a product's life cycle, during which sales fall rapidly

Because most businesses have a product mix consisting of multiple products, a company's destiny is rarely tied to one product. A composite of life-cycle patterns is formed when various products in the mix are at different stages in the cycle. As one product is declining, other products are in the introduction, growth or maturity stage. Marketers must deal with the dual problems of prolonging the life of existing products and introducing new products to meet sales goals.

© NEWSCAST/ALAMY

How companies use product lines to expand. *Firms use the knowledge and expertise they develop producing one product line to develop others. It's much a like a tree in a forest that grows new branches to find sunlight and thrive. This photo shows only a few of Kellogg Company's 20 different cereal brands. The company also produces a wide variety of crackers, bars, beverages, toaster pastries, waffles, pancakes, syrups, and fruit-flavoured snacks.*

MANAGING THE PRODUCT MIX

To provide products that satisfy people in a firm's target market or markets and that also achieve the organisation's objectives, a marketer must develop, adjust, and maintain an effective product mix. Seldom can the same product mix be effective for long. Because customers' product preferences and attitudes change, their desire for a product may diminish or grow. In some cases, a firm needs to alter its product mix to adapt to competition. A marketer may have to eliminate a product from the mix because one or more competitors dominate that product's specific market segment. Similarly, an organisation may have to introduce a new product or modify an existing one to compete more effectively. A marketer may also expand the firm's product mix to take advantage of excess marketing and production capacity. For example, General Mills has a wide product mix consisting of many different brands. It frequently expands its product mix by adding new offerings to its different product lines, such as breakfast cereals. General Mills takes advantage of production capacity for the Cheerios line by increasing its depth with new flavours, such as peanut butter, chocolate, and dulce de leche.* For whatever reason a product mix is altered, the product mix must be managed to bring about improvements in the mix. There are three major ways to improve a product mix: change an existing product, delete a product, or develop a new product.

Managing existing products

A product mix can be changed by deriving additional products from existing ones. This can be accomplished through product modifications and by line extensions.

Product modifications   **Product modification** refers to changing one or more of a product's characteristics. For this approach to be effective, several conditions must be met. First, the product must be modifiable. Second, existing customers must be able to perceive that a modification has been made, assuming that the modified item is still directed at the same target market. Third, the modification should make the product more consistent with customers' desires so that it provides greater satisfaction. For example, General Motors upgraded the structure and cooling systems in the battery for its Chevrolet Volt hybrid car in order to address some consumer hesitations over the battery's safety. Volt owners were encouraged to bring their vehicles to a dealership to receive the new modified battery. In order to publicise the improvement, GM made widespread announcements regarding the change.*

product modification the process of changing one or more of a product's characteristics

Existing products can be altered in three primary ways: in quality, function, and aesthetics. *Quality modifications* are changes that relate to a product's dependability and durability and are usually achieved by alterations in the materials or production process. *Functional modifications* affect

A product-line extension with staying power: Oreo Fudge Cremes. Nabisco, the maker of Oreos, developed a product line extension when it launched Oreo Fudge Cremes. The product, which consists of fudge atop Oreo cream filling, was originally supposed to be produced for just a short time. However, it was so popular Nabisco kept it in its product lineup and later launched mint, peanut butter, and other versions of the treat.

© SUSAN VAN ETTEN

a product's versatility, effectiveness, convenience, or safety; they usually require redesign of the product. Typical product categories that have undergone extensive functional modifications include home appliances, office and farm equipment, and consumer electronics. *Aesthetic modifications* are directed at changing the sensory appeal of a product by altering its taste, texture, sound, smell, or visual characteristics. Because a buyer's purchasing decision is affected by how a product looks, smells, tastes, feels, or sounds, an aesthetic modification may have a definite impact on purchases. Through aesthetic modifications, a firm can differentiate its product from competing brands and perhaps gain a sizable market share if customers find the modified product more appealing.

Line extensions   A **line extension** is the development of a product closely related to one or more products in the existing product line but designed specifically to meet somewhat different customer needs. WD-40, maker of the multi-use lubricant, recently launched its first-ever line extension. The WD-40 Specialist line consists of five different products for industrial and home use, including a rust remover and a waterproofer.*

> **line extension** development of a new product that is closely related to one or more products in the existing product line but designed specifically to meet somewhat different customer needs

Many of the so-called new products introduced each year are in fact line extensions. Line extensions are more common than new products because they are a less-expensive, lower-risk alternative for increasing sales. A line extension may focus on a different market segment or be an attempt to increase sales within the same market segment by more precisely satisfying the needs of people in that segment. Line extensions are also used to take market share from competitors.

Deleting products

To maintain an effective product mix, an organisation often has to eliminate some products. This is called **product deletion**. A weak product costs a company time, money, and resources that could be used to modify other products or develop new ones. In addition, when a weak product generates an unfavourable image among customers, the negative image may rub off on other products sold by the firm.

> **product deletion** the elimination of one or more products from a product line

Most organisations find it difficult to delete a product. Some firms drop weak products only after they have become severe financial burdens. A better approach is to conduct some form of systematic review of the product's impact on the overall effectiveness of a firm's product mix. Such a review should analyse a product's contribution to a company's sales for a given period. It should include

Fan blades 'chop' the airflow, causing buffeting. The new Dyson fan works differently. An annular jet accelerates the surrounding air and amplifies it fifteen times. There are no blades to chop the air so the airflow is smooth – it cools without the unpleasant buffeting.

Blades cause buffeting.

No blades means no buffeting.

dyson air multiplier
No blades. No buffeting.
Learn more at www.dyson.co.uk
Or experience in-store.

COURTESY OF THE ADVERTISING ARCHIVES

You probably won't find a fan like this one in your grandparents' attic. This new type of bladeless fan, developed by Dyson, is called the Air Multiplier. What new-product category do you think the Air Multiplier falls into? Is it an imitation, innovation, or adaptation?

estimates of future sales, costs, and profits associated with the product and a consideration of whether changes in the marketing strategy could improve the product's performance.

A product-deletion programme can definitely improve a firm's performance. For example, T-Mobile recently decided to delete the Sidekick 4G smartphone due to declining sales and customer interest. However, the company announced that it had no plans to discontinue the entire Sidekick line.*

Developing new products

Developing and introducing new products is frequently time consuming, expensive, and risky. Thousands of new products are introduced annually. The overall failure rate for new products is around 50 per cent, although the failure rate in some industries can be much higher.* Although developing new products is risky, failing to introduce new products can be just as hazardous. Successful new products bring a number of benefits to an organisation, including survival, profits, a sustainable competitive advantage, and a favourable public image. Consider the numerous ways that the producers of the products in Table 12.1 have benefited.

TABLE 12.1 Top ten new products since 2000

Rank	Product name	Year introduced
1	iPod	2001
2	Wii	2006
3	Axe	2002
4	$5 Footlong	2008
5	Activia	2006
6	Mini Cooper	2002
7	Crest Whitestrips	2000
8	Guitar Hero	2005
9	Toyota Prius	2000
10	7 For All Mankind	2000

Source: Advertising Age, December 14, 2009, 16. http://adage.com/article?article_id=141032 (accessed February 21, 2012).

SUCCESS STORY

Lego

Europe's largest and the world's fourth largest toy maker, Lego is Danish, family owned and based on strong principles. Lego has five stated values: creativity, innovation, learning, fun and quality.

The basic strategy is one of product development, with Lego developing an enormous number of variations on its basic product theme. Wheels and electric motors

were added in the 1960s. By the mid-1990s some 300 different kits (at a wide range of prices) were available worldwide. Brick colours were selected to appeal to both boys and girls; and the more complex Lego Technic sets were branded and promoted specially to make them attractive to the young teenage market. Well over 200 billion plastic bricks and pieces have been produced since Lego was introduced. More recently, Lego has ventured into the computer games market with CD-based products enabling users to "build" train sets, vehicles, etc., on screen. "Design by Me" allows children to design their own finished Lego piece and then have the required parts shipped to them.

It has also agreed licensing deals for kits based on Bob the Builder, Star Wars and Harry Potter. Lego has constantly sought to diversify its products and it can now add robot toys, theme parks and video games to its brand.

Some believe Lego brought problems on itself by taking some focus away from traditional bricks and experimenting with other products and activities. Yet with reported plans for a Lego MP3 Player and digital camera, Lego is still not quite ready to stop innovating and its enduring success seems to indicate that perhaps this is not a bad thing.

References: *Strategic Management: Awareness and Change* (7th ed.), Thompson, Scott and Martin (2014)

New products are generally grouped into three categories on the basis of their degree of similarity to existing products. *Imitations* are products designed to be similar to—and to compete with—existing products of other firms. Examples are the various brands of whitening toothpastes that were developed to compete with those offered by Rembrandt. *Adaptations* are variations of existing products that are intended for an established market. Product refinements and extensions are the adaptations considered most often, although imitative products may also include some refinement and extension. *Innovations* are entirely new products. They may give rise to a new industry or revolutionise an existing one. The introduction of digital music, for example, has brought major changes to the recording industry. Innovative products take considerable time, effort, and money to develop. They are therefore less common than adaptations and imitations. Google recently announced an innovative new product dubbed Project Glass. It involves a futuristic and ambitious plan to merge online technology with spectacles that users wear. Once finalised, the product will perform the function of many common electronic items. The product will act as a smartphone, day planner, navigation system, and even camera—all in wearable glasses with information showing up as small icons on the lenses. Because this product idea is so new, it has been the target of considerable consumer scrutiny, although many technophiles and early adopters are excited by the possibilities such a product can offer.* As shown in Figure 12.3, the process of developing a new product consists of seven phases.

Idea generation   Idea generation involves looking for product ideas that will help a firm to achieve its objectives. Although some organisations get their ideas almost by chance, firms trying to maximise product-mix effectiveness usually develop systematic approaches for generating new-product ideas.

FIGURE 12.3

Phases of new-product development *Generally, marketers follow these seven steps to develop a new product.*

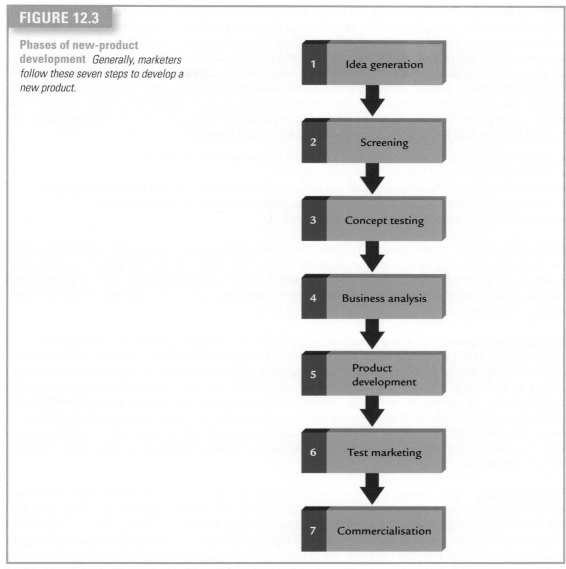

1 Idea generation

2 Screening

3 Concept testing

4 Business analysis

5 Product development

6 Test marketing

7 Commercialisation

Source: William M. Pride and O. C. Ferrell, *Marketing: Concepts and Strategies*, 17th ed. (Mason, OH: South-Western/Cengage Learning, 2014). Adapted with permission.

Ideas may come from managers, researchers, engineers, competitors, advertising agencies, management consultants, private research organisations, customers, salespersons, or top executives. Sometimes, large firms with superior experience and resources may mentor small firms and help them generate ideas to help their businesses grow. Business incubators sprung up around the globe that pair new small businesses with large established ones so that the new business can learn about marketing and branding from experts at established firms. The entrepreneurs can get ideas, help hone their image, and improve marketing strategy.*

Screening During screening, ideas that do not match organisational resources and objectives are rejected. In this phase, a firm's managers consider whether the organisation has personnel with the expertise to develop and market the proposed product. Management may reject a good idea because the company lacks the necessary skills and abilities. The largest number of product ideas are rejected during the screening phase.

Concept testing   Concept testing is a phase in which a product idea is presented to a small sample of potential buyers through a written or oral description (and perhaps a few drawings) to determine their attitudes and initial buying intentions regarding the product. For a single product idea, an organisation can test one or several concepts of the same product. Concept testing is a low-cost means for an organisation to determine consumers' initial reactions to a product idea before investing considerable resources in product research and development (R&D). Product development personnel can use the results of concept testing to improve product attributes and product benefits that are most important to potential customers. The types of questions asked vary considerably depending on the type of product idea being tested. The following are typical questions:

- Which benefits of the proposed product are especially attractive to you?
- Which features are of little or no interest to you?
- What are the primary advantages of the proposed product over the one you currently use?
- If this product were available at an appropriate price, how often would you buy it?
- How could this proposed product be improved?

Business analysis   Business analysis provides tentative ideas about a potential product's financial performance, including its probable profitability. During this stage, the firm considers how the new product, if it were introduced, would affect the firm's sales, costs, and profits. Marketing personnel usually work up preliminary sales and cost projections at this point, with the help of R&D and production managers.

Product development   In the product development phase, the company must find out first if it is technically feasible to produce the product and then if the product can be made at costs low enough to justify a reasonable price. If a product idea makes it to this point, it is transformed into a working model, or prototype. For example, Aptera, an American vehicle manufacturer, recently developed a prototype electric vehicle called the 2e. The 2e is an innovative three-wheeled, two-seat vehicle that uses an electric motor with phosphate-based lithium-ion batteries. The 2e is expected to operate at about 200 MPG and travel about 100 miles on a single charge.14 Often, this step is time-consuming and expensive for the organisation. If a product successfully moves through this step, then it is ready for test marketing.

Test marketing   Test marketing is the limited introduction of a product in several towns or cities chosen to be representative of the intended target market. Its aim is to determine buyers' probable reactions. The product is left in the test markets long enough to give buyers a chance to repurchase the product if they are so inclined. Marketers can experiment with advertising, pricing, and packaging in different test areas and can measure the extent of brand awareness, brand switching, and repeat purchases that result from alterations in the marketing mix. Many companies will trial a new product or service locally to test that the model works before rolling it out nationally or even internationally.

Commercialisation   During commercialisation, plans for full-scale manufacturing and marketing must be refined and completed, and budgets for the project must be prepared. In the early part of the commercialisation phase, marketing management analyses the results of test marketing to find out what changes in the marketing mix are needed before the product is introduced. The results of test marketing may tell the marketers, for example, to change one or more of the product's physical attributes, to modify the distribution plans to include more retail outlets, to alter promotional efforts, or to change the product's price. Products are usually not introduced nationwide overnight. Most new products are marketed in stages, beginning in selected geographic areas and expanding into adjacent areas over a period of time.

Why do products fail?

Despite this rigorous process for developing product ideas, most new products end up as failures. In fact, many well-known companies have produced market failures (see Table 12.2).

TABLE 12.2	Examples of product failures

Company	Product
Gillette	For Oily Hair shampoo
3M	Floptical storage disk
IncrEdibles Breakaway Foods	Push n' Eat
General Mills	Betty Crocker MicroRave Singles
Adams (Pfizer)	Body Smarts nutritional bars
Ford	Edsel
Anheuser-Busch	Bud Dry and Michelob Dry beer
Coca-Cola	New Coke
Heinz	Ketchup Salsa
Noxema	Noxema Skin Fitness

Sources: Robert McMath and Thom Forbes, "What Were They Thinking?," Reed Business Information, 1998; Robert M. McMath, "Copycat Cupcakes Don't Cut It," *American Demographics*, January 1997, 60; Eric Berggren and Thomas Nacher, "Why Good Ideas Go Bust," *Management Review*, February 2000, 32–36.

Why does a new product fail? Mainly because the product and its marketing programme are not planned and tested as completely as they should be. For example, to save on development costs, a firm may market-test its product but not its entire marketing mix. Alternatively, a firm may market a new product before all the "bugs" have been worked out. Or, when problems show up in the testing stage, a firm may try to recover its product development costs by pushing ahead with full-scale marketing anyway. Finally, some firms try to market new products with inadequate financing.

BRANDING, PACKAGING, AND LABELING

Three important features of a product (particularly a consumer product) are its brand, package, and label. These features may be used to associate a product with a successful product line or to distinguish it from existing products. They may be designed to attract customers at the point of sale or to provide information to potential purchasers. Because the brand, package, and label are very real parts of the product, they deserve careful attention during product planning.

What is a brand?

A **brand** is a name, term, symbol, design, or any combination of these that identifies a seller's products and distinguishes it from other sellers' products. A **brand name** is the part of a brand that can be spoken. It may include letters, words, numbers, or pronounceable symbols, such as the ampersand in *Procter & Gamble*. A **brand mark**, on the other hand, is the part of a brand that is a symbol or distinctive design, such as the Nike "swoosh." A **trademark** is a brand name or brand mark that is registered with an official patenting and trademark authority and thus is legally protected from use by anyone except its owner. Whilst there are many international trading standards and regulations in place, different countries do operate different policies and so a patent or trademark registered in one country or region may not necessarily be sufficiently protected in others. Businesses must therefore be aware of the rules and regulations in the countries in which they wish to trade, often taking out multiple patents to protect their branding and intellectual property. Many firms ranging from Gucci to Google are frequently embroiled in disputes to protect the company name and image, and others such Dyson and Lego in protracted lawsuits over alleged patent infringements. Brand protection is discussed in more detail later in the chapter. A **trade name** is the complete and legal name of an organisation, such as Pizza Hut or Cengage Learning (the publisher of this text).

You can easily recognise a manufacturer's brand because it is not sold by just one retailer. This brand was initiated by the manufacturer and is owned and supported by the manufacturer. Duracell batteries are sold in many retail stores.

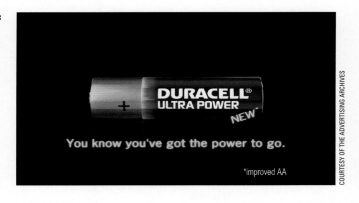

DURACELL® ULTRA POWER NEW

You know you've got the power to go.

*improved AA

> **brand** a name, term, symbol, design, or any combination of these that identifies a seller's products as distinct from those of other sellers
> **brand name** the part of a brand that can be spoken
> **brand mark** the part of a brand that is a symbol or distinctive design
> **trademark** a brand name or brand mark that is registered with an official patenting and trademark authority and thus is legally protected from use by anyone except its owner
> **trade name** the complete and legal name of an organisation

Types of brands

Brands are often classified according to who owns them: manufacturers or stores. A **manufacturer** (or **producer**) **brand**, as the name implies, is a brand that is owned by a manufacturer. Many foods (Kellogg's Frosted Flakes), major appliances (Whirlpool), petrol (Exxon), automobiles (Honda), and clothing (Levi's) are sold as manufacturers' brands. Some consumers prefer manufacturer brands because they are usually nationally known, offer consistent quality, and are widely available.

> **manufacturer (or producer) brand** a brand that is owned by a manufacturer

A **store** (or **private**) **brand** is a brand that is owned by an individual wholesaler or retailer. In the U.K., for example, supermarket chain ASDA has its exclusive George range of clothing, by designer George Davis, whereas Sainsbury's offers its TU range. All the leading supermarkets offer a comprehensive variety of own-branded goods, encompassing everything from pasta sauce and instant coffee to cleaning products. Owners of store brands claim that they can offer lower prices, earn greater profits, and improve customer loyalty with their own brands. Some companies that manufacture private brands also produce their own manufacturer brands. They often find such operations profitable because they can use excess capacity and at the same time avoid most marketing costs. Many private-branded grocery products are produced by companies that specialise in making private-label products. Most supermarkets rely heavily on their store brands because of store brand profitability and could not survive without having store brands. According to the Private Label Manufacturer's Association, the popularity and quality of store brands is on the rise, particularly among consumers who seek out good value without sacrificing quality.*

> **store (or private) brand** a brand that is owned by an individual wholesaler or retailer

Consumer confidence is the most important element in the success of a branded product, whether the brand is owned by a producer or by a retailer. Because branding identifies each product completely, customers can easily repurchase products that provide satisfaction, performance, and quality. Moreover, they can just as easily avoid or ignore products that do not. In supermarkets, the products most likely to keep their shelf space are the brands with large market shares and strong customer loyalty.

A **generic product** (sometimes called a **generic brand**) is a product with no brand at all. Its plain package carries only the name of the product—applesauce, peanut butter, potato chips, or whatever. Generic products, available in supermarkets since 1977, are sometimes made by the major producers that manufacture name brands. Even though generic brands may have accounted for as much as 10 per cent of all grocery sales several years ago, they currently represent less than one-half of 1 per cent.

generic product (or brand) a product with no brand at all

Benefits of branding

Both buyers and sellers benefit from branding. Because brands are easily recognisable, they reduce the amount of time buyers must spend shopping; buyers can quickly identify the brands they prefer. Choosing particular brands, such as Tommy Hilfiger, Polo, Nautica, or Adidas, can be a way of expressing oneself. When buyers are unable to evaluate a product's characteristics, brands can help them to judge the quality of the product. For example, most buyers are not able to judge the quality of stereo components but may be guided by a well-respected brand name such as the innovative Danish audio-visual specialist, Bang & Olufsen. Brands can symbolise a certain quality level to a customer, allowing that perception of quality to represent the actual quality of the item. Brands thus help to reduce a buyer's perceived risk of purchase. Finally, customers may receive a psychological reward that comes from owning a brand that symbolises status. The Bentley luxury motorcar brand is an example.

Because buyers are already familiar with a firm's existing brands, branding helps a firm to introduce a new product that carries the same brand name. Branding aids sellers in their promotional efforts because promotion of each branded product indirectly promotes other products of the same brand. H.J. Heinz, for example, markets many products with the Heinz brand name, such as ketchup, vinegar, vegetarian beans, gravies, barbecue sauce, and steak sauce. Promotion of one Heinz product indirectly promotes the others.

One chief benefit of branding is the creation of **brand loyalty**, the extent to which a customer is favourable toward buying a specific brand. The stronger the brand loyalty, the greater is the likelihood that buyers will consistently choose the brand. There are three levels of brand loyalty: recognition, preference, and insistence. *Brand recognition* is the level of loyalty at which customers are aware that the brand exists and will purchase it if their preferred brands are unavailable or if they are unfamiliar with available brands. This is the weakest form of brand loyalty. *Brand preference* is the level of brand loyalty at which a customer prefers one brand over competing brands. However, if the preferred brand is unavailable, the customer is willing to substitute another brand. *Brand insistence* is the strongest level of brand loyalty. Brand-insistent customers strongly prefer a specific brand and will not buy substitutes. *Brand insistence* is the least common type of brand loyalty. Apple is a brand known for having brand-insistent customers. Every time Apple releases a new product, loyal customers will stand in line for hours just to be among the first to purchase it. Upon the U.K. release of the iPad 3, a couple waited five full days outside a London Apple store.* Brand loyalty in general seems to be declining, partly due to marketers' increased dependence on discounted prices, coupons, and other short-term promotions, and partly because of the enormous array of new products with similar characteristics.

brand loyalty extent to which a customer is favourable toward buying a specific brand

Brand equity is the marketing and financial value associated with a brand's strength in a market. Although difficult to measure, brand equity represents the value of a brand to an organisation. The top ten most highly valued brands in the world are shown in Table 12.3. The four major factors

TABLE 12.3 Top ten most valuable brands in the world

Brand	Brand Value (in billion $)
Coca-Cola	71.9
IBM	69.9
Microsoft	59.1
Google	55.3
GE	42.8
McDonald's	35.6
Intel	35.2
Apple	33.5
Disney	29.0
Hewlett-Packard	28.5

Source: "Best Global Brands," *Interbrand*, http://*interbrand*.com/en/best-global-brands/Best-Global-Brands-2011.aspx (accessed February 21, 2012).

that contribute to brand equity are brand awareness, brand associations, perceived brand quality, and brand loyalty. Brand awareness leads to brand familiarity, and buyers are more likely to select a familiar brand than an unfamiliar one. The associations linked to a brand can connect a personality type or lifestyle with a particular brand. For example, customers associate Michelin tyres with protecting family members; a De Beers diamond with a loving, long-lasting relationship ("A Diamond Is Forever"); and Dr Pepper with a unique taste. When consumers are unable to judge for themselves the quality of a product, they may rely on their perception of the quality of the product's brand. Finally, brand loyalty is a valued element of brand equity because it reduces both a brand's vulnerability to competitors and the need to spend tremendous resources to attract new customers; it also provides brand visibility and encourages retailers to carry the brand. Companies have much work to do in establishing new brands to compete with well-known brands. Sometimes, large firms opt to purchase a well-known brand rather than to compete with it. When Starbucks decided to enter the juice market, it began with acquiring the high-end juice brand Evolution Fresh. After it acquired the brand and expanded its distribution, Starbucks then unrolled a plan to open a chain of its own juice bars.*

 brand equity marketing and financial value associated with a brand's strength in a market

Marketing on the Internet is sometimes best done in collaboration with a better-known Web brand. For instance, Tire Rack, Razor Gator, Audible.com, and Shutterfly all rely on partnerships with Internet retail giant Amazon to increase their sales. Amazon provides special sections on its Web site to promote its partners and their products. As with its own products, Amazon gives users the ability to post online reviews of its partners' products or to add them to an Amazon "wish list" that can be saved or e-mailed to friends. Amazon even labels its partners as "Amazon Trusted" when customers browse their sites, giving even these well-known real-world companies credibility in the online marketplace.*

Choosing and protecting a brand

A number of issues should be considered when selecting a brand name. The name should be easy for customers to say, spell, and recall. Short, one-syllable names such as *Tide* often satisfy this requirement. Words, numbers, and letters are combined to yield brand names such as Motorola's RAZR V3 phone or BMW's Z4 Roadster. The brand name should suggest, in a positive way, the product's uses, special characteristics, and major benefits and should be distinctive enough to set it apart from competing brands. Choosing the right brand name has become a challenge because many obvious product names already have been used.

It is important that a firm select a brand that can be protected through registration, reserving it for exclusive use by that firm. Some brands, because of their designs, are infringed on more easily than others. Depending on the country of registration, the trademark may only be protected for a specific time frame before requiring renewal (such as ten years in the U.S.), and therefore a firm should develop a system for ensuring that its trademarks will be renewed as needed. To protect its exclusive right to the brand, the company must ensure that the selected brand will not be considered an infringement on any existing brand already registered with the official patenting and trademark body of each specific country where it seeks protection. This task may be complicated by the fact that infringement is determined by the courts, which base their decisions on whether a brand causes consumers to be confused, mistaken, or deceived about the source of the product. McDonald's is one company that aggressively protects its trademarks against infringement; it has brought charges against a number of companies with *Mc* names because it fears that the use of the prefix will give consumers the impression that these companies are associated with or owned by McDonald's. Likewise, Apple - known for its instant brand recognition in using the suffix 'i' for its products (iPhone, iPad, iPod, iBook, etc.) - actively pursues any traders seeking to follow suit, frequently suing for brand infringement. Indeed, Apple has often been accused of adopting a bullish approach with its 'iBrand' strategy, allegedly disregarding the rights of existing companies already trading under a name that Apple subsequently wishes to use for a new product. For example, as *The Washington Post* reported in 2011, a company trading as iCloud Communications in Arizon, U.S., filed a complaint against Apple for causing confusion amongst their customer base, citing various damages, when Apple launched its iCloud online storage service. More recently, in June 2013, it was reported that Apple had filed for the the trademark 'iWatch' in Japan, fuelling speculation surrounding the potential new product.

A firm must guard against having its brand name become a generic term that refers to a general product category. Generic terms cannot be legally protected as exclusive brand names. For example, names such as *yo-yo, aspirin, escalator,* and *thermos*—all exclusively brand names at one time—eventually were declared generic terms that refer to product categories. As such, they can no longer be protected. Hoover is another brand name that historically has been used more generically to describe any vacuum cleaner, and is often used as a verb: "I'm doing the hoovering". Whilst, on the one hand it is a flattering testament to a brand's success and widespread appeal that its name eventually becomes a commonplace term, it can have negative connotations as competitors potentially profit through association and the ubiquity of the term. To ensure that a brand name does not become a generic term, the firm should spell the name with a capital letter and use it as an adjective to modify the name of the general product class, as in Jell-O Brand Gelatin. An organisation can deal directly with this problem by advertising that its brand is a trademark and should not be used generically. Firms also can use the registered trademark symbol ® to indicate that the brand is trademarked.

Branding strategies

The basic branding decision for any firm is whether to brand its products. A producer may market its products under its own brands, private brands, or both. A retail store may carry only producer brands, its own brands, or both. Once either type of firm decides to brand, it chooses one of two branding strategies: individual branding or family branding.

Individual branding is the strategy in which a firm uses a different brand for each of its products. For example, Procter & Gamble uses individual branding for its line of bar soaps, which includes Ivory, Camay, Zest, Safeguard, Coast, and Olay. Individual branding offers two major advantages. A problem with one product will not affect the good name of the firm's other products, and the different brands can be directed toward different market segments. For example, Marriott's Fairfield Inns are directed toward budget-minded travelers, whereas Marriott Hotels are aimed toward upscale customers.

 individual branding the strategy in which a firm uses a different brand for each of its products

Family branding is the strategy in which a firm uses the same brand for all or most of its products. Sony, Dell, IBM, and Xerox use family branding for their entire product mixes. A major advantage of family branding is that the promotion of any one item that carries the family brand tends to help all other products with the same brand name. In addition, a new product has a head start when its brand name is already known and accepted by customers.

 family branding the strategy in which a firm uses the same brand for all or most of its products

Brand extensions

A **brand extension** occurs when an organisation uses one of its existing brands to brand a new product in a different product category. Iams, a popular maker of dog food, partnered with VPI Pet Insurance to extend its brand into pet insurance. This brand extension was generally well received, as Iams already had a reputation for offering high-quality products to customers who truly care about their pets. Many considered it a smart move because pet insurance is an industry that is relatively free of major, established competitors; thus, Iams can develop strong market share.* A brand extension should not be confused with a line extension. A *line extension* refers to using an existing brand on a new product in the same product category, such as a new favour or new sizes. For example, Ben & Jerry's ice cream frequently engages in line extension by releasing new flavours, such as Chocolate Therapy and Rocky Roadish. One thing marketers must be careful of, however, is extending a brand too many times or extending too far outside the original product category, which may weaken the brand. Many brands have had to recover from unsuccessful brand extensions, such as Harley Davidson perfume, Fritos lemonade, and Bic disposable underwear.*

 brand extension using an existing brand to brand a new product in a different product category

Packaging

Packaging consists of all the activities involved in developing and providing a container with graphics for a product. The package is a vital part of the product. It can make the product more versatile, safer, or easier to use. Through its shape, appearance, and printed message, a package can influence purchasing decisions.

 packaging all the activities involved in developing and providing a container with graphics for a product

Packaging functions Effective packaging means more than simply putting products in containers and covering them with wrappers. The basic function of packaging materials is to protect the product and maintain its functional form. Fluids such as milk, orange juice, and hair spray need packages that preserve and protect them; the packaging should prevent damage that could affect the product's usefulness and increase costs. Because product tampering has become a problem for marketers of many types of goods, several packaging techniques have been developed to counter this danger. Many sauces and spreads sold in glass jars, for example, have a metal lid that pops up only once the vacuum seal is broken. Pressing the lid before purchase is a quick and simple way for shoppers to check that it hasn't been opened and contaminated. Some packages are also designed to foil shoplifting.

Another function of packaging is to offer consumer convenience. For example, small, aseptic packages—individual-serving boxes or plastic bags that contain liquids and do not require refrigeration—appeal strongly to parents of small children and to young adults with active lifestyles. The size or shape of a package may relate to the product's storage, convenience of use, or replacement rate. Small, single-serving cans of vegetables, for instance, may prevent waste and make storage easier. A third function of packaging is to promote a product by communicating its features, uses, benefits, and image. Sometimes a firm develops a reusable package to make its product more desirable. For example, many packages such as glass jars and plastic tubs are designed to be reused as a food-storage container.

Heinz turns the ketchup bottle on its head. The original design of the ketchup bottle made it difficult for customers to get the ketchup out. To solve this problem, Heinz put the cap on the bottom of the bottle and made the opening larger. In addition, Heinz made the bottle squeezable.

Package design considerations   Many factors must be weighed when developing packages. Obviously, one major consideration is cost. Although a number of packaging materials, processes, and designs are available, some are rather expensive. Although buyers have shown a willingness to pay more for improved packaging, there are limits.

Marketers also must decide whether to package the product in single or multiple units. Multiple-unit packaging can increase demand by increasing the amount of the product available at the point of consumption (in the home, for example). However, multiple-unit packaging does not work for infrequently used products because buyers do not like to tie up their money in an excess supply or to store those products for a long time. However, multiple-unit packaging can make storage and handling easier (as in the case of six-packs used for soft drinks); it can also facilitate special price offers, such as two-for-one sales. In addition, multiple-unit packaging may increase consumer acceptance of a product by encouraging the buyer to try it several times. On the other hand, customers may hesitate to try the product at all if they do not have the option to buy just one. Marketers should also consider the rituals and cultures native to the regions where they are selling their products, particularly when exporting goods overseas, as this may affect the packaging requirements. For example, in Japan products are rarely packaged in sets of four due the association that number and its pronunciation has with death.

Marketers should consider how much consistency is desirable among an organisation's package designs. To promote an overall company image, a firm may decide that all packages must be similar or include one major element of the design. This approach, called *family packaging,* is sometimes used only for lines of products, as with Campbell's soups, Weight Watchers entrées, and Planters nuts. The best policy is sometimes no consistency, especially if a firm's products are unrelated or aimed at vastly different target markets.

Packages also play an important promotional role. Through verbal and nonverbal symbols, the package can inform potential buyers about the product's content, uses, features, advantages, and hazards. Firms can create desirable images and associations by choosing particular colors, designs, shapes, and textures. Many cosmetics manufacturers, for example, design their packages to create impressions of richness, luxury, and exclusiveness. The package performs another promotional function when it is designed to be safer or more convenient to use, especially if such features help to stimulate demand.

Packaging also must meet the needs of intermediaries. Wholesalers and retailers consider whether a package facilitates transportation, handling, and storage. Resellers may refuse to carry certain products if their packages are cumbersome.

Finally, firms must consider the issue of environmental responsibility when developing packages. Companies must balance consumers' desires for convenience against the need to preserve the environment. About one-half of all household waste consists of discarded plastic packaging, such as plastic soft drink bottles and carryout bags. Plastic packaging material is not biodegradable, and paper necessitates destruction of valuable forest lands. Consequently, many companies are exploring packaging alternatives and recycling more materials. Starbucks even holds an annual Cup Summit with packaging leaders in order to discuss issues related to reducing waste and increasing the recyclability of packaging. Many Starbucks locations offer recycling bins for used cups and other refuse in an effort to increase the scale of recycling and to make it more economical.*

Labelling

Labelling is the presentation of information on a product or its package. The *label* is the part that contains the information. This information may include the brand name and mark, the registered trademark symbol ®, the package size and contents, product claims, directions for use and safety precautions, a list of ingredients, the name and address of the manufacturer, and the Universal Product Code (UPC) symbol, which is used for automated checkout and inventory control.

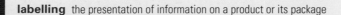

labelling the presentation of information on a product or its package

A number of national and international regulations specify information that *must* be included in the labelling for certain products. For example, some typical requirements include:

- Garments must be labelled with the name of the manufacturer, country of manufacture, fabric content, and cleaning instructions.
- Food labels must contain the most common term for ingredients.
- Any food product for which a nutritional claim is made must have nutrition labelling that follows a standard format.
- Food product labels must state the number of servings per container, the serving size, the number of calories per serving, the number of calories derived from fat, and the amounts of specific nutrients.
- Non-edible items such as shampoos and detergents must carry safety precautions as well as instructions for their use.

Such regulations are aimed at protecting customers from both misleading product claims and the improper (and thus unsafe) use of products. Food manufacturers are not allowed to make misleading health claims about their products. For example, General Mills was ordered to stop making claims about the heart-healthy benefits of Cheerios cereal. Similarly, Vitaminwater was taken to court for leading consumers to believe that the sugary beverage has health benefits. Food, pharmaceutical and product standards bodies have cracked down on such offenses, sending out warning letters to violators.*

Labels also may carry the details of written or express warranties. An **express warranty** is a written explanation of the producer's responsibilities in the event that a product is found to be defective or otherwise unsatisfactory. As a result of consumer discontent (along with some legislation), firms have begun to simplify the wording of warranties and to extend their duration. Apple was forced to clarify the terms of its AppleCare warranty after being fined €1.2 million by Italian regulators for neglecting to fully disclose the terms of the agreement. In response to the fine, Apple posted information pages that outline the warranties and what they cover.*

express warranty a written explanation of the producer's responsibilities in the event that a product is found to be defective or otherwise unsatisfactory

PRICING PRODUCTS

A product is a set of attributes and benefits that has been carefully designed to satisfy its market while earning a profit for its seller. No matter how well a product is designed, however, it cannot help an organisation to achieve its goals if it is priced incorrectly. Somewhere between too high and too low there is a "proper," effective price for each product. Let's take a closer look at how businesses go about determining a product's right price.

The meaning and use of price

The **price** of a product is the amount of money a seller is willing to accept in exchange for the product at a given time and under given circumstances. At times, the price results from negotiations between buyer and seller. In many business situations, however, the price is fixed by the seller. Suppose that a seller sets a price of €10 for a particular product. In essence, the seller is saying, "Anyone who wants this product can have it here and now in exchange for €10."

> **price** the amount of money a seller is willing to accept in exchange for a product at a given time and under given circumstances

Each interested buyer then makes a personal judgment regarding the product's utility, often in terms of some dollar value. A particular person who feels that he or she will get at least €10 worth of want satisfaction (or value) from the product is likely to buy it. If that person can get more want satisfaction by spending €10 in some other way, however, he or she will not buy the product.

Price thus serves the function of *allocator*. First, it allocates goods and services among those who are willing and able to buy them. The answer to the economic question "For whom to produce?" depends primarily on prices.) Second, price allocates financial resources (sales revenue) among producers according to how well they satisfy customers' needs. Third, price helps customers to allocate their own financial resources among various want-satisfying products.

Supply and demand affects prices

The **supply** of a product is the quantity of the product that producers are willing to sell at each of various prices. We can draw a graph of the supply relationship for a particular product, say, a pair of jeans (see the left graph in Figure 12.4). Note that the quantity supplied by producers *increases* as the price increases along this *supply curve*.

> **supply** the quantity of a product that producers are willing to sell at each of various prices

The **demand** for a product is the quantity that buyers are willing to purchase at each of various prices. We can also draw a graph of the demand relationship (see the center graph in Figure 12.4). Note that the quantity demanded by purchasers *increases* as the price decreases along the *demand curve*. The buyers and sellers of a product interact in the marketplace. We can show this interaction by superimposing the supply curve onto the demand curve for our product, as shown in the right graph in Figure 12.4. The two curves intersect at point *E*, which represents a quantity of 15 million pairs of jeans and a price of €30 per pair. Point *E* is on the *supply curve*; thus, producers are willing to supply 15 million pairs at €30 each. Point *E* is also on the demand curve; thus, buyers are willing to purchase 15 million pairs at €30 each. Point *E* represents *equilibrium*. If 15 million pairs are produced and priced at €30, they all will be sold. In addition, everyone who is willing to pay €30 will be able to buy a pair of jeans.

> **demand** the quantity of a product that buyers are willing to purchase at each of various prices

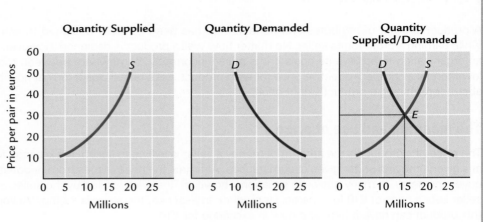

FIGURE 12.4

Supply and demand curves *Supply curve (left): The upward slope means that producers will supply more jeans at higher prices. Demand curve (centre): The downward slope (to the right) means that buyers will purchase fewer jeans at higher prices. Supply and demand curves together (right): Point E indicates equilibrium in quantity and price for both sellers and buyers.*

Price and non-price competition

Before a product's price can be set, an organisation must determine the basis on which it will compete—whether on price alone or some combination of factors. The choice influences pricing decisions as well as other marketing-mix variables.

Price competition occurs when a seller emphasises a product's low price and sets a price that equals or beats competitors' prices. To use this approach most effectively, a seller must have the flexibility to change prices often and must do so rapidly and aggressively whenever competitors change their prices. Price competition allows a marketer to set prices based on demand for the product or in response to changes in the firm's finances. Competitors can do likewise, however, which is a major drawback of price competition. They, too, can quickly match or outdo an organisation's price cuts. In addition, if circumstances force a seller to raise prices, competing firms may be able to maintain their lower prices. The Internet has made it more difficult than ever for sellers to compete on the basis of price, as consumers can quickly and easily conduct comparison-shopping online. Lower-priced competitors for pricy but popular products quickly crop up. For example, the Apple iPad tablet controls nearly three-quarters of the tablet market, but less expensive tablets running on Google's Android operating system are providing consumers with different options with lower price tags.*

> **price competition** an emphasis on setting a price equal to or lower than competitors' prices to gain sales or market share

Non-price competition is competition based on factors other than price. It is used most effectively when a seller can make its product stand out from the competition by distinctive product quality, customer service, promotion, packaging, or other features. Buyers must be able to perceive these distinguishing characteristics and consider them desirable. Once customers have chosen a brand for non-price reasons, they may not be attracted as easily to competing firms and brands. In this way, a seller can build customer loyalty to its brand. A method of non-price competition, **product differentiation**, is the process of developing and promoting differences between one's product and all similar products. Vibram Five Fingers shoes, for example, are sufficiently differentiated from the competition that marketers do not have to compete on price. The shoes have highly distinct styling and are unlike any other shoe on the market. Designed in the silhouette of a foot, tracing the shape of each individual toe, they appeal to athletes who want to protect the soles of their feet while also having a barefoot experience.*

non-price competition competition based on factors other than price
product differentiation the process of developing and promoting differences between one's product and all
  similar products

Buyers' perceptions of price

In setting prices, managers should consider the price sensitivity of people in the target market. How important is price to them? Is it always "very important"? Members of one market segment may be more influenced by price than members of another. For a particular product, the price may be a bigger factor for some buyers than for others. For example, buyers may be more sensitive to price when purchasing petrol than when purchasing running shoes.

Buyers will accept different ranges of prices for different products; that is, they will tolerate a narrow range for certain items and a wider range for others. Consider the wide range of prices that consumers pay for soft drinks—from 15 cents per ounce at the movies down to 1.5 cents per ounce on sale at the grocery store. Management should be aware of these limits of acceptability and the products to which they apply. The firm also should take note of buyers' perceptions of a given product in relation to competing products. A premium price may be appropriate if a product is considered superior to others in its category or if the product has inspired strong brand loyalty. On the other hand, if buyers have even a hint of a negative view of a product, a lower price may be necessary.

Sometimes buyers relate price to quality. They may consider a higher price to be an indicator of higher quality. Managers involved in pricing decisions should determine whether this outlook is widespread in the target market. If it is, a higher price may improve the image of a product and, in turn, make the product more desirable.

PRICING OBJECTIVES

Before setting prices for a firm's products, management must decide what it expects to accomplish through pricing. That is, management must set pricing objectives that are in line with both organisational and marketing objectives. Of course, one objective of pricing is to make a profit, but this may not be a firm's primary objective. One or more of the following factors may be just as important.

Survival

A firm may have to price its products to survive—either as an organisation or as a player in a particular market. This usually means that the firm will cut its price to attract customers, even if it then must operate at a loss. Obviously, such a goal hardly can be pursued on a long-term basis, for consistent losses would cause the business to fail. Even Abercrombie and Fitch (A&F) had to resort to price reductions on its luxury-priced clothing to stay in business during the recent economic downturn. A&F's 2009 first-quarter result was a loss of around €27 million, compared to 2008's income of over €62 million. This drastic difference forced the retailer to adjust prices to better complement customers' smaller budgets.*

Profit maximisation

Many firms may state that their goal is to maximise profit, but this goal is impossible to define (and thus impossible to achieve). What, exactly, is the *maximum* profit? How does a firm know when it has been reached? Firms that wish to set profit goals should express them as either specific dollar amounts, or percentage increases, over previous profits.

What does a product's price communicate to you? How buyers perceive a product is often determined by its price. High prices communicate quality and status—which is why the makers of luxury goods such as Rolex watches are often reluctant to sell them at a discount. The producers of these goods don't want to "cheapen" their brands for a quick sales boost because it could hurt the image of the brand on the longer term.

© LEE HACKER/ALAMY

Target return on investment

The *return on investment* (ROI) is the amount earned as a result of that investment. Some firms set an annual percentage ROI as their pricing goal. ConAgra, the company that produces Healthy Choice meals and a multitude of other products, has a target after-tax ROI of 20 per cent.

Market-share goals

A firm's *market share* is its proportion of total industry sales. Some firms attempt, through pricing, to maintain or increase their market shares. Rivals Coke and Pepsi try to gain market share through aggressive pricing and other marketing efforts.

Status-quo pricing

In pricing their products, some firms are guided by a desire to avoid "making waves," or to maintain the status quo. This is especially true in industries that depend on price stability. If such a firm can maintain its profit or market share simply by meeting the competition—charging about the same price as competitors for similar products—then it will do so.

PRICING METHODS

Once a firm has developed its pricing objectives, it must select a pricing method to reach that goal. Two factors are important to every firm engaged in setting prices. The first is recognition that the market, and not the firm's costs, ultimately determines the price at which a product will sell. The second is awareness that costs and expected sales can be used only to establish some sort of *price floor,* the minimum price at which the firm can sell its product without incurring a loss. In this section, we look at three kinds of pricing methods: cost-based, demand-based, and competition-based pricing.

Cost-based pricing

Using the simplest method of pricing, *cost-based pricing,* the seller first determines the total cost of producing (or purchasing) one unit of the product. The seller then adds an amount to cover additional costs (such as insurance or interest) and profit. The amount that is added is called the **markup.** The total of the cost plus the markup is the product's selling price.

> **markup** the amount a seller adds to the cost of a product to determine its basic selling price

A firm's management can calculate markup as a percentage of its total costs. Suppose, for example, that the total cost of manufacturing and marketing 1,000 DVD players is €100,000, or €100 per unit. If the manufacturer wants a markup that is 20 per cent above its costs, the selling price will be €100 plus 20 per cent of €100, or €120 per unit.

Markup pricing is easy to apply, and it is used by many businesses (mostly retailers and wholesalers). However, it has two major flaws. The first is the difficulty of determining an effective markup percentage. If this percentage is too high, the product may be overpriced for its market; then too few units may be sold to return the total cost of producing and marketing the product. In contrast, if the markup percentage is too low, the seller is "giving away" profit it could have earned simply by assigning a higher price. In other words, the markup percentage needs to be set to account for the workings of the market, and that is very difficult to do.

The second problem with markup pricing is that it separates pricing from other business functions. The product is priced *after* production quantities are determined, *after* costs are incurred, and almost without regard for the market or the marketing mix. To be most effective, the various business functions should be integrated. *Each* should have an impact on all marketing decisions.

Cost-based pricing can also be facilitated through the use of breakeven analysis. For any product, the **breakeven quantity** is the number of units that must be sold for the total revenue (from all units sold) to equal the total cost (of all units sold). **Total revenue** is the total amount received from the sales of a product. We can estimate projected total revenue as the selling price multiplied by the number of units sold.

> **breakeven quantity** the number of units that must be sold for the total revenue (from all units sold) to equal the total cost (of all units sold)
> **total revenue** the total amount received from sales of a product

The costs involved in operating a business can be broadly classified as either fixed or variable costs. A **fixed cost** is a cost incurred no matter how many units of a product are produced or sold. Rent, for example, is a fixed cost; it remains the same whether 1 or 1,000 units are produced. A **variable cost** is a cost that depends on the number of units produced. The cost of fabricating parts for a stereo receiver is a variable cost. The more units produced, the more parts that will be needed, and thus the higher cost of fabricating parts. The **total cost** of producing a certain number of units is the sum of the fixed costs and the variable costs attributed to those units.

> **fixed cost** a cost incurred no matter how many units of a product are produced or sold
> **variable cost** a cost that depends on the number of units produced
> **total cost** the sum of the fixed costs and the variable costs attributed to a product

If we assume a particular selling price, we can find the breakeven quantity either graphically or by using a formula. Figure 12.5 graphs the total revenue earned and the total cost incurred by the sale of various quantities of a hypothetical product. With fixed costs of €40,000, variable costs of €60 per unit, and a selling price of €120, the breakeven quantity is 667 units. To find the breakeven quantity, first deduct the variable cost from the selling price to determine how much money the sale of one unit contributes to offsetting fixed costs. Then divide that contribution into the total fixed costs to arrive at the breakeven quantity. (The breakeven quantity in Figure 12.5 is the quantity represented by the intersection of the total revenue and total cost axes.) If the firm sells more than 667 units at €120 each, it will earn a profit. If it sells fewer units, it will suffer a loss.

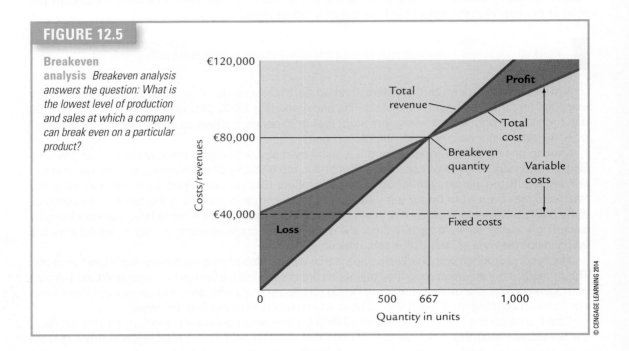

FIGURE 12.5

Breakeven analysis *Breakeven analysis answers the question: What is the lowest level of production and sales at which a company can break even on a particular product?*

© CENGAGE LEARNING 2014

Demand-based pricing

Rather than basing the price of a product on its cost, companies sometimes use a pricing method based on the level of demand for the product: *demand-based pricing*. This method results in a high price when product demand is strong and a low price when demand is weak. Some long-distance telephone companies use demand-based pricing. To use this method, a marketer estimates the amount of a product that customers will demand at different prices and then chooses the price that generates the highest total revenue. Obviously, the effectiveness of this method depends on the firm's ability to estimate demand accurately. In order to address severe problems with parking shortages, the city of San Francisco adopted a demand-based parking meter system. Rates are raised and lowered throughout the day according to demand. The city hopes that the variable fees will help smooth demand for parking spaces and traffic by encouraging people to park outside of congested areas and either walk, bike, or bus to their final destination. The plan is being watched closely by other cities, such as Boston, as a potential market-driven solution to parking and transportation problems.*

A firm may favour a demand-based pricing method called *price differentiation* if it wants to use more than one price in the marketing of a specific product. Price differentiation can be based on such considerations as time of the purchase, type of customer, or type of distribution channel. Sports arenas increasingly use demand-based pricing to sell tickets to events. Seats for single games are priced according to fan demand, meaning that the most popular seats sell for the highest price, no

Why you might have paid twice as much for your plane ticket as the person sitting next to you. *Airlines use demand-based pricing because the number of passengers that can be put on a specific flight is limited. The sophisticated software the companies use constantly re-price seats based on the number of tickets customers are purchasing at any given time as well as historical data.*

matter what the location within the stadium or arena. For price differentiation to work correctly, the company first must be able to segment a market on the basis of different strengths of demand. The company must then be able to keep the segments separate enough so that those who buy at lower prices cannot sell to buyers in segments that are charged a higher price. This isolation can be accomplished, for example, by selling to geographically separated segments.

RESPONSIBLE PRACTICE   Misleading packaging or clever marketing?

There has recently been some controversy regarding Cadbury's re-launch of the Dairy Milk bar. This has been due to the change of the traditional squared bar into a curved shape which, despite looking like a purely aesthetical change, nevertheless means that the chocolate has now shrunk by eight per cent, from 49g to 45g. However, the price has remained the same at 59 pence.

The move is the latest in a series of "stealth price rises" since U.S. food giant Kraft took over the business, which have included the resizing of both the 140g bar of Dairy Milk to 120g and its Roses tin from 975g to 850g.

Cadbury states that these are necessary changes to cope with rising fuel and commodity costs and even though some rival companies, like Mars, have employed similar strategies, this has angered some consumers and critics who claim it is deliberately misleading practice. Confectionary companies are not alone in this practice, and similar stories have echoed throughout the consumer goods trade, incorporating everything from washing detergent (using the same-sized box, despite including less powder) to sandwich spreads.

These recent moves to cut costs at the expense of the consumer raise questions regarding ethical marketing. Should these attempts to cut costs be disguised for marketing purposes as simple product re-launches or should they be openly announced to the consumer?

References: http://www.dailymail.co.uk/news/article-2219775/Cadbury-cuts-size-Dairy-Milk-chocolate-bar-keeps-price-exactly-same.html#ixzz2kL6bfigK

Compared with cost-based pricing, demand-based pricing places a firm in a better position to attain higher profit levels, assuming that buyers value the product at levels sufficiently above the product's cost. To use demand-based pricing, however, management must be able to estimate demand at different price levels, which may be difficult to do accurately.

Competition-based pricing

In using *competition-based pricing,* an organisation considers costs and revenue secondary to competitors' prices. The importance of this method increases if competing products are quite similar and the organisation is serving markets in which price is the crucial variable of the marketing strategy. A firm that uses competition-based pricing may choose to be below competitors' prices, slightly above competitors' prices, or at the same level. Competition-based pricing can help to attain a pricing objective to increase sales or market share. Competition-based pricing may also be combined with other cost approaches to arrive at profitable levels.

PRICING STRATEGIES

A *pricing strategy* is a course of action designed to achieve pricing objectives. Generally, pricing strategies help marketers to solve the practical problems of setting prices. The extent to which a business uses any of the following strategies depends on its pricing and marketing objectives, the markets for its products, the degree of product differentiation, the product's life-cycle stage, and other factors. Figure 12.6 contains a list of the major types of pricing strategies. We discuss these strategies in the remainder of this section.

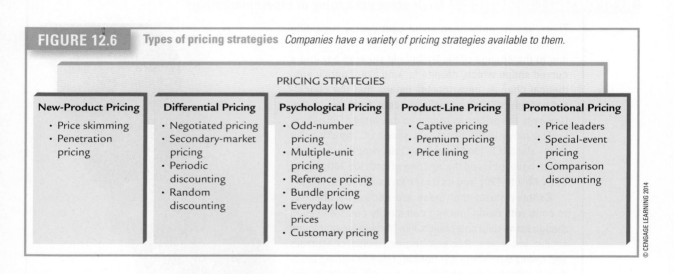

FIGURE 12.6 **Types of pricing strategies** *Companies have a variety of pricing strategies available to them.*

PRICING STRATEGIES

New-Product Pricing	Differential Pricing	Psychological Pricing	Product-Line Pricing	Promotional Pricing
• Price skimming • Penetration pricing	• Negotiated pricing • Secondary-market pricing • Periodic discounting • Random discounting	• Odd-number pricing • Multiple-unit pricing • Reference pricing • Bundle pricing • Everyday low prices • Customary pricing	• Captive pricing • Premium pricing • Price lining	• Price leaders • Special-event pricing • Comparison discounting

© CENGAGE LEARNING 2014

New-product pricing

The two primary types of new-product pricing strategies are price skimming and penetration pricing. An organisation can use either one, or even both, over a period of time.

Price skimming Some consumers are willing to pay a high price for an innovative product either because of its novelty or because of the prestige or status that ownership confers. **Price skimming** is the strategy of charging the highest possible price for a product during the introduction stage of its life-cycle. The seller essentially "skims the cream" off the market, which helps to recover the high costs of R&D more quickly. In addition, a skimming policy may hold down demand for the product, which is helpful if the firm's production capacity is limited during the introduction stage. A danger is that a price-skimming strategy may make the product appear more lucrative than it actually is to potential competitors.

price skimming the strategy of charging the highest possible price for a product during the introduction stage of its life-cycle

Penetration pricing
At the opposite extreme, **penetration pricing** is the strategy of setting a low price for a new product. The main purpose of setting a low price is to build market share for the product quickly. The seller hopes that building a large market share quickly will discourage competitors from entering the market. If the low price stimulates sales, the firm also may be able to order longer production runs, which result in lower production costs per unit. A disadvantage of penetration pricing is that it places a firm in a less flexible position. It is more difficult to raise prices significantly than it is to lower them.

penetration pricing the strategy of setting a low price for a new product

Differential pricing

An important issue in pricing decisions is whether to use a single price or different prices for the same product. A single price is easily understood by both employees and customers. Since many salespeople and customers do not like having to negotiate a price, having a single price reduces the chance of a marketer developing an adversarial relationship with a customer.

Differential pricing means charging different prices to different buyers for the same quality and quantity of product. For differential pricing to be effective, the market must consist of multiple segments with different price sensitivities. When this method is employed, caution should be used to avoid confusing or antagonising customers. Differential pricing can occur in several ways, including negotiated pricing, secondary-market pricing, periodic discounting, and random discounting.

Negotiated pricing **Negotiated pricing** occurs when the final price is established through bargaining between the seller and the customer. Negotiated pricing occurs in a number of industries and at all levels of distribution. Even when there is a predetermined stated price or a price list, manufacturers, wholesalers, and retailers still may negotiate to establish the final sales price. Consumers commonly negotiate prices for houses, cars, and used equipment.

negotiated pricing establishing a final price through bargaining

Secondary-market pricing **Secondary-market pricing** means setting one price for the primary target market and a different price for another market. Often the price charged in the secondary market is lower. However, when the costs of serving a secondary market are higher than normal, secondary-market customers may have to pay a higher price. Examples of secondary markets include a geographically isolated domestic market, a market in a foreign country, and a segment willing to purchase a product during off-peak times (such as "early bird" diners at restaurants and off-peak users of mobile phones).

secondary-market pricing setting one price for the primary target market and a different price for another market

Periodic discounting **Periodic discounting** is the temporary reduction of prices on a patterned or systematic basis. For example, many retailers have annual holiday sales, and some women's apparel stores have two seasonal sales each year—a winter sale in the last two weeks of January and a summer sale in the first two weeks of July. From the marketer's point of view, a major problem with periodic discounting is that customers can predict when the reductions will occur and may delay their purchases until they can take advantage of the lower prices.

periodic discounting temporary reduction of prices on a patterned or systematic basis

Random discounting To alleviate the problem of customers' knowing when discounting will occur, some organisations employ **random discounting.** That is, they reduce their prices temporarily on a nonsystematic basis. When price reductions of a product occur randomly, current users of that brand are unlikely to predict when the reductions will occur; therefore, they will not delay their purchases in anticipation of buying the product at a lower price. Marketers also use random discounting to attract new customers.

random discounting temporary reduction of prices on an unsystematic basis

Psychological pricing

Psychological pricing strategies encourage purchases based on emotional responses rather than on economically rational responses. These strategies are used primarily for consumer products rather than business products.

Odd-number pricing Many retailers believe that consumers respond more positively to odd-number prices such as €4.99 than to whole-euro prices such as €5. **Odd-number pricing** is the strategy of setting prices using odd numbers that are slightly below whole-euro amounts. Nine and five are the most popular ending figures for odd-number prices.

odd-number pricing the strategy of setting prices using odd numbers that are slightly below whole-unit amounts

Sellers who use this strategy believe that odd-number prices increase sales. The strategy is not limited to low-priced items. Auto manufacturers may set the price of a car at €11,999 rather than €12,000. Odd-number pricing has been the subject of various psychological studies, but the results have been inconclusive.

Multiple-unit pricing Many retailers (and especially supermarkets) practice **multiple-unit pricing,** setting a single price for two or more units, such as two cans for 99 cents rather than 50 cents per can. Especially for frequently purchased products, this strategy can increase sales. Customers who see the single price and who expect eventually to use more than one unit of the product regularly purchase multiple units to save money.

multiple-unit pricing the strategy of setting a single price for two or more units

Reference pricing **Reference pricing** means pricing a product at a moderate level and positioning it next to a more expensive model or brand in the hope that the customer will use the higher price as a reference price (i.e., a comparison price). Because of the comparison, the customer is expected to view the moderate price favorably.

reference pricing pricing a product at a moderate level and positioning it next to a more expensive model or brand

Bundle pricing **Bundle pricing** is the packaging together of two or more products, usually of a complementary nature, to be sold for a single price. To be attractive to customers, the single price usually is considerably less than the sum of the prices of the individual products. Being able to buy the bundled combination of products in a single transaction may be of value to the customer as well. Bundle pricing is used commonly for banking and travel services, computers, and automobiles with option packages. Bundle pricing can help to increase customer satisfaction. By bundling slow-moving products with ones with a higher turnover, an organisation can stimulate sales and increase its revenues. Selling products as a package rather than individually also may result in cost savings. It is common for telecommunications providers to sell service bundles of cable, Internet, and phone service for one price. Virgin Media, amongst other providers, offer such services.

 bundle pricing packaging together two or more complementary products and selling them for a single price

Everyday Low Prices (EDLPs) To reduce or eliminate the use of frequent short-term price reductions, some organisations use an approach referred to as **everyday low prices (EDLPs)**. When EDLPs are used, a marketer sets a low price for its products on a consistent basis rather than setting higher prices and frequently discounting them. EDLPs, though not deeply discounted, are set far enough below competitors' prices to make customers feel confident that they are receiving a fair price. EDLPs are employed by retailers such as Walmart and Tesco, and by manufacturers such as Procter & Gamble. A company that uses EDLPs benefits from reduced promotional costs, reduced losses from frequent markdowns, and more stability in its sales. A major problem with this approach is that customers have mixed responses to it. In some instances, customers simply do not believe that EDLPs are what they say they are but are instead a marketing gimmick.

 everyday low prices (EDLPs) setting a low price for products on a consistent basis

Customary pricing In **customary pricing**, certain goods are priced primarily on the basis of tradition. Examples of customary, or traditional, prices would be those set for chocolate bars and chewing gum.

 customary pricing pricing on the basis of tradition

Product-line pricing

Rather than considering products on an item-by-item basis when determining pricing strategies, some marketers employ product-line pricing. *Product-line pricing* means establishing and adjusting the prices of multiple products within a product line. Product-line pricing can provide marketers with flexibility in price setting. For example, marketers can set prices so that one product is quite profitable, whereas another increases market share by virtue of having a lower price than competing products.

When marketers employ product-line pricing, they have several strategies from which to choose. These include captive pricing, premium pricing, and price lining.

Captive pricing When **captive pricing** is used, the basic product in a product line is priced low, but the price on the items required to operate or enhance it are set at a higher level. Two common examples of captive pricing are razor blades and printer ink. The razor handle and the printer are generally priced quite low, but the razor blades and the printer ink replacement cartridges are usually very expensive. Sometimes, a brand will even give away the razor handle because it knows that consumers will then be compelled to buy the requisite razor blades.

 captive pricing pricing the basic product in a product line low, but pricing related items at a higher level

Premium pricing   **Premium pricing** occurs when the highest-quality product or the most-versatile version of similar products in a product line is given the highest price. Other products in the line are priced to appeal to price-sensitive shoppers or to those who seek product-specific features. Marketers that use premium pricing often realise a significant portion of their profits from premium-priced products. Examples of product categories in which premium pricing is common are small kitchen appliances, beer, ice cream, and television cable service.

premium pricing pricing the highest-quality or most-versatile products higher than other models in the product line

Price lining   **Price lining** is the strategy of selling goods only at certain predetermined prices that reflect definite price breaks. For example, a shop may sell men's ties only at €22 and €37. This strategy is used widely in clothing and accessory stores. It eliminates minor price differences from the buying decision—both for customers and for managers who buy merchandise to sell in these stores.

price lining the strategy of selling goods only at certain predetermined prices that reflect definite price breaks

Promotional pricing

Price, as an ingredient in the marketing mix, often is coordinated with promotion. The two variables sometimes are so interrelated that the pricing policy is promotion oriented. Examples of promotional pricing include price leaders, special-event pricing, and comparison discounting.

Price leaders   Sometimes a firm prices a few products below the usual markup, near cost, or below cost, which results in prices known as **price leaders.** This type of pricing is used most often in supermarkets and restaurants to attract customers by giving them especially low prices on a few items. Management hopes that sales of regularly priced products will more than offset the reduced revenues from the price leaders.

price leaders products priced below the usual markup, near cost, or below cost

Special-event pricing   To increase sales volume, many organisations coordinate price with advertising or sales promotions for seasonal or special situations. **Special-event pricing** involves advertised sales or price cutting linked to a holiday, season, or event. If the pricing objective is survival, then special sales events may be designed to generate the necessary operating capital.

special-event pricing advertised sales or price cutting linked to a holiday, season, or event

Comparison discounting   **Comparison discounting** sets the price of a product at a specific level and simultaneously compares it with a higher price. The higher price may be the product's previous price, the price of a competing brand, the product's price at another retail outlet, or a manufacturer's suggested retail price. Customers may find comparative discounting informative, and it can have a significant impact on them. However, because this pricing strategy on occasion has led to deceptive pricing practices, the Federal Trade Commission has established guidelines for comparison discounting. If the higher price against which the comparison is made is the price formerly charged for the product, sellers must have made the previous price available to customers for a reasonable period of time. If sellers present the higher price as the one charged by other retailers in the same trade area, they must be able to demonstrate that this claim is true. When they present the higher price as the manufacturer's suggested retail price, then the higher price must be similar to the price at which a reasonable proportion of the product was sold. Some manufacturers' suggested retail prices are so high that very few products actually are sold at those prices. In such cases, it would be deceptive to use comparison discounting.

comparison discounting setting a price at a specific level and comparing it with a higher price

PRICING BUSINESS PRODUCTS

Many of the pricing issues discussed thus far in this chapter deal with pricing in general. However, setting prices for business products can be different from setting prices for consumer products owing to several factors such as size of purchases, transportation considerations, and geographic issues. We examine three types of pricing associated with business products: geographic pricing, transfer pricing, and discounting.

Geographic pricing

Geographic pricing strategies deal with delivery costs. The pricing strategy that requires the buyer to pay the delivery costs is called *FOB origin pricing*. It stands for "free on board at the point of origin," which means that the price does not include freight charges, and thus the buyer must pay the transportation costs from the seller's warehouse to the buyer's place of business. *FOB destination* indicates that the price does include freight charges, and thus the seller pays these charges.

Transfer pricing

When one unit in an organisation sells a product to another unit, **transfer pricing** occurs. The price is determined by calculating the cost of the product. A transfer price can vary depending on the types of costs included in the calculations. The choice of the costs to include when calculating the transfer price depends on the company's management strategy and the nature of the units' interaction. An organisation also must ensure that transfer pricing is fair to all units involved in the purchases.

transfer pricing prices charged in sales between an organisation's units

Discounting

A **discount** is a deduction from the price of an item. Producers and sellers offer a wide variety of discounts to their customers, including trade, quantity, cash, and seasonal discounts as well as allowances. *Trade discounts* are discounts from the list prices that are offered to marketing intermediaries, or middlemen. *Quantity discounts* are discounts given to customers who buy in large quantities. The seller's per-unit selling cost is lower for larger purchases. *Cash discounts* are discounts offered for prompt payment. A seller may offer a discount of "2/10, net 30," meaning that the buyer may take a 2 per cent discount if the bill is paid within ten days and that the bill must be paid in full within 30 days. A *seasonal discount* is a price reduction to buyers who purchase out of season. This discount lets the seller maintain steadier production during the year. An *allowance* is a reduction in price to achieve a desired goal. Trade-in allowances, for example, are price reductions granted for turning in used equipment, like aircraft, when purchasing new equipment. Table 12.4 describes some of the reasons for using these discounting techniques as well as some examples.

discount a deduction from the price of an item

| TABLE 12.4 | Discounts used for business markets |

Type	Reasons for use	Examples
Trade (functional)	To attract and keep effective resellers by compensating them for performing certain functions, such as transportation, warehousing, selling, and providing credit.	A university bookshop pays about one-third less for a new textbook than the retail price a student pays.
Quantity	To encourage customers to buy large quantities when making purchases and, in the case of cumulative discounts, to encourage customer loyalty.	Numerous companies serving business markets allow a 2 per cent discount if an account is paid within ten days.
Seasonal	To allow a marketer to use resources more efficiently by stimulating sales during off-peak periods.	Hotels provide companies holding national and regional sales meetings with deeply discounted accommodations during the summer months.
Allowance	In the case of a trade-in allowance, to assist the buyer in making the purchase and potentially earn a profit on the resale of used equipment; in the case of a promotional allowance, to ensure that dealers participate in advertising and sales support programmes.	A farm equipment dealer takes a farmer's used tractor as a trade-in on a new one. Nabisco pays a promotional allowance to a supermarket for setting up and maintaining a large end-of-aisle display for a two-week period.

Source: William M. Pride and O. C. Ferrell, *Foundations of Marketing* (Mason, OH: South-Western/Cengage Learning, 2013), 358.

SUMMARY

- Explain what a product is and how products are classified.

A product is everything one receives in an exchange, including all attributes and expected benefits. The product may be a manufactured item, a service, an idea, or some combination of these.

Products are classified according to their ultimate use. Classification affects a product's distribution, promotion, and pricing. Consumer products, which include convenience, shopping, and specialty products, are purchased to satisfy personal and family needs. Business products are purchased for resale, for making other products, or for use in a firm's operations. Business products can be classified as raw materials, major equipment, accessory equipment, component parts, process materials, supplies, and services.

- Discuss the product life-cycle and how it leads to new-product development.

Every product moves through a series of four stages—introduction, growth, maturity, and decline—which together form the product life-cycle. As the product progresses through these stages, its sales and profitability increase, peak, and then decline. Marketers keep track of the life-cycle stage of products in order to estimate when a new product should be introduced to replace a declining one.

- Define *product line* and *product mix* and distinguish between the two.

A product line is a group of similar products marketed by a firm. The products in a product line are related to each other in the way they are produced, marketed, and used. The firm's product mix includes all the products it offers for sale. The width of a mix is the number of product lines it contains. The depth of the mix is the average number of individual products within each line.

- Identify the methods available for changing a product mix.

Customer satisfaction and organisational objectives require marketers to develop, adjust, and maintain an effective product mix. Marketers may improve a product mix by changing existing products, deleting products, and developing new products.

New products are developed through a series of seven steps. The first step, idea generation, involves the accumulation of a pool of possible product ideas. Screening, the second step, removes from consideration those product ideas that do not mesh with organisational goals or resources. Concept testing, the third step, is a phase in which a small sample of potential buyers is exposed to a proposed product through a written or oral description in order to determine their initial reaction and buying intentions. The fourth step, business analysis, generates information about the potential sales, costs, and profits. During the development step, the product idea is transformed into mock-ups and actual prototypes to determine if the product is technically feasible to build and can be produced at reasonable costs. Test marketing is an actual launch of the product in several selected cities. Finally, during commercialisation, plans for full-scale production and marketing are refined and implemented. Most product failures result from inadequate product planning and development.

- Explain the uses and importance of branding, packaging, and labeling.

  A brand is a name, term, symbol, design, or any combination of these that identifies a seller's products as distinct from those of other sellers. Brands can be classified as manufacturer brands, store brands, or generic brands. A firm can choose between two branding strategies—individual branding or family branding. Branding strategies are used to associate (or *not* associate) particular products with existing products, producers, or intermediaries. Packaging protects goods, offers consumer convenience, and enhances marketing efforts by communicating product features, uses, benefits, and image. Labeling provides customers with product information, some of which is required by law.

- Describe the economic basis of pricing and the means by which sellers can control prices and buyers' perceptions of prices.

  Under the ideal conditions of pure competition, an individual seller has no control over the price of its products. Prices are determined by the workings of supply and demand. In our real economy, however, sellers do exert some control, primarily through product differentiation. Product differentiation is the process of developing and promoting differences between one's product and all similar products. Firms also attempt to gain some control over pricing through advertising. A few large sellers have considerable control over prices because each controls a large proportion of the total supply of the product. Firms must consider the relative importance of price to buyers in the target market before setting prices. Buyers' perceptions of prices are affected by the importance of the product to them, the range of prices they consider acceptable, their perceptions of competing products, and their association of quality with price.

- Identify the major pricing objectives used by businesses.

  Objectives of pricing include survival, profit maximisation, target return on investment, achieving market goals, and maintaining the status quo. Firms sometimes have to price products to survive, which usually requires cutting prices to attract customers. ROI is the amount earned as a result of the investment in developing and marketing the product. The firm sets an annual percentage ROI as the pricing goal. Some firms use pricing to maintain or increase their market share. And in industries in which price stability is important, firms often price their products by charging about the same as competitors.

- Examine the three major pricing methods that firms employ.

  The three major pricing methods are cost-based pricing, demand-based pricing, and competition-based pricing. When cost-based pricing is employed, a proportion of the cost is added to the total cost to determine the selling price. When demand-based pricing is used, the price will be higher when demand is higher, and the price will be lower when demand is lower. A firm that uses competition-based pricing may choose to price below competitors' prices, at the same level as competitors' prices, or slightly above competitors' prices.

- Explain the different strategies available to companies for setting prices.

  Pricing strategies fall into five categories: new-product pricing, differential pricing, psychological pricing, product-line pricing, and promotional pricing. Price skimming and penetration pricing are two strategies used for pricing new products. Differential pricing can be accomplished through negotiated pricing, secondary-market pricing, periodic discounting, and random discounting. Types of psychological pricing strategies are odd-number pricing, multiple-unit pricing, reference pricing, bundle pricing, everyday low prices, and customary pricing. Product-line pricing can be achieved through captive pricing, premium pricing, and price lining. The major types of promotional pricing are price-leader pricing, special-event pricing, and comparison discounting.

- Describe three major types of pricing associated with business products.

  Setting prices for business products can be different from setting prices for consumer products as a result of several factors, such as the size of purchases, transportation considerations, and geographic issues. The three types of pricing associated with the pricing of business products are geographic pricing, transfer pricing, and discounting.

EXERCISE QUESTIONS

1 What are the two general categories of products and how do they differ?

2 Describe and give examples of the three levels of product.

3 Why is it so important to manage the product mix?

4 What factors should be considered when choosing a brand name?

5 How can a demand-based pricing method affect consumers?

CASE 12.1

Tata's Nano steers into low pricing

How can a car sell for less than $3,000? That's the price Tata Motors set for its Nano, a four-door, four-seat sub-compact designed specifically for India and introduced in 2009. With a rear-mounted motor, this tiny car initially included absolutely no extras – no radio, no reclining seats, certainly no aircon or electric windows. What the Nano does have, however, is an ultra-low price tag. And that is what makes it very attractive to millions of potential buyers in India. Now "someone who never even dreamed of a car finds it within reach," says Tata's CEO. The range today is more extensive, with various engine options and specifications, but still retails between 140,000 to 210,000 Indian rupees (£2,000 or $3,300 to £2,900 or $4,700).

Racing to develop and market the world's cheapest car has been a challenge, even for a car manufacturer with as much experience as Mumbai-based Tata, which is India's largest automaker and owner of Jaguar and Land Rover in the U.K. The company began working on the Nano in 2003, with the goal of creating a functional yet eye-pleasing design that would fit buyers' lifestyles and tight budgets and, at the same time, be profitable to manufacture and sell. The most essential ingredient was keeping costs in line to keep the car ultra-affordable.

Low price, low costs

The first step in developing the Nano was to establish an upper level for the car's price: roughly one lakh (100,000 Indian rupees), the equivalent of less than £1,400. To sell a car at this price, "you have to cut costs on everything – seats, materials, components – the whole package", says a Tata official. That's exactly what Tata did, using expertise gained from its years of marketing trucks, cars and buses for markets in India, Europe, South America, Southeast Asia, and the Middle East. For instance, Tata sells its Indica compact car for $8,500 in Eastern Europe.

The 330 horsepower engine of the Nano may not win any races, but it can get the car to a top speed of about 80 miles per hour. Thanks to low cost parts and manufacturing, the cost of each engine is only about $700. In contrast, an engine made in the West can be twice as much. By shaving the cost of each part and component, streamlining assembly methods, and offering only a stripped-down basic model, Tata has been able to achieve its low price goal.

What's driving the market?

India's healthy economy is propelling millions of consumers into the middle class and accelerating demand for affordable transportation. As many as 65 million people currently drive small motor scooters in India, often carrying family members on the back. Some of these drivers will be able to trade up to a new car if the price is right.

In fact, sales of small cars are projected to reach 1 million units by 2016. Small wonder that Tata designed its Nano with four doors to appeal to buyers who often have family members and friends riding along. Finally, India's population skews young, with a median age under 25. If Tata can attract young first-time buyers with a low priced model and maintain their loyalty as they trade up to higher priced cars in the years ahead, the company will profit in the long term.

Competition on the roads of India

Competition is fierce at the low end of the car market. Maruti Suzuki India, which sells small cars starting at about $5,000, is the market leader. With its nationwide service network, high brand recognition, and new production facilities in the works, Maruti Suzuki is a formidable competitor.

Other rivals are also expanding to take advantage of this fast-growing segment of the market. Hyundai India, for instance, is opening a global centre for small car manufacturing and adding manufacturing space. Its Santro, which offers both air conditioning and power steering as standard features, sells for about $6,300. Volkswagen's Skoda division offers the low priced Fabia model, among others, in India.

Toyota is designing a no-frills car that will sell in India and other emerging nations for under $7,500. In the process, the company expects to develop new technology that will help it cut costs on other vehicles in its global product mix. Honda has a plant in India and is opening a second plant to support its marketing initiatives in the area. Meanwhile, U.S. carmakers are looking at how they might enter the market in the near future.

Renault-Nissan, working with Indian motorcycle manufacturer Bajaj, is developing a car to be priced around $3,000. The company knows a lot about low cost, low priced cars because since 2004 it has produced its popular $7,000 Logan four-door saloon in Romania and Russia. Nearly half a million Logans are already on the roads of Europe, and even though Renault-Nissan's two plants are operating at full capacity all day and every day, the firm is still struggling to meet ever-growing demand.

To shave costs, Renault-Nissan limited the number of parts that go into the Logan and avoided expensive electronics. To speed development and eliminate the high costs of building prototypes, the company proceeded from digital design directly to production. This alone saved $40 million and is one reason for the CEO's confidence that Renault-Nissan can succeed in the worldwide ultra-low-price segment. "With the Logan, we have the product and we have the lead", he says.

Environmental and safety concerns

As enthusiastic as Tata and other car manufacturers may be about marketing millions of tiny cars with tiny price tags, the car has generated both environmental and safety concerns. Some critics fear that broadening the base of car ownership will only add to the pollution problems in India's largest cities. Where national and local regulations do not require anti-pollution devices, manufacturers are unlikely to install them because of the added costs.

Safety is an issue because more cars on the road mean more traffic congestion and more opportunity for accidents. Cars made by Tata and its competitors comply with all of India's safety standards, but those standards do not require equipment, such as air bags and antilock brakes. Safety advocates worry that people travelling in the smallest, lightest cars will be more vulnerable to serious injury if involved in a traffic accident. For now, the automakers are moving ahead as they monitor the issues and stay alert for possible changes in government regulations.

Getting in gear

Buyers have responded to the Nano's low price tag. Tata received more than 200,000 orders during the 12 months after the car's introduction. Because of limited production capabilities, it has to use a lottery system to select the first 100,000 buyers. Recently, Tata opened a second factory that can produce 250,000 Nanos per year, in an effort to keep up with the expected surge in demand as the Indian economy grows and consumers continue to trade up from motorcycles to cars.

Tata has a long history of good marketing management and above-average profitability. Being based in India gives Tata the advantage of being close to its customers and understanding their needs. Tata's engineers and designers have found creative ways of containing costs to keep the new car ultra-affordable. With increased competition in the super-budget segment, however, Tata will have to get in gear to keep the Nano ahead of the pack.

References: http://tatanano.inservices.tatamotors.com/tatamotors/, July 2011. William M. Pride and O.C. Ferrell, *Marketing* 2012 (Cengage Learning, 2012).

Questions

1 Explain which factors seem to have the greatest influence on Tata's decision about pricing its Nano.

2 What appear to be Tata's primary pricing objectives for the Nano?

3 Assess the level of price competition in India's car industry. What are the implications for Tata's marketing?

CHAPTER REFERENCES

"A Case for Modernising Product Planning," (e-paper) Accept Software Corporation, www.accept360.com/resources/modprodplan, accessed April 2, 2012.

AnandK@TWC, "Google to Discontinue 10 Products, Including Google Desktop, Google Pack," The Windows Club, September 3, 2011, www.thewindowsclub.com/google-discontinue-10-products-including-google-desktop-google-pack.

Apple, http://apple.com accessed February 13, 2012.

Bunkley, Nick, "GM to Reinforce Battery in its Hybrid Car, the Volt," *The New York Times,* January 20, 2012, www. nytimes.com/2012/01/06/business/gm-to-reinforce-battery-in-a-hybrid-car.html.

"Coming Soon: Barq's Root Beer Redesign," Bev Review, February 22, 2012, www.bevreview.com/2012/02/22/coming-soon-barqs-root-beer-redesign/.

"Cup Summit 3," Starbucks, www.starbucks.com/blog/cup-summit-3/1084, accessed March 21, 2012.

Fottrell, Quentin, "New Cheap Alternatives to the iPad 3," *Smart Money*, March 7, 2012, http://blogs.smartmoney.com/advice/2012/03/07/new-cheap-alternatives-to-the-ipad-3/?link=SM_hp_ls4e.

General Mills Cereals, www.generalmills.com/en/Brands/Cereals.aspx, accessed March 30, 2012.

Glazer, Emily and Vranica, Suzanne, "Big Firms Mentor Start-Ups on Their Image," *Wall Street Journal,* March 29, 2012, http://online.wsj.com/article/SB1000142405270 2303816504577309842814468950.html.

Goldstein, Phil, "T-Mobile to Discontinue Sidekick 4G, but May Not Kill Sidekick Brand," Fierce Wireless, March 16, 2012, www.fiercewireless.com/story/t-mobile-discontinue-sidekick-4g-may-not-kill-sidekick-brand/2012-03-16.

Google Project Glass, https://plus.google.com/11162612736 7496192147/posts, accessed April 6, 2012.

Habor, Dominic, "Abercrombie & Fitch Plans Further Price Cuts After 1Q Loss," *TopNews.com*, May 17, 2009, topnews.us/content/25241-abercrombie-fitch-plans-further-price-cuts-after-1q-loss.

Haig, Matt, *Brand Failures: The Truth about the 100 Biggest Branding Mistakes of All Time,* 2011 (Kogan Page Limited, Philadelphia, PA), p. 58, 77, 88

http://amazon.com accessed February 13, 2012.

Jargon, Julie, "Latest Starbucks Concoction: Juice," *Wall Street Journal,* November 11, 2011, http://online.wsj.com/article/SB100014240529702043580045770301121 55716538.html, accessed March 19, 2012; Josh Ozersky, "The Big Gulp," *Time,* March 12, 2012, www.time.com/time/magazine/article/0,9171,2108016,00.html.

Jell-O, www.jello.com, accessed April 2, 2012.

Peña, Joseph, "Aptera Secures Financing, Introduces New 2e Electric Car," *San Diego News Network*, April 14, 2010, sdgln.com/news/2010/04/15/video-aptera-secures-financing-introduces-new-2e-electric-car.

"Pet Insurance," Iams, www.iams.com/pet-health/pet-insurance, accessed April 4, 2012.

Press release, "WD-40 Launches First-Ever Product Line Extension, Introduces New WD-40 Specialist Line of Products," *New York Times,* February 14, 2012, http://markets.on.nytimes.com/research/stocks/news/press_release.asp?docTag=201202141309BIZWIRE_USPRX____BW6491&feedID=600&press_symbol=284382

Procter & Gamble, http://pg.com/en_US/brands/index.shtml accessed February 13, 2012.

SF Park, http://sfpark.org/; Leon Neyfakh, "The Case for the $6 Parking Meter," *The Boston Globe,* January 15, 2012, www.bostonglobe.com/ideas/2012/01/15/the-case-for-parking-meter/H2lh2QJ8wOEgwiMI7yHdVO/story.html.

Slivka, Eric, "Apple Clarifies Warranty Coverage Options for Customers in the European Union," Mac Rumors, March 30, 2012, www.macrumors.com/2012/03/30/apple-clarifies-warranty-coverage-options-for-customers-in-european-union/.

Staff reporter, "Now That's What You Call Brand Loyalty!" *Daily Mail,* March 12, 2012, www.dailymail.co.uk/news/article-2114031/iPad-3-release-date-Pair-sit-head-queue-Apples-new-iPad-5-days-goes-sale.html.

Vibram Five Fingers, www.vibramfivefingers.com/index.htm, accessed April 4, 2012.

"Vitaminwater Accused of Making Misleading Health Claims," Huffington Post, January 3, 2012, www.huffingtonpost.com/2012/01/03/vitaminwater-false-claims_n_1181860.html?ref=food; "Feds Cracking Down on Misleading Labels," National Consumers League, www.nclnet.org/food/85-food-labeling/374-fda-cracking-down-on-misleading-health-claims-on-food-labels, accessed April 1, 2012.

"What Are Store Brands?" PLMA, http://plma.com/storeBrands/factsnew12.html, accessed March 19, 2012; Candace Choi, "Store Brand Groceries Now on Premium Shelves," USA Today, March 25, 2012, www.usatoday.com/money/industries/food/story/2012-03-25/store-brand-groceries/53739828/1.

13 MARKETING CHANNELS

LEARNING OBJECTIVES

Once you complete this chapter, you should be able to:

- Understand the nature of wholesaling in its broadest forms in the marketing channel
- Examine channel players that facilitate wholesaling
- Understand the purpose and function of retailing in the marketing channel
- Describe and distinguish retail locations, major store types and non-store retailing
- Understand how physical distribution activities are integrated into marketing channels and overall marketing strategies, and to examine physical distribution objectives
- Understand about order processing, materials handling and different types of warehousing and their functions
- Appreciate the importance of inventory management and the development of adequate assortments of products for target markets
- Have insight into different transportation methods and how they are selected and coordinated

BUSINESS FOCUS

Multi-channel changes the rules

How did you purchase your last smartphone? From inside a Vodafone or O2 store? A few years ago, this is how most consumers would have selected and acquired their mobile phone upgrade. Teleselling and then the Web enabled an increasing number of consumers to browse selections, read reviews and compare tariffs from the comfort of their homes, receiving their new phone at home in the post. Today's mobile marketing world has further broadened this freedom, so that we are able to select a brand and model while sitting on a train, waiting for friends at a bar or during the break of a sports fixture. While as consumers, new ways of acquiring information and products have been most welcome, opening up an any-time/anywhere purchasing culture, it has presented significant challenges for those businesses supplying our needs and the managers tasked with delivering our products.

In the original business model, Samsung or Nokia had to ensure its products were distributed in a timely fashion to the major retailers'

or mobile phone companies' central warehouses, letting these companies manage distribution out to their stores. Some companies also employed rack jobbers to visit stores directly to stock shelves and store rooms with their handsets. The growth of e-commerce has forced the manufacturers and big mobile phone networks to adopt multi-channel distribution, with home delivery now accounting for more than half of units shipped. Of course, the mobile phone sector is not alone in this growth of home delivery and direct distribution, which has proved good news for City Link, UPS and other delivery firms. The change in consumers' buying behaviour also enabled non-store competitors to emerge, without an expensive store network, instead with single channels of distribution direct to the purchaser's selected address, be it home or workplace.

This growth of mobile commerce, m-commerce, has not only impacted on the channels of distribution, warehousing, inventory management, delivery modes and all aspects

of logistics management, but it has altered the mix of third party suppliers and partners companies rely on in order to do business. Digital selling depends on skills of content providers, social media experts, bloggers and tweeters and a whole set of opinion formers and influencers. So in addition to the physical distribution management players relevant to more traditional channels of distribution, the adoption of a direct channel, digital marketing and direct distribution has necessitated the involvement of a new generation of channel members and facilitating bodies. Multi-channel marketing is now the norm for many manufacturers, brands and retailers, with significant consequences for their channel management and use of third parties to facilitate effective delivery to end-users. Marketers may not be tasked with executing distribution of their products, but they should be aware of the consequences of their channel selection strategies and appreciate the practicalities of managing customers' experiences via the channels they select.

T his chapter examines the roles of wholesaling, retailing and physical distribution management within the marketing channel, without which products would not reach intended users appropriately. Although these areas are normally managed by specialists, marketers must appreciate their importance when developing their marketing programmes.

Wholesaling includes all transactions in which the purchaser intends to use the product for resale, for making other products or for its general business operations. Wholesaling does not include exchanges with the ultimate consumers. Hence, the term wholesaling is used in its broadest sense: intermediaries' activity in the marketing channel between producers and business or trade customers.

Marketers use wholesaling to mean much more than the function of retail wholesalers. The focus is on:

- merchant wholesalers and distributors
- agents and brokers
- manufacturers' own branches and offices
- the "middlemen" in many marketing channels. Retailers are an important part of the marketing channel for many products.

In addition to being part of the distribution channel for a host of products, the characteristics of retailing present retail marketers with many challenges. Retailers are an influential link in the marketing channel because they are both marketers for, and customers of, producers and wholesalers. They perform many marketing activities, such as buying, selling, grading, risk-taking and developing information about consumers' requirements. Of all marketers, retailers are often the most visible to ultimate consumers. They are in a strategic position to gain feedback from consumers, and to relay ideas to producers and intermediaries in the marketing channel. Retailing is an extraordinarily dynamic area of marketing.

Physical distribution is a set of activities that moves products from producers to consumers or end users. These activities include order processing, materials handling, warehousing, inventory management and transportation. While none of these activities would normally be the responsibility of marketing managers, their smooth deployment impacts on customer service levels, customer satisfaction and also customers' perceptions of a brand or business.

The main objective of physical distribution is to decrease costs while increasing customer service. Order processing, the first stage in a physical distribution system, is the receipt and transmission of sales order information. Materials handling, or the physical handling of products, is an important element of physical distribution: packaging, loading, movement and labelling systems must be coordinated to maximise cost reduction and the meeting of customer requirements. Warehousing involves the design and operation of facilities for storing and moving goods. The objective of inventory management is to minimise inventory costs while maintaining a supply of goods adequate for customers' needs. Transportation adds time and place utility to a product by moving it from where it is made to where it is purchased and used. Physical distribution activities should be integrated with marketing channel decisions and adjusted to meet the unique needs of a channel member customer or facilitator.

This chapter addresses wholesalers' and distributors' activities within a marketing channel, the nature of retailing, plus the importance of physical distribution management. Wholesaling is viewed here as *all* exchanges among organisations and individuals in marketing channels, except transactions with ultimate consumers. After examining the role of wholesaling and the major types, the chapter overviews retailing and then turns to physical distribution, its concepts, objectives and techniques: primarily order processing, materials handling, warehousing, inventory management and transportation.

THE NATURE AND IMPORTANCE OF WHOLESALING

Wholesaling comprises all transactions in which the purchaser intends to use the product for resale, for making other products or for general business operations. It does not include exchanges with ultimate consumers. Wholesaling establishments are engaged primarily in selling products directly to industrial, reseller (such as retailers), government and institutional users. This is a broader definition than that applied by the retail trade for cash-and-carry wholesale suppliers.

The term **wholesaling** is used in its broadest sense: intermediaries' activity in the marketing channel between producers and business customers to facilitate the exchange – buying and selling – of goods. A **wholesaler** is an individual or business engaged in facilitating and expediting exchanges that are primarily wholesale transactions. Only occasionally does a wholesaler engage in retail transactions, which are sales to ultimate consumers. A related topic is that of **supply chain management,** which is the orchestration of the channel of distribution – from sourcing supplies, manufacture to delivery to the customer – often with the intention of creating long-term mutually beneficial relationships. Although not part of marketing's remit, those responsible for a business's logistics often focus on the concept of supply chain management.

> **wholesaling** intermediaries' activity in the marketing channel between producers and business customers to facilitate the exchange – buying and selling – of goods
>
> **wholesaler** an individual or business engaged in facilitating and expediting exchanges that are primarily wholesale transactions
>
> **supply chain management** the orchestration of the channel of distribution from sourcing supplies, manufacture to delivery to the customer

THE ACTIVITIES OF WHOLESALERS

In the U.S. and in Europe more than 50 per cent of all products are exchanged, or their exchange is negotiated, through wholesaling institutions. Owing to the strength of large, national retailers in the U.K., wholesaling is not as important in many U.K. consumer markets. There are also far fewer wholesalers. For example, just 27 wholesale companies and buying groups account for 85 per cent of the grocery wholesale market. In Scandinavia, Iberia and much of Eastern Europe, wholesaling companies (or buying groups) account for the bulk of exchanges. Of course, it is important to remember that the distribution of all goods requires wholesaling activities, whether or not a wholesaling institution is involved. Table 13.1 lists the major activities wholesalers perform. The activities are not mutually exclusive; individual wholesalers may perform more or fewer activities than Table 13.1 shows. Wholesalers provide marketing activities for organisations above and below them in the marketing channel.

TABLE 13.1 Major wholesaling activities

Activity	Description
Supply chain management	Creating long-term partnerships among channel members
Wholesale management	Planning, organising, staffing and controlling wholesaling operations
Negotiating with suppliers	Serving as the purchasing agent for customers by negotiating supplies
Promotion	Providing a sales force, advertising, sales promotion, publicity and other promotional mix activity
Warehousing and product handling	Receiving, storing and stock keeping, order processing, packaging, shipping outgoing orders and materials handling
Transport	Arranging and making local and long-distance shipments
Inventory control and data processing	Controlling physical inventory, bookkeeping, recording transactions, keeping records for financial analysis
Security	Safeguarding merchandise
Pricing	Developing prices and providing price quotations
Financing and budgeting	Extending credit, borrowing, making capital investments and forecasting cash flow
Management and marketing assistance to clients	Supplying information about markets and products and providing advisory services to assist customers in their sales efforts

Services for producers

Producers, above wholesalers in the marketing channel, have a distinct advantage when they use wholesalers. Wholesalers perform specialised accumulation and allocation functions for a number of products, thus allowing producers to concentrate on developing and manufacturing products that match business customers' or consumers' wants. Wholesalers provide services to producers as well. By selling a manufacturer's products to retailers and other customers, and by initiating sales contacts with the manufacturer, wholesalers serve as an extension of the producer's sales force. Wholesalers also provide four forms of financial assistance:

1. they often pay the costs of transporting goods
2. they reduce a producer's warehousing expenses and inventory investment by holding goods in inventory
3. they extend credit and assume the losses from buyers who turn out to be poor credit risks
4. when they buy a producer's entire output and pay promptly or in cash, they are a source of working capital.

In addition, wholesalers are conduits for information and market insights within the marketing channel, keeping manufacturers up-to-date on market developments and passing along the manufacturers' promotional plans to other middlemen in the channel.

Ideally, many producers would like more direct interaction with retailers, as close contact with major retail chains may lead to greater shelf-space allocation and higher margins for a producer's goods, there being no middlemen to take a cut. Wholesalers, however, often have close contact with retailers because of their strategic position in the marketing channel. Besides, even though a producer's own sales force is probably more effective in its selling efforts, the costs of maintaining a sales force and performing the activities normally carried out by wholesalers are usually higher than the benefits received from better selling. Wholesalers can also spread their costs over many more products than most producers, resulting in lower costs per product unit. For these reasons, many producers have chosen to control promotion and influence the pricing of products, and have shifted transport, warehousing and financing functions to wholesalers. It must be remembered that the close relationship in the U.K., Benelux, France and Germany between manufacturers and the large retail groups is not typical of much of Europe, where wholesalers tend to act as the manufacturer–retailer interface, particularly in southern, central and eastern Europe.

Services for retailers

Wholesalers help their retailer customers select inventory (stock). In industries where obtaining supplies is important, skilled buying is essential. A wholesaler that buys is a specialist in understanding market conditions and an expert at negotiating final purchases. For example, based on its understanding of local customer needs and market conditions, a building supplies wholesaler purchases inventory ahead of season so that it can provide its retail customers with the building supplies they want when they want them.* A retailer's buyer can thus avoid the responsibility of looking for and coordinating supply sources. Moreover, if the wholesaler makes purchases for several different buyers, expenses can be shared by all customers. A manufacturer's sales people can offer retailers only a few products at a time, but independent wholesalers – or dealers – have a wide range of products always available, often from a variety of producers.

By buying in large quantities and delivering to customers in smaller lots, a wholesaler can perform physical distribution activities – such as transport, materials handling, stock planning, communication and warehousing – more efficiently and can provide more service than a producer or retailer would be able to do with its own physical distribution system. Furthermore, wholesalers can provide quick and frequent delivery even when demand fluctuates. They are experienced in providing fast delivery at low cost, thus allowing the producer and the wholesalers' customers to avoid the risks associated with holding large product inventories.*

Because they carry products for many customers, wholesalers can maintain a wide product line at a relatively low cost. Often wholesalers can perform storage and warehousing activities more efficiently, permitting retailers to concentrate on other marketing activities. When wholesalers provide storage and warehousing, they generally take on the ownership function as well, an arrangement that frees retailers' and producers' capital for other purposes.

Wholesalers are very important in reaching global markets. Approximately 85 per cent of all prescription drugs sold in Europe go through wholesalers that are within national borders. In the future,

SUCCESS STORY

Zara uses technology to streamline operations

Zara, a fashion retailer owned by Inditex and headquartered in Spain, has successfully harnessed the power of information technology as a fundamental part of its business.

In a competitive industry where ordering products months in advance is common, the ability to react quickly to changing trends has transformed Zara into one of the world's biggest clothing retailers. Technology allows the company to monitor inventory, sales patterns, customer buying behaviour and supply chains to give the customer what they want, when they want it.

The fashion giant's marketing success is based on the vertical integration of design, "just-in-time" production, delivery and sales through a fast-expanding chain of stores offering affordable fashion. The designers also keep in touch with Zara store managers to determine the bestsellers. A new product is delivered to stores within five weeks after its design; for a new version of an existing model, this is reduced to only fourteen days. Thanks to this effective method of fine-tuning routes to market Zara is prevented from having to discount slow-selling products, as is common among other retailers.

Zara has over five thousand stores in about 80 nations, 60 per cent of them in Europe. Zara's marketing approach is to open a few test stores in a new country to develop a better insight into local consumers before penetrating further in to that market. It has become the first global retailer to sell fashion products especially for the seasons of the southern hemisphere. Zara has proved that it is possible – and lucrative – to mass market cheap, fast and ethical fashion to maximise customer satisfaction and loyalty.

References: 'Inditex: The future of fast fashion', www.economist.com/node/4086117, June 16, 2005; 'Global stretch. When will Zara hit its limits?', *The Economist*, March 10, 2011; 'Fast fashion: Zara in India', *Forbes*, July 29, 2010; Marion Hume, 'The secrets of Zara's success', *The Telegraph*, 22 June 2011, http://fashion.telegraph.co.uk/newsfeatures/TMG8589217/The-secrets-of-Zarassuccess.html#

© DAVID PEARSON / ALAMY

it is anticipated that more wholesalers will operate across borders, particularly as changing EU regulations and the movement towards European monetary union reduce EU restrictions.*

CLASSIFYING WHOLESALERS

Many types of wholesaler meet the different needs of producers and retailers. In addition, new institutions and establishments develop in response to producers and retail organisations that want to take over wholesaling functions. Wholesalers adjust their activities as the forces of the marketing environment change.

Wholesalers are classified along several dimensions. Whether a wholesaler is owned by the producer – often termed a company-owned dealership – influences how it is classified. Wholesalers are also grouped according to whether they take title to (actually own) the products they handle. The range of services provided is another criterion used for classification. Finally, wholesalers are classified according to the breadth and depth of their product lines. Using these dimensions, this section discusses three general categories, or types, of wholesaling establishment:

1. merchant wholesalers
2. agents and brokers
3. manufacturers' sales branches and offices.

Remember that the term "wholesaling" is used here in its broader context: intermediaries' activity in the marketing channel between producers and business-to-business customers.

Merchant wholesalers

Merchant wholesalers (see Figure 13.1) take title to goods and assume the risks associated with ownership. They are independently owned businesses, buying and reselling products to business or retailer customers. Some are involved with packaging and developing their own-label brands for their retailer customers. Industrial product merchant wholesalers tend to be better established and earn higher profits than consumer goods wholesalers and are likely to have selective distribution arrangements with manufacturers. These wholesalers enable producers to service customers if they have inadequate resources to sell directly. Wholesalers provide the producer with market coverage, making sales contacts, storing stock, handling orders, collecting marketing intelligence and providing customer service.* Merchant wholesalers are referred to by various names: wholesaler, jobber, distributor, assembler, exporter and importer. They fall into two categories: full service or limited service.

merchant wholesalers wholesalers that take title to goods and assume the risks associated with ownership
Merchant wholesalers

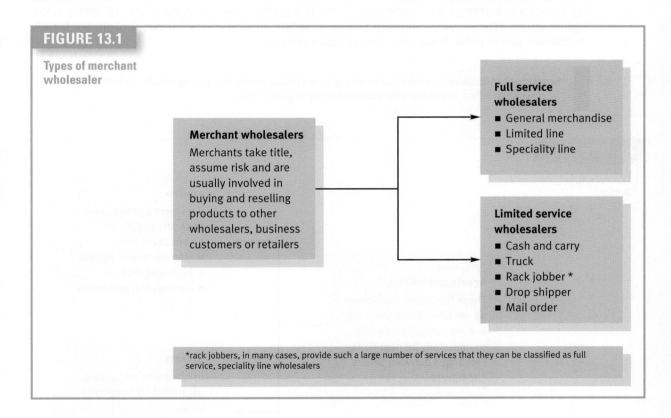

FIGURE 13.1

Types of merchant wholesaler

Merchant wholesalers
Merchants take title, assume risk and are usually involved in buying and reselling products to other wholesalers, business customers or retailers

Full service wholesalers
- General merchandise
- Limited line
- Speciality line

Limited service wholesalers
- Cash and carry
- Truck
- Rack jobber *
- Drop shipper
- Mail order

*rack jobbers, in many cases, provide such a large number of services that they can be classified as full service, speciality line wholesalers

Full service merchant **Full service wholesalers** are middlemen who offer the widest possible range of wholesaling functions. Their business customers rely on them for product availability, suitable assortments, bulk breaking of larger quantities into smaller orders, financial assistance and credit lines, technical advice and after-sales service. Full service wholesalers often provide their immediate customers with marketing support. Grocery wholesalers help smaller retailers with store design and layout, site selection, personnel training, financing, merchandising, advertising, coupon redemption and scanning. Gross margins are high, but so are operating expenses.

full service wholesalers middlemen who offer the widest possible range of wholesaling functions

Limited service merchant wholesalers **Limited service wholesalers** provide only some marketing services and specialise in few functions. The other functions are provided by producers, other middlemen or even by customers. Limited service merchant wholesalers take title to merchandise, but often do not deliver the merchandise, grant credit, provide marketing intelligence, carry stocks or plan ahead for customers' future needs. They earn smaller profit margins than full service merchant wholesalers. Relatively few in number, these wholesalers are important for speciality foods, perishable items, construction supplies and coal.

> **limited service wholesalers** middlemen who provide only some marketing services and specialise in a few functions

Agents and brokers

Agents and brokers (see Figure 13.2) negotiate purchases and expedite sales but do not take title to products. They are **functional middlemen**; intermediaries who perform a limited number of marketing activities in exchange for a commission, which is generally based on the products' selling price. Agents are middlemen who represent buyers or sellers on a permanent basis. Brokers are usually middlemen whom either buyers or sellers employ temporarily.

> **functional middlemen** intermediaries who perform a limited number of marketing activities in exchange for commission sellers, and usually offer customers complete product lines

FIGURE 13.2

Types of agent and broker

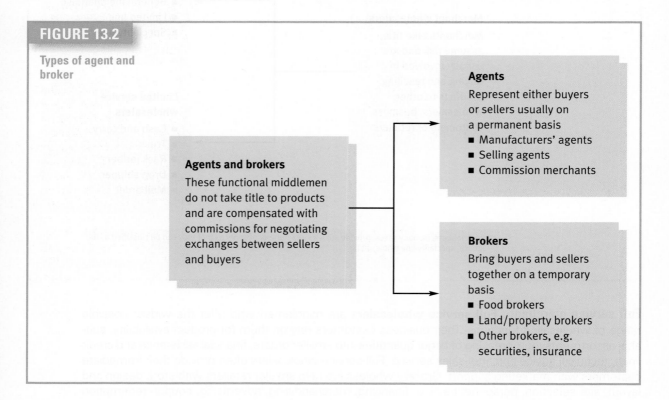

Agents and brokers
These functional middlemen do not take title to products and are compensated with commissions for negotiating exchanges between sellers and buyers

Agents
Represent either buyers or sellers usually on a permanent basis
- Manufacturers' agents
- Selling agents
- Commission merchants

Brokers
Bring buyers and sellers together on a temporary basis
- Food brokers
- Land/property brokers
- Other brokers, e.g. securities, insurance

Table 13.2 summarises the different categories of full service and limited service merchant wholesalers: **general merchandise wholesalers**, including **distributors**, **limited line wholesalers**, **speciality line wholesalers**, plus: **rack jobbers**; **cash and carry wholesalers**; **truck wholesalers**; **drop shippers**; and **mail-order wholesalers**.

general merchandise wholesalers middlemen who carry a wide product mix but offer limited depth within the product lines

distributors companies that buy and sell on their own account but tend to deal in the goods of only certain specified manufacturers

limited line wholesalers wholesalers that carry only a few product lines but offer an extensive assortment of products within those lines

speciality line wholesalers middlemen who carry the narrowest range of products, usually a single product line or a few items within a product line

rack jobbers speciality line wholesalers that own and maintain their own display racks in supermarkets and chemists

cash and carry wholesalers middlemen whose customers will pay cash and provide transport

truck wholesalers limited service wholesalers that transport products direct to customers for inspection and selection

drop shippers intermediaries who take title to goods and negotiate sales but never actually take possession of products

mail-order wholesalers wholesalers that use catalogues instead of sales forces to sell products to retail, industrial and institutional buyers

---

TABLE 13.2 Types of full and limited service merchant wholesalers

Categories of full service merchant wholesalers	Categories of limited service merchant wholesalers
1. General merchandise wholesalers Middlemen who carry a wide product mix but offer limited depth within product lines. Medicines, hardware, non-perishable foods, cosmetics, detergents, tobacco. Develop strong, mutually beneficial relationships with local retail stores, who often buy all their needs from these wholesalers. For industrial customers, these wholesalers provide all supplies and accessories and are often called *industrial distributors* or *mill supply houses.* Distributors are companies which buy and sell on their own account but tend to deal in the goods of only certain specified manufacturers. 2. Limited line wholesalers Wholesalers that carry only a few product lines, such as groceries, lighting fixtures, drilling equipment, construction equipment, but offer an extensive assortment of products within these lines. They provide similar services to general merchandise wholesalers. In business markets, they serve large geographic areas and provide technical expertise. In consumer goods markets, they often supply single or limited line retailers. Some computer limited line wholesalers provide customers with the products of only four or five manufacturers, but for only a limited number of their lines.	1. Cash and carry wholesalers Their customers are retailers or small industrial businesses who provide their own transport and collect from wholesale depots. Some full service wholesalers also set up cash and carry depots in order to reduce their operating costs and boost margins when supplying smaller retailer or business customers. Cash and carry middlemen generally handle a limited line of products with a high turnover rate, such as groceries, building materials, electrical supplies, office supplies. For example, Booker has a network of cash and carry warehouse depots stocking fresh and frozen foods, cigarettes, wines and spirits, meats and provisions. Selling only to the trade, Booker offers bulk discounts to hotels, restaurants, the catering industry and local small shops. Cash and carry operators have little or no expenditures for outside sales staff, marketing, research, promotion, credit or delivery. Their business customers benefit from lower prices and immediate access to products. 2. Truck wholesalers These wholesalers, sometimes called *truck jobbers,* transport a limited line of products directly to customers for on-the-spot inspection and selection. Often small operators who own and drive their own trucks or vans, they tend to have regular routes, calling on retailers and businesses to determine their needs. They may carry items, such as perishables, which other wholesalers do not stock. Meat, service station supplies and tobacco lines are often carried by truck jobbers.

(continued)

TABLE 13.2　Types of full and limited service merchant wholesalers *(Continued)*

Categories of full service merchant wholesalers	Categories of limited service merchant wholesalers
3. Speciality line wholesalers These middlemen carry the narrowest range of products, often only a single product line or a few items within a product line. Shellfish, fruit or cheese wholesalers are speciality line wholesalers. They understand the particular requirements of the ultimate buyer and offer their customers detailed product knowledge and depth of choice. To assist retailers, they may set up displays and arrange merchandise. In industrial markets, they are often better placed than the manufacturer to offer customers technical advice and service. *Rack jobbers* are speciality line wholesalers who own and maintain their display racks in supermarkets and pharmacies. They specialise in non-food items, notably branded, widely advertised products sold on a self-service basis, which retailers prefer not to order or stock themselves because of inconvenience or risk. Health and beauty aids, toys, books, magazines, DVDs, hardware, housewares and stationery are typical products handled by rack jobbers. They send out delivery personnel who set up displays, mark merchandise, stock shelves and keep billing records. The retailer customer only has to provide the space. Most rack jobbers operate on a pay and display basis, taking back any unsold stock from the retailer.	Truck jobbers sell, promote and transport goods, but tend to be classified as limited service merchant wholesalers because they do not provide credit lines. Low volume sales and relatively high levels of customer service result in high operating costs. In eastern and southern Europe, truck jobbers are common marketing channel intermediaries. 3. Drop shippers These intermediaries, also known as *desk jobbers,* take title to goods and negotiate sales, but never take actual possession of products. They forward orders from retailers, industrial buyers or other wholesalers to manufacturers and arrange for large shipments of items to be delivered directly from producers to customers. The drop shipper assumes responsibility for products during the entire transaction, including the costs of any unsold goods. Drop shippers are involved most commonly in the large volume purchases of bulky goods such as coal, coke, oil, chemicals, timber and building materials. Normally sold in wagon loads, these products are expensive to handle and ship relative to their unit value, so it is sensible to minimise unloading. One facet of drop shipping is its use by the large supermarket retailers, direct from manufacturers to the larger supermarket stores. These large supermarkets can each sell an entire lorry load of certain produce. Drop shippers incur no stockholding costs and provide only minimal customer assistance, leading to low operating costs which can be passed on to customers. They do provide planning, credit and personal selling services. 4. Mail order wholesalers These wholesalers use catalogues instead of sales forces to sell to retail, institutional and industrial buyers. Customers use telecommunications, the Internet or post to send orders which are often despatched through courier companies or the postal service. This enables customers in remote, inaccessible areas to be serviced. Mail order in general is growing, and is particularly important for cosmetics, speciality foods, hardware, sporting goods, business and office supplies, car parts, clothing and music. Payment is usually expected up-front by cash or credit card, but discounts may be offered for bulk orders. Mail order wholesalers hold stocks but provide little other service.

References: Louis W. Stern, Barton A. Weitz, 'The revolution in distribution: challenges and opportunities' (Special Issue: The Revolution in Retailing), *Long Range Planning*, December 1997, vol. 30, no. 6, pp. 823–829; Leonard J. Kistner, C. Anthony Di Benedetto, Sriraman Bhoovaraghavan, 'An integrated approach to the development of channel strategy', *Industrial Marketing Management*, October 1994, vol. 23, no. 4, pp. 315–322; Elizabeth Jane Moore, 'Grocery distribution in the UK: recent changes and future prospects', *International Journal of Retail & Distribution Management*, 19 July 1991, pp. 18–24; 'Drop-shipping grows to save depot costs', *Supermarket News*, 1 April 1985, pp. 1, 17.

Although agents and brokers perform even fewer functions than limited service wholesalers, they are usually specialists in particular products or types of customer, and can provide valuable sales expertise. They know their markets well and often form long-lasting associations with customers. Agents and brokers enable manufacturers to expand sales when resources are limited, to benefit from the services of a trained sales force and to hold down personal selling costs. However, despite the advantages they offer, agents and brokers face increased competition from merchant wholesalers, manufacturers' sales branches and offices, and direct sales efforts, including the growing use of the Internet.

This section concentrates on three types of agent:

1. manufacturers' agents
2. selling agents
3. commission merchants

as well as examining the brokers' role in bringing about exchanges between buyers and sellers. Table 13.3 summarises services provided by wholesalers including limited service merchant wholesalers, agents and brokers.

| **TABLE 13.3** | Services provided by wholesalers |

a Various services provided by limited service merchant wholesalers	Cash and carry	Truck wholesaler[a]	Drop shipper[b]	Mail order
Physical possession of merchandise	Yes	Yes	No	Yes
Personal sales calls on customers	No	Yes	No	No
Information about market conditions	No	Yes	Yes	Yes
Advice to customers	No	Yes	Yes	No
Stocking and maintenance of merchandise in customers' stores	No	Yes	No	No
Credit to customers	No	No	Yes	Some
Delivery of merchandise to customers	No	Yes	No	No

b Various services agents and brokers provide	Brokers	Manufacturers' agents	Selling agents	Commission merchants
Physical possession of merchandise	No	Some	No	Yes
Long term relationship with buyers or sellers	No	Yes	Yes	Yes
Representation of competing product lines	Yes	No	No	Yes
Limited geographic territory	No	Yes	No	No
Credit to customers	No	No	Yes	Some
Delivery of merchandise to customers	No	Some	Yes	Yes

[a] Also called truck jobber.
[b] Also called desk jobber.

Agents   Manufacturers' agents – who account for over half of all agent wholesalers – are independent middlemen or distributors who represent two or more sellers and usually offer customers complete product lines. They sell and take orders year round, much as a manufacturer's sales office does. Restricted to a particular territory, a manufacturer's agent handles non-competing and complementary products. The relationship between the agent and each manufacturer is governed by written agreements explicitly outlining territories, selling price, order handling and terms of sale relating to delivery, service and warranties. Manufacturers' agents are commonly used in the sale of clothing and accessories, machinery and equipment, iron, steel, furniture, automotive products, electrical goods and certain food items.

manufacturers' agents independent middlemen or distributors who represent two or more

Although most manufacturers' agents run small enterprises, their employees are professional, highly skilled sales people. The agents' major advantages, in fact, are their wide range of contacts and strong customer relationships. These intermediaries help large producers minimise the costs of developing new sales territories and adjust sales strategies for different products in different locations. Agents are also useful to small producers who cannot afford outside sales forces of their own, because they incur no costs until the agents have actually sold something. By concentrating on a limited number of products, agents can mount an aggressive sales effort that would be impossible with any other distribution method except producer-owned sales branches and offices. In addition, agents are able to spread operating expenses among non-competing products and thus offer each manufacturer lower prices for services rendered.

The chief disadvantage of using agents is the higher commission rate (usually 10 to 15 per cent) they charge for new product sales. When sales of a new product begin to build, total selling costs go up, and producers sometimes transfer the selling function to in-house sales representatives. For this reason, agents try to avoid depending on a single product line; most work for more than one manufacturer. Manufacturers' agents have little or no control over producers' pricing and marketing policies. They do occasionally store and transport products, assist with planning and provide promotional support. Some agents help retailers advertise and maintain a service support organisation. The more services offered, the higher an agent's commission.

Selling agents market either all of a specified product line or a manufacturer's entire output. They perform every wholesaling activity except taking title to products. Selling agents usually assume the sales function for several producers at a time and are often used in place of a marketing department. In contrast to other agent wholesalers, selling agents generally have no territorial limits, and have complete authority over prices, promotion and distribution. They play a key role in the advertising, marketing research and credit policies of the sellers they represent, at times even advising on product development and packaging.

 selling agents agents who market either all of a specified product line or a manufacturer's entire output

Selling agents, who account for about 1 per cent of the wholesale trade, are used most often by small producers or by manufacturers who find it difficult to maintain a marketing department because of seasonal production or other factors. A producer having financial problems may also engage a selling agent. By so doing, the producer relinquishes some control of the business but may gain working capital by avoiding immediate marketing costs. To avoid conflicts of interest, selling agents represent non-competing product lines. The agents play an important part in the distribution of textiles, and they also sometimes handle canned foods, household furnishings, clothing, timber and metal products. In these industries, competitive pressures increase the importance of marketing relative to production, and the selling agent is a source of essential marketing and financial expertise.

Commission merchants are agents who receive goods on consignment from local sellers and negotiate sales in large central markets. Most often found in agricultural marketing, commission merchants take possession of commodities in lorry loads, arrange for any necessary grading or storage, and transport the commodities to auction or markets where they are sold. When sales have been completed, an agent deducts a commission plus the expense of making the sale and then turns over the profits to the producer.

commission merchants agents who receive goods on consignment from local sellers and negotiate sales in large central markets

Sometimes called factor merchants, these agents may have broad powers regarding prices and terms of sale, and they specialise in obtaining the best price possible under market conditions. Commission merchants offer planning assistance and sometimes extend credit, but they do not usually provide promotional support. Because commission merchants deal in large volumes, their per unit costs are usually low. Their services are most useful to small producers who must get products to buyers but choose not to field a sales force or accompany the goods to market themselves. In addition to farm products, commission merchants may handle textiles, art, furniture or seafood products. Businesses – including farms – that use commission merchants have little control over pricing, although the seller can specify a minimum price. Generally, the seller is able to supervise the agent's actions through a check of the commodity prices published regularly in newspapers. Large producers, however, need to maintain closer contact with the market and so have limited need for commission merchants.

Brokers Brokers seek out buyers or sellers and help negotiate exchanges. In other words, brokers' primary purpose is to bring buyers and sellers together. Thus, brokers perform fewer functions than other intermediaries. They are not involved in financing or physical possession, have no authority to set prices and assume almost no risks. Instead, they offer their customers specialised knowledge of a particular commodity and a network of established contacts.

Brokers are especially useful to sellers of certain types of product who market those products only occasionally. Sellers of used machinery, seasonal food products, financial securities and land/property may not know of potential buyers. A broker can furnish them with this information. The party who engages the broker's services – usually the seller – pays the broker's commission when the transaction is completed. Many consumers these days deal with insurance brokers when insuring a car or house contents, or with a mortgage broker when buying a house or moving.

Food brokers – the most common type of broker – are intermediaries who sell food and general merchandise items to retailer-owned and merchant wholesalers, grocery chains, industrial buyers and food processors. Food brokers enable buyers and sellers to adjust to fluctuating market conditions. They also aid in grading, negotiating and inspecting foods, and in some cases they store and deliver products. Because of the seasonal nature of food production, the association between broker and producer is temporary – though many mutually beneficial broker-producer relationships are resumed year after year. Because food brokers provide a range of services on a somewhat permanent basis and in specific geographic territories, they can more accurately be described as manufacturers' agents.

food brokers intermediaries who sell food and general merchandise items to retailer-owned and merchant wholesalers, grocery chains, industrial buyers and food processors

Manufacturers' sales branches and offices

Sometimes called manufacturers' wholesalers or dealerships, manufacturers' sales branches and offices resemble merchant wholesalers' operations. These producer-owned middlemen account for about 9 per cent of wholesale establishments and generate approximately a third (31 per cent) of all wholesale sales.* **Sales branches** are manufacturer-owned middlemen selling products and providing support services to the manufacturer's sales force, especially in locations where large customers are concentrated and demand is high. They offer credit, deliver goods, give promotional assistance and furnish other services. In many cases, they carry inventory, although this practice often duplicates the functions of other channel members and is now declining. Customers include retailers, business buyers and other wholesalers. Branch operations are common in the electrical supplies, plumbing, timber and car parts industries.

sales branches manufacturer-owned middlemen selling products and providing support services to the manufacturer's sales force, especially in locations where large customers are concentrated and demand is high

Sales offices are manufacturer-owned operations that provide support services that are normally associated with agents. Like sales branches, they are located away from manufacturing plants, but unlike branches, they carry no inventory. A manufacturer's sales offices or branches may sell products that enhance the manufacturer's own product line. For example, Hiram Walker, a distiller, imports wine from Spain to increase the number of products its sales offices can offer wholesalers. Most large manufacturers have their own networks of sales branches and sales offices.

> **sales offices** manufacturer-owned operations that provide support services normally associated with agents

Manufacturers may set up sales branches or sales offices so that they can reach customers more effectively by performing wholesaling functions themselves. A manufacturer may also set up these branches or offices when the required specialist wholesaling services are not available through existing middlemen. In some situations, however, a manufacturer may bypass its wholesaling organisation entirely, if the producer decides to serve large retailer customers or even consumers directly. One major distiller bottles own-label spirits for a U.K. grocery chain and separates this operation completely from the company's sales office, which serves other retailers.

FACILITATING AGENCIES

The total marketing channel is more than a chain linking the producer, intermediary and buyer. **Facilitating agencies** – transport companies, insurance companies, advertising agencies, marketing research agencies and financial institutions – may perform activities that enhance channel functions. Note, however, that any of the functions these facilitating agencies perform may be taken over by the regular marketing intermediaries in the marketing channel.

> **facilitating agencies** organisations such as transport companies, insurance companies, advertising agencies, marketing research agencies and financial institutions that perform activities that enhance channel functions

The basic difference between channel members and facilitating agencies is that channel members perform the negotiating functions (buying, selling and taking title), whereas facilitating agencies do not: they perform only the various tasks that are detailed below.* In other words, facilitating agencies assist in the operation of the channel, but they do not sell products. The channel manager may view the facilitating agency as a sub-contractor to which various distribution tasks can be farmed out according to the principle of specialisation and division of labour.*

Channel members (producers, wholesalers, distributors or retailers) may rely on facilitating agencies because they believe that these independent businesses will perform various activities more efficiently and more effectively than they themselves could. Facilitating agencies are functional specialists that perform special tasks for channel members without getting involved in directing or controlling channel decisions. Public warehouses, finance companies, transport companies and trade shows and trade markets are facilitating agencies that expedite the flow of products through marketing channels.

Public warehouses

Public warehouses are storage facilities available for a fee. Producers, wholesalers and retailers may rent space in a warehouse instead of constructing their own facilities or using a merchant wholesaler's storage services. Many warehouses also order, deliver, collect accounts and maintain display rooms where potential buyers can inspect products.

> **public warehouses** storage facilities available for a fee

To use goods as collateral for a loan, a channel member may place products in a bonded warehouse. If it is too impractical or expensive to transfer goods physically, the channel member may arrange for a public warehouser to verify that goods are in the channel member's own facilities and then issue receipts for lenders.* Under this arrangement, the channel member retains possession of the products but the warehouser has control. Many field public warehousers know where their clients can borrow working capital and are sometimes able to arrange low-cost loans.

Finance companies

Wholesalers and retailers may be able to obtain financing by transferring ownership of products to a sales finance company or bank while retaining physical possession of the goods. Often called "floor planning", this form of financing enables wholesalers and retailers – especially car and electrical appliance dealers – to offer a greater selection of products for customers and thus increase sales. Loans may be due immediately upon sale, so products financed this way are usually well known, sell relatively easily and present little risk.

Other financing functions are performed by factors – organisations that provide clients with working capital by buying their accounts receivable or by lending money, using the accounts receivable as collateral. Most factors minimise their own risks by specialising in particular industries, in order to better evaluate individual channel members within those industries. Factors usually lend money for a longer time than banks. They may help clients improve their credit and collection policies, and may also provide management expertise.

Transport companies

Rail, road, air and other carriers are facilitating agencies that help manufacturers and retailers transport products. Each form of transport has its own advantages. Railways ship large volumes of bulky goods at low cost; in fact, outside the U.K., a "unit train" is the cheapest form of overland transport for ore, grain or other commodities. Air transport is relatively expensive but is often preferred for shipping high-value or perishable goods. Trucks, which usually carry short-haul, high-value goods, now carry more and more products because factories are moving closer to their markets. As a result of technological advances, pipelines now transport powdered solids and fluidised solid materials, as well as petroleum and natural gas.

Transport companies sometimes take over the functions of other middlemen. Because of the ease and speed of using air transport for certain types of product, parcel express companies can eliminate the need for their clients to maintain large stocks and branch warehouses. In other cases, freight forwarders perform accumulation functions by combining less than full shipments into full loads and passing on the savings to customers – perhaps charging a wagon rate rather than a less-than-wagon rate.

Trade shows and trade markets

Trade shows and trade markets enable manufacturers or wholesalers to exhibit products to potential buyers, and so help the selling and buying functions. **Trade shows** are industry exhibitions that offer both selling and non-selling benefits.* On the selling side, trade shows let vendors identify prospects; gain access to key decision-makers; disseminate facts about their products, services and personnel; and actually sell products and service current accounts through contacts at the show.* Trade shows

Many consumer durables and food lines depend on sea freight to reach their intended markets

also allow a company to reach potential buyers who have not been approached through regular selling efforts. In fact, many trade show visitors have not recently been contacted by a sales representative of any company within the past year. Many of these individuals are, therefore, willing to travel several hundred miles to attend trade shows to learn about new goods and services. The non-selling benefits include opportunities to maintain the company image with competitors, customers and the industry; gather information about competitors' products and prices; and identify potential channel members.* Trade shows have a positive influence on other important marketing variables, such as maintaining or enhancing company morale, product testing and product evaluation.

 trade shows industry exhibitions that offer both selling and non-selling benefits

Trade shows can permit direct buyer–seller interaction and may eliminate the need for agents. Companies exhibit at trade shows because of the high concentration of prospective buyers for their products. Studies show that it takes, on average, 5.1 sales calls to close an industrial business-to-business sale but less than 1 sales call (0.8) to close a trade show lead. The explanation for the latter figure is that more than half of the customers who purchase a product based on information gained at a trade show order the product by mail or by phone after the show. When customers use these more impersonal methods to gather information, the need for major sales calls to provide such information can be eliminated. Most manufacturers have sales and technical personnel who attend relevant trade shows in key target market territories. Birmingham's National Exhibition Centre (NEC) offers a 240-hectare (600-acre) site, with open display areas, plus 125000 square metres (156000 square yards) of covered exhibition space, hotels, parking for thousands of cars, plus rail and air links. Each year there are toy, fashion, giftware and antique trade fairs at the NEC, when trade customers can select merchandise for their next sales seasons. **Trade markets** are relatively permanent facilities that businesses can rent to exhibit products year round. At these markets, such products as furniture, home decorating supplies, toys, clothing and gift items are sold to wholesalers and retailers.

 trade markets relatively permanent facilities that businesses can rent to exhibit products year round

RETAILING

Retailing includes all transactions in which the buyer intends to consume the product through personal, family or household use. The buyers in retail transactions are the ultimate consumers. A **retailer** is a business that purchases products for the purpose of reselling them to the ultimate consumers, the general public, often from a shop or store, but increasingly also online, adopting a multi-channel strategy. As the link between producers and consumers, retailers occupy an important and highly demanding position in the marketing channel. It is complicated, too: retailers sell other companies' products, yet have to devise their own product/service mixes. They devise their own target market strategies and conduct analyses of marketing opportunities. The merchandise they sell derives from producers that have undertaken their own analysis of marketing opportunities and developed their own target market strategies and brand positioning. These strategies – producers' and retailers' – have to mesh in order for all channel members to make adequate financial returns, while ultimately striving to give satisfaction to the consumer. The growth of retail own-label brands has added to the complexity, with retailers now creating their own brands, products and designs of merchandise, often retailed alongside the proprietary brands of manufacturers.

retailing all transactions in which the buyer intends to consume the product through personal, family or household use
retailer a business that purchases products for the purpose of reselling them to ultimate consumers – the general public – often from a shop or store

By providing assortments of products to match consumers' requirements, retailers create place, time, possession and form utilities:

- *Place utility* means moving products from wholesalers or producers to a location where consumers want to buy them.
- *Time utility* involves maintaining specific business hours to make products available when consumers want them.
- *Possession utility* means facilitating the transfer of ownership or use of a product to consumers.
- In the case of services such as hairdressing, dry cleaning, restaurants and car repairs, retailers themselves develop most of the product utilities. The services of such retailers provide aspects of *form utility* associated with the production process.

Retailers of services usually have more direct contact with consumers and more opportunity to alter the product in the marketing mix.

Retail locations

The traditional hub of most cities and towns is the **central business district (CBD)**, the focus for shopping, banking and commerce, and hence the busiest part of the whole area for traffic, public transport and pedestrians. Examples are London's Oxford and Regent Streets, the Champs Elysées in Paris and Berlin's Kurfürstendamm.* The CBD is sub-divided into zones: generally, retailers are clustered together in a zone; banking and insurance companies locate together; legal offices occupy neighbouring premises; municipal offices and amenities are built on adjoining plots (town hall, library, law courts, art galleries). Within the shopping zone certain streets at the centre of the zone will have the main shops and the highest levels of pedestrian footfall. In this area, known as the **prime pitch**, the key traders or magnets brands will occupy prominent sites, so generating much of the footfall. Other retailers vie to be located close to these key traders so as to benefit from the customer traffic they generate. The highest rents are therefore paid for such sites. Secondary sites are suitable for speciality retailers or discounters, which have either lower margins or lower **customer thresholds**– the number of customers required to make a profit. Figure 13.3 shows the composition of a typical central business district (CBD).

> **central business district (CBD)** the traditional hub of most cities and towns; the focus for shopping, banking and commerce, and hence the busiest part of the whole area
> **prime pitch** the area at the centre of the shopping zone with the main shops and the highest levels of pedestrian footfall
> **customer threshold** the number of customers required to make a profit

Historically, as urban areas expanded during the early part of the twentieth century, they joined and subsequently swallowed up neighbouring towns and villages. The shopping centres of these settlements survived to become the **suburban centres** of the now larger city or town. Where the expansion of the town was planned, suburban centres were created at major road junctions to cater for local shopping needs and reduce demands and congestion in the CBD.* During the 1970s, as rents in the CBD rose and sites sufficient for large, open-plan stores became harder to obtain, retailers looked to the green fields adjacent to outer ring roads for expansion. The superstore era had dawned as the major grocery, carpet and furniture, electrical and DIY retailers opened free-standing "sheds". Needing more space to display stock and sell their goods than they could afford or obtain in the CBD or even suburban centre, but still requiring high traffic levels, they sought sites adjacent to major road arteries into the CBD. Relocating these stores to non-retail areas of the city, and particularly to **edge-of-town sites**, helped redistribute traffic volumes and make use of the latest infrastructure. Retailers no longer had to occupy run-down warehouses; they could acquire undeveloped land on the edge of built-up areas and provide purpose-built stores, parking facilities and amenities for their customers.* The progression of the out-of-town concept and relaxation of planning regulations by local authorities led to the mid-1980s initiation of **retail parks**, in which free-standing superstores,

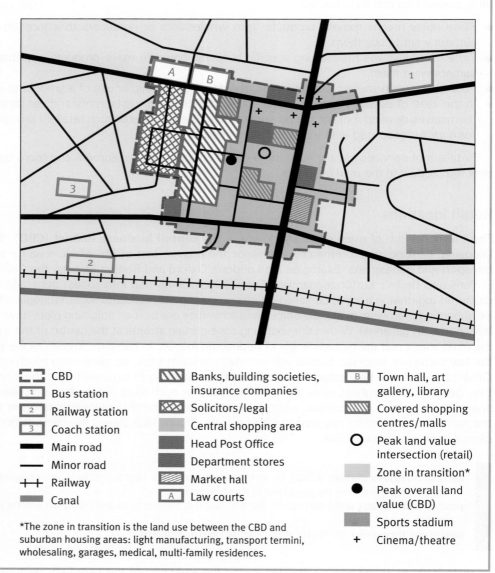

FIGURE 13.3

The composition of a typical central business district (CBD)

Key:

- CBD
- 1 Bus station
- 2 Railway station
- 3 Coach station
- Main road
- Minor road
- ++ Railway
- Canal

- Banks, building societies, insurance companies
- Solicitors/legal
- Central shopping area
- Head Post Office
- Department stores
- Market hall
- A Law courts

- B Town hall, art gallery, library
- Covered shopping centres/malls
- O Peak land value intersection (retail)
- Zone in transition*
- ● Peak overall land value (CBD)
- Sports stadium
- + Cinema/theatre

*The zone in transition is the land use between the CBD and suburban housing areas: light manufacturing, transport termini, wholesaling, garages, medical, multi-family residences.

Source: Lyndon Simkin and Sally Dibb

each over 2500 square metres (27500 square feet) are grouped together to form retail villages or parks. Located close to major roads, they offer extensive free parking.

> **suburban centres** shopping centres created at major road junctions that cater for local shopping needs
> **edge-of-town sites** retail locations on undeveloped land, providing purpose-built stores, parking facilities and amenities for their customers on the edge of a built-up area
> **retail parks** groupings of freestanding superstores, forming a retail village

Major store types

Retail stores are often classified according to width of product mix and depth of product lines. **Department stores** are physically large – around 25,000 square metres (275,000 square feet) – and occupy prominent positions in the traditional heart of the town or city, the central shopping centre. Out-of-town shopping malls, such as Manchester's Trafford Park or Kent's Bluewater, include leading department stores as "anchors" to attract consumers and smaller retail store tenants. Department stores are characterised by wide product mixes in considerable depth for most product lines. Within a department store, related product lines are organised into separate departments such as cosmetics, men's and women's fashions and accessories, house wares, home furnishings, haberdashery and toys. **Variety stores** tend to be slightly smaller and are often more specialised, such as BHS, offering a reduced range of merchandise.

> **department stores** physically large stores that occupy prominent positions in the traditional heart of the town or city, or as anchor stores in out-of-town malls
>
> **variety stores** slightly smaller and more specialised stores than department stores, offering a reduced range of merchandise

In a **catalogue showroom** such as Argos, one item of each product class is on display and the remaining inventory is stored out of the buyers' reach. Using catalogues that have been mailed to their homes or which are available on counters in the store, customers order the goods at their leisure. Shop assistants usually complete the order form and then collect the merchandise from the adjoining warehouse. Such showrooms tend to be in secondary town centre locations or on retail parks.

> **catalogue showroom** outlets in which one item of each product class is on display and the remaining inventory is stored out of the buyers' reach

In the 1960s, grocery retailers – led by Sainsbury's, Tesco and Fine Fare – expanded in to 1,000-square-metre (11,000-square-foot) supermarkets, either in the city centre or within suburban centres. As product ranges grew, self-service requirements called for more space; and as city centre rents rose, the age of the superstore arrived. Size requirements grew further still, and there was an exodus from the city centre. In the 1980s, the average grocery superstore grew from 2,500 square metres to 5,500 square metres (27,500 to 61,000 square feet) and moved away from the suburban centre either to free-standing superstore sites or out-of-town retail parks with plenty of car parking. Now they are often over 6,000 square metres. **Supermarkets** and grocery **superstores** are large, self-service stores that carry a complete line of food products as well as other convenience items, such as cosmetics, non-prescription drugs and kitchenwares. Some, such as ASDA or Tesco, sell clothing and electrical appliances. Grocery superstores are laid out in departments for maximum efficiency in stocking and handling products, but have central checkout facilities by the exits to the ample, free parking. **Category management** is now a core approach to merchandising, inventory control and display in many retailers, with similar lines from several suppliers being controlled by a category manager. S/he is often an employee of one of the major suppliers to the category, giving that supplier significant power over its rivals within the particular retailer account. **Hypermarkets** take the benefits of the superstore even further, using their greater size – over 9,000 square metres (100,000 square feet) – to give the customer a wider range and depth of products.

> **supermarkets and grocery superstores** large, self-service stores that carry a complete line of food products as well as other convenience items
>
> **category management** a core approach to merchandising, inventory control and display in many retailers, with similar lines from several suppliers being controlled by a category manager and managed as a discrete unit
>
> **hypermarkets** stores that take the benefits of the superstore even further, using their greater size to give the customer a wider range and depth of products

The move away from the city or town centre was not confined to multiple grocery retailers. Furniture, carpets and electrical appliances require large display areas, ranges with strength in depth and, if possible, one-floor shopping. The concentration of retailers in the city centre led to limited store opening opportunities – large enough sites were hard to find – and to high rents. Originally freestanding, these 2,000 to 3,500-square-metre (22,000 to 39,000-square-foot) stores are increasingly found in out-of-town retail parks. **Discount sheds** are cheaply constructed, one-storey retail stores with no window displays and few add-on amenities. Oriented towards car-borne shoppers, they have large, free car parks and spacious stock facilities to enable shoppers to take delivery of their purchases immediately.

> **discount sheds** cheaply constructed, one-storey retail stores with no window displays and few add-on amenities; oriented towards car-borne shoppers

Often categorised separately, **category killers** are large stores, tending to be superstore sized, that specialise in a narrow line of merchandise. They are known as category killers – an "Americanism" – because they have a huge selection within a narrow category of merchandise and "kill off" the smaller stores retailing similar lines of merchandise. They require high footfall to be viable and tend to be located in large towns and cities on edge-of-town sites. The expansion of large DIY operators such as B&Q, Castoram and Homebase has led to the closure of many small, traditional hardware stores. Currys (electrical goods), Office World (office supplies) and the superstores of JJB Sports and Allsports (sporting goods) are examples of category killers.

> **category killers** large stores, tending to be superstore sized, which specialise in a narrow line of merchandise

A rapidly growing form of mass merchandising, **warehouse clubs** are large-scale, members-only selling operations combining cash-and-carry wholesaling with discount retailing. For a nominal annual fee, small retailers can purchase products at wholesale prices for business use or for resale. Warehouse clubs also sell to ultimate consumers affiliated with credit unions, schools, hospitals and banks, but instead of paying a membership fee, individual consumers pay about 5 per cent more on each item than do business customers.

> **warehouse clubs** large-scale, members-only selling operations combining cash-and-carry wholesaling with discount retailing

Most shopping centres and towns have a major department store. At the other end of the spectrum is the traditional corner shop. Few small shops these days retail a variety of product groups. In suburban areas, such shops tend to specialise in retailing one convenience product category – newsagents with cigarettes and newspapers, greengrocers, chemists, hair salons and so on. In the town centre (CBD) few retailers of convenience goods, with their low margins, can afford the rents and business tax. Instead, the small store retailers – 250 square metres (2,750 square feet) and under – in the CBD specialise in shopping or comparison items: clothing, footwear, CDs and DVDs, cosmetics, jewellery. **Speciality shops** offer self-service but a greater level of assistance from store personnel than department stores, and carry a narrow product mix with deep product lines. A typical 300-square-metre (3,300-square-foot) footwear or clothing retail store will have window displays to entice passing pedestrians, one or two checkout points, and three or four assistants. Such stores depend on the town centre's general parking facilities and on proximity to a key trader, such as Boots or Marks & Spencer, which will generate pedestrian traffic.

> **speciality shops** stores that offer self-service but a greater level of assistance from store personnel than department stores, and carry a narrow product mix with deep product lines

In most towns there are wholesale **markets** selling meat, greengrocery, fruit, flowers and fish from which speciality retailers make their inventory purchases. Traditional, too, is the general retail market selling to the general public, either in recently refurbished Victorian market halls or in council-provided modern halls adjacent to the town centre shopping malls. Such market halls sell fresh foods, clothing and housewares, and cater for budget-conscious shoppers who typically have a middle and down-market social profile.

> **markets** halls where fresh foods, clothing and housewares are sold, catering for budget-conscious shoppers who typically have a middle and downmarket social profile

As the number of neighbourhood grocery stores declined in the 1960s and 1970s with the expansion of the superstore-based national grocery chains, a niche emerged in the market to be filled by **convenience stores**. These shops – also known as "C-stores" – sell essential groceries, alcoholic drinks, drugs and newspapers outside the traditional 9.00 a.m. to 6.00 p.m. shopping hours. The major superstores extended their opening hours to 8.00 p.m. to facilitate after-work shopping, but no major retailers catered for 'emergency' or top-up shopping. There was a resurgence of the traditional corner shop located in suburban housing estates, offering limited ranges but extended opening hours. Consumers pay a slight price premium but receive convenience in terms of location and opening hours. Tesco Express is an example of retail majors targeting the growth of the C-store.

> **convenience stores** shops that sell essential groceries, alcoholic drinks, drugs and newspapers outside the traditional shopping hours

Retail villages initially sold seconds – imperfect new merchandise – similar to the lines stocked in many factory shops in converted mills or rural locations, in some instances with eight to ten shop units clustered together. Now developers are designing and building out-of-town **factory outlet villages**, such as Cheshire Oaks on Merseyside, for major manufacturers' and branded goods, with up to 20 mini-superstores grouped together. Increasingly, major manufacturers and retailers are using these stores to off-load last season's lines, excess stocks and branded seconds, or to trial new lines. These outlets are very popular for designer-label clothing, linens, crockery and homewares.

> **factory outlet villages** converted rural buildings or purpose-built out-of-town retail parks for manufacturers' outlets retailing branded seconds, excess stocks and last season's lines, or trialling new lines

Cash and carry warehouses, such as Booker or Makro, retail extensive ranges of groceries, tobacco, alcohol, beverages and confectionery to newsagents, small supermarkets and convenience stores and the catering trade (hotels, guest houses, restaurants and cafés). By purchasing from manufacturers in bulk, cash and carry companies can offer substantial price savings to their customers, who in turn can add a retail margin without alienating their customers.

> **cash and carry warehouses** outlets that retail extensive ranges of groceries, tobacco, alcohol, beverages and confectionery to newsagents, small supermarkets and convenience stores, and the catering trade

Non-store retailing

Non-store retailing is the selling of goods or services outside the confines of a retail facility. This form of retailing accounts for an increasing percentage of sales and includes personal sales methods, such as in-home retailing and telemarketing, and non-personal sales methods, such as automatic vending and mail-order retailing (which includes catalogue retailing). Of course, the main source of growth for non-store sales has been the use of the Internet to promote and sell goods and services; orders can be placed online using a credit card from home, office, or, increasingly, while mobile via a smartphone.

non-store retailing the selling of goods or services outside the confines of a retail facility

Certain non-store retailing methods are in the category of **direct marketing**: the use of non-personal media, the Internet or telesales to introduce products to consumers, who then purchase the products by mail, telephone or the Internet. In the case of telephone orders, sales people may be required to complete the sales. Telemarketing, mail-order and catalogue retailing are all examples of direct marketing, as are sales generated by coupons, direct mail and Freephone 0800 numbers and the Internet.

direct marketing the use of non-personal media, the Internet or telesales to introduce products to consumers, who then purchase the products by mail, telephone or the Internet

In-home retailing is selling via personal contacts with consumers in their own homes. Companies such as Avon, Amway and Betterware send representatives to the homes of preselected prospects. A variation of in-home retailing is the home demonstration, or party plan, which companies such as Tupperware and Mary Kay Cosmetics use successfully. One consumer acts as host and invites a number of friends to view merchandise at his or her home, where a sales person is on hand to demonstrate the products.

in-home retailing selling via personal contacts with consumers in their own homes

Many organisations use the telephone to strengthen the effectiveness of traditional marketing methods. **Telemarketing** is the direct selling of goods and services by telephone, based on either a cold canvass of the telephone directory or a pre-screened list of prospective clients. Telemarketing can generate sales leads, improve customer service, speed up collection of overdue accounts, raise funds for not-for-profit groups and gather market data.* In some cases, telemarketing uses advertising to encourage consumers to initiate a call or to request information about placing an order. Such advertisements will include "a call to action" to prompt target consumers to dial an 0800 Freephone number. This type of retailing is only a small part of total retail sales, but its use is growing. Research indicates that telemarketing is most successful when combined with other marketing strategies, such as direct mail or advertising in newspapers, radio and television.

telemarketing the direct selling of goods and services by telephone, based on either a cold canvass of the telephone directory or a pre-screened list of prospective clients

Automatic vending makes use of coin or credit card-operated self-service machines and accounts for less than 1 per cent of all retail sales. However, there are approximately 1.5 million vending machines in the U.K., accounting for sales of around £4 billion.

automatic vending the use of coin or credit card-operated self-service machines to sell small, standardised, routinely purchased products such as chewing gum, sweets, newspapers, cigarettes, soft drinks and coffee

Mail-order retailing involves selling by description, because buyers usually do not see the actual product until it arrives in the mail. Sellers contact buyers through direct mail, catalogues, television, radio, magazines and newspapers and increasingly via the Internet. A wide assortment of products, such as DVDs, books and clothing is sold to consumers through the mail. When **catalogue retailing** – a specific type of mail-order retailing – is used, customers receive their catalogues by mail, or they may pick them up if the catalogue retailer has stores. The *Next Directory* is an example. Although in-store visits result in some catalogue orders, most are placed by mail, telephone or the Internet.

> **mail-order retailing** selling by description because buyers usually do not see the actual product until it arrives in the mail
>
> **catalogue retailing** a type of mail-order retailing in which customers receive their catalogues by mail, or pick them up if the catalogue retailer has stores

PHYSICAL DISTRIBUTION

Wholesalers, in their various guises, are essential "players" in many businesses' marketing channels. Also important is the ability to physically deliver products to customers. **Physical distribution** is a set of activities – consisting of order processing, materials handling, warehousing, inventory management and transportation – used in the movement of products from producers to consumers, or end users. Planning an effective physical distribution system can be a significant decision in developing a marketing strategy. A company that has the right goods in the right place at the right time in the right quantity, and with the right support services is able to sell more than competing businesses that fail to accomplish these goals. Physical distribution is an important variable in a marketing strategy because it can decrease costs and increase customer satisfaction. In fact, speed of delivery, along with service and dependability, is often as important to buyers as cost. In some situations – for example, the emergency provision of a spare part for vital production-line machinery – it may even be the single most important factor. For most companies, physical distribution accounts for about a fifth of a product's retail price.

> **physical distribution** a set of activities –consisting of order processing, materials handling, warehousing, inventory management and transportation – used in the movement of products from producers to consumers or end users

Physical distribution deals with physical movement and inventory holding – the storing and tracking of inventory or stock until it is needed – both within and among marketing channel members. Often, one channel member will arrange the movement of goods for all channel members involved in exchanges. For example, a packing company ships fresh salmon and champagne (often by air) to remote markets on a routine basis. Frequently, buyers are found while the goods are in transit.

The physical distribution system is often adjusted to meet the needs of a channel member. For example, an agricultural equipment dealer who keeps a low inventory of replacement parts requires the fastest and most dependable service when parts not in stock are needed. In this case, the distribution cost may be a minor consideration when compared with service, dependability and promptness. Grocery retailers such as Aldi and ASDA receive some deliveries to central and regional warehouses, whereas other deliveries from manufacturers such as Heinz or Kellogg's go directly to individual stores as required, and insisted upon, by the retail companies. Failure to deliver products to customers where, when and how they demand is likely to lose orders, diminish customer loyalty and provide opportunities for competing suppliers, and is not going to create a mutually satisfying relationship between supplier and customer.

Physical distribution objectives

For most companies, the main **objective of physical distribution** is to decrease costs while increasing customer service.* In the real world, however, few distribution systems manage to achieve these goals in equal measure. The large stock inventories and rapid transport, essential to facilitate high levels of customer service, drive up costs. On the other hand, reduced inventories and slower, cheaper shipping methods cause customer dissatisfaction because of stock-outs or late deliveries. Physical distribution managers strive for a reasonable balance of service, costs and resources. They determine what level of customer service is acceptable yet realistic, develop a "system" outlook of calculating total distribution costs, and trade higher costs at one stage of distribution for savings in another. In this section these three performance objectives are examined more closely.

RESPONSIBLE PRACTICE Lush and environmentally-friendly packaging

© GLYN THOMAS PHOTOGRAPHY / ALAMY

Packaging is one way that a company can boost its environmental credentials. With increasing numbers of consumers becoming more environmentally conscious of the products they choose, it is imperative that businesses seriously consider changing to more eco-friendly and sustainable packaging.

Lush Cosmetics is one company that takes environmental issues very seriously. Lush was formed in the U.K. in 1995 and has since expanded to 830 stores in 51 countries. From the beginning, Lush has refused to buy ingredients from companies who test their products on animals, instead choosing to test on human volunteers and they actively support numerous charities.

Another way in which they care for the environment is by keeping the packaging of their products to an absolute minimum and for roughly 50 per cent of their products there is actually none. Where packaging is unavoidable, for example with liquids such as shampoo and shower gel, Lush uses recyclable plastic bottles, which can be reused by customers, or they can bring them back in to the store so Lush can reuse them.

Lush packaging is 100 per cent recycled material, a move which was not cheap as it added £100,000 to the company's costs. However, founder Mark Constantine does not seem too concerned. Their healthy turnover means that these kinds of changes can easily be accommodated and it is a move that encourages eco-conscious consumers to choose Lush products.

References: http://www.onegreenplanet.org/lifestyle/5-companies-producing-products-with-eco-friendly-packaging/; www.lush.co.uk; http://www.theecologist.org/green_green_living/green_business/684896/green_business_lush.html

---

objective of physical distribution decreasing costs while increasing customer service

Customer service To varying degrees, all businesses attempt to satisfy customer needs and wants through a set of activities known collectively as **customer service**. Many companies claim that service to the customer is their top priority. These companies see service as being as important in attracting customers and building sales as the cost or quality of the companies' products.

customer service customer satisfaction in terms of physical distribution, based on availability, promptness and quality

Customers require a variety of services. At the most basic level, they need fair prices, acceptable product quality and dependable deliveries.* There are many facets of service, as described throughout this book, but in the physical distribution area, availability, promptness and quality are the most important dimensions of customer service. These are the main factors that determine how satisfied customers are likely to be with a supplier's physical distribution activities.* Customers seeking a higher level of customer service may also want sizeable inventories, efficient order processing, availability of emergency shipments, progress reports, post-sale services, prompt replacement of defective items and warranties. Customers' inventory requirements influence the level of physical distribution service they expect. For example, customers who want to minimise inventory storage and shipping costs may require that suppliers assume the cost of maintaining inventory in the marketing channel, or the cost of premium transport.* Because service needs vary from customer to customer, companies must analyse – and adapt to – customer preferences. Attention to customer needs and preferences is crucial to increasing sales and obtaining repeat sales. A company's failure to provide the desired level of service may mean the loss of customers. Without customers there can be no profit.

Companies must also examine the service levels offered by competitors and match those standards, at least when the costs of providing the services can be balanced by the sales generated. For example, companies may step up their efforts to identify the causes of customer complaints or institute corrective measures for billing and shipping errors. In extremely competitive businesses, such as the market for vehicle parts, businesses may concentrate on product availability. To compete effectively, manufacturers may strive for inventory levels and order processing speeds that are deemed unnecessary and too costly in other industries.*

Services are provided most effectively when service standards are developed and stated in terms that are specific, measurable and appropriate for the product – for example, "Guaranteed delivery within 48 hours". Standards should be communicated clearly both to customers and employees, and rigorously enforced. In many cases, it is necessary to maintain a policy of minimum order size to ensure that transactions are profitable: special service charges are added to orders smaller than a specified quantity. A number of carrier or courier companies operate on this basis. Many service policies also spell out delivery times and provisions for back ordering, returning goods and obtaining emergency shipments. The overall objective of any service policy should be to improve customer service just to the point beyond which increased sales would be negated by increased distribution costs.

Total distribution costs   Although physical distribution managers try to minimise the costs of each element in the system – transportation, warehousing, inventory carrying, order entry/customer service and administration – decreasing costs in one area often raises them in another. By using a total cost approach to physical distribution, managers can view the distribution system as a whole, not as a collection of unrelated activities. The emphasis shifts from lowering the separate costs of individual functions to minimising the total cost of the entire distribution system.

The total cost approach calls for analysing the costs of all possible distribution alternatives, even those considered too impractical or expensive. **Total cost analysis** weighs inventory levels against warehousing expenses; materials handling costs against various modes of transport; and all distribution costs against customer service standards. The costs of potential sales losses from lower performance levels are also considered. In many cases, accounting procedures and statistical methods can be used to calculate total costs. Where hundreds of combinations of distribution variables are possible, computer simulations may be helpful. In no case is a distribution system's lowest total cost the result of using a combination of the cheapest functions; instead, it is the lowest overall cost compatible with the company's stated service objectives.

> **total cost analysis** weighs inventory levels against warehousing expenses; and materials handling costs against various modes of transport; and all distribution costs against customer service standards

Cost trade-offs   A distribution system that attempts to provide a specific level of customer service for the lowest possible total cost must use **cost trade-offs** to resolve conflicts about resource allocations. That is, higher costs in one area of the distribution system must be offset by lower costs in another area if the total system is to remain cost-effective.

> **cost trade-offs** the off-setting of higher costs in one area of the distribution system by lower costs in another area, to keep the total system cost-effective

Trade-offs are strategic decisions to combine and recombine resources for greatest cost-effectiveness. When distribution managers regard the system as a network of interlocking functions, trade-offs become useful tools in a unified distribution strategy. The furniture retailer IKEA uses a system of trade-offs. To ensure that each store carries enough inventory to satisfy customers in the area, IKEA groups its retail outlets into regions, each served by a separate distribution centre. In addition, each IKEA store carries a five-week back stock of inventory. Thus, IKEA has chosen to trade higher inventory warehousing costs for improved customer service.*

The remainder of this chapter focuses on order processing, materials handling, warehousing, inventory management and transportation, all of which are essential physical distribution activities. While none of these activities would normally be the responsibility of marketing managers, their smooth deployment impacts on customer service levels, customer satisfaction and also customers' perceptions of a brand or business.

Order processing

Order processing – the first stage in a physical distribution system – is the receipt and transmission of sales order information. Although management sometimes overlooks the importance of these activities, efficient order processing facilitates product flow. Computerised order processing, used now by many businesses, speeds the flow of information from customer to seller.* Indeed, in many industries key suppliers are linked "live" to retailers' or distributors' tills and order books: they are then able to replenish or supply exactly in line with demand and actual sales. When carried out quickly and accurately, order processing contributes to customer satisfaction, repeat orders and increased profits.

 order processing the receipt and transmission of sales order information

Generally, there are three main tasks in order processing:

1. order entry.
2. order handling.
3. order delivery.*

Order entry begins when customers or sales people place purchase orders by mail, telephone, text, fax or computer. In some companies, sales service representatives receive and enter orders personally and also handle complaints, prepare progress reports and forward sales order information.*

The next task, order handling, involves several activities. Once an order has been entered, it is transmitted to the warehouse, where the availability of the product is verified; and to the credit department, where prices, terms and the customer's credit rating are checked. If the credit department approves the purchase, the warehouse begins to fill the order. If the product requested is not in stock, a production order is sent to the factory or the customer is offered a substitute item. Thanks to technology, these various tasks are carried out simultaneously in many businesses and in only a few seconds. When the order has been filled and packed for shipment, the warehouse schedules pick up with an appropriate carrier. If the customer is willing to pay for express service, priority transport, such as an overnight courier, is used. The customer is sent an invoice, inventory records are adjusted and the order is delivered.

Order processing can be done manually or electronically, depending on which method provides greater speed and accuracy within cost limits. Manual processing suffices for a small volume of orders and is more flexible in special situations; electronic processing is more practical for a large volume of orders and lets a company integrate order processing, production planning, inventory, accounting and transport planning into a total information system.* These days, most companies use **electronic data interchange (EDI)**, which uses IT to integrate order processing with production, inventory, accounting and transportation. Many leading retail groups, with products from groceries to electrical goods, have their stores networked to the head office. Suppliers are also linked electronically to the retailers' head offices, so that stock can be ordered electronically.

 electronic data interchange (EDI) the use of IT to integrate order processing with production, inventory, accounting and transportation

Materials handling

Materials handling, or the physical handling of products, is important for efficient warehouse operations, as well as in transport from points of production to points of consumption. The characteristics of the product itself often determine how it will be handled. For example, fresh dairy produce has unique characteristics that determine how it can be moved and stored. Materials handling procedures and techniques should increase the usable capacity of a warehouse, reduce the number of times a good is handled, improve service to customers and increase their satisfaction with the product. Packaging, loading, movement and labelling systems must be coordinated to maximise cost reduction and customer satisfaction.

 materials handling the physical handling of products

The protective functions of packaging are important considerations in product development. Appropriate decisions about packaging materials and methods allow for the most efficient physical handling; most companies employ packaging consultants or specialists to accomplish this important task. Materials handling equipment is used in the design of handling systems. **Unit loading** is grouping one or more boxes on a pallet or skid; it permits movement of efficient loads by mechanical means, such as forklifts, trucks or conveyor systems. **Containerisation** is the practice of consolidating many items into a single large container that is sealed at its point of origin and opened at its destination. Because individual items are not handled in transit, containerisation greatly increases efficiency and security in shipping.

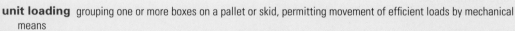 **unit loading** grouping one or more boxes on a pallet or skid, permitting movement of efficient loads by mechanical means
containerisation the practice of consolidating many items into a single large container that is sealed at its point of origin and opened at its destination, greatly increasing efficiency and security in shipping

Warehousing

Warehousing, the design and operation of facilities for storing and moving goods, is an important physical distribution function. Warehousing provides time utility by enabling companies to compensate for dissimilar production and consumption rates. That is, when mass production creates a greater stock of goods than can be sold immediately, companies may warehouse the surplus goods until customers are ready to buy. Warehousing also helps stabilise the prices and availability of seasonal items. There follows a description of the basic functions of warehouses and the different types of warehouse available. Distribution centres, special warehouse operations designed so that goods can be moved rapidly, are also examined.

 warehousing the design and operation of facilities for storing and moving goods

Warehousing functions Warehousing is not limited simply to the storage of goods. When warehouses receive goods by wagon loads or lorry loads, they break the shipments down into smaller quantities for individual customers; when goods arrive in small lots, the warehouses assemble the lots into bulk loads that can be shipped out more economically.* Warehouses perform the following basic distribution functions:

1. *Receiving goods* – the merchandise is accepted, and the warehouse assumes responsibility for the goods.
2. *Identifying goods* – the appropriate stock-keeping units are recorded, along with the quantity of each item received; the item may be marked with a physical code, tag or other label, or it may be identified by an item code (a code on the carrier or container) or by physical properties.
3. *Sorting goods* – the merchandise is sorted for storage in appropriate areas.
4. *Despatching goods to storage* – the merchandise is put away so that it can be retrieved when necessary.
5. *Holding goods* – the merchandise is kept in storage and properly protected until needed.
6. *Recalling and picking goods* – items customers have ordered are retrieved efficiently from storage and prepared for the next step.
7. *Marshalling the shipment* – the items making up a single shipment are brought together and checked for completeness or explainable omissions. Order records are prepared or modified as necessary.
8. *Despatching the shipment* – the consolidated order is packaged suitably and directed to the right transport vehicle; necessary shipping and accounting documents are prepared.*

Types of warehouse   A company's choice of warehouse facilities is an important strategic consideration. By using the right warehouse, a company may be able to reduce transportation and inventory costs or improve its service to customers; the wrong warehouse may drain company resources. For example, a company that produces processed foods must locate its warehousing close to main transport routes to facilitate delivery to supermarkets in different parts of the country. Besides deciding how many facilities to operate and where to locate them, a company must determine which type of warehouse will be most appropriate. Warehouses fall into two general categories: private and public. In many cases, a combination of private and public facilities provides the most flexible approach to warehousing. Many companies operate their own warehousing, whereas others outsource this requirement to specialist inventory management and haulage companies.

Inventory management

Inventory management involves developing and maintaining adequate assortments of products to meet customers' needs. Because a company's investment in inventory usually represents 30 to 50 per cent of its total assets, inventory decisions have a significant impact on physical distribution costs and the level of customer service provided. When too few products are carried in inventory, the result is a **stock-out**, or shortage of products, which results in fewer sales and customers switching to alternative brands. But when too many products or too many slow-moving products are carried, costs increase, as do the risks of product obsolescence, pilferage and damage. The objective of inventory management, therefore, is to minimise inventory costs while maintaining an adequate supply of goods.

> **inventory management** the development and maintenance of adequate assortments of products to meet customers' needs
> **stock-outs** shortages of products resulting from a lack of products carried in inventory

There are three types of inventory cost:

1. *Carrying costs* are holding costs; they include expenditures for storage space and materials handling, financing, insurance, taxes and losses from spoilage of goods.

2. *Replenishment costs* are related to the purchase of merchandise. The price of goods, handling charges and expenses for order processing contribute to replenishment costs.
3. *Stock-out costs* include sales lost when demand for goods exceeds supply, and the clerical and processing expenses of back ordering.

A company must control all the costs of obtaining and maintaining inventory in order to achieve its profit goals. Management must therefore have a clear idea of the level of each type of cost incurred. Customers' expectations of product availability and tolerable delivery lead times will vary between target market segments.

Inventory managers deal with two issues of particular importance. They must know when to reorder and how much merchandise to order. In general, to determine when to order, a marketer calculates the **reorder point,** which is the inventory level that signals that more inventory should be ordered. Three factors determine the reorder point:

> **reorder point** the inventory level that signals the need to order more inventory

1. the **order lead time,** which is the expected time between the date an order is placed and the date the goods are received and made ready for resale to customers

> **order lead time** the average time lapse between placing the order and receiving it

2. the **usage rate** or rate at which a product is sold or used up

> **usage rate** the rate at which a product's inventory is used or sold during a specific time period

3. the quantity of **safety stock** on hand, or inventory needed to prevent stock-outs.

> **safety stock** inventory needed to prevent stock-outs

The reorder point can be calculated using the following formula:

$$\text{reorder point} = (\text{order lead time} \times \text{usage rate}) + \text{safety stock}$$

Thus, if order lead time is 10 days, usage rate is 3 units per day and safety stock is 20 units, the reorder point is 50 units.

The inventory manager faces several trade-offs when reordering merchandise. Large safety stocks ensure product availability and thus improve the level of customer service; they also lower order-processing costs because orders are placed less frequently. Small safety stocks, on the other hand, cause frequent reorders and high order-processing costs but reduce the overall cost of carrying inventory. To quantify this trade-off between carrying costs and order-processing costs, a model for an **economic order quantity (EOQ)** has been developed (see Figure 13.4); it specifies the order size that minimises the total cost of ordering and carrying inventory.* The fundamental relationships underlying the widely accepted EOQ model are the basis of many inventory control systems. However, the objective of minimum total inventory cost must be balanced against the customer service level necessary for maximum profits. Therefore, because increased costs of carrying inventory are usually associated with a higher level of customer service, the order quantity will often lie to the right of the optimal point in the figure, leading to a higher total cost for ordering and larger carrying inventory.

> **economic order quantity (EOQ)** the order size that minimises the total cost of ordering and carrying inventory

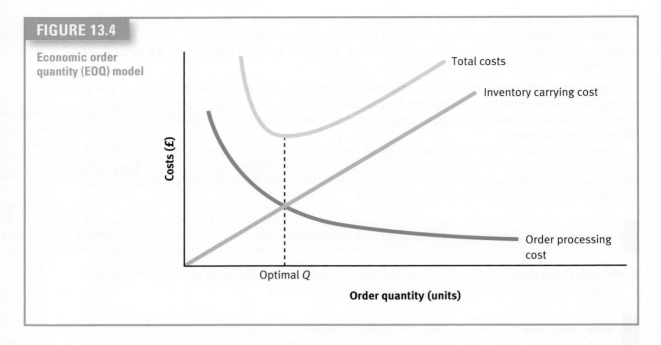

FIGURE 13.4

Economic order quantity (EOQ) model

Fluctuations in demand – for example, in times of economic recession – mean that it is not always easy to predict changing inventory levels. When management miscalculates reorder points or order quantities, inventory problems develop. Warning signs include an inventory that grows at a faster rate than sales, surplus or obsolete inventory, customer deliveries that are consistently late or lead times that are too long, inventory that represents a growing percentage of assets, and large inventory adjustments or write-offs. However, there are several tools for improving inventory control.

From a technical standpoint, an inventory system can be planned so that the number of products sold and the number of products in stock are determined at certain checkpoints. The control may be as simple as tearing off a code number from each product sold so that the correct sizes, colours and models can be tabulated and reordered. Many bookshops insert reorder slips of paper into each item of stock, which can be removed at the checkout. A sizeable amount of technologically advanced electronic equipment is available to assist with inventory management. In many stores, such as Tesco and Toys 'R' Us, checkout terminals connected to central computer systems instantaneously update inventory and sales records. For continuous, automatic updating of inventory records, some companies use pressure-sensitive circuits installed under ordinary industrial shelving to weigh inventory, convert the weight to units and display any inventory changes on a video screen or computer printout.

Various techniques have also been used successfully to improve inventory management. The just-in-time concept calls for companies to maintain low inventory levels and purchase products and materials in small quantities, just at the moment they are needed for production. Ford, for example, sometimes receives supply deliveries as often as every two hours.* Just-in-time inventory management depends on a high level of coordination between producers and suppliers, but the technique enables companies to eliminate waste and reduce inventory costs significantly. Another inventory management technique, the 80/20 rule, holds that fast-moving products should generate a higher level of customer service than slow-moving products, on the theory that 20 per cent of the items account for 80 per cent of the sales. Thus, an inventory manager attempts to keep an adequate supply of fast-selling items and a minimal supply of the slower-moving products. ABC sales: contribution analysis strives to maintain inventory levels while maximising financial returns to the business.

Transportation

Transportation adds time and place utility to a product by moving it from where it is made to where it is purchased and used.* Because product availability and timely deliveries are so dependent on transport functions, a company's choice of transport directly affects customer service and satisfaction. A business may even build its distribution and marketing strategy around a unique transport system if the system ensures on-time deliveries that will give the business a competitive edge. This section considers the principal modes of transport, the criteria companies use to select one mode over another, and several methods of coordinating transport services.

transportation the process of moving a product from where it is made to where it is purchased and used

Transport modes   There are five major **transport modes**, or methods of moving goods: railways, motor vehicles, inland waterways, airways and pipelines. Each mode offers unique advantages; many companies have adopted physical handling procedures that facilitate the use of two or more modes in combination.

transport modes methods of moving goods; these include railways, motor vehicles, inland waterways, airways and pipelines

Criteria for selecting transport   Marketers select a transport mode on the basis of costs, transit time, reliability, capability, accessibility, security and traceability.* It is important to remember that these relationships are approximations and that the choice of a transport mode involves many trade-offs. These attributes all have a significant impact on a customer's perception of customer service levels.

Costs   Marketers compare alternative means of transport to determine whether the benefits from a more expensive mode are worth the higher **costs**. Air freight carriers provide many benefits, such as high speed, reliability, security and traceability, but at higher costs relative to other transport modes. When speed is less important, marketers prefer lower costs. Recently, marketers have been able to cut expenses and increase efficiency. Railways, airlines, road hauliers, barges and pipeline companies have all become more competitive and more responsive to customers' needs. Surveys reveal that in recent years transport costs per tonne and as a percentage of sales have declined, now averaging 7.5 per cent of sales. This figure varies by industry, of course: electrical machinery, textiles and instruments have transport costs of only 3 or 4 per cent of sales, whereas timber products, chemicals and food have transport costs close to 15 per cent of sales.

costs one consideration that helps determine transportation mode, involving comparison of alternative modes to determine whether the benefits of a more expensive mode are worth the higher costs

Transit time   **Transit time** is the total time a carrier has possession of goods, including the time required for pick up and delivery, handling, and movement between the points of origin and destination. Closely related to transit time is frequency, or number of shipments per day. Transit time obviously affects a marketer's ability to provide service, but there are some less obvious implications as well. A shipper can take advantage of transit time to process orders for goods en route, a capability especially important for agricultural and raw materials shippers. Some railways also let shipments that are already in transit be redirected, for maximum flexibility in selecting markets.

transit time the total time a carrier has possession of goods

Reliability   The total **reliability** of a transport mode is determined by the consistency of the service provided. Marketers must be able to count on their carriers to deliver goods on time and in an acceptable condition. Along with transit time, reliability affects a marketer's inventory costs, which include sales lost when merchandise is not available. Unreliable transport necessitates maintaining higher inventory levels to avoid stock-outs. Reliable delivery service, on the other hand, enables customers to save money by reducing inventories; for example, if pharmacists know that suppliers can deliver drugs within hours of ordering, they can carry a smaller inventory.

 reliability the consistency of service provided

Capability **Capability** is the ability of a transport mode to provide the appropriate equipment and conditions for moving specific kinds of goods. For example, many products must be shipped under conditions of controlled temperature and humidity. Other products, such as liquids or gases, require special equipment or facilities for their shipment.

 capability the ability of a transport mode to provide the appropriate equipment and conditions for moving specific kinds of goods

Accessibility A carrier's **accessibility** refers to its ability to move goods over a specific route or network: flights, rail lines, waterways or roads.

 accessibility the ability to move goods over a specific route or network

Security A transport mode's **security** is measured by the physical condition of goods on delivery. A business does not incur costs directly when goods are lost or damaged, because the carrier is usually held liable in these cases. Nevertheless, poor service and lack of security will lead indirectly to increased costs and lower profits for the company, since damaged or lost goods are not available for immediate sale or use. In some cases, companies find it necessary to transport products using courier companies such as UPS or TNT.

 security the measure of the physical condition of goods upon delivery

Traceability **Traceability** is the relative ease with which a shipment can be located and transferred – or found if it is lost. Quick traceability is a convenience that some businesses value highly. Shippers have learned that the ability to trace shipments, along with prompt invoicing and processing of claims, increases customer loyalty and improves a company's image in the marketplace.* Courier companies now offer clients Internet tracking of goods in transit.

 traceability the relative ease with which a shipment can be located and transferred

Physical distribution's importance to marketing

The physical distribution functions discussed in this chapter – order processing, materials handling, warehousing, inventory management and transportation – account for about a third of all marketing costs. Moreover, these functions have a significant impact on customer service and satisfaction, as well as people's perceptions of a brand's or business's image, which are of prime importance to marketers.* Effective marketers accept considerable responsibility for the design and control of the physical distribution system. They work to ensure that the business's overall marketing strategy is enhanced by physical distribution, with its dual objectives of decreasing costs while increasing customer service. Remember, to ensure that customers are satisfied, they must be able to obtain, within reason, the product or service when and where they want it and with a perception of 'no hassle'. The growth of multi-channel marketing has given customers greater flexibility and more options for purchasing and delivery, but places more responsibility on marketers to manage these experiences to ensure customer satisfaction. The growth of multi-channel marketing and home delivery has placed greater importance on channel management to safeguard customer experience and ensure brand experience is similar across channels. The increase in direct delivery and eCommerce has added to the facilitating agents and channel players on which marketers rely to effectively manage their customers.

The strategic importance of physical distribution is evident in all elements of the marketing mix. Product design and packaging must allow for efficient stacking, storage and transport; decisions to differentiate products by size, colour and style must take into account the additional demands that will be placed on warehousing and shipping facilities. Competitive pricing may depend on a company's ability to provide reliable delivery or emergency shipments of replacement parts; a company trying to lower its inventory costs may offer quantity discounts to encourage large purchases. Promotional campaigns must be coordinated with distribution functions so that advertised products are available to buyers; order processing departments must be able to handle additional sales order information efficiently. Distribution planners must consider warehousing and transportation costs, which may influence, for example, the company's policy on stock-outs or its choice to centralise or decentralise its inventory.

No single distribution system is ideal for all situations, and any system must be evaluated continually and adapted as necessary. For instance, pressures to adjust service levels or reduce costs may lead to a total restructuring of the marketing channel relationships; changes in transportation, warehousing, materials handling and inventory may affect speed of delivery, reliability and economy of service. Marketing strategists must consider customers' changing needs and preferences, and recognise that changes in any one of the major distribution functions will necessarily affect all other functions. Consumer-oriented marketers will analyse the various characteristics of their target markets and *then* design distribution systems to provide products at acceptable costs. In many instances, external logistics specialists are subcontracted to handle inventory and physical distribution requirements. The use of third parties may in fact be fully outsourced: **outsourcing** is where a third party is empowered to manage and control a particular activity – such as catering, IT infrastructure management, fleet cars, human resources and recruitment or, as in this case, a company's logistics.

 outsourcing where a third-party organisation is empowered to manage and control a particular activity, such as logistics

SUMMARY

Wholesaling includes all transactions in which the purchaser intends to use the product for resale, for making other products or for general business operations. It does not include exchanges with the ultimate consumers. Hence, the term *wholesaling* is used in its broadest sense: intermediaries' activity in the marketing channel between producers and business-to-business customers to facilitate the exchange – buying and selling – of goods. Marketers use wholesaling to mean much more than the function of retail wholesalers. *Wholesalers* are individuals or businesses that facilitate and expedite primarily wholesale transactions between producers and business-to-business customers. *Supply chain management* has become strategically important in recent years and,

for marketers, this involves an improved appreciation of the role of wholesaling and marketing intermediaries.

Except in many consumer markets, where large multiple retailers dominate, more than half of all goods are exchanged through wholesalers (middlemen in the distribution channel), although the distribution of any product requires that someone must perform wholesaling activities, whether or not a wholesaling institution is involved. For producers, wholesalers perform specialised accumulation and allocation functions for a number of products, letting the producers concentrate on developing and manufacturing the products. For retailers, wholesalers provide buying expertise, wide product lines, efficient distribution and warehousing and storage services.

Various types of wholesaler serve different market segments. How a wholesaler is classified depends on whether the wholesaler is owned by a producer, whether it takes title to products, the range of services it provides and the breadth and depth of its product lines. The three general categories of wholesaler are (1) merchant wholesalers, (2) agents and brokers and (3) manufacturers' sales branches and offices.

Merchant wholesalers are independently owned businesses that take title to goods and assume risk; they account for over half of all wholesale revenues. They are either *full service wholesalers,* offering the widest possible range of wholesaling functions or *limited service wholesalers,* providing only some marketing services and specialising in a few functions. Distributors buy and sell on their own account but tend to deal in the goods of only certain manufacturers. Full service wholesalers include: (1) *general merchandise wholesalers,* which offer a wide but relatively shallow product mix; (2) *limited line wholesalers,* which offer extensive assortments in a few product lines; and (3) *speciality line wholesalers,* which offer great depth in a single product line or in a few items within a line. *Rack jobbers* are speciality line wholesalers that own and service display racks in supermarkets and chemists. There are four types of limited service wholesalers. (1) *Cash-and-carry wholesalers* sell to small businesses, require payment in cash and do not deliver. (2) *Truck wholesalers* transport a limited line of products directly to customers for inspection and selection. (3) *Drop shippers* own goods and negotiate sales but never take possession of products. (4) *Mail-order wholesalers* sell to retail, industrial and institutional buyers through direct mail catalogues.

Agents and brokers, sometimes called *functional middlemen,* negotiate purchases and expedite sales but do not take title to products. They are usually specialists and provide valuable sales expertise. *Agents* represent buyers or sellers on a permanent basis. *Manufacturers' agents* offer customers the complete product lines of two or more sellers; *selling agents* market a complete product line or a producer's entire output, and perform every wholesaling function except taking title to products; *commission merchants* receive goods on consignment from local sellers and negotiate sales in large central markets. *Brokers,* such as *food brokers,* negotiate exchanges between buyers and sellers on a temporary basis.

Manufacturers' sales branches and offices are vertically integrated units owned by manufacturers. *Sales branches* sell products and provide support services for the manufacturer's sales force in a given location. *Sales offices* carry no inventory, and function much as agents do.

Facilitating agencies do not buy, sell or take title but perform certain activities that enhance channel functions. They include *public warehouses,* finance companies, transport companies and *trade shows* and *trade markets.*

In some instances, these organisations eliminate the need for a wholesaling establishment.

Retailing includes all transactions in which the buyer intends to consume the product through personal, family or household use. *Retailers,* businesses that purchase products for the purpose of reselling them to ultimate consumers, are important links in the marketing channel because they are customers for wholesalers and producers. Much retailing takes place inside stores or service establishments, but retail exchanges may also occur outside stores through telemarketing, vending machines, mail order catalogues and the Internet. By providing assortments of products to match consumers' wants, retailers create place, time, possession and form utilities.

Retail stores locate in the *central business district (CBD)* – the traditional centre of the town or the *prime pitch* – or in locations that provide an adequate *customer threshold* – in *suburban centres,* in *edge-of-town sites* or in *retail parks.* The national chains occupy the prime pitch sites in the CBD and the edge-of-town sites. Locally based independent retailers tend to dominate in the suburbs and focus on convenience and some comparison goods.

Retail stores are often classified according to their width of product mix and depth of product lines. The major types of retail store are *department stores, variety stores, catalogue showrooms, supermarkets and superstores, hypermarkets, discount sheds, category killers, warehouse clubs, speciality shops, markets, convenience stores, discounters, factory outlet villages* and *cash and carry warehouses. Category management* is strategically important in marketing, providing a supplier with the opportunity to control a retail account's category. Department stores are characterised by wide product mixes in reasonable depth for most product lines. Their product lines are organised into separate departments that function much as self-contained businesses do. Speciality retailers offer substantial assortments in a few product lines. They include traditional speciality shops, which carry narrow product mixes with deep product lines.

Non-store retailing is the selling of goods or services outside the confines of a retail facility. *Direct marketing* is the use of non-personal media, the Internet or telesales to introduce products to consumers, who then purchase the products by mail, telephone or the Internet. The Internet is becoming increasingly important in direct marketing. Forms of non-store retailing include: *in-home retailing* (selling via personal contacts with consumers in their own homes); *telemarketing* (direct selling of goods and services by telephone based on either a cold canvass of the telephone directory or a pre-screened list of prospective clients); *automatic vending* (selling through machines); *mail-order retailing;* the Internet and *catalogue retailing* (selling by description because buyers usually do not see the actual product until it arrives in the mail).

Physical distribution is a set of activities that moves products from producers to consumers or end users. These activities include order processing, materials handling, warehousing, inventory management and transportation. While none of these activities would normally be the responsibility of marketing managers, their smooth deployment impacts on customer service levels, customer satisfaction and also customers' perceptions of a brand or business. An effective physical distribution system can be an important component of an overall marketing strategy, because it can decrease costs and lead to higher levels of customer satisfaction. Physical distribution activities should be integrated with marketing channel decisions and should be adjusted to meet the unique needs of a channel member. For most companies, physical distribution accounts for about a fifth of a product's retail price.

The main *objective of physical distribution* is to decrease costs while increasing customer service. Physical distribution managers therefore try to balance service, distribution costs and resources. Companies must adapt to customers' needs and preferences, offer service comparable to – or better than – that of their competitors, and develop and communicate desirable *customer service* policies. The costs of providing service are minimised most effectively through the *total cost analysis* approach, which evaluates the costs of the system as a whole rather than as a collection of separate activities. *Cost trade-offs* must often be used to offset higher costs in one area of distribution against lower costs in another area.

Order processing, the first stage in a physical distribution system, is the receipt and transmission of sales order information. Order processing consists of three main tasks: (1) order entry is the placement of purchase orders from customers or sales people by mail, telephone, fax or computer; (2) order handling involves checking customer credit, verifying product availability and preparing products for shipping; and (3) order delivery is provided by the carrier most suitable for a desired level of customer service. Order processing may be done manually or electronically, depending on which method gives greater speed and accuracy within cost limits. *Electronic data interchange (EDI)* helps facilitate order processing.

Materials handling, or the physical handling of products, is an important element of physical distribution. Packaging, loading, movement and labelling systems must be coordinated to maximise cost reduction and customer requirements. Basic handling systems include *unit loading* on pallets or skids, permitting movement by mechanical devices, and *containerisation,* the practice of consolidating many items into a single large container.

Warehousing involves the design and operation of facilities for storing and moving goods. It is important for companies to select suitable warehousing conveniently located close to main transport routes.

The objective of *inventory management* is to minimise inventory costs while maintaining a supply of goods adequate for customers' needs. All inventory costs – carrying, replenishment and stock-out costs – must be controlled if profit goals are to be met. To avoid *stock-outs* without tying up too much capital in inventory, a business must have a systematic method of determining a *reorder point,* the inventory level at which more inventory is ordered. The *order lead time* is lapsed time between order placement and delivery. The *usage rate* is the rate at which inventory is used during a specific period of time. The trade-offs between the costs of carrying larger average *safety stocks* and the costs of frequent orders can be quantified using the *economic order quantity (EOQ)* model. Inventory problems may take the form of surplus inventory, late deliveries, write-offs and inventory that is too large in proportion to sales or assets. Methods for improving inventory management include systems that monitor stock levels continuously, and techniques such as just-in-time management and the 80/20 rule.

Transportation adds time and place utility to a product by moving it from where it is made to where it is purchased and used. The five major *transport modes* are motor vehicles, railways, inland waterways, airways and pipelines. Marketers evaluate transport modes with respect to *costs, transit time, reliability, capability, accessibility, security* and *traceability;* the final selection of a transport mode involves many trade-offs.

Physical distribution affects every element of the marketing mix: product, price, promotion, place/distribution and personnel/customer service. To give customers products at acceptable prices, marketers consider consumers' changing needs and any shifts within the major distribution functions. They then adapt existing physical distribution systems for greater effectiveness. Physical distribution functions account for about a third of all marketing costs and have a significant impact on customer satisfaction. Therefore, effective marketers are actively involved in the design and control of physical distribution systems. Increasingly, many of the logistics activities described in this chapter are subject to *outsourcing.*

The growth of multi-channel marketing and home delivery has placed greater importance on channel management to safeguard customer experience and ensure brand experience is similar across channels. The increase in direct delivery and eCommerce has added to the facilitating agents and channel players on which marketers rely to effectively manage their customers.

EXERCISE QUESTIONS

1 Generically, what services do wholesalers provide to producers and retailers?

2 What are the advantages of using agents to replace merchant wholesalers? What are the disadvantages?

3 What are the principal types of retailers?

4 Describe the most common forms of non-store retailing and what is driving growth for some of these.

5 How can managers improve inventory control? Give specific examples of techniques.

CASE 13.1

Today's cash and carry mega-depots depend on effective stockholding and physical distribution

The wholesale grocery trade is worth £19 billion in the U.K., 47 per cent of which is delivered trade and 53 per cent cash and carry. Cash and carry businesses stock manufacturers' products and have as their customers other businesses, such as small shopkeepers or the hospitality sector, which select merchandise appropriate for their respective target consumers. In order to satisfy the demands of small retail businesses, for example, the leading grocery cash and carry operators have to stock extensive ranges, only a small part of which may be selected by an individual retailer client. Inventory control is particularly important to these cash and carry businesses, but so too are the logistical considerations of receiving deliveries from manufacturers and enabling customers to take out their orders. In the U.K., Booker has 172 depots at an average of 80,000 square feet and Bestway has 51 depots. Makro, however, has 30 depots at an average size of 150,000 square feet. For Makro, the task of replenishing such mighty cash-and-carry depots is a core part of its business proposition.

Although price remains a core trading proposition, service and brand image are increasingly important. Indeed, the cash and carry sector was shaken up by the entry of Holland's Makro, a self-service wholesaler. Makro is part of Metro Group, the world's largest wholesaler, operating in over 30 countries. In the U.K., 30 stores serve the country. Makro's depots have the latest computer systems, customer service points and in-store displays. Makro serves the trade as a cash and carry wholesaler of groceries, fresh foods, wines, spirits, beer and cigarettes, household goods, clothing, toys and sports equipment. The company retails a clutch of own-label brands in these categories, including Aro, Horeca Select (kitchen ware), Rioba (coffee solutions for bars, cafes and hotels), H-Line (hotels and guest houses), Fine Food (for corner shops, kiosks, forecourts) and Sigma (office goods).

In a relatively traditional sector dominated by several long-standing companies, Makro had a major impact in a short time. Its mix of merchandise is more comprehensive than that of its competitors, forcing several – such as Booker and Bestway – to rethink their merchandising strategies. Because depth and breadth of stock within individual product categories are not as extensive as those of U.K. rivals, the industry has been prompted to rethink, and most companies have reduced the number of lines stocked. Although not the first wholesaler with own-label products, Makro's promotion of its own ranges has encouraged its competitors to divert more attention to this area.

Perhaps Makro's biggest impact has been in the sales and marketing techniques it has brought to the U.K. Cash and carry warehouses used to be dowdy depots that paid little attention to layout, upkeep, design or ambience, and demonstrated even less regard for customer service and satisfaction. Price was the name of the game: customers could buy in bulk at a discount but were offered few additional benefits. Makro's philosophy brings to the cash and carry sector the retailing techniques of the hypermarket: carefully controlled branch designs and layouts, high levels of staff training and a significant focus on building ongoing relationships with customers. An emphasis on managing its inventory and the associated need for effective physical distribution are pivotal to Makro's ability to serve its business customers in the retail and catering trades.

Makro's philosophy is encouraging other wholesalers to follow suit. Now customers are being offered better service, together with assistance in building their own company image through local press and television advertising. The leading cash and carry companies are offering marketing support to their key accounts not just to stimulate sales but also to build up those customers' loyalty to their nearby warehouse. Depots have been uprated by the leading groups, with new equipment, better stocking systems and improved physical distribution. They have also initiated sales promotions campaigns and incentive programmes. Computerisation has helped lower costs and improve efficiency. For example, with Germany's Siemens Nixdorf, Booker created MIDAS (management information depot application system), giving each of its depots a comprehensive invoicing, mailing, sales data, customer information and stock control system. This system improved Booker's ability to target customers and monitor stock needs. Systems such as MIDAS have enabled the leading companies to reduce their product lines without alienating customers. For example, Nurdin & Peacock used to carry 60,000 lines but reduced its coverage to 40,000 without losing customers. In most of the leading businesses, branches are being rationalised, both to respond to economic downturns, and to benefit from cost economies and enhanced computer systems. Companies are either consolidating three outdated neighbouring depots into one central, spacious, service-oriented depot, or they are closing a branch while extending and refurbishing a neighbouring one.

References: *Marketing: Concepts and Strategies*, 5th edition; Makro, 2011; www.igd.com, June, 2011; www.makro.co.uk, June, 2011.

Questions

1 How are the major cash and carry companies responding to changing customer needs?

2 In what ways are state-of-the-art inventory management and physical distribution systems important to companies such as Makro or Booker?

RECOMMENDED READINGS

Arikan, A., *Multichannel Marketing: Metrics and Methods for On and Offline Success* (Wiley, 2008).

Christopher, M., *Logistics and Supply Chain Management* (FT/Prentice-Hall, 2010).

Dent, J., *Distribution Channels: Understanding and Managing Channels to Market* (Kogan Page, 2011)

Gattorna, J., ed., *Strategic Supply Chain Alignment: Best Practices in Supply Chain Management* (Gower, 2005).

Harrison, A. and van Hoek, R., *Logistics Management and Strategy: Competing Through the Supply Chain* (FT/Prentice-Hall, 2010).

Hines, T., *Supply Chain Strategies* (Routledge, 2012).

McGoldrick, P. J., *Retail Marketing* (London: McGraw-Hill, 2002).

Rosenbloom, B., *Marketing Channels: A Management View* (South Western, 2012).

Rushton, A., Croucher, P., Oxley J, and Baker, P., *The Handbook of Logistics and Distribution Management* (Kogan Page, 2010).

Varley, R. and Rafiq, M., *Principles of Retail Management* (Palgrave Macmillan, 2012).

Waters, D., *Global Logistics: New Directions in Supply Chain Management* (Kogan Page, 2010).

14 MARKETING COMMUNICATIONS

BUSINESS FOCUS

Škoda has the last laugh

The Czech word Škoda means pity or shame so on seeing a passing Škoda car, Czechs used to say "there goes a shame" – and nobody would argue much. Today Škoda Autos (of the Czech Republic), once a butt of jokes, has now completely overhauled its image. This has been done by clever, playful marketing campaigns making light of the negative image of Škoda previously held in public perception; positive reviews from the motor trade, including TV shows like the popular Top Gear; and successful campaigns in professional motorsports, including rally driving championships.

Now 98 per cent of its drivers say they would recommend Škoda to a friend. Škoda uses this to guide its future strategic development and marketing. Škoda U.K. used this to develop their marketing strategy based on the confident slogan, "the manufacturer of happy drivers" of its brand image. With the help of its German partner Volkswagen who have the controlling share in Škoda, its profitability has consistently grown. The company employs about 4 per cent of the Czech workforce, or 150 000 people, directly or indirectly. In addition to the Czech Republic, Škoda cars are now made in Ukraine, India, Bosnia and Herzegovina, Kazakhstan, China and Russia. Cars are assembled in country from parts and components exported from the Czech Republic and they have worldwide sales of over 700 000.

Productivity in its plants is higher than Western levels and labour costs are much lower than at other VW plants in Europe. Analysts reckon that Škoda is the most successful company from a former Communist region. At time of writing, they produce 700 000 cars and are Central Europe's largest car manufacturer. The growth has been driven by exports. Ten years ago around 30 per cent of Škodas were sold abroad, now over 80 per cent are exported. Its major sales success has been in China, where Škoda has doubled its sales in one year. Its controlled expansion into Western Europe has continued apace, especially into Germany, the firm's biggest Western market. The best selling Škoda model worldwide is the Octavia which sells 158 024 cars a year.

Volkswagen's presence in Central Europe has had three advantages. First, it increased Volkswagen's leadership in Europe through the conquest of local central European markets. Second, it increased competitiveness through local manufacturing and purchases. Third, it has allowed them the possibility of using Škoda to develop its worldwide presence.

References: www.Škoda-auto.com, http://www.thetimes100.co.uk/downloads/Škoda/ and http://www.autoexpress.co.uk/news/ autoexpressnews.

arketers employ multiple promotional methods to create very favourable company and product images in the minds of customers. Skillful use of promotion is of great benefit to many brands.

Promotion is communication about an organisation and its products that is intended to inform, persuade, or remind target-market members. The promotion with which we are most familiar—advertising—is intended to inform, persuade, or remind us to buy particular products. But there is more to promotion than advertising, and it is used for other purposes as well. Charities use promotion to inform us of their need for donations, to persuade us to give, and to remind us to do so in case we have forgotten. Even government revenue services use promotion (in the form of publicity) to remind employees or the self-employed (depending on country) of the national deadline for filing tax returns.

promotion communication about an organisation and its products that is intended to inform, persuade, or remind target-market members

A **promotion mix** (sometimes called a *marketing–communications mix*) is the particular combination of promotional methods a firm uses to reach a target market. The makeup of a mix depends on many factors, including the firm's promotional resources and objectives, the nature of the target market, the product characteristics, and the feasibility of various promotional methods.

> **promotion mix** the particular combination of promotion methods a firm uses to reach a target market

In this chapter, we introduce four promotional methods and describe how they are used in an organisation's marketing plans. First, we examine the role of advertising in the promotion mix. We discuss different types of advertising, the process of developing an advertising campaign, and social and legal concerns in advertising.

Next, we consider several categories of personal selling, noting the importance of effective sales management. We also look at sales promotion—why firms use it and which sales promotion techniques are most effective. Then we explain how public relations can be used to promote an organisation and its products. Also, we illustrate how these four promotional methods are combined in an effective promotion mix. Finally, we discuss the criticisms of promotion.

WHAT IS INTEGRATED MARKETING COMMUNICATIONS?

Integrated marketing communications is the coordination of promotion efforts to ensure their maximal informational and persuasive impact on customers. A major goal of integrated marketing communications is to send a consistent message to customers. This approach fosters not only long-term customer relationships but also the efficient use of promotional resources.

> **integrated marketing communications** coordination of promotion efforts to ensure their maximal informational and persuasive impact on customers

The concept of integrated marketing communications has been increasingly accepted for several reasons. Mass-media advertising, a very popular promotional method in the past, is used less today because of its high costs and unpredictable audience sizes. Marketers now can take advantage of more precisely targeted promotional tools, such as digital TV, direct mail, DVDs, the Internet, special-interest magazines, and podcasts. Database marketing is also allowing marketers to be more precise in targeting individual customers. Mass media advertising used to be much more popular than it is today. It is still widely used, but as only one tool in an expanding toolkit of marketing communication options. Marketers today have access to a wide variety of advertising and promotional options. Marketers can now use a mix of high-tech options. Thanks to online digital media, marketers today can more precisely identify their target audience with affordable advertising campaigns that directly address their customers' needs and wants. Until recently, specialists handled different aspects of marketing communication campaigns. Advertising agencies created advertising campaigns, sales promotion companies handled sales promotion activities, and public relations firms handled public relations issues. Today, firms can rely on organisations that provide one-stop shopping for all marketing and promotion-related activities. Such firms help to reduce coordination problems and improve integration between different functions. This is beneficial because marketing communications can be very expensive and it is important for firms to ensure that promotional resources are used as efficiently as possible. To appeal to consumers while saving money on their advertising budgets, firms are even relying on customers to help develop effective advertisements and to design promotional activities. Companies like Doritos and Pepsi have utilised consumer advertising and promotion ideas with great success. These campaigns generate a lot of buzz and can be produced much more cheaply than a professional campaign. Viral marketing is another way to achieve broad advertising reach via digital channels for minimal cost. Most marketers now acknowledge the importance and power of utilising viral marketing.*

THE ROLE OF PROMOTION

Promotion is commonly the object of two misconceptions. Often, people take note of highly visible promotional activities, such as advertising and personal selling, and conclude that these make up the entire field of marketing. People also sometimes consider promotional activities to be unnecessary, expensive, and the cause of higher prices. Neither view is accurate.

The role of promotion is to facilitate exchanges directly or indirectly by informing individuals, groups, or organisations and influencing them to accept a firm's products or to have more positive feelings about the firm. To expedite exchanges directly, marketers convey information about a firm's goods, services, and ideas to particular market segments. To bring about exchanges indirectly, marketers address interest groups (such as environmental and consumer groups), regulatory agencies, investors, and the general public concerning a company and its products. The broader role of promotion, therefore, is to maintain positive relationships between a company and various groups in the marketing environment.

Marketers frequently design promotional communications, such as advertisements, for specific groups, although some may be directed at wider audiences. Several different messages may be communicated simultaneously to different market segments. For example, BP must address stakeholders concerned about the aftereffects of the 2010 Deepwater Horizon oil leak and subsequent cleanup efforts; inform customers about its products and services; and update investors about financial performance.

Marketers must plan, implement, and coordinate promotional communications carefully to make the best use of them. The effectiveness of promotional activities depends greatly on the quality and quantity of information available to marketers about the organisation's marketing environment (see Figure 14.1). If a marketer wants to influence customers to buy a certain product, for example, the firm must know who these customers are and how they make purchase decisions for that type of product. Marketers must gather and use information about particular audiences to communicate successfully with them. At times, two or more firms partner in joint promotional efforts.

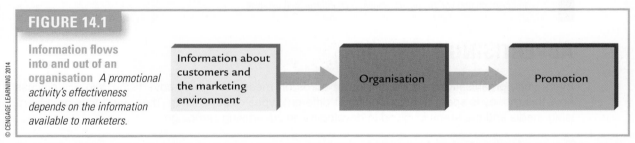

FIGURE 14.1

Information flows into and out of an organisation *A promotional activity's effectiveness depends on the information available to marketers.*

© CENGAGE LEARNING 2014

Source: William M. Pride and O. C. Ferrell, *Marketing: Concepts and Strategies,* 17h ed. (Mason, OH: South-Western/Cengage Learning, 2014). Adapted with permission.

THE PROMOTION MIX: AN OVERVIEW

Marketers can use several promotional methods to communicate with individuals, groups, and organisations. The methods that are combined to promote a particular product make up the promotion mix for that item.

Advertising, personal selling, sales promotion, and public relations are the four major elements in an organisation's promotion mix (see Figure 14.2) While it is possible that only one ingredient may be used, it is likely that two, three, or four of these ingredients will be used together in a promotion mix, depending on the type of product and target market involved.

Advertising is a paid nonpersonal message communicated to a select audience through a mass medium. Advertising is flexible enough that it can reach a very large target group or a small, carefully chosen one. **Personal selling** is personal communication aimed at informing customers and persuading them to buy a firm's products. It is more expensive to reach a consumer through personal selling

FIGURE 14.2

Possible ingredients of a promotion mix *Depending on the type of product and target market involved, one or more of these ingredients are used in a promotion mix.*

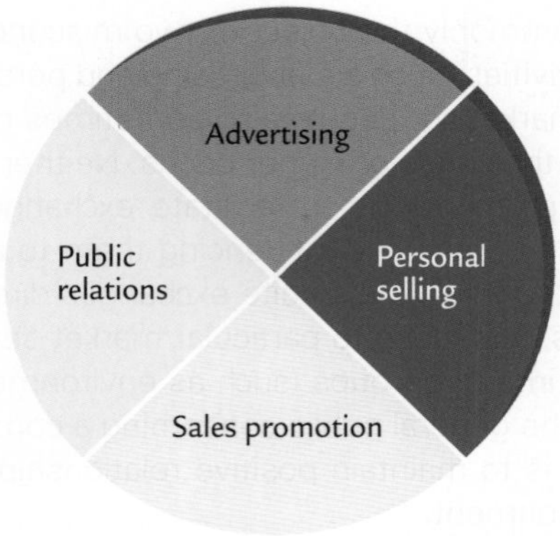

Source: William M. Pride and O. C. Ferrell, *Marketing: Concepts and Strategies*, 17th ed. (Mason, OH: South-Western/Cengage Learning, 2014). Adapted with permission.

than through advertising, but this method provides immediate feedback and often is more persuasive than advertising. **Sales promotion** is the use of activities or materials as direct inducements to customers or salespersons. It adds extra value to the product or increases the customer's incentive to buy the product. **Public relations** is a broad set of communication activities used to create and maintain favourable relationships between an organisation and various public groups, both internal and external.

> **advertising** a paid nonpersonal message communicated to a select audience through a mass medium
> **personal selling** personal communication aimed at informing customers and persuading them to buy a firm's products
> **sales promotion** the use of activities or materials as direct inducements to customers or salespersons
> **public relations** communication activities used to create and maintain favourable relations between an organisation and various public groups, both internal and external

ADVERTISING

Every year, organisations spend billions of euros on measured media advertising. We will discuss how this money is spent by first looking at different types of advertising. Then, we focus on advertising media and the steps involved in developing an advertising campaign.

Types of advertising by purpose

Depending on its purpose and message, advertising may be classified into one of three groups: primary demand, selective demand, or institutional.

Primary-demand advertising **Primary-demand advertising** is advertising aimed at increasing the demand for *all* brands of a product within a specific industry. The British meat industry, for example, has frequently launched campaigns designed to encourage U.K. residents to purchase home-reared beef and lamb.

> **primary-demand advertising** advertising aimed at increasing the demand for all brands of a product within a specific industry

Selective-demand advertising **Selective-demand (or brand) advertising** is advertising that is used to sell a particular brand of product. It is by far the most common type of advertising, and it accounts for the lion's share of advertising expenditures.

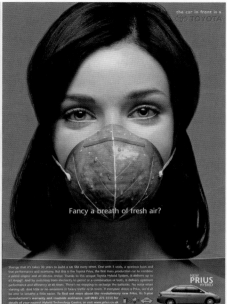

Primary-demand advertising versus selective-demand advertising. The "got milk?" ad is designed to stimulate the demand for all *milk brands. It is an example of primary-demand advertising. In contrast, the Prius ad is designed to stimulate a single *car brand. It is an example of selective-demand advertising.*

---

selective-demand (or brand) advertising advertising that is used to sell a particular brand of product

---

Selective advertising that aims at persuading consumers to make purchases within a short time is called *immediate-response advertising.* Most local advertising is of this type. Often local advertisers promote products with immediate appeal. Selective advertising aimed at keeping a firm's name or product before the public is called *reminder advertising.*

Comparative advertising, which has become more popular over the last three decades, compares specific characteristics of two or more identified brands. Of course, the comparison shows the advertiser's brand to be as good as or better than the other identified competing brands. Consumers sometimes become rather guarded concerning claims based on "scientific studies" and various statistical manipulations. Comparative advertising is unacceptable or illegal in a number of countries.

Institutional advertising **Institutional advertising** is advertising designed to enhance a firm's image or reputation. A positive public image helps an organisation to attract not only customers but also employees and investors. BP's "Still Working, Still Committed" campaign addresses the company's efforts to clean up and maintain the environment in the Gulf of Mexico after the massive Deepwater Horizon oil leak. This ongoing ad campaign seeks to repair BP's damaged image by demonstrating a commitment to cleaning up pollution in the Gulf, showing a commitment to environmentalism, and restoring consumer faith in the company.*

---

institutional advertising advertising designed to enhance a firm's image or reputation

---

Advertising media

The **advertising media** are the various forms of communication through which advertising reaches its audience. The major media are newspapers, magazines, direct mail, Yellow Pages, out-of-home displays, television, radio, the Internet, and social media. Figure 14.3 shows the typical proportion of funds spent on selected media.

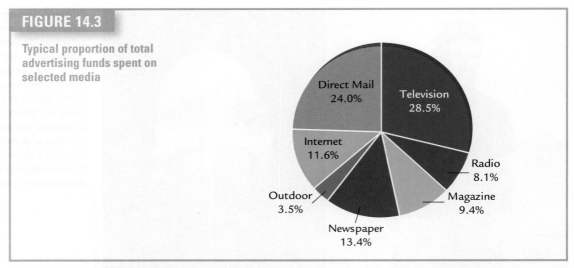

FIGURE 14.3

Typical proportion of total advertising funds spent on selected media

Source: "U.S. Ad Spending Totals," *Advertising Age*, June 20, 2011, p. 18.

advertising media the various forms of communication through which advertising reaches its audience

Newspapers   A very large proportion of newspaper advertising is purchased by local retailers. Retailers use newspaper advertising extensively because it is relatively inexpensive compared with other media. Moreover, since most newspapers provide local coverage, advertising dollars are not wasted in reaching people outside the organisation's market area. It is also timely. Ads usually can be placed just a few days before they are to appear.

There are some drawbacks, however, to newspaper advertising. It has a short life span; newspapers generally are read through once and then discarded. Newspaper readership is declining. Colour reproduction in newspapers is usually not high quality; thus, most ads are run in black and white. Finally, marketers cannot target specific demographic groups through newspaper ads because newspapers are read by such a broad spectrum of people.

Magazines   The amount of money companies spend on magazine advertising has been flat over the last few years. However, advertisers can reach very specific market segments through ads in special-interest magazines. A boat manufacturer has a ready-made consumer audience in subscribers to *Yachting* or *Sail*. A number of magazines such as *Time* and *Cosmopolitan* publish regional editions, which provide advertisers with geographic flexibility as well.

Magazine advertising is more prestigious than newspaper advertising, and it allows for high-quality colour reproduction. In addition, magazine advertisements have a longer life span than those in other media and the ads they contain may be viewed repeatedly.

The major disadvantages of magazine advertising are high cost and lack of timeliness. Because magazine ads normally must be prepared two to three months in advance, they cannot be adjusted to reflect the latest market conditions. Magazine ads—especially full-colour ads—are also expensive. Although the cost of reaching 18 million people may compare favourably with that of other media, the cost of a full-page four-colour ad can be very high—€320,000 in *Time*.*

Direct mail   **Direct-mail advertising** is promotional material mailed directly to individuals. Direct mail is the most selective medium; mailing lists are available (or can be compiled) to reach almost any target audience, from aeroplane enthusiasts to zoologists. The effectiveness of direct-mail advertising can be measured because the advertiser has a record of who received the advertisements and can track who responds to the ads.

***Taking advertising to the streets—and
other places.*** *Out-of-home advertisements are
designed to reach consumers while they are out
of their homes. Promotional messages on buses,
the backs of street benches, in stadiums, and
on backs of the doors of restroom stalls are all
examples of out-of-home advertising.*

direct-mail advertising promotional material mailed directly to individuals

Some organisations are using direct e-mail. To avoid customers receiving unwanted e-mail, a firm should ask customers to complete a request form in order to receive promotional e-mail from the company.

The success of direct-mail advertising depends to some extent on maintaining appropriate and current mailing lists. A direct-mail campaign may fail if the mailing list is outdated and the mailing does not reach the right people. In addition, this medium is relatively costly.

Yellow pages advertising **Yellow Pages advertising** appears in telephone directories that are distributed to millions of customers around the world, as well as online. Customers use Yellow Pages advertising to save time finding products, to find information quickly, and to learn about products and marketers. Unalike other types of advertising media, Yellow Pages advertisements are purchased for one year and cannot be changed.

Yellow Pages advertising simple listings or display advertisements presented under specific product categories
    appearing in print and online telephone directories

Out-of-home advertising **Out-of-home advertising** consists of short promotional messages on hoardings, posters, signs, and transportation vehicles.

out-of-home advertising short promotional messages on hoardings, posters, signs, and transportation vehicles

Sign and hoarding advertising allows the marketer to focus on a particular geographic area; it is also fairly inexpensive. However, because most outdoor promotion is directed toward a mobile audience, the message must be limited to a few words. The medium is especially suitable for products that lend themselves to pictorial display.

Television Television ranks number one in total advertising expenditures. Whilst it naturally varies from country to country, a large proportion of homes in many countries across the world have at least one television set. In the U.K. the Broadcaster's Audience Research Board (BARB) estimates that 26.8 million households, or roughly 97%, have a television. In South Africa, it is closer to 74%.

Television advertising is the primary medium for larger firms whose objective is to reach national or regional markets. A national advertiser may buy *network time*, which means that its message usually will be broadcast by hundreds of local stations affiliated with the network. However, the opportunity to reach extremely large television audiences has been reduced by the increased availability and popularity of online streaming and DVDS (although streaming services have opened up new advertising channels in themselves). Both national and local firms may buy *local time* on a single station that covers a particular geographic area.

Advertisers may *sponsor* an entire show, participate with other sponsors of a show, or buy *spot time* for a single 10-, 20-, 30-, or 60-second commercial during or between programmes. To an extent, they may select their audience by choosing the day of the week and the approximate time of day their ads will be shown. Advertisers often target the specific audience of a particular show or televised event, based on the market segment most likely to be watching. For example, adverts during a children's TV show in the morning are likely to be very different compared those aired during a late night movie, major sporting event, or a cookery show, and so forth.

Laws and regulations do differ from country to country on exactly what can or cannot be shown, and the language that is used, at specific times of day, or targeted at specific market segments. In the U.K. it is illegal to advertise tobacco products via any media at any hour. Likewise rules have tightened on advertising specifically aimed at children. Some countries are more sensitive towards nudity and coarse language than others, depending on various cultural factors.

Marketers also can employ *product placement,* which is paying a fee to have a product appear in a television programme, movie, or music video. The product might appear on a table or counter, or one or more of the actors might be using it. Through channel switching and personal digital video recorders (DVRs), television viewers can avoid watching regular television commercials. By placing the product directly into the programme, viewers are likely to be exposed to the product. Product placement continues to be a stable advertising method for many marketers. Again, different national laws can apply with regard to product placement on television. Music videos are increasingly a venue for product placement, particularly if an artist is a representative for a product. Artists like Lady Gaga, Katy Perry, and Rihanna frequently showcase prominently-displayed products and brand names in their music videos. To facilitate the product placement process in music videos, My Product Placement is a new platform that aims to match musical artists and products.* Recently researchers reported that 90 per cent of all television viewing remains live because more than half of all TV households still do not have access to time-shifting devices (DVRs). Even in households that do have DVRs, only about 20 per cent of the viewing time is shifted.

Another option available to television advertisers is the infomercial. An **infomercial** is a programme-length televised commercial message resembling an entertainment or consumer affairs programme. Infomercials for products such as exercise equipment tell customers why they need the product, what benefits it provides, in what ways it outperforms its competitors, and how much it costs. Currently, infomercials are responsible for marketing over $1 billion worth of products annually. Even some *Fortune* 500 companies are using them.

infomercial a programme-length televised commercial message resembling an entertainment or consumer affairs programme

Television advertising rates are based on the number of people expected to be watching when the commercial is aired. In 2012, the cost of a 30-second during the national American football Super Bowl event was $3.5 million. In the U.S., advertisers typically spend over $500,000 for a 30-second television commercial during a top-rated prime-time programme.*

Radio Like magazine advertising, radio advertising offers selectivity. Radio stations develop programming for—and are tuned in by—specific groups of listeners.

Radio advertising can be less expensive than in other media. Actual rates depend on geographic coverage, the number of commercials contracted for, the time period specified, the station's listener figures, and the wavelength the station transmits on. Even small retailers are able to afford radio advertising, and a radio advertiser can schedule and change ads on short notice. The disadvantages of using radio are the absence of visual images and (because there are so many stations) the small audience size.

Harnessing the power of social media— or not? *Social media allows a business to reach out to customers in a context that is familiar and comfortable to them. Firms attempt to measure the effectiveness of their social media efforts by gathering statistics on the number of followers and fans they have, traffic to their Web sites, and mentions of their products on social networking sites. Whether or not this type of advertising results in additional sales can be difficult to tell.*

Internet   Spending on Internet advertising has increased significantly. Internet advertising can take a variety of forms. The *banner ad* is a rectangular graphic that appears at the top of a Web site. Many Web sites are able to offer free services because they are supported by banner advertisements. Advertisers can use animation and interactive capabilities to draw more attention to their ads. Another type of advertising is *sponsorship* (or *cobranded* ads). These ads integrate a company's brand with editorial content. The goal of this type of ad is to get users to strongly identify the advertiser with the site's mission. For example, a running shoe advertiser such as Puma may choose to place advertisements on a popular lifestyle blog related to running because the site is affiliated with the mission and activities of the firm. Many Web sites display clickable advertisements related to featured articles. Someone browsing articles on windows, for example, would find advertisements for different windows on the site. Such online ads also make it easy for consumers to click over to the company's site to make purchases or browse products.*

Many Internet advertisers choose to purchase keywords on popular search engines such as Google, Bing, Yahoo!, and MSN. For example, Kellogg's purchased the word *cereal* on Google so that every time someone conducts a search using that word, a link to Kellogg's Web site appears. *Interstitial* ads pop up to display a product. For example, users of www.Hulu.com can watch any of the available TV episodes and movies free of charge by viewing commercials periodically throughout each video.

Social media   In the last few years, the use of social media as an advertising medium has increased dramatically. This is largely due to the perception that marketers can target, interact with, and connect more personally with their customers through the different social-media outlets as opposed to more traditional media. Increasingly, customers expect companies to have an online presence. Most firms have a Web site and many also communicate information and relay promotions via Twitter, Facebook, and LinkedIn. Businesses may also post advertisements on social media sites and blogs. Some companies also have their own branded sites that incorporate aspects and features of social media sites, but focus on their own brands and products. Even politicians are increasingly utilising social media to reach out to the electorate directly.

While companies increasingly feel pressure to incorporate digital media, such as social networking sites, into their marketing mixes, research is not clear on the exact benefits of utilising online social media for advertising. Social media can be a very low-cost advertising medium and it can be an excellent means for reaching a targeted audience, but social media sites are not as good at reaching broad or diverse audiences. To contrast, a television ad broadcast during a major sporting event can reach millions of highly diverse viewers at once. Because of the smaller nature of Internet audiences and the problems of whether online customers actually see the promotions, measuring the return on investment of social media advertising remains a challenge. Firms may measure things like followers and fans, traffic to a site, and social media mentions across other digital platforms, but marketers have a hard time translating this data into an estimate on return on investment. Nevertheless, most marketers feel that online social media are important tools and many firms have full-time social media experts on staff.*

Major steps in developing an advertising campaign

An advertising campaign is developed in several stages. These stages may vary in number and the order in which they are implemented depending on the company's resources, products, and audiences. The development of a campaign in any organisation, however, will include the following steps in some form:

1. Identify and analyse the target audience The target audience is the group of people toward whom a firm's advertisements are directed. To pinpoint the organisation's target audience and develop an effective campaign, marketers must analyse such information as the geographic distribution of potential customers; their age, sex, race, income, and education; and their attitudes toward both the advertiser's product and competing products. How marketers use this information will be influenced by the features of the product to be advertised and the nature of the competition. Precise identification of the target audience is crucial to the proper development of subsequent stages and, ultimately, to the success of the campaign itself. Rykä, for example, produces running shoes and accessories aimed at a target audience of female runners. It claims that its products are tailored to fit a woman's foot shape and skeletal structure. As part of its promotional activities, the company partners with exercise programmes, such as Jazzercize, that attract more women than men.*

2. Define the advertising objectives The goals of an advertising campaign should be stated precisely and in measurable terms. The objectives should include the firm's current position, indicate how far and in what direction from that original reference point the company wishes to move, and specify a definite period of time for the achievement of the goals. Advertising objectives that focus on sales will stress increasing sales by a certain percentage or amount or expanding the firm's market share. Communication objectives will emphasise increasing product or brand awareness, improving consumer attitudes, or conveying product information.

3. Create the advertising platform An advertising platform includes the important selling points or features that an advertiser wishes to incorporate into the advertising campaign. These features should be important to customers in their selection and use of a product, and, if possible, they should be features that competing products lack. Although research into what consumers view as important issues is expensive, it is the most productive way to determine which issues to include in an advertising platform. For instance, customer research might indicate to the manufacturer of a cold-symptom reliever that customers want a product that relieves your coughing, stops your nose from running, and keeps your eyes from watering.

4. Determine the advertising appropriation The advertising appropriation is the total amount of money designated for advertising in a given period. This stage is critical to the campaign's success because advertising efforts based on an inadequate budget will understimulate customer demand, and a budget too large will waste a company's resources. Advertising appropriations may be based on last year's (or next year's forecasted) sales, on what competitors spend on advertising, or on executive judgment. Table 14.1 shows some of the biggest advertising spenders. Procter & Gamble is traditionally one of the top spenders.

5. Develop the media plan A media plan specifies exactly which media will be used in the campaign and when advertisements will appear. For example, marketers are not likely to rely on digital media advertising to sell life insurance aimed at retired people because older consumers are not as likely to use the Internet as younger ones. Although cost-effectiveness is not easy to measure, the primary concern of the media planner is to reach the largest number of persons in the target audience for each dollar spent. In addition to cost, media planners must consider the location and demographics of people in the advertising target, the content of the message, and the characteristics of the audiences reached by various media. The media planner begins with general media decisions, selects subclasses within each medium, and, finally, chooses particular media vehicles for the campaign.

TABLE 14.1 Who spends the most on advertising?

Rank	Company	Advertising expenditures (in millions)	Sales (in millions)	Advertising expenditure as a percentage of sales
1	Procter & Gamble Co.	$ 4,615	$ 29,488	15.7
2	AT&T	2,989	123,018	2.4
3	General Motors Co.	2,869	34,514	8.3
4	Verizon Communications	2,451	107,808	2.3
5	American Express Co.	2,223	13,900	16.0
6	Pfizer	2,124	22,504	9.4
7	Walmart Stores	2,055	261,257	0.8
8	Time Warner	2,044	10,960	18.6
9	Johnson & Johnson	2,027	30,330	6.7
10	L'Oreal	1,979	5,742	34.5
11	Walt Disney Co.	1,932	26,389	7.3
12	JPMorgan Chase & Co.	1,917	86,724	2.2
13	Ford Motor Co.	1,915	43,774	4.4
14	Comcast Corp.	1,853	35,996	5.2
15	Sears Holdings Corp.	1,779	36,996	4.8
16	Toyota Motor Corp.	1,736	59,971	2.9
17	Bank of America Corp.	1,553	130,892	1.2
18	Target Corp.	1,508	65,357	2.3
19	Macy's	1,417	23,489	6.0
20	Sprint Nextel Corp.	1,400	32,260	4.3

Source: Reprinted with permission from the June 20, 2011, issue of *Advertising Age.* Copyright Crain Communications Inc., 2011.

6. Create the advertising message The content and form of a message are influenced by the product's features, the characteristics of people in the target audience, the objectives of the campaign, and the choice of media. An advertiser must consider these factors when choosing words and illustrations that will be meaningful and appealing to persons in the advertising target. The copy, or words, of an advertisement will vary depending on the media choice but should attempt to move the audience through attention, interest, desire, and action. Artwork and visuals should complement copy by attracting the audience's attention and communicating an idea quickly. Creating a cohesive advertising message is especially difficult for a company such as eBay that offers such a broad mix of products. eBay developed a "whatever it is" campaign that features a variety of consumers representing all age groups using a variety of products (a car, a television, a dress, and a laptop) all shaped like the letters "it." The tagline, "Whatever *it* is, you can get it on eBay," emphasises the massive range of products available from the site and effectively showcases the service that the company provides its customers.

7. Execute the campaign The execution of an advertising campaign requires extensive planning, scheduling, and coordinating because many tasks must be completed on time. Many people and firms, such as production companies, research organisations, media firms, printers, photoengravers, and commercial artists, may contribute to a campaign. Advertising managers constantly must assess the quality of the work and take corrective action when necessary. Situations may also arise that require a change in plans. Designer Marc Jacobs' marketing team had to scramble to release new advertisements after the initial print ad for its Oh, Lola! perfume was banned in the United Kingdom for being deemed overly inappropriate. Marc Jacobs' marketing team responded by releasing some toned-down advertisements in its place.*

8. Evaluate advertising effectiveness A campaign's success should be measured in terms of its original objectives before, during, and/or after the campaign. An advertiser should at least be able to estimate whether sales or market share went up because of the campaign or whether any change occurred in customer attitudes or brand awareness. Data from past and current sales and responses to coupon offers and customer surveys administered by research organisations are some of the ways in which advertising effectiveness can be evaluated. While most marketers agree that digital media and online social media are essential marketing tools, it can be difficult to gather measurements on the effectiveness of online advertising, such as return on investment.*

Advertising agencies

Advertisers can plan and produce their own advertising with help from media personnel, or they can hire **advertising agencies**. An advertising agency is an independent firm that plans, produces, and places advertising for its clients. Many large ad agencies offer help with sales promotion and public relations as well. The media usually pay a commission of 15 per cent to advertising agencies. Thus, the cost to the agency's client can be quite moderate. The client may be asked to pay for special services that the agency performs. Other methods for compensating agencies are also used.

advertising agency an independent firm that plans, produces, and places advertising for its clients

Firms that do a lot of advertising may use both an in-house advertising department and an independent agency. This approach gives the firm the advantage of being able to call on the agency's expertise in particular areas of advertising. An agency also can bring a fresh viewpoint to a firm's products and advertising plans.

PERSONAL SELLING

Personal selling is the most adaptable of all promotional methods because the person who is presenting the message can modify it to suit the individual buyer. However, personal selling is also the most expensive method of promotion.

Most successful salespeople are able to communicate with others on a one-to-one basis and are strongly motivated. They strive to have a thorough knowledge of the products they offer for sale, and they are willing and able to deal with the details involved in handling and processing orders. Sales managers tend to emphasise these qualities when recruiting and hiring.

Many selling situations demand the face-to-face contact and adaptability of personal selling. This is especially true of industrial sales, in which a single purchase may amount to millions of dollars. Obviously, sales of that size must be based on carefully planned sales presentations, personal contact with customers, and thorough negotiations.

Kinds of salespersons

Because most businesses employ different salespersons to perform different functions, marketing managers must select the kinds of sales personnel that will be most effective in selling the firm's products. Salespersons may be identified as order-getters, order-takers, and support personnel. A single individual can, and often does, perform all three functions.

Order-getters An **order-getter** is responsible for what is sometimes called **creative selling**—selling a firm's products to new customers and increasing sales to current customers. An order-getter must perceive buyers' needs, supply customers with information about the firm's product, and persuade them to buy the product. Order-getting activities may be separated into two groups. In current-customer sales, salespeople concentrate on obtaining additional sales or leads for prospective sales from customers who have purchased the firm's products at least once. In new-business sales, sales personnel seek out new prospects and convince them to make an initial purchase of the firm's product. The real estate, insurance, appliance, heavy industrial machinery, and automobile industries in particular depend on new-business sales.

> **order-getter** a salesperson who is responsible for selling a firm's products to new customers and increasing sales to present customers
>
> **creative selling** selling products to new customers and increasing sales to present customers

Order-takers An **order-taker** handles repeat sales in ways that maintain positive relationships with customers. An order-taker sees that customers have products when and where they are needed and in the proper amounts. *Inside order-takers* receive incoming mail and telephone orders in some businesses; salespersons in retail stores are also inside order-takers. *Outside* (or *field*) *order-takers* travel to customers. Often, the buyer and the field salesperson develop a mutually beneficial relationship of placing, receiving, and delivering orders. Both inside and outside order-takers are active salespersons and often produce most of their companies' sales.

> **order-taker** a salesperson who handles repeat sales in ways that maintain positive relationships with customers

Support personnel **Sales support personnel** aid in selling but are more involved in locating *prospects* (likely first-time customers), educating customers, building goodwill for the firm, and providing follow-up service. The most common categories of support personnel are missionary, trade, and technical salespersons.

> **sales support personnel** employees who aid in selling but are more involved in locating prospects, educating customers, building goodwill for the firm, and providing follow-up service

A **missionary salesperson**, who usually works for a manufacturer, visits retailers to persuade them to buy the manufacturer's products. If the retailers agree, they buy the products from wholesalers, who are the manufacturer's actual customers. Missionary salespersons often are employed by producers of medical supplies and pharmaceuticals to promote these products to retail druggists, physicians, and hospitals.

> **missionary salesperson** a salesperson—generally employed by a manufacturer—who visits retailers to persuade them to buy the manufacturer's products

A **trade salesperson**, who generally works for a food producer or processor, assists customers in promoting products, especially in retail stores. A trade salesperson may obtain additional shelf space for the products, restock shelves, set up displays, and distribute samples. Because trade salespersons usually are order-takers as well, they are not strictly support personnel.

> **trade salesperson** a salesperson—generally employed by a food producer or processor—who assists customers in promoting products, especially in retail stores

A **technical salesperson** assists a company's current customers in technical matters. He or she may explain how to use a product, how it is made, how to instal it, or how a system is designed. A technical salesperson should be formally educated in science or engineering. Computers, steel, and chemicals are some of the products handled by technical salespeople.

> **technical salesperson** a salesperson who assists a company's current customers in technical matters

Marketers usually need sales personnel from several of these categories. Factors that affect hiring and other personnel decisions include the number of customers and their characteristics; the product's attributes, complexity, and price; the distribution channels used by the company; and the company's approach to advertising.

The personal-selling process

No two selling situations are exactly alike, and no two salespeople perform their jobs in exactly the same way. Most salespeople, however, follow the six-step procedure illustrated in Figure 14.4.

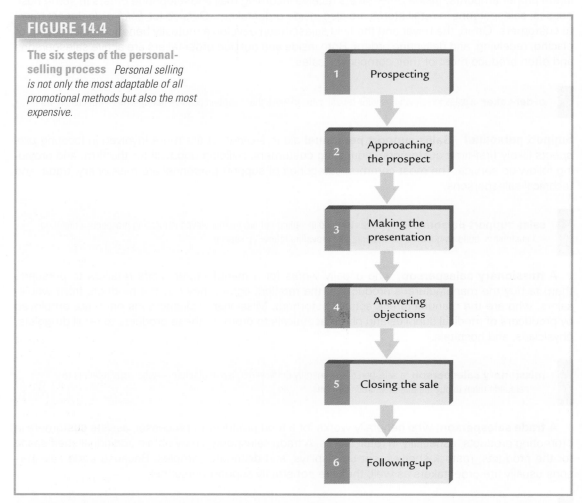

FIGURE 14.4

The six steps of the personal-selling process *Personal selling is not only the most adaptable of all promotional methods but also the most expensive.*

1 Prospecting

2 Approaching the prospect

3 Making the presentation

4 Answering objections

5 Closing the sale

6 Following-up

Source: William M. Pride and O. C. Ferrell, *Marketing: Concepts and Strategies*, 17th ed. (Mason, OH: South-Western/Cengage Learning, 2014). Adapted with permission.

Prospecting The first step in personal selling is to research potential buyers and choose the most likely customers, or prospects. Sources of prospects include business associates and customers, public records, telephone and trade-association directories, and company files. The salesperson concentrates on those prospects that have the financial resources, willingness, and authority to buy the product.

Approaching the prospect First impressions are often lasting impressions. Thus, the salesperson's first contact with the prospect is crucial to successful selling. The best approach is one based on knowledge of the product, of the prospect's needs, and of how the product can meet those needs. Salespeople who understand each customer's particular situation are likely to make a good first impression—and to make a sale.

Making the presentation The next step is actual delivery of the sales presentation. In many cases, this includes demonstrating the product. The salesperson points out the product's features, its benefits, and how it is superior to competitors' merchandise. If the product has been used successfully by other firms, the salesperson may mention this as part of the presentation.

During a demonstration, the salesperson may suggest that the prospect try out the product personally. The demonstration and product trial should underscore specific points made during the presentation.

Answering objections The prospect is likely to raise objections or ask questions at any time. This gives the salesperson a chance to eliminate objections that might prevent a sale, to point out additional features, or to mention special services the company offers.

Closing the sale To close the sale, the salesperson asks the prospect to buy the product. This is considered the critical point in the selling process. Many experienced salespeople make use of a *trial closing,* in which they ask questions based on the assumption that the customer is going to buy the product. The questions "When would you want delivery?" and "Do you want the standard model or the one with the special options package?" are typical of trial closings. They allow the reluctant prospect to make a purchase without having to say, "I'll take it."

Following-up The salesperson must follow up after the sale to ensure that the product is delivered on time, in the right quantity, and in proper operating condition. During follow-up, the salesperson also makes it clear that he or she is available in case problems develop. Follow-up leaves a good impression and eases the way toward future sales. Hence, it is essential to the selling process. The salesperson's job does not end with a sale. It continues as long as the seller and the customer maintain a working relationship.

Managing personal selling

A firm's success often hinges on the competent management of its sales force. Although some companies operate efficiently without a sales force, most firms rely on a strong sales force—and the sales revenue it brings in—for their success.

Sales managers have responsibilities in a number of areas. They must set sales objectives in concrete, quantifiable terms and specify a certain period of time and a certain geographic area. They must adjust the size of the sales force to meet changes in the firm's marketing plan and the marketing environment. Sales managers must attract and hire effective salespersons. They must also develop a training programme and decide where, when, how, and for whom to conduct the training. They must formulate a fair and adequate compensation plan to keep qualified employees. They must motivate salespersons to boost their productivity. They must define sales territories and determine scheduling and routing of the sales force. Finally, sales managers must evaluate the operation as a whole through sales reports, communications with customers, and invoices.

SALES PROMOTION

Sales promotion consists of activities or materials that are direct inducements to customers or salespersons. Are you a member of an airline frequent-flyer programme? Have you recently received a free sample in the mail or at a supermarket? How about a rebate from a manufacturer? Do you use coupons? All these are examples of sales promotion efforts. Sales promotion techniques often are used to enhance and supplement other promotional methods. They can have a significant impact on sales.

The dramatic increase in spending for sales promotion shows that marketers have recognised the potential of this promotional method. Many firms now include numerous sales promotion efforts as part of their overall promotion mix.

Sales promotion objectives

Sales promotion activities may be used singly or in combination, both offensively and defensively, to achieve one goal or a set of goals. Marketers use sales promotion activities and materials for a number of purposes, including:

1. To attract new customers
2. To encourage trial of a new product
3. To invigorate the sales of a mature brand
4. To boost sales to current customers
5. To reinforce advertising
6. To increase traffic in retail stores
7. To steady irregular sales patterns
8. To build up reseller inventories
9. To neutralise competitive promotional efforts
10. To improve shelf space and displays

Sales promotion methods

Most sales promotion methods can be classified as promotional techniques for either consumer sales or trade sales. A **consumer sales promotion method** attracts consumers to particular retail stores and motivates them to purchase certain new or established products. A **trade sales promotion method** encourages wholesalers and retailers to stock and actively promote a manufacturer's product. Incentives such as money, merchandise, marketing assistance, and gifts are commonly awarded to resellers who buy products or respond positively in other ways. Of the combined dollars spent on sales promotion and advertising, about one-half is spent on trade promotions, about one-fourth is spent on consumer promotions, and about one-fourth is spent on advertising.

> **consumer sales promotion method** a sales promotion method designed to attract consumers to particular retail stores and to motivate them to purchase certain new or established products
> **trade sales promotion method** a sales promotion method designed to encourage wholesalers and retailers to stock and actively promote a manufacturer's product

A number of factors enter into marketing decisions about which and how many sales promotion methods to use. Of greatest importance are the objectives of the promotional effort. Product characteristics—size, weight, cost, durability, uses, features, and hazards—and target market profiles—age, gender, income, location, density, usage rate, and buying patterns—likewise must be considered. Distribution channels and availability of appropriate resellers also influence the choice of sales promotion methods, as do the competitive and regulatory forces in the environment. Let's now discuss a few important sales promotion methods.

Rebates A **rebate** is a return of part of the product's purchase price. Usually, this refund is offered to consumers who send in a coupon along with a specific proof of purchase. Rebating is a relatively low-cost promotional method. Once used mainly to help launch new product items, it is now applied to a wide variety of products. Some automakers offer rebates on their vehicles because they have found that many car customers are more likely to purchase a car with a rebate than the same car with a lower price and no rebate. One problem with rebates is that many people perceive the redemption process as too complicated. Only about half of individuals who purchase rebated products actually apply for the rebates.

> **rebate** a return of part of the product's purchase price

Coupons A **coupon** reduces the retail price of a particular item by a stated amount at the time of purchase. They are made available to customers through newspapers, magazines, direct mail, online, and shelf dispensers in stores. Coupons are precisely targeted at customers. Many firms are utilising the Internet to target customers with deals and distribute coupons. This method is a low-cost way of promoting a company's products or services among a customer base that will use and appreciate the service.

coupon an offer that reduces the retail price of a particular item by a stated amount at the time of purchase

Although coupon use had been declining steadily for several years, the recent recession caused coupon usage to increase. 2009 witnessed the highest level of coupon use in 30 years. The largest number of coupons distributed are for household cleaners, condiments, frozen foods, medications and health aids, and paper products. Stores in some areas even deduct double or triple the value of manufacturers' coupons from the purchase price as a sales promotion technique of their own. Coupons also may offer free merchandise, either with or without an additional product purchase.

Samples A **sample** is a free product given to customers to encourage trial and purchase. Marketers use free samples to stimulate the trial of a product, increase sales volume in the early stages of a product's life-cycle, and obtain desirable distribution. Samples may be offered via online coupons, direct mail, or in stores. Many customers prefer to receive their samples by mail. Providing samples remains the most expensive sales promotion technique. Although it is used often to promote new products, it can also be used to promote established brands. For example, cosmetics companies may use samples to attract customers. Coca-Cola often gives out free samples of products such as Vitaminwater at business conventions, concerts, and sporting events. In designing a free sample, organisations must consider such factors as seasonal demand for the product, market characteristics, and prior advertising. If you've ever downloaded a trial version of new software or a new digital game, you've taken advantage of a free sample. This is a great way to try before you buy.

sample a free product given to customers to encourage trial and purchase

Not all samples are free. Some companies have realised that customers will pay a small fee to have regular access to high-end samples. Many online companies have recently popped up, selling boxes containing a variety of high end beauty product samples. One box is sent out to the customer per month, for a small monthly charge of around 10-15 euros.

Premiums A **premium** is a gift that a producer offers a customer in return for buying its product. They are used to attract competitors' customers, introduce different sizes of established products, add variety to other promotional efforts, and stimulate consumer loyalty. Creativity is essential when using premiums; to stand out and achieve a significant number of redemptions, the premium must match both the target audience and the brand's image. Examples include a service station giving a free car wash with a fill-up, a free toothbrush available with a tube of toothpaste, and a free plastic storage box given with the purchase of cheese slices. Premiums also must be easily recognizable

"Try it! You'll like it!" Companies give away coupons to increase the sales of their products and encourage consumers who are unfamiliar with them to give them a try.

and desirable. Premiums are placed on or inside packages and also can be distributed through retailers or through the mail.

> **premium** a gift that a producer offers a customer in return for buying its product

Frequent-user incentives

A **frequent-user incentive** is a programme developed to reward customers who engage in repeat (frequent) purchases. Such programmes are used commonly by service businesses such as airlines, hotels, and auto rental agencies. Frequent-user incentives foster customer loyalty to a specific company or group of cooperating companies because the customer is given an additional reason to continue patronising the business. For example, most major airlines offer frequent-flyer programmes that reward customers who have flown a specified number of miles with free tickets for additional travel. There is significant evidence that airline miles are highly valued by customers. Now, more frequent-flyer miles are awarded by non-airline companies than by airline companies. A high proportion of upper-income customers use frequent-user programmes, whereas moderate-income customers are not as likely to use these programmes. Most supermarket chains now offer a loyalty card scheme, such as the Nectar Card, allowing customers to build up points on purchases that can be redeemed as gifts or money off, as well as receiving special deals tailored to their weekly shop. Whilst helping to retain customers' loyalty, it also enables the supermarket to gather huge amounts of information and produce sophisticated profiles of their customers and their buying behaviour, for market research purposes.

> **frequent-user incentive** a programme developed to reward customers who engage in repeat (frequent) purchases

Point-of-purchase displays

A **point-of-purchase display** is promotional material placed within a retail store. The display is usually located near the product being promoted. It may actually hold merchandise, or it may simply inform customers about what the product offers and encourage them to buy it. Most point-of-purchase displays are prepared and set up by manufacturers and wholesalers.

> **point-of-purchase display** promotional material placed within a retail store

Trade shows

A **trade show** is an industry-wide exhibit at which many sellers display their products. Some trade shows are organised exclusively for dealers—to permit manufacturers and wholesalers to show their latest lines to retailers. Others are events designed to stimulate consumer awareness and interest. Among the latter are boat shows, home shows, and flower shows put on each year in large cities. E3, for example, is the world's largest trade show for electronic games and related products. Tens of thousands attend this trade show each year, including all major producers of gaming products, to see the new products being showcased and to network with professionals in the industry.*

> **trade show** an industry-wide exhibit at which many sellers display their products

Using trade shows to generate interest in products. Trade shows help marketers make their products visible to a large number of businesses and consumers. The shows also allow companies to keep an eye on what their competitors are doing and the new products they are launching.

Buying allowances   A **buying allowance** is a temporary price reduction to resellers for purchasing specified quantities of a product. For example, a laundry detergent manufacturer might give retailers €1 for each case of detergent purchased. A buying allowance may serve as an incentive to resellers to handle new products and may stimulate purchases in large quantities. While the buying allowance is simple, straightforward, and easily administered, competitors can respond quickly by offering a better buying allowance.

> **buying allowance** a temporary price reduction to resellers for purchasing specified quantities of a product

Cooperative advertising   **Cooperative advertising** is an arrangement whereby a manufacturer agrees to pay a certain amount of a retailer's media cost for advertising the manufacturer's products. To be reimbursed, a retailer must show proof that the advertisements actually did appear. A large percentage of all cooperative advertising dollars is spent on newspaper advertisements.

> **cooperative advertising** an arrangement whereby a manufacturer agrees to pay a certain amount of a retailer's media cost for advertising the manufacturer's product

PUBLIC RELATIONS

As noted earlier, public relations is a broad set of communication activities used to create and maintain favourable relationships between an organisation and various public groups, both internal and external. These groups can include customers, employees, stockholders, suppliers, educators, the media, government officials, and society in general.

Types of public-relations tools

Organisations use a variety of public-relations tools to convey messages and to create images. Public-relations professionals prepare written materials such as brochures, newsletters, company magazines, annual reports, and news releases. They also create corporate-identity materials such as logos, business cards, signs, and stationery. Speeches are another public-relations tool. Speeches can affect an organisation's image and therefore must convey the desired message clearly.

Another public-relations tool is event sponsorship, in which a company pays for all or part of a special event such as a concert, sports competition, festival, or play. Sponsoring special events is an effective way for organisations to increase brand recognition and receive media coverage with comparatively little investment.

Some public-relations tools have been traditionally associated with publicity, which is a part of public relations. **Publicity** is communication in news-story form about an organisation, its products, or both. Publicity is transmitted through a mass medium, such as newspapers or radio, at no charge. Organisations use publicity to provide information about products; to announce new product launches, expansions, or research; and to strengthen the company's image. Public-relations personnel

Event sponsorships are intended to promote a positive image of a firm. Event sponsorships are a public-relations tool. They are often used in conjunction with advertising, personal selling, and sales promotions.

©PCN PHOTOGRAPHY/ALAMY

sometimes organise events, such as grand openings with prizes and celebrities, to create news stories about a company.

> **publicity** communication in news-story form about an organisation, its products, or both

The most widely used type of publicity is the **news release**. It is generally one typed page of about 300 words provided by an organisation to the media as a form of publicity. The release includes the firm's name, address, phone number, and contact person. Table 14.2 lists some of the issues news releases can address. There are also several other kinds of publicity-based public-relations tools. A **feature article**, which may run as long as 3,000 words, is usually written for inclusion in a particular publication. For example, a software firm might send an article about its new product to a computer magazine. A **captioned photograph**, a picture accompanied by a brief explanation, is an effective way to illustrate a new or improved product. A **press conference** allows invited media personnel to hear important news announcements and to receive supplementary textual materials and photographs. Finally, letters to the editor, special newspaper or magazine editorials, and videos may be prepared and distributed to appropriate media for possible use.

> **news release** a typed page of about 300 words provided by an organisation to the media as a form of publicity
> **feature article** a piece (of up to 3,000 words) prepared by an organisation for inclusion in a particular publication
> **captioned photograph** a picture accompanied by a brief explanation
> **press conference** a meeting at which invited media personnel hear important news announcements and receive supplementary textual materials and photographs

TABLE 14.2   Possible issues for news releases

Use of new information technology	Packaging changes
Support of a social cause	New products
Improved warranties	Creation of new software
Reports on industry conditions	Research developments
New uses for established products	Company's history and development
Product endorsements	Launching of new Web site
Winning of quality awards	Award of contracts
Company name changes	Opening of new markets
Interviews with company officials	Improvements in financial position
Improved distribution policies	Opening of an exhibit
Global business initiatives	History of a brand
Sponsorship of events	Winners of company contests
Visits by celebrities	Logo changes
Reports of new discoveries	Speeches of top management
Innovative marketing activities	Merit awards to the organisation
Economic forecasts	Anniversaries of inventions

© CENGAGE LEARNING 2014

The uses of public relations

Public relations can be used to promote people, places, activities, ideas, and even countries. Public relations focuses on enhancing the reputation of the total organisation by making people aware of a company's products, brands, or activities and by creating specific company images such as that of innovativeness or dependability. Social media sites, YouTube, and Twitter can all be great low-cost tools for connecting with consumers and engaging in a dialogue. However, the social media landscape is changing fast. Public relations experts and other marketers must keep track of a growing list of small, niche social media sites. Smaller social media sites that focus on a specific area of interest can be an easy way to target a specific audience. For instance, Tennisopolis is a social media site for

SUCCESS STORY

Viral marketing and the power of YouTube hits

Although only a relatively new concept, "viral" marketing – like the name suggests – has rapidly spread around the world, quickly becoming an established and extremely valuable asset in the marketer's toolbox. Often distributed via video link, viewers are quite happy to watch a shaky or poor quality video clip, as long as it is easily accessed and portrays a message they can relate to, or simply makes them laugh. The rise of viral marketing and the popularity of YouTube are closely linked, and together they have revolutionised the way content is created, delivered and absorbed.

One particularly interesting aspect of viral marketing is that it has brought innovation and creation back to the forefront of the message, rather than the level of resources at the marketer's disposal. In other words, the quality of the *idea* is much more important than the quality of the *production*. The band OK Go, for example, have enjoyed a successful career largely through fresh and inventive music videos. Their most popular track, "Here It Goes Again", featuring band members dancing in choreographed formation on treadmills, has racked up almost 19 million hits on YouTube, despite being made for almost nothing.

Anyone with a cheap and relatively basic mobile phone or digital camera can now record videos and upload them almost instantaneously to YouTube, Vimeo or any of the other streaming services that are cropping up. If it connects with the mass consciousness, whether showing a cat doing backflips or a baby drooling, soon it will rack up millions of hits. Enterprising individuals and small business ventures soon realised the potential of this new media as a marketing tool to promote themselves, whether wannabe stars or small start-up businesses, utilising YouTube's commercial capacity to good effect.

This "levelling of the playing field" has enabled many successful marketing campaigns to be carried out, on relatively scarce resources. Indeed, sometimes the more amateur the footage looks the better! Many consumers put off by large, expensive-looking corporate messages devised by focus groups have enjoyed the bespoke, often spontaneous, and more immediately relatable videos online. This has led to large multinationals actually commissioning material that looks cheaply produced to tap into this winning formula.

Extreme sportswear and surfing brand Quiksilver cleverly combined both "big budget" and "handmade" in a short video that professes to be real amateur footage showing surfers throwing dynamite off a city bridge into the river below before using the ensuing wave from the explosion to surf on. Although staged and digitally altered, the video went viral. Most major brands from Nike to Burger King have now utilised viral marketing in some form in their campaigns, often to great effect.

References: B. Verhage, *Marketing: A Global Perspective*, (Cengage Learning EMEA 2014), Damian Kulash Jr., 'The New Rock-Star Paradigm', *The Wall Street Journal*, December 17, 2010.

© ALEX SEGRE / ALAMY

---

tennis enthusiasts and Lookk is a site for fashion enthusiasts and designers. Advertising on sites like these help a brand establish its image and reach its specific target audience. These sites can also be good resources for marketers looking to discover customer needs and wants and new trends.*

PROMOTION PLANNING

A **promotional campaign** is a plan for combining and using the four promotional methods—advertising, personal selling, sales promotion, and public relations—in a particular promotion mix to achieve one or more marketing goals. When selecting promotional methods to include in promotion mixes, it is important to coordinate promotional elements to maximise the total informational and promotional impact on customers. Integrated marketing communication requires a marketer to look at the broad perspective when planning promotional programmes and coordinating the total set of communication functions.

> **promotional campaign** a plan for combining and using the four promotional methods—advertising, personal selling, sales promotion, and publicity—in a particular promotion mix to achieve one or more marketing goals

In planning a promotional campaign, marketers must answer these two questions:

1. What will be the role of promotion in the overall marketing mix?
2. To what extent will each promotional method be used in the promotion mix?

The answer to the first question depends on the firm's marketing objectives because the role of each element of the marketing mix—product, price, distribution, and promotion—depends on these detailed versions of the firm's marketing goals. The answer to the second question depends on the answer to the first, as well as on the target market.

Promotion and marketing objectives

Promotion is naturally better suited to certain marketing objectives than to others. For example, promotion can do little to further a marketing objective such as "reduce delivery time by one-third." It can, however, be used to inform customers that delivery is faster. Let's consider some objectives that *would* require the use of promotion as a primary ingredient of the marketing mix.

Providing information   This is, of course, the main function of promotion. It may be used to communicate to target markets the availability of new products or product features. It may alert them to special offers or give the locations of retailers that carry a firm's products. In other words, promotion can be used to enhance the effectiveness of each of the other ingredients of the marketing mix.

Increasing market share   Promotion can be used to convince new customers to try a product while maintaining the product loyalty of established customers. Comparative advertising, for example, is directed mainly at those who might—but presently do not—use a particular product. Advertising that emphasises the product's features also assures those who *do* use the product that they have made a smart choice. Nature Valley, maker of granola bars, unveiled a new campaign that seeks to increase its already dominant share of the granola bar market. The campaign features a Web site called Nature Valley Trail View, which allows users to virtually hike trails in national parks. This new promotional campaign is aimed at capturing greater market share by further aligning the Nature Valley brand name with a healthy outdoor lifestyle. Nature Valley gained a 3.9 per cent market share and now commands a 41.6 per cent share of the market.*

Positioning the product   The sales of a product depend, to a great extent, on its competition. The stronger the competition, the more difficult it is to maintain or increase sales. For this reason, many firms go to great lengths to position their products in the marketplace. **Positioning** is the development of a product image in buyers' minds relative to the images they have of competing products.

> **positioning** the development of a product image in buyers' minds relative to the images they have of competing products

Promotion is the prime positioning tool. A marketer can use promotion to position a brand away from competitors to avoid competition. Promotion also may be used to position one product directly against another product. For example, in hopes of providing legitimate competition to Apple's iPhone, Motorola is offering the Droid. Looking at its advertising, there is no doubt which phone it is competing against. With statements about its competition like "iDon't have a real keyboard, iDon't allow open development, and iDon't take pictures in the dark," it is very clear that the Droid is positioned head to head with the iPhone.*

Stabilising sales   Special promotional efforts can be used to increase sales during slack periods, such as the "off season" for certain sports equipment. By stabilising sales in this way, a firm can use its production facilities more effectively and reduce both capital costs and inventory costs. Promotion is also used frequently to increase the sales of products that are in the declining stage of their life-cycles. The objective is to keep them going for a little while longer.

Developing the promotion mix

Once the role of promotion is established, the various methods of promotion may be combined in a promotional campaign. As in so many other areas of business, promotion planning begins with a set of specific objectives. The promotion mix then is designed to accomplish these objectives.

Marketers often use several promotion mixes simultaneously if a firm sells multiple products. The selection of promotion-mix ingredients and the degree to which they are used depend on the organisation's resources and objectives, the nature of the target market, the characteristics of the product, and the feasibility of various promotional methods.

The amount of promotional resources available in an organisation influences the number and intensity of promotional methods that marketers can use. A firm with a limited budget for promotion probably will rely on personal selling because the effectiveness of personal selling can be measured more easily than that of advertising. An organisation's objectives also have an effect on its promotional activities. A company wishing to make a wide audience familiar with a new convenience item probably will depend heavily on advertising and sales promotion. If a company's objective is to communicate information to consumers—on the features of worktop appliances, for example—then the company may develop a promotion mix that includes some advertising, some sales promotion to attract consumers to stores, and a lot of personal selling.

The size, geographic distribution, and socioeconomic characteristics of the target market play a part in the composition of a product's promotion mix. If the market is small, personal selling probably will be the most important element in the promotion mix. This is true of organisations that sell to small industrial markets and businesses that use only a few wholesalers to market their products. Companies that need to contact millions of potential customers, however, will emphasise sales promotion and advertising because these methods are relatively inexpensive. The age, income, and education of the target market also will influence the choice of promotion techniques. For example, with less-educated consumers, personal selling may be more effective than ads in newspapers or magazines.

In general, industrial products require a considerable amount of personal selling, whereas consumer goods depend on advertising. This is not true in every case, however. The price of the product also influences the composition of the promotion mix. Because consumers often want the advice of a salesperson on an expensive product, high-priced consumer goods may call for more personal selling. Similarly, advertising and sales promotion may be more crucial to marketers of seasonal items because having a year-round sales force is not always appropriate.

The cost and availability of promotional methods are important factors in the development of a promotion mix. Although national advertising and sales promotion activities are expensive, the cost per customer may be quite small if the campaign succeeds in reaching large numbers of people. In addition, local advertising outlets—newspapers, magazines, radio and television stations, and outdoor displays—may not be that costly for a small local business. In some situations, a firm may find that no available advertising medium reaches the target market effectively.

RESPONSIBLE PRACTICE   Using ambush marketing to profit from major events

Sponsorship is big business. Individual corporations spend millions – if not billions – of euros every year on sponsorship of major events across the world, whether music festivals, motoring championships, or large sporting tournaments. Companies invest huge sums of money to have their brand associated with these tournaments and events. The Wimbledon tennis championships, for example, have long been associated with the fruit cordial and beverages brand, Robinson's.

Firstly, sponsorship creates a huge amount of exposure for the brand through press conferences backdropped by screens brandishing the company logo, widespread TV and Internet coverage, and often (if the brand name itself has been incorporated into the event's official title) through repeated exposure to the name every time a commentator refers to the event. England's top flight football league, for instance, is officially known as the Barclays Premier League, whereas the European UEFA Champions League is sometimes referred to as the Mastercard Champions League, and their respective logos are used extensively in promotional materials.

Secondly, association with the specific event is intended to be a reflection of the brand's own core values and aspirations. Aligning a brand with the Olympics, where individuals and teams push themselves to be the very best in the world in their particular field, implies that the brand also aspires to be the best; to be a world leader in its field; to strive for perfection and never give up in the face of defeat or adversity.

So when brands spend so much money on sponsorship through legitimate channels, is it right that others should profit using other means? A growing concern is "ambush marketing", when companies use underhand, if often playful, techniques to gain exposure during an event, without paying for an official endorsement. During the 2012 London Olympics, athletes were handed out free headphones from Dr Dre's "Beats" brand, which they would then be inadvertently snapped wearing whilst out and about in the Olympic village, or in preparation for the next race, much to the annoyance of the official sponsors. Often ambush marketing relies on a sensational and unexpected stunt designed to create a buzz that will later "trend" on social media sites such as Twitter, or go viral on YouTube. These stunts can lead to repercussions from regulatory bodies, offset by the huge publicity in the media. The great irony is that, often, the more that regulators try to clamp down on illicit marketing, the more press coverage it creates.

Is the practice of ambush marketing unethical or simply a new and acceptable phenomenon of today's social world, where there are so many opportunities to communicate freely?

References: *Marketing: A Global Perspective*, B. Verhage (2014); Vanessa Kortekaas, 'Olympic sponsors seek podium for brands', *Financial Times*, September 3-4, 2011, p. 12; 'London Eye: Dr Dre beats the brand ban – for a while', *The Independent*, August 3rd, 2012.

CRITICISMS OF PROMOTION

Even though promotional activities can help customers to make informed purchasing decisions, social scientists, consumer groups, government agencies, and members of society in general have long criticised promotion. There are two main reasons for such criticism: Promotion does have some flaws, and it is a highly visible business activity that pervades our daily lives. Although people almost universally complain that there is simply too much promotional activity, several more specific issues have been raised. Promotional efforts have been called deceptive. Promotion has been blamed for increasing prices. Other criticisms of promotion are that it manipulates consumers into buying products they do not need, that it leads to a more materialistic society, that customers do not benefit sufficiently from promotion to justify its high costs, and that promotion is used to market potentially harmful products. These issues are discussed in Table 14.3.

TABLE 14.3	Criticisms of promotion	
Issue	**Discussion**	
Is promotion deceptive?	Although no longer widespread, some deceptive promotion still occurs; laws, government regulations, and industry self-regulation have helped to decrease intentionally deceptive promotion; however, customers may be unintentionally misled because some words have diverse meanings.	
Does promotion increase prices?	When promotion stimulates demand, higher production levels may result in lower per-unit production costs, which keeps prices lower; when demand is not stimulated, however, prices increase owing to the added costs of promotion; promotion fuels price competition, which helps to keep prices lower.	
Does promotion create needs?	Many marketers capitalise on consumers' needs by basing their promotional appeals on these needs; however, marketers do not actually create these needs. If there were no promotion, consumers would still have basic needs.	
Does promotion encourage materialism?	Because promotion creates awareness and visibility for products, it may contribute to materialism in the same way that movies, sports, theatre, art, and literature may contribute to materialism; if there were no promotion, it is likely that there would still be materialism among some groups, as evidenced by the existence of materialism among some ancient groups of people.	
Does promotion help customers without costing too much?	Customers learn about products and services through promotion, allowing them to make more intelligent buying decisions.	
Should potentially harmful products be promoted?	Some critics suggest that the promotion of possibly unhealthy products should not be allowed at all; others argue that as long as it is legal to sell such products, promoting those products should be allowed.	

Source: William M. Pride and O. C. Ferrell, *Foundations of Marketing* (Mason, OH: South-Western/Cengage Learning, 2011), 389.

SUMMARY

- Describe integrated marketing communications.

Integrated marketing communications is the coordination of promotion efforts to achieve the maximum informational and persuasive impact on customers.

- Understand the role of promotion.

Promotion is communication about an organisation and its products that is intended to inform, persuade, or remind target-market members. The major ingredients of a promotion mix are advertising, personal selling, sales promotion, and public relations. The role of promotion is to facilitate exchanges directly or indirectly and to help an organisation maintain favourable relationships with groups in the marketing environment.

- Explain the purposes of the three types of advertising.

Advertising is a paid nonpersonal message communicated to a specific audience through a mass medium. Primary-demand advertising promotes the products of an entire industry rather than just a single brand. Selective-demand advertising promotes a particular brand of product. Institutional advertising is image-building advertising for a firm.

- Describe the advantages and disadvantages of the major advertising media.

The major advertising media are newspapers, magazines, direct mail, out-of-home displays, television, radio, the Internet, and social media. Newspapers are relatively inexpensive compared with other media, reach only people in the market area, and are timely. Disadvantages include a short life span, poor colour reproduction, and an inability to target specific demographic groups. Magazine advertising can be quite prestigious. In addition, it can reach very specific market segments, can provide high-quality colour reproduction, and has a relatively long life span. Major disadvantages are high cost and lack of timeliness. Direct mail is the most selective medium, and its effectiveness is measured easily. The disadvantage of direct mail is that if the mailing list is outdated and the advertisement does not reach the right people, then the campaign cannot be successful. Yellow Pages advertising allows customers who use it to save time in finding products, to find information quickly, and to learn about products and marketers. Unlike other types of advertising media, Yellow Pages advertisements are purchased for one year and cannot be changed. Out-of-home advertising allows marketers to focus on a particular geographic area and is relatively inexpensive. Messages, though, must be limited to a few words because the audience is usually in transit.

Television accounts for the largest share of advertising expenditures. Television offers marketers the opportunity to broadcast a firm's message nationwide. However, television advertising can be very expensive and has a short life span. In addition, cable channels and home videos have reduced the likelihood of reaching extremely large audiences. Radio advertising offers selectivity, can be less expensive than other media, and is flexible for scheduling purposes. Radio's limitations include no visual presentation and fragmented, small audiences. Benefits of using the Internet as an advertising medium include the growing number of people using the Internet, which means a growing audience, and the ability to precisely target specific customers. Disadvantages include the relatively simplistic nature of the ads that can be produced, especially in comparison with television, and the lack of evidence that net browsers actually pay attention to the ads. Social media appear to allow marketers the ability to target, interact, and connect more personally with customers through sites such as Twitter, Facebook, and brand-specific Web sites. Drawbacks are that the audience is restricted to followers, marketers are still unsure of the usefulness and return on investment, and companies must have employees dedicated to real-time activity.

- Identify the major steps in developing an advertising campaign.

An advertising campaign is developed in several stages. A firm's first task is to identify and analyse its advertising target. The goals of the campaign also must be clearly defined. Then the firm must develop the advertising platform, or statement of important selling points, and determine the size of the advertising budget. The next steps are to develop a media plan, to create the advertising message, and to execute the campaign. Finally, promotion managers must evaluate the effectiveness of the advertising efforts before, during, and/or after the campaign.

- Recognise the various kinds of salespersons, the steps in the personal-selling process, and the major sales management tasks.

Personal selling is personal communication aimed at informing customers and persuading them to buy a firm's products. It is the most adaptable promotional method because the salesperson can modify the message to fit each buyer. Three major kinds of salespersons are order-getters, order-takers, and support personnel. The six steps in the personal-selling process are prospecting, approaching the prospect, making the presentation, answering objections, closing the sale, and following up. Sales managers are involved directly in setting sales force objectives; recruiting, selecting, and training salespersons; compensating and motivating sales personnel; creating sales territories; and evaluating sales performance.

- Describe sales promotion objectives and methods.

Sales promotion is the use of activities and materials as direct inducements to customers and salespersons. The primary objective of sales promotion methods is to enhance and supplement other promotional methods. Methods of sales promotion include rebates, coupons, samples, premiums, frequent-user incentives, point-of-purchase displays, trade shows, buying allowances, and cooperative advertising.

- Understand the types and uses of public relations.

Public relations is a broad set of communication activities used to create and maintain favourable relationships between an organisation and various public groups, both internal and external. Organisations use a variety of public-relations tools to convey messages and create images. Brochures, newsletters, company magazines, and annual reports are written public-relations tools. Speeches, event sponsorship, and publicity are other public-relations tools. Publicity is communication in news-story form about an organisation, its products, or both. Types of publicity include news releases, feature articles, captioned photographs, and press conferences. Public relations can be used to promote people, places, activities, ideas, and even countries. It can be used to enhance the reputation of an organisation and also to reduce the unfavourable effects of negative events.

- Identify the factors that influence the selection of promotion-mix ingredients.

A promotional campaign is a plan for combining and using advertising, personal selling, sales promotion, and publicity to achieve one or more marketing goals. Campaign objectives are developed from marketing objectives. Then the promotion mix is developed based on the organisation's promotional resources and objectives, the nature of the target market, the product characteristics, and the feasibility of various promotional methods.

- Identify and explain the criticisms of promotion.

Promotion activities can help consumers to make informed purchasing decisions, but they also have evoked many criticisms. Promotion has been accused of deception. Although some deceiving or misleading promotions do exist, laws, government regulation, and industry self-regulation minimise deceptive promotion.

Promotion has been blamed for increasing prices, but it usually tends to lower them. When demand is high, production and marketing costs decrease, which can result in lower prices. Promotion also helps to keep prices lower by facilitating price competition. Other criticisms of promotional activity are that it manipulates consumers into buying products they do not need, that it leads to a more materialistic society, and that consumers do not benefit sufficiently from promotional activity to justify its high cost. Finally, some critics of promotion suggest that potentially harmful products, especially those associated with violence, sex, and unhealthy activities, should not be promoted at all.

EXERCISE QUESTIONS

1   What is the major task of promotion?

2   What is communication? Describe the communication process. Is it possible to communicate without using all of the elements in the communication process?

3   How does publicity differ from advertising?

4   Identify and briefly describe the major promotional methods that can be included in an organisation's promotional mix.

5   Assume that a company is planning to promote a cereal to both adults and children. Along what major dimensions would these two promotional efforts have to be different?

CASE 15.1

Häagen-Dazs – Discover Indulgence

Häagen-Dazs makes the best-selling super-premium ice cream in North America. Its luscious ingredients include chocolate from Belgium, vanilla from Madagascar, coffee from Brazil, strawberries from Oregon, and nuts from Hawaii. The packaging serenely asserts that it is the world's best ice cream.

London's Leicester Square shop served close to one million ice cream lovers in its first year. The success of the Victor Hugo Plaza shop in Paris, now the company's second busiest, led to the establishment of its first European factory in France. Häagen-Dazs shops have opened in Italy, Spain, Benelux and Scandinavia, among other countries. The appealing flavours can now be found not only in the company's shops but also at airports, in cafés and in carefully selected delicatessens, with rapidly growing popularity.

The product's high quality has been essential in maintaining a loyal customer following, but it was promotional work that led to the successful take-off of what was previously an unheard-of brand in Europe. Sales promotion in the guise of free tasting was a major part of the promotional mix: over 5 million free cupfuls of ice cream were given away during the company's European launch. Thousands of retailers, cafés and delis were supplied with branded freezers both to display and carefully look after the new premium ice cream. As part of its European launch, Häagen-Dazs spent £30 million on advertising, stressing the deluxe ingredients, unusual flavours and novelty of its product. Europeans currently eat 25 per cent of the 3 billion gallons of ice cream each year consumed worldwide. Häagen-Dazs plans to increase consumption by appealing to more than traditional ice cream-loving children.

The summer afternoon stroll with an ice cream cornet, the family trip to a fun park or beach, a snack during a film or concert, the sticky climax of a birthday party feast had long been the core market for Wall's and Nestlé. Ice Cream Mars changed all that by creating an ice cream bar suitable for any occasion and particularly attractive to adults. Häagen-Dazs went further. Award-winning press adverts, artistically shot, often in black and white, featured lithe, semi-nude couples entwined in exotic poses while feeding each other Häagen-Dazs ice cream. The appeal of vanilla ice cream bars hand-dipped in Belgian chocolate and rolled in roasted almonds now seems hard to resist for adults everywhere. The advertising imagery promotes an adult, upmarket, glamorous positioning for this super-premium ice cream.

The Häagen-Dazs range has grown, expanding to include frozen yoghurts, sorbets and now ice cream novelties, such as the ice cream sandwich made with cookies. Formats, too, have evolved, from sharing tubs to minis, stick-bars to novelty lines. Product development and quality controls are important to Häagen-Dazs' brand positioning as an upmarket, indulgent treat for adults, but so is the company's innovative promotional mix and the messages at the heart of its advertising. Industry observers suggest that despite the exceptional quality and novel flavours, without marketing communications Häagen-Dazs would not have been so successful. Certainly its current campaign, Win A Date with well-known heart-throb celebrities, promoted on-line and via blogs, has captured the attention of many adults seeking indulgence.

Questions

1 Why did the London launch of Häagen-Dazs utilise more than just advertising?

2 Why did Häagen-Dazs target the adult market rather than families or children?

3 Was the 'adult' positioning and promotional execution risky? Why did Häagen-Dazs deploy this positioning strategy?

References: Sainsbury's, 2004–11; 'Dairy produce', *Campaign*, 15 March 1996, p. 34; 'Häagen-Dazs cinema first', *Campaign*, 26 March 1995, p. 5; 'Pillsbury's global training plan', *Crossborder Monitor*, 19 April 1995, p. 9; G. Mead, 'Sex, ice and videod beer', *Financial Times*, 26 September 1992, p. 5; 'Saucy way to sell a Knicker-bocker Glory – Häagen-Dazs' new ice cream campaign',

Financial Times, 8 August 1991, p. 8; 'Häagen-Dazs is using sex to secure an up market niche in Britain's £400m ice cream market', *Observer*, 4 August 1991, p. 25; M. Carter, 'The luxury ice cream market', *Marketing Week*, 22 May 1992, p. 30; www.haagen-dazs.com, July 2004, January, 2008 and June, 2011; www. haagen-dazs.co.uk, June, 2011.

CHAPTER REFERENCES

"2012 U.S. National Edition Rates," *Time*, http://timemediakit. com/us/rates-specs/national.html accessed February 22, 2012; Nielsen Wire, "TV Usage Trends: Q3 and A4 2010-Timeshifted Viewing Grows in U.S.," March 10, 2011, http://blog.nielsen.com/nielsenwire/media_entertainment/ tv-usage-trends-q3-and-q4-2010/; Nielsen Wire, "Nielsen Estimates Number of U.S. Television Homes to be 114.7 Million," May 3, 2011, http://blog.nielsen.com/ nielsenwire/media_entertainment/Nielsen-estimates- number-of-u-s-television-homes-to-be-114-7-million/.

"About E3 2012," www.e3expo.com/show-info/1101/about- e3/, accessed April 1, 2012.

Company Web site llbean.com accessed February 13, 2012; "Photobrand 25 Ranks ESPN, GE, and Dunkin' Donuts as New England's Most Powerful Brands for 2010," *PR Newswire,* June 1, 2010, http://prnewswire. com/news-releases/protobrand-25-ranks-espn-ge- and-dunkin-donuts-as-new-englands-most-powerful- brands-for-2010-95310399.html; Michael Arndt, "Cus- tomer Service Champs: L.L. Bean Follows Its Shoppers to the Web," *Bloomberg BusinessWeek*, February 18, 2010, http://businessweek.com/magazine/content/10_09/ b4168043788083.htm; interviews with L.L. Bean employ- ees and the video, "L.L. Bean Employs a Variety of Pro- motion Methods to Communicate with Customers."

DIY Network, www.diynetwork.com/, accessed April 1, 2012.

Goldwert, Lindsay, "Dakota Fanning Oh, Lola! Perfume Ad Banned," *New York Daily News*, November 9, 2011, http://articles.nydailynews.com/2011-11-09/news/ 30379945_1_perfume-ad-lola-elle-fanning.

Guest, Peter, "Facebook, Friend of Foe?" *Wall Street Journal,* March 12, 2012, http://online.wsj.com/article/ SB10001424052970203358704577235213738850008.html.

Hampp, Andrew, "How David Guetta is Helping EMI Improve its Product Placement" Billboard Biz, March 27, 2012, www.billboard.biz/bbbiz/industry/branding/how-david- guetta-is-helping-emi-improve-1006581152.story.

http://www.tvlicensing.co.uk/about/foi-licences-facts- and-figures-AB18/, accessed 8th November 2013;

'Census: More TVs than fridges in SA homes', *IOL news*, http://www.iol.co.za/news/south-africa/census-more- tvs-than-fridges-in-sa-homes-1.1414075, accessed 8th November 2013.

Mershon, Phil "5 Social Media Marketing Trends: New Research," Social Media Examiner, February 29, 2012, www.socialmediaexaminer.com/5-social-media- marketing-trends-new-research-2/.

Neher, Krista, "4 Unique Approaches for Measur- ing Social Media ROI," ClicZ, February 15, 2012, www.clickz.com/clickz/column/2152418/unique- approaches-measuring-social-media-roi.

Newman, Andrew Adam, "Marketers Promoting a Gran- ola Bar Hit the Trails in National Parks," *The New York Times,* March 8, 2012, www.nytimes.com/2012/03/08/ business/media/virtual-hikes-promote-nature-valley- granola-bars.html.

O'Grady, Jason D., "Verizon Droid Ad Attacks iPhone on Features," *ZDNet*, October 19, 2009, http://zdnet. com/blog/apple/verizon-droid-ad-attacks-iphone- on-features/5055.

Rykä, www.ryka.com, accessed April 1, 2012.

"Still Working, Still Committed," BP, www.bp.com/ sectionbodycopy.do?categoryId=41&contentId= 7067505, accessed April 1, 2012.

Superbowlcommericals.tv, "2012 Super Bowl Commercial Lineup," November 25, 2011, http://superbowl-commercials. org/3850.html.

Verhage, B., *Marketing: A Global Perspective* (Cengage Learning, 2014).

Wisnefski, Kenneth C., "'Kony 2012' Offers Business Lessons on Viral Marketing," *Washington Post*, March 9, 2012, www. washingtonpost.com/business/on-small-business/ kony-2012-offers-businesses-lessons-on-viral-marketing/ 2012/03/09/gIQAGBsh1R_story.html.

www.marketingcharts.com/television/politics-olympics-to- drive-almost-half-of-12-us-ad-revenue-growth-20894/ May 23, 2012.

15 SOCIAL MEDIA AND E-BUSINESS

BUSINESS FOCUS

Monitoring social media postings

Many companies have adapted and responded to the meteoric rise of social media, quickly recognising the huge marketing potential waiting to be tapped into. Twitter spreads the latest trends across the globe almost instantaneously. Facebook has huge advertising capability; intelligent mapping personalises specific promotions to individual users depending on demographic character traits determined by their profile settings, geographic location, search history and social groups. Understanding the "Zeitgeist" or general consensus on a subject, event or product has never been easier.

Marketers now use sophisticated programming to gather data, identify and analyse trends, and build instant profiles on almost any subject, categorised by age, gender, and socioeconomic background. Following a major sporting or television event, many people will inevitably go online to comment upon it. Whether or not they realise it, through posting personal opinions into the public domain, the populous are inadvertently contributing to one big, continuous marketing research exercise.

Social media analytics company Netbase obtained a lucrative business contract with a consumer products company worth millions of euros, through overcoming a challenge to determine why many young men have stubble. The research question, submitted to over one hundred market research companies, was addressed by mining a large number of male postings on Facebook, Twitter and other social media sites. With software enabling them to examine three million sentences per hour, Netbase identified over 75,000 online references to stubble in seconds. And within an hour of analysis, they had positioned and categorised the main motives. Not surprisingly, the foremost reason for wearing stubble was a perception that it looked appealing.

The real insight from this exercise was not regarding facial hair, but rather the researchers' capability to gather and analyse a stunning amount of online information quickly and methodically; scrutinising thousands of social media posts, then selecting the most relevant ones to help marketers identify and evaluate major trends and intelligence. As a result, the global business of collecting and decoding online chatter is growing fast.

What consumers really think about marketing-related issues remains an intriguing question for customer-focused firms. Today, corporations are spending over €800 million euros per year for online data to better satisfy their customers' needs. Major marketing research companies are rapidly acquiring firms that specialise in monitoring social media, providing instant insights into consumers' beliefs, attitudes and behaviour. Likewise, corporations are allocating an ever increasing part of their marketing communication budgets to advertising via social media. In the U.S. alone, advertisers are spending over $2 billion per year to reach consumers through Facebook and similar sites.

Monitoring networks and blogs also helps to limit the damage of failed new product introductions, ineffective advertising campaigns or other marketing mistakes. As Elaine Boxer, a marketing strategist in the healthcare sector recently asserted, "The Internet is the world's largest instant focus group". While managers cannot control this consumer input, they do have the option to engage in the dialogue and to promptly act in response to the customer feedback.

References: Verhage, *Marketing: A Global Perspective* (2014); Ryan Flinn, 'The Big Business of Sifting Through Social Media Data', *Bloomberg Businessweek*, October 31, 2010, pp. 20–22; 'We hear you! How companies respond to user feedback', *South Source*, November 2012

Take a moment to think about how social media and technology affect your own life. In just a few short years, it has changed the way we communicate with each other, it has changed the way we meet people, and it has changed the way we shop. In this chapter, we explore how these trends affect both individuals and businesses.

We begin this chapter by examining why social media is important for both individuals and business firms. Next, we discuss how companies can use social media to build relationships with customers, the goals for social media usage, and the steps required to build a social media plan and measure the effectiveness of a firm's social media activities. In the last part of this chapter, we take a close look at how firms use technology to conduct business on the Internet and what growth opportunities and challenges affect both social media and e-businesses.

WHY IS SOCIAL MEDIA IMPORTANT?

What is social media and how popular is it?

Today, there are many definitions of social media because it is still developing and continually changing. For our purposes, **social media** represents the online interactions that allow people and businesses to communicate and share ideas, personal information, and information about products and services. Simply put: Social media is about people. It is about a culture of participation, meaning that people can now discuss, vote, create, connect, and advocate much easier than ever before. For example, you can post your plans for a weekend trip on Facebook. Then you can share a travel itinerary and chronicle your trip through videos, photos, and ratings on Facebook. People can also use Twitter to raise awareness about bone-marrow donations in order to help a friend find a match. While it's hard to imagine, many popular social media sites like Facebook and Twitter were just created in the past decade (see Figure 15.1).

> **social media** the online interactions that allow people and businesses to communicate and share ideas, personal information, and information about products and services

So how popular is social media? A recent Pew Internet Research study showed that more than two-thirds of online adults use some sort of social media platform like Facebook, LinkedIn, or Twitter. Most of them say staying in touch with family and friends is their primary reason for using social media and roughly half say that reconnecting with old friends is a major reason why they use social media. Other reasons like connecting with people who share interests, making new friends, and reading comments by public figures are less important.*

Why businesses use social media

Social media has completely changed the business environment. Early on, companies saw potential in the sheer number of people using social media and that made using social media a top priority for many business firms. By using social media, companies could share information about their products and services and improve customer service. To date (and by the time you read this, the number will be higher), Facebook has not only one of the largest social networks with more than 1.15 billion users (as of March 2013), but also one of the "stickiest" Web sites, meaning that a lot of people spend a lot of time on Facebook.* As a result, many companies have flocked to build Facebook pages, develop contests, create Facebook ads, and find ways to get as many people as possible to "like" them on Facebook. Coca-Cola, for example, is one of the most effective marketers using Facebook, with more than 41 million likes to date.* For more information about why businesses use social media (and the benefits for a business), see Figure 15.2.

The fact that so many people are actively sharing information about themselves and their likes and dislikes online for all to see was a driving force behind many companies' attempts to develop a social media presence. Unalike social media, traditional marketing messages were top down—meaning that companies used television and magazine ads to promote their product to a large audience without any opportunity for feedback. Discussions about products were limited to consumers' immediate circle of friends and family. With social media, this is no longer the case. If a person has a bad experience with a product or service, they tend to post it on their blog or on Facebook, or tweet about it. A few years ago, Dell, Inc., experienced the wrath of a customer when blogger Jeff Jarvis posted a series of rants called "Dell Hell" after purchasing a Dell laptop. The post caught the attention of others who experienced similar problems; these consumers then

FIGURE 15.1

Timeline of major technology events and social media *Like computer technology, developments in social media have been not only rapid, they have also changed the way people connect.*

TECHNOLOGY BREAKTHROUGH

Year	Technology Breakthrough
1966	• E-mail
1969	• Advanced Research Projects Agency Network (ARPANET), Compuserve
1979	• USENET
1986	• LISTSERV
1991	• AOL
1995	• Classmates.com; Yahoo
1996	• AOL instant messenger
1998	• MoveOn.org, Google
1999	• Napster, Blogger, Epinions, LiveJournal
2001	• Wikipedia, StumbleUpon
2002	• Friendster, Technorati
2003	• LinkedIn, Wordpress, MySpace, Hi5, Photobucket, Delicious
2004	• Gmail, Flickr, Facebook, Yelp, Digg, Orkut
2005	• YouTube, Mashable, Reddit, Bebo
2006	• Twitter, Ustream
2007	• Tumblr
2008	• Apple's App Store
2009	• Foursquare, Google Wave
2010	• Pinterest,
2011	• Google +
2012	• Facebook sells stock to the public
The Future	• Who knows what the next generation of social media will mean for both individuals and business?

© CENGAGE LEARNING 2014

proceeded to voice their own Dell Hell stories. As a result, more people knew about the company's mistakes than ever before. Jarvis continued to voice his experience with Dell's customer service department, which at the time was not very effective or responsive. After the story hit the mainstream press and their customer service ratings began to suffer, Dell finally developed a corporate initiative aimed at listening to customers and fixing its customer service problems.* Now Dell is considered a leader in monitoring social media and listening to customers. The bottom line: Because of social media, companies no longer have much control over what is said about their products or services, and many are not yet comfortable with the new roles set forth by a consumer-dominated culture.

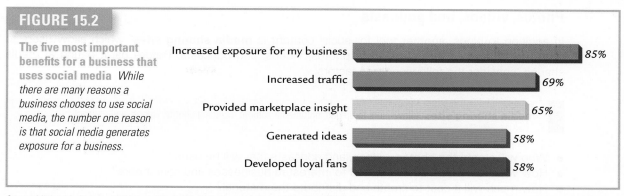

FIGURE 15.2

The five most important benefits for a business that uses social media *While there are many reasons a business chooses to use social media, the number one reason is that social media generates exposure for a business.*

Increased exposure for my business — 85%
Increased traffic — 69%
Provided marketplace insight — 65%
Generated ideas — 58%
Developed loyal fans — 58%

Source: Michael A. Stelzner, "2012 Social Media Marketing Industry Report," The SocialMediaExaminer.com Web site at www.socialmediaexaminer.com, accessed August 14, 2012.

SOCIAL MEDIA TOOLS FOR BUSINESS USE

For a business, part of what makes social media so challenging is the sheer number of ways to interact with other businesses and both existing and potential consumers. Companies are using social media because it allows the company to

- connect with customers;
- listen to its main stakeholders (including but not limited to customers);
- provide another means of customer service;
- develop content that is valuable to customers; and
- engage customers in product development and formulation.

Social content sites allow companies to create and share information about their products and services via blogs, videos, photos, and podcasts. For businesses selling to other businesses, social content sites can also include webinars and online informational promotional materials. For an overview of how businesses can use social media tools, take another look at Figure 15.2.

> **social content sites** allow companies to create and share information about their products and services

Business use of blogs

For businesses, blogs have become one of the most widely used tools for the effective use of social media. A **blog** is a Web site that allows a company to share information in order to increase customers' knowledge about its products and services, as well as to build trust. Once a story or information is posted, customers can provide feedback through comments, which is one of the most important ways of creating a conversation between business firms and consumers. Some experts believe that every company should have a blog that speaks to current and potential customers, not as customers, but as people.*

> **blog** a Web site that allows a company to share information in order to not only increase the customer's knowledge about its products and services, but also to build trust

Blogs are effective at developing better relationships with customers, attracting new customers, telling stories about the company's products or services, and providing an active forum for testing new ideas. By including information about webinars and promotional materials, blogs are also effective for businesses that are selling to other businesses.

Photos, videos, and podcasts

In addition to blogs, another tool for social content is **media sharing sites**, which allow users to upload multimedia content including photos, videos, and podcasts. Before participating in media sharing, consider the following three factors.

media sharing sites allow users to upload multimedia content including photos, videos, and podcasts

- Who will create the photos, videos, and podcasts that will be used?
- How will the content be distributed to interested businesses and consumers?
- How much will it cost to create and distribute the material?

Today, photo sharing provides a method for companies to tell a compelling story about its products or services through postings on either the company's Web site or a social media site.

Videos have also gained popularity because of their inherent ability to tell stories. Entertainment companies, for example, now traditionally use YouTube as a way to showcase movie trailers. Companies know that YouTube, Flickr, and others sites are useful because they are already recognised by other businesses and consumers as a source of both entertainment and information. YouTube is not only large (in terms of visitors), but the characteristics of its users are evenly split among different age groups and sexes.

Podcasts are digital audio or video files that people listen to or watch online on tablets, computers, MP3 players, or smartphones. Think of podcasts as radio shows that are distributed through various means (like iTunes) and not linked to a scheduled time period. The great thing about podcasts is that they are available for download at any time.

podcasts digital audio or video files that people listen to or watch online on tablets, computers, MP3 players, or smartphones

Social media ratings

Social media enables shoppers to access opinions, recommendations, and referrals from others within and outside of their own social circles. This type of information is available via a social media site and can include reviews and ratings, as well as information on sales promotions programmes like Groupon and LivingSocial. Both of these sites provide information about companies that offer deep discounts to customers that redeem an offer.

Sites for ratings and reviews are based on the idea that consumers trust the opinions of others when it comes to purchasing products and services. According to Nielsen Media Research, more than 70 per cent of consumers said that they trust online consumer opinions.* This statistic was much higher when compared with the same type of research for traditional advertising. Based on the early work of Amazon and eBay, new sites have sprung up allowing consumers to rate local businesses or compare products and services. One of the most popular, Yelp, combines customer ratings with social networking and is now the largest local review directory on the Web.

Social games

Social games are another area of growth in social media. A **social game** is "a multiplayer, competitive, goal-oriented activity with defined rules of engagement and online connectivity among a community of players."* One of the most important aspects of social media is entertainment and games like Angry Birds and World of Warcraft serve that purpose. Indeed, research shows that the "gamification" of social media is a huge trend because people like the competition, social status, and rewards that they can earn through social gaming.* For businesses that create games, it can be very profitable. Rovio Entertainment, the parent company of Angry Birds, rings up more than $100 million every year from global sales of game-related goods and services. While some businesses elect to create their own games, others choose to place advertising into a game. For example, the search engine Bing placed ads within the Facebook game FarmVille and gained several hundred thousand Facebook fans as a result.*

> **social game** a multiplayer, competitive, goal-oriented activity with defined rules of engagement and online connectivity among a community of players

ACHIEVING BUSINESS OBJECTIVES THROUGH SOCIAL MEDIA

Although the popularity of social media is a recent phenomenon, many businesses are already using it to achieve important objectives. Some of these goals are long-term—such as building brand awareness and brand reputation—while others are more short-term—such as increasing Web site traffic or generating sales leads. Regardless of how social media is used, there are a lot of business opportunities. In this section, we explore a few ways that companies have used social media effectively to achieve business objectives.

Social media communities

For a business, social media can be used to build a community. **Social media communities** are social networks based on the relationships among people.* These electronic communities encourage two-way communication, allow for people to develop profiles, and identify other people to connect with by using technology and the Internet. People in each community can be called friends, fans, followers, or connection. Popular social networking sites include Facebook (the largest), LinkedIn (for professionals), Twitter, Google+, YouTube, Pinterest, and many others. To see how many businesses use the top four social media community sites, see Figure 15.3.

> **social media communities** social networks based on the relationships among people

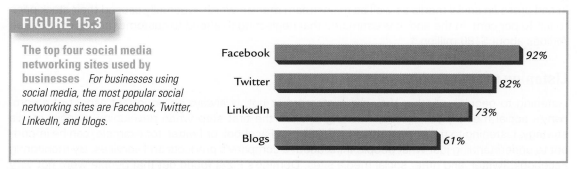

FIGURE 15.3

The top four social media networking sites used by businesses *For businesses using social media, the most popular social networking sites are Facebook, Twitter, LinkedIn, and blogs.*

Facebook — 92%
Twitter — 82%
LinkedIn — 73%
Blogs — 61%

Source: Michael A. Stelzner, "2012 Social Media Marketing Industry Report," The SocialMediaExaminer.com Web site at www.socialmediaexaminer.com, accessed August 14, 2012.

There are social communities for every interest, ethnic group, and lifestyle. Different types of social communities include forums and wikis. Forums were perhaps the earliest form of social community. A **forum** is an interactive version of a community bulletin board that focuses on threaded discussions. These are particularly popular with people who share a common interest such as video games. Another community based on social media is a wiki. A **wiki** is a collaborative online working space that enables members to contribute content that is then sharable with other people. With wikis, members of the community are the editors and gatekeepers ensuring that the content is correct and updated. Wikipedia—the free online encyclopaedia—is perhaps the most widely-recognised example of a wiki. A community of unpaid experts voluntarily keeps the content on the Wikipedia Web site as updated and accurate as possible.

> **forum** an interactive version of a community bulletin board that focuses on threaded discussions
> **wiki** a collaborative online working space that enables members to contribute content that is then sharable with other people

The whole purpose of social networks is to build communities and develop connections. Today, many companies are using social media to build communities with other businesses and consumers in order to achieve business objectives. Recently, Pepsi used social media to showcase its commitment to real-world communities by shifting the $20 million typically spent on Super Bowl advertising to a Web site that allowed customers to post ideas for helping their own communities in areas like education and the environment. The driving force behind its "Refresh Everything" campaign was the belief that the company needed to "walk the walk" and really do something to make an impact. The Pepsi Refresh Project allowed people to upload their ideas or vote for their favourites. Pepsi then funded projects with the most votes. More than 57 million customers voted on different ideas—all designed to improve communities. For Pepsi, this social media project enabled the soft-drink giant to engage its customers who are heavy social media users.*

Crisis and reputation management

One of the most important reasons for listening to stakeholders is to determine whether there is a crisis brewing. A majority of companies believe that their company is less than a year away from some potential crisis moment and monitor social media for conversations that may predict a crisis.*

United Airlines recently found out the hard way what happens when customers voice their grievances with a service using social networks. Guitarist Dave Carroll accused United Airlines of breaking his guitar during baggage handling. After months of moving through the traditional channels and getting nowhere, Dave wrote a song, filmed a video, and posted it on YouTube. He also had friends send out the link to their networks. Soon the video had thousands of views and people started sharing their own negative United Airlines stories. United did try to control the damage on Twitter, but most people saw it as an empty promise to improve customer service. Soon the company was embroiled in bad press (in social media as well as mainstream media), which eventually caused their stock price to fall 10 per cent. In the end, it is estimated that neglecting to attend to customer needs cost United Airlines about $180 million.*

Listening to stakeholders

Listening to people, whether they are customers or not, is always an important aspect of a company's social media plan. Indeed, listening is often the first step when developing a social media strategy. Listening to the conversations unfolding on Facebook or Twitter, for example, can be important to understanding just what people think about a company's products and services. By monitoring Facebook, Twitter, and other social media sites, Domino's Pizza found out that people were not very happy with its product quality. Customers described the sauce as "tasting like ketchup" and the crust as "tasting like cardboard." Unfortunately, there were enough comments of a similar nature for the company to use traditional marketing research to verify this information. They found the sentiment to be true and the company then developed a plan to reinvent every aspect of the company—and its pizza products. Did the plan work? Same store sales increased more than 14 per cent.*

Targeting customers

Many companies are using social media to increase awareness and build their brand among customers. It is especially valuable in targeting the Millennials. **Millennials** are tech-savvy digital natives born after 1980. When Ford wanted to introduce its subcompact car, the Fiesta, to Millennials, it used social media. Ford chose to target Millennials because, as a group, they are also more likely than older consumers to purchase a subcompact car. For this social media promotion, Ford recruited 100 social media users, dubbed "agents," who were given a Ford Fiesta to drive for six months. The only requirement was that each agent talked about the car on social media—using video, posts on Facebook and Twitter, and other social media sites. Initially, Ford set a goal of attracting 144,000 Web site visitors, but by the end of the promotion more than 300,000 people had viewed the Web site. Additional results showed that Ford's social media marketing promotion for the Fiesta worked well and social media could be used to build brand recognition with a specific group of people.*

Millennials tech-savvy digital natives born after 1980

In some cases, awareness is not a problem, but the ability to connect with the customer is. Social media can be used to build that connection. Consider the case of Old Spice. Once thought of as an "old man's" cologne, Old Spice struggled to gain attention for its body wash product in an industry dominated by newcomers like Axe—a brand that had done a very good job of connecting with Millennial men. Old Spice decided to use social media to reposition its body wash with a video launched on YouTube. The video was launched online, and then later on television. The results were so positive that Old Spice followed up with a campaign using online videos based on comments from customers posted on Twitter and Facebook.*

Social media marketing

Studies show that Increasingly more companies are using social media in marketing.* **Social media marketing** is the "utilisation of social media technologies, channels, and software to create, communicate, deliver and exchange offerings that have value for an organisation."* As companies become more comfortable with social media, we can expect even more companies to use social media to market products and services to their customers. Already, research indicates that companies are shifting their advertising money from traditional marketing (like television and magazines) to digital marketing (like Internet search engines and social media). Experts now predict that social media will account for 26 per cent of all online spending by 2016.* The primary reason is simple. People are spending more time online.* Often the first step for a business that wants to use social media is to go to LinkedIn, Facebook, or Twitter. As you can tell from the information in Figure 15.4, companies like LinkedIn make using their technology as easy as possible to connect with potential or existing customers.

social media marketing the utilisation of social media technologies, channels, and software to create, communicate, deliver, and exchange offerings that have value for an organisation

Today, many companies have been quite successful using social media marketing not only to develop customer awareness, but also to obtain sales leads and increase actual sales. HubSpot, for example, is a software company that helps small and medium-sized companies develop inbound marketing programmes. **Inbound marketing** is a marketing term that describes new ways of gaining attention, and ultimately, customers, by creating content on a Web site that pulls customers in. Tools used for inbound marketing programmes include search engine optimisation, blogging, videos, and social media. In order to market its software products, the software company HubSpot shunned traditional advertising and began to practice what it preached. First, the company developed its own inbound marketing programme by creating valuable content and marketing information that was then distributed through social media and search engine Web sites. Companies interested in HubSpot's software were required to enter contact information (name, phone number, and e-mail address) in order to view the information. People provided contact information because they believed the

FIGURE 15.4

LinkedIn's marketing solutions for other businesses *Like many popular social media communities, LinkedIn's marketing tools make it easy to connect with potential or existing customers.*

company's software could help them improve their marketing activities. As a result of HubSpot's inbound marketing programme, the cost of generating new sales leads was five to seven times less than leads generated by more traditional marketing activities and as a bonus they gained thousands of new customers.*

> **inbound marketing** a marketing term that describes new ways of gaining attention and ultimately customers by creating content on a Web site that pulls customers in

Dell also uses social media to sell its computer and technology products. Unalike other companies experimenting with social media, Dell decided to be more visible and actively use social media to increase sales by using Twitter. The company has sold computers valued at more than $6.5 million by including links in its Twitter account to the DellOutlet Web site. While this represents a tiny percentage of total sales, it does show that products can be sold through social media.*

As important as social media is, it is only one aspect of digital marketing. Indeed, digital marketing or online marketing is comprised of several areas, including

- online public relations—developing social media press kits;
- search engine optimisation—using keywords in the Web site in order to rank higher in search engine results;
- search engine marketing—buying ads like Google's AdWords to increase traffic to a company's Web site;
- display advertising—buying banner ads;
- e-mail marketing—targeting customers through opt-in email campaigns; and
- content marketing—developing photos, videos, podcasts, blog posts, and other tools to increase the value to the customer.

© AP PHOTO/ZEF NIKOLIA/DSPD

The face of social media. While many people use Facebook to connect with friends and relatives, the world's largest social media site is so much more! For many businesses, Facebook has created new ways to market their products and services and connect with potential or existing customers. Experts predict that the use of social media sites like Facebook will only increase in the future because people are spending more time online.

Generating new product ideas

Companies can use social media to conduct much of their consumer-based research. Using insight gained from Facebook or Twitter, for example, allows a company to modify existing products and services and develop new ones. **Crowdsourcing** involves outsourcing tasks to a group of people in order to tap into the ideas of the crowd. In some cases valuable information can be obtained by crowd voting.

crowdsourcing outsourcing tasks to a group of people in order to tap into the ideas of the crowd

Companies can even build communities for specific brands in order to obtain information and new ideas from consumers. A few years ago, Starbucks built a network called Mystarbucksidea.com that allowed customers to post ideas about how the company could improve. Since the creation of

SUCCESS STORY

Global brand localises Facebook content

Adidas Originals' Facebook page currently has more than 1.9m global fans. However, they wanted to make their pages more useful to their fans and more appealing for Adidas advertising. The solution Adidas and Facebook came up with was more localisation of the campaigns and e-commerce links. As a result they have introduced a new tab to its fan page that tailors advertising content according to the location of the Facebook user.

There are now a number of localised versions for countries including the U.S., U.K., France, Italy, Japan and South Africa. Facebook are currently developing localised versions for cities and a regional Latin America version.

Tara Moss, Adidas global head of digital marketing, said: "Facebook is a global platform and, as Adidas is a brand that celebrates originality, it was important for us to be relevant in our engagement with all of our consumers worldwide. Innovation is in our DNA and is what consumers expect from Adidas. Innovation coupled with the connection that social media is how we'll continue to get closer to our consumers and build meaningful relationships with them online and beyond."

How important is it for global brands such as Adidas to localise their communications given the global nature of its brand platform?

References: www.guardian.co.uk, Monday June 1 2009 and McEleny, C., 'Adidas Originals ramps up localised content on Facebook fan page', *News Media Age*, 2 June 2009 and www.hedgehogs.net/

How do companies find the right employee? Answer: More and more companies are using social media sites to recruit employees. Sites like LinkedIn, the largest social network for professionals, are often used by both large and small companies to advertise current job openings and reach out to potential employees located not only in the United States, but also in other parts of the world.

the Web site, thousands of ideas have been posted about Starbucks products, the customer's store experience, and the company's community involvement. The site also enables people to vote on the best ideas, many of which Starbucks has already implemented. For example, getting a free coffee on your birthday if you are a Gold Member or developing a VIP programme were both originally customer ideas. In cases such as this one, customers appreciate the ability to share their ideas with a company to whom they are loyal, only to receive reciprocal loyalty when the company implements their ideas.*

Recruiting employees

For years, companies have used current employees to recruit new employees based on the theory that "birds of a feather flock together." The concept is simple: Current employees' friends and family may prove to be good job candidates. Social media takes that concept to a whole new level. LinkedIn, the largest social network for professionals, has been used quite effectively by both large and small companies to recruit employees. Indeed, more than half of *Fortune* 100 companies use LinkedIn to recruit future employees. Using LinkedIn is beneficial for companies because it saves time and lowers recruiting costs. And using a site like LinkedIn also allows employers to see more information about candidates. Companies like Accenture, Home Depot, IBM, and Oracle have all had success with LinkedIn.

DEVELOPING A SOCIAL MEDIA PLAN

Before developing a plan to use social media, it is important to determine how social media can improve the organisation's overall performance and how it "fits" with a company's other operational and promotional activities. For example, if a social media plan attempts to improve customer service, it needs to link to the company's overall organisational efforts to improve customer service.

Steps to build a social media plan

Once it is determined how social media links to the company's other activities, there are several steps that should be considered.

Step 1: Listen to determine opportunities Often social media is used to "listen" to what customers like and don't like about a company's products or services. For example, reading comments on social media sites can yield some insight into how consumers are reacting to a price increase or decrease for an existing product or service. Monitoring social media sites also allows managers and employees to enter the conversation and tell the company's side of the story. In addition, companies can monitor social media sites to gather information about competitors as well as what is being said about the industry.

After the listening phase, it is important to analyse the information to identify the company's strengths and weaknesses. For a company, it is also important to identify opportunities and threats before taking the next step—setting objectives.

Step 2: Establish social media objectives After listening to and analysing the information obtained from social media sites, it is important to use that information to develop specific objectives. For social media, an objective is a specific statement about what a social media plan should accomplish. Each objective should be specific, measurable, achievable, realistic, and oriented toward the future.

For most companies, the most popular objectives are increasing brand awareness, acquiring new customers, introducing new products, retaining current customers, and gaining customer insight.* Other objectives that are often important include improving search engine ranking, showcasing public relations activities, increasing Web site traffic, and generating sales leads.* All objectives need to be clear and linked to specific actions that can be used to accomplish each objective.

Step 3: Segment and target the social customer Ideally, a company will have developed a customer profile that describes a typical customer in terms of age, income, gender, ethnicity, etc. When segmenting or targeting customers, it also helps to know how they think, how they spend their time, how much they buy, and how often they buy. In fact, more information about potential customers will help you develop a social media plan to achieve a company's objectives. Lack of information about customers can lead to wasted time and money and the inability to successfully achieve the firm's social media objectives. For example, most companies feel that they must use Facebook and Twitter. But if their core customer does not use these social media sites, then it does not make sense to use them. Additionally it is important to really understand how customers use social media.

- Do they create content like photos, videos, blog posts, etc?
- Do they use social media for ratings and reviews?
- Do they post product reviews and ratings on Facebook accounts?
- Do they spend a lot of time using social media?

According to Forrester Research, there are six types of individuals that use social media. Individuals can be classified as creators, critics, collectors, joiners, spectators, or inactives. In addition to the Forrester classifications of social media users, additional information that can help you target just the "right" social media customer is illustrated in Figure 15.5.

Step 4: Select social media tools The search for the right social media tool(s) usually begins with the company's objectives, outlined in Step 2. It also helps to review the target customer or segment of the market the company is trying to reach (Step 3). With this information, the next step is to choose the right social media tools to reach the right customers. A company can use social communities, blogs, photos, videos, podcasts, or games to reach potential or existing customers. For example, if the goal is to recruit college students for college entry-level jobs, LinkedIn may be a good choice. Remember, it is not necessary (or even advisable) to use all of the above tools. It also helps to remember that social media is not free and can be quite expensive because it costs both time and money.

Step 5: Implement and integrate the plan Once social media tools have been identified, a company can implement and integrate the social media plan. Because a social media plan doesn't necessarily have a start and stop date, it is different from traditional advertising campaigns. Some social media activities continue and have a life of their own. Some companies, on the other hand, feel that it is important to have a mix of short- and long-term social media promotion. In this case, it is important to develop each social media activity to make sure that it is as effective as it can be. For example, if a company is running a Facebook promotion, it is important to consider issues like developing a branded page, updating the page frequently, and providing fresh content to keep customers coming back to the Facebook site. If the same or similar social media activity is used on Twitter, the company must make changes to make sure it works on the Twitter site.

To increase the effectiveness of social media, companies will often integrate online promotions with more traditional or offline promotions. For example, it is not unusual to see the Twitter icon at the

FIGURE 15.5

Types of information that can help target different social media customers *The more information you have about social media customers, the easier it is to develop a social media plan that targets the "right" customer.*

General Information
- Age, income, gender, ethnicity, education, occupation, family size, religion, etc.

Identifying Factors
- What do they consider important?
- How do they spend their time?
- What do they buy and how often do they buy?

Social Media Usage
- How often do they use social media?
- Do they use Facebook, Twitter, YouTube, and other social media sites?
- Do they create videos, Web pages, or other content?
- Do they read ratings and reviews?
- What other factors can help you identify potential social customers?

POTENTIAL SOCIAL MEDIA CUSTOMERS

© CENGAGE LEARNING 2014

end of a television commercial. This signals to consumers that more information about the product or service is provided on Twitter. Indeed, as companies increase the amount of money spent on digital marketing and social media, they will attempt to tie online and offline promotions together to make the message go further.

Measuring and adapting a social media plan

Because social media is a relatively new method of reaching customers, many companies struggle when attempting to measure social media. Often companies use the same measurements that have been used with long-established media channels like television and radio to determine the effect of social media on the customer's awareness of the company or a specific brand and if sales (and profits) are increasing. Based on this information, the company may try to determine if it is getting a positive return on its investment in social media. Generally, there are two types of social media measurement. While both quantitative and qualitative measurements can be used, most companies tend to use quantitative measurements.

Technology that satisfies needs online.
Both large and small businesses are using social media to sell products and services to customers 24 hours a day and seven days a week. As an added bonus, today's technology can reach potential and existing customers any place in the world as long as customers have access to the Internet.

©DAVID J. GREEN-LIFESTYLE 2/ALAMY

Quantitative social media measurement **Quantitative social media measurement** consists of using numerical measurements, such as counting the number of Web site visitors, number of fans and followers, number of leads generated, and the number of new customers. Table 15.1 shows a few popular quantitative ways to measure social media.

quantitative social media measurement using numerical measurements, such as counting the number of Web site visitors, number of fans and followers, number of leads generated, and the number of new customers

TABLE 15.1 Quantitative measurements for selected social media web sites

Type of social media	Typical measuremens
Blogs	• Unique visitors • Number of views • Ratio of visitors to posted comments
Twitter	• Number of followers • Number of tweets and retweets • Click through rate (CTR) of tweeted links • Visits to Web site from tweeted links
Facebook	• Number of fans • Number of likes • Number of comments • Growth of wall response • Visits to Web sites from Facebook links
YouTube	• Number of videos • Number of visitors • Ratio of comments to the number of videos uploaded • Number of embedded links

© CENGAGE LEARNING 2014

Because a company must invest both time and money when it uses social media, it is important to measure the success and make adjustments if needed. In addition to the quantitative measurements already mentioned, a number of companies are using key performance indicators. **Key performance indicators (KPIs)** are measurements that define and measure the progress of an organisation toward achieving its objectives. Generally, KPIs are *quantitative* (based on numbers like the number of Twitter followers).

key performance indicators (KPIs) measurements that define and measure the progress of an organisation toward achieving its objectives

If measuring the success or failure of social media activities with KPIs, the first step is to connect KPIs with objectives. The second step is to set a benchmark—a number that shows what success should look like. For example, Ford said that if 144,000 people visited the Ford Fiesta Web site within a specified time, it would indicate that the company's social media plan to introduce the new subcompact car to Millennials was successful. When measured, more than 300,000 people had visited the Web site. Simply put: The company's social media plan was successful because it surpassed the original benchmark. It is also possible to compare the company's social media KPIs to its benchmarks over time. When trend comparison is used to measure the effectiveness of social media, the trend may be more important than the actual percentage of increase or decrease for just one measurement period.

Qualitative social media measurement **Qualitative social media measurement** is the process of accessing the opinions and beliefs about a brand. This process primarily uses sentiment analysis to categorise what is being said about a company. **Sentiment analysis** is a measurement that uses technology to detect the mood, attitudes, or emotions of people who experience a social media activity. Other measurements for determining customer sentiment include:

> **qualitative social media measurement** the process of accessing the opinions and beliefs about a brand and primarily uses sentiment analysis to categorise what is being said about a company
>
> **sentiment analysis** a measurement that uses technology to detect the moods, attitudes, or emotions of people who experience a social media activity

- *Customer satisfaction score*—defined as the relative satisfaction of customers.
- *Issue resolution rate*—the percentage of customer service inquiries resolved satisfactorily using social media.
- *Resolution time*—defined as the amount of time taken to resolve customer service issues.

When compared to quantitative measurement, it should be noted that many of these qualitative social media measurements are more subjective in nature.

Regardless of the type of measurement used, one of the most powerful aspects of social media—and indeed digital marketing—is the ability to tie the objectives of a social media plan to the results that were achieved. After reviewing results for social media activities against pre-established benchmarks and analysing trends, changes can be made to increase the effectiveness of social media activities.

Social media is particularly important to businesses that use e-business to sell their products and services online. In the next section, we take a close look at how e-business firms are organised, satisfy needs online, and earn profits.

DEFINING E-BUSINESS

In a simple sense, **e-business**, or **electronic business**, can be defined as the organised effort of individuals to produce and sell, for a profit, the products and services that satisfy society's needs *through the facilities available on the Internet.* Sometimes people use the term *e-commerce* instead of *e-business*. In a strict sense, e-business is used when you're talking about all business activities and practices conducted on the Internet by an individual firm or industry. On the other hand, e-commerce is a part of e-business and usually refers only to buying and selling activities conducted online. In this chapter, we generally use the term *e-business* because of its broader definition and scope. As you will see in the remainder of this chapter, e-business is transforming key business activities.

> **e-business (electronic business)** the organised effort of individuals to produce and sell, for a profit, the products and services that satisfy society's needs *through the facilities available on the Internet*

Organising e-business resources

To be organised, a business must combine *human, material, informational,* and *financial resources.* This is true of e-business, too (see Figure 15.6), but in this case, the resources may be more specialised than in a typical business. For example, people who can design, create, and maintain Web sites are only a fraction of the specialised human resources required by e-businesses. Material resources must include specialised computers, sophisticated equipment and software, and high-speed Internet connection. Computer programs that track the number of customers who view a firm's Web site are generally among the specialised informational resources required. Financial resources, the money required to start and maintain the firm and allow it to grow, usually reflect greater participation by individual entrepreneurs, venture capitalists, and investors willing to invest in a high-tech firm instead of conventional financial sources such as banks.

In an effort to reduce the cost of specialised resources that are used in e-business, many firms have turned to outsourcing. **Outsourcing** is the process of finding outside vendors and suppliers that

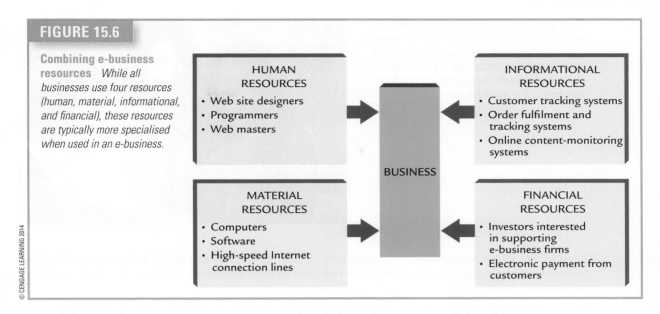

FIGURE 15.6

Combining e-business resources *While all businesses use four resources (human, material, informational, and financial), these resources are typically more specialised when used in an e-business.*

HUMAN RESOURCES
• Web site designers
• Programmers
• Web masters

INFORMATIONAL RESOURCES
• Customer tracking systems
• Order fulfilment and tracking systems
• Online content-monitoring systems

BUSINESS

MATERIAL RESOURCES
• Computers
• Software
• High-speed Internet connection lines

FINANCIAL RESOURCES
• Investors interested in supporting e-business firms
• Electronic payment from customers

© CENGAGE LEARNING 2014

provide professional help, parts, or materials at a lower cost. For example, a firm that needs special-ised software to complete a project may turn to an outside firm located in another part of the world.

> **outsourcing** the process of finding outside vendors and suppliers that provide professional help, parts, or materials at a lower cost

Satisfying needs online

Think for a moment about this question: "Why do people use the Internet?" As pointed out in the first part of this chapter, more and more people are using computers, the Internet, and social media as a way to connect with people. The Internet can also be used to purchase products or services. Today, more people use the Internet to satisfy these needs than ever before. Let's start with two basic assumptions.

● The Internet has created some new customer needs that did not exist before the creation of the Internet.
● e-Businesses can satisfy those needs, as well as more traditional ones.

©BLOOMBERG VIA GETTY IMAGES

Google—the number 1 search engine. When Google created its now-famous Web site, the developers chose a rather simple opening screen with just the Google name, a search box, and very little else. Users loved the simple format and used the search engine to find information about products and services, investment research, new movies, the current weather, and the latest news stories. Now Google has used its early success to develop new services, including Google Earth, Google+, and mobile apps.

These days, you can find e-businesses that sell almost anything. Many will help you recognise a new need by offering free trials of apps, games, or other digital products. This is a great way to find out whether the digital product is useful, convenient, and worth buying.

©CHRIS ROUT/ALAMY

At eBay's global auction site, customers can, for a small fee, buy and sell almost anything. In addition to purchasing products, the Internet can be used by both individuals and business firms to obtain information. For example:

- Internet users can access newspapers, magazines, and radio and television programming at a time and place convenient to them.
- The Internet provides the opportunity for two-way interaction between an Internet firm and the viewer. For example, many news-content sites encourage dialogue among users.
- Customers can respond to information on the Internet by requesting more information or posing specific questions, which may lead to purchasing a product or service.
- Finally, the Internet allows customers to choose the content they are offered. Knowing the interests of a customer allows an Internet firm to direct appropriate, smart advertising to a specific customer. For the advertiser, knowing that its advertisements are being directed to the most likely customers represents a better way to spend advertising dollars.

Creating e-business profit

Business firms can increase profits either by increasing sales revenue or by reducing expenses through a variety of e-business activities.

Increasing sales revenue   Each source of sales revenue flowing into a firm is referred to as a **revenue stream**. One way to increase revenues is to sell merchandise on the Internet. Online merchants can reach a global customer base 24 hours a day, seven days a week, because the opportunity to shop on the Internet is virtually unrestricted. However, shifting revenues earned from customers inside a real store to revenues earned from these same customers online does not create any real new revenue for a firm. The goal is to find *new customers* and generate *new sales* so that *total revenues are increased.*

 revenue stream   a source of revenue flowing into a firm

Intelligent information systems also can help to generate sales revenue for Internet firms such as Amazon.com. Such systems store information about each customer's purchases, along with a variety of other information about the buyer's preferences. Using this information, the system can assist the customer the next time he or she visits the Web site. For example, if the customer has bought a book by J.K. Rowling in the past, the system might suggest books by similar authors who write in the same genre.

Although some customers may not make a purchase online, the existence of the firm's Web site and the services and information it provides may lead to increased sales in the firm's physical stores.

Using Facebook to reach online customers. *Today many retailers are using Facebook and other social network sites to reach consumers. It's just one more way to provide information to consumers that may want to purchase the firm's products or services.*

For example, Honda's Web site can provide basic comparative information for shoppers so that they are better prepared for their visit to an automobile showroom.

In addition to selling products or services online, e-business revenue streams are created by advertising placed on Web pages and by subscription fees charged for access to online services and content. For example, Hoover's, a comprehensive source for company and industry information, makes some of its online content free for anyone who visits the site, but more detailed information is available only by paid subscription. In addition, Hoover's receives revenue from companies acting as sponsors who advertise their products and services on the site.

Many Internet firms that distribute news, magazine and newspaper articles, and similar content generate revenue from commissions earned from sellers of products linked to the site. Online shopping malls, for example, now provide groups of related vendors of electronic equipment and computer hardware and software with a new method of selling their products and services. In many cases, the vendors share online sales revenues with the site owners.

Reducing expenses Reducing expenses is the second major way in which e-business can help to increase profitability. Providing online access to information that customers want can reduce the cost of dealing with customers. Sprint Nextel (www.sprint.com), for instance, is just one company that maintains an extensive Web site where potential customers can learn more about products and services, and where current customers can access personal account information, send questions to customer service, and purchase additional products or services. With such extensive online services, many retailers can reduce the amount of physical shops and hence the associated costs such as rent and rates.

FUNDAMENTAL MODELS OF E-BUSINESS

One way to get a better sense of how businesses are adapting to the opportunities available on the Internet is to identify e-business models. A **business model** represents a group of common characteristics and methods of doing business to generate sales revenues and reduce expenses. Each of the models discussed in the following text represents a primary e-business model. Regardless of the type of business model, planning often depends on if the e-business is a new firm or an existing firm adding an online presence—see Figure 15.7. It also helps to keep in mind that in order to generate sales revenues and earn profits, a business—especially an e-business—must meet the needs of its customers.

business model represents a group of common characteristics and methods of doing business to generate sales revenues and reduce expenses

FIGURE 15.7

Planning for a new internet business or building an online presence for an existing business *The approach taken to creating an e-business plan will depend on whether you are establishing a new Internet business or adding an online component to an existing business.*

SUCCESSFUL E-BUSINESS PLANNING

Starting a new Internet business

- Will the new e-business provide a product or service that meets customer needs?
- Who are the new firm's potential customers?
- How do promotion, pricing, and distribution affect the new e-business?
- Will the potential market generate enough sales and profits to justify the risk of starting an e-business?

Building an online presence for an existing business

- Is going online a logical way to increase sales and profits for the existing business?
- Are potential online customers different from the firm's traditional customers?
- Will the new e-business activities complement the firm's traditional activities?
- Does the firm have the time, talent, and financial resources to develop an online presence?

© CENGAGE LEARNING 2014

Business-to-business (B2B) model

Many e-businesses can be distinguished from others simply by their customer focus. For instance, some firms use the Internet mainly to conduct business with other businesses. These firms are generally referred to as having a **business-to-business (or B2B) model**.

business-to-business (or B2B) model a model used by firms that conduct business with other businesses

When examining B2B firms, two clear types emerge. In the first type, the focus is simply on facilitating sales transactions between businesses. For example, Dell manufactures computers to specifications that customers enter on the Dell Web site (www.dell.com). A large portion of Dell's online orders are from corporate clients who are well informed about the products they need and are looking for fairly priced, high-quality computer products that will be delivered quickly. Basically, by building only what is ordered, Dell reduces storage and carrying costs and rarely is stuck with unsold

A new way to reach business customers around the globe. Alibaba.com is a business-to-business (B2B) global trade site that makes it easy for millions of importers and exporters to buy and sell products and services online. Because it meets the needs of its customers, Alibaba.com has become a successful company with offices in more than 70 cities around the globe.

© M4OS/ALAMY

RESPONSIBLE PRACTICE   The integrity of online reviews

In 2009, The Daily Background (a blog run by student Arlen Parsa) ran a story that became a brief sensation. Parsa was looking for work on Mechanical Turk, a site owned by Amazon where users are paid small sums to do tasks that can't be done automatically by software.

Parsa noticed an advert titled "Write a Positive 5/5 Review for Product on Web site". It was looking for well-written review of a Belkin router giving 100 per cent ratings; while also asking people to mark negative reviews as "unhelpful".

It was clear from the advert that these reviews were meant to be from "customers" – the description gave instructions that ranged from making up a story about needing and using the product to how to create an account on the site.

Wondering about the ethics of this, Parsa researched who the advert had come from – a man who was listed on LinkedIn as the Business Development Representative at Belkin.

In a statement released just days after this story, Belkin assured readers that this was an isolated incident; that they were working to remove these reviews; and that they were sorry for it.

This story raised a number of questions, especially when it became clear that this practice is used by a number of businesses, who haven't received the same amount of bad press as Belkin. Is this an example of unethical marketing, or just something to be expected on online reviews? Is it more unethical for a large business to "buy" reviews than a small one to write their own?

References: Arlen Parsa, 'Exclusive: Belkin's Development Rep is Hiring People to Write Fake Positive Amazon Reviews' (January 16th, 2009), accessed on 4th September 2013 at http://www.thedailybackground.com/2009/01/16/exclusivebelkins-development-rep-is-hiring-people-to-write-fakepositive-amazon-reviews/); Justin Mann, 'Belkin issues apology for paid review scandal', techspot.com (January 19th 2009), accessed on 4th September 2013 at http://www.techspot.com/news/33257-belkin-issues-apology-for-paid-review-scandal.html

inventory. By dealing directly with Dell, customers eliminate costs associated with wholesalers and retailers, thereby helping to reduce the price they pay for equipment.

A second, more complex type of B2B model involves a company and its suppliers. Today, suppliers use the Internet to bid on products and services they wish to sell to a customer and learn about the customer's rules and procedures that must be followed. For example, Ford has developed a B2B model to link thousands of suppliers that sell the automobile maker parts, supplies, and raw materials worth millions of dollars each year. Although the B2B site is expensive to start and maintain, there are significant savings for Ford. Given the potential savings, it is no wonder that many other manufacturers and their suppliers are beginning to use the same kind of B2B systems that are used by the automaker. In fact, suppliers know that to be a "preferred" supplier for a large firm that may purchase large quantities of parts, supplies, or raw materials, they must be tied into the purchaser's B2B system.

Business-to-consumer (B2C) model

In contrast with the B2B model, firms such as Barnes and Noble (www.barnesandnoble.com) and online retailer Lands' End (www.landsend.com) clearly are focused on individual consumers. These companies are referred to as having a **business-to-consumer (or B2C) model**. In a B2C situation, understanding how consumers behave online is critical to a firm's success. Typically, a business firm that uses a B2C model must answer the following questions:

> **business-to-consumer (or B2C) model** a model used by firms that focus on conducting business with individual consumers

- Will consumers use Web sites merely to simplify and speed up comparison shopping?
- Will consumers purchase services and products online or end up buying at a traditional retail store?
- What sorts of products and services are best suited for online consumer shopping?

In addition to providing round-the-clock global access to all kinds of products and services, B2C firms often attempt to build long-term relationships with their customers. Often, firms will make a special effort to make sure that the customer is satisfied and that problems, if any, are solved quickly. Specialised software also can help build good customer relationships. Tracking the decisions and buying preferences as customers navigate a Web site, for instance, helps management to make well-informed decisions about how best to serve online customers. In essence, this is Orbitz's online selling approach. By tracking and analysing customer data, the online travel company can provide individualised service to its customers. Although a "little special attention" may increase the cost of doing business for a B2C firm, the customer's repeated purchases will repay the investment many times over.

Today, B2B and B2C models are the most popular business models for e-business. And yet, there are other business models that perform specialised e-business activities to generate revenues. Most of the business models described in Table 15.2 are modified versions of the B2B and B2C models.

TABLE 15.2 **Other business models that perform specialised e-business activities** *Although modified versions of B2B or B2C, these business models perform specialised e-business activities to generate revenues.*

Advertising e-business model	Advertisements that are displayed on a firm's Web site in return for a fee. Examples include pop-up and banner advertisements on search engines and other popular Internet sites.
Brokerage e-business model	Online marketplaces where buyers and sellers are brought together to facilitate an exchange of goods and services. One example is eBay, which provides a site for buying and selling virtually anything.
Consumer-to-consumer model	Peer-to-peer software that allows individuals to share information over the Internet. Examples include Bit Torrent, which allows users to exchange digital media files.
Subscription and pay-per-view e-business models	Content that is available only to users who pay a fee to gain access to a Web site. Examples include investment information provided by Standard & Poor's and business research provided by Forrester Research, Inc.

© CENGAGE LEARNING 2014

THE FUTURE OF THE INTERNET, SOCIAL MEDIA, AND E-BUSINESS

Since the beginning of commercial activity on the Internet, developments in computer technology, social media, and e-business have been rapid and formidable with spectacular successes such as Google, eBay, and Pinterest. However, a larger-than-usual number of technology companies struggled or even failed during the economic crisis. Today, most firms involved in the Internet, social media, and e-business use a more intelligent approach to development. The long-term view held by the vast majority of analysts is that the Internet, social media, and e-business will continue to expand to meet the needs of businesses and consumers.

Internet growth potential

To date, only a small percentage of the global population uses the Internet. At the beginning of 2012, estimates suggest that about 2.3 billion of the nearly 7 billion people in the world use the Web.* Clearly, there is much more growth opportunity. The other hand, the number of Internet users in the world's developing countries is expected to increase dramatically.

Although the number of global Internet users is expected to increase, that's only part of the story. Perhaps the more important question is why people are using the Internet. Primary reasons for using the Internet include the ability to connect with other people, to obtain information, or to purchase a firm's products or services. Of particular interest to business firms is the growth of social media. The number of Facebook users, for example, increased from 664 million to 835 million in the 12-month period from March 2011 to March 2012, and then onto 1.15 billion only a year later. And the number of Facebook users is expected to continue to increase for years to come.* The number of users for other social media sites like LinkedIn, Twitter, Pinterest, are also expected to increase.

Experts also predict that the number of companies using e-business to increase sales and reduce expenses will continue to increase. Firms that adapt existing business models to an online environment will continue to dominate development. For example, books, CDs, clothing, hotel accommodations, car rentals, and travel reservations are products and services well suited to online buying and selling. These products or services will continue to be sold in the traditional way, as well as in a more cost-effective and efficient fashion over the Internet.

Ethical and legal concerns

The social and legal concerns for the Internet, social media, and e-business extend beyond those shared by all businesses. Essentially, the Internet is a new "frontier" without borders and without much control by governments or other organisations.

Ethics and social responsibility   Socially responsible and ethical behaviour by individuals and businesses on the Internet are major concerns. For example, an ethically questionable practice in cyberspace is the unauthorised access and use of information discovered through computerised tracking of users once they are connected to the Internet. Essentially, a user may visit a Web site and unknowingly receive a small piece of software code called a **cookie**. This cookie can track where the user goes on the Internet and measure how long the user stays at any particular Web site. Although this type of software may produce valuable customer information, it also can be viewed as an invasion of privacy, especially since users may not even be aware that their movements are being monitored.

 cookie   a small piece of software sent by a Web site that tracks an individual's Internet use

Besides the unauthorised use of cookies to track online behaviour, there are several other threats to users' privacy and confidentiality. Monitoring an employee's computer usage may be intended to help employers police unauthorised Internet use on company time. However, the same records can also give a firm the opportunity to observe what otherwise might be considered private and confidential information. Today, legal experts suggest that, at the very least, employers need to disclose the level of surveillance to their employees and consider the corporate motivation for monitoring employees' behaviour.

Some firms also practice data mining. **Data mining** refers to the practice of searching through data records looking for useful information. Customer registration forms typically require a variety of information before a user is given access to a site. Based on an individual's information, data mining analysis can then provide what might be considered private and confidential information about individuals. For instance, assume an individual frequents a Web site that provides information about

Lululemon Develops Lasting Legacies.
Lululemon has built an online presence based on demand for their technical athletic apparel for yoga, dancing, and running. Viewing efficiency and waste reduction as good business, the company is focused on eliminating waste in their factories, stores, and support centres. Lululemon has an embedded core culture, "Personal responsibility creates global change," that reaches every aspect of the business.

a life-threatening disease. If this information is sent to an insurance company, the company might refuse to insure this individual, thinking that there is a higher risk associated with someone who wants more information about this disease.

> **data mining** the practice of searching through data records looking for useful information

Internet Crime Because the Internet is often regarded as an unregulated frontier, both individuals and business users must be particularly aware of online risks and dangers. For example, a general term that describes software designed to infiltrate a computer system without the user's consent is **malware**. Malware is often based on the creator's criminal or malicious intent and can include computer viruses, spyware, deceptive adware, and other software capable of criminal activities. A more specific term used to describe disruptive software is computer virus. A **computer virus**, which can originate anywhere in the world, is a software code designed to disrupt normal computer activities. The potentially devastating effects of both malware and computer viruses have given rise to a software security industry.

> **malware** a general term that describes software designed to infiltrate a computer system without the user's consent
> **computer virus** a software code designed to disrupt normal computer operations

In addition to the risk of computer viruses, identity theft is one of the most common computer crimes that impacts both individuals and business users. Most consumers are also concerned about fraud. Because the Internet allows easy creation of Web sites, access from anywhere in the world, and anonymity for the creator, it is almost impossible to know with certainty that the Web site, organisation, or individuals that you believe you are interacting with are what they seem. As always, caveat emptor ("let the buyer beware") is a good suggestion to follow whether on the Internet or not.

Future challenges for computer technology, social media, and e-business

Today, more information is available than ever before. Although individuals and business users may think we are at the point of information overload, the amount of information will only increase in the future. In order to obtain more information in the future, both individuals and business users must consider the cost of obtaining information and computer technology. For a business, the ability to obtain information or sell products or services with a simple click or touch is expensive. In an effort to reduce expenses and improve accessibility, some companies and individuals are now using cloud computing. **Cloud computing** is a type of computer usage in which services stored on the Internet are provided to users on a temporary basis. When cloud computing is used, a third party makes processing power, software applications, databases, and storage available for on-demand use from anywhere. Instead of running software and storing data on their employer's computer network or their individual computers, employees log onto the third party's system and use (and pay for) only the applications and data storage they actually need. In addition to just cost, there are a number of external and internal factors that a business must consider.

> **cloud computing** a type of computer usage in which services stored on the Internet is provided to users on a temporary basis

Although the environmental forces at work are complex, it is useful to think of them as either *internal* or *external* forces that affect how a business uses computer technology. Internal environmental forces are those that are closely associated with the actions and decisions taking place within a firm. As shown in Figure 15.8, typical internal forces include a firm's planning activities, organisational structure, human resources, management decisions, information database, and available financing. A shortage of skilled employees needed for a specialised project, for instance, can undermine a firm's ability to sell its services to clients. Unlike the external environmental forces affecting the firm, internal forces such as this one are more likely to be under the direct control of management. In this case, management can either hire the needed staff or choose to pass over a prospective project. In addition to the obvious internal factors that affect how a company operates, a growing number of firms are concerned about how their use of technology affects the environment. The term **green IT** is now used to describe all of a firm's activities to support a healthy environment and sustain the

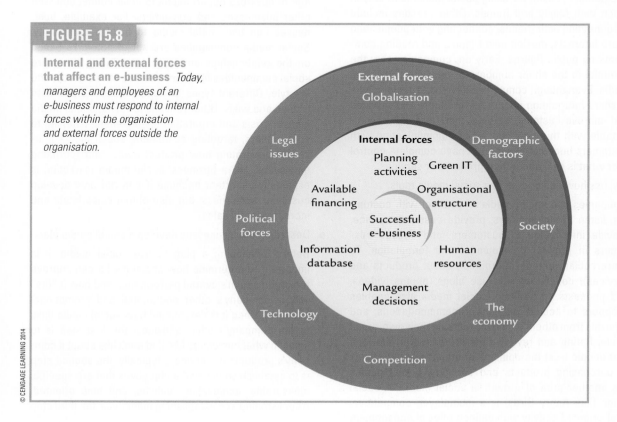

FIGURE 15.8

Internal and external forces that affect an e-business *Today, managers and employees of an e-business must respond to internal forces within the organisation and external forces outside the organisation.*

External forces
Globalisation
Legal issues
Demographic factors
Internal forces
Planning activities
Green IT
Available financing
Organisational structure
Political forces
Successful e-business
Society
Information database
Human resources
Management decisions
Technology
The economy
Competition

planet. Many offices, for example, are reducing the amount of paper they use by storing data and information on computers.

 green IT   a term used to describe all of a firm's activities to support a healthy environment and sustain the planet

In contrast, external environmental forces affect a company's use of technology and originate outside the organisation. These forces are unlikely to be controllable by a company. Instead, managers and employees of a company generally will react to these forces, attempting to shield the organisation from any undue negative effects and finding ways to take advantage of opportunities in an ever-changing technology environment. The primary external environmental forces affecting a company's use of technology include globalisation, demographic, societal, economic, competitive, technological, and political and legal forces.

SUMMARY

- Examine why it is important for a business to use social media.

  Millions of people of all ages use social media to interact with people and share ideas, personal information, and information about products and services. Today, more than two-thirds of online adults use some sort of social media platform like Facebook, LinkedIn, or Twitter, according to a recent Pew Internet Research Study. The primary reason for using social media is to stay in touch with family and friends. Other reasons include reconnecting with friends, connecting with people who share interests, making new friends, and reading comments by public figures. Early on, companies saw the potential in the sheer numbers of people using social media. Even though companies have used social media to share information about their products and services and improve customer service, many are still uncomfortable with this new method of communicating with customers because they do not have complete control over what is said about their products or services.

- Discuss how businesses use social media tools.

  Companies use social media to connect with customers, listen to stakeholders, provide customer service, provide information to customers, and engage customers in product development and formulation. To share social content (information about products and services), companies can use blogs, photos, videos, and podcasts. In addition, social media also enables shoppers to access opinions, recommendations, and referrals from others within and outside their own social circle. Rating and review sites are based on the idea that people trust the opinions of others when it comes to purchasing products and services. Social games are another area of growth in social media. A social game (like Angry Birds) is a multiplayer, competitive, goal-oriented activity with defined rules of engagement

  and online connectivity among a community of players. While some businesses elect to create their own game, others choose to place advertising into a game.

- Explain the business objectives for using social media.

  Although its popularity is a recent phenomenon, many businesses are already using social media to achieve important goals and objectives. In fact, there are many ways for businesses to use social media to take advantage of business opportunities to build connection with other businesses and consumers. For example, businesses can use social media to build a community. Social media communities are social networks based on the relationships among people. Today, there are social communities for every interest, ethnic group, and lifestyle. Different types of communities include both forums and wikis. Other reasons for using social media include crisis and reputation management, listening to stakeholders, targeting customers, social media marketing, generating new product ideas, and recruiting employees. For a business, social media marketing is especially important because it can not only develop customer awareness, but also obtain sales leads and increase actual sales.

- Describe how businesses develop a social media plan.

  Before developing a plan to use social media, it is important to determine how social media can improve the organisation's overall performance and how it "fits" with a company's other operational and promotional activities. Once it is determined how social media links to the company's other activities, the first step is to listen to what customers like and don't like about a company's products or services. Typically, the second step is to establish social media objectives that are specific, measurable, achievable, realistic, and time oriented. After listening and establishing objectives, the third step is to identify the customer or market segment a business is trying to reach with a social media promotion. The fourth step is to select the social media tool that will be used to reach customers. While it is not necessary (or even advisable) to use all of the available tools, a company can use social media communities, blogs, photos, videos, podcasts, or games to reach potential or existing customers. Once social media tools have been identified, a company can implement and integrate the social media plan.

Both quantitative and qualitative measurements can be used to determine the effectiveness of a social media plan. Quantitative social media measurement consists of using numerical measurements. Key performance indicators (KPIs), for example, are quantitative measurements. Qualitative measurement is the process of accessing the opinions and beliefs about a brand and primarily uses sentiment analysis to categorise what is being said about a company.

- Explain the meaning of e-business.

e-Business, or electronic business, can be defined as the organised effort of individuals to produce and sell, for a profit, the goods and services that satisfy society's needs *through the facilities available on the Internet*. The human, material, information, and financial resources that any business requires are highly specialised for e-business. In an effort to reduce the cost of e-business resources, many firms have turned to outsourcing.

Using e-business activities, it is possible to satisfy new customer needs created by the Internet as well as traditional ones in unique ways. Meeting customer needs is especially important when an e-business is trying to earn profits by increasing sales and reducing expenses. Each source of revenue flowing into the firm is referred to as a revenue stream.

- Understand the fundamental models of e-business.

e-Business models focus attention on the identity of a firm's customers. Firms that use the Internet mainly to conduct business with other businesses generally are referred to as having a business-to-business, or B2B, model. When examining B2B firms, two clear types emerge. In the first type of B2B, the focus is simply on

facilitating sales transactions between businesses. A second, more complex type of the B2B model involves a company and its suppliers. In contrast to the focus of the B2B model, firms such as Amazon or eBay clearly are focused on individual buyers and are thus referred to as having a business-to-consumer, or B2C, model. In a B2C situation, understanding how consumers behave online is critical to the firm's success. Successful B2C firms often make a special effort to build long-term relationships with their customers. While B2B and B2C models are the most popular e-business models, there are other models that perform specialised e-business activities to generate revenues (see Table 15.2).

- Identify the factors that will affect the future of the Internet, social media, and e-business.

Since the beginning of commercial activity on the Internet, developments in computer technology, social media, and e-business have been rapid and formidable. Although a number of technology companies struggled or even failed during the recent economic crisis, most firms involved in computer technology, social media, and e-business today use a more intelligent approach to development. The long-term view held by the vast majority of analysts is that use of the Internet will continue to expand along with related technologies. Only 2.3 billion of the nearly 7 billion people in the world use the Web. Clearly, the number of Internet users in the world's developing countries is expected to increase dramatically.

The future of computer technology and the Internet will be influenced by advances in technology, the increasing popularity of social media, and the increasing use of e-business. Other factors including ethics, social responsibility, and Internet crime will all impact the way that businesses and consumers use computer technology and the Internet. Although the environmental forces at work are complex, it is useful to think of them as either internal or external forces that affect how businesses use computer technology. Internal environmental forces are those that are closely associated with the actions and decisions taking place within a firm. In contrast, external environmental forces are those factors affecting an e-business originating outside an organisation.

EXERCISE QUESTIONS

1 How has the development of social media affected consumer behaviour?

2 Imagine you own a company that sells camping equipment. Devise a marketing strategy using social media.

3 Is there a downside to allowing customers to share their opinions and suggestions for company improvement publicly?

4 How can social media negatively impact the recruitment process?

5 There are two types of social media measurement, which one would you choose for your business and why?

CASE 15.1

Social networking – searching for a new advertising model

Social networking became the global phenomenon that changed the advertising industry for ever, as two thirds of the Internet population visited a social network or blogging site. It overtook email to become the fourth most popular sector after search, portals and PC software applications, accounting for 10 per cent of all Internet time spent. It is interesting to see the different patterns of development. For example, Germany and Switzerland were quite late to embrace the phenomenon, perhaps due to natural German reserve in disclosing personal data.

Facebook, the market leaders, did not immediately launch a German language interface and by the time they did, five local start-up competitors were already more popular.

Facebook started out as a service for university students and the early dramatic growth was driven by younger people, but its appeal to a wider age group brought about a demographic change such that its 35–49 year old audience outstripped its 18–34 audience. MySpace, focused more on music and video entertainment, and self expression, (with customizable profile pages), so appealing more to teenagers and young adults, but in countries outside of the U.S., it is regarded as a niche player. Local players became leaders in many markets, for example, Google-owned Orkut in Brazil, Wer-kennt-wen in Germany and Mixi in Japan. The particular mix of factors in each country provides a challenge for the international players. Because the global growth of social networking was so rapid in many countries these local players established themselves, forming partnerships with the portals, before the international players had time to enter the market. For example in China the different language and regulatory issues of doing business, and the mindset needed for running a Chinese social network that understands the cultural nuances and network behaviour, made the strong local players such as the leading social network 51.com more likely winners. In Japan Mixi is an invite only system that appeals more to the "humble" Japanese mindset. Facebook, which launched without effective local leadership and sensitivity to the local culture failed to make an impact.

The social networking players whether local or global constantly face new challenges as new network models, such as Twitter become the next global phenomenon or fad, and consumers are increasing their demands and expectations for easier mobile social networking.

The challenge for advertisers

For advertisers social networking provides the potential opportunity for targeting all demographic groups in a focused way and achieving high levels of engagement with the audience, but so far advertising on social networking sites has not been successful. Unlike traditional media where they simply consume content, members of social networks both consume and supply content. The sense of ownership they feel over the content means that advertising is intrusive and less acceptable. A well used analogy is that it is like gate crashing a party. The personal data of consumers available on networks is attractive to advertisers as it allows highly targeted ads, but consumers see this as invading their privacy. Research by Nielsen suggests that consumers are becoming less tolerant of online advertising and the term they most closely associate with advertising is "false".

Bearing in mind these factors advertising on social networks must be through conversation, rather than by using a "push model". Authentic, candid and humble messages similar to "word of mouth" approaches are needed to overcome the lack of trust. Nielsen suggest that standard "ad" formats are not acceptable, different approaches, trial and error and a closer relationship between the advertisers and the social networks than is common in traditional media advertising will be essential.

Social networks are a communication channel like traditional media, and advertisers have to understand the nature of engagement and new approaches to connect with consumers. Consumers are keen to offer opinion and co-create content so advertisers can no longer simply push content to the audience and sit back and wait for a reaction. They must genuinely interact and crucially they must think of their consumers as people with whom they want a dialogue.

References: 'Global faces and networked places', Nielsen, March 2009 accessed at: www.nielsen.com.

Questions

1 Will advertising in social media become acceptable? Explain your answer.

2 Imagine that you work for a global e-business which sells clothing aimed at teenage girls. What social media advertising strategy would you suggest, and how would it change from country to country?

3 Do some research into the "Ads" and "Sponsored stories" types of advertising on Facebook. Which do you think would be more effective for the above company?

CHAPTER REFERENCES

Barker, Melissa, Barker Donald, Bormann, Nicolas and Neher, Krista E., *Social Media Marketing: A Strategic Approach* (Mason, OH: Cengage Publishing, 2103), 29, 31.

Chaffey, Dave, "2011 Marketing Trends," the Smart Insights Web site at www.smartinsights.com/digital-p.marketing-strategy/online-marketing-mix/2011-digital-marketing-trends/, accessed March 1, 2012.

"Consumers Spend Less Time with Traditional Media: US Interactive Marketing Forecast 2011 to 2016," the Forrester Research Web site at www.forrester.com, accessed August 24, 2011.

Deighton, John and Kornfeld, Leora, "The Ford Fiesta," *Harvard Business School*, June 20, 2011, 1–24.

Deighton, John and Kornfeld, Leora, "United Breaks Guitars" *Harvard Business School*, August 11, 2011, p. 1–13.

Hempel, Jessi, "Why Bing Loves Farmville," the CNNMoney Web site at http://tech.fortune.cnn.com/2010/03/09/why-bing-loves-farmville/, accessed March 9, 2010.

Mayar, Vipin and Ramsey, Geoff, *Digital Impact: The Two Secrets to Online Marketing Success* (Hoboken, New Jersey: John Wiley & Sons, 2011), 141–143, 147.

Miller, Michael, *The Ultimate Web Marketing Guide* (Indianapolis: QUE, 2011), 315.

Norton, Michael and Avery, Jill, "The Pepsi Refresh Project: A Thirst for Change," *Harvard Business School*, November 14, 2011, 1–24.

Ostrow, Adam, (2009, December 8) "Dell Rides Twitter to $6.5 Million in Sales," the Mashable Social Media Web site at www.mashable.com, accessed April 1, 2012.

Rosendahl, Stephanie, "Top 5 Tips for Reputation Management through Social Media," the Articlebase Web site at http://articlebase.com/internet-marketing-articles/top-5-tips-for-reputation-managmenet-through-social-media-4997832.html, accessed July 7, 2011.

Smith, Aaron, "Why Americans Use Social Media, Pew Internet and American Life Project," the Pew Web site at www.pewinternet.org, accessed November 14, 2011.

Steenburgh, Thomas, Avery, Jill and Dahoud, Naseem, "Hubspot: Inbound Marketing and Web 2.0," *Harvard Business School*, January 24, 2011, 1–21.

The Coca-Cola Facebook Web site at www.facebook.com/cocacola, accessed April 23, 2012.

The Facebook Web site at www.facebook.com, accessed April 23, 2012.

The Internet World Stats Web site at www.internetworldstats.com, accessed April 29, 2012.

The Starbucks Idea Web site at www.mystarbucksidea.com, accessed April 27, 2012.

Tuten, Tracy L. and Solomonm, Michael R., *Social Media Marketing* (Upper Saddle River, New Jersey: Pearson Publishing, 2013), 5, 147.

"US Interactive Marketing Forecast 2011 to 2016," the Forrester Research Web site at wwwforrester.com, accessed August 24, 2011.

Wasserman, Todd, "How Old Spice Revived a Campaign that No One Wanted to Touch" the Mashable Social Media Web site at http://mashable.com/2011/11/01/old-spice-campaign, accessed November 1, 2011.

Williams, Kim, "Dell Hell: The Impact of Social Media on Corporate Communication" at https://learningspaces.njit.edu/elliot/content/dell-hell-impact-social-media-corporate-communication, accessed March 12, 2009.

York, Emily Bryson, "Domino's Reports 14 Percent Same-Store Sales Hike for First Quarter," the Advertising Age Web site at www.advertisingage.com, accessed April 1, 2012.

© ISAK55 / SHUTTERSTOCK

PART 6
ACCOUNTING, FINANCE AND INVESTMENT

In this part, we look at another business resource—money. First, we discuss accounting, then the functions of money and the financial institutions that are part of our banking system. Then we examine the concept of financial management and investing for both business firms and individuals.

16 INTRODUCTION TO MANAGEMENT ACCOUNTING

BUSINESS FOCUS

Accounting information for human resource professionals

People Management, the journal of the Chartered Institute of Personnel and Development (CIPD), provides an example of the importance of accounting information to human resources (HR) professionals. The article touts the oft-cited expression "people are our greatest asset", but questions how many HR professionals appreciate the full costs of people in an organisation. According to Vanessa Robinson of the CIPD, HR professions shouldn't merely say "people are our greatest asset", but look at the income statement and see what they cost! The problem is

that many HR professionals may not have sufficient basic accounting knowledge to understand basic accounting principles. They need to be familiar with the basic financial statements – the income statement, statement of financial position and the statement of cash flows – as well as understand basic cost concepts. What this article tells us is something that accountants already know – that accounting is a communication medium, a language indeed, that not everyone understands. Having said that, while HR professionals may not think they require fluency in accounting,

they do need to make business decisions which are underpinned by sound financial information, e.g. recruit and retain staff. Having an understanding of accounting information (rather than just accepting it from the accountants) will benefit HR and other professionals in an organisation.

What kind of accounting information would you communicate to HR professionals? What format would you use?

References: 'You do the match', *People Management*, 30/7/2009, available at http://www.peoplemanagement.co.uk/pm/articles/2009/07/you-do-the-math.htm

There are many definitions of accounting, but the one that captures the theme of this chapter is the definition formulated by the American Accounting Association. It describes accounting as:

the process of identifying, measuring and communicating economic information to permit informed judgements and decisions by users of the information.

In other words, accounting is concerned with providing both financial and non-financial information that will help decision-makers to make good decisions. In order to understand accounting, you need to know something about the decision-making process, and also to be aware of the various users of accounting information.

During the past two decades many organisations in both the manufacturing and service sectors have faced dramatic changes in their business environment. Deregulation and extensive competition from overseas companies in domestic markets has resulted in a situation where most companies now operate in a highly competitive global market. At the same time there has been a significant reduction in product life cycles arising from technological innovations and the need to meet increasingly discriminating customer demands. To succeed in today's highly competitive environment, companies have made customer satisfaction an overriding priority. They have also adopted new management approaches and manufacturing companies have changed their manufacturing systems and invested in new technologies. These changes have had a significant influence on management accounting systems.

The aim of this chapter is to give you the background knowledge that will enable you to achieve a more meaningful insight into the issues and problems of cost and management accounting. We begin by looking at the users of accounting information and identifying their requirements. This is followed by a description of the decision-making process and the changing business environment. Finally, the different functions of management accounting are described.

Accounting is used to make good business decisions

© ZADOROZHNYI VIKTOR / SHUTTERSTOCK

THE USERS OF ACCOUNTING INFORMATION

Accounting is a language that communicates economic information to various parties (known as stakeholders) who have an interest in the organisation. Stakeholders fall into several groups (e.g. managers, shareholders and potential investors, employees, creditors and the government) and each of these groups has its own requirements for information:

- Managers require information that will assist them in their decision-making and control activities; for example, information is needed on the estimated selling prices, costs, demand, competitive position and profitability of various products/services that are provided by the organisation.
- Shareholders require information on the value of their investment and the income that is derived from their shareholding.
- Employees require information on the ability of the firm to meet wage demands and avoid redundancies.
- Creditors and the providers of loan capital require information on a firm's ability to meet its financial obligations.
- Government agencies such as the Central Statistical Office collect accounting information and require such information as the details of sales activity, profits, investments, stocks (i.e. inventories), dividends paid, the proportion of profits absorbed by taxation and so on. In addition, government taxation authorities require information on the amount of profits that are subject to taxation. All this information is important for determining policies to manage the economy.

The need to provide accounting information is not confined to business organisations. Individuals sometimes have to provide information about their own financial situation; for example, if you want to obtain a mortgage or a personal loan, you may be asked for details of your private financial affairs. Non-profit-making organisations such as churches, charitable organisations, clubs and government units such as local authorities, also require accounting information for decision-making, and for reporting the results of their activities. For example, a tennis club will require information on the cost of undertaking its various activities so that a decision can be made as to the amount of the annual subscription that it will charge to its members. Similarly, municipal authorities, such as local government and public sector organisations, need information on the costs of undertaking specific activities so that decisions can be made as to which activities will be undertaken and the resources that must be raised to finance them.

As you can see, there are many different users of accounting information who require information for decision-making. The objective of accounting is to provide sufficient information to meet the needs of the various users at the lowest possible cost. Obviously, the benefit derived from using an information system for decision-making must be greater than the cost of operating the system.

The users of accounting information can be divided into two categories:

1. internal users within the organisation;
2. external users such as shareholders, creditors and regulatory agencies, outside the organisation.

It is possible to distinguish between two branches of accounting, which reflect the internal and external users of accounting information. **Management accounting** is concerned with the provision of information to people within the organisation to help them make better decisions and improve the efficiency and effectiveness of existing operations, whereas **financial accounting** is concerned with the provision of information to external parties outside the organisation. Thus, management accounting could be called internal reporting and financial accounting could be called external reporting. This chapter concentrates on management accounting.

> **management accounting** accounting concerned with the provision of information to people within the organisation to aid decision-making and improve the efficiency and effectiveness of existing operations
> **financial accounting** accounting concerned with the provision of information to parties that are external to the organisation

DIFFERENCES BETWEEN MANAGEMENT ACCOUNTING AND FINANCIAL ACCOUNTING

The major differences between these two branches of accounting are:

- Legal requirements. There is a statutory requirement for public limited companies to produce annual financial accounts, regardless of whether or not management regards this information as useful. Management accounting, by contrast, is entirely optional and information should be produced only if it is considered that the benefits it offers management exceed the cost of collecting it.
- Focus on individual parts or segments of the business. Financial accounting reports describe the whole of the business, whereas management accounting focuses on small parts of the organisation; for example, the cost and profitability of products, services, departments, customers and activities.
- Generally accepted accounting principles. Financial accounting statements must be prepared to conform with the legal requirements and the generally accepted accounting principles established by the regulatory bodies such as the Financial Accounting Standards Board (FASB) in the U.S., the Accounting Standards Board (ASB) in the U.K. and the International Accounting Standards Board. These requirements are essential to ensure uniformity and consistency, which make inter-company and historical comparisons possible. Financial accounting data should be verifiable and objective. In contrast, management accountants are not required to adhere to generally accepted accounting principles when providing managerial information for internal purposes. Instead, the focus is on the serving management's needs and providing information that is useful to managers when they are carrying out their decision-making, planning and control functions.
- Time dimension. Financial accounting reports what has happened in the past in an organisation, whereas management accounting is concerned with future information as well as past information. Decisions are concerned with future events and management, therefore, requires details of expected future costs and revenues.
- Report frequency. A detailed set of financial accounts is published annually and less detailed accounts are published semi-annually. Management usually requires information more quickly than this if it is to act on it. Consequently, management accounting reports on various activities may be prepared at daily, weekly or monthly intervals.

SUCCESS STORY

BuyCostumes.com uses managerial accounting information to improve operations

The greatest benefit of managerial accounting is also its biggest challenge – to provide managers with information that improves decisions and creates organisational values. This information helps inform managers about the impact of various strategic and operational decisions on key nonfinancial performance measures and their eventual impact on the organisation's financial performance.

The information is challenging to prepare and analyse because it requires an understanding of all value chain components that affect the organisation including research and development, production, marketing, distribution, and customer service.

Since its inception in 1999, BuyCostumes.com has blended the right managerial accounting information and an innovative business model to provide costumes to customers in over 50 countries. Using the Internet and marketing creativity, BuyCostumes.com serves a market of 150 million U.S. consumers who spend $3.6 billion on costumes each year.

According to CEO Jalem Getz, BuyCostumes.com measures key

performance indicators to guide its decision making. For example, managerial accountants analyse measures of customer satisfaction, average time between order placement and costume arrival for each shipping method, and the profitability of individual customer types. As customer trends change, competitors emerge, and technological advances occur, BuyCostumes.com's managerial accounting information adapts to provide crucial insight into the company's performance and how its strategy should evolve to remain the world's largest Internet costumer retailer.

References: Mowen *et al, Cornerstones of Managerial Accounting*, South Africa Edition (2014)

THE DECISION-MAKING PROCESS

Information produced by management accountants must be judged in the light of its ultimate effect on the outcome of decisions. It is therefore important to have an understanding of the decision-making process. Figure 16.1 presents a diagram of the decision-making, planning and **control process**. The first four stages represent the decision-making or planning process. The final two stages represent the control process, which is the process of measuring and correcting actual performance to ensure the alternatives that are chosen and the plans for implementing them are carried out. We will now examine the stages in more detail.

> **control process** the process of setting targets or standards against which actual results are measured

Identifying objectives

Before good decisions can be made there must be some guiding aim or direction that will enable the decision-makers to assess the desirability of choosing one course of action over another. Hence, the first stage in the decision-making process should be to specify the company's goals or organisational objectives.

This is an area where there is considerable controversy. Economic theory normally assumes that firms seek to maximise profits for the owners of the firm or, more precisely, the maximisation of

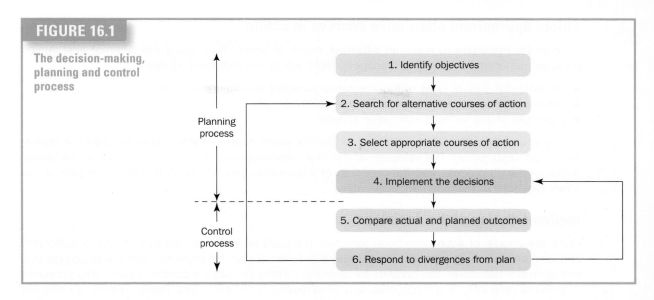

FIGURE 16.1

The decision-making, planning and control process

Planning process

1. Identify objectives
2. Search for alternative courses of action
3. Select appropriate courses of action
4. Implement the decisions

Control process

5. Compare actual and planned outcomes
6. Respond to divergences from plan

shareholders' wealth. Some writers (e.g. Simon, 1959) believe that many managers are content to find a plan that provides satisfactory profits rather than to maximise profits.

Clearly it is too simplistic to say that the only objective of a business firm is to maximise profits. Some managers seek to establish a power base and build an empire. Another common goal is security, and the removal of uncertainty regarding the future may override the pure profit motive. Organisations may also pursue more specific objectives, such as producing high quality products or being the market leader within a particular market segment. Nevertheless, the view adopted in this book is that, broadly, firms seek to maximise future profits. There are two reasons for us to concentrate on this objective:

1. It is unlikely that any other objective is as widely applicable in measuring the ability of the organisation to survive in the future.
2. It is unlikely that maximising future profits can be realised in practise, but by establishing the principles necessary to achieve this objective you will learn how to increase profits.

The search for alternative courses of action

The second stage in the decision-making model is a search for a range of possible courses of action (or **strategies**) that might enable the objectives to be achieved. If the management of a company concentrates entirely on its present product range and markets, and market shares and profits are allowed to decline, there is a danger that the company will be unable to survive in the future. If the business is to survive, management must identify potential opportunities and threats in the current environment and take specific steps now so that the organisation will not be taken by surprise by future developments. In particular, the company should consider one or more of the following courses of action:

 strategies courses of action designed to ensure that objectives are achieved

1. developing new products for sale in existing markets;
2. developing new products for new markets;
3. developing new markets for existing products.

The search for alternative courses of action involves the acquisition of information concerning future opportunities and environments; it is the most difficult and important stage of the decision-making process.

Select appropriate alternative courses of action

In order for managers to make an informed choice of action, data about the different alternatives must be gathered. For example, managers might ask to see projected figures on:

- the potential growth rates of the alternative activities under consideration;
- the market share the company is likely to achieve;
- projected profits for each alternative activity.

The alternatives should be evaluated to identify which course of action best satisfies the objectives of an organisation. The selection of the most advantageous alternative is central to the whole decision-making process and the provision of information that facilitates this choice is one of the major functions of management accounting.

Implementation of the decisions

Once the course of action has been selected, it should be implemented as part of the budgeting and longterm planning process. The **budget** is a financial plan for implementing the decisions that management has made. The budgets for all of the various decisions a company takes are expressed in terms of cash inflows and outflows, and sales revenues and expenses. These budgets are merged together into a single unifying statement of the organisation's expectations for future periods. This statement is known as a **master budget** and consists of budgeted profit and cash flow statements. The budgeting process communicates to everyone in the organisation the part that they are expected to play in implementing management's decisions.

> **budget** a financial plan for implementing management decisions
> **master budget** a single unifying statement of an organisation's expectations for future periods comprising budgeted profit and cash flow statements

Comparing actual and planned outcomes and responding to divergencies from plan

The final stages in the process outlined in Figure 16.1 involve comparing actual and planned outcomes and responding to divergencies from plan. The managerial function of **control** consists of the measurement, reporting and subsequent correction of performance in an attempt to ensure that the firm's objectives and plans are achieved.

> **control** a managerial function that consists of the measurement, reporting and subsequent correction of performance in order to achieve the organisation's objectives

To monitor performance, the accountant produces **performance reports** and presents them to the managers who are responsible for implementing the various decisions. These reports compare actual outcomes (actual costs and revenues) with planned outcomes (budgeted costs and revenues) and should be issued at regular intervals. Performance reports provide feedback information and should highlight those activities that do not conform to plans, so that managers can devote their limited time to focusing mainly on these items. This process represents the application of **management by exception**. Effective control requires that corrective action is taken so that actual outcomes conform to planned outcomes. Alternatively, the plans may require modification if the comparisons indicate that the plans are no longer attainable.

> **performance reports** regular reports to management that compare actual outcomes with planned outcomes
> **management by exception** a situation where management attention is focused on areas where outcomes do not meet targets

The process of taking corrective action or modifying the plans if the comparisons indicate that actual outcomes do not conform to planned outcomes, is indicated by the arrowed lines in Figure 16.1 linking stages 6 and 4 and 6 and 2. These arrowed lines represent "feedback loops". They signify that the process is dynamic and stress the interdependencies between the various stages in the process. The feedback loop between stages 6 and 2 indicates that the plans should be regularly reviewed, and if they are no longer attainable then alternative courses of action must be considered for achieving the organisation's objectives. The second loop stresses the corrective action taken so that actual outcomes conform to planned outcomes.

THE IMPACT OF THE CHANGING BUSINESS ENVIRONMENT ON MANAGEMENT ACCOUNTING

During the last few decades global competition, deregulation, growth in the service industries, declines in product life cycles, advances in manufacturing and information technologies, environmental issues and a competitive environment requiring companies to become more customer driven, have changed the nature of the business environment. These changes have significantly altered the ways in which firms operate, which in turn, have resulted in changes in management accounting practices.

Global competition

During the last few decades reductions in tariffs and duties on imports and exports, and dramatic improvements in transportation and communication systems, have resulted in many firms operating in a global market. Prior to this, many organisations operated in a protected competitive environment. Barriers of communication and geographical distance, and sometimes protected markets, limited the ability of overseas companies to compete in domestic markets. There was little incentive for firms to maximise efficiency and improve management practices, or to minimise costs, as cost increases could often be passed on to customers. During the 1990s, however, organisations began to encounter severe competition from overseas competitors that offered high-quality products at low prices. Manufacturing companies can now establish global networks for acquiring raw materials and distributing goods overseas, and service organisations can communicate with overseas offices instantaneously using video conferencing technologies. These changes have enabled competitors to gain access to domestic markets throughout the world. Nowadays, organisations have to compete against the best companies in the world. This new competitive environment has increased the demand for cost information relating to cost management and profitability analysis by product lines and geographical locations.

Growth in the service industry

In many countries the service sector exceeds 50 per cent of GDP. For example, in 2010 the service sector in the U.K. and U.S. was approximately 75 per cent of GDP. Before the 1990s many service organisations, such as those operating in the airlines, utilities and financial service industries, were either government-owned monopolies or operated in a highly regulated, protected and non-competitive environment. These organisations were not subject to any great pressure to improve the quality and efficiency of their operations or to improve profitability by eliminating services or products that were making losses. Prices were set to cover operating costs and provide a predetermined return on capital. Hence cost increases could often be absorbed by increasing the prices of the services. Little attention was therefore given to developing cost systems that accurately measured the costs and profitability of individual services. Privatisation of government-controlled companies and deregulation have completely changed the competitive environment in which service companies operate. Pricing and competitive restrictions have been virtually eliminated. Deregulation, intensive competition and an expanding product range create the need for service organisations to focus on cost management and develop management accounting information systems that enable them to understand their cost base and determine the sources of profitability for their products, customers and markets. One of the major features of the business environment in recent decades has been the growth in the service sector and the growth of management accounting within service organisations.

Changing product life cycles

A **product's life cycle** is the period of time from initial expenditure on research and development to the time at which support to customers is withdrawn. Intensive global competition and technological innovation, combined with increasingly discriminating and sophisticated customer demands, have resulted in a dramatic decline in product life cycles. To be successful companies must now speed up the rate at which they introduce new products to the market. Being later to the market than the competitors can have a dramatic effect on product profitability.

> **product's life cycle** the period of time from initial expenditure on research and development to the withdrawal of support to customers

In many industries a large fraction of a product's life cycle costs are determined by decisions made early in its life cycle. This has created a need for management accounting to place greater emphasis on providing information at the design stage because many of the costs are committed or locked in at this time. Therefore, to compete successfully, companies must be able to manage their costs effectively at the design stage, have the capability to adapt to new, different and changing customer requirements and reduce the time to market of new and modified products.

Advances in manufacturing technologies

Excellence in manufacturing can provide a competitive weapon to compete in sophisticated world-wide markets. In order to compete effectively, companies must be capable of manufacturing innovative products of high quality at a low cost, and also provide a first-class customer service. At the same time, they must have the flexibility to cope with short product life cycles, demands for greater product variety from more discriminating customers and increasing international competition. World-class manufacturing companies have responded to these competitive demands by replacing traditional production systems with **lean manufacturing systems** that seek to reduce waste by implementing just-in-time (JIT) production systems, focusing on quality, simplifying processes and investing in advanced manufacturing technologies (AMTs). The major features of these new systems and their implications for management accounting is a topic for further study.

> **lean manufacturing systems** systems that seek to reduce waste in manufacturing by implementing just-in-time production systems, focusing on quality, simplifying processes and investing in advanced technologies

The impact of information technology

During the past two decades the use of information technology (IT) to support business activities has increased dramatically and the development of electronic business communication technologies known as **e-business, e-commerce** or **Internet commerce** have had a major impact. For example, consumers are more discerning in their purchases because they can access the internet to compare the relative merits of different products. Internet trading also allows buyers and sellers to undertake transactions from diverse locations in different parts of the world. E-commerce (such as bar coding) has allowed considerable cost savings to be made by streamlining business processes and has generated extra revenues from the adept use of online sales facilities (such as ticketless airline bookings and internet banking). The proficient use of e-commerce has given many companies a competitive advantage.

e-business the use of information and communication technologies to support any business activities, including buying and selling

e-commerce the use of information and communication technologies to support the purchase, sale and exchange of goods

Internet commerce the buying and selling of goods and services over the Internet

One advanced IT application that has had a considerable impact on business information systems is **enterprise resource planning systems (ERPS)**. An ERPS comprises a set of integrated software applications modules that aim to control all information flows within a company. Users can use their personal computers (PCs) to access the organisation's database and follow developments almost as they happen. Using real time data enables managers to analyse information quickly and thus continually improve the efficiencies of processes. A major feature of ERPS systems is that all data are entered only once, typically where they originate.

enterprise resource planning system (ERPS) a set of integrated software application modules that aim to control all information flows within a company

The introduction of ERPS has the potential to have a significant impact on the work of management accountants. In particular, it substantially reduces routine information gathering and the processing of information. Instead of managers asking management accountants for information, they can access the system to derive the information they require directly and do their own analyses. This has freed accountants to adopt the role of advisers and internal consultants to the business. Management accountants have now become more involved in interpreting the information generated from the ERPS and providing business support for managers.

Environmental issues

Customers are no longer satisfied if companies simply comply with the legal requirements of undertaking their activities. They expect company managers to be more proactive in terms of their social responsibility, safety and environmental issues. Environmental management accounting is becoming increasingly important in many organisations. There are several reasons for this. First, environmental costs can be large for some industrial sectors. Second, regulatory requirements involving huge fines for non-compliance have increased significantly over the past decade. Therefore, selecting the least costly method of compliance has become a major objective. Third, society is demanding that companies focus on being more environmentally friendly. Companies are finding that becoming a good social citizen and being environmentally responsible improves their image and enhances their ability to sell their products and services.

These developments have created the need for companies to develop systems of measuring and reporting environmental costs, the consumption of scarce environmental resources and details of hazardous materials used or pollutants emitted to the environment. Knowledge of environmental costs, and their causes, provides the information that managers need to redesign processes to minimise the usage of scarce environmental resources and the emission pollutants and to also make more sensitive environmental decisions.

Customer orientation

In order to survive in today's competitive environment companies have had to become more customer-driven and to recognise that customers are crucial to their future success. This has resulted in companies making customer satisfaction an overriding priority and to focus on identifying and achieving the key success factors that are necessary to be successful in today's competitive environment. These key success factors are discussed in the next section.

FOCUS ON CUSTOMER SATISFACTION AND NEW MANAGEMENT APPROACHES

The key success factors which organisations must concentrate on to provide customer satisfaction are cost, quality, reliability, delivery and the choice of innovative new products. In addition, firms are attempting to increase customer satisfaction by adopting a philosophy of continuous improvement to reduce costs and improve quality, reliability and delivery.

Cost efficiency

Keeping costs low and being cost efficient provides an organisation with a strong competitive advantage. Increased competition has also made decision errors, due to poor cost information, more potentially hazardous to an organisation. Many companies have become aware of the need to improve their cost systems so that they can produce more accurate cost information to determine the cost of their products and services, monitor trends in costs over time, pinpoint loss-making activities and analyse profits by products, sales outlets, customers and markets.

Quality

In addition to demanding low costs, customers are demanding high quality products and services. Most companies are responding to this by focusing on **total quality management (TQM)**. TQM is a term used to describe a situation where all business functions are involved in a process of continuous quality improvement that focuses on delivering products or services of consistently high quality in a timely fashion. The emphasis on TQM has created fresh demands on the management accounting function to measure and evaluate the quality of products and services and the activities that produce them.

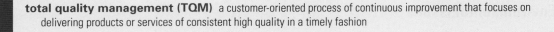

total quality management (TQM) a customer-oriented process of continuous improvement that focuses on delivering products or services of consistent high quality in a timely fashion

Time as a competitive weapon

Organisations are also seeking to increase customer satisfaction by providing a speedier response to customer requests, ensuring 100 per cent on-time delivery and reducing the time taken to develop and bring new products to market. For these reasons management accounting systems now place more emphasis on time-based measures, such as **cycle time**. This is the length of time from start to completion of a product or service. It consists of the sum of processing time, move time, wait time and inspection time. Only processing time adds value to the product, and the remaining activities are **non-value added activities** in the sense that they can be reduced or eliminated without altering the product's service potential to the customer. Organisations are therefore focusing on minimising cycle time by reducing the time spent on such activities. The management accounting system has an important role to play in this process by identifying and reporting on the time devoted to value added and non-value added activities. Cycle time measures have also become important for service organisations. For example, the time taken to process mortgage loan applications by financial organisations can be considerable, involving substantial non-value added waiting time. Reducing the time to process applications enhances customer satisfaction and creates the potential for increasing sales revenue.

cycle time the length of time from start to completion of a product or service and is the sum of processing time, move time, wait time and inspection time
non-value added activities activities that can be reduced or eliminated without altering the product's service potential to the customer

Innovation and continuous improvement

To be successful companies must develop a steady stream of innovative new products and services and have the capability to adapt to changing customer requirements. Management accounting information systems have begun to report performance measures relating to innovation. Examples include:

- the total launch time for new products/services;
- an assessment of the key characteristics of new products relative to those of competitors;
- feedback on customer satisfaction with the new features and characteristics of newly introduced products and the number of new products launched.

Organisations are also attempting to enhance customer satisfaction by adopting a philosophy of **continuous improvement**. Traditionally, organisations have sought to study activities and establish standard operating procedures. Management accountants developed systems and measurements that compared actual results with predetermined standards. This process created a climate whereby the predetermined standards represented a target to be achieved and maintained. In today's competitive environment, companies must adopt a philosophy of continuous improvement, an ongoing process that involves a continuous search to reduce costs, eliminate waste and improve the quality and performance of activities that increase customer value or satisfaction. Management accounting supports continuous improvement by identifying opportunities for change and then reporting on the progress of the methods that have been implemented.

> **continuous improvement** an ongoing search to reduce costs, eliminate waste and improve the quality and performance of activities that increase customer value or satisfaction

Benchmarking is a technique that is increasingly being adopted as a mechanism for achieving continuous improvement. It is a continuous process of measuring a firm's products, services or activities against the other best performing organisations, either internal or external to the firm. The objective is to ascertain how the processes and activities can be improved. Ideally, benchmarking should involve an external focus on the latest developments, best practice and model examples that can be incorporated within various operations of business organisations. It therefore represents the ideal way of moving forward and achieving high competitive standards.

> **benchmarking** a mechanism for achieving continuous improvement by measuring products, services or activities against those of other best performing organisations

In their quest for the continuous improvement of organisational activities, managers have found that they need to rely more on the people closest to the operating processes and customers, to develop new approaches to performing activities. This has led to employees being provided with relevant information to enable them to make continuous improvements to the output of processes. Allowing employees to take such actions without the authorisation by superiors has come to be known as **employee empowerment**. It is argued that by empowering employees and giving them relevant information they will be able to respond faster to customers, increase process flexibility, reduce cycle time and improve morale. Management accounting is therefore moving from its traditional emphasis on providing information to managers to monitor the activities of employees, to providing information to employees to empower them to focus on the continuous improvement of activities.

> **employee empowerment** providing employees with relevant information to allow them to make continuous improvements to the output of processes without the authorisation by superiors

---

RESPONSIBLE PRACTICE Management accounting and ethical behaviour

Earlier in this chapter it was suggested that management accounting practices were developed to provide information that assists managers to maximise future profits. It was, however, pointed out that it is too simplistic to assume that the only objective of a business firm is to maximise profits. The profit maximisation objective should be constrained by the need for firms to also give high priority to their social responsibilities and ensure that their employees adopt high standards of ethical behaviour. A code of ethics has now become an essential part of corporate culture.

Identification of what is acceptable ethical behaviour has attracted much attention in recent years. Performance measurement systems are widely used to financially reward managers on the basis of their performance in reducing costs or increasing sales or profits. This has resulted in many managers in the financial services sector taking actions to increase sales or profits when such actions have resulted in providing high risk loans that caused the financial crises in the banking sector. Many would argue that they were motivated by personal greed to increase the reported sales revenues and profits and thus their bonus, without considering the adverse long-term implications of their actions. It could be argued, however, that they were engaging in organisationally desirable behaviour by seeking to maximise profits because the reward system strongly encouraged them to increase sales or profits. An alternative view is that they were engaging in unethical actions. So where should the blame be assigned? Is the reward system at fault or the unethical behaviour? Or both?

Professional accounting organisations also play an important role in promoting a high standard of ethical behaviour by their members. Both of the professional bodies representing management accountants, in the U.K. (Chartered Institute of Management Accountants), and in the U.S. (Institute of Management Accountants), have issued a code of ethical guidelines for their members and established mechanisms for monitoring and enforcing professional ethics. The guidelines are concerned with ensuring that accountants follow fundamental principles relating to:

- integrity (being honest and not being a party to any falsification);
- objectivity (not being biased or prejudiced);
- confidentiality and professional competence and due care (maintaining the skills required to ensure a competent professional service);
- compliance with relevant laws and regulations.

You can view the Chartered Institute of Management Accountants code of ethics at www.cimaglobal.com/professional-ethics/ethics/

INTERNATIONAL CONVERGENCE OF MANAGEMENT ACCOUNTING PRACTICES

Management accounting practices generally do not differ across national borders. Granlund and Lukka (1998) argue that there is a strong current tendency towards global homogenisation of management accounting practices within the industrialised parts of the world.

Granlund and Lukka distinguish between management accounting practices at the macro and micro levels. The macro level of management accounting practices relates to concepts and techniques. In contrast, the micro level is concerned with the behavioural patterns relating to how management accounting information is actually used. At the macro level, Granlund and Lukka suggest that the convergence of management accounting practices in different countries has occurred because of intensified global competition, developments in information technology, the increasing tendency of transnational companies to standardise their practices, the global consultancy industry and the use of globally applied textbooks and teaching.

Firms throughout the world are adopting similar integrated enterprise resource planning systems or standardised software packages that have resulted in the standardisation of data collection formats and reporting patterns of accounting information. In multinational companies this process has resulted in the standardisation of the global flow of information, but it has also limited the ability to generate locally relevant information. Besides the impact of integrated IT systems, it is common for the headquarters/parent company of a transnational enterprise to force foreign divisions to adopt similar accounting practices to those of the headquarters/parent company. A large global consultancy industry has recently emerged that tends to promote the same standard solutions globally. The consultancy industry also enthusiastically supports mimetic processes. Granlund and Lukka describe mimetic processes as processes by which companies, under conditions of uncertainty, copy publicly known and appreciated models of operation from each other, especially from successful companies that have a good reputation. Finally, the same textbooks are used globally and university and professional accounting syllabuses tend to be similar in different countries.

At the micro level, Granlund and Lukka acknowledge that differences in national and corporate culture can result in management accounting information being used in different ways across countries. For example, there is evidence to suggest that accounting information is used in a more rigorous/rigid manner to evaluate managerial performance in cultures exhibiting certain national traits, and in a more flexible way in cultures exhibiting different national traits. At the macro level Granlund and Lukka argue that the impact of national culture is diminishing because of the increasing emerging pressures to follow national trends to secure national competitiveness.

FUNCTIONS OF MANAGEMENT ACCOUNTING

A cost and management accounting system should generate information to meet the following requirements.

It should:

1. allocate costs between cost of goods sold and inventories for internal and external profit reporting;
2. provide relevant information to help managers make better decisions;
3. provide information for planning, control, performance measurement and continuous improvement.

Financial accounting rules require that we match costs with revenues to calculate profit. Consequently, any unsold finished goods inventories (or partly completed work in progress) will not be included in the cost of goods sold, which is matched against sales revenue during a given period. In an organisation that produces a wide range of different products it will be necessary, for inventory valuation purposes, to charge the costs to each individual product. The total value of the inventories of completed products and work in progress, plus any unused raw materials, forms the basis for determining the inventory valuation to be deducted from the current period's costs when calculating profit. This total is also the basis for determining the inventory valuation for inclusion in the balance sheet. Costs are therefore traced to each individual job or product for financial accounting requirements, in order to allocate the costs incurred during a period between cost of goods sold and inventories. This information is required for meeting external financial accounting requirements, but most organisations also produce internal profit reports at monthly intervals. Thus, product costs are also required for periodic internal profit reporting. Many service organisations, however, do not carry any inventories and product costs are therefore not required by these organisations for valuing inventories.

The second requirement of a cost and management accounting system is to provide relevant financial information to managers to help them make better decisions. Information is required relating to the profitability of various segments of the business such as products, services, customers and distribution channels, in order to ensure that only profitable activities are undertaken. Information is also required for making resource allocation and product/service mix and discontinuation decisions. In some situations information extracted from the costing system also plays a crucial role in determining selling prices, particularly in markets where customised products and services that do not have readily available market prices are provided.

Management accounting systems should also provide information for planning, control, performance measurement and continuous improvement. Planning involves translating goals and objectives into the specific activities and resources that are required to achieve them. Companies develop both long-term and short-term plans and the management accounting function plays a critical role in this process. Short-term plans, in the form of the budgeting process, are prepared in more detail than the longer-term plans and are one of the mechanisms used by managers as a basis for control and performance evaluation. The control process involves the setting of targets or standards (often derived from the budgeting process) against which actual results are measured. The management accountant's role is to provide managers with feedback information in the form of periodic reports, suitably analysed, to enable them to determine if operations for which they are responsible are proceeding according to plan, and to identify those activities where corrective action is necessary. In particular, the management accounting function should provide economic feedback to managers to assist them in controlling costs and improving the efficiency and effectiveness of operations.

It is appropriate at this point to distinguish between cost accounting and management accounting. **Cost accounting** is concerned with cost accumulation for inventory valuation to meet the requirements of external reporting and internal profit measurement, whereas management accounting relates to the provision of appropriate information for decision-making, planning, control and performance evaluation. However, a study of the literature reveals that the distinction between cost accounting and management accounting is not clear cut and the two terms are often used synonymously.

cost accounting accounting concerned with cost accumulation for inventory valuation to meet the requirements of external reporting and internal profit measurement

You should now be aware that a management accounting system serves multiple purposes. The emphasis is that costs must be assembled in different ways for different purposes. Most organisations record cost information in a single database, with costs appropriately coded and classified, so that relevant information can be extracted to meet the requirements of different users.

A BRIEF HISTORICAL REVIEW OF MANAGEMENT ACCOUNTING

The origins of today's management accounting can be traced back to the Industrial Revolution of the nineteenth century. According to Johnson and Kaplan (1987), most of the management accounting practices that were in use in the mid-1980s had been developed by 1925, and for the next 60 years there was a slow-down, or even a halt, in management accounting innovation. They argue that this stagnation can be attributed mainly to the demand for product cost information for external financial accounting reports. The separation of the ownership and management of organisations created a need for the owners of a business to monitor the effective stewardship of their investment. This need led to the development of financial accounting, which generated a published report for investors and creditors summarising the financial position of the company. Statutory obligations were established requiring companies to publish audited annual financial statements. In addition, there was a requirement for these published statements to conform to a set of rules known as Generally Accepted Accounting Principles (GAAP), which were developed by regulators.

The preparation of published external financial accounting statements required that costs be allocated between cost of goods sold and inventories. Cost accounting emerged to meet this requirement. Simple procedures were established to allocate costs to products that were objective and verifiable for financial accounting purposes. Such costs, however, were not sufficiently accurate for decision-making purposes and for distinguishing between profitable and unprofitable products and services. Johnson and Kaplan argue that the product costs derived for financial accounting purposes were also being used for management accounting purposes. They conclude that managers did not have to yield the design of management accounting systems to financial accountants and auditors. Separate systems could have been maintained for managerial and financial accounting purposes, but the high cost of information collection meant that the costs of maintaining two systems exceeded the additional benefits. Thus, companies relied primarily on the same information as that used for external financial reporting to manage their internal operations.

Johnson and Kaplan claim that, over the years, organisations had become fixated on the cost systems of the 1920s. Furthermore, when the information systems were automated in the 1960s, the system designers merely automated the manual systems that were developed in the 1920s. Johnson and Kaplan conclude that the lack of management accounting innovation over the decades, and the failure to respond to its changing environment, resulted in a situation in the mid-1980s where firms were using management accounting systems that were obsolete and no longer relevant to the changing competitive and manufacturing environment.

During the late 1980s, criticisms of current management accounting practices were widely publicised in the professional and academic accounting literature. In 1987 Johnson and Kaplan's book entitled *Relevance Lost: The Rise and Fall of Management Accounting*, was published. An enormous amount of publicity was generated by this book as a result of the authors' criticisms of management accounting.

Many other commentators also concluded that management accounting was in crisis and that fundamental changes in practice were required.

Since the mid-1980s management accounting practitioners and academics have sought to modify and implement new techniques that are relevant to today's environment which will ensure that management accounting regains its relevance. By the mid-1990s Kaplan (1994a) stated that:

> The past 10 years have seen a revolution in management accounting theory and practice. The seeds of the revolution can be seen in publications in the early to mid-1980s that identified the failings and obsolescence of existing cost and performance measurement systems. Since that time we have seen remarkable innovations in management accounting; even more remarkable has been the speed with which the new concepts have become widely known, accepted and implemented in practice and integrated into a large number of educational programmes.

SUMMARY

- Distinguish between management accounting and financial accounting.

Management accounting differs from financial accounting in several ways. Management accounting is concerned with the provision of information to internal users to help them make better decisions and improve the efficiency and effectiveness of operations. Financial accounting is concerned with the provision of information to external parties outside the organisation. Unlike financial accounting there is no statutory requirement for management accounting to produce financial statements or follow externally imposed rules. Furthermore, management accounting provides information relating to different parts of the business whereas financial accounting reports focus on the whole business. Management accounting also tends to be more future oriented and reports are often published on a daily basis whereas financial accounting reports are published semi-annually.

- Identify and describe the elements involved in the decision-making, planning and control process.

The following elements are involved in the decision-making, planning and control process: (a) identify the objectives that will guide the business; (b) search for a range of possible courses of action that might enable the objectives to be achieved; (c) select appropriate alternative courses of action that will enable the objectives to be achieved; (d) implement the decisions as part of the planning and budgeting process; (e) compare actual and planned outcomes; and (f) respond to divergencies from plan by taking corrective action so that actual outcomes conform to planned outcomes, or modify the plans if the comparisons indicate that the plans are no longer attainable.

- Justify the view that a major objective of commercial organisations is to broadly seek to maximise future profits.

The reasons for identifying maximising future profits as a major objective are: (a) it is unlikely that any other objective is as widely applicable in measuring the ability of the organisation to survive in the future; (b) although it is unlikely that maximising future profits can be realised in practice it is still important to establish the principles necessary to achieve this objective; and (c) it enables shareholders as a group in the bargaining coalition to know how much the pursuit of other goals is costing them by indicating the amount of cash distributed among the members of the coalition.

● Explain the factors that have influenced the changes in the competitive environment.

The factors influencing the change in the competitive environment are: (a) globalisation of world trade; (b) deregulation in various industries; (c) growth of the service sector; (d) changing product life cycles; (e) advances in manufacturing and information technologies; (f) focus on environmental issues; and (g) the need to become more customer-driven.

● Outline and describe the key success factors that directly affect customer satisfaction.

The key success factors are: cost efficiency, quality, time and innovation and continuous improvement. Keeping costs low and being cost efficient provides an organisation with a strong competitive advantage. Customers also demand high quality products and services and this has resulted in companies making quality a key competitive variable. Organisations are also seeking to increase customer satisfaction by providing a speedier response to customer requests, ensuring 100 per cent on-time delivery and reducing the time taken to bring new products to the market. To be successful companies must be innovative and develop a steady stream of new products and services and have the capability to rapidly adapt to changing customer requirements.

● Identify and describe the functions of a cost and management accounting system.

A cost and management accounting system should generate information to meet the following requirements: (a) allocate costs between cost of goods sold and inventories for internal and external profit reporting and inventory valuation; (b) provide relevant information to help managers make better decisions; and (c) provide information for planning, control and performance measurement.

● Provide a brief historical description of management accounting.

Most of the management accounting practices that were in use in the mid-1980s had been developed by 1925, and for the next 60 years there was virtually a halt in management accounting innovation. By the mid-1980s firms were using management accounting systems that were obsolete and no longer relevant to the changing competitive and manufacturing environment. During the late 1980s, criticisms of current management accounting practices were widely publicised in the professional and academic accounting literature. In response to the criticisms, considerable progress has been made in modifying and implementing new techniques that are relevant to today's environment and that will ensure that management accounting regains its relevance.

EXERCISE QUESTIONS

1   Identify and describe the different users of accounting information.

2   Explain each of the elements of the decision-making, planning and control process.

3   Explain how the business environment that businesses face has changed over the past decades and discuss how this has had an impact on management accounting.

4   Describe the different functions of management accounting.

5   Explain why management accounting practices tend not to differ across countries.

CASE 16.1

PricewaterhouseCoopers Innovates Through PowerPitch

How do you get accounting and consulting specialists to think creatively about future business possibilities? With 766 offices in 158 nations, New York–based PricewaterhouseCoopers (now known as PwC) is one of the industry-leading "Big Four" accounting firms. It offers a wide range of accounting, auditing, consulting, and tax services—all designed to provide information to clients in many industries, including almost 90 per cent of the *Fortune Global* 500 companies. From a one-person operation in 1849, PwC has grown into a multinational giant with more than 169,000 employees.

To keep annual revenue growing beyond $30 billion, the company is looking for cutting-edge ideas as the foundation of future multimillion-dollar businesses. It recently held a contest called "PowerPitch," inviting teams of U.S. employees to pitch their best ideas for new businesses. The reward: $100,000 to the winning team, bragging rights, and the opportunity to shepherd the idea through the development process.

During the contest's first stage, hundreds of PwC teams submitted a grand total of 779 business proposals. Then all U.S. employees and a panel of PwC partners reviewed and voted on them. Of those proposals, 25 were chosen as semifinalists, and the five most promising moved on to become finalists. The finalist teams traveled to New York City to pitch to PwC's top executives (with thousands of colleagues watching via live webcast). After some discussion, the judges chose a grand prize winner. In a surprise move, they also backed all five of the finalist proposals for further development and sent the semi-finalist proposals to an incubation group for further study. Just as important, PowerPitch proved that PwC welcomes and rewards bold new ideas—"the kind of programme that becomes a talent magnet," says the U.S. chairman.

Meanwhile, PwC is already expanding into new services that will help corporate clients achieve their goals. For example, it now conducts "green" audits, examining a client's environmental activities at regular intervals. The audits show how much progress the client is making toward long-term sustainability targets such as conserving natural resources and energy, reducing emissions, and making products and processes as eco-friendly as possible.

The 21st-century PwC is nothing like the small accounting practice that Samuel Lowell Price set up in London during the mid-19th century. Relying on the knowledge and experience of its global workforce, PwC offers a wide variety of auditing, accounting, and tax services. Its industry specialists also provide expert advice and guidance to banks, law firms, retailers, hospitals, energy firms, travel companies, and many other types of companies, as well as educational institutions, government agencies, and nonprofit groups.

PwC has some very glamorous clients, although its role is behind the scenes rather than on the red carpet. For example, PwC collects and counts the votes for the Academy Awards. Thanks to the firm's extreme measures to ensure secrecy, nobody knows who won until the famous presenters step into the spotlight and make their announcements to the world.

References: PwC Web site at www.pwc.com, accessed April 12, 2012; Alison Overholt, "American Idol: Accounting Edition," Fortune, October 17, 2011, pp. 101–106; Dena Aubin, "Going Green, Big Business Hires Auditors for Proof," Reuters, November 23, 2011, www.reuters.com; Alex Spence, "PwC Reclaims the Lead in Global Consulting's Four-Horse Race," *The Times*, October 4, 2011, www.thetimes.co.uk.

Questions

1 When an accounting firm like PwC has been hired to examine and sign off on a public corporation's annual report, should it limit its consulting work to avoid being influenced by financial ties to the client? Explain your answer.

2 Why would the Academy of Motion Picture Arts and Sciences hire PwC instead of having its own employees count votes for the Academy Awards?

17 MONEY AND THE BANKING SYSTEM

BUSINESS FOCUS

Two high street banks with very different strategies

Strategy is fundamental to why a customer continues to buy and experience a product and service over time, and it should differentiate an organisation's value from that offered by its competitors. Value is the satisfaction and benefits customers (and other stakeholders) receive in return for buying and using products and services.

The secret of success is not to excel equally in everything, but — and especially — in those things that are vital to the *unique* value that an organisation creates for its customers. This is important to nearly all organisations. Take for example the difference in service offered by retail banks by the U.K. brands, NatWest and HSBC.

NatWest has a locally pitched strategy based on "helpful banking" and the "local bank", and the importance of its branches is paramount for an attentive service based on a Customer Charter prominently displayed at every branch outlet. At HSBC strategy is linked to "celebrating global diversity", which emphasises the importance of customer convenience, and the importance to this of flexible, internationally organised but cost saving online processes. This difference has been characterised as "bricks versus clicks" competition.

Of course, all retail banks provide a basic universal banking service and have also encouraged the convenience of Internet-based services, which in turn has encouraged some banks to reduce costs by closing branches. However, HSBC has followed this path more than most and has gone further to automate service at its remaining branches.

At NatWest, strategy is all about personal service, while at HSBC strategy is about product based on convenience and cost.

References: Witcher and Chau, *Strategic Management: Principles and Practice*, 2nd ed. (2014)

Most people regard a bank, like NatWest or HSBC, as a place to deposit or borrow money. When you deposit money in a bank, you *receive* interest. When you borrow money from this bank or any financial institution or lender, you must *pay* interest. You may borrow to buy a home, a car, or some other high-cost item. In this case, the resource that will be transformed into money to repay the loan is the salary you receive for your labour.

Businesses also transform resources into money. A business firm (even a new one) may have a valuable asset in the form of an idea for a product or service. If the firm (or its founder) has a good credit history and the idea is a good one, a bank like Umpqua or other lenders may lend it the money to develop, produce, and market the product or service. The loan—with interest—will be repaid out of future sales revenue. In this way, both the firm and the lender will earn a reasonable profit.

In each of these situations, the borrower needs the money now and will have the ability to repay it later. Although the decision to borrow money from a bank or other financial institution should always be made after careful deliberation, the fact is that responsible borrowing enables both individuals and business firms to meet specific needs.

THE MONETARY SYSTEM

When you walk into a restaurant to buy a meal, you receive something of value: the enjoyment of the food together with the experience of eating the meal in a pleasant environment and being waited upon. To pay for this service, you might hand the restaurateur several pieces of brightly coloured paper decorated with portraits of recognisable national figures, swirly symbols and industrial buildings. Or you might hand them a small, rectangular piece of coloured plastic with a magnetic strip and a small computer chip set into it, which the restaurateur will later return to you. You might even hand them a single piece of paper with the name of a bank and your signature. Whether you pay by cash, debit card, credit card or cheque, the restaurateur is happy to work hard to satisfy your gastronomic desires either in exchange for pieces of paper that, in and of themselves, are worthless, or in exchange for borrowing an equally worthless small piece of plastic from you for a few minutes.

To anyone who has lived in a modern economy, this social custom is not at all odd. Even though paper money has no intrinsic value, the restaurateur is confident that, in the future, some third person will accept it in exchange for something that the restaurateur does value. And that third person is confident that some fourth person will accept the money, with the knowledge that yet a fifth person will accept the money ... and so on. To the restaurateur and to other people in our society, your cash represents a claim to goods and services in the future. If you paid by debit card, the restaurateur is happy because they know that money has been transferred more or less instantly to their bank account from your bank account, and the figures on their bank balance also represent a claim to goods and services produced by the economy. Similarly, if you paid by cheque, they know that money will be transferred between accounts as soon as the cheque is processed – usually within a few days. If you paid with a credit card, they know that their account has been credited with the money that you have borrowed on the credit card in order to pay the restaurant bill.

The social custom of using money for transactions is extraordinarily useful in a large, complex society. Imagine, for a moment, that there was no item in the economy widely accepted in exchange for goods and services. People would have to rely on a **barter system** – the exchange of one good or service for another – to obtain the things they need. To get your restaurant meal, for instance, you would have to offer the restaurateur something of immediate value. You could offer to wash some dishes, clean their car or give them the secret recipe for your family's favourite dish. An economy that relies on barter will have trouble allocating its scarce resources efficiently. In such an economy, trade is said to require the *double coincidence of wants* – the unlikely occurrence that two people each have a good or service that the other wants.

> **barter system** a system of exchange in which goods or services are traded directly for other goods or services

The existence of money makes trade easier. The restaurateur does not care whether you can produce a valuable good or service for them. They are happy to accept your money, knowing that other people will do the same for them. Such a convention allows trade to be roundabout. The restaurateur accepts your money and uses it to pay the chef; the chef uses their salary to send their child to the crèche; the crèche uses this money to pay a teacher; and the teacher hires you to child-mind when he goes to the cinema on a Saturday evening. As money flows from person to person in the economy, it facilitates production and trade, thereby allowing each person to specialise in what he or she does best and raising everyone's standard of living.

In this chapter we begin to examine the role of money in the economy. We discuss what money is, the various forms that money takes, how the banking system helps create money, and how the central bank controls the quantity of money in circulation.

THE MEANING OF MONEY

What is money? This might seem like an odd question. When you read that Mark Zuckerberg, one of the co-founders of Facebook, is a billionaire and has a lot of money, you know what that means: he is so rich that he can buy almost anything he wants. In this sense, the term money is used to mean wealth.

Economists, however, use the word in a more specific sense: **money** is the set of assets in the economy that people regularly use to buy goods and services from other people. The cash in your wallet is money because you can use it to buy a meal at a restaurant or a shirt at a clothes shop. By contrast, if you happened to own part of Facebook, as Mark Zuckerberg does, you would be wealthy, but this asset is not considered a form of money. You could not buy a meal or a shirt with this wealth without first obtaining some cash. According to the economist's definition, money includes only those few types of wealth that are regularly accepted by sellers in exchange for goods and services.

money the set of assets in an economy that people regularly use to buy goods and services from other people

The functions of money

Money has three functions in the economy: it is a medium of exchange, a unit of account and a store of value. These three functions together distinguish money from other assets in the economy, such as stocks, bonds, residential property and art. Let's examine each of these functions of money in turn.

A **medium of exchange** is an item that buyers give to sellers when they purchase goods and services. When you buy a shirt at a clothes shop, the shop gives you the shirt and you give the shop your money. This transfer of money from buyer to seller allows the transaction to take place. When you walk into a shop, you are confident that the shop will accept your money for the items it is selling because money is the commonly accepted medium of exchange.

 medium of exchange an item that buyers give to sellers when they want to purchase goods and services

A **unit of account** is the yardstick people use to post prices and record debts. When you go shopping in South Africa, for example, you might observe that a shirt is priced at R200 and a ham-and-cheese sandwich at R20. Even though it would be accurate to say that the price of a shirt is 10 sandwiches and the price of a sandwich is 1/10 of a shirt, prices are never quoted in this way. Similarly, if you take out a loan in rand from a bank, the size of your future loan repayments will be measured in rand, not in a quantity of goods and services. When we want to measure and record economic value, we use money as the unit of account.

 unit of account the yardstick people use to post prices and record debts

A **store of value** is an item that people can use to transfer purchasing power from the present to the future. When a seller accepts money today in exchange for a good or service, that seller can hold the money and become a buyer of another good or service at another time. Of course, money is not the only store of value in the economy, for a person can also transfer purchasing power from the present to the future by holding other assets. The term *wealth* is used to refer to the total of all stores of value, including both money and non-monetary assets.

 store of value an item that people can use to transfer purchasing power from the present to the future

Important characteristics of money

Money must be easy to use, trusted, and capable of performing the three functions just mentioned. To meet these requirements, money must possess the following five characteristics.

Divisibility The standard unit of money must be divisible into smaller units to accommodate small purchases and large ones. The U.K. pound, the euro and the U.S. dollar are all made up of 100 "cents" or "pence". Coins are produced for smaller day-to-day purchases, such as 5 cents, 10 cents and so on.

Portability Money must be small enough and light enough to be carried easily. For this reason, paper currency is issued in larger denominations, for example, 5-, 10-, 20-, 50-, and 100-euro notes.

Stability Money should retain its value over time. When it does not, people tend to lose faith in their money. When money becomes extremely unstable, people may turn to other means of storing value, such as gold and jewels, works of art, and property.

Inflation isn't just an economic indicator—it means that you'll pay more for many goods and services. If you're saving to buy a car or a home, the money you put aside won't go as far when prices are on the rise.

© RICHARD B. LEVINE/ALAMY

Durability The objects that serve as money should be strong enough to last through reasonable use. To increase the life expectancy of paper currency, most nations use special paper with a high fibre content.

Difficulty of counterfeiting If a nation's currency were easy to counterfeit—that is, to imitate or fake—its citizens would be uneasy about accepting it as payment. In an attempt to make paper currency more difficult to counterfeit, the government periodically redesign paper currency and use both watermarks and intricate designs to discourage counterfeiting.

Liquidity

Economists use the term **liquidity** to describe the ease with which an asset can be converted into the economy's medium of exchange. Because money is the economy's medium of exchange, it is the most liquid asset available. Other assets vary widely in their liquidity. Most stocks and bonds can be sold easily with small cost, so they are relatively liquid assets. By contrast, selling a car or a Pierneef painting requires more time and effort, so these assets are less liquid.

> **liquidity** the ease with which an asset can be converted into the economy's medium of exchange

When people decide in what form to hold their wealth, they have to balance the liquidity of each possible asset against the asset's usefulness as a store of value. Money is the most liquid asset, but it is far from perfect as a store of value. When prices rise, the value of money falls. In other words, when goods and services become more expensive, each euro or pound in your wallet can buy less. This link between the price level and the value of money will turn out to be important for understanding how money affects the economy.

Kinds of money

When money takes the form of a commodity with intrinsic value, it is called **commodity money**. The term *intrinsic value* means that the item would have value even if it were not used as money. One example of commodity money is gold. Gold has intrinsic value because it is used in industry and in the making of jewellery. Although today we no longer use gold as money, historically gold has been a common form of money because it is relatively easy to carry, measure, and verify for impurities. When an economy uses gold as money (or uses paper money that is convertible into gold on demand), it is said to be operating under a *gold standard*.

> **commodity money** money that takes the form of a commodity with intrinsic value

Although gold has, historically, been the most common form of commodity money, other commodity monies have been used from time to time. For example, in the hyperinflation in Zimbabwe in the early 2000s the country's people began to lose faith in the Zimbabwean dollar; people began to trade goods and services with one another using cigarettes as the store of value, unit of account and medium of exchange.

Money without intrinsic value is called **fiat money**. A fiat is simply an order or decree, and fiat money is established as money by government decree.

> **fiat money** money without intrinsic value that is used as money because of government decree

Although governments are central to establishing and regulating a system of fiat money (by prosecuting counterfeiters, for example), other factors are also required for the success of such a monetary system. To a large extent, the acceptance of fiat money depends as much on expectations and social convention as on government decree. Zimbabweans preferred to accept cigarettes (or American dollars) in exchange for goods and services, because they were more confident that these alternative monies would be accepted by others in the future.

Money in the economy

The quantity of money circulating in the economy, called the money stock, has a powerful influence on many economic variables. But before we consider that, we need to ask a preliminary question: what is the quantity of money? In particular, suppose you were given the task of measuring how much money there is in the economy of South Africa. What would you include in your measure?

The most obvious asset to include is **currency** – the paper notes and metal coins in the hands of the public. Currency is clearly the most widely accepted medium of exchange in a modern economy. There is no doubt that it is part of the money stock.

> **currency** the paper banknotes and coins in the hands of the public

Yet currency is not the only asset that you can use to buy goods and services. Most businesses also accept payment by debit card, which allows money to be transferred electronically between your current account and the current account of the business. Another, more old fashioned way of transferring money between current accounts is to write a personal cheque, and personal cheques are indeed still widely accepted as a means of payment (though rapidly being replaced by debit cards).

So is a debit card or a cheque money? Not really – it is the bank account on which the cheque or debit card draws which contains the money. A debit card is just a *means* of transferring money between accounts. The same is true of a cheque. Although a cheque may seem to be similar in some ways to paper money – it is also written on paper and is made out for a certain sum of money – it is only accepted by a business because it is a *means* of transferring money from your bank account to his.

What about credit cards? We need to think about these even more carefully, because credit cards are not really a method of payment but a method of *deferring* payment. When you buy a meal with a credit card, the bank that issued the card pays the restaurant what it is due – you have effectively borrowed from the bank. At a later date, you will have to repay the bank (perhaps with interest). When the time comes to pay your credit card bill, you will probably do so by direct transfer from your current account (or possibly by writing a cheque against your current account). The balance in this current account is part of the economy's stock of money. Notice that credit cards are very different from debit cards, which automatically withdraw funds from a bank account to pay for items bought. Why does the restaurateur accept payment by credit card? Because he gets his money immediately by having his bank account credited for the price of the meal even though you do not have to pay the credit card company back immediately. Again, however, it is the underlying movement in the restaurateur's bank balance that matters.

Thus, although a debit card, a cheque and a credit card can each be used to settle the restaurant bill, none of them are money – they are each a method of transferring money between bank accounts. In the case of a debit card or a cheque, money is transferred from your account to the restaurateur's account more or less immediately or with a very short lag. In the case of a credit card, the restaurateur gets his money in his account more or less immediately and you will then have to settle up with the bank issuing the credit card later by drawing on your bank account. In every case, the true movement in money occurs when bank balances change.

Wealth held in your current account is almost as convenient for buying things as wealth held in your wallet. To measure the money stock, therefore, you might want to include **demand deposits** – balances in bank accounts that depositors can access *on demand* simply by using their debit card or writing a cheque. Once you start to consider balances in current accounts as part of the money stock, you are led to consider the large variety of other accounts that people hold at banks and other financial institutions. Bank depositors usually cannot write cheques or use their debit cards against the balances in their savings accounts, but they can (mostly) easily transfer funds from savings into current accounts. In addition, depositors in money market funds can often write cheques and use debit cards against their balances. Thus, these other accounts should plausibly be counted as part of the money stock.

> **demand deposits** balances in bank accounts that depositors can access on demand by using a debit card or writing a cheque

For our purposes, we need not dwell on the differences between the various measures of money. The important point is that the money stock for an advanced economy includes not just currency but also deposits in banks and other financial institutions that can be readily accessed and used to buy goods and services.

THE ROLE OF CENTRAL BANKS

Whenever an economy relies on a system of fiat money–as all modern advanced economies do – some agency must be responsible for regulating the system. This agency is generally known as the **central bank** – an institution designed to regulate the quantity of money made available in the economy, called the **money supply**. The central bank in South Africa is the South African Reserve Bank (SARB). Other important central banks are the European Central Bank the Bank of England, the U.S. Federal Reserve and the Bank of Japan. We'll take a closer look at examples in a moment. Before then, however, we can look at some features of central banks in general.

> **central bank** an institution designed to regulate the quantity of money in the economy
> **money supply** the quantity of money available in the economy

The central bank of an economy has the power to increase or decrease the amount of currency in that economy. The set of actions taken by the central bank in order to affect the money supply is known as **monetary policy**. In simple metaphorical terms, you can imagine the central bank printing up banknotes and dropping them by helicopter. Similarly, you can imagine the central bank using a giant vacuum cleaner to suck banknotes out of people's wallets. Although in practice the central bank's methods for changing the money supply are more complex and subtle than this, the helicopter-vacuum metaphor is a good first approximation to the meaning of monetary policy.

> **monetary policy** the set of actions taken by the central bank in order to affect the money supply

Many texts and studies show how the central bank actually changes the money supply, but it is worth noting here that an important tool that the central bank can use is **open-market operations** – the purchase and sale of nonmonetary assets from and to the banking sector. For example, if the central bank decides to increase the money supply, it can do this by creating currency and using it to buy bonds from the public in the bond market. After the purchase, the extra currency is in the hands of the public. Thus, an open-market purchase of bonds by the central bank increases the money supply. Conversely, if the central bank decides to decrease the money supply, it can do this by selling bonds from its portfolio to the public. After the sale, the currency it receives for the bonds is out of the hands of the public. Thus an open-market sale of bonds by the central bank decreases the money supply.

> **open-market operations** the purchase and sale of non-monetary assets from and to the banking sector by the central bank

The central bank of an economy is an important institution because changes in the money supply can profoundly affect the economy. One of the *Ten Principles of Economics* is that prices rise when too much money is printed. Another of the *Ten Principles of Economics* is that society faces a short-run tradeoff between inflation and unemployment. The power of the central bank rests on these principles. The central bank's policy decisions have an important influence on the economy's rate of inflation in the long run and the economy's employment and production in the short run. In particular, because of the link between the amount of money in the economy and the inflation rate (the rate of increase of prices), the central bank is often seen as the guardian of price stability in a modern economy and at least two of the central banks we shall look at are specifically charged with the duty to maintain inflation at or near an inflation target. To be precise, the central bank should perhaps be thought of as the guardian of inflation stability, rather than price stability, since even with a constant, low rate of inflation, prices are by definition rising. Still, if inflation is low and stable, prices might be said to be rising in a stable fashion.

The European Central Bank and the Eurosystem

The **European Central Bank** (ECB), located in Frankfurt, Germany, was officially created on 1 June 1998 as a number of European countries had decided that they wished to enter European Monetary Union (EMU) and have the same currency – the euro – circulating among them. If a group of countries has the same currency, then it makes sense for the countries in the group to have a common monetary policy, and the ECB was set up for precisely this purpose. There were originally 11 countries making up the euro area: Belgium, Germany, Spain, France, Ireland, Italy, Luxembourg, the Netherlands, Austria, Portugal and Finland. By 2010, there were 16 countries, the new additions being Greece, Cyprus, Slovakia, Slovenia and Malta.

> **European Central Bank (ECB)** the overall central bank of the 16 countries comprising the European Monetary Union

The primary objective of the ECB is to promote price stability throughout the euro area and to design and implement monetary policy that is consistent with this objective. The ECB operates with the assistance of the national central banks in each of the euro area countries, such as the Banque de France, the Banca d'Italia, the Bank of Greece and the German Bundesbank. The network made up of the ECB together with the 16 euro area national central banks is termed the **Eurosystem**.

> **Eurosystem** the system made up of the ECB plus the national central banks of each of the 16 countries comprising the European Monetary Union

The implementation of monetary policy by the ECB is under the control of the Executive Board, which comprises the President and Vice-President of the ECB and four other people of high standing in the banking profession. While the Executive Board – as the name suggests – is responsible for *executing* monetary policy, the monetary policy of the ECB is actually designed by the Governing Council, which comprises the whole of the Executive Board plus the governors of the national central banks in the Eurosystem (22 people in total). The Governing Council, which meets twice a month in Frankfurt, is the most important decision-making body of the ECB and decides, for example, on the level of the ECB's key interest rate, the refinancing rate. The Governing Council also decides how to interpret its duty to achieve price stability. In October 1998 it agreed that price stability should be defined as a "year-on-year increase in prices of less than 2 per cent as measured by the annual change in a harmonized index of consumer prices throughout the euro area". A problem with this definition of price stability, however, is that "less than 2 per cent" is a little vague – an annual inflation rate of 1 per cent and an annual inflation rate of 0 per cent are both less than 2 per cent. In fact, some people were worried that the ECB might even aim for falling prices or negative inflation in order to achieve its target of less than 2 per cent. As we discuss more fully in the coming chapters, this would tend sharply to reduce output and employment in the economy, especially in the short to medium run. In May 2003, therefore, the Governing Council confirmed its official definition thus: *"in the pursuit of price stability, it aims to maintain inflation rates below but close to 2% over the medium term"*.

An important feature of the ECB and of the Eurosystem in general is its independence. When performing Eurosystem-related tasks, neither the ECB, nor a national central bank, nor any member of their decision-making bodies is allowed to seek or take instructions from any external body, including any member governments or any European Union institutions.

The President of the ECB and other members of the Executive Board are appointed for a minimum non-renewable term of office of eight years (although a system of staggered appointments was used for the first Executive Board for members other than the President in order to ensure continuity) and the governors of the 16 national central banks in the Eurosystem are appointed for a minimum renewable term of office of five years.

The Bank of England

The **Bank of England** was founded in 1694, although it is not the oldest European central bank (the Swedish Riksbank was founded in 1668). Arguably the most significant event in the Bank of England's 300-hundred-year history was when the U.K. government granted it independence in the setting of interest rates in 1997, which was formalised in an Act of Parliament in 1998. The important body within the Bank that makes the decision on the level at which to set the Bank's key interest rate, the **repo rate**, is the Monetary Policy Committee (MPC). The MPC consists of the Governor and two Deputy Governors of the Bank of England, two other members appointed by the Bank after consultation with the Chancellor of the Exchequer (the U.K. finance minister) and four other members appointed by the Chancellor. The Governor and the two Deputy Governors serve five-year renewable terms of office, while other MPC members serve three-year renewable terms. The MPC meets monthly and its interest rate decision is announced immediately after the meeting.

> **Bank of England** the central bank of the United Kingdom
> **repo rate** the interest rate at which the central bank lends on a short-term basis to the banking sector

Like the ECB, one of the Bank of England's primary duties is to deliver price stability. Also in common with the ECB, it enjoys independence in the setting of monetary policy – and in particular interest rates – in order to achieve the objective of price stability. Unlike the ECB, however, the Bank of England does not have the freedom to define for itself precisely what "price stability" means in this context. This is done by the U.K. government and, in particular, by the Chancellor of the Exchequer. In fact, the 1998 Bank of England Act requires that the Chancellor write to the Governor of the Bank of England once a year to specify what price stability is to be defined as. Currently, the inflation target of 2 per cent is expressed in terms of an annual rate of inflation based on the consumer prices index (CPI). If the target is missed by more than 1 percentage point on either side – i.e. if the annual rate of CPI inflation is more than 3 per cent or less than 1 per cent – the Governor of the Bank of England must write an open letter to the Chancellor explaining the reasons why inflation has increased or fallen to such an extent and what the Bank proposes to do to ensure inflation comes back to the target.

In changes made to financial regulation in the U.K. in June 2010, the Chancellor of the Exchequer announced that the Bank of England would have new responsibilities focusing on monetary policy and financial stability. The new system led to the Bank of England getting additional responsibilities for financial stability, macro-prudential supervision and oversight of micro-prudential supervision. These regulatory functions are overseen by four main groups, the Prudential Regulatory Authority (not its final name) which is responsible for day-to-day supervision of bank safety and soundness (micro-prudential policy), the Financial Policy Committee, charged with preventing credit and asset bubbles and overall financial stability, the Economic Crime Agency focusing on serious economic crime such as corporate fraud, market-fixing and insider trading and the Consumer Protection and Markets Authority which manages protection of investors, market supervision and regulation and the conduct of banks and financial services. A Banking Commission was also created which looks at ways to reduce systemic risk in the banking system and investigate the possibility of splitting the retail and investment divisions of banks.

The South African Reserve Bank

The SARB is responsible for maintaining price stability in South Africa, which is its primary role. However it also has other functions which include issuing banknotes and coins, acting as lender of last resort (which tends to occur in times of financial crisis when liquidity in the banking system has dried up), acting as a banker to the government, supervising the banking sector, managing gold and foreign currency reserves and for administering exchange controls (South Africa still has some controls over the amount of currency that can be brought into and taken out of the country). Putting all these responsibilities together the SARB, like other central banks, plays an important role in maintaining financial stability in the country, something which is vital to the smooth running of the economy.

The SARB was set up in 1920 and its activities are now governed by legislation passed in the South African Reserve Banking Act 1989. By setting a primary aim of achieving and maintaining price stability, the SARB also plays a role in helping to set the conditions under which sustainable economic growth can take place. The SARB has been granted independence by the legislation which means that it is able to make decisions free from political interference. In setting interest rates (which the South African Reserve calls the repo or repurchase rate) to target inflation this is vital although the SARB is still ultimately accountable to parliament.

The SARB responsibility for monetary policy sees it operating policy to achieve an inflation target set, at the time of writing, at a range of 3 – 6 per cent as measured by the consumer prices index (CPI). Policy is set by the Monetary Policy Committee (MPC) which meets at set dates throughout the year announced in advance. In 2012, for example, the meetings were held every other month starting in January. The meetings are chaired by the Governor of the SARB and consists of 8 people, the Governor, three deputy governors and four senior officials of the Bank. The MPC are briefed on the state of the economy and study data related to economic growth, prices and the financial markets and have a free vote on the interest rate which, in their opinion, will be most likely to bring about the target inflation rate desired.

Monetary policy is set within a framework of a cash reserve system requirement of the banking system. The SARB sets the interest rate or repo rate (see explanation above) for lending funds to the banking system which in turn determines the structure of interest rates throughout the economy. The SARB also conducts open market operations to manage liquidity in the financial system. By setting the interest rate and influencing the structure of interest rates in commercial banks, the exchange rate, bond and equity prices and expectations, the real economy is influenced. This means that the level of aggregate demand in the economy, import and export prices, investment and wage a price increases are all influenced and in turn the inflation rate. This process is known as the **transmission mechanism.**

> **transmission mechanism** the process by which monetary policy decisions is transmitted throughout the economy to the inflation rate.

The Federal Reserve System

The U.S. **Federal Reserve** was created in 1913. The Fed is run by its Board of Governors, which has seven members appointed by the U.S. president. Six of the governors have 14-year terms to give them independence from short-term political pressures when they formulate monetary policy, although the Chairman has a four-year term.

> **Federal Reserve (Fed)** the central bank of the United States

The Federal Reserve System is made up of the Federal Reserve Board in Washington, D.C., and 12 regional Federal Reserve Banks located in major cities around the U.S.

At the Federal Reserve, monetary policy is made by the Federal Open Market Committee (FOMC). The FOMC meets about every six weeks in Washington, DC, to discuss the condition of the economy and consider changes in monetary policy, including the setting of its key interest rate, the discount rate. The FOMC is made up of the seven members of the Board of Governors and five of the 12 regional bank presidents. All 12 regional presidents attend each FOMC meeting, but only five get to vote. The five with voting rights rotate among the 12 regional presidents over time. The President of the New York Fed always gets a vote, however, because New York is the traditional financial centre of the U.S. economy and because all Fed open-market operations are conducted at the New York Fed's trading desk.

BANKS AND THE MONEY SUPPLY

In general, a central bank has three main tools in its monetary toolbox: open-market operations, the refinancing rate and reserve requirements.

Open-market operations

If the central bank wants to increase the money supply, it can create currency and use it to buy bonds from the public in the bond market. After the purchase, the extra currency is in the hands of the public. Thus, an open-market purchase of bonds by the central bank increases the money supply. If, on the other hand, the central bank wants to decrease the money supply, it can sell bonds from its portfolio to the public. After the sale, the currency it receives for the bonds is out of the hands of the public. Thus an open-market sale of bonds by the central bank decreases the money supply. To be precise, the open-market operations discussed in these simple examples are called **outright open-market operations**, because they each involve an outright sale or purchase of non-monetary assets to or from the banking sector without a corresponding agreement to reverse the transaction at a later date.

> **outright open-market operations** the outright sale or purchase of nonmonetary assets to or from the banking sector by the central bank without a corresponding agreement to reverse the transaction at a later date

The refinancing rate

The central bank of an economy will set an interest rate at which it is willing to lend to commercial banks on a short-term basis. Note that the name of this interest rate differs across central banks, although for the purpose of this chapter, as with other texts, we shall refer to it as the **refinancing rate**.

 refinancing rate the interest rate at which a central lends on a short-term basis to the banking sector

The way in which the central bank lends to the banking sector is through a special form of open-market operations. In the previous paragraph we discussed the use of *outright* open-market operations. Although outright open-market operations have traditionally been used by central banks to regulate the money supply, central banks nowadays more often use a slightly more sophisticated form of open-market operations that involves buying bonds or other assets from banks and at the same time agreeing to sell them back later. When it does this, the central bank has effectively made a loan and taken the bonds or other assets as collateral or security on the loan. The central bank will have a list of eligible assets that it will accept as collateral – "safe" assets such as government bonds or assets issued by large corporations, on which the risk of default by the issuer is negligible. The interest rate that the central bank charges on the loan is the refinancing rate. Because the central bank has bought the assets but the seller has agreed to buy them back later at an agreed price, this kind of open-market operation is often called a **repurchase agreement** or "repo" for short. To see how central bank's use repos as a means of controlling the money supply and how this is affected by the refinancing rate, we need to look a little more closely at the way commercial banks lend money to one another and borrow from the central bank.

 repurchase agreement (repo) the sale of a non-monetary asset together with an agreement to repurchase it at a set price at a specified future date

Banks need to carry enough reserves to cover their lending and will generally aim for a certain ratio of reserves to deposits, known as the reserve ratio. The minimum reserve ratio may be set by the central bank, but even if it isn't, banks will still have a reserve ratio that they consider prudent. Now, because deposits and withdrawals at banks can fluctuate randomly, some banks may find that they have an excess of reserves one day (i.e. their reserve ratio is above the level the bank considers prudent or above the minimum reserve ratio, or both), while other banks may find that they are short of reserves and their reserve ratio is too low. Therefore, the commercial banks in an economy will generally lend money to one another on a short-term basis – overnight to a couple of weeks – so that banks with excess reserves can lend them to banks who have inadequate reserves to cover their lending. This market for short-term reserves is called the **money market**. If there is a *general* shortage of liquidity in the money market (because the banks together have done a lot of lending), then the short-term interest rate at which they lend to one another will begin to rise, while it will begin to fall if there is excess liquidity among banks. The central bank closely monitors the money market and may intervene in it in order to affect the supply of liquidity to banks, which in turn affects their lending and hence affects the money supply.

money market the market in which the commercial banks lend money to one another on a short-term basis

Suppose, for example, that there is a shortage of liquidity in the market because the banks have been increasing their lending and they need to increase their reserves. A commercial bank may then attempt to obtain liquidity from the central bank by selling assets to the central bank and at the same time agreeing to purchase them back a short time later. As we said before, in this type of open-market operation the central bank effectively lends money to the bank and takes the assets as collateral on the loan. Because the commercial bank is legally bound to repurchase the assets at a set price, this is called a "repurchase agreement" and the difference between the price the bank sells the assets to the central bank and the price at which it agrees to buy them back, expressed as an annualized percentage of the selling price, is called the repurchase or repo rate and (as noted) represents the rate at which the central bank will lend to the banking sector.

In the example given, the central bank added liquidity to the banking system by lending reserves to banks. This would have the effect of increasing the money supply. Because the loans made through open-market operations are typically very short term, with a maturity of at most two weeks, however, the banks are constantly having to repay the loans and borrow again, or "refinance" the loans. If the central bank wants to mop up liquidity it can simply decide not to renew some of the loans. In practice, however, the central bank will set a reference rate of interest – the repo rate or the refinancing rate – and will conduct open-market operations, adding to or mopping up liquidity, close to this reference rate.

In the U.S. the interest rate at which the Federal Reserve lends to the banking sector (corresponding to the refinancing rate or the repo rate used by the South African Reserve Bank) is called the **discount rate**.

 discount rate the interest rate at which the Federal Reserve lends on a short-term basis to the U.S. banking sector

Now we can see why the setting of the central bank's refinancing rate is the key instrument of monetary policy. If the central bank raises the refinancing rate, commercial banks will try and rein in their lending rather than borrow reserves from the central bank, and so the money supply will fall. If the central bank lowers the refinancing rate, banks will feel freer to lend, knowing that they will be able to borrow more cheaply from the central bank in order to meet their reserve requirements, and so the money supply will tend to rise.

Reserve requirements

The central bank may also influence the money supply with **reserve requirements**, which are regulations on the minimum amount of reserves that banks must hold against deposits. Reserve requirements influence how much money the banking system can create with each euro of reserves. An increase in reserve requirements means that banks must hold more reserves and, therefore, can lend out less of each euro that is deposited; as a result, it raises the reserve ratio, lowers the money multiplier and decreases the money supply. Conversely, a decrease in reserve requirements lowers the reserve ratio, raises the money multiplier and increases the money supply.

 reserve requirements regulations on the minimum amount of reserves that banks must hold against deposits

Central banks have traditionally tended to use changes in reserve requirements only rarely because frequent changes would disrupt the business of banking. When the central bank increases reserve requirements, for instance, some banks find themselves short of reserves, even though they have seen no change in deposits. As a result, they have to curtail lending until they build their level of reserves to the new required level.

Following the financial crisis negotiations have taken place on improving banks' reserves to avoid the problems faced during the crisis. The so-called Basel III negotiations between 27 countries set new reserve requirements in September 2010. The new rules will come into force in 2013 and then be phased in over a period of six years. The regulations mean that banks will have to have higher reserves to support lending; for every R50 of lending banks will have to have R3.50 of reserves compared to R1 prior to the Basel III agreement. This obviously more than triples the amount of reserves that banks will have to keep. If banks do not adhere to the new regulations then they risk seeing the authorities placing restrictions on their activities including paying out dividends to shareholders and bonuses to staff.

Problems in controlling the money supply

Through the setting of its refinancing rate and the associated open-market operations, the central bank can exert an important degree of control over the money supply. Yet the central bank's control of the money supply is not precise. The central bank must wrestle with two problems, each of which arises because much of the money supply is created by the system of fractional-reserve banking.

The first problem is that the central bank does not control the amount of money that households choose to hold as deposits in banks. The more money households deposit, the more reserves banks have, and the more money the banking system can create. And the less money households deposit, the less reserves banks have, and the less money the banking system can create. To see why this is a problem, suppose that one day people begin to lose confidence in the banking system and, therefore, decide to withdraw deposits and hold more currency. When this happens, the banking system loses reserves and creates less money. The money supply falls, even without any central bank action.

The second problem of monetary control is that the central bank does not control the amount that bankers choose to lend. When money is deposited in a bank, it creates more money only when the bank lends it out. Because banks can choose to hold excess reserves instead, the central bank cannot be sure how much money the banking system will create. For instance, suppose that one day bankers become more cautious about economic conditions and decide to make fewer loans and hold greater reserves. In this case, the banking system creates less money than it otherwise would. Because of the bankers' decision, the money supply falls.

Hence the amount of money in the economy depends in part on the behaviour of depositors and bankers. Because the central bank cannot control or perfectly predict this behaviour, it cannot perfectly control the money supply.

Commercial banks

A **commercial bank** is a profit-making organisation that accepts deposits, makes loans, and provides related services to its customers. Like other businesses, the bank's primary goal—its mission—is to meet its customers' needs while earning a profit.

> **commercial bank** a profit-making organisation that accepts deposits, makes loans, and provides related services to its customers

Because they deal with money belonging to individuals and other business firms, banks must meet certain requirements before they receive a charter, or permission to operate, from government banking authorities.

Other financial institutions

In addition to commercial banks, at least eight other types of financial institutions perform either full or limited banking services for their customers.

Savings and loan associations   A **savings and loan association (S&L)** is a financial institution that offers current and savings accounts and certificates of deposit (CDs) and that invests most of its assets in home mortgage loans and other consumer loans.

> **savings and loan association (S&L)** a financial institution that offers current and savings accounts and CDs and that invests most of its assets in home mortgage loans and other consumer loans

Credit unions   A **credit union** is a financial institution that accepts deposits from, and lends money to, only those people who are its members. Usually, the membership consists of employees of a particular firm, people in a particular profession, or those who live in a community served by a local credit union. Credit unions may pay higher interest on deposits than commercial banks and S&Ls, and they may provide loans at lower cost.

> **credit union** a financial institution that accepts deposits from, and lends money to, only the people who are its members

Organisations that perform banking functions   Six other types of financial institutions are involved in banking activities. Although not actually full-service banks, they offer customers some banking services.

- *Mutual savings banks* are financial institutions that are owned by their depositors and offer many of the same services offered by banks, S&Ls, and credit unions, including current accounts, savings accounts, and CDs. Like other financial institutions, they also fund home mortgages, commercial loans, and consumer loans. Unalike other types of financial institutions, the profits of a mutual savings bank go to the depositors, usually in the form of dividends or slightly higher interest rates on savings.
- *Insurance companies* provide long-term financing for office buildings, shopping centres, and other commercial property projects throughout the United States. The funds used for this type of financing are obtained from policyholders' insurance premiums.
- *Pension funds* are established by employers to guarantee their employees a regular monthly income on retirement. Contributions to the fund may come from the employer, the employee, or both. Pension funds earn additional income through generally conservative investments in corporate stocks, corporate bonds, and government securities, as well as through financing property developments.
- *Brokerage firms* offer combination savings and current accounts that pay higher-than-usual interest rates. Many people have switched to these accounts because they are convenient and to get slightly higher rates.
- *Finance companies* provide financing to individuals and business firms that may not be able to get financing from banks, S&Ls, or credit unions. Lenders such as Ace Cash Express, Inc., provide short-term loans to individuals. The interest rates charged by these lenders may be higher than the interest rates charged by other financial institutions.
- *Investment banking firms* are organisations that assist corporations in raising funds, usually by helping sell new issues of stocks, bonds, or other financial securities. Although these firms do not accept deposits or make loans like traditional banking firms, they do help companies raise millions of euros.

Careers in the banking industry

The banking industry employs millions of people across the world. In the U.S., 1,2 million people are employed by just seven banks alone!

To be successful in the banking industry, employees for a bank, S&L, credit union, or other financial institution must possess the following traits:

1. *You must be honest.* Because you are handling other people's money, many financial institutions go to great lengths to discover dishonest employees.
2. *You must be able to interact with people.* A number of positions in the banking industry require that you possess the interpersonal skills needed to interact not only with other employees but also with customers.
3. *You need a strong background in accounting.* Many of the routine tasks performed by employees in the banking industry are basic accounting functions. For example, a cashier must post deposits or withdrawals to a customer's account and then balance out at the end of the day to ensure accuracy.
4. *You need to appreciate the relationship between banking and finance.* Bank officers must interview loan applicants and determine if their request for money is based on sound financial principles.

Above all, loan officers must be able to evaluate applicants and their loan requests to determine if the borrower will be able to repay a loan.

5. *You should possess basic computer skills.* Almost all employees in the banking industry use a computer for some aspect of their work on a daily basis.

Depending on qualifications, work experience, and education, starting salaries generally are between €18,000 and €30,000 a year, but it is not uncommon for university graduates to earn €35,000 a year or more.

TRADITIONAL SERVICES PROVIDED BY FINANCIAL INSTITUTIONS

To determine how important banking services are to you, ask yourself just three simple questions:

- How many cheques did you write last month?
- Do you have a credit or debit card? If so, how often do you use it?
- How many times did you visit an ATM last month?

If you are like most people and business firms, you would find it hard to live a normal life without the services provided by banks and other financial institutions. Typical services provided by a bank or other financial institution are illustrated in Figure 17.1.

The most important traditional banking services for both individuals and businesses are described in this section. Online banking, electronic transfer of funds, and other significant and future developments are discussed in the next section.

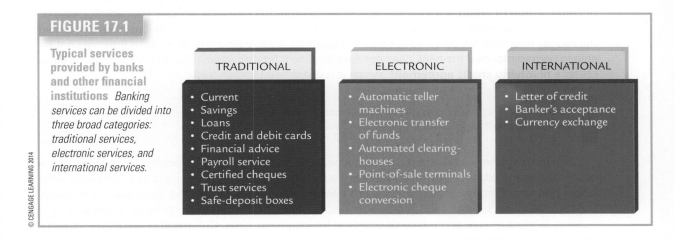

FIGURE 17.1

Typical services provided by banks and other financial institutions *Banking services can be divided into three broad categories: traditional services, electronic services, and international services.*

© CENGAGE LEARNING 2014

TRADITIONAL
- Current
- Savings
- Loans
- Credit and debit cards
- Financial advice
- Payroll service
- Certified cheques
- Trust services
- Safe-deposit boxes

ELECTRONIC
- Automatic teller machines
- Electronic transfer of funds
- Automated clearing-houses
- Point-of-sale terminals
- Electronic cheque conversion

INTERNATIONAL
- Letter of credit
- Banker's acceptance
- Currency exchange

Current or transactional accounts

Firms and individuals deposit money in current (or transactional or checking) accounts (demand deposits) so that they can write cheques to pay for purchases. A **cheque** is a written order for a bank or other financial institution to pay a stated amount to the business or person indicated on the face of the cheque. Today, some financial institutions offer free checking; others charge activity fees (or service charges) for current accounts. Charges for business accounts are often higher than those for individual accounts.

cheque   a written order for a bank or other financial institution to pay a stated amount to the business or person indicated on the face of the cheque

Although banks and other financial institutions may pay low interest rates on current accounts, even small earnings are better than no earnings. In addition to interest rates, be sure to compare monthly fees before opening a current account for your personal use or a business.

Savings accounts

Savings accounts (time deposits) provide a safe place to store money and a very conservative means of investing.

A depositor who is willing to leave money on deposit with a bank for a set period of time can earn a higher rate of interest. To do so, the depositor buys a certificate of deposit. A **certificate of deposit (CD)** is a document stating that the bank will pay the depositor a guaranteed interest rate on money left on deposit for a specified period of time. The interest rate always depends on how much is invested and for how long. Generally, the rule is: The longer the period of time until maturity, the higher is the rate. Depositors are penalised for early withdrawal of funds invested in CDs.

> **certificate of deposit (CD)** a document stating that the bank will pay the depositor a guaranteed interest rate on money left on deposit for a specified period of time

Short- and long-term loans

Banks, S&Ls, credit unions, and other financial institutions provide short- and long-term loans to both individuals and businesses. *Short-term business loans* must be repaid within one year or less. Typical uses for the money obtained through short-term loans include solving cash-flow problems, purchasing inventory, monthly expenses, and meeting unexpected emergencies.

To help ensure that short-term money will be available when needed, many firms establish a line of credit. A **line of credit** is a loan that is approved before the money is actually needed. Because all the necessary paperwork is already completed and the loan is pre-approved, the business can obtain the money later without delay, as soon as it is required. Even with a line of credit, a firm may not be able to borrow money if the bank does not have sufficient funds available. For this reason, some firms prefer a **revolving credit agreement**, which is a guaranteed line of credit.

> **line of credit** a loan that is approved before the money is actually needed
> **revolving credit agreement** a guaranteed line of credit

Long-term business loans are repaid over a period of years. The average length of a long-term business loan is generally three to seven years but sometimes as long as 15 years or in a few cases even longer periods of time. Long-term loans are used most often to finance the expansion of buildings and retail facilities, mergers and acquisitions, replacement of equipment, or product development.

Most lenders require some type of collateral for long-term loans. **Collateral** is real estate or property (stocks, bonds, equipment, or any other asset of value) pledged as security for a loan. For example, when an individual obtains a loan to pay for a new Audi A4, the automobile is the collateral for the loan. If the borrower fails to repay the loan according to the terms specified in the loan agreement, the lender can repossess the car.

> **collateral** real estate or property pledged as security for a loan

Repayment terms and interest rates for both short- and long-term loans are arranged between the lender and the borrower. For businesses, repayment terms may include monthly, quarterly, semi-annual, or annual payments. Repayment terms and interest rates for personal loans vary depending on how the money will be used and what type of collateral, if any, is pledged. However, individuals typically make monthly payments to repay personal loans. Borrowers always should "shop" for a loan, comparing the repayment terms and interest rates offered by competing financial institutions.

How do you pay for your purchases?
Today more and more people are using credit and debit cards to pay for their purchases. For consumers, "plastic cards" are convenient and fast. For the merchant, credit and debit card transactions can be converted to cash and improve a firm's cash flow.

Credit card and debit card transactions

Why have credit cards become so popular?

For a merchant, the answer is obvious. By depositing charge slips in a bank or other financial institution, the merchant can convert credit card sales into cash. In return for processing the merchant's credit card transactions, the financial institution charges a fee that generally ranges between 1.5 and 4 per cent. Let's assume that you use a Visa credit card to purchase a microwave oven for €300 from a retailer in Aachen. At the end of the day, the retailer deposits your charge slip, along with other charge slips, cheques, and currency collected during the day, at its bank. If the bank charges the retailer 4 per cent to process each credit card transaction, the bank deducts a processing fee of €12 (€300 × 0.04 = €12) for your credit card transaction and immediately deposits the remainder (€288) in the retailer's account. Typically, small businesses pay more than larger businesses. The number of credit card transactions, the total euro amount of credit sales, and how well the merchant can negotiate the fees the bank charges determine actual fees.

Do not confuse debit cards with credit cards. Although they may look alike, there are important differences. A **debit card** electronically subtracts the amount of your purchase from your bank account at the moment the purchase is made. (By contrast, when you use your credit card, the credit card company extends short-term financing, and you do not make payment until you receive your next statement.) Debit cards are used most commonly to obtain cash at ATMs and to purchase products and services from retailers.

> **debit card** a card that electronically subtracts the amount of your purchase from your bank account at the moment the purchase is made

INNOVATIVE BANKING SERVICES

Today, many individuals, financial managers, and business owners are finding it convenient to do their banking electronically. Let's begin by looking at how banking will change in the future.

Changes in the banking industry

While the experts may not be able to predict with 100 per cent accuracy the changes that will affect banking, they all agree that banking *will* change. The most obvious changes the experts do agree on are as follows:

- More emphasis on evaluating the credit-worthiness of loan applicants as a result of the recent economic crisis
- An increase in government regulation of the banking industry

Now you can bank with a click of a computer's mouse. With improved technology, bank customers can now deposit cheques without leaving their office or home, obtain current account balances, and pay bills online. In fact, many of the traditional banking services that used to require a trip to the bank can now be completed online. Why not take a look at your bank's Web site to see how online banking can help you manage your finances?

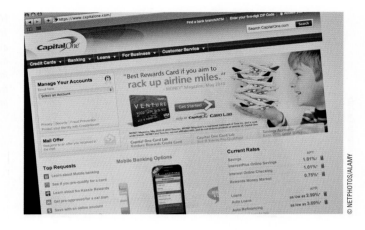

© NETPHOTOS/ALAMY

- A reduction in the number of banks, S&Ls, credit unions, and financial institutions because of consolidation and mergers
- Globalisation of the banking industry as the economies of individual nations become more interrelated
- The importance of customer service as a way to keep customers from switching to competitors
- Increased use of credit and debit cards and a decrease in the number of written cheques
- Continued growth in online and mobile banking

Online, mobile, and international banking

Online banking allows you to access your bank's computer system from home, the office, or even while you are travelling. For the customer, online banking offers a number of advantages, including the following:

- The ability to obtain current account balances
- The capability to deposit cheques without leaving your home or office

SUCCESS STORY

Vying to run your digital wallet

Cash isn't going away any time soon, but Google, PayPal, Visa, and other big companies are already competing to run the digital wallet that could replace your leather wallet in the future. The idea is to speed up transactions and make them as convenient as the one-click payments many online businesses accept. Instead of handing notes and coins to a cashier or waiting for change, you use your digital wallet (typically, your mobile phone) to transfer money electronically to the business you're buying

from. Your digital wallet might even alert you to special deals or earn you rewards for certain purchases.

The Google Wallet, for example, uses a wireless technology called near field communication to let your mobile phone app "talk" to a cash register and arrange payment (charged to your credit card or another card) with just a tap of the phone. Subway sandwich shops were among the first businesses to accept Google Wallet payments. PayPal's system, which works as an

app and online, has an interesting feature: After you pay, you have several days to decide where the money will come from—a store credit card or a bank debit card, for example. Billions of euros in cash transactions are going cashless every year. Is a digital wallet in your future?

References: Olga Kharif, "Google Said to Rethink Wallet Strategy," *Bloomberg,* March 21, 2012, www.bloomberg.com; Edward C. Baig, "Mobile Wallet Competition Heats Up," *USA Today,* February 28, 2012, www.usatoday.com; Deirdre van Dyk, "The End of Cash," *Time,* January 9, 2012, pp. 48–49.

- The convenience of transferring funds from one account to another
- The ability to pay bills
- The convenience of seeing which cheques have cleared
- Simplified loan application procedures

Online banking provides a number of advantages for the financial institution. Probably the most important advantage is the lower cost of processing large numbers of transactions. Lower costs often lead to larger profits. In addition to lower costs and increased profits, financial institutions believe that online banking offers increased security because fewer people handle fewer paper documents.

In addition to online banking, many banks now offer mobile banking via text message or apps (software applications) downloaded to mobile phones and other electronic devices. The goal is to let customers use technology to check account balances, transfer money, and track deposits at any time, from anywhere. This is especially convenient for busy businesspeople who don't live or work next door to a bank branch and can't always get to a computer to use online banking.

Electronic funds transfer (EFT)   An **electronic funds transfer (EFT) system** is a means of performing financial transactions through a computer terminal or telephone hookup. The following four EFT applications are changing how banks do business:

> **electronic funds transfer (EFT) system**   a means of performing financial transactions through a computer terminal or telephone hookup

1. *Automatic teller machines (ATMs).* An ATM or "cash machine" is an electronic bank cashier—a machine that provides almost any service a human cashier can provide. Once the customer is properly identified, the machine dispenses cash from the customer's current or savings account or makes a cash advance charged to a credit card. ATMs are located in the wall outside high street banks, supermarkets, pharmacies, and even petrol stations. Customers have access to them at all times of the day or night. There may be a fee for each transaction.
2. *Automated clearinghouse (ACH).* Designed to reduce the number of paper cheque, an automated clearinghouse processes state benefits, tax payments, recurring bill payments, payments for Internet sales, and employee salaries. For example, many large companies use the ACH network to transfer wages and salaries directly into their employees' bank accounts, thus eliminating the need to make out individual paychecks.
3. *Point-of-sale (POS) terminals.* A POS terminal is a computerised cash register located in a retail store and connected to a bank's computer. Assume you want to pay for purchases at a Carrefour Supermarket. You begin the process by pulling your credit or debit card through a magnetic card reader. A central processing centre notifies a computer at your bank that you want to make a purchase. The bank's computer immediately adds the amount to your account for a credit card transaction. In a similar process, the bank's computer deducts the amount of the purchase from your bank account if you use a debit card. Finally, the amount of your purchase is added to the retailer's account. The Carrefour store then is notified that the transaction is complete, and the cash register prints out your receipt.

Why is a French bank in the United States? Because it makes perfect business sense in a world where national boundaries blur and multinational firms operate in many different countries. Actually, the number of U.S. banks that operate overseas and the number of foreign banks that operate in the United States are both increasing. For banks, the world is becoming smaller and much more competitive.

4. *Electronic cheque conversion (ECC).* Electronic cheque conversion is a process used to convert information from a paper cheque into an electronic payment for merchandise, services, or bills. When you give your completed cheque to a cashier at a store, the cheque is processed through an electronic system that captures your banking information and the amount of the cheque. Once the cheque is processed, you are asked to sign a receipt, and you get a voided (cancelled) cheque back for your records. Finally, the funds to pay for your transaction are transferred into the store's account. ECC also can be used for cheques you mail to pay for a purchase or to pay on an account.

Bankers and business owners generally are pleased with online banking and EFT systems. Both online banking and EFT are fast, and they eliminate the costly processing of cheques. However, many customers are reluctant to use online banking or EFT systems. Some simply do not like "the technology," whereas others fear that the computer will garble their accounts.

International banking services For international businesses, banking services are extremely important. Depending on the needs of an international firm, a bank can help by providing a letter of credit or a banker's acceptance.

A **letter of credit** is a legal document issued by a bank or other financial institution guaranteeing to pay a seller a stated amount for a specified period of time—usually 30 to 60 days. With a letter of credit, certain conditions, such as delivery of the merchandise, may be specified before payment is made.

> **letter of credit** a legal document issued by a bank or other financial institution guaranteeing to pay a seller a stated amount for a specified period of time

A **banker's acceptance** is a written order for a bank to pay a third party a stated amount of money on a specific date. With a banker's acceptance, no conditions are specified. It is simply an order to pay guaranteed by a bank without any strings attached.

> **banker's acceptance** a written order for a bank to pay a third party a stated amount of money on a specific date

Both a letter of credit and a banker's acceptance are popular methods of paying for import and export transactions. For example, imagine that you are a business owner in the United Arab Emirates who wants to purchase some leather products from a small business in Florence, Italy. You offer to pay for the merchandise with your company's cheque drawn on a bank based in the U.A.E., but the Italian business owner is worried about payment. To solve the problem, your bank can issue either a letter of credit or a banker's acceptance to guarantee that payment will be made. In addition to a letter of credit and a banker's acceptance, banks also can use EFT technology to speed international banking transactions.

One other international banking service should be noted. Banks and other financial institutions provide for currency exchange. If a Spanish citizen places an order for merchandise valued at €50,000 from a company in Japan, how do they pay for the order? Do they use euros or Japanese yen? To solve this problem, they can use a bank's currency-exchange service. To make payment, they can use either currency. If necessary, the bank will exchange one currency for the other to complete the transaction.

EFFECTIVE CREDIT MANAGEMENT

One of the most important activities of any financial institution or business is making wise decisions regarding to whom it will extend credit. **Credit** is immediate purchasing power that is exchanged for a promise to repay borrowed money, with or without interest, at a later date. For example, suppose that you obtain a bank loan to buy a €150,000 home. You, as the borrower, obtain immediate purchasing power. In return, you agree to certain terms imposed by the lender. Generally, the lender requires that you make a down payment, make monthly payments, pay interest, and purchase insurance to protect your home until the loan is paid in full.

> **credit** immediate purchasing power that is exchanged for a promise to repay borrowed money, with or without interest, at a later date

Banks and other financial institutions lend money because they are in business for that purpose. The interest they charge is what provides their profit. Other businesses extend credit to their customers for at least three reasons.

Some customers simply cannot afford to pay the entire amount of their purchase immediately, but they *can* repay credit in a number of smaller payments stretched out over some period of time. Some firms are forced to sell goods or services on credit to compete effectively when other firms offer credit to their customers.

Finally, firms can realise a profit from interest charges that a borrower pays on some credit arrangements.

Getting money from a bank or lender after the economic crisis

While lenders need interest from loans to help pay their business expenses and earn a profit, they also want to make sure that the loans they make will be repaid. As a borrower, your job is to convince the lender that you are able and willing to repay the loan. After the recent economic crisis, bankers, lenders and suppliers, and credit card companies are much more careful when evaluating credit applications.

For individuals, the following suggestions may be helpful when applying for credit:

- Obtain a loan application and complete it at home. At home, you have the information needed to answer *all* the questions on the loan application.
- Be prepared to describe how you will use the money and how the loan will be repaid.
- For most loans, an interview with a loan officer is required. Here again, preparation is the key. Think about how you would respond to questions a loan officer might ask.
- If your loan request is rejected, try to analyse what went wrong. Ask the loan officer why you were rejected. If the rejection is based on incorrect information, supply the correct information and reapply.

© BLEND IMAGES/SHUTTERSTOCK

No one likes to pay more than they have to for anything. And yet, many consumers often pay more for loans than necessary. Factors that increase the amount of interest you pay for credit cards, an auto loan, or a home mortgage include how well you have paid your bills in the past, the amount of debt you currently have, and your credit score. It also helps to compare rates for different types of consumer credit. Even a one per cent lower interest rate for a home mortgage, for example, can save you thousands of dollars over the life of a home loan.

Business owners in need of financing may find the following additional tips helpful:

- It is usually best to develop a relationship with your banker before you need financing.
- Help the banker understand what your business is and how you may need future financing for expansion, cash-flow problems, or unexpected emergencies.
- Apply for a pre-approved line of credit or revolving credit agreement even if you do not need the money. View the application as another way to showcase your company and its products or services.
- In addition to the application, supply certified public accountant (CPA)-prepared financial statements and business tax returns for the last three years. If your business is small, you may want to supply your own personal financial statements and tax returns for the same period.
- Update your business plan in case the lender wants to review your plan. Be sure the sales estimates and other projections are realistic.
- Write a cover letter describing how much experience you have, whether you are operating in an expanding market, or any other information that would help convince the banker to provide financing.

RESPONSIBLE PRACTICE   Short-term loans – helping the needy or preying on the vulnerable?

Almost everyone has experienced it at some point in their lives: payday is still a week away but you've already spent all your money for this month. Do you dip into your savings (assuming you have some) which you promise yourself to repay later? Borrow some money from a friend or family member to tide you over the next few days? Ask your boss if they can give you a "sub", or advance, before pay day? Another option that people are increasingly turning to is the plethora of short-term, or "payday", loan services available. Various services offer cash to those in need, on a short-term basis, regardless of the borrower's personal financial status.

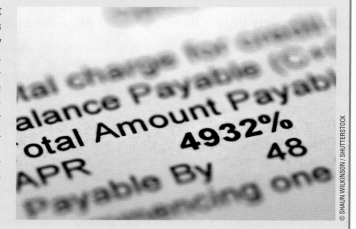

© SHAUN WILKINSON / SHUTTERSTOCK

For those who find themselves temporarily short of money, these lenders could be seen to be providing a very useful service. However, one could also argue that this is simply a "quick-fix", and using such services could encourage and even promote poor money management and spending beyond means. One service, Wonga, for example, notes prominently on its Web site that it can send "£400 within 5 minutes" of the loan being approved. Furthermore, the interest rates, whilst on a short term, are staggering, with representative 5853% APR on a typical loan. Meanwhile, missed payment fees of £30 are arguably disproportionate the amount of money originally lent.

Nevertheless, if a payday loan service is just relied upon on a one-off occasion and the loan is paid off promptly, then surely there's no problem? Not necessarily. Another potential longer-term issue is that payday loans can affect your credit rating. Even if the loan *has* been repaid promptly, the very fact that it was taken out in the first place is enough for some traditional lenders to refuse credit, on the basis that it suggests that the borrower is unable to manage their finances.

Wonga does pride itself on being upfront and transparent without hidden charges; it clearly displays information on responsible lending on its Web site, and has won awards for customer service. Whether justified or not, it certainly has a battle on its hands to tackle the negative press that such services receive.

References: www.wonga.com; www.moneysavingexpert.com; 'Wonga wrote to my son, 12, urging him to take a payday load', *The Telegraph*, November 16th, 2013

The five Cs of credit management

When a business extends credit to its customers, it must face the fact that some customers will be unable or unwilling to pay for their credit purchases. To help determine if an individual or business is a good credit risk, lenders often examine a business firm's financial statements. Individuals may be asked to complete a credit application. Most lenders will also consider the five Cs of credit, described in Table 17.1.

TABLE 17.1 **The five Cs of credit** *Lenders often use the five Cs of credit to determine which credit or loan requests will be approved and which will be rejected.*

Factor to consider	Description of why this factor is important
Character	The borrower's attitude toward credit obligations
Capacity	The financial ability to meet credit obligations—that is, to make regular loan payments.
Capital	The term *capital* as used here refers to the borrower's assets or the net worth of the individual or business applying for a loan.
Collateral	Real estate or property including stocks, bonds, equipment, or any other asset pledged as security for a loan.
Conditions	General economic conditions that can affect a borrower's ability to repay a loan or other credit obligation.

© Cengage Learning 2014

Checking credit information

The five Cs of credit are concerned mainly with information supplied by the applicant. But how can a lender determine whether this information is accurate? This depends on whether the potential borrower is a business or an individual consumer.

Credit information concerning businesses can be obtained from the following four sources:

- *Global credit-reporting agencies.* D&B (formerly Dun & Bradstreet) is the world's leading credit-reporting agency. Their reports present detailed credit information about specific companies.
- *Local credit-reporting agencies.* These agencies may require a monthly or yearly fee for providing information on a continual basis.
- *Industry associations.* These associations may charge a service fee.
- *Other firms.* This refers to other firms that have given the applicant credit.

A number of government regulations even the playing field between consumers and credit card companies and lenders.

THE MAIN DIFFERENCES BETWEEN ISLAMIC AND CONVENTIONAL BANKS

Throughout this chapter, we have focused exclusively on the "Western" banking system. This section looks specifically at Islamic banking, which is currently experiencing a growing international profile.

There are many similarities between Islamic and conventional banks. An Islamic bank is expected to perform the same activities as a conventional bank and carries out the role of a financial intermediary. Unlike conventional banks, Islamic banks are not allowed to borrow and lend funds based on interest. The assets of an Islamic bank include funds on a profit-and–loss sharing basis usually coming from equity financing, asset financing, and lease financing. On the liabilities side, Islamic banks mobilise funds on the basis of agency contract. It can accept current, saving and investment deposits which are treated again on the basis of profit and loss sharing. Table 17.2 summarises the main differences between Islamic and conventional banks.

TABLE 17.2 The main differences between Islamic and conventional banks

Criteria	Islamic banking system	Conventional banking system
Operations	Based on Shariah principal. For example, banks cannot finance a business that involves selling cigarettes or alcohol.	Based on secular principles. Banks may finance any legal activity.
Interest charging	Financing is not interest (*Riba*) oriented and should be based on risk-and-reward sharing.	Financing is interest oriented, both fixed and variable rates can be charged for the use of money.
Interest on deposits	Account holders do not receive interest (*Riba*) but may share risk and rewards of investments made by the Islamic bank.	Depositors receive interest and a guarantee of principal repayment
Risk sharing in equity financing	Islamic banks offer equity financing with risk sharing for a project.	Risk sharing is not offered.
Penalty on default	Islamic banks are not allowed to charge penalties. They may impose conditions and collateral to face late payment or fraud.	Conventional banks normally charge additional money (compound interest) in case of late payments or defaults.
Avoidance of Gharar	Transactions with elements of gambling or speculation are forbidden.	Speculative investments are allowed.
Customer relationships	The status of an Islamic bank in relation to its clients is that of partner and investor.	The status of a traditional bank in relation to its clients is one of creditor and debtor.
Shariah supervisory board	Each Islamic bank must have a supervisory board to ensure that all its business activities are in line with Shariah requirements.	Conventional banks have no such requirement but are beholden to their shareholders (which may, in some cases be a government).

SUMMARY

- Identify the functions and characteristics of money.

Money is anything a society uses to purchase products, services, or resources. Money must serve as a medium of exchange, a measure of value, and a store of value. To perform its functions effectively, money must be divisible into units of convenient size, light and sturdy enough to be carried and used on a daily basis, stable in value, and difficult to counterfeit. The M_1 supply of money is made up of coins and notes (currency) and deposits in current accounts (demand deposits). The M_2 supply includes M_1 plus savings accounts, certain money-market securities, and certificates of deposits.

- Describe the organisations involved in the banking industry.

Most everyone has been affected in one way or another by the nation's economic problems. To help resolve the major problems that led to the economic crisis, Congress passed and the president signed the Dodd–Frank Wall Street Reform and Consumer Protection Act that provides new protection for consumers and increased regulation of the financial industry.

A commercial bank is a profit-making organisation that accepts deposits, makes loans, and provides related services to customers. Commercial banks are chartered by the federal government or state governments. Savings and loan associations and credit unions offer the same basic services that commercial banks provide. Mutual savings banks, insurance companies, pension funds, brokerage firms, finance companies, and investment banking firms provide some limited banking services. A large number of people work in the banking industry because of the number of banks and other financial institutions.

- Identify the services provided by financial institutions.

Banks and other financial institutions offer today's customers a tempting array of services. Among the most important banking services for both individuals and businesses are current accounts, savings accounts, short- and long-term loans, and processing credit card and debit card transactions. Other traditional services include financial advice, payroll services, certified cheques, trust services, and safe-deposit boxes.

- Understand how financial institutions are changing to meet the needs of domestic and international customers.

  Competition among banks, brokerage firms, insurance companies, and other financial institutions has increased. The use of technology will also increase as financial institutions continue to offer online and mobile banking. Increased use of electronic funds transfer systems (automated teller machines, automated clearinghouses, point-of-sale terminals, and electronic cheque conversion) also will change the way people bank. For firms in the global marketplace, a bank can provide letters of credit and banker's acceptances that will reduce the risk of nonpayment for sellers. Banks and financial institutions also can provide currency exchange to reduce payment problems for import or export transactions.

- Discuss the importance of credit and credit management.

  Credit is immediate purchasing power that is exchanged for a promise to repay borrowed money, with or without interest, at a later date. Banks lend money because they are in business for that purpose. Businesses sell goods and services on credit because some customers cannot afford to pay cash and because they must keep pace with competitors who offer credit. Businesses also may realise a profit from interest charges.

  Decisions on whether to grant credit to businesses and individuals usually are based on the five Cs of credit: character, capacity, capital, collateral, and conditions. Credit information can be obtained from various credit-reporting agencies, credit bureaus, industry associations, and other firms. A number of government regulations even the playing field between consumers and credit card companies and lenders.

- Understand some of the main similarities and differences between Islamic and conventional banks.

  There are many similarities between Islamic and conventional banks. An Islamic bank is expected to perform the same activities as a conventional bank and carries out the role of a financial intermediary. However, there are some notable differences (discussed in Table 17.2). The Islamic banking system is governed by Shariah law.

EXERCISE QUESTIONS

1 What distinguishes money from other assets in the economy?

2 What are the three functions of money in the economy?

3 What are the main functions of a national Reserve Bank such as the South African Reserve Bank?

4 If the central bank wants to increase the money supply with outright open market operations, what does it do?

5 Why can't central banks control the money supply perfectly?

CASE 17.1

First direct's innovative banking channels

With our 1st Account you'll get £100 for switching and a £250 interest-free overdraft comes as standard. Discover how simple our Easyswitch team make moving your account and just how refreshing it is to talk to real people 24 7 365. We're sure you'll love us.

www1.firstdirect.com, June 2011

Most consumers have a bank cheque account from which cash is drawn, bills are paid and cheques written, and into which salaries, pensions or student loan cheques are paid. For many consumers, the bank is a high-street or shopping-centre office – imposing, formal and often intimidating. Whether it's NatWest, Barclays or Lloyds TSB in the U.K. or ABN AMRO or Rabobank in the Netherlands, each high-street bank is fairly alike, with similar products

and services, personnel, branch layouts, locations and opening hours.

Differentiation has been difficult to achieve and generally impossible to maintain over any length of time as competitors have copied rivals' moves. Promotional strategy and brand image have been the focus for most banking organisations, supported with more minor tactical changes in, for example, opening hours or service charges. For many bank account holders, however, the branch – with its restricted openings, formal ambience and congested town-centre location – is the only point of contact for the bulk of transactions.

First direct, owned by HSBC but managed separately, broke the mould in 1989. Launched with a then massive £6 million promotional campaign, first direct bypassed the traditional marketing channel. First direct has no branches and no branch overhead and operating costs. It provides free banking, unlike its high-street competitors with their systems of bank charges combined with interest paid on positive balances. First direct is a telephone and online banking service that offers full banking, mortgage, loan, investment/saving, insurance, foreign currency and credit card services, plus ATM 'hole in the wall' cash cards through HSBC's international service-till network. All normal banking transactions can be completed over the telephone or online.

Initial reactions were positive, with many non-HSBC account holders switching to the innovative new style of banking. The more traditional consumer – who equates the marbled halls of the Victorian branches with heritage, security and traditional values – has been less easily converted. For the targeted, more financially aware and independent income earner, first direct is proving very popular. Research shows that first direct is the most recommended bank with the most satisfied customers.

First direct's services and products are not new, but the chosen marketing channels are innovative: no branches, only telephone call centres, online banking and texting. Customers no longer have to reach inaccessible, parked-up, town-centre branches with queues and restricted opening hours. The company is fast to adopt evolving technologies and opportunities to interact with its customers digitally:

We're always trying to figure out new ways to make our customers' lives easier so as you'd expect, we're at the forefront of new technologies. We offer you Mobile Banking, Text Message Banking, award-winning online Podcasts and Vodcasts and on top of all that we create online spaces for you to communicate with us and other customers, inviting you to become part of our community and give voice to your thoughts. Check out Little Black Book, Talking Point and Social Media Newsroom.

www1.firstdirect.com, Jun 2011

First direct has introduced a service, alien to some more traditional tastes perhaps, that is more readily available and with fewer costs. Hundreds of thousands of consumers have welcomed the launch of this new option, but millions have preferred to bank the traditional way. For HSBC, this is fine: its HSBC proposition caters for those consumers preferring the more traditional banking format, while first direct caters for the new breed of telephone, online and texting customers.

References: www1.firstdirect.com, June 2011.

Questions

1 Why was first direct different from its rivals?

2 What gave it differentiation when it first launched?

3 Why might some potential customers of first direct have reservations about the innovative nature of the service?

CHAPTER REFERENCES

"The Economy: Crisis & Response," The Federal Reserve Board of San Francisco Web site at www.frsb.org, accessed April 1, 2012.

The Federal Reserve Board at www.federalreserve.gov, accessed March 30, 2012.

The Federal Trade Commission Web site at www.ftc.gov, accessed March 27, 2012.

The Investopedia.com Web site at www.investopedia.com, accessed March 30, 2012.

The Office of the Comptroller of the Currency Web site at www.occ.gov, accessed March 31, 2012.

"The Quarterly Banking Profile for December 31, 2011," The Federal Deposit Insurance Corporation Web site at www.fdic.gov, accessed March 31, 2012.

The United States Senate Committee on Banking, Housing, and Urban Affairs Web site at banking.senate.gov, accessed June 15, 2010.

U.S. Census Bureau, *Statistical Abstract of the United States*, 2012 (Washington, DC: U.S. Government Printing Office), table 1183.

"Wall Street Reform," the White House Web site at www.whitehouse.gov, accessed June 20, 2010.

18 FINANCIAL MANAGEMENT

LEARNING OBJECTIVES

Once you complete this chapter, you should be able to:

- Understand why financial management is important in today's uncertain economy
- Identify a firm's short- and long-term financial needs
- Summarise the process of planning for financial management
- Describe the advantages and disadvantages of different methods of short-term debt financing
- Evaluate the advantages and disadvantages of equity financing
- Evaluate the advantages and disadvantages of long-term debt financing

BUSINESS FOCUS

Woolworths

The ubiquitous and universally known high street chain Woolworths went into administration towards the end of 2008. Did it have a future as a going concern, or had the business deteriorated beyond the point of return? If it was finished as a business, there would be a large number of store closures and staff redundancies. Realistically the business had lost focus; it had an image problem and no positive unique qualities.

Various organisations asked for information but no serious buyer came forward and a closing down sale was introduced. The subsidiary business (Entertainment UK) which supplies music and DVDs to supermarkets and independent retailers) would also close down. Some of the retail units enjoy prime high street positions and were eventually likely to be taken up by various rivals and supermarket chains – but this would not save jobs in the short term.

Woolworths was introduced into the U.K. from America in 1909 when a store was opened in Liverpool. The stores sold a huge range of household goods at very affordable prices. The real growth came between the two world wars when Woolworths arrived in every town or city of any size.

Many older U.K. shoppers have very fond memories of Pick n Mix sweets, but that is only part of the story. The stores sold a huge and eclectic range – including toys, music, electrical goods, household items and some food products as well as sweets and chocolate. Recorded music was once a key product, with Woolworth being the leading music retailer in the U.K.

Traditionally the counters were piled high with an incredible array of goods to meet almost any need. But in retail it is critical to get the product range, the displays and the service "right". Woolworths didn't and arguably lost focus - thus opening itself to competition from chains such as Wilkinson and Toys R Us, let alone the supermarkets such as Asda and Tesco with their growing ranges of non-food items. Music sales were affected by Amazon and then downloading.

The company was probably too slow to engineer the changes it needed to make. For a lengthy period, and throughout the 1980s and 1990s, it had been part of the Kingfisher Group, which also incorporated Superdrug and B&Q DIY – but the group was split up, with Woolworth eventually being the main loser. It also had something of an image problem. To many it was always perceived to be relatively "downmarket" when compared to Marks & Spencer, for example. Whilst there might always have been a huge affection for Woolworths – in part this might be because it had always been there – this did not bring in high spending shoppers in sufficient numbers. In the end the company could not service its debts – "the charm of everything under one roof" had finally worn off.

Was the demise of Woolworths basically inevitable in a steep recession?

Unfortunately, as was the case with Woolworths in the U.K., many cash-strapped businesses struggled to find the funds they needed to operate during the recent economic crisis. In fact, the crisis was a wake-up call for most corporate executives, managers, and business owners because one factor became obvious. The ability to borrow money (debt capital) or obtain money from the owners of a business (equity capital) is necessary for the efficient operation of a business firm *and* the economic system.

In this chapter we examine why financial management is important in an uncertain economy. Then, we discuss how firms find the financing required to meet two needs of all business organisations: the need for money to start a business and keep it going, and the need to manage that money effectively. We also look at how firms develop financial plans and evaluate financial performance. Then we compare various methods of obtaining short-term and long-term financing.

WHY FINANCIAL MANAGEMENT?

Question: How important is financial management for a business firm?

To answer that question, consider the recent financial problems of the motorcar industry. Both General Motors and Chrysler filed for bankruptcy protection during the recent economic crisis, but Ford had the financial fuel to keep going, despite sagging sales and worldwide economic turmoil. Executives at Ford used aggressive financial planning to anticipate the automaker's need for financing. To avoid the same fate as General Motors and Chrysler—bankruptcy—Ford's financial managers borrowed money in anticipation of a downturn in the company's sales and profits. Ford also sold both stocks and bonds to raise the money it needed to keep the company operating during the crisis and even build for the future. Did that financial plan work? The answer: A definite yes! Today, Ford is selling more cars, developing environmentally friendly engines, creating concept cars for the future, and has returned to profitability. Although there are many factors that account for Ford's success, most experts agree that the firm's financial planning enabled it to weather the economic storm and build for the future.

Although most managers and employees have been affected by the economic crisis, the years since the end of 2007 have been especially difficult for financial managers. After all, they are the ones that must be able to raise the money needed to pay bills and expenses to keep a company's doors open. During the recent economic crisis, many financial managers and business owners found it was increasingly difficult to use many of the traditional sources of short- and long-term financing described later in this chapter. In some cases, banks stopped making loans even to companies that had always been able to borrow money. For example, both GE and AT&T—two corporations with a huge global presence—could not get the financing they needed.* Furthermore, the number of corporations selling stock for the first time to the general public decreased because investors were afraid to invest in new companies. The worst-case scenario: There was an increase in the number of businesses that filed for bankruptcy during the crisis. Fortunately, there were many more business firms that were able to weather the economic storm and keep operating because of their ability to manage their finances. And now that the world economy is improving, the number of bankruptcies is beginning to decline.

The need for financial management

Financial management consists of all the activities concerned with obtaining money and using it effectively. To some extent, financial management can be viewed as a two-sided problem. On one side, the uses of funds often dictate the type or types of financing needed by a business. On the other side, the activities a business can undertake are determined by the types of financing available. Financial managers must ensure that funds are available when needed, that they are obtained at the lowest possible cost, and that they are used as efficiently as possible. In addition, proper financial management must also ensure that:

 financial management all the activities concerned with obtaining money and using it effectively

- Financing priorities are established in line with organisational goals and objectives.
- Spending is planned and controlled.
- Sufficient financing is available when it is needed, both now and in the future.
- A firm's credit customers pay their bills on time, and the number of past due accounts is reduced.
- Bills are paid promptly to protect the firm's credit rating and its ability to borrow money.
- The funds required for paying the firm's taxes are available when needed to meet tax deadlines.
- Excess cash is invested in certificates of deposit (CDs), government securities, or conservative, marketable securities.

How do managers decide how much inventory is needed? One of the most perplexing problems financial managers must deal with is the amount of inventory a retail store needs. If a retailer has too much inventory, then too much money is tied up in merchandise that is not selling. If a retailer has too little inventory, it may not have enough merchandise to meet consumer demand.

© CHRIS HOWES/WILDPLACESPHOTOGRAPHY/ALAMY

Financial reform after the economic crisis

The job of financial managers became a bit easier as the economy stabilised. Still, it became apparent that something needed to be done to stabilise the financial system and prevent future economic meltdowns. In the wake of the crisis that affected both business firms and individuals across the globe, a cry for more regulations and reforms became a high priority. Hence governments around the world debated the need for greater checks and balances and in some cases enacted new laws in response to growing concerns over the continued stability of the economy, both at home and internationally. In the U.S., for example, President Obama signed the Dodd–Frank Wall Street Reform and Consumer Protection Act into law on July 21, 2010. Even with the new regulations, some experts say the law did not go far enough while others argue it went too far. Although the U.S. Senate and House of Representatives debate additional regulations, the goals are to hold Wall Street firms accountable for their actions, end taxpayer bailouts, tighten regulations for major financial firms, and increase government oversight. There has also been debate about limiting the amount of executive pay and bonuses, limiting the size of the largest financial firms, and curbing speculative investment techniques that were used by banks before the crisis.

New regulations aim to protect families from unfair, abusive financial and banking practices. For business firms, the impact of new regulations could increase the time and cost of obtaining both short- and long-term financing.

Careers in finance

After reading the material in the last section, you might be thinking why anyone would want a job in finance. And yet, a career in finance can be rewarding.

Today, there are many different types of positions in finance. At the executive level, most large business firms have a chief financial officer for financial management. A **chief financial officer (CFO)** is a high-level corporate executive who manages a firm's finances and reports directly to the company's chief executive officer or president. Some firms prefer to use the titles vice president of financial management, treasurer, or controller instead of the CFO title for executive-level positions in the finance area.

chief financial officer (CFO) a high-level corporate executive who manages a firm's finances and reports directly to the company's chief executive officer or president

Although some executives in finance do make €300,000 a year or more, many entry-level and lower-level positions that pay quite a bit less are available. Banks, insurance companies, and investment firms obviously have a need for workers who can manage and analyse financial data. So do businesses involved in manufacturing, services, and marketing. Colleges and universities, not-for-profit organisations, and government entities at all levels also need finance workers.

People in finance must have certain traits and skills. One of the most important priorities for someone interested in a finance career is honesty. Be warned: Investors, lenders, and other corporate executives expect financial managers to be above reproach. Moreover, government entities have enacted legislation to ensure that corporate financial statements reflect the "real" status of a firm's financial position. In addition to honesty, managers and employees in the finance area must:

1. Have a strong background in accounting or mathematics.
2. Know how to use a computer to analyse data.
3. Be an expert at both written and oral communication.

Typical job titles in finance include bank officer, consumer credit officer, financial analyst, financial planner, loan officer, insurance analyst, and investment account executive. Depending on qualifications, work experience, and education, starting salaries generally begin at €25,000 to €35,000 a year, but it is not uncommon for university graduates to earn higher salaries. In addition to salary, many employees have attractive benefits and other perks that make a career in financial management attractive.

THE NEED FOR FINANCING

Money is needed both to start a business and to keep it going. The original investment of the owners, along with money they may have borrowed, should be enough to open the doors. After that, ideally sales revenues should be used to pay the firm's expenses and provide a profit as well.

This is exactly what happens in a successful firm—over the long run. However, income and expenses may vary from month to month or from year to year. Temporary financing may be needed when expenses are high or sales are low. Then, too, situations such as the opportunity to purchase a new facility or expand an existing plant may require more money than is currently available within a firm.

Short-term financing

Short-term financing is money that will be used for one year or less. As illustrated in Table 18.1, there are many short-term financing needs, but three deserve special attention. First, certain business practices may affect a firm's cash flow and create a need for short-term financing. **Cash flow** is the movement of money into and out of an organisation. The goal is to have sufficient money coming into the firm in any period to cover the firm's expenses during that period. This goal, however, is not always achieved. For example, Callaway Golf offers credit to retailers and wholesalers that carry the firm's golf clubs, balls, clothing, and golf accessories. Credit purchases made by Callaway's retailers generally are not paid until 30 to 60 days (or more) after the transaction. Callaway therefore may need short-term financing to pay its bills until its customers have paid theirs.

TABLE 18.1 **Comparison of short- and long-term financing** *Whether a business seeks short- or long-term financing depends on what the money will be used for.*

Corporate cash needs

Short-term financing needs	Long-term financing needs
Cash-flow problems	Business start-up costs
Speculative production	Mergers and acquisitions
Current inventory needs	New product development
Monthly expenses	Long-term marketing activities
Short-term promotional needs	Replacement of equipment
Unexpected emergencies	Expansion of facilities

© Cengage Learning 2014

Business success often begins with a financial plan. *Before the merchandise in this IKEA warehouse can be sold, it must be purchased from manufacturers or suppliers and then stored until it is needed in the retailer's stores.* Successful *businesses often use sound financial planning built on the firm's goals and objectives, different types of budgets, and available sources of funds to make sure financing is available to purchase inventory and other necessities needed to operate a business.*

short-term financing money that will be used for one year or less
cash flow the movement of money into and out of an organisation

A second major need for short-term financing is speculative production. **Speculative production** refers to the time lag between the actual production of goods and when the goods are sold. Consider what happens when a firm such as Draper Tools begins to manufacture electric tools and small appliances for sale during the Christmas season. Manufacturing begins in February, March, and April, and the firm negotiates short-term financing to buy materials and supplies, to pay wages and rent, and to cover inventory costs until its products eventually are sold to wholesalers and retailers later in the year. Take a look at Figure 18.1. Although the tool manufacturer produces and sells finished products all during the year, expenses peak during the first part of the year. During this same period, sales revenues are low. Once the firm's finished products are shipped to retailers and wholesalers and payment is received (usually within 30 to 60 days), sales revenues are used to repay short-term financing.

speculative production the time lag between the actual production of goods and when the goods are sold

FIGURE 18.1

Cash flow for a manufacturing business *Manufacturers often use short-term financing to pay expenses during the production process. Once goods are shipped to retailers and wholesalers and payment is received, sales revenues are used to repay short-term financing.*

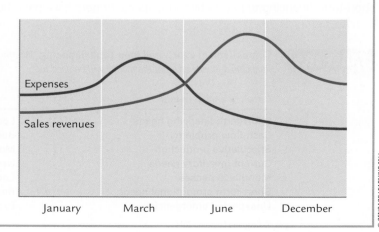

Expenses

Sales revenues

January   March   June   December

A third need for short-term financing is to increase inventory. Retailers that range in size from large international supermarket chains to the local pharmacy need short-term financing to build up their inventories before peak selling periods. For example, a garden centre must increase the number of shrubs, trees, and flowering plants that it makes available for sale during the spring and summer growing seasons. To obtain this merchandise inventory from growers or wholesalers, it may use short-term financing and then repay the loans when the merchandise is sold.

Long-term financing

Long-term financing is money that will be used for longer than one year. Long-term financing obviously is needed to start a new business. As Table 19.1 shows, it is also needed for business mergers and acquisitions, new product development, long-term marketing activities, replacement of equipment that has become obsolete, and expansion of facilities.

> **long-term financing** money that will be used for longer than one year

The amounts of long-term financing needed by large firms can seem almost unreal. The 3M Company—a large multinational corporation known for research and development—has invested more than €7 billion over the last five years to develop new products designed to make people's lives easier and safer.*

The risk–return ratio

According to financial experts, business firms will find it more difficult to raise both short- and long-term financing in the future for two reasons. First, financial reform and increased regulations will lengthen the process required to obtain financing. Second, both lenders and investors are more cautious about who receives financing. As a result of these two factors, financial managers must develop a strong financial plan that describes how the money will be used and how it will be repaid. When developing a financial plan for a business, a financial manager must also consider the risk–return ratio when making decisions that affect the firm's finances.

The **risk–return ratio** is based on the principle that a high-risk decision should generate higher financial returns for a business. On the other hand, more conservative decisions (with less risk) often generate lesser returns. Although financial managers want higher returns, they often must strive for

Take a moment to write down your short-term and long-term financing needs. Paying for college is a long-term need, for example, as is buying a home. What kinds of short-term financing needs do you have? What can you do to meet your short- and long-term needs in the coming months and years.

a balance between risk and return. For example, an energy company such as EDF Energy or BP may consider investing millions of euros to fund research into new solar technology that could enable the company to use the sun to generate electrical power. Yet, financial managers (along with other managers throughout the organisation) must determine the potential return before committing to such a costly research project.

> **risk–return ratio** a ratio based on the principle that a high-risk decision should generate higher financial returns for a business and more conservative decisions often generate lower returns

PLANNING—THE BASIS OF SOUND FINANCIAL MANAGEMENT

Earlier in the book, we defined a *plan* as an outline of the actions by which an organisation intends to accomplish its goals and objectives. A **financial plan**, then, is a plan for obtaining and using the money needed to implement an organisation's goals and objectives.

> **financial plan** a plan for obtaining and using the money needed to implement an organisation's goals and objectives

Developing the financial plan

Financial planning (like all planning) begins with establishing a set of valid goals and objectives. Financial managers must then determine how much money is needed to accomplish each goal and objective. Finally, financial managers must identify available sources of financing and decide which to use. The three steps involved in financial planning are illustrated in Figure 18.2.

Establishing organisational goals and objectives A *goal* is an end result that an organisation expects to achieve over a one- to ten-year period. An *objective* is a specific statement detailing what an organisation intends to accomplish over a shorter period of time. If goals and objectives

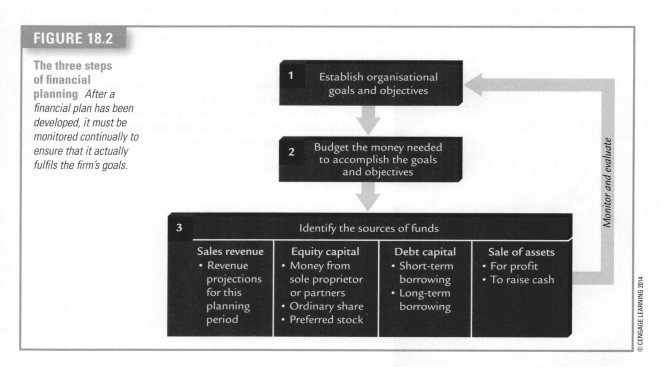

FIGURE 18.2

The three steps of financial planning *After a financial plan has been developed, it must be monitored continually to ensure that it actually fulfils the firm's goals.*

are not specific and measurable, they cannot be translated into costs, and financial planning cannot proceed. For large corporations, both goals and objectives can be expensive. For example, have you ever wondered how much McDonald's spends on advertising? Well, to reach the nearly 68 million customers it serves each day, the world's most famous fast-food restaurant chain spends over €685 million each year.*

Budgeting for financial needs Once planners know what the firm's goals and objectives are for a specific period—say, the next calendar year—they can construct a budget that projects the costs the firm will incur and the sales revenues it will receive. Specifically, a **budget** is a financial statement that projects income, expenditures, or both over a specified future period.

> **budget** a financial statement that projects income, expenditures, or both over a specified future period

Usually, the budgeting process begins with the construction of departmental budgets for sales and various types of expenses. Financial managers can easily combine each department's budget for sales and expenses into a company-wide cash budget. A **cash budget** estimates cash receipts and cash expenditures over a specified period. Notice in the cash budget for Holbein Clothing, shown in Figure 18.3, sales receipts and collections are listed at the top for each calendar quarter. Payments for purchases and routine expenses are listed in the middle section. Using this information, it is possible to calculate the anticipated cash gain or loss at the end of each quarter for this retail clothing store.

> **cash budget** a financial statement that estimates cash receipts and cash expenditures over a specified period

FIGURE 18.3   Cash budget for Holbein Clothing   *A company-wide cash budget projects sales, collections, purchases, and expenses over a specified period to anticipate cash surpluses and deficits.*

HOLBEIN CLOTHING
Cash Budget   From January 1, 2013 to December 31, 2013

	First Quarter (€)	Second Quarter (€)	Third Quarter (€)	Fourth Quarter (€)	Total (€)
Cash sales and collections	150,000	160,000	150,000	185,000	645,000
Less payments					
Purchases	110,000	80,000	90,000	60,000	340,000
Wages/salaries	25,000	20,000	25,000	30,000	100,000
Rent	10,000	10,000	12,000	12,000	44,000
Other expenses	4,000	4,000	5,000	6,000	19,000
Taxes	8,000	8,000	10,000	10,000	36,000
Total payments	157,000	122,000	142,000	118,000	539,000
Cash gain or (loss)	(7,000)	38,000	8,000	67,000	106,000

© CENGAGE LEARNING 2014

Most firms today use one of two approaches to budgeting. In the *traditional* approach, each new budget is based on the dollar amounts contained in the budget for the preceding year. These amounts are modified to reflect any revised goals, and managers are required to justify only new expenditures. The problem with this approach is that it leaves room for padding budget items to protect the (sometimes selfish) interests of the manager or his or her department. This problem is essentially eliminated through zero-base budgeting. **Zero-base budgeting** is a budgeting approach in which every expense in every budget must be justified.

> **zero-base budgeting** a budgeting approach in which every expense in every budget must be justified

To develop a plan for long-term financing needs, managers often construct a capital budget. A **capital budget** estimates a firm's expenditures for major assets, including new product development, expansion of facilities, replacement of obsolete equipment, and mergers and acquisitions.

> **capital budget** a financial statement that estimates a firm's expenditures for major assets and its long-term financing needs

Identifying sources of funds The four primary sources of funds, listed in Figure 18.2, are sales revenue, equity capital, debt capital, and proceeds from the sale of assets. Future sales revenue generally provides the greatest part of a firm's financing. Figure 18.3 shows that for Holbein Clothing, sales for the year are expected to cover all expenses and to provide a cash gain of €106,000. However, Holbein has a problem in the first quarter, when sales are expected to fall short of expenses by €7,000. In fact, one of the primary reasons for financial planning is to provide management with adequate lead time to solve this type of cash-flow problem.

A second type of funding is **equity capital.** For a sole proprietorship or partnership, equity capital is provided by the owner or owners of the business. For a corporation, equity capital is money obtained from the sale of shares of ownership in the business. Equity capital is used almost exclusively for long-term financing.

> **equity capital** money received from the owners or from the sale of shares of ownership in a business

A third type of funding is **debt capital**, which is borrowed money. Debt capital may be borrowed for either short- or long-term use—and a short-term loan seems made to order for Holbein Clothing's shortfall problem. The firm probably would borrow the needed €7,000 (or perhaps a bit more) at some point during the first quarter and repay it from second-quarter sales revenue.

> **debt capital** borrowed money obtained through loans of various types

Proceeds from the sale of assets are the fourth type of funding. Selling assets is a drastic step. However, it may be a reasonable last resort when sales revenues are declining and equity capital or debt capital cannot be found. Assets also may be sold to increase a firm's cash balance or when they are no longer needed or do not "fit" with the company's core business.

Monitoring and evaluating financial performance

It is important to ensure that financial plans are implemented properly and to catch potential problems before they become major ones. Despite efforts to raise additional financing, reduce expenses,

After 40 years, U.S. bookseller Borders closed all of its stores. The firm filed for bankruptcy in early 2011 and was forced to close a large number of stores in order to reorganise. Then in the summer of 2011, the bookseller was forced to liquidate its inventory and remaining stores despite revised financial plans, new financial goals, and its reorganisational efforts. Simply put: A buyer could not be found for the bankrupt firm.

and increase sales to become profitable, retail and online bookseller Borders filed for bankruptcy protection in 2011. Eventually, the firm was forced to liquidate its inventory and close all its stores because a buyer could not be found for the bankrupt firm.

To prevent such problems, financial managers should establish a means of monitoring financial performance. Interim budgets (weekly, monthly, or quarterly) may be prepared for comparison purposes. These comparisons point up areas that require additional or revised planning—or at least areas calling for a more careful investigation. Budget comparisons can also be used to improve the firm's future budgets.

SOURCES OF SHORT-TERM DEBT FINANCING

Typically, short-term debt financing is money that will be repaid in one year or less. During the economic crisis, many business firms found that it was much more difficult to borrow money for short periods of time to purchase inventory, buy supplies, pay salaries, and meet everyday expenses. Today the amount of available short-term financing has increased.

The decision to borrow money does not necessarily mean that a firm is in financial trouble. On the contrary, astute financial management often means regular, responsible borrowing of many different kinds to meet different needs. In this section, we examine the sources of *short-term debt financing* available to businesses. In the next two sections, we look at long-term financing options: equity capital and debt capital.

Sources of unsecured short-term financing

Short-term debt financing is usually easier to obtain than long-term debt financing for three reasons:

1. For the lender, the shorter repayment period means less risk of non-payment.
2. The unit amounts of short-term loans are usually smaller than those of long-term loans.
3. A close working relationship normally exists between the short-term borrower and the lender.

Most lenders do not require collateral for short-term financing. If they do, it is usually because they are concerned about the size of a particular loan, the borrowing firm's poor credit rating, or the general prospects of repayment.

Unsecured financing is financing that is not backed by collateral. A company seeking unsecured short-term financing has several options.

> **unsecured financing** financing that is not backed by collateral; unsecured short-term financing offers several options

Trade credit Manufacturers and wholesalers often provide financial aid to retailers by allowing them 30 to 60 days (or more) in which to pay for merchandise. This delayed payment, known as **trade credit**, is a type of short-term financing extended by a seller who does not require immediate payment after delivery of merchandise. It is the most popular form of short-term financing, because most manufacturers and wholesalers do not charge interest for trade credit. In fact, from 70 to 90 per cent of all transactions between businesses involve some trade credit.

> **trade credit** a type of short-term financing extended by a seller who does not require immediate payment after delivery of merchandise

Let us assume that Calais Budget Tyres receives a shipment of tyres from a manufacturer. Along with the merchandise, the manufacturer sends an invoice that states the terms of payment. Calais Budget Tyres now has two options for payment. First, the retailer may pay the invoice promptly and take advantage of any cash discount the manufacturer offers. Cash-discount terms are specified on

Entrepreneurs can always use more capital. *Even though Body Rest Mattress Company in St. Petersburg, Florida was successful, Carl and Emma Calhoun found that obtaining short-term financing was difficult during the economic crisis. Traditional sources of financing—banks and other financial institutions—tightened the requirements for obtaining unsecured loans or in many cases rejected loan requests.*

© BRIAN BLANCO MCT/MCT VIA GETTY IMAGES

the invoice. For instance, "2/10, net 30" means that the customer—Calais Budget Tyres—may take a "2" per cent discount if it pays the invoice within ten days of the invoice date. Let us assume that the euro amount of the invoice is €200,000. In this case, the cash discount is €4,000 (€200,000 × 0.02 = €4,000). If the cash discount is taken, Calais Budget Tyres only has to pay the manufacturer $196,000 (€200,000 − €4,000 = €196,000).

A second option is to wait until the end of the credit period before making payment. If payment is made between 11 and 30 days after the date of the invoice, Calais Budget Tyres must pay the entire amount. As long as payment is made before the end of the credit period, the retailer maintains the ability to purchase additional merchandise using the trade-credit arrangement.

Promissory notes issued to suppliers   A **promissory note** is a written pledge by a borrower to pay a certain sum of money to a creditor at a specified future date. Suppliers uneasy about extending trade credit may be less reluctant to offer credit to customers who sign promissory notes. Unlike trade credit, however, promissory notes usually require the borrower to pay interest. Although repayment periods may extend to one year, most short-term promissory notes are repaid in 60 to 180 days.

> **promissory note** a written pledge by a borrower to pay a certain sum of money to a creditor at a specified future date

A promissory note offers two important advantages to the firm extending the credit.

1. A promissory note is legally binding and an enforceable contract.
2. A promissory note is a negotiable instrument.

Because a promissory note is negotiable, the manufacturer, wholesaler, or company extending credit may be able to discount, or sell, the note to its own bank. If the note is discounted, the dollar amount received by the company extending credit is slightly less than the maturity value because the bank charges a fee for the service. The supplier recoups most of its money immediately, and the bank collects the maturity value when the note matures.

Unsecured bank loans   Banks and other financial institutions offer unsecured short-term loans to businesses at interest rates that vary with each borrower's credit rating. The **prime interest rate** is the lowest rate charged by a bank for a short-term loan. Organisations with good to high credit ratings may pay the prime rate plus "2" per cent. Firms with questionable credit ratings may have to pay the prime rate plus "4" per cent. (The fact that a banker charges a higher interest rate for a higher-risk loan is a practical application of the risk–return ratio discussed earlier in this chapter.) Of course, if the banker believes that loan repayment may be a problem, the borrower's loan application may well be rejected.

prime interest rate the lowest rate charged by a bank for a short-term loan

When a business obtains a short-term bank loan, interest rates and repayment terms may be negotiated. As a condition of the loan, a bank may require that a *compensating balance* be kept on deposit at the bank. Compensating balances, if required, are typically 10 to 20 per cent of the borrowed funds. The bank may also require that every commercial borrower *clean up* (pay off completely) its short-term loans at least once each year and not use it again for a period of 30 to 60 days.

Commercial paper Large firms with excellent credit reputations like Microsoft, Procter & Gamble, and Caterpillar can raise large sums of money quickly by issuing commercial paper. Commercial paper is a short-term promissory note issued by a large corporation. The maturity date for commercial paper is normally 270 days or less.

Commercial paper is secured only by the reputation of the issuing firm; no collateral is involved. The interest rate a corporation pays when it sells commercial paper is tied to its credit rating and its ability to repay the commercial paper. In most cases, corporations selling commercial paper pay interest rates slightly below the interest rates charged by banks for short-term loans. Thus, selling commercial paper is cheaper than getting short-term financing from a bank.

Although it is possible to purchase commercial paper in smaller denominations, larger amounts—€100,000 or more—are quite common. Money obtained by selling commercial paper is most often used to purchase inventory, finance a firm's accounts receivables, pay salaries and other necessary expenses, and solve cash-flow problems.

Sources of secured short-term financing

If a business cannot obtain enough money through unsecured financing, it must put up collateral to obtain additional short-term financing. Almost any asset can serve as collateral. However, *inventories* and *accounts receivable* are the assets most commonly pledged for short-term financing. Even when it is willing to pledge collateral to back up a loan, a firm that is financially weak may have difficulty obtaining short-term financing.

Loans secured by inventory Normally, manufacturers, wholesalers, and retailers have large amounts of money invested in finished goods. In addition, manufacturers carry raw materials and work-in-process inventories. All three types of inventory may be pledged as collateral for short-term loans. However, lenders prefer the much more salable finished merchandise to raw materials or work-in-process inventories.

A lender may insist that inventory used as collateral be stored in a public warehouse. In such a case, the receipt issued by the warehouse is retained by the lender. Without this receipt, the public warehouse will not release the merchandise. The lender releases the warehouse receipt—and the merchandise—to the borrower when the borrowed money is repaid. In addition to paying the interest on the loan, the borrower must pay for storage in the public warehouse. As a result, this type of loan is more expensive than an unsecured short-term loan.

Loans secured by receivables *Accounts receivable* are amounts owed to a firm by its customers. A firm can pledge its accounts receivable as collateral to obtain short-term financing. A lender may advance 70 to 80 per cent of the euro amount of the receivables. First, however, it conducts a thorough investigation to determine the *quality* of the receivables. (The quality of the receivables is the credit standing of the firm's customers, coupled with the customers' ability to repay their credit obligations when they are due.) If a favourable determination is made, the loan is approved. When the borrowing firm collects from a customer whose account has been pledged as collateral, generally it must turn the money over to the lender as partial repayment of the loan. An alternative approach is to notify the borrowing firm's credit customers to make their payments directly to the lender.

Factoring accounts receivable

Accounts receivable may be used in one other way to help raise short-term financing: They can be sold to a factoring company (or factor). A **factor** is a firm that specialises in buying other firms' accounts receivable. The factor buys the accounts receivable for less than their face value; however, it collects the full euro amount when each account is due. The factor's profit thus is the difference between the face value of the accounts receivable and the amount the factor has paid for them. Generally, the amount of profit the factor receives is based on the risk the factor assumes. Risk, in this case, is the probability that the accounts receivable will not be repaid when they mature. In the aftermath of the economic crisis and because of the reluctance of some banks to provide short-term financing, some large financial firms, including CIT Group and GE Capital, are providing additional factoring services to both old and new firms that sell their accounts receivables.*

> **factor** a firm that specialises in buying other firms' accounts receivable

Even though the firm selling its accounts receivable gets less than face value, it does receive needed cash immediately. Moreover, it has shifted both the task of collecting and the risk of non-payment to the factor, which now owns the accounts receivable. Generally, customers whose accounts receivable have been factored are given instructions to make their payments directly to the factor.

Cost comparisons

Table 18.2 compares the various types of short-term financing. As you can see, trade credit is the least expensive. Factoring of accounts receivable is typically the highest-cost method shown.

For many purposes, short-term financing suits a firm's needs perfectly. At other times, however, long-term financing may be more appropriate. In this case, a business may try to raise equity capital or long-term debt capital.

TABLE 18.2 Comparison of short-term financing methods

Type of financing	Cost	Repayment period	Businesses that may use it	Comments
Trade credit	Low, if any	30–60 days	All businesses with good credit	Usually no finance charge
Promissory note issued to suppliers	Moderate	One year or less	All businesses	Usually unsecured but requires legal document
Unsecured bank loan	Moderate	One year or less	All businesses	Promissory note is required and compensating balance may be required
Commercial paper	Moderate	270 days or less	Large corporations with high credit ratings	Available only to large firms
Secured loan	High	One year or less	Firms with questionable credit ratings	Inventory or accounts receivable often used as collateral
Factoring	High	None	Firms that have large numbers of credit customers	Accounts receivable sold to a factor

© Cengage Learning 2014

Just a piece of paper—or is it? In fact, a piece of paper can be worth a lot of money when it is a stock certificate. A corporation sells stock to raise needed financing for expansion and to pay for other long-term financial needs. On the other hand, investors purchase stock because they can profit from their investment if the price of the corporation's stock increases and a corporation pays dividends.

SOURCES OF EQUITY FINANCING

Sources of long-term financing vary with the size and type of business. As mentioned earlier, a sole proprietorship or partnership acquires equity capital (sometimes referred to as *owners' equity*) when the owner or partners invest money in the business. For corporations, equity-financing options include the sale of stock and the use of profits not distributed to owners. All three types of businesses can also obtain venture capital and use long-term debt capital (borrowed money) to meet their financial needs.

Selling stock

Some equity capital is used to start every business—sole proprietorship, partnership, or corporation. In the case of corporations, stockholders who buy shares in the company provide equity capital.

Initial public offering and the primary market An **initial public offering (IPO)** occurs when a corporation sells ordinary share to the general public for the first time. To raise money, the social networking site Groupon used a 2011 IPO to raise €700 million that it could use to fund expansion and other business activities.* In another 2011 IPO, LinkedIn—one of the world's largest social media companies—raised over €350 million.* In mid-2012, Facebook used an IPO to raise capital, and it was one of the largest IPOs in recent history. And at the time of the publication of your text, there are more social media and technology IPOs planned for 2012. Corporations in other industries also use IPOs to raise money. In fact, as illustrated in Figure 18.4, the largest IPOs—Visa, General Motors, AT&T Wireless, Kraft Foods, and United Parcel Service—for U.S. companies involve companies from a number of different industries.

> **initial public offering (IPO)** occurs when a corporation sells ordinary share to the general public for the first time

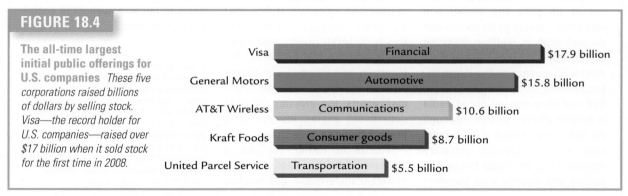

FIGURE 18.4

The all-time largest initial public offerings for U.S. companies *These five corporations raised billions of dollars by selling stock. Visa—the record holder for U.S. companies—raised over $17 billion when it sold stock for the first time in 2008.*

Visa — Financial	$17.9 billion
General Motors — Automotive	$15.8 billion
AT&T Wireless — Communications	$10.6 billion
Kraft Foods — Consumer goods	$8.7 billion
United Parcel Service — Transportation	$5.5 billion

Source: Renaissance Capital, Greenwich, CT (www.renaissancecapital.com), accessed February 28, 2012.

Established companies that plan to raise capital by selling subsidiaries to the public can also use IPOs. In addition to using an IPO to increase the cash balance for the parent company, corporations often sell shares in a subsidiary when shares can be sold at a profit or when the subsidiary no longer fits with its current business plan. Finally, some corporations will sell a subsidiary that is growing more slowly than the rest of the company's operating divisions.

When a corporation uses an IPO to raise capital, the stock is sold in the primary market. The **primary market** is a market in which an investor purchases financial securities (via an investment bank) directly from the issuer of the securities. An **investment banking firm** is an organisation that assists corporations in raising funds, usually by helping to sell new issues of stocks, bonds, or other financial securities.

> **primary market** a market in which an investor purchases financial securities (via an investment bank) directly from the issuer of those securities
>
> **investment banking firm** an organisation that assists corporations in raising funds, usually by helping to sell new issues of stocks, bonds, or other financial securities

Although a corporation can have only one IPO, it can sell additional stock after the IPO, assuming that there is a market for the company's stock. Even though the cost of selling stock (often referred to as *flotation costs*) is high, the *ongoing* costs associated with this type of equity financing are low for two reasons. First, the corporation does not have to repay money obtained from the sale of stock because the corporation is under no legal obligation to do so. If you purchase corporate stock and later decide to sell your stock, you may sell it to another investor—not the corporation.

A second advantage of selling stock is that a corporation is under no legal obligation to pay dividends to stockholders. A *dividend* is a distribution of earnings to the stockholders of a corporation. For any reason (e.g., if a company has a bad year), the board of directors can vote to omit dividend

SUCCESS STORY

Improving investor relations using social media

Tweeting about earnings? Increasingly, public corporations are communicating with their investors via Twitter, Facebook, YouTube, LinkedIn, and other social media. Companies still publish annual reports (in print and online) and hold annual meetings (in person and via webcast). In addition, because stockholders and potential investors want easy access to the latest financial news, companies like Alcoa, Dell, and eBay now use social media to provide official updates. Although the timing and content of these messages must comply with regulatory requirements, the ability to connect quickly and directly with investors

is vital at a time when rumours can fly around the world at the click of a mouse.

Alcoa, for example, uses its Facebook page to announce quarterly earnings figures and link to executive webcasts. It also uses its Twitter account to call attention to specific results and invite comments from its followers. For investors who want to dig deeper into quarterly or annual financial reports, the investor relations department shares its electronic presentations on SlideShare.

Thanks to Twitter, YouTube, a dedicated investor relations blog, and other social media, Dell reaches

more than five million people when it presents its quarterly financial results. And the online auction site eBay live-tweets earnings results as the CEO announces them. Watch for corporate investor relations departments to become even more social in the years ahead.

References: Rachel Koning Beals, "Investors Increasingly Tap Social Media for Stock Tips," *U.S. News & World Report*, January 31, 2012, http://money.usnews.com/money; Dominic Jones, "Social Media Investor Relations Reaches Tipping Point," *IR Web Report*, April 14, 2011, http://irwebreport.com; Dave Hogan, "Investor Relations and Social Media: Together at Last," *PR News Online*, May 9, 2011, www.prnewsonline.com; Jennifer Van Grove, "Investor Relations Tool Helps Fortune 500 Companies Get Social," *Mashable*, June 8, 2011, www.mashable.com.

payments. Earnings then are retained for use in funding business operations. Of course, corporate management may hear from unhappy stockholders if expected dividends are omitted too frequently.

The secondary market   Although a share of corporate stock is only sold one time in the primary market, the stock can be sold again and again in the secondary market. The **secondary market** is a market for existing financial securities that are traded between investors. Although a corporation does not receive money each time its stock is bought or sold in the secondary market, the ability to obtain cash by selling stock investments is one reason why investors purchase corporate stock. Without the secondary market, investors would not purchase stock in the primary market because there would be no way to sell shares to other investors. Usually, secondary-market transactions are completed through a securities exchange or the over-the-counter (OTC) market.

 secondary market a market for existing financial securities that are traded between investors

A **securities exchange** is a marketplace where member brokers meet to buy and sell securities. Generally, securities issued by larger corporations are traded at the Stock Exchange, or at regional exchanges, depending on the country in question. The securities of very large corporations may be traded at more than one of these exchanges. Securities of firms also may be listed on foreign securities exchanges—in Tokyo or Frankfurt, for example.

 securities exchange a marketplace where member brokers meet to buy and sell securities

Stocks issued by several thousand companies are traded in the OTC market. The **over-the-counter (OTC) market** is a network of dealers who buy and sell the stocks of corporations that are not listed on a securities exchange. The term *over-the-counter* was coined more than 100 years ago when securities actually were sold "over the counter" in stores and banks. Most OTC securities today are traded through an *electronic* exchange such as the Nasdaq (pronounced "nazzdack"). The term Nasdaq stands for National Association of Securities Dealers Automated Quotations. The Nasdaq is now one of the largest securities markets in the world. Today, the Nasdaq is known for its forward-looking, innovative, growth companies, including Intel, Microsoft, Cisco Systems, and Dell Computer.

 over-the-counter (OTC) market a network of dealers who buy and sell the stocks of corporations that are not listed on a securities exchange

There are two types of stock: common and preferred. Each type has advantages and drawbacks as a means of long-term financing.

Ordinary share   A share of **ordinary share** represents the most basic form of corporate ownership. In return for the financing provided by selling ordinary share, management must make certain concessions to stockholders that may restrict or change corporate policies. Every corporation must hold an annual meeting, at which the holders of ordinary share may vote for the board of directors. Often, stockholders are also asked to approve or disapprove of major corporate actions by voting on the following:

 ordinary share stock whose owners may vote on corporate matters but whose claims on profits and assets are subordinate to the claims of others

1. Amendments to the corporate charter or corporate by-laws
2. Sale of certain assets

3. Mergers and acquisitions
4. New issues of preferred stock or bonds
5. Changes in the amount of ordinary share issued

Few investors will buy ordinary share unless they believe that their investment will increase in value.

Preferred stock   The owners of **preferred stock** must receive their dividends before holders of ordinary share receive theirs. Also, preferred stockholders know the unit amount of their dividend because it is stated on the stock certificate. When compared to ordinary shareholders, preferred stockholders also have first claim (after creditors) on assets if the corporation is dissolved or declares bankruptcy. Even so, as with ordinary share, the board of directors must approve dividends on preferred stock, and this type of financing does not represent a debt that must be legally repaid. In return for preferential treatment, preferred stockholders generally give up the right to vote at a corporation's annual meeting.

> **preferred stock**   stock whose owners usually do not have voting rights but whose claims on dividends and assets are paid before those of ordinary share owners

Although a corporation usually issues only one type of ordinary share, it may issue many types of preferred stock with varying dividends or dividend rates.

RESPONSIBLE PRACTICE   Improving the image of the financial sector

Earlier in the book we addressed the issue of irresponsible investing and the need for checks and balances to deter unsavoury practices. It is fair to say that in recent years, as a result of the global economic downturn, the banking and financial sectors have received an extremely bad press.

Bankers and those working "in the city" have often been demonised in media coverage, frequently parodied by comedians and political commentators, and – in more extreme examples – depicted as greedy, arrogant, overly-powerful, out of touch with their stakeholders, and reckless with other people's money. Detractors were also angered by huge bonuses received by many.

But is this view too simplistic? Apologists might argue that bankers and investors need to have a certain degree of autonomy to operate efficiently and that it is in the best interest of all parties for banks to enjoy prosperity.

Whether justified or not, this protracted criticism has necessitated some damage limitation and bridge building to restore faith and trust in the industry in wider public perception, not only in terms of greater transparency and regulation.

Indeed many organisations in the sector – both high street and investment firms – have recognised the need to go one step further, through actively portraying an approachable, friendly, and even "cuddly" image in corporate messages and advertising campaigns.

In 2010, the Business Finance Taskforce was set up in the U.K., with the full participation of leading high street banks including Barclays, HSBC, Lloyds and Santander, specifically aimed at rebuilding relations with small businesses and aiding regrowth in the public sector.

More recently, a new U.K. high street bank, Metro Bank, has arrived, proffering to "revolutionise" banking. The CEO has promised "a focus on service" and "the end of stupid bank rules".

Meanwhile, a 2012 report published by the Boston Consulting Group highlighted the "tall challenge" to both "improve profits and polish image" of investment banking.

Mutual trust does seem to be gradually returning, but time will tell if this represents a permanent transformation of the financial sector's image.

References: S. Thewlis, 'Is Metro Bank the new, friendly face of banking?', http://www.bitterwallet.com/is-metro-bank-the-new-friendly-face-of-banking/67041 (accessed November 19th, 2013); The Boston Consulting Group, http://www.bcg.com/media/PressReleaseDetails.aspx?id=tcm:12-104472 (accessed November 19th, 2013).

Retained earnings

Most large corporations distribute only a portion of their after-tax earnings to stockholders. The portion of a corporation's profits *not* distributed to stockholders is called **retained earnings.** Because they are undistributed profits, retained earnings are considered a form of equity financing.

 retained earnings the portion of a corporation's profits not distributed to stockholders

The amount of retained earnings in any year is determined by corporate management and approved by the board of directors. Most small and growing corporations pay no cash dividend—or a very small dividend—to their stockholders. All or most earnings are reinvested in the business for research and development, expansion, or the funding of major projects. Reinvestment tends to increase the value of the firm's stock while it provides essentially cost-free financing for the business. More mature corporations may distribute 40 to 60 per cent of their after-tax profits as dividends. Utility companies and other corporations with very stable earnings often pay out as much as 80 to 90 per cent of what they earn. For a large corporation, retained earnings can amount to a hefty bit of financing.

Venture capital and private placements

To establish a new business or expand an existing one, an entrepreneur may try to obtain venture capital. *Venture capital* is money invested in firms, often small and sometimes struggling, that have the potential to become very successful. Most venture capital firms do not invest in the typical small business—a neighbourhood convenience store or a local dry cleaner—but in firms that have the potential to become extremely profitable. Today, most venture capital firms are investing in companies that build the nation's infrastructure, develop computer software, or provide consumer information or social media services.

Generally, a venture capital firm consists of a pool of investors, a partnership established by a wealthy family, or a joint venture formed by corporations with money to invest. In return for financing, these investors generally receive an equity or ownership position in the business and share in its profits. Venture capital firms vary in size and scope of interest. Some offer financing for start-up businesses, whereas others finance only established businesses. Although venture capital firms are willing to take chances, they have also been more selective about where they invest their money after the recent economic crisis.

Another method of raising capital is through a private placement. A **private placement** occurs when stock and other corporate securities are sold directly to insurance companies, pension funds, or large institutional investors. When compared with selling stocks and other corporate securities to the public, there are often fewer government regulations and the cost is generally less when the securities are sold through a private placement. Typically, terms between the buyer and seller are negotiated when a private placement is used to raise capital.

 private placement occurs when stock and other corporate securities are sold directly to insurance companies, pension funds, or large institutional investors

SOURCES OF LONG-TERM DEBT FINANCING

As pointed out earlier in this chapter, businesses borrow money on a short-term basis for many valid reasons other than desperation. There are equally valid reasons for long-term borrowing. In addition to using borrowed money to meet the long-term needs listed in Table 18.1, successful businesses often use the financial gearing it creates to improve their financial performance. **Financial gearing** is the use of borrowed funds to increase the return on owners' equity. The principle of financial gearing works as long as a firm's earnings are larger than the interest charged for the borrowed money.

> **financial gearing** the use of borrowed funds to increase the return on owners' equity

To understand how financial gearing can increase a firm's return on owners' equity, study the information for Berlin-based Klaus Plastics presented in Table 18.3. Hans Klaus, the owner of the firm, is trying to decide how best to finance a €100,000 purchase of new high-tech manufacturing equipment.

- He could borrow the money and pay 7 per cent annual interest.
- He could invest an additional €100,000 in the firm.

TABLE 18.3 Analysis of the effect of additional capital from debt or equity for Klaus Plastics, Inc.

Additional debt		Additional equity	
Owners' equity	€ 500,000	Owners' equity	€ 500,000
Additional equity	+ 0	Additional equity	+ 100,000
Total owner's equity	€ 500,000	Total owner's equity	€ 600,000
Loan (@ 7%)	+ 100,000	No loan	+ 0
Total capital	€ 600,000	Total capital	€ 600,000
		Year-end earnings	
Gross profit	€95,000	Gross profit	€ 95,000
Less loan interest	– 7,000	No interest	– 0
Operating profit	€88,000	Operating profit	€ 95,000
Return on owners' equity	17.6%	Return on owners' equity	15.8%
(€88,000 ÷ €500,000 = 17.6%)		(€95,000 ÷ €600,000 = 15.8%)	

© Cengage Learning 2014

Assuming that the firm earns €95,000 a year and that annual interest for this loan totals €7,000 (€100,000 × 0.07 = €7,000), the return on owners' equity for Klaus Plastics would be higher if the firm borrowed the additional financing. Return on owners' equity is determined by dividing a firm's net income by the euro amount of owners' equity. Based on the calculations illustrated in Table 18.3, Klaus Plastics' return on owners' equity equals 17.6 per cent if Hans borrows the additional €100,000. The firm's return on owners' equity would decrease to 15.8 per cent if Hans invests an additional €100,000 in the business.

The most obvious danger when using financial gearing is that the firm's earnings may be lower than expected. If this situation occurs, the fixed interest charge actually works to reduce or eliminate the return on owners' equity. Of course, borrowed money eventually must be repaid.

For a small business, long-term debt financing is generally limited to loans. Large corporations have the additional option of issuing corporate bonds.

Long-term loans

Many businesses satisfy their long-term financing needs with loans from commercial banks, insurance companies, pension funds, and other financial institutions. Manufacturers and suppliers of heavy machinery may also provide long-term debt financing by granting credit to their customers.

Term-loan agreements A **term-loan agreement** is a promissory note that requires a borrower to repay a loan in monthly, quarterly, semiannual, or annual instalments. Although repayment may be as long as 15 to 20 years, long-term business loans normally are repaid in 3 to 7 years.

> **term-loan agreement** a promissory note that requires a borrower to repay a loan in monthly, quarterly, semiannual, or annual instalment

Assume that Hans Klaus, the owner of Klaus Plastics, decides to borrow €100,000 and take advantage of the principle of financial gearing illustrated in Table 18.3. Although the firm's return on owners' equity does increase, interest must be paid each year and, eventually, the loan must be repaid. To pay off a €100,000 loan over a three-year period with annual payments, Klaus Plastics must pay €33,333 on the loan balance plus €7,000 annual interest, or a total of €40,333 the first year. Although the amount of interest decreases each year because of the previous year's payment on the loan balance, annual payments of this amount are still a large commitment for a small firm such as Klaus Plastics.

The interest rate and repayment terms for term loans often are based on factors such as the reasons for borrowing, the borrowing firm's credit rating, and the value of collateral. Although long-term loans occasionally may be unsecured, the lender usually requires some type of collateral. Acceptable collateral includes land and property, stocks, bonds, equipment, or any asset with value. Lenders may also require that borrowers maintain a minimum amount of working capital.

The basics of getting a loan   According to many financial experts, preparation is the key when applying for a long-term business loan. In reality, preparation begins before you ever apply for the loan. To begin the process, you should get to know potential lenders before requesting debt financing. Although there may be many potential lenders that can provide the money you need, the logical place to borrow money is where your business does its banking. This fact underscores the importance of maintaining adequate balances in the firm's bank accounts. Before applying for a loan, you may also want to check your firm's credit rating.

Typically, business owners will be asked to fill out a loan application. In addition to the loan application, the lender will also want to see your current business plan. Be sure to explain what your business is, how much funding you require to accomplish your goals, and how the loan will be repaid. Most lenders insist that you submit current financial statements that have been prepared by an independent certified public accountant. Then compile a list of references that includes your suppliers, other lenders, or the professionals with whom you are associated. You may also be asked to discuss the loan request with a loan officer. Hopefully, your loan request will be approved. If not, try to determine why your loan request was rejected. Think back over the loan process and determine what you could do to improve your chances of getting a loan the next time you apply.

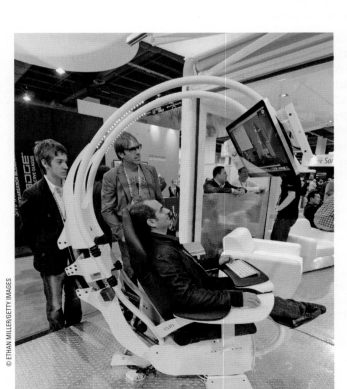

© ETHAN MILLER/GETTY IMAGES

The office of the future. While this product may look like something that should be on the next spaceship to the moon, it is a state-of-the-art office chair designed for people who spend long hours in front of computer monitors. The chair was created by Modern Work Environment (MWE) Lab. Companies that develop innovative products like this one need financing, and they generally have two choices. They can obtain financing from owners and investors or they can borrow money.

As CFO of your life, you should put your financial house in order before you apply for any loan. Be sure to check your credit report in advance to see how it looks, and think about how you'll repay the loan. Apply only when you know your finances are ready for the spotlight.

Corporate bonds

In addition to loans, large corporations may choose to issue bonds in denominations of €1,000 to €50,000. Although the usual face value for corporate bonds is €1,000, the total face value of all the bonds in an issue usually amounts to millions of euros. In fact, one of the reasons why corporations sell bonds is so that they can borrow a lot of money from a lot of different bondholders and raise larger amounts of money than could be borrowed from one lender. A **corporate bond** is a corporation's written pledge that it will repay a specified amount of money with interest. Interest rates for corporate bonds vary with the financial health of the company issuing the bond. Specific factors that increase or decrease the interest rate that a corporation must pay when it issues bonds include

> **corporate bond** a corporation's written pledge that it will repay a specified amount of money with interest

- The corporation's ability to pay interest each year until maturity.
- The corporation's ability to repay the bond at maturity.

For bond investors, the interest rate on corporate bonds is an example of the risk–return ratio discussed earlier in this chapter. Simply put: Investors expect more interest if there is more risk with more speculative bond issues—see Figure 18.5.

The **maturity date** is the date on which the corporation is to repay the borrowed money. Today, most corporate bonds are registered bonds. A **registered bond** is a bond registered in the owner's name by the issuing company. Many corporations do not issue actual bonds. Instead, the bonds are recorded electronically, and the specific details regarding the bond issue, along with the current owner's name and address, are maintained by computer. Computer entries are safer because they cannot be stolen, misplaced, or destroyed, and make it easier to transfer when a bond is sold.

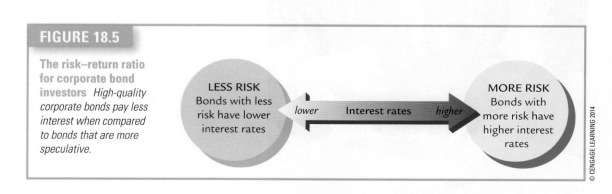

FIGURE 18.5

The risk–return ratio for corporate bond investors *High-quality corporate bonds pay less interest when compared to bonds that are more speculative.*

LESS RISK Bonds with less risk have lower interest rates

lower Interest rates *higher*

MORE RISK Bonds with more risk have higher interest rates

> **maturity date** the date on which a corporation is to repay borrowed money
> **registered bond** a bond registered in the owner's name by the issuing company

Until a bond's maturity, a corporation pays interest to the bond owner at the stated rate. On the maturity date, a registered owner will receive cash equaling the face value of the bond.

Types of bonds Corporate bonds are generally classified as debentures, mortgage bonds, or convertible bonds. Most corporate bonds are debenture bonds. A **debenture bond** is a bond backed only by the reputation of the issuing corporation. To make its bonds more appealing to investors, a corporation may issue mortgage bonds. A **mortgage bond** is a corporate bond secured by various assets of the issuing firm. Typical corporate assets that are used as collateral for a mortgage bond include real estate, machinery, and equipment that is not pledged as collateral for other debt obligations. The corporation can also issue convertible bonds. A **convertible bond** can be exchanged, at the owner's option, for a specified number of shares of the corporation's ordinary share. An Advanced Micro Devices (AMD) bond that matures in 2015 is convertible: Each bond can be converted to 35.6125 shares of AMD ordinary share.* A corporation can gain in three ways by issuing convertible bonds. First, convertibles usually carry a lower interest rate than nonconvertible bonds. Second, the conversion feature attracts investors who are interested in the speculative gain that conversion to ordinary share may provide. Third, if the bondholder converts to ordinary share, the corporation no longer has to redeem the bond at maturity.

> **debenture bond** a bond backed only by the reputation of the issuing corporation
> **mortgage bond** a corporate bond secured by various assets of the issuing firm
> **convertible bond** a bond that can be exchanged, at the owner's option, for a specified number of shares of the corporation's ordinary share

Repayment provisions for corporate bonds Maturity dates for bonds generally range from 10 to 30 years after the date of issue. Some bonds are callable before the maturity date; that is, a corporation can buy back, or redeem, them. For these bonds, the corporation may pay the bond owner a call premium. The amount of the call premium, if any, is specified, along with other provisions, in the bond indenture. The **bond indenture** is a legal document that details all the conditions relating to a bond issue.

> **bond indenture** a legal document that details all the conditions relating to a bond issue

Before deciding if bonds are the best way to obtain corporate financing, managers must determine if the company can afford to pay the interest on the corporate bonds. It should be obvious that the larger the bond issue, the higher the euro amount of interest that must be paid each year. For example, assume that a firm issues bonds with a face value of €100 million. If the interest rate is 4.875 per cent, the interest on this bond issue is €4,875,000 (€100 million × 0.04875 = €4,875,000) each year until the bonds are repaid. In addition, the firm's corporate bonds must all be redeemed for their face value (€100 million) at maturity. If the corporation defaults on (does not pay) either interest payments or repayment of the bond at maturity, owners of bonds can force the firm into bankruptcy and their claims take precedence over the claims of both common and preferred stockholders.

A corporation may use one of three methods to ensure that it has sufficient funds available to redeem a bond issue. First, it can issue the bonds as **serial bonds**, which are bonds of a single issue that mature on different dates. For example, a company may use a 25-year €50 million bond issue to finance its expansion. None of the bonds mature during the first 15 years. Thereafter, 10 per cent of the bonds mature each year until all the bonds are retired at the end of the 25th year. Second, the corporation can establish a sinking fund. A **sinking fund** is a sum of money to which deposits are made each year for the purpose of redeeming a bond issue. Third, a corporation can pay off an old bond issue by selling new bonds. Although this may appear to perpetuate the corporation's long-term debt, a number of utility companies use this repayment method.

> **serial bonds** bonds of a single issue that mature on different dates
> **sinking fund** a sum of money to which deposits are made each year for the purpose of redeeming a bond issue

A corporation that issues bonds must also appoint a **trustee**, an individual or an independent firm that acts as the bond owner's representative. A trustee's duties are handled most often by a commercial bank or other large financial institution. The corporation must report to the trustee periodically regarding its ability to make interest payments and eventually redeem the bonds. In turn, the trustee transmits this information to the bond owners, along with its own evaluation of the corporation's ability to pay.

> **trustee** an individual or an independent firm that acts as a bond owner's representative

Cost comparisons

Table 18.4 compares some of the methods that can be used to obtain long-term equity *and* debt financing. Although the initial flotation cost of issuing stock is high, selling ordinary share is generally a popular option for most financial managers. Once the stock is sold and upfront costs are paid, the *ongoing* costs of using stock to finance a business are low. The type of long-term financing that generally has the highest *ongoing* costs is a long-term loan (debt).

To a great extent, firms are financed through the investments of individuals—money that people have deposited in banks or have used to purchase stocks, mutual funds, and bonds.

TABLE 18.4   **Comparison of long-term financing methods**

Type of financing	Repayment	Repayment period	Cost/Dividends interest	Businesses that may use it
Equity				
Ordinary share	No	None	High initial cost; low ongoing costs because dividends not required	All corporations that sell stock to investors
Preferred stock	No	None	Dividends not required but must be paid before ordinary shareholders receive any dividends	Large corporations that have an established investor base of ordinary shareholders
Debt				
Long-term loan	Yes	Usually 3–7 years	Interest rates between 3.25 and 12 per cent depending on economic conditions and the financial stability of the company requesting the loan	All firms that can meet the lender's repayment and collateral requirements
Corporate bond	Yes	Usually 10–30 years	Interest rates between 3 and 9 per cent depending on the financial stability of the company issuing the bonds and economic conditions	Large corporations that are financially healthy

SUMMARY

- Understand why financial management is important in today's uncertain economy.

The last few years have been especially difficult for financial managers. Financial managers have had to deal with a downturn in sales and profits. In some cases, banks stopped making loans even to companies that had always been able to borrow money. And the number of companies selling stock for the first time to the general public decreased. The worst-case scenario: There was an increase in the number of businesses that filed for bankruptcy during the crisis. Fortunately, there were many more business firms that were able to weather the economic storm and keep operating because of their ability to manage their finances.

Financial management consists of all activities concerned with obtaining money and using it effectively. Financial management can be viewed as a two-sided problem. On one side, the uses of funds often dictate the type or types of financing needed by a business. On the other side, the activities a business can undertake are determined by the types of financing available. Financial managers must ensure that funds are available when needed, that they are obtained at the lowest possible cost, and that they are used as efficiently as possible. In the wake of the economic crisis, governments enacted new laws to increase the level of checks and balances. And today, there is an ongoing debate if more regulations are needed. Still, there are a number of rewarding jobs in finance for qualified job applicants.

- Identify a firm's short- and long-term financial needs.

Short-term financing is money that will be used for one year or less. There are many short-term needs, but cash flow, speculative production, and inventory are three for which financing is often required. Long-term financing is money that will be used for more than one year. Such financing may be required for a business start-up, for a merger or an acquisition, for new product development, for long-term marketing activities, for replacement of equipment, or for expansion of facilities. According to financial experts, business firms will find it more difficult to raise both short- and long-term financing in the future because of increased regulations and more cautious lenders. Financial managers must also consider the risk–return ratio when making financial decisions. The risk–return ratio is based on the principle that a high-risk decision should generate higher financial returns for a business. On the other hand, more conservative decisions generate lesser returns.

- Summarise the process of planning for financial management.

A financial plan begins with an organisation's goals and objectives. Next, a firm's goals and objectives are "translated" into departmental budgets that detail expected income and expenses. From these budgets, which may be combined into an overall cash budget, the financial manager determines what funding will be needed and where it may be obtained. Whereas departmental and cash budgets emphasise short-term financing needs, a capital budget can be used to estimate a firm's expenditures for major assets and its long-term financing needs. The four principal sources of financing are sales revenues, equity capital, debt capital, and proceeds from the sale of assets. Once the needed funds have been obtained, the financial manager is responsible for monitoring and evaluating the firm's financial activities.

- Describe the advantages and disadvantages of different methods of short-term debt financing.

Most short-term financing is unsecured; that is, no collateral is required. Sources of unsecured short-term financing include trade credit, promissory notes issued to suppliers, unsecured bank loans, and commercial paper. Sources of secured short-term financing include loans secured by inventory and accounts receivable. A firm may also sell its receivables to factors. Trade credit is the least-expensive source of short-term financing. The cost of financing through other sources generally depends on the source and on the credit rating of the firm that requires the financing. Factoring is generally the most expensive approach.

- Evaluate the advantages and disadvantages of equity financing.

A corporation can raise equity capital by selling either common or preferred stock. The first time a corporation sells stock to the general public is referred to as an initial public offering (IPO). With an IPO, the stock is sold in the primary market. Once sold in the primary market, investors buy and sell stock in the secondary market. Usually, secondary market transactions are completed through a securities exchange or the over-the-counter market. Ordinary share is voting stock; holders of ordinary share elect the corporation's directors and often must approve changes to the corporate charter. Holders of preferred stock must be paid dividends before holders of ordinary share are paid any dividends. Another source of equity funding is retained earnings, which is the portion of a business's profits *not* distributed to stockholders. Venture capital—money invested in small (and sometimes struggling) firms that have the potential to become very successful—is yet another source of equity funding. Finally, a private placement can be used to sell stocks and other corporate securities.

- Evaluate the advantages and disadvantages of long-term debt financing.

  For a small business, debt financing is generally limited to loans. Large corporations have the additional option of issuing corporate bonds. Regardless of whether the business is small or large, it can take advantage of financial gearing. Financial gearing is the use of borrowed funds to increase the return on owners' equity. The rate of interest for long-term loans usually depends on the financial status of the borrower, the reason for borrow-

ing, and the kind of collateral pledged to back up the loan. Long-term business loans are normally repaid in 3 to 7 years but can be as long as 15 to 20 years. Money realised from the sale of corporate bonds must be repaid when the bonds mature. In addition, the corporation must pay interest on that money from the time the bonds are sold until maturity. The interest rate the corporation must pay often depends on the financial health of the firm issuing bonds. Maturity dates for bonds generally range from 10 to 30 years after the date of issue. Three types of bonds—debentures, mortgage bonds, and convertible bonds—are sold to raise debt capital. When comparing the cost of equity and debt long-term financing, the ongoing costs of using stock (equity) to finance a business are low. The most expensive is a long-term loan (debt).

EXERCISE QUESTIONS

1 What does the acronym "CFO" stand for and what is its function in a business?

2 List the main sources of equity financing.

3 What is the "maturity date"?

4 Consider the *Responsible Practice* feature in this chapter. How successful do you think the financial sector has been in improving its image?

5 What other steps could be carried out to improve the image of the financial sector in public opinion?

CASE 18.1

The Global Financial Crisis: a Question of Leadership?

The global financial crisis of 2008 was precipitated by rising interest rates in the sub-prime lending sector of the housing market in the United States. Mortgage lenders had advanced loans to people with bad credit histories and insecure sources of income; many borrowers had bought properties on the expectation that house values would rise to enable them to refinance their mortgages at a profit. Rising interest rates, however, dampened the housing market, and many people found themselves with negative equity and unable to sustain interest payments.

The risk to lenders had been spread by selling loans on as repackaged securities to other banks. However, the scale of the sub-prime market collapse took the financial securities market by surprise, and substantial bank assets were down-valued and written off, to a point where inter-bank lending dwindled to almost nothing (the so-called "credit crunch").

The "repackaging" of securities is part of a bigger picture of expanding financial markets stimulated by new sophisticated financial products. This includes securitization, which involves pooling and repackaging cash flow producing assets, like mortgages, into securities for reselling to

investors. These assets are derivatives, in the sense that they are financial instruments whose values are derived from something else (such as mortgages). This activity has been encouraged by western governments, which in recent years have moved to remove banking restrictions and relax regulation.

What role did leadership and the strategic management of the financial institutions play in the failure of the banks?

It is not that people did not see the dangers. Stefan Stern, reporting in the *Financial Times*, cites the influential Paul Volcker, an ex-chairman of the American Federal Reserve, speaking in February, 2005:

> *"Circumstances seem to be as dangerous and intractable as any I can remember, and I can remember quite a lot. What really concerns me is that there should be so little willingness or capacity to do anything about it."*

Stern alleges there has been a turning away from good management. He follows the Hopper brothers who cite Alfred Chandler's view that the great growth of modern capitalism had been achieved through "*...making administrative decisions...that favoured the long-term stability and growth of their enterprises to those that maximised short-term profits,*". Stern omits Chandler's next sentence, which more telling: "*For salaried managers the continuing existence of their enterprises was essential to their lifetime careers.*" It is some time since, that top managers, especially in the financial sector, have thought in terms of 'lifetime careers'; especially as the tenure of a chief executive is growing ever shorter.

The failures of strategy and risk management suggest that the strategic management of banks have not been as rigorous in overseeing its business models as it might have been. There has been a perfect storm of a strategy-operations disconnect. The traditional model for banking was based on retail business, but a new investment bank model seems to have taken over.

A question was asked in an internal memo at Lehman Brothers, dated just weeks before the collapse of the bank: "*Why did we allow ourselves to be so exposed?*"

According to Dick Fuld (in 2005), Lehman's then chief executive, the answer seems to have been: "*I expect everyone at the firm to be a risk manager. All 12 of us* [on the executive committee] *are focused on all parts of the business. It's all about risk management. If it's just me then we're in trouble.*"

Stern concludes his article that the banks were: "*Always chasing the next deal, too many businesses neglect the boring but crucial issue of management. As Tom Stewart, the former Harvard Business Review editor and now chief marketing and knowledge officer for consultants Booz & Co, points out, the current financial crisis has its origins in plain bad management.*

"*It's no accident that Goldman Sachs – which of all the investment banks is the one that appears to value management most – has survived this crisis best,*" he says. "*I bet that each of the players and victims in this credit crisis began to small the rot in their mortgage-derivatives books at about the same time, within weeks, even days of each other. But who managed the crisis – and who just looked for a deal that would save the year?*

... Yes, greed is bad, and stupidity is bad, but bad management is worst of all."

The Royal Bank of Scotland

In March 2009, the Royal Bank of Scotland (RBS), announced the biggest corporate loss in British history, and the British Government was preparing to underwrite its (rather dodgy) assets to a value of £325 billion (the government now holds a majority of the bank's shares). Much attention has been focused on the role of Sir Fred Goodwin, the former chief executive. Concerns have been raised about the culture that developed within the bank and way in which decisions were made.

In 1998, when Sir Fred joined as deputy chief executive, the RBS was a modest Scottish high street bank and by 2008 it was the fifth largest bank in the world by market capitalisation. Within three years Sir Fred had masterminded a takeover of the U.K.'s largest retain bank, NatWest. By 2001 he was chief executive and the bank embarked on a series of acquisitions, including leveraged buyouts (in 2008 it had lent more than 49.3 billion, more than double its nearest rival). The last high profile acquisition was the Dutch bank, ABN Amro, in 2007.

The takeover involved a consortium of banks, including Santander of Spain, and the Belgo-Dutch Fortis group. ABN was broken up, with the RBS taking the American operations. Thus the bank had transformed itself over two decades from a provincial niche player, to a diversified global financial services provider. Its alliance with other banks, such as Spain's Bank of Santander, has enabled it to build an awareness of European banking with a minimal capital outlay. However, in the words of the then chairman, Sir Tom McKillop, the investment is now worthless. Sir Tom had been chief executive of AstraZeneca, the U.K.'s largest pharmaceutical company, from 1999 until 2005. He is a chemist and had no banking background, until he became chairman of the RBS.

The ABN acquisition at the time met with general acclaim from shareholders, that the bank had outmanoeuvred its U.K. rival Barclays, which had wanted to buy ABN, and there was a feeling that the bank was repeating its success with NatWest. But scepticism started to rise. "*There was a feeling that the bank had a very powerful CEO and the board couldn't stand up to him,*".

Sir Fred had put out statements saying that RBS do not do sub-prime, but traders were buying sub-prime assets. It is uncertain to what extent the board really knew what was happening. RBS began buying up about $34 billion of sub-prime assets as U.S. banks were off-loading the mortgages and RBS was unable to sell the assets on as planned.

There is evidence from the U.K. consumer magazine, *Which*, that during this time almost half of bank retail customers were unhappy about the interest rates offered on their savings, and that the banks tried to sell them financial products that they did not wish to take on. There were other complaints about long queues in branches, high unauthorised bank charges, small print that is hard to understand, customer call centres located outside the U.K., and the closure of local branches.

References: Witcher and Chau, *Strategic Management: Principles and Practice* (2010); Stern S. (2009), Whitehouse needs a competent manager, *Financial Times*, February; Hopper K. and Hopper W. (2009), *The Puritan Gift; Reclaiming the American Dream Amidst Global Financial Chaos,* London: I. B. Tauris & Co.; Candler Jr., A. D. (1977), *The Visible Hand: The Managerial Revolution in American Business,* London: Belknap; *Euromoney Magazine* (2005), July; Winnett R. (2009), RBS traders hid toxic debt, *Daily Telegraph*, March 23; Winnett R. and Corrigan T. (2009), RBS was disaster waiting to happen, *Daily Telegraph*, March 23; Burgess K. (2009), Culpability debate intensifies, *Financial Times*, January 20, 2; Larsen P. T. (2007), Aiming to repeat NatWest purchase trick, *Financial Times*, October 17, 26.

Questions

1 Consider if the global financial crisis owed a lot to bad management at an organisational level.

2 Can effective risk management live within a transformational and visionary organisational culture?

3 How important was leadership style at the Royal Bank of Scotland?

CHAPTER REFERENCES

3M Corporation Web site at www.3m.com, accessed February 24, 2012.

Bartiromo, Maria, "BlackRock's Peter Fisher on When the Pan Will End," the *BusinessWeek* Web site, accessed October 8, 2008.

"CIT, GE Capital Add to Factoring Businesses," the Reuters Web site at www.reuters.com, accessed March 29, 2010.

Levy, Ari and Spears, Lee, "LinkedIn Retains Most Gains Second Day After Surging in Initial Offering," the

Bloomberg Web site at www.bloomberg.com, accessed May 20, 2011.

McDonald's Corporate Web site at www.aboutmcdonalds. com, accessed February 27, 2012.

Pepitone, Julianne, "Groupon IPO Opens at $28," the Fidelity.com Web site at https://fidelity.com/news, accessed November 4, 2011.

The Advanced Micro Devices corporate Web site at www. amd.com, accessed February 25, 2012.

19 PERSONAL FINANCES AND INVESTMENTS

LEARNING OBJECTIVES

Once you complete this chapter, you should be able to:

- Explain why you should manage your personal finances and develop a personal investment programme
- Describe how the factors of safety, risk, income, growth, and liquidity affect your investment programme
- Recognise how you can reduce investment risk and increase investment returns
- Explain the reasons people choose conservative investments including bank accounts and bonds
- Identify the advantages and disadvantages of stocks, mutual funds, bought, and more speculative investments
- Use financial information to evaluate investment alternatives
- Understand how different investments are bought and sold

BUSINESS FOCUS

The Vanguard group thinks low-cost and high-tech

The Vanguard Group helps investors make the most of their money by offering low-cost investments and high-tech access. From its early days, the company focused not on individual stocks or bonds but on selling shares in mutual funds, pools of money invested in a select group of stocks or bonds. Vanguard was a pioneer in establishing mutual funds tied to a specific group of ordinary shares or bonds in a particular financial index. Before Vanguard launched its Vanguard 500 Index Fund, individual investors had no way to buy this type of indexed mutual fund directly from an investment company. Today, Vanguard offers hundreds of mutual funds and many other securities for every type of investor and every investment goal, short- and long-term.

Because the Vanguard Group is owned by the different funds it manages, it has a long tradition of operating mutual funds "at cost." As a result, investors pay lower mutual fund fees, and more of their money remains invested to earn returns year after year. Exactly how low is low? By Vanguard's calculations, its average expense ratio is, on average, one-fifth of the industry average. To dramatize this difference, Vanguard recently sent an "At-Cost Café" food lorry on tour selling coffee at 28 cents per cup—just one-fifth of the usual price. "The concept of at-cost investing can be difficult to explain," says a Vanguard spokesperson, "so we are trying to help investors 'experience' it through something tangible, such as a routine daily purchase like coffee."

Vanguard also uses the latest technology to let customers check on their accounts and investigate new investment possibilities at any hour, from any place. In addition to its Web site, which offers detailed financial information, online trading, and much more, the company provides downloadable apps for mobile phones and tablet computers. Whether investors are just starting out or have a lot of investing experience, they can use the technology of their choice to see their recent transactions, analyse investment performance, buy or sell securities, read Vanguard's research reports, subscribe to its electronic newsletter, and watch its educational videos—all at the touch of a finger or the click of a mouse.

References: Chris Flood, "Vanguard ETF Assets Surge to Top $200 bn," *Financial Times*, March 25, 2012, www.ft.com; Jackie Noblett, "Vanguard Drives Home Low-Cost Mantra, in a Mobile Café," *Financial Times*, March 21, 2012, www.ft.com; Jason Kephart, "Vanguard Steps Up Efforts to Woo Advisers," *Investment News*, March 12, 2012, p. 2; Robert Steyer, "Providers Going Big with Technology," *Pensions & Investments*, October 31, 2011, p. 2; www.vanguard.com.

As the saying goes, "I've been rich and I've been poor, but believe me, rich is better." Yet, just dreaming of being rich does not make it happen. Although being rich does not guarantee happiness, managing your personal finances and beginning an investment programme are both worthy goals. Many firms offer an array of services to help people manage their personal finances, research investments, and buy and sell stocks, bonds, mutual funds, and other securities. Nevertheless, you must be willing to invest the time and effort required to manage your personal finances and become a good investor. Furthermore, do not underestimate how important you are when it comes to managing your money. No one is going to make you manage your money. No one is going to make you save the money you need to fund an investment programme. These are your decisions—important decisions that literally can change your life.

Many people ask the question: Why begin an investment programme now? To answer that question, you must understand that personal finance experts agree that the best investment programme is one that stresses long-term growth over a 20- to 40-year period. As you will see later in this chapter, the unit value of your investments may decrease over a short time period, but historically the value of quality securities has usually increased over a long time period.

A second compelling reason to start an investment programme is that the sooner you start an investment programme, the more time your investments have to work for you. So why do people wait to begin investing? In most cases, there are two reasons. First, they do not have the money needed to fund an investment programme. However, once you begin managing your personal finances and get your spending under control, you will be able to save the money needed to fund an investment programme. The second reason people do not begin investing is because they do not know anything about investing. Again, this chapter provides the basics to get you started.

We begin this chapter by examining everyday money management activities and outlining the reasons for developing a personal investment plan. Next we discuss important factors to consider when choosing investments and describe both traditional and high-risk (or speculative) investments. Then, we explain how to use information to evaluate potential investments. Finally, we examine the methods used to buy and sell investments.

It is time! Take the first step, and begin managing your personal finances.

MANAGING YOUR PERSONAL FINANCES

Most people begin by making sure that their "financial house" is in order. In this section, we examine several steps for effective money management that will help you to prepare for an investment programme.

Step 1: Tracking your income, expenses, assets, and liabilities

Many personal finance experts recommend that you begin the process of managing your money by determining your current financial condition. Often the first step is to construct a personal income statement and balance sheet. A *personal income statement* lists your income and your expenses for a specific period of time—usually a month. By subtracting expenses from income, you can determine if you have a surplus or a deficit at the end of the time period. Surplus funds can be used for savings, investing, or for any purpose that you feel is important. On the other hand, if you have a deficit, you must take actions to reduce spending and pay down any debts you may have that will keep you from starting an investment programme.

To get another picture of your current financial condition, you should construct a personal balance sheet. A *personal balance sheet* lists your assets and liabilities on a specific date. By subtracting your total liabilities from your total assets, you can determine your net worth. For an individual, **net worth** is the difference between the value of your total assets and your total liabilities. Over time, the goal is to increase the value of your assets (items of value that you own) and decrease liabilities (your debts).

 net worth the difference between the value of your total assets and your total liabilities

Based on the information contained in these two statements, you can determine your current financial condition and where you spend your money. You can also take the next step: Construct a personal budget.

Step 2: Developing a budget that works

A **personal budget** is a specific plan for spending your income. You begin by estimating your income for a specific period—for example, next month. For most people, their major source of income is their salary. The second step is to list expenses for the same time period. Typical expenses include savings and investments, housing, food, transportation, entertainment, and so on. For most people, this is the area where you can make choices and increase or decrease the amount spent on different items listed in your budget. For example, you may decide to reduce the dollar amount spent on entertainment to increase the amount for savings. Above all, it is important to balance your budget so that your income is equal to the money you spend, save, or invest each month. For help managing your money and constructing a realistic budget, there are various services available for free on the Internet that can help you take the necessary steps to improve your personal finances.

personal budget a specific plan for spending your income

After you have constructed your personal budget, you will need to compare the amounts included in your budget with your actual income and expenses. The goal is that the estimated income and expenses are correct and that you have a surplus at the end of the budgeting period. If income is less than anticipated or expenses are more than budgeted, then you will need to take corrective actions to get your budget back on track. Often one change will affect other areas of your budget as well. An increase in your monthly rent payment, for instance, may mean that you have to reduce the amount spent on entertainment to balance your budget. *Caution*: Avoid the temptation to spend more than you make by using credit cards or borrowing money.

Step 3: Managing credit card debt

Unfortunately, many individuals spend more than they make. They purchase items on credit and then make monthly payments and pay finance charges ranging from 10 to 21 per cent or more. It makes no sense to start an investment programme until payments for credit card and installment purchases, along with the accompanying finance charges, are reduced or eliminated.

Although all cardholders have reasons for using their credit cards, the important point to remember is that it is *very easy* to get in trouble by using your credit cards. Watch for the following five warning signs.

1. Don't fall behind on payments. One of the first warning signs is the inability to pay your entire balance each month.
2. Do not use your credit cards to pay for many small purchases during the month. This can often lead to a "real surprise" when you open your credit card statement at the end of the month.
3. Do not use the cash advance provision that accompanies most credit cards. The reason is simple: The interest rate is usually higher for cash advances.
4. Think about the number of cards you really need. Most experts recommend that an individual have one or two cards and use these cards for emergencies.
5. Get help if you think you are in trouble. There are many organisations available to help you work out a plan for paying off credit card debt.

By reducing or eliminating credit purchases, eventually the amount of cash remaining after the bills are paid will increase and can be used to start a savings and investment programme that will help you obtain your investment goals.

Investment goals

Personal investment is the use of your personal funds to earn a financial return. Thus, in the most general sense, the goal of investing is to earn money with money. However, such a goal is completely useless for the individual because it is so vague.

 personal investment the use of your personal funds to earn a financial return

In reality, an investment goal must be specific and measurable. It must be tailored to you so that it takes into account your particular financial needs. It must also be oriented toward the future because investing is usually a long-term undertaking. By investing small amounts of money each year over a 20- to 40-year period, you can accumulate money for emergencies and retirement. In addition, if you choose quality investments, the value of your investments will grow over a long period of time. Finally, an investment goal must be realistic in terms of current economic conditions and available investment opportunities.

Some financial planners suggest that investment goals should be stated in terms of money: "By January 1st, 2022, I will have total assets of €80,000." Others believe that people are more motivated to work toward goals that are stated in terms of the particular things they desire: "By May 1st, 2024, I will have accumulated enough money so that I can take a year off from work to travel around the

What are your personal, professional, and investment goals? Just like a successful business, you should be looking ahead to what you want to achieve in the next few years and writing down specific goals for yourself. If one goal is to start an investment programme, for example, it will help to think about how much you'll need to start investing and how much you will want to accumulate by a specific date.

world." Like the goals themselves, the way they are stated depends on you. The following questions can be helpful in establishing valid investment goals:

1. What financial goals do you want to achieve?
2. How much money will you need, and when?
3. What will you use the money for?
4. Is it reasonable to assume that you can obtain the amount of money you will need to meet your investment goals?
5. Do you expect your personal situation to change in a way that will affect your investment goals?
6. What economic conditions could alter your investment goals?
7. Are you willing to make the necessary sacrifices to ensure that your investment goals are met?

Keep in mind the investment goals you develop may be affected by your career choice. If you choose a career that provides above-average financial rewards, you can develop more challenging investment goals. If you choose a career that provides average or below-average financial rewards, it is still possible to develop an investment programme by carefully managing your personal finances. Simply put: You must control spending and manage debt regardless of how much money you make.

A personal investment programme

Once you have formulated specific goals and have some money to invest, investment planning is similar to planning for a business. It begins with the evaluation of different investment opportunities—including the potential return and risk involved in each. At the very least, this process requires some careful study and maybe some expert advice. Investors should beware of people who call themselves "financial planners" but who are in reality nothing more than salespersons for various financial investments, tax shelters, or insurance plans.

A true **financial planner** has had at least two years of training in investments, insurance, taxation, retirement planning, and estate planning and has passed a rigorous examination.

> **financial planner** an individual who has had at least two years of training in investments, insurance, taxation, retirement planning, and estate planning and has passed a rigorous examination

Many financial planners suggest that you accumulate an "emergency fund"—a certain amount of money that can be obtained quickly in case of immediate need—before beginning an investment programme. The amount of money that should be salted away in a savings account varies from person to person. Most financial planners agree that an amount equal to at least three months' living expenses is reasonable. However, you may want to increase your emergency fund in anticipation of a crisis.

Managing your personal finances can improve a relationship! *Often money problems can cause relationships to sour and can even lead to divorce for some couples. On the other hand, managing your personal finances can lead to financial stability, peace of mind, and a more stable personal relationship.*

After the emergency account is established, you may invest additional funds according to your investment programme. Some additional funds may already be available, or money for further investing may be saved out of earnings. For suggestions to help you obtain the money needed to fund your investment programme, see Table 19.1.

Monitoring the value of your investment programme

The recent world economic crisis had many causes, including a banking and financial crisis, a downturn in home sales, lower consumer spending, and high unemployment rates. Although the economy shows signs of improving at the time of publication, and the **Dow Jones Industrial Average** is just over 13,000 at the time of publication, a crisis could happen again.

> **Dow Jones Industrial Average** an average of 30 leading U.S. corporations that reflect the U.S. stock market as a whole

Although monitoring your investment programme and re-evaluating your investment choices are always important, the recent economic crisis underscores the importance of managing your personal finances *and* your investment programme. Because of the global economic problems, many people were caught off guard. Moreover, some individuals were forced to sell some or all of their investments at depressed prices just to pay for everyday necessities.

TABLE 19.1 Suggestions to help you accumulate the money needed to fund an investment programme

1. *Pay yourself first*. Many financial experts recommend that you (1) pay your monthly bills, (2) save a reasonable amount of money, and (3) use whatever money is left over for personal expenses.
2. *Take advantage of employer-sponsored pensions*. Many employers will match part or all of the contributions you make to a 401(k) or 403(b) retirement account.
3. *Participate in an elective savings programme*. Elect to have money withheld from your pay each payday and automatically deposited in a savings or investment account.
4. *Make a special savings effort one or two months each year*. By cutting back to the basics, you can obtain money for investment purposes.
5. *Take advantage of gifts, inheritances, and windfalls*. During your lifetime, you likely will receive gifts, inheritances, salary increases, year-end bonuses, or income tax returns. Instead of spending these windfalls, invest these funds.

Source: Jack R. Kapoor, Les R. Dlabay, and Robert J. Hughes, *Focus on Personal Finance*, 3rd ed. Copyright © 2010 by The McGraw Hill Companies Inc. Reprinted with permission of The McGraw Hill Companies Inc.

SUCCESS STORY

Smart investing

Don't you wish you had invested in Facebook or Twitter in their infantile stages? Well some intuitive investors did just that.

Venture capital firms make no secret of where they're looking to invest, and these days they're investing heavily in information technology. Venture capitalist, Marc Andreessen, is a partner in California-based Andreessen Horowitz—arguably one of the most successful venture capitalist firms in the world. Since the venture capital firm was founded, his firm has invested money in many very recognisable and profitable firms including Facebook, Twitter, and Pinterest.

To avoid the type of problems just described, you must monitor your investment programme and, if necessary, modify it. Always bear in mind that your circumstances and economic conditions are both subject to change.

IMPORTANT FACTORS IN PERSONAL INVESTMENT

How can you (or a financial planner) tell which investments are "right" for your investment programme and which are not? One way to start is to match potential investments with your investment goals in terms of safety, risk, income, growth, and liquidity.

Safety and risk

Safety and risk are two sides of the same coin. *Safety* in an investment means minimal risk of loss; *risk* in an investment means a measure of uncertainty about the outcome. If you want a steady increase in value over an extended period of time, choose safe investments, such as certificates of deposit (CDs), highly rated government and corporate bonds, and the stocks of highly regarded corporations—sometimes called blue-chip stocks. A **blue-chip stock** is a safe investment that generally attracts conservative investors. Blue-chip stocks are generally issued by corporations that are industry leaders and have provided their stockholders with stable earnings and dividends over a number of years. Selected mutual funds and property may also be very safe investments.

 blue-chip stock a safe investment that generally attracts conservative investors

If you want higher euro returns on investments, you must generally give up some safety. In general, *the potential return should be directly related to the assumed risk.* That is, the greater the risk you assume, the higher the potential monetary reward. As you will see shortly, there are a number of speculative—and potentially profitable—investments.

Often beginning investors are afraid of the risk associated with many investments. However, it helps to remember that without risk, it is impossible to obtain larger returns that really make your investment programme grow. In fact, some investors often base their investment decision on projections for rate of return. You can also use the same calculation to determine how much you actually earn on an investment over a specific period of time. To calculate **rate of return**, the total euro amount of return you receive on an investment over a specific period of time is divided by the amount invested. For example, assume that you invest €5,000 in Unilever stock, you receive €108 in dividends, and the stock is worth €5,300 at the end of one year. Your rate of return is 8.2 per cent, as illustrated here.

> **rate of return** the total dollar amount of return you receive on an investment over a specific period of time divided by the amount invested

Step 1: *Subtract the investment's initial value from the investment's value at the end of the year.*

€5,300 − €5,000 = €300

Step 2: *Add the dividend amount to the amount calculated in step 1.*

€108 + €300 = €408

Step 3: *Divide the total euro amount of return calculated in step 2 by the original investment.*

€408 ÷ €5,000 = 0.082 = 8.2 per cent

Note: If an investment decreases in value, the steps used to calculate the rate of return are the same, but the answer is a negative number. With this information, it is possible to compare the rate of return for different investment alternatives that offer more or less risk.

__Purchasing stocks is one way to invest.__
Since 1926, stocks have returned just below 10 per cent a year—a larger return than most other investment alternatives. So why not just pick a bunch of stocks and begin investing? The truth is that an investment programme should begin with a financial checkup to make sure that you are ready to invest and the creation of investment goals before you purchase any investment.

© STEPHEN COBURN/SHUTTERSTOCK

Investment income

Investors sometimes purchase certain investments because they want a predictable source of income. For example, CDs, corporate and government bonds, and certain stocks pay interest or dividends each year. Some mutual funds and real estate may also offer steady income potential. Such investments are generally used by conservative investors or retired individuals who need a predictable source of income.

When purchasing investments for income, most investors are concerned about the issuer's ability to continue making periodic interest or dividend payments. Investors in CDs and bonds know exactly how much income they will receive each year. The dividends paid to stockholders can and do vary, even for the largest and most stable corporations. As with dividends from stock, the income from mutual funds and real estate may also vary from one year to the next.

Investment growth

To investors, *growth* means that their investments will increase in value. For example, growing corporations such as Monster Beverage, Adobe Systems, and Silicon Motion Technology usually pay a small cash dividend or no dividend at all. Instead, profits are reinvested in the business (as retained earnings) to finance additional expansion. In this case, the value of the stock increases as the corporation expands.

Other investments that may offer growth potential include selected mutual funds and property. For example, many mutual funds are referred to as growth funds or aggressive growth funds because of the growth potential of the individual securities included in the fund.

Investment liquidity

Liquidity, as touched upon earlier in the book, is the ease with which an investment can be converted into cash. Investments range from cash or cash equivalents (such as investments in government securities or money-market accounts) to the other extreme of frozen investments, which you cannot convert easily into cash.

> **liquidity** the ease with which an investment can be converted into cash

Although you may be able to sell stock, mutual-fund, and corporate-bond investments quickly, you may not regain the amount of money you originally invested because of market conditions, economic conditions, or many other reasons. It may also be difficult to find buyers for property. Furthermore, finding a buyer for investments in certain types of collectibles may also be difficult.

FACTORS THAT CAN IMPROVE YOUR INVESTMENT DECISIONS

We begin this section with an overview of how portfolio management can reduce investment risk and factors that you should consider to choose "just the right" investments. Then in the next two sections, we describe how the investments listed in Table 19.2 can help you to reach your investment goals.

Portfolio management

"How can I choose the right investment?" That's a good question! Unfortunately, there are no easy answers because your investment goals, age, tolerance for risk, and financial resources are different

TABLE 19.2   Investment alternatives   *Traditional investments involve less risk than speculative or high-risk investments.*

Traditional investments
Bank accounts
Corporate and government bonds

More speculative investments
Ordinary share
Preferred stock
Mutual funds
Property

The most speculative investments
Short transactions
Margin transactions
Share options
Derivatives
Commodities
Precious metals
Gemstones
Coins
Antiques
Collectibles

© Cengage Learning 2014

from those of the next person. To help you to decide what investment is right for you, consider the following: Since 1926, as measured by the Standard and Poor's 500 Stock Index, stocks have returned on average just below 10 per cent a year. The **Standard & Poor's 500 Stock Index** is an index that contains 500 different stocks that reflect increases or decreases in value for the U.S. stock market as a whole. During the same period, U.S. government bonds have returned about 6 per cent.* Therefore, why not just invest all your money in stocks or mutual funds that invest in stocks? After all, they offer the largest potential return. In reality, stocks may have a place in every investment portfolio, but there is more to investing than just picking a bunch of stocks or stock mutual funds.

> **Standard & Poor's 500 Stock Index** an index that contains 500 different stocks that reflect increases or decreases in value for the U.S. stock market as a whole

Asset allocation, the time factor, and your age

Asset allocation is the process of spreading your money among several different types of investments to lessen risk. Although the term *asset allocation* is a fancy way of saying it, simply put, it really

> **asset allocation** the process of spreading your money among several different types of investments to lessen risk

means that you need to diversify and avoid the pitfall of putting all of your eggs in one basket—a common mistake made by investors. Asset allocation is often expressed in percentages. For example, what percentage of my assets do I want to put in stocks and mutual funds? What percentage do I want to put in more conservative investments such as CDs and government bonds? In reality, the answers to these questions are determined by:

- The time your investments have to work for you
- Your age
- Your investment objectives
- Your ability to tolerate risk
- How much you can save and invest each year
- The euro value of your current investments
- The outlook for the economy
- Several other factors

Two factors—the time your investments have to work for you and your age—are so important they deserve special attention.

The time factor   The amount of time you have before you need your investment money is crucial. If you can leave your investments alone and let them work for five to ten years or more, then you can invest in stocks, mutual funds, and property. On the other hand, if you need your investment money in two years, you probably should invest in short-term government bonds, highly rated corporate bonds, or CDs. By taking a more conservative approach for short-term investments, you reduce the possibility of having to sell your investments at a loss because of depressed market value or a staggering economy. For example, during the recent economic crisis, many retirees who were forced to sell stocks and mutual funds to pay for everyday living expenses lost money. On the other hand, many young investors with long-term investment goals could afford to hold their investments until the price of their securities recovered.

Your age   You also should consider your age when developing an investment programme. Younger investors tend to invest a large percentage of their nest egg in growth-oriented investments. On the other hand, older investors tend to choose more conservative investments. As a result, a smaller percentage of their nest egg is placed in growth-oriented investments. While no investor regardless of age likes to lose money on an investment, the fact is that younger investors have more time for an investment to recover its original value and even increase in value.

How much of your portfolio should be in growth-oriented investments? Personal financial expert Suze Orman suggests that you subtract your age from 110, and the difference is the percentage of your assets that should be invested in growth investments. For example, if you are 30 years old, subtract 30 from 110, which gives you 80. Therefore, 80 per cent of your assets should be invested in growth-oriented investments, whereas the remaining 20 per cent should be kept in safer conservative investments.*

Your role in the investment process

Investors want large returns, yet they are often unwilling to invest the time required to become a good investor. They would not buy a car without a test drive or purchase a home without comparing different homes, but for some unknown reason they invest without doing their homework. The suggestions given here will help you choose investments that will increase in value.

- *Evaluate potential investments.* Keep in mind that successful investors evaluate their investments before making investment decisions. Often, it is useful to keep copies of the material you used to evaluate each investment. Then, when it is time to re-evaluate an existing investment, you will know where to begin your search for current information. Much of the information in this chapter in the section "Sources of Financial Information" will help you learn how to evaluate different investment opportunities.
- *Monitor the value of your investments.* Would you believe that some people invest large sums of money and do not know what their investments are worth? They do not know if their investments have increased or decreased in value and if they should sell their investments or continue to hold them. A much better approach is to monitor the value of your investments.
- *Keep accurate and current records.* Accurate record keeping can help you spot opportunities to maximise profits, reduce euro losses when you sell your investments, and help you decide whether you want to invest additional funds in a specific investment. For tax purposes, you should keep purchase records for each of your investments that include the actual euro cost of the investment, plus any commissions or fees you paid, along with records of dividends, interest income, or rental income you received.

CONSERVATIVE INVESTMENT ALTERNATIVES

Typically investors who are afraid of the risk associated with stocks, mutual funds, and other investment alternatives, beginning investors, investors that need a predictable source of income, or people worried about a downturn in the economy will often invest their money in bank accounts, government bonds, or corporate bonds.

Bank accounts

Bank accounts that pay interest—and therefore are investments—include passbook savings accounts, money-market accounts, CDs, and other interest-bearing accounts. The interest paid on bank accounts can be withdrawn to serve as income, or it can be left on deposit and increase the value of the bank account and provide for growth. At the time of this publication, one-year CDs were paying between 0.50 and 1 per cent. Although CDs and other bank accounts are risk-free for all practical purposes, many investors often choose other investments because of the potential for larger returns.

Corporate and government bonds

Investors generally choose bonds because they provide a predictable source of income.

Government bonds   Despite concerns about national debt through the world, many investors still consider government bonds to be risk-free. The other side of the coin is that these bonds pay lower interest than most other investments.

RESPONSIBLE PRACTICE   Invest in green bonds?

Should investors choose green bonds? The World Bank issues green bonds to pay for sustainability projects such as water purification, solar installations, and reforestation. Since 2008, it has issued €3.3 billion worth of green bonds, in 17 currencies, with a range of maturities from 2 to 10 years. For example, Bank of America Merrill Lynch offers World Bank green bonds with 10-year maturities starting with a €1,000 investment. Because repayment is not tied to the performance of the projects they finance, these bonds are rated as low-risk and carry relatively low interest rates.

COURTESY OF HTTP://YESINVESTING.COM

Nobody questions the need to fund sustainability projects. In fact, some institutional investors see green bonds as a way to support environmental action while diversifying their portfolios. One issue, however, is that the money goes into a World Bank account designated for environmental projects—and investors don't know which project they're supporting. As a result, money from an investor who hopes to preserve the rainforest may actually be used for mass transportation improvements that reduce pollution. Another issue is liquidity. Demand for green bonds is unproven, and they aren't traded as widely or as often as, say, U.S. Treasury bonds. In fact, lack of liquidity may be a real problem for investors who have to sell prior to maturity. So should investors choose green bonds?

Green Investing

Interested in earning some profit while you're saving the planet? Maybe green investing is for you! Green investing involves choosing to invest in companies that are involved in operations aimed at improving the environment, such as alternative energy sources, clean air and water projects, or companies that provide environmentally friendly products. Socially Responsible Investing is an organization that provides information about green investing, including green stock investment choices, green mutual funds, and tips for investors. Take a look at http://yesinvesting.com/.

References: Sally Bakewell, "Green Bond Bankers in Japan, Sweden Beat U.S. to €7 Billion," *Bloomberg,* January 24, 2012, www.bloomberg.com; "A Modest, But Important, Addition to Climate Finance," *Economist,* October 29, 2011, www.economist.com; Sonia Kolesnikov-Jessop, "A Change of Heart on Investing in the Climate," *New York Times,* November 27, 2011, www.nytimes.com; Elizabeth O'Brien, "Now Bonds Are Going Green Too," *Smart Money,* October 25, 2011, www.smartmoney.com; www.worldbank.org.

A **municipal bond**, sometimes called a *muni,* is a debt security issued by a state or local government. Municipal bonds are especially attractive to wealthy investors because interest income from municipal bonds may be tax exempt from federal taxes. Whether or not the interest on municipal bonds is tax-exempt often depends on how the funds obtained from their sale are used. *Caution: It is your responsibility, as an investor, to determine whether or not the interest paid by municipal bonds is taxable. It is also your responsibility to evaluate municipal bonds.* Although most municipal bonds are relatively safe, defaults have occurred in recent years.

 municipal bond sometimes called a *muni,* a debt security issued by a state or local government

Corporate bonds Because they are a form of long-term debt financing that must be repaid, investment-grade corporate bonds are generally considered a more conservative investment than either stocks or mutual funds that invest in stocks. One of the principal advantages of corporate bonds is that they are primarily long-term, income-producing investments. Between the time of purchase and the maturity date, the bondholder will receive interest payments—usually semiannually, or every six months. Assume that you purchase a €1,000 bond—the typical face value for a corporate bond—issued by a large transportation corporation, for example, and that the interest rate for this bond is 6 per cent. In this situation, you receive interest of €60 (€1,000 × 0.06 = €60) a year from the corporation. For corporate bonds, interest is usually paid semiannually or every six months. In the case of the bond just described, a bondholder will receive two €30 interest payments each year.

Most beginning investors think that a €1,000 bond is always worth €1,000. In reality, the price of a bond may fluctuate until its maturity date. Changes in the overall interest rates in the economy are the primary cause of most bond price fluctuations. When overall interest rates in the economy increase, the market value of existing bonds with a fixed interest rate typically declines. For example, the value of the transportation corporation bond with a fixed 6 per cent interest rate will decline if interest rates in the economy or interest rates for comparable bonds increase. When a bond's price declines, it may be purchased for less than its face value. By holding the bond until maturity, bond owners can redeem the bond for more than they paid for it.

A corporate bond with a fixed interest rate can also increase in value if overall interest rates in the economy decline. In this situation, a bond like the transportation corporation bond with a 6 per cent fixed interest rate will increase in value. The difference between the purchase price and the selling price is profit and is in addition to annual interest income.

Before you invest in bonds, remember that the price of a corporate bond can decrease and that interest payments and eventual repayment may be a problem for a corporation that encounters financial difficulty. To compare potential risk and return on corporate bond issues, many investors rely on the bond ratings provided by financial services.

Convertible corporate bonds   Some corporations prefer to issue convertible bonds because they carry a lower interest rate than nonconvertible bonds—by about 1 to 2 per cent. In return for accepting a lower interest rate, owners of convertible bonds have the opportunity for increased investment growth. For example, assume that you purchase an Advanced Micro Devices €1,000 corporate bond that is convertible to 35.6125 shares of the company's ordinary share. This means that you could convert the bond to ordinary share. whenever the price of the company's stock is €28.08 (€1,000 ÷ 35.6125 = €28.08) or higher.* However, owners may opt not to convert their bonds to ordinary share even if the market value of the ordinary share does increase to €28.08 or more. The reason for not exercising the conversion feature is quite simple. As the market value of the ordinary share increases, the price of the convertible bond also increases. By not converting to ordinary share, bondholders enjoy interest income from the bond in addition to the increased bond value caused by the price movement of the ordinary share.

MORE SPECULATIVE INVESTMENTS

Earlier in this chapter, we discussed the concepts of safety and risk. Before you examine more speculative investment alternatives, it may help to review the basic rule: *The potential return should be directly related to the assumed risk.* While all investors want larger returns, you must consider the risk involved with each of the following investments. Above all, keep in mind that returns for the more speculative investments described in this section are not guaranteed.

Ordinary share

Corporations issue ordinary share to finance their business start-up costs and help pay for expansion and their ongoing business activities. Before investing in stock, keep in mind that corporations do not have to repay the money a stockholder pays for stock. Usually, a stockholder may sell her or his stock to another individual.

How do you make money by buying ordinary share? Basically, there are three ways: through dividend payments, through an increase in the value of the stock, or through stock splits.

Should you invest in Cheerios? *While the Cheerios brand is widely recognised, did you know that the famous cereal is manufactured and marketed by General Mills? Often you have to dig deeper if you want to invest in a corporation that produces a famous product or service to determine if the "parent" company is a quality investment that will help you obtain your financial goals.*

Dividend payments   One of the reasons why many stockholders invest in ordinary share is *dividend income*. Generally, dividends are paid on a quarterly basis. Although corporations are under no legal obligation to pay dividends or can reduce dividends if the company experiences financial difficulties, most corporate board members like to keep stockholders happy (and prosperous). A corporation may pay stock dividends in place of—or in addition to—cash dividends. A **stock dividend** is a dividend in the form of additional stock. It is paid to shareholders just as cash dividends are paid—in proportion to the number of shares owned.

> **stock dividend**   a dividend in the form of additional stock

Increase in Euro value   Another way to make money on stock investments is through a capital gain that occurs when you sell stock. A **capital gain** is the difference between a security's purchase price and its selling price. To earn a capital gain, you must sell when the market value of the stock is higher than the original purchase price you paid for the stock. The **market value** is the price of one share of a stock at a particular time. Let's assume that on March 8th, 2009, you purchased 100 shares of Kellogg ordinary share at a cost of €37 a share and that you paid €25 in commission charges, for a total investment of €3,725. Let's also assume that you held your 100 shares until March 8, 2012, and then sold the Kellogg stock for €52. Your total return on investment is shown in Table 19.3. You realised a profit of €1,925 because you received dividends totaling €4.75 a share during the three-year period and because the stock's market value increased by €15 a share. Of course, if the stock's

TABLE 19.3   **Sample ordinary share transaction for Kellogg** *Assumptions: 100 shares of ordinary share purchased on March 8, 2009, for €37 a share; 100 shares sold on March 8, 2012, for €52 a share; dividends for three years total €4.75 a share.*

Cost when purchased		Return when sold	
100 shares @ €37	€3,700	100 shares @ €52	€5,200
Plus commission	+25	Minus commission	−25
Total investment	€3,725	Total return	€5,175
Transaction summary			
Total return	€5,175		
Minus total investment	−3,725		
Profit from stock sale	€1,450		
Plus total dividends (three years)	+475		
Total return for this transaction	€1,925		

Source: Price data and dividend amounts were taken from the Yahoo Finance Web site, http://finance.yahoo.com (accessed March 8, 2012).

market value had decreased, or if the firm's board of directors had voted to reduce or omit dividends, your return would have been less than the total dollar return illustrated in Table 19.3.

> **capital gain** the difference between a security's purchase price and its selling price
> **market value** the price of one share of a stock at a particular time

Stock splits Directors of many corporations feel that there is an optimal price range within which their firm's stock is most attractive to investors. When the market value increases beyond that range, they may declare a *stock split* to bring the price down. A **stock split** is the division of each outstanding share of a corporation's stock into a greater number of shares.

> **stock split** the division of each outstanding share of a corporation's stock into a greater number of shares

The most ordinary share splits result in one, two, or three new shares for each original share. For example, in November 2011, the board of directors of Estée Lauder, the company known for skin care, cosmetics, fragrances, and hair-care products, approved a two-for-one stock split. After this split, a stockholder who originally owned 100 shares owned 200 shares. The value of an original share was proportionally reduced. In the case of Estée Lauder, the market value per share was reduced to half the stock's value before the two-for-one stock split. There is no evidence to support that a corporation's long-term performance is improved by a stock split; however, some investors do profit from stock splits on a short-term basis. *Be warned: There are no guarantees that the stock will increase in value after a split.* However, the stock may be more attractive to the investing public because of the potential for a rapid increase in euro value. This attraction is based on the belief that most corporations split their stock only when their financial future is improving and on the upswing.

Preferred stock

A firm's preferred stockholders must receive their dividends before ordinary shareholders are paid any dividends. Moreover, the preferred-stock dividend amount is specified on the stock certificate. In addition, the owners of preferred stock have first claim, after bond owners and general creditors, on corporate assets if the firm is dissolved or enters bankruptcy. These features make preferred stock a more conservative investment with an added degree of safety and a more predictable source of income when compared with ordinary share.

In addition, owners of preferred stock may gain through special features offered with certain preferred-stock issues. Owners of *cumulative* preferred stocks are assured that omitted dividends will be paid to them before ordinary shareholders receive any dividends. Owners of *convertible* preferred stock may profit through growth as well as dividends. When the value of a firm's ordinary share increases, the market value of its convertible preferred stock also increases. Convertible preferred stock thus combines the lower risk of preferred stock with the possibility of greater speculative gain through conversion to ordinary share.

Mutual funds and exchange-traded funds

For many investors, mutual funds are the investment of choice. There are plenty of funds from which to choose. In 1970, there were only about 400 mutual funds. In January 2012, there were over 10,000 funds.*

According to the Mutual Fund Education Alliance (www.mfea.com), a **mutual fund** pools the money of many investors—its shareholders—to invest in a variety of different securities.* The major advantages of a mutual fund are its *professional management* and its *diversification*, or investment in a wide variety of securities. Most investment companies do everything possible to convince you that they can do a better job of picking securities than you can. In reality, mutual funds are managed by professional fund managers who devote large amounts of time to picking just the "right" securities for their funds' portfolios. *Be warned:* Even the best portfolio managers make mistakes. So you, the investor, must be careful and evaluate different funds before investing. Diversification spells safety because an occasional loss incurred with one security is usually offset by gains from other investments.

 mutual fund pools the money of many investors—its shareholders—to invest in a variety of different securities

Mutual-fund basics   There are basically three types of mutual funds: (1) open-end funds, (2) closed-end funds, and (3) exchange-traded funds (ETFs). The investment company sponsoring an *open-end fund* issues and sells new shares to any investor who requests them. It also buys back shares from investors who wish to sell all or part of their holdings. A *closed-end fund* sells shares in the fund to investors only when the fund is originally organised. Once all the shares are sold, an investor must purchase shares from some other investor who is willing to sell them. The investment company is under no obligation to buy back shares from investors.

An **exchange-traded fund (ETF)** is a fund that generally invests in the stocks or securities contained in a specific stock or securities index. There are many different types of ETFs available that attempt to track all kinds of indexes including different types of stocks, bonds, and even commodities. Exchange-traded funds tend to mirror the performance of a specific index, moving up or down as the individual stocks or securities contained in the index move up or down.

 exchange-traded fund (ETF) a fund that generally invests in the stocks or other securities contained in a specific stock or securities index

Like a closed-end fund, shares of an exchange-traded fund are traded on a securities exchange or in the over-the-counter market at any time during the business day. Although exchange-traded funds are similar to closed-end funds, there is an important difference. Most closed-end funds are actively managed, with portfolio managers making the selection of stocks and other securities contained in a closed-end fund. Almost all exchange-traded funds, on the other hand, normally invest in the stocks, bonds, or securities included in a specific index. Therefore, there is less need for a portfolio manager to make investment decisions. Because of passive management, fees associated with owning shares are generally less when compared to both closed-end and open-end funds. Although increasing in popularity, there are only about 1,100 exchange-traded funds.*

The share value for any mutual fund is determined by calculating its net asset value. **Net asset value (NAV)** per share is equal to the current market value of the mutual fund's portfolio minus the mutual fund's liabilities divided by the number of outstanding shares. For most mutual funds, NAV is calculated once a day and is reported in newspapers and financial publications and on the Internet. Because ETFs and closed-end funds trade like stocks, their shares trade at the current market value, which can be more or less than a closed-end fund's or ETF's NAV.

 net asset value (NAV) current market value of a mutual fund's portfolio minus the mutual fund's liabilities divided by the number of outstanding shares

Mutual-fund sales charges and fees   With regard to costs, there are two types of mutual funds: load and no-load funds. An individual who invests in a *load fund* pays a sales charge every time he or she purchases shares. This charge may be as high as 8.5 per cent. Although many exceptions exist, the average load charge for mutual funds is between 3 and 5 per cent. Instead of charging investors a fee when they purchase shares in a mutual fund, some funds charge a *contingent deferred sales fee*. Generally, this fee ranges from 1 to 5 per cent of the amount withdrawn during the first five to seven years. Typically, the amount of the contingent deferred sales fee declines each year that you own the fund until there is no withdrawal fee.

The purchaser of shares in a *no-load fund* pays no sales charges at all. Although some fund salespeople claim that load funds outperform no-load funds, there is no significant performance

How do you choose the right investment and financial company to help you obtain your financial goals? *Beginning investors often see the investment world as a jungle because of the different investment alternatives and the large number of companies that want to help you invest. In reality, all investments and the companies that want to help you should be evaluated before you make any decisions on how and where to invest.*

difference between funds that charge load charges (commissions) and those that do not.* Because no-load funds offer the same type of investment opportunities as load funds, you should investigate them further before deciding which type of mutual fund is best for you.

Mutual funds also collect a yearly management fee of about 0.25 to 1.5 per cent of the total dollar amount of assets in the fund. Although fees vary considerably, the average management fee is between 0.50 and 1 per cent of the fund's assets. Finally, some mutual funds charge a 12b-1 fee (sometimes referred to as a *distribution fee*) to defray the costs of advertising and marketing the mutual fund. Annual 12b-1 fees are calculated on the value of a fund's assets and cannot exceed 1 per cent of the fund's assets. Unlike the one-time sales fees that some mutual funds charge to purchase *or* sell mutual-fund shares, the management fee and the 12b-1 fee are ongoing fees charged each year.

Together, all the different management fees; 12b-1 fees, if any; and additional operating costs for a specific fund are referred to as an **expense ratio**. As a guideline, many financial planners recommend that you choose a mutual fund with an expense ratio of 1 per cent or less.

> **expense ratio** all the different management fees; 12b-1 fees, if any; and additional operating costs for a specific fund

Today, mutual funds can also be classified as A, B, or C shares. With A shares, investors pay commissions when they purchase shares in the mutual fund. With B shares, investors pay commissions when money is withdrawn or shares are sold during the first five to seven years. With C shares, investors often pay no commissions to buy or sell shares but usually must pay higher ongoing management and 12b-1 fees.

Managed funds versus indexed funds Most mutual funds are managed funds. In other words, there is a professional fund manager (or team of managers) who chooses the securities that are contained in the fund. The fund manager also decides when to buy and sell securities in the fund.

Instead of investing in a managed fund, some investors choose to invest in an index fund. Why? The answer to this question is simple: Over many years, index funds have outperformed managed funds. If the individual securities included in an index increase in value, the index goes up. Because an index fund contains the same securities as the index, the dollar value of a share in an index fund also increases when the index increases. Unfortunately, the reverse is also true. A second reason why investors choose index funds is the lower fees charged by these passively managed funds.

Types of mutual-fund investments Based on the type of securities they invest in, mutual funds generally fall into three broad categories: stocks, bonds, and other. The majority of mutual funds are *stock funds* that invest in stocks issued by small, medium-size, and large corporations that provide investors with income, growth, or a combination of income and growth. *Bond funds* invest in corporate, government, or municipal bonds that provide investors with interest income. The third category includes funds that stress asset allocation and money-market investments or strive for a balance between stocks and bonds. In most cases, the name of the category gives a pretty good clue to the type of investments included in the fund. Typical fund names include:

- Aggressive growth stock funds
- Balanced funds
- Global stock funds
- Growth stock funds
- High-yield (junk) bond funds
- Income stock funds
- Index funds
- Life cycle funds
- Long-term bond funds
- Regional funds
- Sector stock funds
- Socially responsible funds
- Small-cap stock funds

To help investors obtain their investment objectives, most investment companies now allow shareholders to switch from one fund to another fund within the same family of funds. A **family of funds** exists when one investment company manages a group of mutual funds. Generally, investors may give instructions to switch from one fund to another fund within the same family either in writing, over the telephone, or via the Internet. Charges for exchanges, if any, are small for each transaction.

family of funds a group of mutual funds managed by one investment company

Land and property

Property and land ownership represents one of the best hedges against inflation, but like all investments it has its risks. A piece of property in a poor location, for example, can actually decrease in value. Table 19.4 lists some of the many factors you should consider before investing in property or land.

 TABLE 19.4   **Real estate checklist** *Although property offers one of the best hedges against inflation, not all property increases in value. Many factors should be considered before investing in property.*

Evaluation of property	Inspection of the surrounding area	Other factors
Is the property priced competitively with similar property?	What are the present zoning requirements?	Why are the present owners selling the property?
What type of financing, if any, is available?	Is the neighbourhood's population increasing or decreasing?	How long will you have to hold the property before selling it to someone else?
How much are the taxes?	What is the average income of people in the area?	How much profit can you reasonably expect to obtain?
How much will it cost to repair or remodel a property?	What is the state of repair of surrounding property? Do most of the buildings and homes need repair?	Is there a chance that the property value will decrease?

There are, of course, disadvantages to any investment, and land or property is no exception. If you want to sell your property, you must find an interested buyer with the ability to obtain enough money to complete the transaction. Finding such a buyer can be difficult if loan money is scarce, the property market is in a decline, or you overpaid for a piece of property. For example, many investors were forced to hold some properties longer than they wanted because buyers could not obtain financing during the recent economic crisis. If you are forced to hold your investment longer than you originally planned, taxes, interest, and instalment payments can be a heavy burden. As a rule, property increases in value and eventually sells at a profit, but there are no guarantees. The degree of your success depends on how well you evaluate different alternatives.

The most speculative investment techniques

A **high-risk investment** is one made in the uncertain hope of earning a relatively large profit in a short time. Although all investments have some risk, some investments become high-risk because of the methods used by investors to earn a quick profit. These methods can lead to large losses as well as to impressive gains. They should not be used by anyone who does not fully understand the risks involved. We begin this section with a discussion of selling short. Then we examine margin transactions and other high-risk investments.

high-risk investment an investment made in the uncertain hope of earning a relatively large profit in a short time

Selling short   Normally, you buy stocks expecting that they will increase in value and then can be sold at a profit. This procedure is referred to as **buying long**. However, many securities decrease in value for various reasons. The market value for a share of a corporation's stock, for example, can decrease when sales and profits are lower than expected. When this type of situation occurs, you can use a procedure called selling short to make a profit when the price of an individual stock is falling. **Selling short** is the process of selling stock that an investor does not actually own but has borrowed from a brokerage firm and will repay at a later date. The idea is to sell at today's higher price and then buy later at a lower price. To make a profit from a short transaction, you must proceed as follows:

buying long buying a stock with the expectation that it will increase in value and then can be sold at a profit
selling short the process of selling stock that an investor does not actually own but has borrowed from a brokerage firm and will repay at a later date

1. Arrange to borrow a certain number of shares of a particular stock from a brokerage firm.
2. Sell the borrowed stock immediately, assuming that the price of the stock will drop in a reasonably short time.
3. After the price drops, buy the same number of shares that were sold in step 2.
4. Give the newly purchased stock to the brokerage firm in return for the stock borrowed in step 1.

Your profit is the difference between the amount received when the stock is sold in step 2 and the amount paid for the stock in step 3. For example, assume that you think Barnes & Noble stock is overvalued at €18 a share. You also believe that the stock will decrease in value over the next three to four months. In this example, you can make money with a short transaction—*if the stock's value does decline*. On the other hand, if the market value for a share of Barnes & Noble increases, you lose.

Buying stock on margin   An investor buys stock *on margin* by borrowing part of the purchase price, usually from a stock brokerage firm. The **margin requirement** is the portion of the price of a stock that cannot be borrowed.

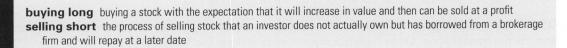

margin requirement the portion of the price of a stock that cannot be borrowed

Is gold a conservative or a high-risk investment? *Good question. When purchased from reputable dealers, gold can be a conservative investment—especially in troubled economic times. And yet, there are many unscrupulous dealers who sell worthless gold-plated coins to unsuspecting investors who want to make money quickly. The final answer: Consider the potential risks for a conservative or high-risk investment before investing your money.*

© ANAKENM2012/SHUTTERSTOCK

Today, the current margin requirement is 50 per cent, which means you can borrow up to 50 per cent of the cost of a stock purchase. Some securities exchanges and brokerage firms may impose other restrictions and require that you deposit more cash, which reduces the percentage that can be borrowed. However, why would investors want to buy stock on margin? Simply because they can buy up to twice as much stock that way. Suppose that an investor expects the market price of a share of ordinary share of an energy company to increase in the next three to four months. Assume you have enough money to purchase 200 shares of the stock. However, if you buy on margin, you can purchase an additional 200 shares for a total of 400 shares. If the price of the energy company's stock increases by €8 per share, your profit will be €1,600 (€8 × 200 = €1,600) if you pay cash. But it will be €3,200 (€8 × 400 = €3,200) if you buy the stock using margin. By buying more shares on margin, you will earn more profit (less the interest you pay on the borrowed money and customary commission charges).

Note that the stock purchased on margin serves as collateral for the borrowed funds. Before you become a margin investor, you should consider two factors. First, if the market price of the purchased stock does not increase as quickly as expected, interest costs mount and eventually drain your profit. Second, if the price of the margined stock falls, your euro loss will be greater because you own more shares.

If the value of a stock you bought on margin decreases to approximately 60 per cent of its original price, you may receive a *margin call* from the brokerage firm. You then must provide additional cash or securities to serve as collateral for the borrowed money. If you cannot provide additional collateral, the stock is sold, and the proceeds are used to pay off the loan and commissions. Any funds remaining after the loan and commissions are paid off are returned to you.

Other high-risk investments   We have already discussed two high-risk investments—selling short and margin transactions. Other high-risk investments include the following:

- Share options
- Derivatives
- Commodities
- Precious metals
- Gemstones
- Coins
- Antiques and collectibles

Without exception, investments of this kind are normally referred to as high-risk investments for one reason or another. For example, the gold market has many unscrupulous dealers who sell worthless gold-plated lead coins to unsuspecting, uninformed investors. It pays to be careful. *Although investments in this category can lead to large gains, they should not be used by anyone who does not fully understand all the potential risks involved.*

SOURCES OF FINANCIAL INFORMATION

A wealth of information is available to investors. Sources include the Internet, professional advisory services, newspapers, brokerage firm reports, business periodicals, corporate reports, and securities averages.

The Internet

By using the Internet, investors can access a wealth of information on most investment and personal finance topics. For example, you can obtain interest rates for CDs; current price information for stocks, bonds, and mutual funds; and experts' recommendations to buy, hold, or sell an investment. You can even trade securities online.

Because the Internet makes so much information available, you need to use it selectively. One of the Web search engines such as Yahoo! or Google can help you locate the information you really need. These search engines allow you to do a word search for the personal finance topic or investment alternative you want to explore. Why not take a look? Type in a key term such as *personal finance* or *financial planning* and see the results. In addition to using a search engine to locate information, you can also obtain information from a number of investment sites.

Corporations; brokerage firms; investment companies that sponsor mutual funds; property agents; and national and local governments also have Web sites where you can obtain valuable investment information. You may want to explore the information available on the Internet for two reasons. First, these sites are easily accessible. Second, the information on these sites may be more up-to-date than printed material obtained from published sources. Today, many of the above sources of information also use social media to connect with investors.

In addition, you can access professional advisory services—a topic discussed in the next section— for information on stocks, bonds, mutual funds, and other investment alternatives. Although some of the information provided by these services is free, there is a charge for the more detailed information you may need to evaluate an investment.

Professional advisory services

For a fee, various professional advisory services provide information about investments. Information from these services may also be available at university and public libraries.

Each investor service provides detailed financial reports. A number of professional advisory services provide detailed information on mutual funds. Although some information may be free, a fee is generally charged for more detailed research reports. In addition, various mutual-fund newsletters supply financial information to subscribers for a fee.

Financial coverage of securities transactions

Many local newspapers carry several pages of business news, including reports of securities transactions. The *Wall Street Journal* (published on weekdays) and *Barron's* (published once a week) are devoted almost entirely to financial and economic news. Both include coverage of transactions on major securities exchanges. *The Financial Times* also provides the latest information on the FTSE 100 index.

Because transactions involving stocks, bonds, and mutual funds are reported differently, we examine each type of report separately.

© YURI ARCURS/SHUTTERSTOCK

You must "invest" the time needed to research stocks, bonds, mutual funds, and other alternatives before you invest your money. And in order to be a "best" investor, you'll need to continue to evaluate each investment. Continued evaluation can help you decide if you want to hold, sell, or buy more of each investment in your investment portfolio.

FIGURE 19.1

Reading stock quotations *Reproduced at the top of the figure is a portion of the stock quotations listed in the* Wall Street Journal. *At the bottom is an enlargement of the same information. The numbers above each of the enlarged columns correspond to the numbered entries in the list of explanations that appears in the middle of the figure.*

STOCK	(SYM)	CLOSE	NET CHG
ABB ADS	ABB	18.33	–0.45
ACE Ltd	ACE	68.41	–0.96
AES Cp	AES	11.72	–0.14
Aflac	AFL	42.89	–0.89

1. Name (often abbreviated) of the corporation: Aflac
2. Ticker symbol or letters that identify a stock for trading: AFL
3. Close is the price paid in the last transaction of the day: $42.89
4. Difference between the price paid for the last share sold today and the price paid for the last share sold on the previous day: –0.89 (in Wall Street terms, Aflac "closed down $0.89" on this day).

1	2	3	4
STOCK	(SYM)	CLOSE	NET CHG
ABB ADS	ABB	18.33	–0.45
ACE Ltd	ACE	68.41	–0.96
AES Cp	AES	11.72	–0.14
Aflac	AFL	42.89	–0.89

Source: The *Wall Street Journal*, December 13, 2011, C8.

Common and preferred stocks Stock transactions are reported in tables that usually look like the top section of Figure 19.1. Stocks are listed alphabetically. Your first task is to move down the table to find the stock you are interested in. To read the stock quotation, you read across the table. The highlighted line in Figure 19.1 gives detailed information about ordinary share issued by Aflac—the insurance company with the talking duck.

Bonds Although some newspapers and financial publications provide limited information on certain corporate and government bond issues, it is usually easier to obtain more detailed information on a greater number of bond issues by accessing the Internet. Regardless of the source, bond prices are quoted as a percentage of the face value. Thus, to find the current price, you must multiply the face value (say, €1,000) by the quotation. For example, a price quoted as 84 translates to a selling price of €840 (€1,000 × 84% = €840). Detailed information obtained from the Yahoo! Finance Web site for a €1,000 AT&T corporate bond, which pays 5.50 per cent interest and matures in 2018, is provided in Figure 19.2.

Mutual funds Purchases and sales of shares of mutual funds are reported in tables like the one shown in Figure 19.3. As in reading stock quotations, your first task is to move down the table to find the mutual fund you are interested in. Then, to find the mutual-fund price quotation, read across the table. The first line in Figure 19.3 gives information for the Vanguard 500 Index mutual fund.

Other sources of financial information

In addition to the Internet, professional advisory services, and financial and newspaper coverage, other sources, which include brokerage firm reports, business periodicals, corporate reports, and securities averages offer information about investment alternatives.

Brokerage firm analysts' reports Brokerage firms employ financial analysts to prepare detailed reports on individual corporations and their securities. Such reports are based on the corporation's sales, profits or losses, management, and planning, plus other information on the company, its industry, demand for its products, its efforts to develop new products, and the current economic

FIGURE 19.2

Reading bond quotations
Reproduced at the top of the figure is bond information obtained from the Yahoo! Finance Web site. The numbers beside each line correspond to numbered entries in the list of explanations that appears at the bottom of the figure.

AT&T INC	
OVERVIEW	
1. Price	112.28
2. Coupon (%)	5.500
3. Maturity Date	1-Feb-2018
4. Yield to Maturity (%)	3.447
5. Current Yield (%)	4.899
6. Fitch Ratings	A
7. Coupon Payment Frequency	Semi-annual
8. First Coupon Date	1-Aug-2008
9. Type	Corporate
10. Callable	No

1. Price quoted as a percentage of the face value: $1,000 × 112.28% = $1,122.80
2. Coupon (%) is the rate of interest: 5.500 per cent
3. Maturity Date is the date when bondholders will receive repayment: February 1, 2018
4. Yield to Maturity (%) takes into account the relationship among a bond's maturity value, the time to maturity, the current price, and the amount of interest: 3.447 per cent
5. Current Yield (%) is determined by dividing the dollar amount of annual interest by the current price of the bond: ($55 ÷ $1,122.80 ÷ 0.04899 = 4.899 per cent)
6. Fitch Ratings is used to assess risk associated with this bond: A
7. Coupon Payment Frequency tells bondholders how often they will receive interest payments: Semi-annual
8. First Coupon Date: August 1, 2008
9. Type: Corporate
10. Callable: No

Source: The Yahoo! Finance bond Web site at http://bonds.yahoo.com (accessed March 12, 2012).

environment. The reports, which may include buy or sell recommendations, are usually provided free to the clients of full-service brokerage firms. Brokerage firm reports may also be available from discount brokerage firms, although they may charge a fee.

Business periodicals Business magazines such as *Bloomberg Businessweek*, *Fortune*, and *Forbes* provide not only general economic news but also detailed financial information about individual corporations. Trade or industry publications such as *Advertising Age* include information about firms in a specific industry. News magazines such as *Time* and *Newsweek* feature financial news regularly. *Money, Kiplinger's Personal Finance Magazine, Smart Money*, and similar magazines provide information and advice designed to improve your investment skills. These periodicals are available at libraries and are sold at newsstands and by subscription. Many of these same periodicals sponsor an online Web site that may contain all or selected articles that are contained in the print version.

Corporate reports Publicly held corporations must publish annual reports which include a description of the company's performance, information about the firm's products or services, and detailed financial statements that readers can use to evaluate the firm's actual performance. There should also be a letter from the accounting firm that audited the corporation. An audit does not guarantee that a company has not "cooked" the books, providing misleading information, but it does imply that the company has followed generally accepted accounting principles to report revenues, profits, assets, liabilities, and other financial information.

In addition, a corporation issuing a new security must—by law—prepare a prospectus and ensure that copies are distributed to potential investors. A **prospectus** is a detailed, written description

FIGURE 19.3

Reading mutual-fund quotations *Reproduced at the top of the figure is a portion of the mutual-fund quotations as reported by the Wall Street Journal. At the bottom is an enlargement of the same information. The numbers above each of the enlarged columns correspond to numbered entries in the list of explanations that appears in the middle of the figure.*

FUND	NAV	NET CHG	YTD %RET
Vanguard 500 Index	126.74	+0.46	9.4
TotBd	11.01	–	0.6
TotIntl	14.60	-0.04	11.8
TotSt	34.44	+0.16	10.1

1. The name of the mutual fund: Vanguard 500 Index
2. The net asset value (NAV) is the value of one share of the Vanguard 500 Index Fund: $126.74
3. The difference between the net asset value today and the net asset value on the previous trading day: +0.46 (in Wall Street terms, the "Vanguard 500 Index fund closed up $0.46" on this day)
4. The YTD% RET gives the total return for the Vanguard 500 Index fund for the year to date: 9.4%

1	2	3	4
FUND	NAV	NET CHG	YTD %RET
Vanguard 500 Index	126.74	+0.46	9.4
TotBD	11.01	–	0.6
TotIntl	14.60	-0.04	11.8
TotSt	34.44	+0.16	10.1

Source: The *Wall Street Journal,* March 10, 2012, B14.

of a new security, the issuing corporation, and the corporation's top management. A corporation's prospectus and its annual reports are available to the general public. You can request both an annual report and a prospectus by mail or telephone. In addition you can obtain an annual report, prospectus, or other financial information online. It's simple: Go to the corporation's Web site and click on "Investor Relations."

prospectus a detailed, written description of a new security, the issuing corporation, and the corporation's top management

Security averages

Investors often gauge the stock market through the security averages reported in newspapers and on television news programmes. A **security average (or security index)** is an average of the current market prices of selected securities. For example, the Dow Jones Industrial Average and the Standard & Poor 500 Stock Index are both used by investors to track the U.S. stock market. Today, there are averages for not only stocks, but also averages for bonds, U.S. Treasury securities, mutual funds, real estate, commodities, natural resources, and many popular investments. Over a period of time, these averages indicate price trends, but they do not predict the performance of individual investments. At best, they can give the investor a "feel" for what is happening to investment prices.

security average (or security index) an average of the current market prices of selected securities

HOW INVESTMENTS ARE BOUGHT AND SOLD

Think back over the material that was covered in this chapter. We began by discussing why it is important to examine your current financial situation and the need to manage your money. Next we talked about the factors that influence your choice of investments, how successful investors are involved in their investment programme, and conservative and speculative investment alternatives. Then, in the last section, we discussed how you can evaluate different investment alternatives in order to make an informed decision to buy or sell an investment. Once you understand the information in the previous sections and have researched a potential investment, you can use the options described in this section to buy or sell an investment.

Purchasing stocks and bonds

To purchase a Burberry jumper, you simply walk into a store that sells these jumpers, choose one, and pay for it. To purchase stocks and bonds, you work through a brokerage firm. In turn, an employee of the brokerage firm buys or sells securities for you.

Brokerage firms and account executives An **account executive**—sometimes called a *stockbroker* or *registered representative*—is an individual who buys and sells securities for clients. Before choosing an account executive, you should have already determined your investment goals. Then you must be careful to communicate these goals to the account executive so that she or he can do a better job of advising you. You must also decide whether you need a *full-service* broker or a *discount* broker. A full-service broker usually charges higher commissions when compared to a discount broker. To help decide if you should use a full-service or a discount brokerage firm, you should consider how much help you need when making an investment decision. Many full-service brokerage firms argue that you need a professional to help you make important investment decisions. Although this may be true for some investors, most account executives employed by full-service brokerage firms are too busy to spend unlimited time with you on a one-on-one basis, especially if you are investing a small amount. On the other side, many discount brokerage firms argue that you alone are responsible for making your investment decisions. Furthermore, they argue that discount brokerage firms have both the personnel and research materials to help you to become a better investor.

 account executive an individual, sometimes called a *stockbroker* or *registered representative,* who buys and sells securities for clients

The mechanics of a transaction Once you decide on a particular stock or bond, you can telephone your account executive or use the Internet to place a market or limit order. A **market order** is a request that a security be purchased or sold at the current market price. Figure 19.4 illustrates one method of executing a market order to sell a stock listed on the New York Stock Exchange (NYSE) at its current market value. It is also possible for a brokerage firm to match a buy order for a security for one of its customers with a sell order for the same security from another of its customers. Matched orders are not completed through a security exchange or the over-the-counter market. Regardless of how the security is bought or sold, payment for stocks, bonds, and many other financial securities generally is required within three business days of the transaction.

market order a request that a security be purchased or sold at the current market price

A **limit order** is a request that a security be bought or sold at a price equal to or better than (lower for buying, higher for selling) some specified price. Suppose that you place a limit order to *sell* Coca-Cola ordinary share at €70 per share. Your broker's representative sells the stock only if the price is €70 per share or *higher*. If you place a limit order to *buy* Coca Cola at €70, the representative buys it

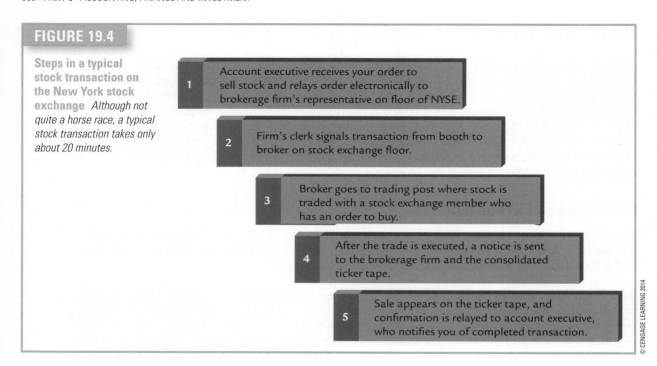

FIGURE 19.4

Steps in a typical stock transaction on the New York stock exchange *Although not quite a horse race, a typical stock transaction takes only about 20 minutes.*

1. Account executive receives your order to sell stock and relays order electronically to brokerage firm's representative on floor of NYSE.

2. Firm's clerk signals transaction from booth to broker on stock exchange floor.

3. Broker goes to trading post where stock is traded with a stock exchange member who has an order to buy.

4. After the trade is executed, a notice is sent to the brokerage firm and the consolidated ticker tape.

5. Sale appears on the ticker tape, and confirmation is relayed to account executive, who notifies you of completed transaction.

© CENGAGE LEARNING 2014

only if the price is €70 per share or *lower*. Usually, a limit order is good for one day, one week, one month, or good until cancelled.

limit order a request that a security be bought or sold at a price that is equal to or better than some specified price

Commissions Most brokerage firms have a minimum commission typically ranging from €7 to €25 for buying and selling stock. Additional commission charges are based on the number of shares and the value of stock bought and sold.

Generally, online transactions are less expensive when compared with the costs of trading securities through a full-service brokerage firm. As a rule of thumb, full-service brokerage firms charge as much as 1 to 2 per cent of the transaction amount. Commissions for trading bonds, commodities, and options are usually lower than those for trading stocks.

Purchasing mutual funds, real estate, and other investments

The method used to buy or sell mutual funds depends on the type of fund you choose. Open-end funds, for example, can be purchased or sold directly from the investment company that sponsors the fund on any business day. Both closed-end funds and exchange-traded funds can be purchased or sold on any business day through a securities exchange or the over-the-counter market. The amount of sales charge also depends on the type of fund you purchase. The sales charge for load funds can be as high as 8 $\frac{1}{2}$ per cent. For a load fund, the sales charge can be charged when you make a purchase or when you withdraw money from the fund. If you purchase a no-load fund, there is no sales charge. When purchasing shares in a load fund, you usually pay commission to buy *or* sell shares—but not to buy *and* sell shares. Reminder: For fund investments, you will also pay other fees that are usually assessed each year.

Although it is possible to buy or sell property without an estate agent or broker, these professionals are involved in most transactions. Finding an agent or broker that can help you to either buy or sell an investment is especially important because she or he can provide professional advice, realistic market values for different properties, and help completing the transaction. You should expect to pay commissions when you sell a property.

A broker (or account executive) is usually involved in the purchase or sale of the most speculative investment alternatives. For example, brokers can help you purchase commodities and precious metals. It is especially important to "know" the person you are dealing with when purchasing many of the speculative investments because of the potential for fraud and misrepresentation. It pays to be careful.

It should be apparent that vast sums of money are involved in securities trading. In an effort to protect investors from unfair treatment, both governments have acted to regulate securities trading.

Regulation of securities trading

Government regulation of securities was begun as a response to abusive and fraudulent practices in the sale of stocks, bonds, and other financial securities. Today, with so many news reports of banks with a portfolio of bad loans and of corporations that are in "hot water" over financial reporting problems that range from simple mistakes to out-and-out fraud, the concerns of both government officials and investors have grown.

Today, governments across the world have enacted various pieces of legislation to regulate the system, protect investors and ensure responsible practice and trading. **Full disclosure** means that investors should have access to all important facts about stocks, bonds, and other securities so that they can make informed decisions. This also requires that corporations issuing new securities file a registration statement and publish a prospectus. Many governments have passed legislation to curb insider-trading abuses. **Insider trading** occurs when insiders—board members, corporate managers, and employees—buy and sell a corporation's stock. Although insiders can buy and sell a corporation's stock, they must disclose their trading activities to the public.

> **full disclosure** requirement that investors should have access to all important facts about stocks, bonds, and other securities so that they can make informed decisions
> **insider trading** the practice of board members, corporate managers, and employees buying and selling a corporation's stock

A fundamental aspect in ensuring responsible practice is self-regulation by securities exchanges and brokerage firms. According to the NYSE, self-regulation—the way the securities industry monitors itself to create a fair and orderly trading environment—begins here.* To provide guidelines of ethical behaviour, various stock exchanges have published rules, policies, and standards of conduct. These standards are applied to every member in the stock exchange's investment community. They also conduct a thorough examination of each member firm that does business with the public at least once a year.* In addition, there are hundreds of brokerage firms that buy and sell securities for their customers. These firms are responsible for ensuring that their employees are highly trained and meet rigorous ethical standards.

Before they can start investing, most people have to decide on a career and obtain a job that will provide the money needed to finance an investment programme.

SUMMARY

- Explain why you should manage your personal finances and develop a personal investment programme

Many personal finance experts recommend that you begin the process of managing your money by determining your current financial condition. The first step often is to construct a personal income statement sheet and a personal balance sheet. You can also construct a personal budget. Before you begin investing, you must manage your credit card debts. For most people, the next step is to formulate realistic investment goals. A personal investment programme then is designed to implement these goals. Many financial planners also suggest that the investor should establish an emergency fund equivalent to at least three months' living expenses. However, you may want to increase your emergency fund in anticipation of a crisis. Then additional funds may be invested according to the investment programme. Finally, all investments should be monitored carefully, and if necessary, the investment programme should be modified.

- Describe how the factors of safety, risk, income, growth, and liquidity affect your investment programme

Depending on their particular investment goals, investors seek varying degrees of safety, risk, income, growth, and liquidity from their investments. Safety is, in essence, freedom from the risk of loss. Generally, the greater the risk, the greater should be the potential return on an investment. To determine how much risk you are willing to assume, many investors calculate the rate of return. It is also possible to compare the rate of return for different investments that offer more or less risk. Income is the periodic return from an investment. Growth is an increase in the value of the investment. Liquidity is the ease with which an asset can be converted to cash.

- Recognise how you can reduce investment risk and increase investment returns

The investments in your investment portfolio should be tailored to your goals, age, tolerance for risk, and financial resources. Asset allocation is the process of spreading your money among several different types of investments to lessen risk. Two other factors—the time your investments have to work for you and your age—should also be considered before deciding where to invest your money. To reduce investment risk and increase the returns on your investments, you should evaluate potential investments before investing your money, monitor the value of your investments on a regular basis, and keep accurate and current records.

- Explain the reasons people choose conservative investments including bank accounts and bonds

In this section, we examined traditional investments that include bank accounts, government bonds, and corporate bonds. Although bank accounts and bonds can provide investment growth, they are generally purchased by investors who seek a predictable source of income. Both government and corporate bonds are a form of debt financing. As a result, bonds are generally considered a more conservative investment than stocks, mutual funds, or other more speculative investments.

- Identify the advantages and disadvantages of stocks, mutual funds, property, and more speculative investments.

With stock investments, investors can make money through dividend payments, an increase in the market value of the stock, or stock splits. The major advantages of mutual-fund investments are professional management and diversification. Today, there are mutual funds to meet just about any conceivable investment objective. The success of land and property investments is often tied to how well each investment alternative is evaluated. High-risk investment techniques can provide greater returns, but they also entail greater risk of loss. You can make money by selling short when the market value of a financial security decreases. An investor can also buy stock on margin by borrowing part of the purchase price, usually from a stock brokerage firm. Because you can purchase up to twice as much stock by using margin, you can increase your return on investment as long as the stock's market value increases. Other high-risk investments include share options, derivatives, commodities, gemstones, precious metals, antiques, coins, and collectibles.

- Use financial information to evaluate investment alternatives.

Today, there is a wealth of information on stocks, bonds, and other securities and the firms that issue them. There is also a wealth of investment information on other types of investments, including mutual funds, real estate, and high-risk investment alternatives. Two popular sources—the Internet and newspapers—report daily securities transactions. The Internet can also be used to obtain detailed research information about different investment alternatives. Often, the most detailed research information about securities—and the most expensive—is obtained from professional advisory services. In addition, brokerage firm reports, business periodicals, and corporate reports can also be used to evaluate different investment alternatives. Finally, there are a number of security indexes or averages that indicate price trends but reveal nothing about the performance of individual securities.

- Understand how different investments are bought and sold.

If you invest in stocks and bonds, chances are that you will use the services of an account executive who works for a brokerage firm. It is also possible to use a discount broker or trade securities online with a computer. Both a market order and a limit order can be used to purchase stocks on a securities exchange or in the over-the-counter market. Full-service brokerage firms usually charge higher commissions than discount brokerage firms. With the exception of mutual funds and property, you generally pay a commission to buy *and* sell stocks, bonds, commodities, and most other investments.

The method used to buy or sell mutual funds depends on the type of fund you choose. Open-end funds, for example, can be purchased or sold directly from the investment company that sponsors the fund on any business day. Both closed-end funds and exchange-traded funds can be purchased or sold on any business day through a securities exchange or the over-the-counter market. While it is possible to buy or sell land or property without the help of an agent or broker, most investors rely on the professional advice provided by agents and brokers to help complete an estate transaction.

Governments have put in place legislation to regulate the system, protect investors and ensure ethical practice

EXERCISE QUESTIONS

1 Why should you get your personal finances in order before investing?

2 Describe exactly how you would go about checking and ensuring that your personal finances are in order and how would you maintain this?

3 Can anybody purchase stocks and bonds? Describe the typical processes involved.

4 Where can you look to find information on financial trading and companies to invest in?

5 Describe the relationship between safety and risk in regard to investing.

CASE 19.1

Fidelity Helps Investors Prepare for Their Financial Future

Boston-based Fidelity Investments wants its 20 million customers to be able to manage their money and receive responsive assistance from anywhere at any time. Whether customers use an iPad or Android app, tweet for customer service, transfer money electronically, use online chat for service, call a broker, or place orders through the company's Web site, Fidelity is ready to help around the clock.

Founded in 1946, Fidelity now has 39,000 employees worldwide and offers 524 mutual funds that hold a total of €3.6 trillion in assets from individuals and institutional investors. Its mutual funds fall into four main categories: money market, stocks, bonds, and international securities. Fidelity is best known for its managed funds, such as the Contrafund and the Magellan Fund, although it also offers many indexed stock and bond funds. Over the years, it has expanded into a wide range of other financial services, including discount brokerage services, college savings accounts, credit cards, current accounts, and online bill payment. Fidelity is also the country's largest administrator of 401(k) retirement accounts, handling retirement plans for more than 19,000 corporations, educational institutions, and nonprofit groups.

When the financial markets are open, Fidelity completes 345,000 securities trades per day for its customers. More than 3 million customers click on its user-friendly Web site every day to read analysts' reports, learn about investment and account options, view market update webinars, monitor their portfolios, or place a trade. For in-person service and advice, customers can visit one of the 168 Fidelity Investor Centres around the United States or attend a local seminar featuring Fidelity's investment experts.

Technology has always been one of Fidelity's strengths, so it's not surprising that the company has a Facebook page with 55,000 "likes" and a Twitter account with 48,000 followers. "Our expectation is that over time, we'll be interacting with not tens of thousands, but millions of people on these channels," says Fidelity's head of digital distribution. On the company's Web site, customers are invited to rate brokerage products and services for convenience, value, and features on a scale of one to five stars. In addition, they can write detailed reviews of what they like and don't like. This allows investors to see what other investors think, as well as giving Fidelity vital feedback and fresh ideas for new products.

Given Fidelity's diverse menu of offerings, "The time has arrived when a lot of people can do very well with a firm like Fidelity for all of their cash management [needs]," says a senior executive. For example, customers can deposit cheques to non-retirement accounts using a smart phone app, and withdraw money from any local bank's ATM—Fidelity pays the ATM fee. In fact, customers now click to make 7 million transfers of money to or from Fidelity accounts every year, a number that is growing as customers shift more of their personal finances to Fidelity.

Are young people going to have the money they need to enjoy retirement decades in the future? Fidelity's research shows that, thanks to new U.S. laws, more employees are being automatically enrolled in their employers' retirement plans. The earlier people begin to build their savings, the more money they will have when they reach retirement age. Among the plans that Fidelity administers, more than half of company employees now participate in the plan—triple the number of employees who participated in 2006. When these people need help with other financial matters, Fidelity will be ready.

References: John McCrank, "E-Brokerages Tap Social Media for Faster Service," *Reuters*, April 5, 2012, www.reuters.com; Stephen Miller, "Pension Protection Act Changes Plan Design, Motivates Saving," *HR Magazine*, February 2012, p. 14; Dan McCrum, "Original US Fidelity Business Thrives," *Financial Times*, April 11, 2012, www.ft.com; Ari I. Weinberg, "Coming to Your 401(k): Fidelity ETFs?" *Wall Street Journal*, January 3, 2012, www.wsj.com; William Baldwin, "Who Needs Bank Branches?" *Forbes*, August 3, 2011, www.forbes.com; www.fidelity.com.

Questions

1 Why would Fidelity offer 524 mutual funds? What are the advantages to the company and to investors?

2 What are the pros and cons of having a current account with Fidelity rather than with a local bank or credit union?

3 If you were trying to evaluate a specific mutual fund, where would you obtain the research information needed to choose the right fund? Assuming that you have found the right fund, would you prefer to invest online or talk with a Fidelity broker to complete the transaction?

CHAPTER REFERENCES

Barker, Bill, "Loads," the Motley Fool Web site at www.fool.com, accessed March 8, 2012. "Money 101 Lesson 4: Basics of Investing," the CNN/Money Web site at www.money.cnn.com, accessed March 8, 2012.

Orman, Suze, *The Road to Wealth* (New York: Riverbend Books, 2001), 371.

The 2010 Advanced Micro Devices Annual Report, the Advanced Micro Devices Web site at www.amd.com, accessed March 8, 2012.

The Investment Company Institute Web site at www.ici.org, accessed August 21, 2012.

The Mutual Fund Education Alliance Web site at www.mfea.com accessed March 8, 2012.

"The Regulatory Pyramid," the New York Stock Exchange Web site, accessed March 10, 2012.

GLOSSARY

absolute advantage the ability to produce a specific product more efficiently than any other nation

accessibility the ability to move goods over a specific route or network

accessory equipment Tools and equipment used in production or office activities that do not become part of the final physical product

accountability the obligation of a worker to accomplish an assigned job or task

account executive an individual, sometimes called a stockbroker or *registered representative*, who buys and sells securities for clients

actual product a composite of the features and capabilities offered in a product, quality and durability, design and product styling, packaging and brand name

ad hoc committee a committee created for a specific short-term purpose

administrative manager a manager who is not associated with any specific functional area but who provides overall administrative guidance and leadership

advertising agency an independent firm that plans, produces, and places advertising for its clients

advertising a paid nonpersonal message communicated to a select audience through a mass medium

advertising media the various forms of communication through which advertising reaches its audience

analytical process a process in operations management in which raw materials are broken into different component parts

analytic skills the ability to identify problems correctly, generate reasonable alternatives, and select the "best" alternatives to solve problems

Asia-Pacific Economic Cooperative (APEC) aims to promote trade between its members: the six ASEAN members plus the United States, Australia, Canada, New Zealand, Japan, China, South Korea, Hong Kong and Taiwan

asset allocation the process of spreading your money among several different types of investments to lessen risk

Association of South East Asian Nations (ASEAN) formed in 1967 with the intention of building trade and other links among its six members: Brunei, Indonesia, Malaysia, the Philippines, Singapore and Thailand

augmented product support aspects of a product, including customer service, warranty, delivery and credit, personnel, installation and after-sales support

authority the power, within an organisation, to accomplish an assigned job or task

automatic vending the use of coin or credit card-operated self-service machines to sell small, standardised, routinely purchased products such as chewing gum, sweets, newspapers, cigarettes, soft drinks and coffee

automation the total or near-total use of machines to do work

balance of payments the total flow of money into a country minus the total flow of money out of that country over some period of time

balance of trade the total value of a nation's exports minus the total value of its imports over some period of time

banker's acceptance a written order for a bank to pay a third party a stated amount of money on a specific date

Bank of England the central bank of the United Kingdom

barter an exchange in which goods or services are traded directly for other goods or services without using money

barter system a system of exchange in which goods or services are traded directly for other goods or services

behaviour modification a systematic programme of reinforcement to encourage desirable behaviour

benchmarking a mechanism for achieving continuous improvement by measuring products, services or activities against those of other best performing organisations; a process used to evaluate the products, processes, or management practices of another organisation that is superior in some way in order to improve quality

blog a Web site that allows a company to share information in order to not only increase the customer's knowledge about its products and services, but also to build trust

blue-chip stock a safe investment that generally attracts conservative investors

board of directors the top governing body of a corporation, the members of which are elected by the stockholders

bond indenture a legal document that details all the conditions relating to a bond issue

brand a name, term, symbol, design, or any combination of these that identifies a seller's products as distinct from those of other sellers

brand equity marketing and financial value associated with a brand's strength in a market

brand extension using an existing brand to brand a new product in a different product category

brand loyalty extent to which a customer is favourable toward buying a specific brand

brand mark the part of a brand that is a symbol or distinctive design

brand name the part of a brand that can be spoken

breakeven quantity the number of units that must be sold for the total revenue (from all units sold) to equal the total cost (of all units sold)

budget a financial plan or statement that projects income, expenditures, or both over a specified future period for implementing management decisions.

bundle pricing packaging together two or more complementary products and selling them for a single price

business the organised effort of individuals to produce and sell, for a profit, the goods and services that satisfy a society's needs

business cycle the recurrence of periods of growth and recession in a nation's economic activity

business model represents a group of common characteristics and methods of doing business to generate sales revenues and reduce expenses

business plan a carefully constructed guide for the person starting a business

business-to-business (or B2B) model a model used by firms that conduct business with other businesses

business-to-consumer (or B2C) model a model used by firms that focus on conducting business with individual consumers

buying allowance a temporary price reduction to resellers for purchasing specified quantities of a product

buying long buying stock with the expectation that it will increase in value and then can be sold at a profit

capability the ability of a transport mode to provide the appropriate equipment and conditions for moving specific kinds of goods

capacity the amount of products or services that an organisation can produce in a given time

capital budget a financial statement that estimates a firm's expenditures for major assets and its long-term financing needs

capital gain the difference between a security's purchase price and its selling price

capital-intensive technology a process in which machines and equipment do most of the work

capitalism an economic system in which individuals own and operate the majority of businesses that provide goods and services

captioned photograph a picture accompanied by a brief explanation

captive pricing pricing the basic product in a product line low, but pricing related items at a higher level

cash and carry warehouses outlets that retail extensive ranges of groceries, tobacco, alcohol, beverages and confectionery to newsagents, small supermarkets and convenience stores, and the catering trade

cash and carry wholesalers middlemen whose customers will pay cash and provide transport

cash budget a financial statement that estimates cash receipts and cash expenditures over a specified period

cash flow the movement of money into and out of an organisation

catalogue retailing a type of mail-order retailing in which customers receive their catalogues by mail, or pick them up if the catalogue retailer has stores

catalogue showroom outlets in which one item of each product class is on display and the remaining inventory is stored out of the buyers' reach

category killers large stores, tending to be superstore sized, which specialise in a narrow line of merchandise

category management a core approach to merchandising, inventory control and display in many retailers, with similar lines from several suppliers being controlled by a category manager and managed as a discrete unit

cause-related marketing the practice of linking products to a particular social cause on an ongoing or medium-term basis

Central and Eastern Europe (CEE) encompasses the Commonwealth of Independent States (formerly the Soviet Union), the Czech and Slovak Republics, Hungary, Poland, Slovenia, Croatia, Bosnia and Herzegovina, Serbia and Montenegro, Bulgaria, FYR Macedonia and Albania

central bank an institution designed to regulate the quantity of money in the economy

central business district (CBD) the traditional hub of most cities and towns; the focus for shopping, banking and commerce, and hence the busiest part of the whole area

centralised organisation an organisation that systematically works to concentrate authority at the upper levels of the organisation

certificate of deposit (CD) a document stating that the bank will pay the depositor a guaranteed interest rate on money left on deposit for a specified period of time

chain of command the line of authority that extends from the highest to the lowest levels of an organisation

charismatic or visionary leadership is a personalised form of strategic leadership based on a leader's vision about purpose and behaviour of the organisation that helps condition an organisation's culture and strategic management.

cheque a written order for a bank or other financial institution to pay a stated amount to the business or person indicated on the face of the cheque

chief financial officer (CFO) a high-level corporate executive who manages a firm's finances and reports directly to the company's chief executive officer or president

citizenship marketing the adoption of a strategic focus for fulfilling the economic, legal, ethical and philanthropic social responsibilities expected by stakeholders

closed corporation a corporation whose stock is owned by relatively few people and is not sold to the general public

cloud computing a type of computer usage in which services stored on the Internet are provided to users on a temporary basis

codes of conduct formalised rules and standards that describe what the company expects of its employees

collateral real estate or property pledged as security for a loan

command economy an economic system in which the government decides what goods and services will be produced, how they will be produced, for whom available goods and services will be produced, and who owns and controls the major factors of production

commercial bank a profit-making organisation that accepts deposits, makes loans, and provides related services to its customers

commission a payment that is a percentage of sales revenue

commission employees (usually salespeople) are paid a percentage of the value of what they have sold by way of reward.

commission merchants agents who receive goods on consignment from local sellers and negotiate sales in large central markets

commodity money money that takes the form of a commodity with intrinsic value

Commonwealth of Independent States (CIS) the CIS unites Azerbaijan, Armenia, Belarus, Georgia, Kazakhstan, Kyrgyzstan, Moldova, Russia, Tajikistan, Turkmenistan, Ukraine and Uzbekistan in a trading bloc

communication skills the ability to speak, listen, and write effectively

community interest company (CIC) a limited company set to function as a social enterprise, which adheres to strict statutory requirements for adhering to social purposes

comparable worth a concept that seeks equal compensation for jobs requiring about the same level of education, training, and skills

comparative advantage the ability to produce a specific product more efficiently than any other product

comparison discounting setting a price at a specific level and comparing it with a higher price

compensation the payment employees receive in return for their labour

compensation system the policies and strategies that determine employee compensation

competition rivalry among businesses for sales to potential customers

component parts parts that become a part of the physical product and are either finished items ready for assembly or products that need little processing before assembly

computer-aided design (CAD) the use of computers to aid in the development of products

computer-aided manufacturing (CAM) the use of computers to plan and control manufacturing processes

computer-integrated manufacturing (CIM) a computer system that not only helps to design products but also controls the machinery needed to produce the finished product

computer virus a software code designed to disrupt normal computer operations

conceptual skills the ability to think in abstract terms

consumable supplies supplies that facilitate production and operations but do not become part of the finished product

consumer price index (CPI) a monthly index that measures the changes in prices of a fixed basket of goods purchased by a typical consumer in an urban area

consumer products items purchased to satisfy personal or family needs

consumer sales promotion method a sales promotion method designed to attract consumers to particular retail stores and to motivate them to purchase certain new or established products

consumer-to-consumer (C2C) communication consumer-to-consumer (C2C) communication is now routine, enabled by the digital era and social media in particular. Consumers readily and rapidly share views, experiences and information with each other. A positive or negative customer experience is tweeted instantly, blogged or shared on Facebook with potentially very many fellow consumers.

containerisation the practice of consolidating many items into a single large container that is sealed at its point of origin and opened at its destination, greatly increasing efficiency and security in shipping

contingency plan a plan that outlines alternative courses of action that may be taken if an organisation's other plans are disrupted or become ineffective

continuous improvement an ongoing search to reduce costs, eliminate waste and improve the quality and performance of activities that increase customer value or satisfaction.

continuous process a manufacturing process in which a firm produces the same product(s) over a long period of time

contract manufacturing the practice of hiring a foreign company to produce a designated volume of product to a set specification

control a managerial function that consists of the measurement, reporting and subsequent correction of performance in order to achieve the organisation's objectives.

controlling the process of evaluating and regulating ongoing activities to ensure that goals are achieved

control process the process of setting targets or standards against which actual results are measured.

convenience products items purchased to satisfy Inexpensive, frequently purchased and rapidly consumed items that demand only minimal purchasing effort

convenience stores shops that sell essential groceries, alcoholic drinks, drugs and newspapers outside the traditional shopping hours

convertible bond a bond that can be exchanged, at the owner's option, for a specified number of shares of the corporation's ordinary share

cookie a small piece of software sent by a Web site that tracks an individual's Internet use

cooperative advertising an arrangement whereby a manufacturer agrees to pay a certain amount of a retailer's media cost for advertising the manufacturer's product

core competencies approaches and processes that a company performs well that may give it an advantage over its competitors

core product the level of a product that provides the perceived or real core benefit or service

corporate bond a corporation's written pledge that it will repay a specified amount of money with interest

corporate culture the inner rites, rituals, heroes, and values of a firm

corporate officers the chairman of the board, president, executive vice presidents, corporate secretary, treasurer, and any other top executive appointed by the board of directors

corporation an artificial person created by law with most of the legal rights of a real person, including the rights to start and operate a business, to buy or sell property, to borrow money, to sue or be sued, and to enter into binding contracts

cost accounting accounting concerned with cost accumulation for inventory valuation to meet the requirements of external reporting and internal profit measurement.

costs one consideration that helps determine transportation mode, involving comparison of alternative modes to determine whether the benefits of a more expensive mode are worth the higher costs

cost trade-offs the off-setting of higher costs in one area of the distribution system by lower costs in another area, to keep the total system cost-effective

coupon an offer that reduces the retail price of a particular item by a stated amount at the time of purchase

creative selling selling products to new customers and increasing sales to present customers

credit immediate purchasing power that is exchanged for a promise to repay borrowed money, with or without interest, at a later date

credit union a financial institution that accepts deposits from, and lends money to, only the people who are its members

critical marketing critical marketing involves challenging orthodox views that are central to the core principles of the discipline. Sometimes this involves promoting radical philosophies and theories in relation to the understanding of economies, society, markets and consumers, which may have implications for the practice of marketing. Critical marketing is connected with the growing area of critical management.

cross-functional team a team of individuals with varying specialties, expertise, and skills that are brought together to achieve a common task

crowdsourcing outsourcing tasks to a group of people in order to tap into the ideas of the crowd

cultural (or workplace) diversity differences among people in a workforce owing to race, ethnicity, and gender

currency the paper banknotes and coins in the hands of the public

currency devaluation the reduction of the value of a nation's currency relative to the currencies of other countries

customary pricing pricing on the basis of tradition

customer satisfaction a state that results when an exchange meets the needs and expectations of the buyer

customer service customer satisfaction in terms of physical distribution, based on availability, promptness and quality

customer threshold the number of customers required to make a profit

cycle time the length of time from start to completion of a product or service and is the sum of processing time, move time, wait time and inspection time.

data mining the practice of searching through data records looking for useful information

debenture bond a bond backed only by the reputation of the issuing corporation

debit card a card that electronically subtracts the amount of your purchase from your bank account at the moment the purchase is made

debt capital borrowed money obtained through loans of various types

decentralised organisation an organisation in which management consciously attempts to spread authority widely in the lower levels of the organisation

decision making the act of choosing one alternative from a set of alternatives

decline stage the last stage of a product's life cycle, during which sales fall rapidly

deflation a general decrease in the level of prices

delegation assigning part of a manager's work and power to other workers; giving authority to lower levels of management so they have the power to use the business's resources to produce and deliver goods and services.

demand deposits balances in bank accounts that depositors can access on demand by using a debit card or writing a cheque

demand the quantity of a product that buyers are willing to purchase at each of various prices

departmentalisation the process of grouping jobs into manageable units

departmentalisation by customer grouping activities according to the needs of various customer populations

departmentalisation by function grouping jobs that relate to the same organisational activity

departmentalisation by location grouping activities according to the defined geographic area in which they are performed

departmentalisation by product grouping activities related to a particular product or service

department stores physically large stores that occupy prominent positions in the traditional heart of the town or city, or as anchor stores in out-of-town malls

depression a severe recession that lasts longer than a typical recession and has a larger decline in business activity when compared to a recession

depth (of product mix) the number of different products offered in each product line

design planning the development of a plan for converting an idea into an actual product or service

digital marketing the use of particularly the Web and mobile phones, as well as radio, TV and any other form of digital media to attract, engage and build relationships with customers and other target audiences.

directing the combined processes of leading and motivating

direct-mail advertising promotional material mailed directly to individuals

direct marketing the use of non-personal media, the Internet or telesales to introduce products to consumers, who then purchase the products by mail, telephone or the Internet

discount a deduction from the price of an item

discount rate the interest rate at which the Federal Reserve lends on a short-term basis to the U.S. banking sector

discount sheds cheaply constructed, one-storey retail stores with no window displays and few add-on amenities; oriented towards car-borne shoppers

distributors companies that buy and sell on their own account but tend to deal in the goods of only certain specified manufacturers

dividend a distribution of earnings to the stockholders of a corporation

domestic system a method of manufacturing in which an entrepreneur distributes raw materials to various homes, where families process them into finished goods to be offered for sale by the merchant entrepreneur

Dow Jones Industrial Average an average of 30 leading U.S. corporations that reflect the U.S. stock market as a whole

drop shippers intermediaries who take title to goods and negotiate sales but never actually take possession of products

dumping exportation of large quantities of a product at a price lower than that of the same product in the home market

e-business (electronic business) the organised effort of individuals to produce and sell through the Internet, for a profit, the products and services that satisfy society's needs; the use of information and communication technologies to support any business activities, including buying and selling.

e-commerce the use of information and communication technologies to support the purchase, sale and exchange of goods.

economic order quantity (EOQ) the order size that minimises the total cost of ordering and carrying inventory

economics the study of how wealth is created and distributed

economy the way in which people deal with the creation and distribution of wealth

edge-of-town sites retail locations on undeveloped land, providing purpose-built stores, parking facilities and amenities for their customers on the edge of a built-up area

electronic data interchange (EDI) the use of IT to integrate order processing with production, inventory, accounting and transportation

electronic funds transfer (EFT) system a means of performing financial transactions through a computer terminal or telephone hookup

embargo a complete halt to trading with a particular nation or of a particular product

emotional intelligence is an individual's ability to recognise their own emotions and those of others, and act to take these into account in relationships.

employee benefit a reward in addition to regular compensation that is provided indirectly to employees

employee empowerment providing employees with relevant information to allow them to make continuous improvements to the output of processes without the authorisation by superiors.

employee ownership a situation in which employees own the company they work for by virtue of being stockholders

employee training the process of teaching operations and technical employees how to do their present jobs more effectively and efficiently

empowerment giving employees greater control by providing them with decision-making powers that have an effect on their working lives.

enterprise resource planning system (ERPS) a set of integrated software application modules that aim to control all information flows within a company.

entrepreneur a person who risks time, effort, and money to start and operate a business

entrepreneurial leadership is characterised by the personality, usually of a single owner-manager, or sometimes of a few collaborating individuals, who impose their view on the business in ways that are characteristically innovative.

equity capital money received from the owners or from the sale of shares of ownership in a business

equity theory a theory of motivation based on the premise that people are motivated to obtain and preserve equitable treatment for themselves

ethical issue an identifiable problem, situation or opportunity requiring a choice between several actions that must be evaluated as right or wrong, ethical or unethical

European Central Bank (ECB) the overall central bank of the 16 countries comprising the European Monetary Union

European Union (EU) the major grouping in Western Europe, the EU has 27 members: Austria, Belgium, Denmark, Finland, France, Germany, Greece, Ireland, Italy, Luxembourg, the Netherlands, Portugal, Spain, Sweden and the United Kingdom have been joined by Bulgaria, Cyprus, the Czech Republic, Estonia, Hungary, Latvia, Lithuania, Malta, Poland, Romania, Slovakia and Slovenia

Eurosystem the system made up of the ECB plus the national central banks of each of the 16 countries comprising the European Monetary Union

everyday low prices (EDLPs) setting a low price for products on a consistent basis

exchange the provision or transfer of goods, services and ideas in return for something of value

exchange-traded fund (ETF) a fund that generally invests in the stocks or other securities contained in a specific stock or securities index

expectancy theory a model of motivation based on the assumption that motivation depends on how much we want something and on how likely we think we are to get it

expense ratio all the different management fees; 12b-1 fees, if any; and additional operating costs for a specific fund

exporting selling and shipping raw materials or products to other nations; use of an intermediary that performs most marketing functions associated with selling to other countries; entails the minimum effort, cost and risk involved in international marketing

express warranty a written explanation of the producer's responsibilities in the event that a product is found to be defective or otherwise unsatisfactory

external recruiting the attempt to attract job applicants from outside an organisation

facilitating agencies organisations such as transport companies, insurance companies, advertising agencies, marketing research agencies and financial institutions that perform activities that enhance channel functions

factor a firm that specialises in buying other firms' accounts receivable

factors of production resources used to produce goods and services

factory outlet villages converted rural buildings or purpose-built out-of-town retail parks for manufacturers' outlets retailing branded seconds, excess stocks and last season's lines, or trialling new lines

factory system a system of manufacturing in which all the materials, machinery, and workers required to manufacture a product are assembled in one place

family branding the strategy in which a firm uses the same brand for all or most of its products

family of funds a group of mutual funds managed by one investment company

feature article a piece (of up to 3,000 words) prepared by an organisation for inclusion in a particular publication

Federal Reserve (Fed) the Central Bank of the United States

fiat money money without intrinsic value that is used as money because of government decree

financial accounting accounting concerned with the provision of information to parties that are external to the organisation.

financial gearing the use of borrowed funds to increase the return on owners' equity

financial management all the activities concerned with obtaining money and using it effectively

financial manager a manager who is primarily responsible for an organisation's financial resources

financial plan a plan for obtaining and using the money needed to implement an organisation's goals and objectives

financial planner an individual who has had at least two years of training in investments, insurance, taxation, retirement planning, and estate planning and has passed a rigorous examination

first-line manager a manager who coordinates and supervises the activities of operating employees

fiscal policy government influence on the amount of savings and expenditures; accomplished by altering the tax structure and by changing the levels of government spending

fixed cost a cost incurred no matter how many units of a product are produced or sold

flexible benefit plan compensation plan whereby an employee receives a predetermined amount of benefit money to spend on a package of benefits he or she has selected to meet individual needs

flexible manufacturing system (FMS) a single production system that combines electronic machines and computer-integrated manufacturing

flexitime a system in which employees set their own work hours within employer-determined limits

flotation the process of offering a company's shares for sale on the stock market for the first time

food brokers intermediaries who sell food and general merchandise items to retailer-owned and merchant wholesalers, grocery chains, industrial buyers and food processors

foreign direct investment (FDI) a long-term commitment to marketing in a foreign nation through direct ownership of a foreign subsidiary or division

foreign-exchange control a restriction on the amount of a particular foreign currency that can be purchased or sold

forum an interactive version of a community bulletin board and focuses on threaded discussions

four competences of leadership are management of attention; management of meaning; management of trust and management of self.

franchise a license to operate an individually owned business as though it were part of a chain of outlets or stores

franchisee a person or organisation purchasing a franchise

franchising a form of licensing granting the right to use certain intellectual property rights, such as trade names, brand names, designs, patents and copyrights

franchising the actual granting of a franchise

franchisor an individual or organisation granting a franchise

free enterprise the system of business in which individuals are free to decide what to produce, how to produce it, and at what price to sell it

frequent-user incentive a programme developed to reward customers who engage in repeat (frequent) purchases

fringe benefits payments to workers in a non-monetary form, such as company cars or private health care.

full disclosure requirement that investors should have access to all important facts about stocks, bonds, and other securities so that they can make informed decisions

full service wholesalers middlemen who offer the widest possible range of wholesaling functions

functional middlemen intermediaries who perform a limited number of marketing activities in exchange for commission sellers, and usually offer customers complete product lines

Gantt chart a graphic scheduling device that displays the tasks to be performed on the vertical axis and the time required for each task on the horizontal axis

General Agreement on Tariffs and Trade (GATT) an agreement between countries to reduce worldwide tariffs and increase international trade

general merchandise wholesalers middlemen who carry a wide product mix but offer limited depth within the product lines

generic product (or brand) a product with no brand at all

goal an end result that an organisation is expected to achieve over a one- to ten-year period

goal-setting theory a theory of motivation suggesting that employees are motivated to achieve goals that they and their managers establish together

good a physical entity that can be touched

grapevine the informal communications network within an organisation

green IT a term used to describe all of a firm's activities to support a healthy environment and sustain the planet

green marketing the specific development, pricing, promotion and distribution of products that do not harm the natural environment

gross domestic product (GDP) the total value of all goods and services produced by all people within the boundaries of a country during a one-year period

growth stage the stage at which a product's sales rise rapidly and profits reach a peak, before levelling off into maturity

high-risk investment an investment made in the uncertain hope of earning a relatively large profit in a short time

hostile takeover a situation in which the management and board of directors of a firm targeted for acquisition disapprove of the merger

hourly wage a specific amount of money paid for each hour of work

human resources management (HRM) all the activities involved in acquiring, maintaining, and developing an organisation's human resources

human resources manager a person charged with managing an organisation's human resources programmes

human resources planning the development of strategies to meet a firm's future human resources needs

hypermarkets stores that take the benefits of the superstore even further, using their greater size to give the customer a wider range and depth of products

ideas a concept, philosophy, image or issue

import duty (tariff) a tax levied on a particular foreign product entering a country

importing purchasing raw materials or products in other nations and bringing them into one's own country

import quota a limit on the amount of a particular good that may be imported into a country during a given period of time

inbound marketing a marketing term that describes new ways of gaining attention and ultimately customers by creating content on a Web site that pulls customers in

incentive payment a payment in addition to wages, salary, or commissions

individual branding the strategy in which a firm uses a different brand for each of its products

industrial/business services the intangible products that many organisations use in their operations, including financial, legal, marketing research, computer programming and operation, caretaking and printing services

industrial or business products items bought for use in a company's operations or to make other products

inflation a general rise in the level of prices

infomercial a programme-length televised commercial message resembling an entertainment or consumer affairs programme

informal group a group created by the members themselves to accomplish goals that may or may not be relevant to an organisation

informal organisation the pattern of behaviour and interaction that stems from personal rather than official relationships

in-home retailing selling via personal contacts with consumers in their own homes

initial public offering (IPO) occurs when a corporation sells ordinary share to the general public for the first time

insider trading the practice of board members, corporate managers, and employees buying and selling a corporation's stock

inspection the examination of the quality of work-in-process

institutional advertising advertising designed to enhance a firm's image or reputation

integrated marketing communications coordination of promotion efforts to ensure their maximal informational and persuasive impact on customers

intermittent process a manufacturing process in which a firm's manufacturing machines and equipment are changed to produce different products

internal recruiting considering present employees as applicants for available positions

international business all business activities that involve exchanges across national boundaries

International Monetary Fund (IMF) an international bank with 188 member nations that makes short-term loans to developing countries experiencing balance-of-payment deficits

International Organisation for Standardisation (ISO) a network of national standards institutes and similar organisations from over 160 different countries that is charged with developing standards for quality products and services that are traded throughout the globe

internet commerce the buying and selling of goods and services over the internet.

interpersonal skills the ability to deal effectively with other people

introduction stage a product's first appearance in the marketplace, before any sales or profits have been made

inventory control the process of managing inventories in such a way as to minimise inventory costs, including both holding costs and potential stock-out costs

inventory management the development and maintenance of adequate assortments of products to meet customers' needs

investment banking firm an organisation that assists corporations in raising funds, usually by helping to sell new issues of stocks, bonds, or other financial securities

invisible hand a term created by Adam Smith to describe how an individual's personal gain benefits others and a nation's economy

job analysis a systematic procedure for studying jobs to determine their various elements and requirements

job description a list of the elements that make up a particular job

job enlargement expanding a worker's assignments to include additional but similar tasks

job enrichment a motivation technique that provides employees with more variety and responsibility in their jobs

job evaluation the process of determining the relative worth of the various jobs within a firm

job redesign a type of job enrichment in which work is restructured to cultivate the worker–job match

job rotation the systematic shifting of employees from one job to another

job sharing an arrangement whereby two people share one full-time position

job specialisation the separation of all organisational activities into distinct tasks and the assignment of different tasks to different people

job specification a list of the qualifications required to perform a particular job

joint venture a partnership between a domestic company and a foreign company or government; cooperating firms create a legally independent firm in which they invest and from which they share any profits that are created

just-in-time inventory system a system designed to ensure that materials or supplies arrive at a facility just when they are needed so that storage and holding costs are minimised

key performance indicators (KPIs) measurements that define and measure the progress of an organisation toward achieving its objectives

labeling the presentation of information on a product or its package

labour-intensive technology a process in which people must do most of the work

leader a person, who by influencing others, has an ability to take the organisation forward to serve a common purpose.

leadership the ability to influence others

leading the process of influencing people to work toward a common goal

lean manufacturing a concept built on the idea of eliminating waste from all of the activities required to produce a product or service

lean manufacturing systems systems that seek to reduce waste in manufacturing by implementing just-in-time production systems, focusing on quality, simplifying processes and investing in advanced technologies.

licensing system in which a licensee pays commissions or royalties on sales or supplies used in manufacturing

limited liability a situation where the liability (responsibility) of the owner/s of a business is limited to the amount that they have agreed to subscribe/invest

limited liability partnership (LLP) a partnership in which some or all partners (depending on the jurisdiction) have limited liability

limited line wholesalers wholesalers that carry only a few product lines but offer an extensive assortment of products within those lines

limited service wholesalers middlemen who provide only some marketing services and specialise in a few functions

limit order a request that a security be bought or sold at a price that is equal to or better than some specified price

line-and-staff structure an organisational structure that utilises the chain of command from a line structure in combination with the assistance of staff managers

line extension development of a new product that is closely related to one or more products in the existing product line but designed specifically to meet somewhat different customer needs

line manager a position in which a person makes decisions and gives orders to subordinates to achieve the organisation's goals

line of credit a loan that is approved before the money is actually needed

line structure an organisational structure in which the chain of command goes directly from person to person throughout the organisation

liquidity the ease with which an asset can be converted into the economy's medium of exchange

lockout a firm's refusal to allow employees to enter the workplace

long-term financing money that will be used for longer than one year

maastricht treaty the treaty, signed in 1992, that established the European Union

macroeconomics the study of the national economy and the global economy

mail-order retailing selling by description because buyers usually do not see the actual product until it arrives in the mail

mail-order wholesalers wholesalers that use catalogues instead of sales forces to sell products to retail, industrial and institutional buyers

major equipment large tools and machines used for production purposes

malware a general term that describes software designed to infiltrate a computer system without the user's consent

management the process of coordinating people and other resources to achieve the goals of an organisation

management accounting accounting concerned with the provision of information to people within the organisation to aid decision-making and improve the efficiency and effectiveness of existing operations.

management by exception a situation where management attention is focused on areas where outcomes do not meet targets.

management by objectives (MBO) a motivation technique in which managers and employees collaborate in setting goals

management development the process of preparing managers and other professionals to assume increased responsibility in both present and future positions

manufacturer (or producer) brand a brand that is owned by a manufacturer

manufacturers' agents independent middlemen or distributors who represent two or more

margin requirement the portion of the price of a stock that cannot be borrowed

market economy an economic system in which businesses and individuals decide what to produce and buy, and the market determines quantities sold and prices

marketing concept the philosophy that an organisation should try to provide products that satisfy customers' needs through a coordinated set of activities that also allows the organisation to achieve its goals

marketing environment external changing forces within the trading environment: laws, regulations, political activities, societal pressures, economic conditions and technological advances

marketing era in which the focus is not only on expediting the single transaction but on developing ongoing relationships with customers to maintain lifetime share of wallet

marketing era the period in which product and aggressive selling were no longer seen to suffice if customers either did not desire a product or preferred a rival brand, and in which customer needs were identified and satisfied

marketing ethics principles and standards that define acceptable marketing conduct as determined by various stakeholders, including the public, government, regulators, private interest groups, consumers, industry and the organisation itself

marketing individual and organisational activities that facilitate and expedite satisfying exchange relationships in a dynamic environment through the creation, distribution, promotion and pricing of goods, services and ideas

marketing management a process of planning, organising, implementing and controlling marketing activities to facilitate and expedite exchanges effectively and efficiently

marketing manager a manager who is responsible for facilitating the exchange of products between an organisation and its customers or clients

marketing mix the tactical "toolkit" of the marketing programme; product, place/distribution, promotion, price and people variables that an organisation can control in order to appeal to the target market and facilitate satisfying exchange

marketing opportunity one that exists when circumstances allow an organisation to take action towards reaching a particular group of consumer or business customers

marketing orientation a marketing-oriented organisation devotes resources to understanding the needs and buying behaviour of customers, competitors' activities and strategies, and of market trends and external forces – now and as they may shape up in the future; inter-functional coordination ensures that the organisation's activities and capabilities are aligned to this marketing intelligence

marketing strategy the selection of which marketing opportunities to pursue, identification of associated target market(s), creation of a basis for competing and 'wow' positioning, and the development and maintenance of an appropriate marketing mix to satisfy those in the target market(s)

market order a request that a security be purchased or sold at the current market price

market price the price at which the quantity demanded is exactly equal to the quantity supplied

markets halls where fresh foods, clothing and housewares are sold, catering for budget-conscious shoppers who typically have a middle and downmarket social profile

market value the price of one share of a stock at a particular time

markup the amount a seller adds to the cost of a product to determine its basic selling price

mass production a manufacturing process that lowers the cost required to produce a large number of identical or similar products over a long period of time

master budget a single unifying statement of an organisation's expectations for future periods comprising budgeted profit and cash flow statements

materials handling the physical handling of products

materials requirements planning (MRP) a computerised system that integrates production planning and inventory control

matrix structure an organisational structure that combines vertical and horizontal lines of authority, usually by superimposing product departmentalisation on a functionally departmentalised organisation

maturity date the date on which a corporation is to repay borrowed money

maturity stage the stage during which a product's sales curve peaks and starts to decline, and profits continue to decline

media sharing sites allow users to upload multimedia content including photos, videos, and podcasts

medium of exchange an item that buyers give to sellers when they want to purchase goods and services

merchant wholesalers wholesalers that take title to goods and assume the risks associated with ownership Merchant wholesalers

merger the purchase of one corporation by another

microeconomics the study of the decisions made by individuals and businesses

middle manager a manager who implements the strategy and major policies developed by top management

millennials tech-savvy digital natives born after 1980

mission a statement of the basic purpose that makes an organisation different from others

missionary salesperson a salesperson—generally employed by a manufacturer—who visits retailers to persuade them to buy the manufacturer's products

mixed economy an economy that exhibits elements of both capitalism and socialism

monetary policies central bank decisions that determine the size of the supply of money in the nation and the level of interest rates

monetary policy the set of actions taken by the central bank in order to affect the money supply

money market the market in which the commercial banks lend money to one another on a short-term basis

money supply the quantity of money available in the economy

money the set of assets in an economy that people regularly use to buy goods and services from other people

monopolistic competition a market situation in which there are many buyers along with a relatively large number of sellers who differentiate their products from the products of competitors

monopoly a market (or industry) with only one seller, and there are barriers to keep other firms from entering the industry

morale an employee's feelings about his or her job and superiors and about the firm itself

mortgage bond a corporate bond secured by various assets of the issuing firm

motivating the process of providing reasons for people to work in the best interests of an organisation

motivation the desire, interest or drive to want to work; the individual internal process that energises, directs, and sustains behaviour; the personal "force" that causes you or me to behave in a particular way

MRO items consumable supplies in the subcategories of maintenance, repair and operating (or overhaul) supplies

multilateral development bank (MDB) an internationally supported bank that provides loans to developing countries to help them grow

multinational corporations (MNC) companies who own and control operations in more than one country

multinational enterprise a company with operations or subsidiaries in many countries

multiple-unit pricing the strategy of setting a single price for two or more units

municipal bond sometimes called a muni, a debt security issued by a state or local government

mutual fund pools the money of many investors—its shareholders—to invest in a variety of different securities

natural monopoly an industry requiring huge investments in capital and within which any duplication of facilities would be wasteful and thus not in the public interest

negotiated pricing establishing a final price through bargaining

net asset value (NAV) current market value of a mutual fund's portfolio minus the mutual fund's liabilities divided by the number of outstanding shares

network structure an organisational structure in which administration is the primary function, and most other functions are contracted out to other firms

net worth the difference between the value of your total assets and your total liabilities

news release a typed page of about 300 words provided by an organisation to the media as a form of publicity

non-price competition competition based on factors other than price

non-store retailing the selling of goods or services outside the confines of a retail facility

nontariff barrier a nontax measure imposed by a government to favor domestic over foreign suppliers

non-value added activities activities that can be reduced or eliminated without altering the product's service potential to the customer.

North American Free Trade Agreement (NAFTA) implemented in 1994, and designed to eliminate all tariffs on goods produced and traded between Canada, Mexico and the United States, providing for a totally free trade area by 2009

objective a specific statement detailing what an organisation intends to accomplish over a shorter period of time

objective of physical distribution decreasing costs while increasing customer service

odd-number pricing the strategy of setting prices using odd numbers that are slightly below whole-unit amounts

oligopoly a market (or industry) in which there are few sellers

open corporation a corporation whose stock can be bought and sold by any individual

open-market operations the purchase and sale of non-monetary assets from and to the banking sector by the central bank

operational plan a type of plan designed to implement tactical plans

operations management all the activities required to produce goods and services

operations manager a manager who manages the systems that convert resources into goods and services

opportunity a favourable set of conditions that limit barriers or provide rewards

order-getter a salesperson who is responsible for selling a firm's products to new customers and increasing sales to present customers

order lead time the average time lapse between placing the order and receiving it

order processing the receipt and transmission of sales order information

order-taker a salesperson who handles repeat sales in ways that maintain positive relationships with customers

ordinary share stock owned by individuals or firms who may vote on corporate matters but whose claims on profits and assets are subordinate to the claims of others

organisation a group of two or more people working together to achieve a common set of goals

organisational (corporate) culture a set of values, beliefs, goals, norms and rituals that members of an organisation share

organisational height the number of layers, or levels, of management in a firm

organisation chart a diagram that represents the positions and relationships within an organisation

organising the grouping of resources and activities to accomplish some end result in an efficient and effective manner

orientation the process of acquainting new employees with an organisation

out-of-home advertising short promotional messages on hoardings, posters, signs, and transportation vehicles

outright open-market operations the outright sale or purchase of nonmonetary assets to or from the banking sector by the central bank without a corresponding agreement to reverse the transaction at a later date

outsourcing the process of finding outside vendors and suppliers that provide professional help, parts, or materials at a lower cost; where a third-party organisation is empowered to manage and control a particular activity, such as logistics

over-the-counter (OTC) market a network of dealers who buy and sell the stocks of corporations that are not listed on a securities exchange

packaging all the activities involved in developing and providing a container with graphics for a product

participative or backroom leadership lowprofile, self-effacing, and aims to involve colleagues in taking and forming decisions on purpose, objectives and strategy; they lead quietly from the backroom to build up a disciplined sense of core values.

partnership when you go into business with someone else (more commonly associated with professional services such as accountants, solicitors and doctors)

part-time work permanent employment in which individuals work less than a standard work week

penetration pricing the strategy of setting a low price for a new product

people variable the aspect of the marketing mix that reflects the level of customer service, advice, sales support and after-sales back-up required, involving recruitment policies, training, retention and motivation of key personnel

perfect (or pure) competition the market situation in which there are many buyers and sellers of a product, and no single buyer or seller is powerful enough to affect the price of that product

performance appraisal the evaluation of employees' current and potential levels of performance to allow managers to make objective human resources decisions

performance-related pay an incentive scheme that is used to motivate employees by linking their pay to the achievement of pre-agreed performance targets.

performance reports regular reports to management that compare actual outcomes with planned outcomes.

periodic discounting temporary reduction of prices on a patterned or systematic basis

personal budget a specific plan for spending your income

personal investment the use of your personal funds to earn a financial return

personal selling personal communication aimed at informing customers and persuading them to buy a firm's products

PERT (programme evaluation and review technique) a scheduling technique that identifies the major activities necessary to complete a project and sequences them based on the time required to perform each one

physical distribution a set of activities – consisting of order processing, materials handling, warehousing, inventory management and transportation – used in the movement of products from producers to consumers or end users

piece rate a method of paying employees for each unit of output they produce.

place/distribution variable the aspect of the marketing mix that deals with making products available in the quantities desired to as many customers as possible and keeping the total inventory, transport and storage costs as low as possible

plan an outline of the actions by which an organisation intends to accomplish its goals and objectives

planning establishing organisational goals and deciding how to accomplish them

planning horizon the period during which an operational plan will be in effect

plant layout the arrangement of machinery, equipment, and personnel within a production facility

podcasts digital audio or video files that people listen to or watch online on tablets, computers, MP3 players, or smartphones

point-of-purchase display promotional material placed within a retail store

positioning the development of a product image in buyers' minds relative to the images they have of competing products

preferred stock stock whose owners usually do not have voting rights but whose claims on dividends and assets are paid before those of common-stock owners

premium a gift that a producer offers a customer in return for buying its product

premium pricing pricing the highest-quality or most-versatile products higher than other models in the product line

press conference a meeting at which invited media personnel hear important news announcements and receive supplementary textual materials and photographs

price the amount of money a seller is willing to accept in exchange for a product at a given time and under given circumstances

price competition an emphasis on setting a price equal to or lower than competitors' prices to gain sales or market share

price leaders products priced below the usual markup, near cost, or below cost

price lining the strategy of selling goods only at certain predetermined prices that reflect definite price breaks

price skimming the strategy of charging the highest possible price for a product during the introduction stage of its life-cycle

price variable the aspect of the marketing mix that relates to activities associated with establishing pricing policies and determining product prices

primary-demand advertising advertising aimed at increasing the demand for all brands of a product within a specific industry

primary market a market in which an investor purchases financial securities (via an investment bank) directly from the issuer of those securities

prime interest rate the lowest rate charged by a bank for a short-term loan

prime pitch the area at the centre of the shopping zone with the main shops and the highest levels of pedestrian footfall

private placement occurs when stock and other corporate securities are sold directly to insurance companies, pension funds, or large institutional investors

problem-solving team a team of knowledgeable employees brought together to tackle a specific problem

problem the discrepancy between an actual condition and a desired condition

process materials materials used directly in the production of other products, but not readily identifiable

producer price index (PPI) an index that measures prices that producers receive for their finished goods

product a good, service or idea

product deletion the elimination of one or more products from a product line

product design the process of creating a set of specifications from which a product can be produced

product differentiation the process of developing and promoting differences between one's products and all competitive products

product everything one receives in an exchange, including all tangible and intangible attributes and expected benefits; it may be a good, a service, or an idea

production era the period of mass production following industrialisation

product item a specific version of a product that can be designated as a distinct offering among a business's products

productivity the average level of output per worker per hour

product life cycles the four major stages through which products move: introduction, growth, maturity and decline

product line a group of closely related product items that are considered a unit because of marketing, technical or end-use considerations

product mix the composite group of products that a company makes available to customers

product modification the process of changing one or more of a product's characteristics

product's life cycle the period of time from initial expenditure on research and development to the withdrawal of support to customers.

product variable the aspect of the marketing mix that deals with researching consumers' product wants and designing a product with the desired characteristics

profit-sharing the distribution of a percentage of a firm's profit among its employees

profit what remains after all business expenses have been deducted from sales revenue

promissory note a written pledge by a borrower to pay a certain sum of money to a creditor at a specified future date

promotional campaign a plan for combining and using the four promotional methods—advertising, personal selling, sales promotion, and publicity—in a particular promotion mix to achieve one or more marketing goals

promotion communication about an organisation and its products that is intended to inform, persuade, or remind target-market members

promotion mix the particular combination of promotion methods a firm uses to reach a target market

promotion variable the aspect of the marketing mix that relates to marketing communications used to inform one or more groups of people about an organisation and its products

prospectus a detailed, written description of a new security, the issuing corporation, and the corporation's top management

proxy a legal form listing issues to be decided at a stockholders' meeting and enabling stockholders to transfer their voting rights to some other individual or individuals

proxy fight a technique used to gather enough stockholder votes to control a targeted company

publicity communication in news-story form about an organisation, its products, or both

Public Limited Company (PLC) a limited company whose shares may be purchased by the public and traded freely on the open market and whose share capital is not less than a statutory minimum (for the U.K. – a company registered under the Companies Act (1980) as a public company)

public relations communication activities used to create and maintain favourable relations between an organisation and various public groups, both internal and external

public warehouses storage facilities available for a fee

purchasing all the activities involved in obtaining required materials, supplies, components, and parts from other firms

qualitative social media measurement the process of accessing the opinions and beliefs about a brand and primarily uses sentiment analysis to categorise what is being said about a company

quality circle a team of employees who meet on company time to solve problems of product quality

quality control the process of ensuring that goods and services are produced in accordance with design specifications

quantitative social media measurement using numerical measurements, such as counting the number of Web site visitors, number of fans and followers, number of leads generated, and the number of new customers

rack jobbers speciality line wholesalers that own and maintain their own display racks in supermarkets and chemists

random discounting temporary reduction of prices on an unsystematic basis

rate of return the total amount of return you receive on an investment over a specific period of time divided by the amount invested

raw materials the basic materials that become part of physical products

rebate a return of part of the product's purchase price

recession two or more consecutive three-month periods of decline in a country's GDP

recruiting the process of attracting qualified job applicants

reference pricing pricing a product at a moderate level and positioning it next to a more expensive model or brand

refinancing rate the interest rate at which a central lends on a short-term basis to the banking sector

registered bond a bond registered in the owner's name by the issuing company

reinforcement theory a theory of motivation based on the premise that rewarded behaviour is likely to be repeated, whereas punished behaviour is less likely to recur

reliability the consistency of service provided

reorder point the inventory level that signals the need to order more inventory

replacement chart a list of key personnel and their possible replacements within a firm

repo rate the interest rate at which the central bank lends on a short-term basis to the banking sector

repurchase agreement (repo) the sale of a non-monetary asset together with an agreement to repurchase it at a set price at a specified future date

research and development (R&D) a set of activities intended to identify new ideas that have the potential to result in new goods and services

reserve requirements regulations on the minimum amount of reserves that banks must hold against deposits

reshoring a situation in which manufacturers bring manufacturing jobs back to domestic soil

responsibility the duty to do a job or perform a task

retailer a business that purchases products for the purpose of reselling them to ultimate consumers – the general public – often from a shop or store

retailing all transactions in which the buyer intends to consume the product through personal, family or household use

retail parks groupings of freestanding superstores, forming a retail village

revenue stream a source of revenue flowing into a firm

revolving credit agreement a guaranteed line of credit

risk–return ratio a ratio based on the principle that a high-risk decision should generate higher financial returns for a business and more conservative decisions often generate lower returns

robotics the use of programmable machines to perform a variety of tasks by manipulating materials and tools

safety stock inventory needed to prevent stock-outs

salary a specific amount of money paid for an employee's work during a set calendar period, regardless of the actual number of hours worked

sales branches manufacturer-owned middlemen selling products and providing support services to the manufacturer's sales force, especially in locations where large customers are concentrated and demand is high

sales era the period from the mid-1920s to the early 1950s when competitive forces and the desire for high sales volume led a company to emphasise selling and the sales person in its business strategy

sales offices manufacturer-owned operations that provide support services normally associated with agents

sales promotion the use of activities or materials as direct inducements to customers or salespersons

sales support personnel employees who aid in selling but are more involved in locating prospects, educating customers, building goodwill for the firm, and providing follow-up service

sample a free product given to customers to encourage trial and purchase

savings and loan association (S&L) a financial institution that offers current and savings accounts and CDs and that invests most of its assets in home mortgage loans and other consumer loans

scheduling the process of ensuring that materials and other resources are at the right place at the right time

secondary market a market for existing financial securities that are traded between investors

secondary-market pricing setting one price for the primary target market and a different price for another market

securities exchange a marketplace where member brokers meet to buy and sell securities

security average (or security index) an average of the current market prices of selected securities

security the measure of the physical condition of goods upon delivery

selection the process of gathering information about applicants for a position and then using that information to choose the most appropriate applicant

selective-demand (or brand) advertising advertising that is used to sell a particular brand of product

self-managed teams groups of employees with the authority and skills to manage themselves

selling agents agents who market either all of a specified product line or a manufacturer's entire output

selling short the process of selling stock that an investor does not actually own but has borrowed from a brokerage firm and will repay at a later date

sentiment analysis a measurement that uses technology to detect the moods, attitudes, or emotions of people who experience a social media activity

serial bonds bonds of a single issue that mature on different dates

service economy an economy in which more effort is devoted to the production of services than to the production of goods

service The application of human and mechanical efforts to people or objects in order to provide intangible benefits to customers

share ownership similar to a profit-share scheme except that employees gain shares in the company and then receive a share of profits via dividend distribution.

shopping products items chosen more carefully than convenience products; consumers will expend effort in planning and purchasing these items

short-term financing money that will be used for one year or less

sinking fund a sum of money to which deposits are made each year for the purpose of redeeming a bond issue

Six Sigma a disciplined approach that relies on statistical data and improved methods to eliminate defects for a firm's products and services

skills inventory a computerised data bank containing information on the skills and experience of all present employees

small business one that is independently owned and operated for profit and is not dominant in its field

social audit a comprehensive report of what an organisation has done and is doing with regard to social issues that affect it

social content sites allow companies to create and share information about their products and services

social enterprise an enterprise which lies somewhere between the for-profit and not-for-profit organisation, aiming to make money, but using it mainly for social causes

social game a multiplayer, competitive, goal-oriented activity with defined rules of engagement and online connectivity among a community of players

social marketing use of tools and techniques from commercial marketing to encourage positive behavioural changes, such as quitting smoking, reducing alcohol consumption, minimising anti-social behaviours or reducing carbon footprint.

social marketing use of tools and techniques from commercial marketing to encourage positive behavioural changes, such as quitting smoking, reducing alcohol consumption, minimising anti-social behaviours or reducing carbon footprint. The health and well-being of individuals, society and the planet are at the core of social marketing.

social media the online interactions that allow people and businesses to communicate and share ideas, personal information, and information about products and services

social media communities social networks based on the relationships among people

social media marketing the utilisation of social media technologies, channels, and software to create, communicate, deliver, and exchange offerings that have value for an organisation

social responsibility an organisation's obligation to maximise its positive impact and minimise its negative impact on society

sole trader a type of business entity which legally has no separate existence from its owner (the limitations of liability benefited from by a corporation, and limited liability partnerships, do not apply to sole traders) – the simplest form of business

span of management (or span of control) the number of workers who report directly to one manager

special-event pricing advertised sales or price cutting linked to a holiday, season, or event

specialisation the separation of a manufacturing process into distinct tasks and the assignment of the different tasks to different individuals

speciality line wholesalers middlemen who carry the narrowest range of products, usually a single product line or a few items within a product line

speciality products items that possess one or more unique characteristics; consumers of speciality products plan their purchases and will expend considerable effort to obtain them

speciality shops stores that offer self-service but a greater level of assistance from store personnel than department stores, and carry a narrow product mix with deep product lines

speculative production the time lag between the actual production of goods and when the goods are sold

staff manager a position created to provide support, advice, and expertise within an organisation

staff retention this measures a business's ability to keep its employees.

stakeholders all the different people or groups of people who are affected by the policies and decisions made by an organisation; constituents who have a "stake", or claim, in some aspect of a company's products, operations, markets, industry and outcomes

standard of living a loose, subjective measure of how well off an individual or a society is, mainly in terms of want satisfaction through goods and services

Standard & Poor's 500 Stock Index an index that contains 500 different stocks that reflect increases or decreases in value for the U.S. stock market as a whole

standing committee a relatively permanent committee charged with performing some recurring task

stock the shares of ownership of a corporation

stock dividend a dividend in the form of additional stock

stockholder a person who owns a corporation's stock

stock-outs shortages of products resulting from a lack of products carried in inventory

stock split the division of each outstanding share of a corporation's stock into a greater number of shares

store of value an item that people can use to transfer purchasing power from the present to the future

store (or private) brand a brand that is owned by an individual wholesaler or retailer

strategic alliance a partnership formed to create competitive advantage on a worldwide basis

strategic leaders leaders who are dispersed across the organisation, who influence and empower others to participate in strategic management.

strategic leadership the style and general approach used by a senior management to articulate purpose, objectives and strategy, to influence implementation and execution of these through the organisation.

strategic philanthropy the synergistic use of organisational core competencies and resources to address key stakeholders' interests, and achieve both organisational and social benefits

strategic plan an organisation's broadest plan, developed as a guide for major policy setting and decision making

strategic planning process the establishment of an organisation's major goals and objectives and the allocation of resources to achieve them

strategies courses of action designed to ensure that objectives are achieved.

suburban centres shopping centres created at major road junctions that cater for local shopping needs

supermarkets and grocery superstores large, self-service stores that carry a complete line of food products as well as other convenience items

supply chain management the orchestration of the channel of distribution from sourcing supplies, manufacture to delivery to the customer

supply the quantity of a product that producers are willing to sell at each of various prices

sustainability meeting the needs of the present without compromising the ability of future generations to meet their own needs; the potential for the long term well-being of the natural environment, including all biological entities, as well as the interaction among nature and individuals, organisations and business strategies

SWOT analysis the identification and evaluation of a firm's strengths, weaknesses, opportunities, and threats

synthetic process a process in operations management in which raw materials or components are combined to create a finished product

tactical plan a smaller scale plan developed to implement a strategy

task force a committee established to investigate a major problem or pending decision

team two or more workers operating as a coordinated unit to accomplish a specific task or goal

technical salesperson a salesperson who assists a company's current customers in technical matters

technical skills specific skills needed to accomplish a specialised activity

telecommuting working at home all the time or for a portion of the work week

telemarketing the direct selling of goods and services by telephone, based on either a cold canvass of the telephone directory or a pre-screened list of prospective clients

tender offer an offer to purchase the stock of a firm targeted for acquisition at a price just high enough to tempt stockholders to sell their shares

term-loan agreement a promissory note that requires a borrower to repay a loan in monthly, quarterly, semiannual, or annual instalments

Theory X a concept of employee motivation generally consistent with Taylor's scientific management; assumes that employees dislike work and will function only in a highly controlled work environment

Theory Y a concept of employee motivation generally consistent with the ideas of the human relations movement; assumes responsibility and work toward organisational goals, and by doing so they also achieve personal rewards

Theory Z the belief that some middle ground between type A and type J practices is best for business

time rates employees are paid a set rate for a specific length of time, for example, per hour or per shift.

top manager an upper-level executive who guides and controls the overall fortunes of an organisation

total cost analysis weighs inventory levels against warehousing expenses; and materials handling costs against various modes of transport; and all distribution costs against customer service standards

total cost the sum of the fixed costs and the variable costs attributed to a product

total quality management (TQM) a customer-oriented process of continuous improvement that focuses on delivering products or services of consistent high quality in a timely fashion; the coordination of efforts directed at improving customer satisfaction, increasing employee participation, strengthening supplier partnerships, and facilitating an organisational atmosphere of continuous quality improvement

total revenue the total amount received from sales of a product

traceability the relative ease with which a shipment can be located and transferred

trade credit a type of short-term financing extended by a seller who does not require immediate payment after delivery of merchandise

trade deficit a negative balance of trade

trademark a brand name or brand mark that is registered with an official patenting and trademark authority and thus is legally protected from use by anyone except its owner

trade markets relatively permanent facilities that businesses can rent to exhibit products year round

trade name the complete and legal name of an organisation

trade salesperson a salesperson—generally employed by a food producer or processor—who assists customers in promoting products, especially in retail stores

trade sales promotion method a sales promotion method designed to encourage wholesalers and retailers to stock and actively promote a manufacturer's product

trade show an industry-wide exhibit at which many sellers display their products

trade shows industry exhibitions that offer both selling and non-selling benefits

trading company a company that provides a link between buyers and sellers in different countries

traditional specialty store a store that carries a narrow product mix with deep product lines

transactional leadership centred on mission and explicit management systems, which clarify expectations, agreements, and utilise constructive feedback about performance.

transfer pricing prices charged in sales between an organisation's units

transformational leadership charismatic leadership which works to associate individual self-interest with the larger vision of the organisation by inspiring people with a sense of collective vision.

transit time the total time a carrier has possession of goods

transmission mechanism the process by which monetary policy decisions is transmitted throughout the economy to the inflation rate.

transportation the process of moving a product from where it is made to where it is purchased and used

transport modes methods of moving goods; these include railways, motor vehicles, inland waterways, airways and pipelines

truck wholesalers limited service wholesalers that transport products direct to customers for inspection and selection

trustee an individual or an independent firm that acts as a bond owner's representative

unemployment rate the percentage of a nation's labour force unemployed at any time

unit loading grouping one or more boxes on a pallet or skid, permitting movement of efficient loads by mechanical means

unit of account the yardstick people use to post prices and record debts

unlimited liability a situation where the owner of a business is legally responsible for all the debts of the business

unsecured financing financing that is not backed by collateral; unsecured short-term financing offers several options

unsought products items that are purchased when a sudden problem arises or when aggressive selling is used to obtain a sale that would not otherwise take place

usage rate the rate at which a product's inventory is used or sold during a specific time period

value-based marketing value-based marketing recognises that marketing must prove its long term financial worth and be accountable to organisations, which involves showing that marketing enables both the creation of short-term customer value and longer-term value for shareholders.

variable cost a cost that depends on the number of units produced

variety stores slightly smaller and more specialised stores than department stores, offering a reduced range of merchandise

virtual team a team consisting of members who are geographically dispersed but communicate electronically

wage survey a collection of data on prevailing wage rates within an industry or a geographic area

warehouse clubs large-scale, members-only selling operations combining cash-and-carry wholesaling with discount retailing

warehousing the design and operation of facilities for storing and moving goods

wholesaler an individual or business engaged in facilitating and expediting exchanges that are primarily wholesale transactions

wholesaling intermediaries activity in the marketing channel between producers and business customers to facilitate the exchange – buying and selling – of goods

width (of product mix) the number of product lines a company offers

wiki a collaborative online working space that enables members to contribute content that is then sharable with other people

Wold Trade Organisation (WTO) an entity that promotes and facilitates free trade between member states

Yellow Pages advertising simple listings or display advertisements presented under specific product categories appearing in print and online telephone directories

zero-base budgeting a budgeting approach in which every expense in every budget must be justified

INDEX